MICHAEL DAVIES
AN EVALUATION

"To the best of my knowledge, no one has been able to point out a theological error in any of my books."

(Michael Davies, *The Angelus*, March 1984)

"All my writing is governed by one criterion only, the truth."

(Michael Davies, *The Remnant*, 30th November 1988)

"I have now written four books, fourteen pamphlets, and countless articles, exposing the deficiencies of the post-Vatican II liturgical revolution. No one has, as yet, been able to point out any factual or doctrinal error in any of them."

(Michael Davies, *The Remnant*, 15th May 1989)

MICHAEL DAVIES
AN EVALUATION

NEW EDITION

JOHN S. DALY

First edition 1989
This edition © copyright John S. Daly 2015
ISBN 978-2-917813-52-2

TRADIBOOKS
Rouchas Sud
47180 Saint-Sauveur de Meilhan, France
http://www.tradibooks.com – *tradibooks@orange.fr*

CONTENTS

CONTENTS	VII
INTRODUCTION TO THE NEW 2015 EDITION	IX
INTRODUCTION	XI
I. DAVIES'S ATTITUDE TO AUTHORITY	23
II. SHOCKINGLY SLIPSHOD SCHOLARSHIP	55
III. THE VACANCY OF THE HOLY SEE	92
APPENDIX: SUAREZ ON THE HERETICAL POPE	148
IV. DISHONESTY, INCONSISTENCY AND ARROGANCE	164
V. WHICH SIDE IS MICHAEL DAVIES ON?	191
VI. MISCELLANEOUS DOCTRINAL ERRORS	255
VII. THE SOCIETY OF ST. PIUS X	273
VIII. DAVIES AS AN ANARCHIST	290
IX. ERRORS OF SACRAMENTAL THEOLOGY	314
(A) THE ORDERS OF ARCHBISHOP LEFEBVRE	316
(B) THE 1968 NEW RITE OF ORDINATION	355
(C) VALIDITY AND "SIGNIFICATIO EX ADJUNCTIS"	396
(D) VALIDITY OF THE NOVUS ORDO MISSÆ	409
X. THE ALLEGED FALL OF POPE LIBERIUS	427
XI. SALVATION OUTSIDE THE CHURCH?	482
XII. DOCTRINAL EVOLUTION?	537
XIII OPEN LETTER TO MR. MICHAEL DAVIES	553
ALSO BY JOHN S. DALY	585

INTRODUCTION TO THE NEW 2015 EDITION

The book you have before you is a considerably revised version of the original edition published in 1989. The passage of precisely half of its author's lifetime with its attendant progress in study, thought and approach, together with the death of its subject, Michael Treharne Davies (1936-2004), have made it appropriate that *Michael Davies – An Evaluation* should be republished, but inevitable that the new edition should require revision.

I have made no attempt to bring the book up to date in the sense of analysing Davies's *later* writings, but I have added a great deal of new information and sources on the subjects already covered, verified my theological and historical authorities, weeded out any irrelevancies, toned down some youthful excesses, and, as a rule, preferred understatement to any risk of its opposite. Doubtless some traces of callowness remain from the first edition,[1] but, as Gustavo Corção has observed, *quod scripsi scripsi*[2] is the harsh law of the irreversibility of the written word once committed to the presses.

I am often asked whether Michael Davies ever made any answer to this *Evaluation* and in particular to the "Open Letter" which comprises its final chapter, which has struck many readers as its most devastating part. The answer is No. Moreover, in a letter of 30th June 1990 to an enquirer Davies said "I have done no more than glance through the first few

---

[1] I was twenty-six when it appeared.
[2] "What I have written I have written."

pages of the Daly diatribe." And challenged in person on the subject by philosopher Dr. David S. Oderberg, Davies stated that he still had not read it but, under pressure, vaguely undertook to do so when he should retire, though there is no sign that he ever did so. Two postgraduate students who had visited Davies and discussed with him a number of the issues raised in the *Evaluation* wrote to him afterwards in the following terms:

> Neither of us will deny that, at one time, we valued your writings very highly indeed. Concerned for truth, for the authentic voice of tradition, we naturally gravitated to your works, recommended to us as they were by people of equal good will and fervour for the truth. Neither of us can say this now. All we can do is *urge* you, in the strongest possible terms, to address yourself to the *Open Letter* addressed to you by Mr. Daly at the end of his *Evaluation*. If, as you say, its contents are spurious, then your refutation of the allegations in it should require a minimal expenditure of time and of intellectual effort.[3]

But no amount of pressure, even from persons whose intelligence and status did not allow them to be easily dismissed, ever induced Davies to depart from the line he had taken of ignoring rather than evaluating or answering.

Michael Davies himself is now beyond the reach of any help save our charitable prayers for his soul, but it not too late for his disciples. If they deign to read they will swiftly see that the entire edifice of traditional Catholicism as erected and championed by Davies is built on falsified facts and falsified theology. Once the facts and the theology are corrected, a synthesis very different from the one they are accustomed to imposes itself.

Michael Davies – An Evaluation remains not only an unanswered indictment of Davies as a Catholic scholar, but a standing refutation of the entire ecclesiology of those who believe it possible for an orthodox Catholic to reject the

---

[3] Letter of 13th January 1991.

doctrinal errors and reformed rites spawned by Vatican II without calling into doubt the legitimacy of recent papal claimants and the validity of the new sacraments.

John S. Daly
Feast of St. Andrew, 2015

INTRODUCTION

If a random group of traditional Catholics were asked to name the most important English-language periodicals defending the Church against the Modernist onslaught, the answers would probably be diverse. No doubt *The Remnant*, *Christian Order*, *The Angelus*, *Approaches/À Propos* and *The Roman Catholic* would all get a mention. By contrast, if such a group were asked to name the most important English-language *author* on the anti-revolution side, there can be no doubt that the name of Mr. Michael Davies would top the ballot by a large margin and that even many who disagree with his position would vote for him. That is a measure of his significance.

Another, perhaps even more telling, gauge of Mr. Davies's influence would be to tot up the total number of copies of each of his works printed in England and America.[1] The result would compare very favourably, not only with the publication figures of any other author in the traditional Catholic movement, but also with those of most of the leading lights of what Mr. Davies calls "the liturgical revolution", despite the fact that, thanks to the adulation of the media, many of them are much better known to the general public than he is; and it is not unfair to conjecture that each copy of Mr. Davies's books and pamphlets is probably *read* on average much more than those written by his opponents who favour the "revolution".

Nor, I suggest, is even this a sufficient gauge of the importance of Mr. Davies's writings: for it should not be overlooked that for many thousands of his readers Mr. Davies's books constitute more or less the *only* serious theological

---

[1] Even disregarding the translations of his works into languages such as Spanish and French.

literature they have ever read. Many of those who swell the ranks at "traditionalist" Mass centres on Sundays have reached their convictions concerning the present state of the Church largely because they have come across the writings of Mr. Davies in periodicals or in book form and have allowed him to sort out for them the reality underlying what they had recognized only by instinct as a series of "changes in the Church" that jarred with their Catholic instinct. Their knowledge of the history of the Catholic liturgy and of the theological facts needed to defend their stance has been derived almost exclusively from his works. It is upon him that they rely for their views on the significance of Paul VI's liturgical changes or the status of the decrees of Vatican II. It is upon him that they rely as they insist to their traditionally-inclined fellow-parishioners that the constitution *Missale Romanum* did not abrogate the bull *Quo Primum,* and as they berate their harassed parish priests for not being able to distinguish between the "substance" of a sacrament and its essential form, or for failing to state correctly the Church's position in relation to *"per saltum"* Ordinations. And of course it is upon him that they rely for their authority in resisting the not infrequent temptation to wonder whether the Johns and the Pauls have really been popes at all.

I do not think that any of this is an exaggeration. Before the Council very few laymen had studied the niceties of sacramental theology, and the fact that a large proportion of the traditional Catholic movement now knows more about that subject than the clergy that run their respective parishes must be due more to the writings of Mr. Davies than to any other single cause. It is therefore true to say that, for a by no means insignificant number of people, Michael Davies has something approaching a theological monopoly. The writings of the heavyweight theologians are open to the great mass of traditional Catholic layfolk only to the extent that Mr. Davies quotes from them or summarises their doctrines in his books, pamphlets and articles.

Add to that the fact that Mr. Davies handles his pen skilfully, has a commendable grasp of many of the topics of which he writes, and explains them lucidly and persuasively in readable prose with a popular style, and it is easy to explain the esteem in which Mr. Davies is widely held. It would hardly be an overstatement to say that in the eyes of some of his readers Mr. Davies is an object of hero-worship and is considered to be endowed almost with infallibility, for his authority is not infrequently invoked as conclusive evidence to settle theological disputes – a fact which is illustrated in this *Evaluation*.

In view of Mr. Davies's uniquely influential position in the Catholic world today, a candid examination of his writings to assess to what extent his facts, theology and reasoning can be relied upon seems to be an appropriate undertaking. That is what this *Evaluation* sets out to achieve by subjecting Mr. Davies's writings to careful analysis in the light of Catholic authority.

V

The author of this *Evaluation* subscribes to a very different analysis of the present crisis from that defended by Michael Davies. *It is by no means necessary for readers to agree with his views before beginning to* read, but it will be useful to be aware of the main issues which divide him from Davies. In summary, his position is that:

(i) Heresy, strictly so-called, is found in several documents of the synod held in 1962-1965 known as the Second Vatican Council, in the texts of the revised liturgy introduced in the Council's wake and in many of the pronouncements of those who have apparently succeeded Pope Pius XII.

(ii) By Divine law and Canon Law all those who manifest conscious assent to heresy automatically (*ipso facto*) cease to be members of the Catholic Church, forfeit whatever offices they may once have had in her, and have no more valid authority over Catholics than the Dalai Lama, the Chief Rabbi, the President of the United States or the kinglet of an undiscovered heathen island in the South Pacific.

(iii) This clearly applies to the papal claimants of the Vatican II era and to the great bulk of the Vatican II hierarchy and clergy.

(iv) The new sacramental formulæ used by the Conciliar Church for the Eucharist (vernacular versions), episcopal "Ordination", and Extreme Unction ("sacrament of the sick") are invalid, and in the case of diaconal and priestly Ordination, the Eucharist (Latin version) and Confirmation, *probably* invalid also.

(v) Movements and initiatives among those known as traditional Catholics are often wanting in any doctrinal foundation, fail to understand even the basics of the current situation in the Church, claim a lawfulness that is entirely unfounded and are not infrequently so far infected with heresy or schism as to be little better than the Conciliar Church from which they pose as a refuge.

(vi) All the foregoing can be demonstrated from indisputable Catholic authorities.

Whether or not readers agree at this stage with this analysis, it will be well worth their while to read on with an open mind, for in examining and refuting Mr. Davies's opinions on all these issues (and many others) the evidence opposing his position and supporting the author's will be set out in considerable detail.

I made the acquaintance of Mr. Davies in 1979-80 while I was still a student, met him on several occasions, and knew his son Adrian well when both of us were studying at Cambridge University. Mr. Davies gave me considerable and generous assistance towards attempting to work out where the truth lay in respect of the changes in the Church, and I was in broad agreement with Mr. Davies's position during the years between 1978 and 1982.

In early 1983, however, I concluded that Mr. Davies was in error on the six points outlined above and on many others – a position I adopted despite considerable repugnance and only in the light of evidence which appeared then and still appears today to be entirely conclusive. After several years of study and work in Catholic publishing I reached the conclusion that an *Evaluation* such as this was necessary in order to accomplish three main objectives:

(i)   To refute the gravely erroneous positions of Mr. Davies on the six points already mentioned, as well as on many others in which his assertions have been responsible for leading many souls astray in matters upon which salvation may quite literally depend.

(ii) To show by careful analysis that Mr. Davies is a grossly unreliable author whose statements about Catholic doctrine should never be accepted without verification from genuine Catholic authorities.

(iii) To set out in a single study the main points of disagreement among those commonly referred to as traditional Catholics, allowing both sides to state their case, and showing by rigorous demonstration in each case where the truth lies.

This task has been carried out by locating relevant passages in Mr. Davies's writings, arranging them systematically, and comparing them with the teaching of approved sources. The conclusions reached in this *Evaluation* are that Mr. Davies is a shameless purveyor of false doctrine, sometimes reaching actual heresy; intensely ignorant even on many elementary points of theology as well as on matters of historical fact and general Catholic knowledge; not infrequently guilty of downright dishonesty; an execrable scholar; arrogant and foolish; a source of huge scandal and, in fine, an utter disgrace to the name of Catholic. Naturally these conclusions are far from savoury. My only justification for reaching them is that they are inescapably true, and my justification for publishing them is that the good of souls demands that so great a source of danger be exposed as publicly as possible.

For some readers it may seem shocking that Catholics should, for whatever reason, subject anyone to a head-on public attack on both his beliefs and his morals[2] so perhaps a little more explanation is called for. This explanation is best given, not in my own words, but in those of Fr. Felix Sarda y Salvany, in his wonderful book *What is Liberalism?* This work was scrutinized by the Sacred Congregation of the Index and was reported (10th January 1887) not only to contain nothing contrary to sound doctrine, but to merit great praise. And the extracts I shall now quote amply justify any member of the faithful competent to do so in (a) firmly and ruthlessly attacking false doctrine, (b), when the common good requires it, no less firmly and ruthlessly attacking the persons of those who obstinately purvey it, rather than restricting himself to an abstract dissertation against the errors. Indeed they do not merely justify, they exhort.

> "The propagators and abettors of heresy as well as its authors have at all times been called heretics. As the Church has always considered heresy a very grave evil, so has she always called its adherents evil and perverted. Run over the list of ecclesiastical writers – you will then see how the Apostles treated the first heretics, how the Fathers, and modern controversialists, and the Church herself in her official language, have pursued them. There is, then, no sin against charity in calling evil evil; nor in calling its authors, abettors and disciples bad; nor in calling all their acts, words and writings iniquitous, wicked, malicious.
>
> "In short, the wolf has always been called the wolf; and in so calling it, no one ever believed that injury was done to the flock and the shepherd.
>
> "If the propagation of good and the necessity of combating evil require the use of harsh terms against error and its supporters, this is certainly not against charity. It is a corollary or consequence of the

---

[2] By "morals" I am referring exclusively to Mr. Davies's conduct as a researcher and writer – his private life is so far as I know irreproachable and it certainly has no relevance to the subjects discussed in these pages.

principle we have just demonstrated. We *must* render evil odious and detestable. We cannot attain this result without pointing out the dangers of evil, without showing how and why it is odious, detestable and contemptible. Christian oratory of all ages has ever employed the most vigorous and emphatic rhetoric in the arsenal of human speech against impiety. In the writings of the great athletes of Christianity the use of irony, imprecation, execration and of the most crushing epithets is continual. Hence the only rule is that of opportuneness and truth.

"But there is another justification for such an usage. Apologetics that are intended for popular consumption cannot be couched in elegant and constrained academic forms. In order to convince the people we must speak to their heart and their imagination, which can be touched only by ardent, fiery, and impassioned language. To be impassioned is not reprehensible, when the emotion is stirred up by the holy ardour of truth.[3]

"'It is fair enough to make war on abstract doctrines,' some may say, 'but in combating error, be it ever so evident, is it proper to make an attack upon the *persons* of those who uphold it?' We reply that very often it is – and not only proper, but at times even indispensable and meritorious before God and men.

"The accusation of indulging in personalities is not spared to Catholic apologists, and when liberals and those tainted with liberalism have hurled it at our heads they imagine that we are overwhelmed by the charge. But they deceive themselves. We are not so easily thrust into the background. We have reason, and substantial reason, on our side. In order to combat and discredit false ideas, we must inspire contempt and horror in the hearts of the multitude for those who seek to seduce and debauch them. A disease is inseparable from the persons of the diseased. The cholera

---

[3] In defence of such strong language as may occur in this *Evaluation* (and any that is present is intended to make a serious and valid point rather than to deride), it could also be remarked that that Mr. Davies can be quite as acerbic towards those who take a contrary view to his. Anyone who accuses his opponents of, for instance, "writing the most utter drivel one can possibly imagine" (*The Remnant*, 15th January 1987) – language which borders on the hysterical – can have no objection to the harsh but accurate terms used in this *Evaluation*.

threatening a country comes in the persons of the infected. If we wish to exclude it, we must exclude them. Now just as ideas do not generate themselves, neither do they spread or propagate themselves. Left to themselves, if it be possible to imagine them apart from those who conceive them, they would never produce all the evil from which society suffers. It is only in the concrete that they are effective; when they animate the behaviour of those who conceive them. They are like the arrows and the bullets which would hurt no one if they were not shot from the bow or the gun. It is the archer and the gunner to whom we should give our attention if we want to put an end to their murderous assaults. Any other method of warfare would be liberal, admittedly, but it would be opposed to common-sense.

"The authors and propagators of heretical doctrines are soldiers with poisoned weapons in their hands. Their arms are the book, the newspaper, the lecture, their personal influence. Is it sufficient to dodge their blows? Not at all; the first thing necessary is to demolish the combatant himself. When he is 'hors de combat', he can do no more mischief.

"It is therefore perfectly proper not only to discredit any book, newspaper or discourse of the enemy, but also, in certain cases, to discredit his person; for in warfare, beyond question, the principal element is the person engaged, as the gunner is the principal factor in an artillery fight, and not the cannon, the powder and the bomb. It is thus lawful, in certain cases, to expose the crimes of a liberal opponent, to bring his habits into contempt, and to drag his name in the mire. Yes, this is permissible; permissible in prose, in verse, in caricature, in a serious vein or in badinage, by every means and method within reach. The only restriction is not to employ a lie in the service of righteousness. This never. Under no pretext may we sully the truth, not by one iota. As Crétineau-Joly has remarked: "'Truth is the only charity allowed in history,' and, we may add, in the defence of religion and society.

"The Fathers of the Church support this thesis. The very titles of their works clearly show that, in their contests with heresy, their first blow was against the heresiarchs. The works of St. Augustine almost always bear the name of the author of the heresy against which they are written: *Contra Fortunatum Manichoeum*; *Adversus*

Adamanctum; *Contra Felicem*; *Contra Secundinum*; *Quis fuerit Petilianus?*; *De gestis Pelagii*; *Quis fuerit Julianus?*, etc. Thus the greater part of the polemics of this great doctor was personal, aggressive, biographical, as well as doctrinal, a hand-to-hand struggle with heretics as well as with heresy."[4]

---

[4] Perhaps one final objection needs to be answered, namely whether it is appropriate even for layfolk, as well as priests and bishops, to defend the Church in this manner. My answer here is that the laity not only may, but sometimes must, do so, and that when it is their duty to defend the Church they are entitled to use precisely the same literary weapons as the highest ecclesiastics might choose to use in writings of controversy. Certainly, when possible, they should write under the guidance of their pastors, but there can undoubtedly be exceptions to this. The history of the Church furnishes a multitude of instances illustrating these principles, of which the case of the layman Eusebius as recounted by Dom Guéranger is justly celebrated:

"In the very year of his exaltation, on Christmas Day 428, Nestorius, taking advantage of the immense concourse which had assembled in honour of the Virgin Mother and her Child, pronounced from the episcopal pulpit the blasphemous words: 'Mary did not bring forth God; her Son was only a man, the instrument of the Divinity.' The multitude shuddered with horror. *Eusebius, a simple layman, rose to give expression to the general indignation, and protested against this impiety.* Soon a more explicit protest was drawn up and disseminated in the name of the members of this grief-stricken Church, launching an anathema against anyone who should dare to say: 'The Only-begotten Son of the Father and the Son of Mary are different persons.' *This generous attitude was the safeguard of Byzantium, and won the praise of Popes and Councils. When the shepherd becomes a wolf the first duty of the flock is to defend itself.* It is usual and regular, no doubt, for doctrine to descend from the bishops to the faithful, and those who are subject in the Faith are not to judge their superiors. But in the treasure of revelation *there are essential doctrines which all Christians, by the very fact of their title as such, are bound to know and defend. The principle is the same whether it be a question of belief or conduct, dogma or morals.* Treachery like that of Nestorius is rare in the Church, but it may happen that some pastors keep silence for one reason or another in circumstances when religion is at stake. *The true children of Holy Church at such times* are those who walk by the light of their baptism, *not the cowardly souls who, under the specious pretext of submission to the powers that be, delay their opposition to the enemy in the hope of receiving instructions which are neither necessary nor desirable.*" (*Liturgical Year*: 9th February)

That my criticisms of Mr. Davies and the doctrines which he propounds do not exceed the bounds of these canons I am confident. But it may still be objected that such ruthless tactics are appropriate only in the warfare against the Church's *main* enemies, who are currently so numerous and are spreading their pestilential errors without restraint. Should not our attacks be aimed against a Küng or a Schillebeeckx, a Rahner or even a Wojtyła, rather than against someone who is professedly anti-Modernist and who does his best to defend the Church even if he makes certain mistakes in doing so? To this I would answer that the writings of Michael Davies are vastly more pernicious in their effects than those of Küng, Schillebeeckx *et al.*, because, whereas the latter have been sowing the seed of error on receptive ground and leading astray from the Church those who "heap to themselves teachers, having itching ears, and will indeed turn away their hearing from the truth, but will be turned unto fables" (2 Timothy 4:3-4), it is Mr. Davies's role (however unwittingly) to lead astray those who have some genuine concern for the truth, and thereby "to deceive (if possible) even the elect." (Matthew 24:24) Why such writers can be more pernicious than more blatant purveyors of false doctrine emerges clearly from the words of Pope Leo XIII in his encyclical *Satis Cognitum* (1896):

> There can be *nothing more dangerous* than those heretics who admit *nearly the whole series of doctrine*, and yet *by one word*, as with a drop of poison, taint the real and simple Faith taught by Our Lord and handed down by Apostolic tradition. [Emphases added.]

In view of these authoritative pronouncements, I think that no objection can be made to the nature of my critique provided that I am correct in my estimation of the reality and gravity of Mr. Davies's departures from orthodoxy. The reader will be able to assess this only by reading my case.

And yet, perhaps there is one other objection that could be made – why did I not privately draw Mr. Davies's attention to his errors and invite him to retract them voluntarily rather than exposing him in public? To this I reply that I *have*, on a *number* of occasions, drawn various of Mr. Davies's errors to his attention, and have also seen copies of correspondence in which others have done the same. In each case the response has been identical; not only is no retraction made[5] but the objector is either fobbed off with specious excuses, or he is promised a reply which never comes, or his communication is simply ignored. This has been the experience not only of the present writer but also of many other critics in England, America, Australia and Canada. Despite all their remonstrances, Mr. Davies has gone so far as to make the following claim:

> To the best of my knowledge, no one has been able to point out a theological error in any of my books. (*The Angelus*, March 1984).

When he has read this *Evaluation*, the reader will be in a position to assess whether that boast is well-founded.

It is perhaps also worth forestalling at this stage the obvious objection that might be made in Mr. Davies's defence if he gives "the silent treatment" to the documented catalogue of extremely numerous theological errors on his part which comprise this *Evaluation* – namely, that there is simply so much of it that a busy man would not have time to assess all its points, let alone rectify the deficiencies they catalogue. However, to neutralise this difficulty, I have appended as the last chapter of this *Evaluation* an *Open Letter to Mr. Michael Davies* in which I draw attention to a handful of the most serious errors for which he has been responsible and call upon him either to substantiate his assertions from pre-Vatican II authorities (any approved theological authority would suffice) or to withdraw them. *I am happy to let the validity of my case be gauged by his response to this Open Letter.* If Mr. Davies is able to substantiate his

---

[5] Mr. Davies is certainly well aware of the grave duty of retracting theological error as publicly as one has stated it, because he has protested at the failure of others to comply with this duty, for instance in *The Remnant* for 31st October 1984.

positions from genuine Catholic authority[6] on the handful of questions covered in it, I am prepared to acknowledge that this would be sufficient evidence of the weakness of my case and that he would be under no obligation to devote any more time to answering the rest of the contents of this *Evaluation*. If, on the other hand, he is unable to refute my charges on these fundamental questions, I feel confident that readers will agree that Mr. Davies will then be bound not only to retract his position on these questions but also carefully to address all the remaining criticisms made, either answering them satisfactorily from genuine Catholic authorities or recognising their validity.

V

---

[6] Naturally to quote a post-Vatican II theological source would amount to begging the question, while a lightweight pre-Conciliar writer would also not constitute sufficient evidence. An approved theological manualist would generally be quite sufficient and should be available in his defence if I am wrong in accusing Mr. Davies of error on these fundamental points. The works of approved theological manualists are easily distinguished from less reliable works, because most of them carry Roman approbation; and even those which do not, make it clear that they are widely authorized as seminary textbooks.

CHAPTER ONE
DAVIES'S ATTITUDE TO AUTHORITY

"He that taketh authority to himself unjustly shall be hated." (Ecclesiasticus 20:8)

What is the Catholic Attitude to Authority?

Michael Davies has written a great deal. Where is the best place to begin an analysis of what he has written?

Of all the tests that can be applied to assess what confidence can justifiably be placed in an author who writes on matters pertaining to the holy Catholic religion, there can be no better, more certain or easier way to distinguish someone who writes in a Catholic way from a writer imbued with the erroneous attitudes of the age than by his attitude to authority. It is here that I shall start, therefore, and at once it can be said that this crucial test readily exposes Davies as a man whose whole attitude and character are at variance with the mind of the Catholic Church.

In order to apply the test fairly and accurately, it is necessary first to establish what the attitude of a Catholic to authority should be. This can appropriately be done by looking at some of the necessary characteristics of a good Catholic, seven of which, obviously relevant to our examination, I now offer:

(i) A faithful Catholic is always loath to give his personal opinion without the clear support of authority. "A true disciple of Christ," says Fr. Alban Butler in his *Lives of the Saints*, February 26, "by a sincere spirit of humility and distrust in himself, is, as it were, naturally inclined to submission to all authority appointed by God, in which he finds his peace, security and joy. This happy disposition of his soul is his secure fence against the illusions of self-sufficiency and blind pride, which easily betray men into the most fatal errors."

(ii) When authority is lacking and he is forced by real need to express his personal view, he always makes it clear that what he is saying is not founded on the voice of authority and he invariably supplies his justifying reasons for the view which he holds, stating his position to be only provisional and written subject to correction. "In all that I say in this book, I submit to what is taught by Our Mother, the Holy Roman Church; if there is anything in it contrary to this, it will be without my knowledge. Therefore, for the love of Our Lord, I beg the learned men who are to revise it to look at it very carefully and to amend any faults of this nature which there may be in it and the many others which it will have of other kinds. If there is anything good in it, let this be to the glory and honour of God and in the service of His most sacred Mother, our Patroness and Lady, whose habit, though all unworthily, I wear," protested St. Teresa of Avila in *The Way of Perfection*. (So fundamental and well-known was the distinction between authority and opinion in the Ages of Faith that it is familiarly referred to, right at the beginning of her "Prologue", by Chaucer's "Wife of Bath", though she makes no pretence to theological erudition.)

(iii) In using authorities, he quotes frequently from those sources recognized by the Church as the ultimate sources of truth, and invariably accepts what these sources say as final – the sources in question being Holy Scripture and Tradition as interpreted by the Church, the definitions of the Holy See, the definitions of councils, the consensus of the Fathers, the unanimous doctrine of approved theologians, etc. "Some enumerate more theological sources, and some fewer, but there are ten mentioned by

Melchior Cano, namely: (i) Sacred Scripture; (ii) tradition; (iii) the authority of the Church; (iv) general, or particular, councils, approved by the Roman Pontiff; (v) decisions of the Roman Pontiff speaking '*ex cathedra*'; (vi) the authority of the Holy Fathers; (vii) the authority of theologians; (viii) natural reason; (ix) the authority of the philosophers; (x) the authority of history. Of these, the first seven are theological sources properly so called, and intrinsically so: Scripture and Divine-Apostolic tradition as containing the deposit of revelation, and the other five as testifying some truth to be contained in Scripture or tradition. The last three listed are sources improperly so called, external and not necessary; for '*per se*' their object is purely natural." (Fr. J. Herrmann C.SS.R.: *Institutiones Theologiæ Dogmaticæ*, Prolegomena, n. 15)

(iv) He shows the greatest respect and deference to the other genuine authorities regarded as such by the Church, even though not regarded by the Church as infallible – the Fathers and Doctors speaking alone, the saints and popes expressing their private views, writings approved by high authority in the Church or by long tradition, etc. "They are not judges whose decision is authoritative and final, but they are witnesses who testify to the doctrine of the Church in their time, and their witness has been examined and found to be truthful." (Sylvester J. Hunter S.J.: *Outlines of Dogmatic Theology*, n. 101)

(v) He quotes what might be called the "semi-authorities" with respect, but always remembers that their weight, is ultimately no greater than whatever reasons they adduce to support their position, and that theological manualists, although generally reliable, are not only often too brief in their exposition of particular points to cover all the possibilities but sometimes make clear mistakes which may or may not have been picked up and corrected by other writers.

> The agreement of a number of scholastics [i.e. dogmatic theologians] on some doctrine, if some of note, though they be only a few, disagree, is of no greater weight than the reasons which they rely on. (The unknown author of the treatise *Institutiones de Locis Theologicis*, published with ecclesiastical approval at Rome, 1771, p. 565)

> Sometimes ... authors have not sufficiently examined the foundations of their opinions, and subsequent authors, blindly following their lead, have merely transcribed what their predecessors wrote. (Claudius Lacroix S.J.: *Theologia Moralis*, tom. I, lib. I, n. 149)

(vi) Rarely, if ever, will he quote in support of a theological position the view of a private individual who has not even been regarded by the Church as an approved author;[1] and should he quote such a one, he will invariably point out that the view expressed is not an authoritative one.

> "Quotations and testimonies of profane writers or authors should be used only with the utmost discernment; much more so the statements of heretics, apostates and infidels; but *never* should living persons be adduced as authorities. Faith and Christian moral integrity have no need of such supporters and defenders." (The decree *Ut Quæ* of the Sacred Consistorial Congregation, listing norms for preachers, 28th June 1917)[2]

(vii) In explaining why he has chosen to quote some writers rather than others, he will be cautious lest he give his readers a false impression of the weight carried by certain private individuals. "Opinions are like coins, the value of

---

[1] The great writers of pagan antiquity – Aristotle, Plato, Cicero, etc. – are in a special category since, although by no means Catholics and often wrong in their beliefs, their colossal wisdom is so universally recognized as to make them suitable quasi-authorities on many topics and they have often been quoted as such by the popes and saints.

[2] Evidently these principles are not universally binding except for preachers, but, no less evidently, those principles which the Church requires to be observed by her preachers are a trustworthy guide for the general practice of all those who address theological topics, whether orally or in writing.)

which is reckoned not by their number but by their weight and the amount of precious metal in them. Thus opinions are not commended by the number of authors who maintain them, but by the quality of reason, truth and prudence which support them. Otherwise the fools would ever be victorious, as there are more of them than of the wise." (Cardinal Sfondratus: *In Reg. Sacerd.*, lib. 1, n. 20 and lib. 2, n. 14§6)

The Consistent Practice of Michael Davies

There is not a single one of these tests which Davies does not fail miserably. But if one were to select the most glaringly anti-Catholic feature of his writing, this must surely be the way in which he (a) quotes writers, scholars and theologians of this century or the last who have little or no weight or authority at all as though they were to be regarded as oracles of greater value than the Extraordinary Magisterium, and (b) credits them with a wildly exaggerated status in order to brow-beat his readers into accepting what they say even though a Catholic has no greater obligation to defer to their opinions than he has to defer to the opinions of the man who delivers his milk or sweeps the street in which he lives.

Davies's reading is by no means as wide as it might appear from a casual glance over the bibliography to his books. He is familiar with the writings of certain scholars of recent times and has studied these fairly carefully, accumulating an index of valuable quotations which he uses and reuses whenever necessary. Other authorities he can look up as he needs them, but he is evidently not at all well read in the Fathers or the great theologians of the Middle Ages. Consequently, a glance through the index of his books reveals many quotations from his repertory of favoured writers and comparatively few from other much greater authorities. This technique, which gives an impression of much greater learning than he possesses, is backed up by very frequent appeals to the authority of certain friends and acquaintances of his who he assures us are eminent theologians who have told him such and such, or expressed this or that opinion, but whom, for reasons best known to himself, he refuses to name.

Let us now consider some examples of these un-Catholic attitudes to authority.

Instances of Hero Worship

One of the writers whom Davies most frequently quotes is Dietrich von Hildebrand, an American layman whose name would probably be mentioned in a footnote or appendix to a reasonably comprehensive history of twentieth century philosophy – a man who had no significant theological status and simply wrote his opinions on Vatican II and its revolution as a private individual just as Davies does and just as the present writer is doing. Here are some of the ways in which Davies introduces him:

(i) From *Pope Paul's New Mass*, p. 193:

The last word on the Children's Directory must go to Dietrich von Hildebrand, the most profound thinker in the American Church this century. This great theologian and philosopher would not have expressed himself so strongly without good reason ....

(ii) From *Pope Paul's New Mass*, p. 30:

Dietrich von Hildebrand has rightly condemned this anomaly ....

(iii) *An Open Lesson to a Bishop*, pp. 2-3:

This deplorable state of affairs ... has been well described by Dietrich von Hildebrand, almost certainly the most courageous, erudite, and respected layman in the English-speaking world since World War II. Professor von Hildebrand was second to no one in his loyalty to the Holy See, he was made a papal knight for his defence of *Humanæ Vitæ*,[3] but he would not allow human

---

[3] It is noteworthy that the sole evidence Davies offers for von Hildebrand's status is the fact that he was awarded a dignity by the very man – Montini – who is more responsible than anyone else for the ecclesiastical revolution of

respect to silence him when the Faith was endangered ... Professor von Hildebrand also expresses the belief that bishops who tolerate liturgical pluralism lose the right to claim obedience in disciplinary matters ... I would suggest that any bishop who reads these words ponder them carefully. The opinion of so great a philosopher and theologian is not to be set aside lightly.

(iv) From *Pope Paul's New Mass*, p. 590

Dietrich von Hildebrand was of the opinion that nothing should be forbidden unless it was evidently wrong or harmful.

Whether von Hildebrand had the grace to blush at Davies's virtual canonisation of him will not be known in this world, for it is now some years since his death, but it is hard to understand how any Catholic could take such words seriously.

Of the many objectionable features of this conjuring with von Hildebrand's name, the most serious is the fact that Davies is fraudulently pressuring his readers into thinking that he has independent and weighty authority for his assertions when in fact von Hildebrand can lend no weight to Davies's words because we have only Davies's own authority for the fact that von Hildebrand is worthy of credence with regard to the matters in question. But it must also be stressed that whether one holds the view that von Hildebrand was a pretentious buffoon or the greatest philosopher in history, the fact remains that he is *not* a theological authority and that Davies treats him with more deference than he treats Fathers, Saints or popes. No, this is not an exaggeration: the very last quotation taken from von Hildebrand in the above selection, for instance, is one in which he is cited in support of an opinion, which is such a commonplace that it needs no authority to defend it anyhow,[4] but, if any authority were to be cited for it, one would naturally choose an authority of great weight. In matters of *opinion* (the

---

which Davies himself complains.

[4] There can be no question, however, but that by attributing the principle to von Hildebrand Davies is *intending* to lend authority to what he says and expecting the authority to be considered conclusive.

word Davies uses), Catholics are not even obliged to agree with St. Thomas Aquinas, yet Davies quotes von Hildebrand as if his words could not but command his readers' assent. It is as if a political commentator had quoted as a conclusive argument against anarchism the fact that a little known politician had once at a cocktail party expressed the view that for a country to have one or two laws and maybe a small police force is not such a bad thing. The opinion is merely trite; the authority cited for it is not an authority at all and the status implicitly attributed to him by writing as if his say-so were both necessary and sufficient to prove the point is so disproportionate to the reality as to be laughable.

The Truth About Dietrich von Hildebrand

Let us take a moment to examine the phenomenon of Dietrich von Hildebrand (1889-1977) in the world of Catholic thought. This will enable us not only to appreciate the gravity of Davies's misrepresentation, but also to pinpoint one major intellectual malaise in the world of traditional Catholicism.

If we approach von Hildebrand via his life-story, while the man of action may appeal to us for his courageous intellectual opposition to Nazism, it is a disappointment to discover the extent to which he was influenced by unsound sources among those who were striving to reconcile Catholicism with the Revolution, with Socialism or with "progressive" social doctrines. Notable among these was Marc Sangnier, whose political theories were denounced and condemned by Pope St. Pius X in *Notre Charge Apostolique*. It is greatly to be feared that von Hildebrand's opposition to Hitler was in part due to social and political convictions which owed much more to his dubious friends than to the teaching of the encyclicals and which, for instance in the form of the "Catholic" contribution to France's *Front Populaire* in the 1930s, presented at least as great a threat to social justice and order as Nazism did.

Approaching von Hildebrand as a philosopher (his chosen profession), we also find von Hildebrand keeping disquieting company – in the "phenomenological" school to which we are indebted for rendering the intelligence of Karol Wojtyła irreparably impermeable to orthodox Catholic doctrine. The strange mercy by which we see von Hildebrand entering the Church (in 1914) apparently through the same door which his apostate friend Max Scheler had left it by, surely owes more to grace than to any connaturality between the Faith and the unhappy pseudo-philosophy of Husserl.

Where does von Hildebrand stand in the field of philosophical thought? To answer the question, let us divide into four groups those who have endeavoured in recent times to cross the Kantian Sea between the Island of Apprehension and the Continent of Reality. The first group is of those doomed forever to pace the near bank without ever getting closer to their destination, though often becoming highly expert on the flora and fauna of Apprehension Cliffs. The second is of those who have ventured a rash leap and fallen into the maelstrom infested by many man-eating sharks. The third comprises the thinkers who have paid the toll of humility at the Bridge of St. Thomas, obtaining the only true right of access. Finally comes the fourth group: those whom we saw yesterday still on the Island, sucking their fingers and gazing seaward and whom we discover today on the continent with no coherent explanation of how they got there.

Whereas his Catholic Faith ought to have pointed him towards the third group, we find that von Hildebrand in fact belongs to the fourth. His distinctive philosophy of "realistic phenomenology", offers an entirely illusory solution to a difficulty satisfactorily solved by the Angelic Doctor more than seven centuries ago.

There is no trace of any real contribution to *theology* by von Hildebrand unless we so class his lifelong attempts to justify the ethical teaching of the Church in terms of this false philosophy.

The malaise referred to above is relevant here. For von Hildebrand was one of the many whose adherence to the Church's direct teaching, at least in its main points, was too strong for him be dragged into the Modernist apostasy precipitated by Vatican II, but whose underlying philosophical thought was too far from the mind of the Church for him to accept the account given by the Church herself of the metaphysics underpinning her doctrines.

Von Hildebrand's epistemology and ontology were not merely weakened by accidental error, but entirely vitiated. Using experience and intuition to replace our knowledge of essences von Hildebrand raised on the Kantian quicksands an edifice of what he calls "values" in the stead of natural law and the common good. From this he attempted to safeguard the *conclusions* of Catholic teaching, especially in the field of ethics, by finding what are in reality entirely new reasons for them. In other words he attempted to reach the answers required by the Church, while entirely rejecting the reasoning on which the Church herself bases them. Thus, to take a single instance, we find him in the vanguard of those who reprobate fornication and contraception, *not* because they violate the natural law by frustrating the finality of a faculty, but because they fail in an alleged, but indefinable, duty of *self-giving*, allegedly discovered via experience and depending on the *heart* for its verification.

It is hardly astonishing that these forlorn voluntaristic attempts to "save the appearances" of Catholic doctrine and morality have massively failed to convince and indeed have merely exacerbated the tidal wave of unnatural practices within and without marriage which has engulfed the masses of those who mistakenly still think of themselves as Catholic. Nor is it astonishing to find them enthusiastically endorsed by von Hildebrand's intellectual fellow-traveller Karol Wojtyła.

What is much harder to explain is why so many traditional Catholics, instead of blaming anti-scholastic intellectuals like von Hildebrand for leaving the Church defenceless against her enemies by unilaterally abandoning the Thomistic arsenal, should instead uncritically hail them as allies and shower them with unmerited eulogies whenever they dissent from any of the consequences of the Revolution they made possible.

Nor is it reassuring to be informed *ad nauseam* that Pope Pius XII described von Hildebrand as a doctor of the Church when we discover that the only verifiable source for the claim is von Hildebrand himself![5]

Pride Before a Fall

Once the reader of Davies's writings has noticed that Davies, on his own authority, has invested Dietrich von Hildebrand with quasi-infallible status, he may well, if he is alert, be wondering how long it will be before our author is led by the nose into error by his chosen mentor. After all, when someone persuades himself with no sufficient reason that a private individual is a credible authority on matters of great moment simply because he *likes* what that person says, would it not be a wholly appropriate consummation of this process of self-deceit if master and disciple both foundered together, in accordance with Our Lord's dictum that "if the blind lead the blind, both fall into the pit"? (Matthew 15:14) Well, how long it took I have not bothered to check, but certainly it had happened by the time Davies laid his pamphlet *An Open Letter to a Bishop* before the public; for the passage I have just quoted from that work contains as clear an

---

[5] Gustavo Corção closes his *O Século do Nada* with a pitiless dissection of the essentially false perspective which vitiates the analysis of the crisis in the Church presented by von Hildebrand in his *Trojan Horse in the City of God*. The Brazilian intellectual explains why it is unacceptable to present the deviations of the "progressives" as reactions to allegedly comparable deviations, ossifications or archeologisms on the part of the "right" which allegedly dominated in the pre-conciliar period.

Readers interested in a more general analysis of von Hildebrand from the standpoint of sound philosophy are referred to Dr. Francisco J. Romero Carrasquillo's 2007 article "Von Hildebrand... What Do We Make of Him?"

example of grave theological error, affirmed by "the most profound thinker in the American Church this century," as one could want – or, rather, not want.

I refer to Professor von Hildebrand's belief, cited with approval by Davies, that "bishops who tolerate liturgical pluralism lose the right to claim obedience in disciplinary matters." The context in which it first appeared does not in any way temper this remarkable assertion. Since von Hildebrand evidently believed that the bishops in question did *not* forfeit their offices automatically, he appears to be declaring, in effect, that it can be permissible for a Catholic to disobey lawfully constituted authority, not only on a particular matter where the authority commands something intrinsically evil, but always, habitually and invariably, purely on the basis of some particular offence which the bishop has committed on one occasion. And this can only be appropriately described as a travesty of Catholic doctrine.

As has already been pointed out, it is correct Catholic doctrine that bishops, like all other clerics, forfeit their offices automatically, and are therefore no longer entitled to obedience, if they fall into heresy or into schism;[6] but the doctrine that the same applies to bishops who "tolerate liturgical pluralism," i.e. fail to condemn liturgical abuses, is an astonishing one. It seems impossible to see how a bishop could "lose the right to claim obedience in disciplinary matters" without losing his office. The only basis I can think of for the notion is the teaching of Wycliffe and Hus that clerics lose their offices for any mortal sin whatsoever – a doctrine which the Church has twice solemnly condemned. (Dz. 595 and 656.) If this is not what von Hildebrand had in mind, I cannot see how Davies's citation of his words admits of any more orthodox interpretation.

---

[6] Some Catholic authorities believe that a pure *schismatic* does not necessarily lose his offices automatically, but all agree that public *heretics* do.

More Heroes

Von Hildebrand is not, however, the only writer whom Davies has elevated to a position of authority vastly beyond what can reasonably be claimed for anyone who is neither a pope nor a canonised saint. I draw attention to some further instances.

In *Pope Paul's New Mass*, on p. 32, Davies introduces as an authority the late Mr. Douglas Woodruff, who was, until 1967, editor of *The Tablet*, which was the "high-brow" English Catholic weekly from its foundation in the 1840s until it degenerated during the 1970s into the organ of the tiny number of intellectual members of the clique of rabid liberals. Here is how Davies introduces him: "Douglas Woodruff, probably England's most erudite layman ..." The reader should beware of adopting this opinion as his own, for even Davies appeared to have abandoned it between writing that section of *Pope Paul's New Mass* and writing his pamphlet, *An Open Lesson to a Bishop*; since on p. 13 of the latter Mr. Woodruff has been demoted to only " ...possibly England's most erudite layman ..." But in either case Davies is taking upon himself a judgement which few in even the most exalted academic circles would make so confidently – a judgement which necessarily presupposes considerable erudition in the person making it, unless he quotes some authority to back it up, which Davies certainly does not. It is another example of brow-beating the reader in order to bolster up his case in a way that is wholly artificial.

Dom David Knowles, the Benedictine monk who incurred excommunication for abandoning his cloister at Downside without permission in the 1930s and eventually came to occupy the Chair of Mediæval History at Cambridge University,[7] seems to have been a rival to Woodruff's erudition – on p. 320 of *Pope Paul's New Mass* he is described as, "Fr. David Knowles,

---

[7] See the biography of Knowles entitled *David Knowles: a Memoir* by Dom Adrian Morey, 1979.

probably England's greatest Catholic scholar until his death in 1974 ...".

On p. 159 of *Pope John's Council,* Rudolph Graber, named bishop of Regensburg in 1962, receives Davies's highest commendation. As the brow-beating is stepped up, the prudent reader ought to ask himself with even greater urgency such questions as whether he thinks it might be just possible that Davies's fulsome praises are really justified in respect of a bishop who has complicity with what Davies calls "the liturgical revolution" or whether the praises are not thrown in to bolster the credibility of a man whose slim volume Davies quotes from nine times in this one book and who might otherwise be looked at askance by most traditional Catholics. Here, without further comment, is some of what Davies deems it appropriate to write about a bishop cheerfully presiding over a diocese of the Conciliar Church in which, as in other post-Vatican II dioceses, Almighty God is freely and extravagantly insulted in what purports to be Catholic worship and catechesis:

> ... the Church on the road to atheism? That this is indeed the case is the thesis of a book by Dr. Rudolph Graber, consecrated Bishop of Regensburg by Pope John XXIII in 1962. (The fact that this book has been written by a German bishop is, like the presence of theologians of irreproachable orthodoxy among the *periti* [theological experts], a warning against making sweeping generalizations.) Bishop Graber is one of the outstanding theologians in the German episcopate and his stature is such that the German government wished to honour him with its Order of Merit in 1974. He declined to receive any honour from a government which had approved such anti-Christian abortion laws. His book provides one of the very rare instances to which the overworked adjective 'sensational' could be applied with perfect accuracy.

Readers of Graber's rather humdrum little booklet will find that, apart form one or two occasional shafts of light shed on the conspiratorial action against the Church – which, however, could have been found in a number of other places better set out and better substantiated – it is no more worthy of Davies's eulogy than is its author, and of no more value than one would expect of a book intended to expose the conspiracy against the Church which has been written by someone who is – albeit let us hope unconsciously – carrying out the very work which the conspirators have imposed on him in order to destroy the Church!

Again, on p. 67 of the same work, a footnote informs us that "Philip Hughes' three-volume work, *The Reformation in England* and Francis Clark's *Eucharistic Sacrifice and the Reformation* are examples of scholarship of the highest possible level." Note: not just scholarship of a very high level, but scholarship of *the highest possible level*. The technique is always the same. Davies selects in support of his views writers with no official status and whose reliability is, generally speaking, open to debate, and compels his readers to assent to their judgements by his blusteringly exaggerated account of their credentials.

Newmanolatry

Other writers whom Davies "canonizes" include, not surprisingly, his greatest hero, Cardinal Newman. Despite the widespread belief that Newman was a great and orthodox Catholic thinker of the 19th century, nothing could be further from the truth. It may come as a surprise to some readers – but certainly will not do so to all – to learn that Newman was in fact a subversive, a defender of multiple heresies, and has rightly been hailed by Conciliar authors as the "father" of Vatican II; yet such is the case. Want of space precludes expansion on this until a later chapter, but readers will doubtless be satisfied in principle by one clear example of a grave theological error championed by Newman but condemned by the Magisterium and this is provided by the specific condemnation of one of Newman's most distinctive views by Pope St. Pius X in the anti-Modernist Syllabus *Lamentabili Sane* (Proposition 25).[8] Those who wish to study the subject of Newman, his doctrines and his pernicious influence in greater depth, are referred to Richard Sartino's 50-page study entitled *Another Look at John Henry Cardinal Newman* which contains a penetrating assessment, in the light of orthodox Catholic theology, of Newman's grosser falsifications of the Catholic Faith.

On p. 596 of *Pope Paul's New Mass*, Davies writes: "Cardinal Newman stresses that if a man is sincerely convinced that 'what his superior commands is displeasing to God, he is not bound to obey.'" It seems to have eluded him that, whether or not the opinion which he expresses is correct, the fact that Cardinal Newman once stressed it is wholly beside the point. If Davies thinks that the opinion which he is defending needs some support, his duty is to supply *genuine* authority – an extract from St. Thomas would surely have been appropriate. But in Davies's perverse mind Cardinal Newman seems to carry greater weight than St. Thomas![9] Once again, this forces Davies to blind

---

[8] In *The Grammar of Assent*, p. 411, Newman writes as follows:
> It is pleasant ... to follow a theological writer such as Amort who has dedicated to the great pope, Benedict XIV, what he calls 'a new, modest and easy way of demonstrating the Catholic Religion.' ... He adopts the argument merely of the greater probability; I prefer to rely on that of an accumulation of various probabilities; but we both hold (that is, I hold with him), that from probabilities we may construct legitimate proof, sufficient for certitude.

St. Pius X condemned this doctrine in the following, summarized, but unmistakably identical form:
> "The assent of faith is ultimately based on an accumulation of probabilities." (*Assensus fidei ultimo innititur in congerie probabilitatum.*)

Newman confirms his adhesion to this doctrine by restating it in slightly different form but still with definite verbal echoes, in the *Apologia Pro Vita Sua*, p. 199 of Longman's 1877 edition, and on p. 8 of his *Two Essays on Biblical and Ecclesiastical Miracles*, 1890.

[9] Doubtless Davies would deny this if taxed with it; and doubtless he *will* deny it when he reads these words. But no one acquainted with much of his writing can doubt that it is true in practice. To give just one classic example of his completely topsy-turvy attitude to the relative weight carried by various writers, on p. 18 of his *Divine Constitution*, he writes: "Fr. R.L.

himself to Newman's obvious defects – in the very extract from which he quotes from Newman, the controversial convert writes: "Certainly ... I shall drink – to the pope, if you please, still, to Conscience first, and to the pope afterwards." A less Catholic sentiment could hardly be imagined. its natural effect will be to encourage the reader to trust his own instinctive "sense of direction" as of greater value than map, compass or guide; it amounts to honouring the lifeboat before the captain! A Catholic stares in disbelief at such a sentiment uttered as if it were orthodox, debating whether its author could seriously have been ignorant of the fact that the pope, in settling a moral dilemma, is a Divinely appointed judge, exercising Divine authority, with Divine guidance, whereas the conscience of an individual is no more than a reasoned judgement of a fallible, non-authoritative, unassisted human mind as to the moral implications of a situation. All in all, the most convincing explanation of Newman's absurd toast seems to be that he was so theologically illiterate – as Cardinal Lépicier states of him in slightly milder terms in his *De Stabilitate* ... (p. 187) – as to think that "conscience" was a faculty favoured by special Divine enlightenment of a kind denied to an external authority such as the pope. Whatever the nature of his misapprehension, it is quite evident that Davies enthusiastically holds the same error – and Chapters 11 and 12 will examine how, by trusting Cardinal Newman[10] and his infallible "conscience" in preference to the

---

Bruckberger O.P. has warned us that the Church may one day be reduced to a handful of inflexible Catholics." Thus, in order to reinforce a truth emphatically taught by men such as St. Athanasius, we are referred *not* to any of the countless *genuine* authorities available, but to a still living French Dominican journalist who, as is related in his autobiography, no longer functions as a priest and has for many years co-habited with a series of mistresses!

[10] Newman's doctrine of the primacy of conscience over the voice of ecclesiastical authority was attacked and refuted by Dr. W.G. Ward in the *Dublin Review* for January 1876.

popes and their teachings, Davies has been led by the nose into two heresies.

More Newmanolatry occurs on p. 370 of the same book. Here Davies writes: "Some Catholic apologists have attempted to prove that Liberius neither confirmed the excommunication of Athanasius nor subscribed to one of the formulæ of Sirmium. But Cardinal Newman has no doubt that the fall of Liberius is an historical fact." We shall be analysing the alleged fall of Pope Liberius at length in Chapter 10 of this *Evaluation,* but the point of quoting this extract here is to draw attention once again to the fact that, on a matter which is fiercely disputed among Catholic authorities, Davies evidently regards the word of Cardinal Newman as definitive. And what is the value of Newman's opinion? It is entirely dependent upon the degree of his historical learning, the soundness of his judgement and his honesty, just as is the opinion of any other historian on this topic; and his learning, sound judgement and honesty would have to be proved, either by internal evidence or by reference to statements made by unquestionably competent Catholic judges, before one would even think of using him as Davies does.

However Davies goes even further than this. Indeed he seems to go so far as to regard Newman as an authority worth heeding considerably before his (Newman's) reception into the Catholic Church, for under the title *Newman Against the Liberals* he edited a selection of Newman's sermons delivered while Newman was still an Anglican.

The Question of Credibility

It has already been pointed out that the principal objection to Davies's use of these nonentities or suspected subversives as if they were infallible authorities – rather than because they happen to phrase an already proved truth particularly well, which as mentioned earlier, may be perfectly proper – is not the fact that they are often, in reality, of no great status at all, and indeed not infrequently of doubtful orthodoxy, but simply the fact that, even if they were all the greatest scholars in their respective fields of research, their word would still carry little real weight. This is because popes, Fathers, Doctors and saints are officially recognized as trustworthy representatives of authentic Catholic doctrine by the Church, whereas theologians – apart from those specifically commended by the Holy See – do not have such recognition except to the extent that a particular bishop may have appointed them to a theological office or a particular diocesan censor may have approved their works for publication.

It is now necessary to come back to this characteristic of Davies, because it is not irrelevant to inquire whether he is actually sincere – whether he really believes he is telling the truth – in the extravagant superlatives with which he adorns every mention of his chosen "authorities".

Certainly there are places where it is particularly difficult to believe that he is. On p. 628 of *Pope Paul's New Mass*, for instance, he advises his readers that "the four-volume series *Moral and Pastoral Theology* by H. Davis S.J. is one of the best standard manuals on this subject [i.e. sacramental theology]." And, quite simply, this is blatantly false. Davis's *Moral and Pastoral Theology* is, of all the works on moral theology published prior to the Second Vatican Council by purportedly Catholic writers which were not censured by the Church, probably the *worst*. So objectionable is it that even a fairly liberal seminary such as the Beda College in Rome (the English college for late vocations) forbade seminarians to read it. There are literally hundreds of manuals of moral theology of higher status, the vast majority being in Latin, and it seems quite evident that the real reason that Davies chose to cite this one, rather than, for example, that of St. Alphonsus, which obviously carries the greatest weight, is that it is one of comparatively few comprehensive works of moral theology written in English and of these, though easily the worst,[11] it does happen to be the most readily obtainable in England. The assertion that it is "one of the best standard manuals" is accounted for simply by the fact that Davies cannot bring himself to state honestly that he is merely quoting from *a* manual or *a* theologian, but has to insist that the manual or theologian in question is the best one available whether or not this has any foundation in reality.

Karl Rahner S.J. – an Authority?

The examples so far given are bad enough, but it should not be thought that Davies is not capable of quoting *much* more unlikely "authorities" than even these. One particularly striking example is Karl Rahner S.J. For those not already aware of it, it should be pointed out that probably the four writers who carry the greatest responsibility for having prepared the ground for, and brought about the realization of, the collapse of the institutional Catholic Church in the last three decades – and who are notorious in traditional Catholic circles for having done so – have been M. Jacques Maritain[12] and the priests Hans Küng, Pierre Teilhard de Chardin S.J., and Karl Rahner S.J.[13] Rahner studied under Heidegger, a lapsed Catholic, who was one of the early proponents of the heretical pseudo-philosophy of "existentialism" and eventually became the expositor of a weird form of paganism, lying somewhere between atheism and pantheism. The following quotations, which indicate the extent of Rahner's subversive influence, are taken from *The Church Learned and the Revolt of the Scholars* by Philip Trower, a work offering a thorough analysis of the causes and effects of the Vatican II revolution in the world of Catholic learning,[14] though

---

[11] Examples of much better manuals on moral theology in English, both quite modern, are Jone's *Moral Theology* and McHugh and Callan's *Moral Theology*.

[12] On logic and philosophy Maritain sometimes wrote soundly, but none of the four is ever trustworthy on theology.

[13] Perhaps Fr. John Courtney Murray S.J. (1904-1967) should have been included too.

[14] This quotation from Philip Trower furnishes a convenient opportunity to

it suffers from the defect that its author, despite being considerably more aware than most of the extent of the corruption of authentic Catholic doctrine even prior to the Council, has allowed himself to be deceived by the authorities of the Conciliar Church in their claim to be the hierarchy of the Catholic Church.

> Such is the system of ideas, or view of life ... which the German theologian Fr. Karl Rahner and his followers have been trying to push and haul into place so that it can be made the philosophical foundation for the teaching and preaching of the Catholic faith and the training of Catholic priests. It is to replace not only the philosophy of St. Thomas but all the natural categories of philosophic thought ... Fr. Rahner's particular brand of existentialism is called 'transcendental Thomism'. What they are doing is shifting the faith from a philosophical foundation of concrete onto a bed of sand and silt.
>
> Fr. Rahner ... was one of the principal theologians whose ideas were censured by Pius XII in *Humani Generis* ... He has been doing for existentialism what Père Teilhard has done for evolutionary progress religion. It would be difficult to say which of these two men is responsible for the most damage. It is the introduction of existentialist terminology and categories of thought which has enabled the theological revolutionaries to make it seem as if all Catholic doctrine were dissolving in a mist of doubt, and to persuade people that their innovations are 'developments of doctrine' instead of the heresies they actually are ...

---

illustrate and underline the difference between legitimate and illegitimate use of sources which are not specifically approved by the Church. The reason why it is appropriate to quote Trower is twofold: (a) I am not in fact using him as an *authority*, i.e. to corroborate a disputed assertion concerning Rahner and co., but simply to *voice* facts which can be confirmed from countless sources and are not indeed seriously contested even by the liberals; and (b) in summarizing Trower's credentials I have drawn attention to the bad as well as the good and made it clear that my assessment of him is a personal one. This is not the same as the fraudulent technique of selecting a dubious "authority" to *confirm the accuracy* of a dubious assertion and then guaranteeing the status of the "authority", not by any objective gauge, but simply by one's own rhetoric.

Fr. Rahner ... is more than the champion of a doubtful system of philosophy. Using existentialism as his base, he has played an active role in the destruction of Catholic belief, functioning as the revolution's heavy artillery. He moves slowly forward, keeping well behind the lines, and fires over the heads of the advancing troops (Fathers Küng, Schillebeeckx, Häring, Schoonenberg *et al.*) so as to weaken in advance the dogmatic positions they are about to assault. He rarely himself attacks a doctrine directly. His method is to sow doubts in the mind about it by putting a question .... Having put the question he moves cumbrously round it, peers at it as if it presented insoluble difficulties, then stands back, sucks his forefinger and wonders. At last, when he has given the impression that the answer must be 'yes' and that the Church will have to accept whichever of these heterodox opinions he is pushing, he retreats behind a smoke screen of qualifications and affirmations of orthodoxy, leaving the questions still hanging in the air, and the doubts fixed like barbs in his readers' minds.

This is the man that Davies considers suitable to quote as a Catholic theologian without giving his readers the smallest warning or indication that he is anything other than a theologian of the first rank in orthodoxy and erudition.

Most readers will have appreciated even from that short extract that Trower is a penetrating scholar and that, despite being partially deceived by the imposture of the Conciliar Church, he is nonetheless a capable expositor of his subject. To appreciate fully the brilliance of his analysis, however, the reader would have to read for himself some of Rahner's works – a course from which I would dissuade him, since, if the *Index of Forbidden Books* were still kept up to date, Rahner's name would certainly figure prominently on it. Let us look at some examples of Davies's attitude to Rahner.

In *Pope Paul's New Mass*, p. 597, he writes: "The subtitle appears on p. 394 of Karl Rahner's book *Studies in Modern Theology* which was published in English in 1965. Fr. Rahner makes an important distinction between what is legally valid and what is morally licit." Again, on p. 599 of the same work Davies says: "Fr. Rahner also uses a similar example to illustrate a morally illicit papal act," and at the bottom of the next page he goes so far as to put him on a par with the great Jesuit Suarez, the Church's "*Doctor Eximius*".[15]

Rahner is also favoured with three references in the index to *Apologia Pro Marcel Lefebvre* Volume I, and four in the index to *Pope John's Council*, while on p. 47 of the latter work, Davies gives his only indication that Rahner may not quite be suitable material for canonisation, when he writes, with reference to a public manifesto signed by a number of priests of the Conciliar Church protesting against *Humanæ Vitæ*:

> It is of great significance that among the most prominent agitators against *Humanæ Vitæ* were some of the most prominent *periti* [theological experts] of Vatican II. It is sad to note that Karl Rahner himself is included in their number. It is astonishing to find a theologian of his calibre, one who could not normally be classified with such men as Hans Küng or Gregory Baum, following their example and informing Catholics that they are not being disobedient if they ignore a Sovereign Pontiff when he reiterates a point of consistently taught Catholic moral teaching....

Notice that even when Davies is criticising Rahner he does everything in his power to palliate his crimes and insists on representing Rahner's grossly un-Catholic position that a Catholic – or, indeed, anyone else – may be entitled to use artificial contraception as an astonishing lapse in an otherwise admirable theologian, rather than a typical piece of subversion and immorality from one of the Church's more prominent enemies, which, as the quotation from Trower points out and illustrates, is the truth of the matter. Although it is at first bewildering to see a "traditionalist" writer doing his best to

---

[15] He does this by referring to "the example of papal interference with liturgical custom, chosen by Fathers Rahner and Suarez" as though these two Jesuits were of equal weight and the fact that an example had been chosen by Fr. Suarez was no more significant than that Fr. Rahner selected the same example.

whitewash and even glorify a notorious liberal subversive, an obvious explanation of this anomaly is available. Davies, it seems, was at one stage, if not an out-and-out progressive, at least a middle-of-the-roader with distinct leanings in favour of some of the new liturgical and theological initiatives of the 1960s.[16] Presumably it was during this period that Davies read Rahner, and, being not yet alerted to the subversive activities of Rahner and his school, admitted him into his gallery of heroes. When it became apparent to everyone else that Rahner had simply been yet another forerunner of the Revolution, Davies was evidently either too stubborn or too proud to admit his error and change his position.

More Unlikely Theological Sources

Even less explicable is Davies's consistent use of the malodorous *New Catholic Encyclopædia* (1967) as a source throughout his deplorable pamphlet entitled *The True Voice of Tradition*. As many readers will already be aware, the original *Catholic Encyclopædia*, published in 1913, was – notwithstanding some unmistakable and serious blemishes such as are inevitable in a work compiled by a large number of contributors – a remarkable and generally trustworthy source of Catholic scholarship. In 1967, however, a *New Catholic Encyclopædia* was published to incorporate the fruits of twentieth-century studies and to furnish a reference work comparable in scope to its predecessor but brought up to date and into line with the developments of Vatican II. Needless to say, in common with all similar revisions, the new version was stuffed with heresy and subversion and, as a generality, has been prudently avoided by traditional Catholic writers, who are

---

[16] Davies makes it clear on p. 91 of *Pope Paul's New Mass* that he was completely taken in by the first stage of the post-Conciliar liturgical renewal and was so enthusiastic in his support for the changes that he even used to leave his own parish to attend "Mass" in a neighbouring parish which was more up-to-date in introducing liturgical innovations.

usually sufficiently alert to realise that any book on theological subjects published in the 1960s with the word "new" in the title will inevitably repay its readers by subtly – or not so subtly – attacking and undermining their faith at every opportunity. Nor indeed does Davies seem to have been unaware of this commonplace, for in his book *Pope Paul's New Mass* it is the 1913 *Catholic Encyclopædia* which he cites; and even in the bibliography to his *The True Voice of Tradition*, in addition to listing the *New Catholic Encyclopædia* on which he draws throughout that pamphlet, he goes out of his way to mention also the 1913 *Catholic Encyclopædia*, despite the fact that nowhere in the pamphlet does he quote from it and that it does not appear to have contributed in any way to assisting his efforts.

To understand why this should be, one needs to know that the pamphlet in question concerns the historical episode of Pope Liberius and St. Athanasius. In an endeavour to establish a parallel between that episode and the present condition of the Church, Davies alleges that Pope Liberius subscribed to false doctrine and excommunicated St. Athanasius, who, notwithstanding, stood firm and was eventually canonized while Liberius had to recant and died in ignominy.

And the straightforward truth about this story which Davies has widely popularised among traditional Catholics is that it is historically unfounded. The truth is that Pope Liberius, like Athanasius, remained orthodox (and was therefore sent into exile by the emperor), never condemned Athanasius, never recanted anything, died gloriously, and was officially recognized as a saint. The rumours impugning his orthodoxy originated among the Arians and Semi-Arians, who, assisted by the schismatic Luciferians, so far succeeded in poisoning the wells of history that even some orthodox Catholic historians, well-intentioned towards the papacy, were deceived in the period just after the Reformation when scholarly historiography of the early Christian era was in its infancy. But it was not long before the truth was brought to light and Liberius was vindicated. And after that the ancient calumnies were no longer peddled by any reputable Catholic historians, and became almost exclusively the preserve of the Church's enemies, whether Protestants or lukewarm Catholics disaffected towards the Holy See, both of whom, of course, had and have a vested interest in maintaining the hoax.

All these facts are copiously demonstrated in Chapter 10 of this *Evaluation* and no attempt is made to duplicate at this point the evidence that will be found there. Suffice it for now to say that the article in the 1913 *Catholic Encyclopædia* by Dom John Chapman comes down in favour of Liberius's orthodoxy and, although perhaps giving more credence than is necessary to some of the lesser crimes imputed to Liberius, on balance undoubtedly opposes the version of history which Davies in his pamphlet sets down as if it were the only one admitted. By contrast, it will come as no surprise to anyone to learn that the updated, post-Vatican II *New Catholic Encyclopædia* dug up and recycled all the old anti-Liberian calumnies.

And, as already indicated, Davies selected the latter as the source for his pamphlet, and deliberately suppressed the contrary view of the much sounder 1913 encyclopædia, unless, of course, he included the 1913 *Catholic Encyclopædia* in his bibliography without ever having read what it had to say on the subject. What is quite certain is that Davies's decision to side with the enemies of the Church (pre-Vatican II Protestants or Gallicans and post-Vatican II liberals) on this subject against the vast mass of solid, orthodox Catholic scholarship cannot have been founded upon either a balanced weighing of the credibility of the rival schools or upon an independent assessment of the evidence. It can only have been due to his having already decided, before he assessed the evidence, what side he *needed* to take in order to present a convincing historical parallel in favour of Archbishop Lefebvre's position and against the position of those who claim that the Holy See is vacant. And finding that in order to maintain this version of history he would have to align himself with the Church's enemies, misrepresent her defenders and rely upon utterly untrustworthy source material in preference to readily available reliable sources, he cheerfully did precisely that.

The Cult of Anonymity

This accumulation of fraudulent pseudo-authorities, however, is nothing compared with a practice of Davies's which is so unscholarly and shows such contempt for his readers that it is amazing that he has dared to "try it on" to the extent that he has. This is the practice of quoting, as authorities in support of whatever position he is maintaining, "theologians" *whom he refuses to name*, but who are, he insists, of such high repute that what they say must be accepted. Those who follow Davies's articles or have read his books will have come across countless instances of this dishonest technique, but in order to make this *Evaluation* self-contained, a few examples will now be quoted:

(i) "One of Britain's most respected theologians provided me with the following comment on this explanation ...." ("The ICEL Betrayal", *The Angelus,* August 1980)

(ii) "I have consulted an outstanding traditionalist theologian on this point, a professor of theology and author of twelve books, who says only the Tridentine Mass." (*The Angelus*, December 1984)

(iii) " ... The typescript was vetted by a number of well-qualified priests who assured me that it is free from any doctrinal or moral error." (*Pope John's Council*, p. xv)

(iv) "I am much indebted to the theologian who has examined the text with great care and assured me that it contains no error." (*Pope Paul's New Mass*, p. xxvi)

(v) "Competent theologians have presented me with reasons which I found so convincing that they left me with no alternative but to conclude that I must accept the new Ordination rite ...." (*The Roman Catholic*, 1981)

(vi) "The theologians who have examined it [the form of the new Ordination rite] at my request have confirmed a definite [but *not* invalidating – J.S.D.] deficiency ...." (*The Roman Catholic*, 1981)

(vii) "The old Code of Canon Law does not state this specifically, but an eminent theologian has assured me that this was the case in practice." (*The Divine Constitution and Indefectibility of the Church*, p. 24, supplement to *Approaches*, N° 93)

(viii) "In compiling what follows in this article, I consulted the three theologians who helped with *The Order of Melchisedech* [named in the introduction to *that* book as van der Ploeg, Lawson and Flanagan – one of whom said the Novus Ordo till his death and the other two of whom have been happy to attend it and approve its being said and attended by others – J.S.D.], a canonist [almost certainly the Rev. Dr. Thomas Glover, the then professor of Canon Law at Écône who was ordained in the new rite – J.S.D.], a fourth theologian who is a scholar of world repute on the subject of sacramental theology [any guesses?], and a number of other priests .... I also obtained the advice of a leading authority on Christian Latin [Davies told the present writer during a telephone conversation in 1983 that the scholar in question is Dr. Christine Mohrmann who had been a professor at the universities of Nijmegen and Amsterdam]." (*The Roman Catholic*, 1981)

(ix) "I have consulted well qualified priests as to the orthodoxy of your 'different paths to the top of the mountain' analogy." (*The Remnant*, 15th November 1987)

The reason that writers on complex and controversial subjects generally cite authorities is to ensure that sceptical readers do not have to rely on the author's word, but instead can see that his view is reinforced by the opinion of those most competent in the relevant field. Naturally, this purpose of using authorities is frustrated by the refusal to name the authorities and give their credentials. In effect, those who doubt that Michael Davies can be relied upon to give a correct statement of Catholic doctrine on, say, sacramental theology, are being told that their doubts ought to be dispelled by the fact that theologians agree with him – theologians of high repute. *But* the man who hand-picks the theologians, and guarantees that they *are* of high repute and *do* agree with him, is Michael Davies himself. So there is a vicious circle by which the word of Michael Davies is reinforced by the word of Michael Davies. This should not be taken to imply that Davies actually invents the "theologians" who support his more controversial positions, but what he certainly *does* is to judge by his own standards which theologians are "reputable" and which are not. And, of course, a theologian who disagreed with whatever position he was maintaining would automatically become disreputable. Nor is this mere conjecture, since, as is shown in the section of his article dealing with the questions of the alleged lapse into heresy of Pope St. Liberius and his alleged excommunication of St. Athanasius, Davies has been prepared to disregard some of the weightiest Catholic authorities that there are rather than admit any degree of doubt in one of the opinions which he has espoused, despite the fact that it is demonstrably[17] false.

It is worth mentioning in passing that, whenever the identity of Davies's anonymous sources comes to light, they generally turn out to be *very* unimpressive individuals. In his *Random Thoughts* column in *The Angelus* for March 1984, Davies revealed that "Monsignor Flanagan was one of a number of theologians who have helped me with my books." The late Mgr. Philip Flanagan (who died on 22nd November 1983) was

---

[17] Although based on a historical evidence which, in disputed matters, rarely generates certitude of the same kind as a mathematical proof, I do not think that the adjective I use is too strong a description of the force of evidence in favour of the innocence of St. Liberius of the charges made against him. Readers will be able to make their own assessment when they come to Chapter 10.

certainly a learned priest and had been rector of a seminary, but surely Davies's readers are entitled to be informed that he had no objections to the Novus Ordo, which he was happy to use, that he was a functioning parish priest of the Conciliar Church, that he wrote a catechism based on texts from Vatican II, and that he did not consider himself to be a traditionalist.

When asked directly, on the telephone, to name one of the theologians who advised him, Davies told the present writer that one of the main ones was Fr. William Lawson S.J. A few days later this writer's colleague Mr. N.M. Gwynne had occasion to telephone Fr. Lawson about something else and asked him if he was one of the theologians cited anonymously by Davies. Fr. Lawson replied that Davies did occasionally *consult* him, but never asked permission to *quote* him as a theologian, and that he would not have given it as he did not consider himself a theologian at all! Hence Davies's anonymous but *highly trustworthy* theological sources turn out to consist of persons considerably compromised with the Conciliar Church, persons with an axe to grind on the very subjects concerning which they are quoted as objective, ignoramuses, self-avowed non-theologians, and, to cap it all, do not even know that he is quoting them!

Catholic Theologians – An Extinct Breed?

What is quite certain is that there are no living, traditionalist theologians who are remotely comparable in erudition with the great theologians of the past. It goes without saying that no one living can compare with the early Fathers, the great popes and Doctors, St. Thomas Aquinas, St. Alphonsus Liguori, etc., of course; but even the nineteenth century and the early part of our own have been able to boast truly great theologians of a kind now wholly extinct – Cardinal Franzelin, Cardinal Lépicier, Cardinal Billot, Fr. Perrone, Fr. Ballerini, Fr. de la Taille, Fr. Scheeben, and countless others. Today, however, as just mentioned, there is no one – *no one* – whose theological learning is remotely comparable with that of any of these great figures of the recent past; and it follows from this that Davies's choice of living authorities to support his position on especially controverted points unmistakably implies that he is unable to find authority for what he is maintaining among the great writers of the past who would truly be worthy of his readers' esteem.

But whoever these theologians – so called – may be, *why* is it that Davies breaks two thousand years of tradition in the handling of controversial issues and will not tell us their identity?

Of course, at least part of the reason may simply be that he has a predilection for citing anonymous sources; and, quite seriously, there *is* some evidence of that, for he not infrequently refuses to give names without any apparent reason, even though this on occasion has the effect of destroying the value, as evidence, of whatever information he is recording since it is impossible to confirm it. This feature of his writing is so extraordinary and so contrary to the rules of all scholarship, both theological and secular, and to plain common sense[18] that it is perhaps as well to give an example or two of it. On p. 643 of *Pope Paul's New Mass*, for instance, he writes:

> I had a letter from another priest who says that in his diocese the 'Abbey X has been concelebrating (225 priests a day) with invalid matter (milk and honey substituted for the water) for about four years.'

Now why are we not privileged to be told the identity of the Abbey in question? Is it that Davies does not wish to embarrass

---

[18] A reviewer writing in the *American Quarterly Review*, Vol. IV (1879) p. 381, in criticism of a controversial pamphlet by the canonist Dr. S.B. Smith in which Smith employed similar tactics to Davies's, wrote as follows:
> By the way, the reverend author should not have been allowed to allege anonymous authority so freely in his pamphlet. We are treated to long extracts from great theologians, distinguished canonists, learned friends, all anonymous, not one of them having either name or habitat. *Such testimony is worthless and must be ruled out of court.* (Emphasis added.)

the diocesan bishop or the abbot? It can scarcely be that he thinks that his account is of the same value as it would have been if he had included the Abbey's name.

Again, on p. 631 of the same work he writes:

> In April 1980, I mentioned to the Cardinal Prefect of a Roman Congregation that, as in some dioceses of the United States of America invalid matter is being used for the Sacrament of the Eucharist, many American Catholics are worshipping not God the Son but bread. 'Not bread,' he corrected me, 'cake. What they are using is cake.'

If one were to quote that passage to a member of the Conciliar Church as evidence against his religious position, one would obviously meet the retort, "How do I know it's true?" Such a question would be perfectly reasonable and would leave one without an available reply. For as things stand, the only basis upon which we can possibly know that Davies's allegation is true is the fact that he has made it,[19] whereas if he had condescended to tell us the name of the cardinal in question and the name of his Congregation, we should be able to point out (a) that no writer in his senses would have invented the episode lest the cardinal in question deny the facts, and (b) that, if the account were not true, the cardinal would indeed almost

---

[19] The validity of this objection is quite independent of any question marks which hang over Davies's integrity. Admittedly anyone who reaches the end of this *Evaluation* without admitting the reality of such question marks would be showing a considerable disregard for evidence, but, even leaving that consideration aside, it remains true that there can be no justification for the citation of spurious authorities, or anonymous authorities, in what purport to be serious writings of theological controversy, any more than that there could be for the complete omission of authorities. This is amply confirmed by the fact that popes and saints – whose testimony is evidently much more worthy of credence than anyone else's – are punctilious in relying heavily upon trustworthy Catholic authorities in all that they write, and no less so in furnishing detailed references for them. The same practice is universally observed by Catholic theologians and even by non-Catholic academics writing on secular topics; it is, in short, a custom which, for altogether obvious and excellent reasons, is universal.

certainly have denied it to protect his reputation with the liberal mafia. For the benefit of any readers who are interested, I am able to reveal that the cardinal was in fact Cardinal Šeper, the Prefect of the Conciliar Church's Congregation for the Doctrine of the Faith.[20]

Yet another example of the same idiosyncrasy is found in Davies's pamphlet *An Open Lesson to a Bishop*, written in response to an article by an English bishop which deceitfully misrepresented the traditionalist position and was also dishonest concerning the history of the Roman liturgy. Davies wrote:

> One English-speaking bishop recently wrote an article in a Catholic journal with the clear object of exposing what he believed to be the ignorance of those fighting to preserve the Tridentine Mass .... In order to preclude any suggestion that this pamphlet is intended to be a personal attack upon a particular bishop, the author of the article will not be named.

That may *sound* all very well. Unfortunately, however, in the first place, it takes away a large part of the value of the pamphlet, since, once again, it cannot be used as evidence. And in the second place, Davies's reason for extending anonymity to the guilty bishop is completely invalid. He could easily have given the bishop's name at the beginning and pointed out at once that he did not intend the pamphlet as a personal attack, but merely to draw a general lesson. But anyhow, *why* is he so averse to giving the impression of a "personal attack"? Does he

---

[20] Davies was quite happy to give this information in conversation with the author and others back in 1980, and he confirmed it in *The Remnant*, 31st July 1983, after Šeper's death. His first detailed account of what took place at his meeting with Šeper appeared in *Apologia Pro Marcel Lefebvre*, Vol. III, which was published in 1988 when the information it contained was of no more than historical value. His change of policy after Šeper's death suggests that the reason for preserving this anonymity during his lifetime was a desire not to offend or upset this scapegrace who presided over the Roman congregation responsible for the Conciliar Church's doctrinal orthodoxy, thus conniving at every heresy which failed to elicit prompt denunciation from the Vatican.

not believe that heretics and liars who are seeking to destroy the Faith by deceiving those committed to their care are suitable objects for "personal attack"? Is he not aware that those who have taken it upon themselves to defend the Faith in time of crisis have commonly regarded it as *necessary* to launch "personal attacks" on the Church's enemies? Did not Our Lord and St. John the Baptist launch the most scathing, hurtful and completely public "personal attacks" on many even of their co-religionists (the Scribes and Pharisees) whom they deemed to be enemies of souls? Did not St. Alphonsus Liguori, Doctor of the Church, in his attack on King Henry VIII go much further than criticizing Henry's publicly infamous actions against religion and dwell also on his filthy personal life, and even indicate – despite the absence (for obvious reasons) of conclusive evidence – his conviction that the revolting king's second "wife", Anne Boleyn, was also his illegitimate daughter? (*History of Heresies*, p. 330) The fact is that here, as in so many other areas, Davies has taken it upon himself to rewrite the Catholic principles on how the sort of issue he is purporting to deal with *should* be dealt with – a typical symptom exhibited by those infected with liberalism.

Communist Techniques?

Although Davies considers himself entitled to invoke the authority of his hand-picked gurus to settle any point, this does not prevent him from being prompt to denounce the same tactics on the part of others. Consider the following excerpt taken from Davies's *Open Letter to the Editor of the 'Universe'* printed in *Christian Order* for May 1982:

Madam

(...)

You conclude your circular letter with a paragraph which is breathtaking in its impertinence and contempt for your readers. Because you happen to prefer the new rite of Mass, you take it as a self-evident truth that it is vastly superior to the old one. You therefore conclude that those who do not share your enthusiasm fail to do so only because 'the new rite was not sympathetically introduced and the various changes explained as well as they could have been. As part of the *Universe*'s attempt to help with this problem, we are running a series on the Liturgy by Fr. Edward Matthews, senior lecturer at Allen Hall, the Westminster Diocesan Seminary – I hope you will find this series useful.' It is as if an imprisoned Pole had written to General Jaruzelski complaining of the deprivation, misery, and great damage done to the future of Poland by the military takeover, and received in turn a letter from the General stating that he was sorry his military régime had not been sympathetically introduced, and the various changes not explained as well as they could have been, and that he had asked one of his commissars to write a series of articles in the Party paper which he hoped the imprisoned Pole would find helpful.

Davies's point, made with admirable crispness and vividness, is surely a valid one. But why do the objections which he raises to the use of Fr. Edward Matthews as an authority not apply equally to his own "authorities"? The editor of the *Universe* was acting as if her readers were under the same obligation to recognize that senior seminary lecturer as an infallible source of truth. For this Davies rightly rebukes her, observing that her attitude was like that of a Communist leader invoking the infallible authority of one of his commissars. Even judged against this background alone, and setting aside just for the moment the background of Catholic tradition and of common sense, is there the remotest possibility that it could be out of order, or in any way unfair, to make the same reproach to Davies himself over his use of his own favourite authors – private individuals like himself – as if their having made an assertion put the facts beyond dispute? – let alone private sources which are unnamed, so that the reader has no independent means of verifying this credibility? It is insufficient to argue that Fr. Edward Matthews is both ignorant and dishonest (which, having myself clashed with him in public debate, I am in a position to confirm) and that Davies's sources often tell the truth (which they do). The point is that they still have no more *authority* than Davies himself, or Fr. Matthews, or the present writer, and cannot therefore be treated as if they were popes or authorities entitled to any recognition as such whatever. And it follows from this that introducing them into his writings as though they strengthen what he is saying, rather than either, (a) using *proper* authorities,[21] or, (b) exposing his own logic nakedly and uncamouflaged and inviting it to be publicly examined and criticized, amounts to nothing short of fraud.

---

[21] Of course it would be quite impossible for Davies to supply genuine authorities for many of the propositions he defends, because – as this *Evaluation* comprehensively illustrates and proves – much of what he writes is expressly contradicted by the relevant authorities; but one of the main reasons that Catholic writers are obliged to cite their authorities is precisely so that any errors to which they fall prey are exposed – by the absence of any authorities supporting them – before they find their way into print.

CHAPTER TWO
THE SHOCKINGLY SLIPSHOD SCHOLARSHIP OF MICHAEL DAVIES

"Seek not the things that are too high for thee, and search not into things above thy ability." (Ecclesiasticus 3:22)

The Good Points

Not excluding even those who disagree with Davies on many points, almost everyone regards his scholarship as beyond criticism. Few would disagree that his reputation could fairly be summed up as follows:

(i) He is an extremely learned man.
(ii) He has indefatigably devoted his estimable intellectual powers to accumulating and digesting a vast quantity of material concerning traditional Catholic theology and the recent revolution in the Church.
(iii) The fruits of his efforts and dedication have been the production by him of a series of books, booklets, newspaper articles and published letters, providing in total: (a) a historical record of the revolution at every stage which, at least in terms of accuracy and clarity, could scarcely be improved upon and which, comparing, with painstaking care, the new, post-conciliar teachings and practices with traditional theology, demonstrates the revolution to have been unnecessary and un-Catholic; and (b) a chronicle of the progress of the forces of counter-revolution as led by Archbishop Lefebvre.

There may be those who think that there are other important favourable features which should be included in this summary of

Davies's reputation, but surely few would contest those just mentioned. And while it would be churlish not to give wholehearted acknowledgement to these qualities in Davies if they really existed, even stronger is the obligation to refute the illusion if Davies's scholarship is in fact fictitious. This is because, while the duty to give credit where credit can be given is a general duty to fairness and truth, the duty to attack and bring to light an utterly false reputation for sound learning and good scholarship is in addition a duty of charity towards our neighbour – in fact very many "neighbours" indeed – who have been, and otherwise might continue to be, grossly misled, with disastrous results that, in some instances, could endure for as long as eternity continues.

And the truth, to put it bluntly, is that Davies is a very mediocre scholar indeed.

This is not to deny that he has done a great deal of hard work. Nor is it to deny that this hard work has resulted in his having accumulated material which has enabled him to produce what is, up to the present time, much the most complete summary in the English language of the progress of the apostasy of the Conciliar Church. Nor is it to deny that Davies has written copiously and often with an admirable lucidity, and that his books will always be useful source material for those who wish to research the same subjects. But those points once admitted, there is little if anything else to his credit that can truthfully be conceded.

The Bad Points

The most obvious and glaring of the shocking deficiencies in Davies's scholarship can be conveniently summarized as follows:

(i) Much though he has written, his books are by no means exhaustive, and this neither through accidental omissions nor through lack of space. There is sufficient evidence in his writings that, when it suits him to do so, he sidles round matters which he would find it uncomfortable to address.

(ii)   Although he is generally reliable when giving historical facts, he is not always so.

(iii) As is demonstrated at considerable length in other parts of this *Evaluation*, when it comes to theological matters he is unreliable to a degree which almost defies belief.

(iv)   Only very rarely indeed is his reading and use of source material extensive enough to give a balanced treatment of the subjects which he addresses; and even when he does read sufficiently in a particular subject to represent it correctly, his lack of a wider and more general knowledge of connected topics often lets him down. This is a point which marks the difference between first-rate and second-rate scholarship, and has the effect of leaving him open to attack by his Modernistic adversaries. (Perhaps it would be more appropriate to say his *more* Modernistic adversaries, since, as is shown elsewhere in this document, there is much of the Modernist in Davies also.)

These assertions will now be justified with some examples.

The Question of "Intention"

First, his lack of sufficient reading should be considered. Those who have read Davies carefully will have observed that he repeatedly quotes the same authorities, whom he assures us are regarded as the highest authorities in their field. And, because few of his readers will be sufficiently expert in the subject to know differently, it is inevitable that his assurances are generally accepted unquestioningly.

Seldom, however, is this justified. Let us examine a typical instance.

In *The Order of Melchisedech* he spends a considerable time treating the question of the intention necessary to confer a sacrament validly, and the same subject is addressed in his article in *Approaches* N° 72 (Lent 1981) concerning the question of whether Archbishop Lefebvre's orders can be regarded as valid in view of his having been ordained and consecrated by a high degree Freemason. And these are the authorities which he tells us, on p. 130 of *The Order of Melchisedech*, that he has used for forming his position on ministerial intention: *Moral and Pastoral Theology* by Henry Davis S.J.; *Fundamentals of Catholic Dogma* by Ludwig Ott; Addis and Arnold's *Catholic Dictionary*; *The Teaching of the Catholic Church* edited by Canon G. Smith; *A Catholic Dictionary of Theology* edited by Fr. Crehan; and the works of St. Thomas Aquinas.

And in relation to these authorities the following facts are pertinent:

(i) As mentioned earlier, Davis's *Moral and Pastoral Theology*, notwithstanding much in it that is perfectly sound, is almost certainly the most liberal text-book of moral theology published in English before Vatican II. Readers do not have to rely on the author's judgement over this, because it was banned in some seminaries at that time.[1]

(ii) Ott's *Fundamentals of Catholic Dogma* is the shortest complete text-book of dogmatic theology available in English, and considers no subject in depth, never allowing more than a sentence or two for summaries of conflicting opinions on disputed points (such as the question of ministerial intention).

(iii) Addis and Arnold's *Catholic Dictionary* has only a very brief treatment of the question of ministerial intention in relation to the validity of the sacraments.

(iv) Canon Smith's book is a work which would be suitable for teaching teenagers in high school but is certainly not an authority worthy of being quoted by someone attempting a comprehensive treatment of a complex part of sacramental theology.

(v) Crehan's work was published in three volumes appearing in 1962, 1967 and 1971 respectively – that is, during and after

---

[1] For instance, at the Pontifical Beda College in Rome on the instruction of its noted moral theologian Dom Peter Flood O.S.B.

Vatican II – and is again very general even where it is sound, which is by no means everywhere. Crehan's attack on St. Alphonsus Liguori's doctrine of conflicting intention, for instance, in the very article on which Davies relies, seems to the present writer to betray not only disrespect to the Holy Doctor, but a complete misconception of the point at issue.

(vi) And the extract from St. Thomas, although obviously of the highest authority and value, touches upon only one part of the matter which Davies is discussing.

By contrast with these authorities – if, other than St. Thomas, they can fairly be called that – there is a book in English, which although not in print is fairly readily available, which devotes sixty-two very learned pages to the precise question of ministerial intention in cases where the correct matter and form are used, and which considers it from every angle, quoting all major opinions on the subject with abundant references, while clearly disagreeing with a number of points made by Davies. This is Fr. Bernard Leeming's *Principles of Sacramental Theology*. Did Davies neglect it because he had not heard of it, or avoid it because he did not wish to draw attention to its contents in view of their opposition to his position? I do not know and it does not matter. Either way, its absence from his bibliography suffices to demonstrate that his scholarship is extremely shoddy. In fact what is evident, both here and in many other places in his books, is that he has cobbled his opinions together from reading a few articles in encyclopædias and dictionaries summarizing the state of Catholic theological opinion, without systematically reading what the theologians themselves say in their full-length treatments. The fact that, for instance, he sees fit to cite no moral theologian in his articles on sacramental intention other than Henry Davis could perhaps fairly be described as thoroughly remarkable, were it not for the even more striking fact that *nowhere*, in *any* of his indexed works, does he quote the Church's great Doctor of moral theology, St. Alphonsus Liguori.

I shall not give examples here of the rest of the most conspicuous and unacceptable defects in Davies's scholarship, for a very great abundance of such examples is to be found in other places throughout this *Evaluation*; but I *shall* cite a few of his errors which, while not significant enough to be considered under any other heading, certainly demand consideration in view of the misplaced trust which many of his devotees have in his infallibility – and indeed would be even more significant if they had been committed by an author who had not dwarfed them with more atrocious errors such as those regularly perpetrated by Davies.[2]

The Wrong Council

In *Cranmer's Godly Order* on p. 63, he says that St. Pius X, in his encyclical *Pascendi Dominici Gregis*, "found it necessary to repeat the condemnation of the Council of Nicæa ..." But he does not say *which* Council of Nicæa, and inevitably those of his readers who trust what he says at all will assume that the condemnation, which he goes on to quote, was taken from the *first* Council of Nicæa in 325 A.D. – the great general council which first defined the consubstantiality of God the Son with God the Father. In reality, however, the Council in question was the *second* Council of Nicæa, a much less significant council – in fact perhaps the least of the Church's ecumenical councils – held in 787 A.D., the canons of which were almost all disciplinary in nature.

---

[2] *Not* included in the catalogue which follows are errors which could be the fault of printers, such as Davies's statement on p. 21 of *The Goldfish Bowl* that Vatican II began in 1965 (rather than in 1962). No writer is immune to such gremlins and few of us are impeccable proof-readers.

The Wrong Words of Consecration

On p. 104 of the same work, he asserts that the Latin word "*benedixit*" occurs "in the Consecration formula" – i.e. of the Mass. In fact of course it *precedes* the essential form for the consecration of the chalice but does not occur *in* it.

Active Falsification

On p. 177 of *Pope Paul's New Mass*, Davies tells us:

> It is important to note that as regards our participation in the Mass, Vatican II did not actually use the word 'active' (Latin – '*activus*'), but the word '*actuosus*' – which requires a participation involving a full, sincere and interior cooperation with the action of Christ our '*leitourgos*' in His Mass, which we are privileged to make ours. Such a '*participatio actuosa*' can be expressed fittingly in such external forms as word and gesture .... All are valid and valuable external manifestations of our *interior* participation.

Davies is asserting, in short, that the council was faced with the choice of recommending that the participation of the laity in the Mass be either "*activus*" – which is substantially external, Protestant-type participation – or "*actuosus*" – which is substantially internal, Catholic-type participation. Alas for those poor readers who embrace and swallow trustingly his every word. The truth that they must now face up to is that the distinction which he has told them it is "important to note" is an entirely spurious one, the genuine distinction of meaning between the two terms being quite different. Let us consult the standard Latin dictionary used by classical scholars, that of Lewis and Short. In it, "*actuosus*" is defined as "full of activity, very active (with the accessory idea of zeal, subjective impulse ....)". "*Activus*", by contrast, is defined as "active, practical (opposed to contemplative)". Nor, as can be confirmed by referring to Du Cange's exhaustive glossary of later Latin, did these words change their meaning in later centuries.

On the one hand, therefore, we have the fact that, of the two available Latin words for "active", the Council appears to have decided to select the one which indicates the need for vigorous, external, even impulsive activity, by preference to the word which is more restrained and general in meaning. And on the other hand, we have Davies's didactic assurance to his readers that there is a difference in meaning between the two words which is *almost the opposite* of what it really is, and that the word which the council chose is more appropriate to denote the traditional devotional practice of the faithful at Mass than to denote the *principally external* participation which characterizes the de-spiritualized Novus Ordo.

Ultra Vires

Even this ignorance of Latin, however, leaves us unprepared for p. 589 of the same book, in which we find that Davies is ignorant of the true meaning of the phrase *"ultra vires"*, which is commonly used even in English. Here are his words:

> Simply because an action is legal it does not follow that it is right. It is possible for a person in authority, even a pope, to act '*ultra vires*'.

In other words, he is telling us that an action which is *"ultra vires"* is *legal*, but is *not right*.

In fact, it is the other way round. It is certainly possible for one in authority to posit an action which is within his *legal* powers but not *morally* correct. If, for instance, a pope were to command that statues of a particular saint were to be removed from all Catholic churches, the pope would undoubtedly sin by giving the order; but he would be completely *within* his powers, and, because it would not be intrinsically sinful for the parish priests to comply with the instruction, they would be obliged to do so. But in giving such a command the pope would *not* be acting *"ultra vires"*. For a pope – or any other person in authority – to act *"ultra vires"* would involve his giving an order or performing an action which he had no *power* to give or do, such as if a pope were to abolish the Mass or a parish priest were to promulgate a new dogma. In such a case, the action would indeed be *"ultra vires"*, but it would certainly *not* be "legal".

Davies seems to be under the impression that any action can be termed *"ultra vires"* if it is sinful for the person giving the command, even if it be within his legal rights; but this is certainly not the case. The words *"ultra vires"* mean "beyond one's *power"* – *not* "beyond one's *right"*. An action which is *"ultra vires" cannot* be legal.

Another Wrong Translation

Latin gives Mr. Davies more trouble on p. 591 of *Pope Paul's New Mass*. There he quotes the following words which he attributes to St. Thomas (*Summa Theologiæ*, II – II, Q. 33, A. 8, ad 5):

> ... *ipse peccaret præcipiens, et ei obediens, quasi contra præceptum Domini agens* ....

and then translates them as:

> [anybody obeying him] would sin just as certainly as if he disobeyed a Divine command.

Certainly this error is more excusable than the previous one, in that the word "quasi" does sometimes have the force which Mr. Davies translates it as having in this passage. But that does not excuse someone who holds himself out to be competent to teach his readers for making it, for to anyone acquainted with the Latin of St. Thomas there could be no doubt that the passage should be rendered:

> [anyone obeying him] would sin *in view of the fact that* he *would* be disobeying a command of Our Lord.

Nor is the mistranslation by Davies inconsequential. On the contrary, it seriously distorts St. Thomas's meaning, since it implies that St. Thomas permits disobedience to an authority in a case when obedience would not automatically entail disobedience to a Divine command and that he recognizes parity between a case in which someone disobeys a pope because to obey him would involve disobeying God and a case in which someone disobeys a papal instruction which Divine law does *not* forbid him to comply with – which is the very opposite of his position. St. Thomas permits disobedience to (properly constituted) human authority *only* when this authority gives a command obedience to which would necessarily entail disobedience to a Divine command.

It should also be noted that Davies's reference is incorrect. Indeed the *Summa Theologiæ*, II-II, Q. 33, A. 8 does not even contain 5 objections, and I have been unable to trace where St. Thomas in fact *does* say what Davies attributes to him. The extreme carelessness manifested by a wrong translation coupled with a wrong reference characterizes the entire appendix in which it occurs, where Davies says that the duty to disobey a prelate who commands something contrary to a Divine precept is an example of the automatic revocation of a law – a claim which is considerably weakened by the fact that a prelate's command contrary to a Divine precept is *not* a law at all (a command differs essentially from a law), and is not automatically revoked either, as it never had any binding force in the first place!

Another Gaffe

He is in no better form on p. 132 of the same work, in which he carelessly refers to a letter written by Pope Pius VII to "the Bishop of Boulogne" entitled *Post Tam Diuturnitas*. In fact, the last word of the title of the letter should be "*Diuturnas*" and the bishop to whom it was addressed was really the Bishop of Troyes – his *surname* was "de Boulogne".[3] One might ask what the point of giving a reference is, if, by making a mistake in *both* of the two details by which he identifies his source, the author

---

[3] Étienne-Marie de Boulogne (1747-1825), Archbishop of Troyes.

makes it almost impossible for his readers to verify the reference.

"It's the Mass that Matters"

One of the most remarkable instances of Davies's unscholarly approach occurs on pages 29-30 of *Cranmer's Godly Order*, where he writes:

> One of the most outstanding and perceptive contemporary [i.e. of the Reformation era] champions of the Mass was the German theologian John Cochlæus (1479-1552). He rightly pointed out that in attacking the Mass Luther was attacking Christ himself 'since He is the true founder and perfecter of the Mass, the true High Priest of the Mass and also the One who is sacrificed as all Christian teachers acknowledge.' With equal accuracy he diagnosed the contradiction which lay at the heart of the heresiarchs' claim to be 'reformers'. 'They are justly deemed guilty of heresy who instead of seeking remedies for what is amiss set themselves to abolish the very substance on account of the abuse.' He warned his fellow Catholic apologists not to concentrate their *main efforts on defending the primacy of the pope but on defending the Mass*, a task which was far more vital, for 'thereby Luther threatens to tear out the heart from the body of the Church.'

Doubtless among Davies's readers there will have been many who have not studied the polemical writers of the "Reformation" in depth and could name few champions of the Catholic position during those years other than the obvious ones such as St. Thomas More, St. John Fisher, Blessed Edmund Campion, Cardinal Allen, Fr. Robert Parsons S.J. and Fr. Thomas Stapleton (and, among the non-British, St. Robert Bellarmine, Suarez and Melchior Cano). And they will surely have been as startled as the present writer was to learn that this "outstanding and perceptive" defender of the Church against the "reformers" advised Catholic polemicists to defend the Mass at the expense of the papacy.

After all, every Catholic is obliged to know and to acknowledge that the Mass depends on the Church and is of no value outside the Church, even when celebrated validly. And every Catholic is equally obliged to know and acknowledge that the Church is built on the papacy. Consequently, one who defends the Mass at the expense of the papacy would appear to be in the same position as a man who insists on standing in his attic guarding his treasure chest when his enemies are beating down his door. By defending the door he could have saved his treasure, but when the door is gone the treasure will inevitably be lost. By defending the papacy one is automatically defending the Mass, while to have retained the Mass at the expense of losing the papacy would have achieved nothing at all.

And yet ... is there perhaps some flaw in these assertions about Catholic obligations? Who would dare to doubt it, when the contrary is held by a man who was, we are assured, at the time of the Reformation, "one of the most outstanding and perceptive contemporary champions of the Mass" – and presumably, therefore, a trustworthy Catholic authority?

The reality, of course, is that Davies has made up his own mind that defence of the Mass rather than the papacy is in order today, and to support this erroneous position has, relying on his expert knowledge of the "Reformation" period (a period in which, as a historian, he specializes), dredged up the nearest thing he could find to a Catholic authority who held this position at the time of the "Reformation". Naturally he has had to pass swiftly over such authorities as Doctors of the Church and canonized martyrs in his search, but he has succeeded in producing someone who, though wholly unknown to probably all his readers, was at least officially a member of the Catholic Church.

Cochlæus is *not* a trustworthy Catholic authority, however, but evidently a member of that class of people – of which the late Fr. Leonard Feeney was a notable example – whose zeal to defend the Church against her enemies is so unbalanced if not hysterical that they themselves are brought either into, or to the very brink of, a heresy opposite to the one they are attacking.

The *Dictionnaire de Théologie Catholique* has an article on him (entitled "Cochlée, Jean" and contributed by C. Toussaint) from which the following pertinent details about his theological career can be gleaned.

In the Diet of Worms he challenged Luther to a public debate – the loser of which was to be burnt. (Luther in fact publicly accepted the challenge, but both parties were dissuaded by their friends from actually embarking on the debate.) In 1512 he wrote a book in which, by gathering texts from various parts of Scripture, he demonstrated that Jesus Christ is not God. And in 1528 he wrote another in which, by the same procedure, he demonstrated that men owe obedience to the devil and that Our Lady lost her virginity.

Now Cochlæus did not in fact himself believe any of these positions, and wrote the books only to demonstrate that the method of controversy relying upon the random use of Scriptural texts was not to be trusted; but this is neither here nor there, whether from the point of view of the use Davies sees fit to make of him or from any other point of view. It is scandalous in the highest degree for a Catholic to write such works and shows a completely unbalanced approach to the very question – that of how to repel the assaults on the Church – which is the subject upon which Davies assures us that he is an authority to be heeded.

Oh, and it should be added that some of his writings were placed on the *Index of Forbidden Books* and that the (1913) *Catholic Encyclopædia* observes of his countless polemical pamphlets that "almost all of these publications ... were written in haste and bad temper, without the necessary revision and theological thoroughness, consequently they produced no effect on the masses."

Such are the true credentials of this "outstanding and perceptive contemporary champion of the Mass."[4]

---

[4] No one is denying that Cochlæus was a learned polemicist and capable on

Liturgical Dancing – or How to Use the Infallible Word to Sabotage Truth

Let us now turn to p. 246 of *Pope Paul's New Mass*, where Davies is in the process of countering Scriptural arguments put forward by Fr. Joseph Champlin in favour of liturgical dancing.

Fr. Champlin had adduced the incident recorded in 2 Kings 6:14 when "David danced with all his might before the Lord", and to answer this point Davies says:

> This is no more than an isolated instance of a spontaneous outburst by an individual which could scarcely have been less liturgical.

That much is defensible. But then he proceeds:

> Indeed David was rebuked for it by Michol, the daughter of Saul, who said: 'How glorious was the King of Israel today, uncovering himself before the handmaids of his servants, and was naked,[5] as if one of the buffoons should be naked.'

What Davies is indicating, in other words, is that King David's dancing was inappropriate and that Michol rightly rebuked him. But his reliability in attributing the correct meaning to well-known Scriptural passages is no greater than his reliability in all other theological matters, it seems. Not only was Michol's sarcastic rebuke wholly inappropriate, and David's dance perfectly appropriate and pleasing to God, but only seven verses later in the very same chapter, it is recorded that Michol was cursed by God and made barren for life, *in punishment of the very reproof which Davies quotes with approval!*

The irony of the wretched business is increased to an extent which even writers of comic fiction might hesitate to risk, by the

---

occasion of arguing very cogently in defence of the Church. He was, and was hailed as such by St. Robert Bellarmine. The point is simply that he is grossly unreliable and cannot therefore be invoked to settle a point which is self-evidently controversial.

[5] David was not completely naked, but had removed his regal outer garments and wore only a "linen ephod".

use that Davies then makes of his "refutations" of Fr. Champlin. For he follows them with a pained protest at the way that "liturgical revolutionaries ... never miss an opportunity of stressing their own alleged scholarship and the ignorance of the traditionalists" despite their "intellectual bankruptcy." And, as either Fr. Champlin or any other liturgical revolutionary would be perfectly justified in pointing out, Davies's reply is itself as good an illustration as could possibly be wanted of "the ignorance of the traditionalists," and of evident "intellectual bankruptcy" on their – that is, the traditionalists' – part, not to mention, in his attempt to interpret Holy Scripture, of showing off "alleged scholarship". The plain reality is, of course, that Davies's scholarship is not one whit better than Champlin's. To say that a non-liturgical dance is liturgical, as Champlin did, is certainly no greater offence against scholarship than to say that King David's dancing was worthy of rebuke when Michol had been cursed precisely for making it the object of a rebuke.

Humanism

Further embarrassing confusion occurs on p. 6 of *The Goldfish Bowl*, where Davies instructs his readers on the nature of humanism. Under the subtitle "The Divinisation of Man", this is what he writes:

> [The word 'renaissance'] refers to the rebirth of interest in classical studies which began in Italy in the fourteenth century. Those engaged upon these studies became known as humanists, as their researches were concerned with purely human topics, whereas in Europe until that time, God had been the focus of almost every aspect of scholarship and art ....
> In his book *Christian Humanism*, Professor Thomas Molnar provides us with the following definition: 'Humanism was a doctrine, or network of doctrines, putting man in place of God, and endowing him with virtues he was inevitably to abuse.'

The picture Davies paints is that the "humanism" of the Renaissance era is essentially the same thing as the atheistic cult today known as "humanism", or more exactly "secular humanism". Despite his apparent assurance, this picture is grossly misleading; indeed it would be nearer the truth to say that the only relationship between what is today called *humanism* and the humanist intellectual and cultural movement of the Renaissance years is the use of the same term to denote them. Hence Davies quotes Professor Molnar, apparently speaking of one species of humanism,[6] and places his words in a context which refers them to the other – a confusion as great as would be the introduction of a quotation about "classical" music into a discussion of classical languages.

The truth of the matter is that the humanism of the Renaissance era was a cultural and educational movement centred upon the classical tongues. Its object was certainly not directly theological, any more than medicine is directly theological, but so far removed was this humanism from any conflict with theology that many of the great humanists were also great theologians and some of them, like St. Thomas More and St. John Fisher, have even been canonized. Indeed the Catholic Church has to some extent officially embraced humanism, an obvious manifestation of this fact, for instance, being the adoption by the popes, from the end of the Middle Ages onwards, of the humanistic practice of couching their encyclical letters in Ciceronian Latin.[7]

The movement *today* known as humanism or *secular humanism* is today so powerful and widespread – it would be difficult to find a field of human activity not affected by it – that

---

[6] If by any chance Professor Molnar was referring, in the words Davies quotes, to the movement of humanistic studies which flourished in the fifteenth century, this means only that Davies has chosen as his source someone as ignorant as himself – but I have no reason to think that this is the case and as Davies quotes no page number I have been unable to track down the passage in Molnar's book.

[7] Humanism also revived interest in the Fathers of the Church *quite* as much as in the pagan classics. See *Humanism and the Church Fathers* by C.L. Stinger, Albany, State Univ. of N.Y. Press – 1977.

the possession of *some* knowledge of it is indispensable. Indeed it is quite simply the godless religion imposed by the controlled media and taken for granted in the world of politics, letters and science. One useful source for information about it is Professor James Hitchcock's 1982 study *What Is Secular Humanism? Why Humanism Became Secular and How It Is Changing Our World*. As a corrective to Davies's error and with particular respect to Renaissance humanism, the following lucid exposition by Professor Revilo P. Oliver, formerly of the University of Illinois at Urbana, could scarcely be improved upon.

> 'Humanism', properly speaking, designates the cultural system introduced by the scholars who initiated the Renaissance, thus ending the Middle Ages and making possible most of modern civilization. That meaning was derived from Cicero, who did not invent, but did use and give authority to the terms '*studium humanitatis*' and '*artes humanitatis*' (or, in clear contexts, simply '*humanitas*') to designate the cultivation of the human mind through the historical, philosophical, literary, and rhetorical studies which, it was believed, gave men of ability the perception and wisdom requisite for a high civilization, and thereby enabled them most fully to realize their potentiality as human beings. Those studies, naturally, were conducted in Greek and Latin.
>
> The humanists of the Renaissance – Petrarch and his successors – revived the intensive study of Greek and Latin literature (including history and philosophy), and they also revived the use of classical Latin as the common and, so to speak, native language of Western civilization. That is why the ability to write fluent and accurate Latin has always been the hallmark of a true humanist. The strictly correct definition of humanism is that given by the eminent American scholar and former President of Oberlin College, Ernest H. Wilkins:
>
> 'Humanism is a scholarly and initially reactive enthusiasm for classical culture, accompanied by creative writing in Latin on classic lines.'
>
> As is obvious from the definition – as well as from the fact that any list of prominent humanists will include Pope Pius II, Cardinal

Bembo, Erasmus, Sir Thomas More, Melanchthon, Beza, and Milton – *the word 'humanist' no more indicates a man's religious belief than does 'philologist' or 'astronomer'.* The only consideration that is at all relevant in this connection is that the humanist necessarily acquires an extensive, and sometimes profound, knowledge of Græco-Roman antiquity, and necessarily respects the accumulated experience of mankind. It is very probable, therefore, that he will judge human institutions and human nature in the light of all history, particularly that of Western civilization, but not excluding such other civilizations as are known to him.

From the early Renaissance until recently, the humanists' conception of what studies were most conducive to human excellence was taken for granted throughout the West. That is why we still speak of 'humane learning'; why colleges eager to cash in on the prestige of such studies profess to teach 'the humanities'; and why in some of the older universities, such as St. Andrews, the senior Latinist bears the title, Professor of Humanity.

Until the early years of the present century, a humanistic education, which meant proficiency in Latin and Greek and their literatures and history, was the most highly prized and respected cultural attainment, and the word 'humanism' thus had a potent and almost magic connotation of excellence and superiority that it still retains even in the minds of persons who have forgotten precisely what it means and so can read the *Times*'[8] editorial drivel without laughter or disgust. (*America's Decline*, p. 283)

A Very Slovenly Review

Our path through Davies's *œuvre* on the track of his slapdash scholarship now brings us to a review, which he contributed to *The Angelus* in May 1982, of a book entitled *The Destruction of the Christian Tradition* by Dr. Rama Coomaraswamy – a work with which some readers of this *Evaluation* will doubtless be familiar. Briefly, Coomaraswamy's book is an analysis from a

---

[8] An American, Professor Oliver is referring to the *New York Times*; his parting shot would be equally valid, however, in respect of the London *Times*.

traditional standpoint of the recent revolution in the Catholic Church which argues persuasively for the invalidity of the new rituals and for the duty of resisting "the changes". In places it supports Archbishop Lefebvre, but is generally somewhat more "extreme" than that prelate; in particular, the book recognizes the illegitimacy of recent pontificates, though only in an unobtrusive footnote.

The book is certainly defective, failing to distinguish adequately between the Conciliar Church and the Catholic Church, and contains also a number of other errors, some of which its author has since recognized, and others of which, alas, he has not. But despite its defects it is a book which has quite as much claim to significance in its analysis of recent events as any of Davies's, or indeed as all of them put together.

With this background in place, we are now ready to consider Davies's review of Dr. Coomaraswamy's book, a review which might almost be said to constitute as definite a milestone in the history of half-baked pseudo-scholarship as is the *Summa Theologiæ* of St. Thomas in the history of genuine scholarship; a review, also, which is far from devoid of the irony to be found very often in Davies's polemical writings, in that it reaches its most pitiful depths, which are extravagant even by the standards that Davies manages so consistently to maintain, precisely when it attempts to convict Coomaraswamy of crimes of which its own author, i.e. Davies himself, is patently, and embarrassingly, guilty.

The first page of the review consists of irrelevant frivolity on completely secular subjects with not even the faintest connection with the matter under review. Having thus warmed his pen, Davies turns to theological topics and starts by offering the following for his readers' consideration:

> I have been particularly saddened at the defection of a young priest of the Society of St. Pius X who [sic] I knew as a seminarian and had visited me in my home. He has been deluded by those claiming that we no longer have a pope and that the New Mass is

intrinsically invalid, and he now denounces the Archbishop as a traitor because he rejects these crazy, diabolically crazy, theories. Indeed the very idea of recently ordained priests considering themselves competent to make a credible contribution to speculative theology is absurd to the point of being grotesque.

Readers who have hacked their way through the undergrowth of hysterically hostile adjectives to the meaning of that passage will have gathered that Davies is deploring the temerity of a priest in believing the following:

(a) that John-Paul II is a manifest heretic and therefore not a valid pope;
(b) that the New Mass, either by the changes in its essential form or by the absence of a true offertory, is invalid; and
(c) that Archbishop Lefebvre, who ordained him, is betraying the Church by forbidding members of his Society to hold these convictions.

He will also have learnt that Davies considers that such opinions fall under the heading of "speculative theology", and that young priests should learn their place and leave such subjects to their elders and betters.

While detailed discussion of the positions of the young priest is to be found in the next chapter it is worth anticipating slightly what is covered there, by mentioning, briefly, the following facts, which are simply not open to dispute:

(i) The Consecration formula of the Novus Ordo, even in Latin, omits words which St. Thomas Aquinas (*Summa Theologiæ*, III, Q. 78, A. 3) teaches to be essential to validity.

(ii) Pope Paul IV teaches explicitly[9] that one guilty of heresy before his election to the supreme pontificate would be invalidly elected and could *never* become pope, no matter who and how many believed he was pope, and for no matter how long the situation prevailed.

---

[9] In his Constitution *Cum Ex Apostolatus*, 1559.

(iii) On the subjects of ecumenism, religious liberty and a number of others, a *prima facie* case of heresy against John-Paul II remains to be adequately answered.

The first two of these facts do not even belong to the realm of opinion: anyone can confirm them by checking the references given, and the third is admitted by Davies himself, for instance in his article *The Sedevacantists* (*Christian Order*, November 1982) in which he shows that he is aware of the case against John-Paul II, based on his acceptance of religious liberty, but neither explains how religious liberty, as taught by John-Paul II is orthodox, nor refers to anyone else who has explained it. So, although fuller discussion of each point is reserved for later chapters, it is legitimate, even at this stage, to present them as facts rather than opinions. And in the light of these facts the first thing to be said, surely, is that Davies's *tone*, which might be justifiable in the case of a dangerous and obstinate purveyor who has been comprehensively exposed as defiantly adhering to wholly indefensible claims – in short which might well be justifiable in a discussion about Davies himself – is in the case in question intemperate, uncalled for, and offensive. And, that said, what of the *subject matter* of which this needlessly vitriolic language is the clothing? What, for instance, of the charge that young priests ought not to venture within the realms of speculative theology?

Let us begin by finding out exactly what speculative theology is.

In the introduction to his *Dialectics*, Mgr. P. Glenn, author of a standard series of textbooks of Catholic philosophy, explains the following distinction:

> A science that presents facts which enrich knowledge, but which do not directly imply laws or norms for the guidance of thought or action, is called a 'speculative' science. A science which presents facts from which directive norms or laws are immediately derived is called a 'practical' science.

Hence, since theology is just as much a science as any other science, we must expect *speculative* theology to be that part of theology which relates to religious *truths* but does not relate directly to *behaviour*; in other words, the kind of theology commonly known as "dogmatic theology". Hence it is no surprise that Fr. J. Herrmann in Article II of the Introduction to his *Institutiones Theologiæ Dogmaticæ* should use the two terms interchangeably:

> 'Speculative' or 'dogmatic' theology consists in the contemplation of revealed truths.

The scope of speculative theology is explained as follows by Drs. Wilhelm and Scannel (*Manual of Catholic Theology*, p. xviii):

> When theology expounds and co-ordinates the dogmas themselves, and demonstrates them from Scripture and Tradition, it takes the name of Positive Theology. When it takes the dogmas for granted, and penetrates into their nature and discovers their principles and consequences, it is designated Speculative Theology, and sometimes Scholastic Theology ... Positive Theology and Speculative Theology cannot be completely separated.

Using the synonymous term "scholastic theology", Fr. Sylvester J. Hunter S.J. remarks in his *Outline of Dogmatic Theology* (Vol. I, p. 6) that "the difference between Positive and Scholastic Theology is then a difference of method, not of doctrine."

Now if speculative theology is identical in doctrine to dogmatic theology, and embraces the whole of theology except for those points which relate to morals, the spiritual life and law, being characterized and distinguished from "positive theology" by its penetrative rather than expository method, it is remarkable that Davies should consider that it falls outside the competence of a simple priest; for without grappling with dogmatic or speculative theology, how would it be possible to preach, or to teach catechism or even to recite the Creed? And it is even more remarkable that he should express his conviction in such extravagant language.

In fact, however, it becomes clear to anyone who reads his review as a whole that the question this issue invites should not be "Is Davies correct?" but "Does Davies have the least idea what he is talking about?". Earlier in the review he has told his readers that a simple priest may "preach sound doctrines," and yet it is evident that he sees no contradiction between this and his assertion, just a few lines away, of the arrant nonsense that:

> The number of priests who are competent to engage in speculative theology is as limited as that of scientists who invent moon-rockets.

However, if one makes allowance for his theological illiteracy and adopts as a working assumption the hypothesis that his acquaintance with Catholic terminology is too limited to allow him to say what he means, it is, in fact, possible to locate a reasoning underneath his incoherent effusions, which, though certainly erroneous, is nevertheless at least comprehensible. Probably he has appropriated the term "speculative theology", which he has doubtless come across from time to time during the course of his reading, to mean *theological speculation* (in the modern sense of the word "speculation") – i.e. consideration of theological questions which (a) are unsettled by the Magisterium, (b) are highly theoretical, and (c) afford learned men matter on which to sharpen their intellects without risk of falling foul of the authority of the Church.

But, even assuming that this assessment is correct, it does not help Davies much, for of course it still remains utterly untrue to say that simple priests or even layfolk are not permitted to engage in this sphere of theology. And when a matter of *practical* moment arises, such as whether a man is or is not the pope, it ceases to be even a matter of its being merely *permitted*. A genuine obligation may arise. And we need no more hesitate either in broaching the topic, or in expressing publicly our conclusions if they are certainly true, than did the illiterate St.

Catherine of Siena when she encountered a not incomparable situation in which there were simultaneously more than one claimant to the papacy.[10]

Be all this as it may, one thing that *is* clear if we cut through Davies's terminological confusion is his position that for a simple priest to comment on such subjects, let alone for a layman like Dr. Coomaraswamy to do so, is something which is automatically out of court and a crime which brands its perpetrator as unworthy to be taken seriously. And this he immediately confirms, for he goes on to say:

> I hope most sincerely that I will cause no offence in [sic] the remark I am about to make. This is certainly not my intention. As far as I know, there is not a single priest within the traditionalist movement in the English-speaking world who is qualified to engage in speculative theology.

Of course if we take "speculative theology" literally, Davies's words will not cause offence but, rather, embarrassed laughter; but if he means the study of theological questions not defined by the Church and requiring solid theological grounding for their correct understanding, the position is hardly any better. No, Mr. Davies, this branch of theology is *not* an activity restricted by the Church to "qualified" priests. You do not quote any authority to support your dogmatic assertion – and if what you

---

[10] Here is a typical extract from the letter that St. Catherine wrote in her letter to the cardinals who had elected Antipope Clement VII in opposition to Pope Urban VI:

"Rather than the angels on earth you ought to be, set to snatch us from the path of Hell's demon and undertake the angelic office of leading sheep back into the fold of obedience to Holy Church, you have assumed the task of devils, wishing to infect us, also, with the evil you have in yourselves, by drawing us, too, away from our obedience to Christ-on-earth and into obedience to anti-Christ that limb of the devil which is what you are too, for as long as you persist in this heresy... This is no blindness due to ignorance...no, for you know what the truth is...and now you wish to corrupt this truth and convince us of the opposite... And what shows me that your lives are disordered? The poison of heresy..."

said were true, century after century would have been peppered with condemnations of "unqualified" priests and laymen who have studied such matters. Nor will you be able to find such an authority. The branch of theology to which you are presumably referring is quite open to all, and indeed for much of the Church's history – a particularly famous period being, for instance, the early Byzantine era – such topics were the principal matter for conversation in Christian society, in place of our current typical fare, of politics, eroticism, money and the latest novel or television programme. The only restrictions are that, on any point which is not already certain, (a) we must be ready to submit our judgement to future pronouncements of the Church if they should be made, and (b) we may not suggest that our opinion binds others, except to the extent that they evidently follow by immediate logical necessity from points already settled by the Church. *In all other circumstances*, as Fr. Herrmann tells us in article IV of his Introduction, "the opinions of theologians *are of as much weight as the reasons which support them*." (Emphases added)

A little later Davies clarifies his last sentence quoted above, with the following words:

> All I am claiming ... is that we do not have the good fortune to possess a theologian of repute among our ranks.[11]

Davies is of the conviction, therefore, that a "theologian of repute" is fit to pronounce upon matters of what he calls "speculative theology", but no one else. And a "theologian of repute" is ...? Davies now proceeds to describe him:

---

[11] I have no idea how Davies reconciles this with his assertion in *The Angelus* for December 1987 that he knows "an *outstanding traditionalist theologian* ... a professor of theology ... who says only the Tridentine Mass." The distinction between an "outstanding traditionalist theologian" of which he knows one, and a "theologian of repute ... within the traditionalist movement" of which he denies the existence, is much too subtle for this writer and he prefers not to speculate on the subject, while inviting Mr. Davies to offer any clarification he may deem appropriate.

Now what do I mean by a theologian of repute? He would normally be a priest of mature years who had earned one or more higher degrees in theology, taught theology in pontifical universities or at least seminaries, contributed to learned periodicals, and, perhaps, written books on theology. Above all, his orthodoxy would be above suspicion. If there are any such priests within the traditionalist movement, I would certainly like to learn of them.

Well, readers may by now have legitimate doubts as to whether Davies is a competent judge of whose orthodoxy is "above suspicion" and whose is not, but it is hard to see why he should exclude from the status of "theologians of repute" men such as Fr. Michel-Louis Guérard des Lauriers O.P. (1898-1988), Fr. Reginald Ginns O.P. (1893-1987), or Bishop de Castro Mayer (1904-1991), all of whom seem to match very closely the criteria he assigns for membership as he himself would assess them. True most of these were not native to the English-speaking world, but then neither was the "young priest of the Society of St. Pius X" whose "defection" had inspired Davies to set pen to paper in the first place. Whatever qualifications may be necessary to assess the legitimacy of John-Paul II's claim to the papacy, the ability to speak English is clearly *not* one of them.

However the relevance of the existence of such men is surely diminished by the fact that Davies seems to be simply making up his criteria as he goes along. Let us consider them for a moment. Does St. Thomas Aquinas match Davies's requirements? To the best of the present writer's knowledge, he died before the age of fifty – so hardly "of mature years"; he never "contributed to learned periodicals"; and his orthodoxy, though widely recognized in most quarters, was so far from being "above suspicion" that his doctrines were condemned and forbidden by several of the great Catholic universities. At best he is a borderline case!

And evidently St. Peter and St. Paul meet none of the criteria at all, except as being priests who eventually reached relatively mature years. And yet this no more prevented them from pronouncing on what Davies calls "speculative theology" than it did St. Thomas Aquinas.

The criteria, I repeat, are invented. And the purpose of the invention, of course, is to nullify the effect produced by laymen[12] and priests who, without laying claim to vast erudition, are able to perform the relatively simple task of referring to relevant Catholic authorities and applying the teachings of those authorities to an existing concrete situation.

Although Davies would have us reject this as presumptuous, those who follow his lead by doing so are rejecting it solely on the basis of Davies's authority; and they submit to his dictate at their peril, because in fact what he forbids is far from presumptuous. Anyone, even the most lowly layman, may reach firm conviction on such topics, provided he remembers that his conclusions are, in the words of Fr. Herrmann, "of as much weight as the reasons which support them." Indeed Cardinal Billot, whose theology forms the basis of Pope Pius XII's encyclical *Mystici Corporis*, went so far as to quote at considerable length, in one of his renowned theological works, from the "free-thinking" (i.e. non-Christian) layman Charles Maurras on a topic in which scholastic theology rubs shoulders with social science.

In other words, if Davies's insistence that only "theologians of repute" may pronounce on such topics is true, one of the greatest theologians of recent times was unaware of it.

Readers are now invited to recall Davies's explicit admission that he knows of no "theologian of repute" who is a "traditionalist" and to read on; for this admission is not without

---

[12] A layman may perfectly well be a weighty theologian, as was, for instance, W.G. Ward (1812-1882). But more important is the fact that one no more needs to be a *weighty theologian* to find legitimate grounds for prudent rejection of Karol Wojtyła's papal claims than one needs to be a *weighty biologist* to find legitimate grounds for prudent rejection of Darwin's theory of evolution.

interest in connection with Davies's next move, which is to anticipate the objections of those who might say that he pronounces on such topics himself without being a "theologian of repute". To anyone who might feel tempted to make this accusation, his reply is:

> I do happen to have spent three years in a Catholic college and received a degree entitling me to teach Catholic doctrine and philosophy, and this is what I confine myself to doing. I make a practice of never indulging[13] in speculative theology if I can avoid it, and where I do, I obtain the advice of theologians of repute.

That does it! Davies has completely given himself away! Forget the insufferable arrogance. Overlook the fact that his degree from a teacher training college prepared him to teach only at primary or secondary school level. Pardon the questionable claim that Davies avoids "speculative theology" if he can. Just concentrate on those last words: "Where I do ['indulge' in 'speculative theology'] *I obtain the advice of theologians of repute.*"

But, Mr. Davies, there *aren't* any "traditionalist" theologians of repute. You have already admitted it. So you are finally – accidentally – letting your naive readers into the secret that, when you regale them with the opinions of your erudite theologian friends and sing their praises, insisting that their orthodoxy is beyond reproach, etc., etc., these hand-picked "authorities" of yours are not even what you call "traditionalists". In short, they are, *even on your own terms*, members of the enemy camp. They say the Novus Ordo which you admit that, were you a priest, you could not say and which you do not attend. Not even the horrific blasphemies, doctrinal dilution and all the rest that it contains have enlightened them on this most crucial topic, but you have the effrontery to require us to bow and scrape before these wretched renegades. Indeed you

---

[13] As the article proceeds, "speculative theology" sounds increasingly like a risky leisure activity rather than a supernatural science.

even quote their opinions on such subjects as the validity of the Novus Ordo without so much as letting on that the Novus Ordo is the "Mass" *that they themselves say*. If this is not dishonesty and hypocrisy, it is hard to imagine what is.

A little later Davies writes:

> I hope therefore, that I am not guilty of arrogance in preferring my own opinion to that of certain priests. The reason is that it is not my own opinion, but that of learned theologians.

Presumably "learned theologians" is synonymous with "reputable theologians", so we must admire both Davies's humility and his prudence in restricting his role, allegedly, to that of mere mouthpiece for those properly qualified to give their opinion and to be listened to with submissive hearts and wills.

Or must we? Let us put our feet back firmly on the ground. What, in Heaven's name, are we to make of Davies's claim when the clearest example of an "opinion" that Davies has preferred "to that of certain priests" is that the right course for him to take in respect of the Vatican II revolution is to champion, and publicly champion, the traditionalist[14] cause? Does it fall within the scope of Davies's college degree in Catholic doctrine and philosophy? Clearly it does not. So where *does* it fall? If his claim as just quoted is true, it follows that he maintains his traditionalist stance, not because his own intellect can recognize its truth – for so much audacity on his part would be as reprehensible as that of the poor young priest who was lambasted earlier in the review – *but because it is the view of learned (or reputable) theologians.*

But it is *not*. It cannot be – because Davies avows that he is not aware of any reputable theologian who holds the traditionalist stance.

---

[14] I take this word to mean the position of those who refuse the recent doctrinal and liturgical innovations though usually recognizing in theory the authority of those who introduced them.

So, once again, Davies is lying.

And this lie is a trivial one. It enables him to give an *appearance* of humility in his approach and an *appearance* of objectivity in his conclusions, assuring his readers that it is not on his views that they are being invited to rely but on the views of the reputable theologians, while *in fact*:

(a) he is perfectly happy to follow his own opinion in the face of such "authorities" where he feels confident that he is right, *but*

(b) he does not want his readers to feel confident enough to enjoy the same liberty.

In short, dear admirers of Michael Davies – if any of you are reading this *Evaluation* – his position is that on one occasion and one occasion only may you use your own intellect by preference to that of "reputable theologians", namely to arrive at the "traditionalist" position which, as there are no reputable theologians who defend it, you must accept without theological guidance; but having got there, you may never again have the effrontery to use your own God-given brain, but must humbly submit to the opinions of ... well, Davies calls them *"learned theologians"* – but at any rate, theologians channelled to you by means of the pen of Michael Davies who, as an expert on the subject,

(a) handpicks the theologians for you to ensure that only the most "reputable" are selected, and

(b) conceals their names from you lest you should be presumptuous enough to wish to conduct an independent examination of their credentials and "reputability".

V

At this juncture it has clearly become important to ensure that all readers are fully aware of the correct Catholic position on the use of one's intellect to assess theological questions on which the Church does not teach the answers directly and explicitly.

There are three major pitfalls to be avoided: obvious enough when they are pointed out, they are:

(i)   Sitting on the fence when it is obligatory to take a position.
(ii)   Insisting that a position is obligatory when it is no more than a private opinion.
(iii) Blindly accepting the opinions of others where there is no guarantee that their opinions will be correct.

It boils down to the fact that Catholics must be acutely aware of their obligation to distinguish between, on the one hand, judgements which are definitely correct and upon which it is necessary to insist, and, on the other hand, private opinions; and that they must be no less aware of *how* to make this distinction in any given case, for otherwise they will not be able to avoid one or more than one of these pitfalls.

Under this heading, one of Davies's most prominent errors, repeated whenever the opportunity arises, is the assumption that any judgement made by *a private individual* – as opposed to one made officially by *the Church* – is a "private judgement", in the sense used to describe the principle on which all the various manifestations of the Protestant "religion" are based. Let us tackle this confusion first, by noting that:

(i)   "Private judgement" is simply another term for "opinion".[15]

---

[15] "There are five states of the mind with regard to its acquisition of truth," we are informed by Fr. J.S. Hickey in his *Summula Philosophiæ Scholasticæ*, Vol. 1, n. 159, "namely: ignorance, doubt, suspicion, opinion and certitude." And "objective evidence is the ultimate criterion of truth and motive of certitude." (*Ibid.*, n. 258) The word "evidence" here does not denote a collection of suggestive indications, but rather the quality of *evident-ness* – of being visibly true. But private judgement is an intellectual act by which assent, at least provisional, is given to a proposition in the *absence* of this motive of certitude. Or, as the influential nineteenth century American writer Dr. Orestes Brownson put it: "Private judgement is only when the matters judged lie out of the range of reason, and when its principle is not the common reason of mankind, nor a Catholic or public authority, but the fancy,

(ii) An opinion is a judgement not truly certain, and therefore,

    (a) at least to some extent, and perhaps to a very great extent, liable to error,[16] and

    (b) as a result of (a) necessarily *provisional*.

(iii) But the intellect of a private individual *is* capable, under certain conditions, of making judgements which are *not* liable to error, *because within due limits the human intellect is infallible*.[17]

And this third point, although the reader will certainly not have found it anywhere in Davies's writings, is of course of the greatest importance. And if any Catholic thinks about it for a moment, it must become fully apparent to him that it is true. If it were otherwise, Catholics could have nothing with which to reproach Protestants in the fact that they attempt to save their souls in accordance with their own *opinions* rather than with some objective standard, *because the infallibility of the Church herself would be no more than our opinion if we were liable to error in establishing it*. As it is, however, the difference between Catholics and Protestants is that:

(a) Catholics can establish with *certainty*, by objective criteria, the fact that the Church is infallible and then listen in docility to her teachings;[18] and at no point does mere opinion play any part in the procedure; whereas

---

the caprice, the prejudice or the idiosyncracy of the individual forming it." (*Brownson's Quarterly Review*, October 1851; *Brownson's Works*, Vol. 1, p. 347.)

Hence none of these "principles" mentioned by Dr. Brownson is capable of generating an assent firmer than that of "opinion".

[16] Scholastic philosophers distinguish opinion from certainty by the presence of some degree of *formido errandi* – fear that one may be mistaken.

[17] "The intellect is *per se* infallible, although *per accidens* it can err ...(albeit only where evidence is lacking.)" (Fr. Hickey: *op. cit.*, Vol. I, n. 184)

[18] The virtue of faith by which we believe without doubt all that the Church presents to us for belief as divinely revealed is not a *mere* logical conclusion based on the evidence of the Church's credibility, for it is a supernatural and infused certainty. But the acquisition of supernatural faith by one who does

(b) Protestants *opine* that Holy Scripture is Divinely revealed (this cannot be proved without the Church); they *opine* that it is to be interpreted by each individual for himself; they *opine* that their opinion as to its meaning will be sufficient for their salvation; and each and every interpretation they make of its meaning (except where no conceivable doubt exists from the text) is no more than an *opinion*.

And of course this distinction between the intellectual grounds of Catholicism and Protestantism necessarily presupposes that our recognition of the Church God has founded to teach us is *not* a mere opinion or private judgement but something that the intellect can know, *by its own efforts, with infallible certainty.*

And once this is granted, how can the intellect be denied the capacity to recognize *other* truths with certainty on the basis of objective and inescapable evidence? And how is it possible to reject in advance of all consideration the possibility that such truths may include the proposition that the Holy See is at present not occupied by a legitimate and Catholic occupant?[19]

The following passage, once again by famous nineteenth-century American convert Dr. Orestes Brownson writing in the enormously influential *Brownson's Quarterly Review*, explains these points admirably:

> Here is the error of our Protestant friends. They recognize no distinction between reason and private judgement. Reason is

---

not already possess it normally presumes the prior recognition (with true certainty), by the ordinary natural process of reason, that God has indeed established the Church as His infallible mouthpiece upon earth. The ordinary course of apologetics used by the Church to lead men to the act of faith establishes by convincing and certain argumentation conclusions that grace will later make *supernaturally* certain. "Before the acceptance of faith, reason can and must know with certainty (apart from the fact of revelation) the motives of credibility." (Denzinger: *Index Systematicus*, I, D.)

[19] Of course, even if this cannot be known with infallible certainty and is only an opinion, it is impossible to dismiss it at once as unworthy of consideration without weighing the evidence in its favour.

common to all men; private judgement is the special act of an individual .... In all matters of this sort there is a criterion of certainty beyond the individual, and evidence is adducible which ought to convince the reason of every man, and which, when adduced, does convince every man of ordinary understanding, unless through his own fault. Private judgement is not so called ... because it is a judgement of an individual, but because it is a judgement rendered by virtue of a private rule or principle of judgement .... The distinction here is sufficiently obvious, *and from it we may conclude that nothing is to be termed 'private judgement' which is demonstrable from reason or provable from testimony.* (*Brownson's Quarterly Review*, October 1852, p. 482-3. Emphasis added.)

Indeed. And it is precisely this writer's contention (as it is that of Dr. Coomaraswamy, from the review of whose book by Davies we are digressing), that it is "demonstrable from reason" and "provable from testimony" that the Conciliar Church is an essentially different society from that founded by Our Divine Saviour and that its new sacramental formulæ are at best of doubtful validity. If Davies can refute the reasoning by which Dr. Coomaraswamy, or others including the present writer, have demonstrated these contentions, let him do so, and he will find no one more grateful than ourselves; but to refuse to broach the subject as though there were something sinful in using one's God-given intellect to apply Catholic principles to a concrete situation is not a permissible manner of debate.[20] The number of

---

[20] Under a subtitle "Judgements of the simple human reason, duly enlightened", Fr. Felix Sarda y Salvany, on p. 201 of the French edition of his *Le Libéralisme est un Péché*, a work approved by the Holy See, remarks:
Yes, reader, reason is itself, as the theologians would say, a theological source ('*locus theologicus*') ... Reason must be subordinate to ... faith in all respects, but it is false to allege that reason is impotent on its own. It is therefore permitted, and even obligatory, for the layman to rationalize his faith, to infer its consequences, to apply it and to deduce parallels and analogies from it. The simple layman can thus distrust, at first sight, a novel doctrine presented to him insofar as he sees it to be in conflict with another, defined doctrine. If this conflict is clear, he can fight it as evil, and

"reputable theologians" who side with us on a question of *opinion* is worth considering; but where the facts are already definite, it is irrelevant.

It should be noticed also that in this matter Davies, not untypical, *is not true to his own principles*. Although the subject of whether the vernacular form of the Novus Ordo is invalid is one which Davies has indicated to be part of "speculative theology", yet in his book *Pope Paul's New Mass* he *does* discuss it, and comes to a conclusion in favour of its validity. And Davies cannot justifiably claim that he is merely citing the opinions of "reputable" theologians, for:

(a) he quotes *no* theologian who supports his personal position on the subject;

(b) he employs reasoning on the topic which is evidently his own; and

(c) he conceals from his readers the existence of theologians such as St. Thomas Aquinas – who, though not meeting Davies's criteria, many of his readers might consider at least *semi*-reputable! – and St. Pius V (who meets even Davies's home-made criteria for "reputability") who firmly maintain the opposite view.

Let us return to Davies's review. It continues:

The two most pernicious errors prevailing within the traditionalist movement today, undermining it, destroying it, and making it ridiculous to those outside with a modicum of theological competence, are that one or more of the new sacramental rites is intrinsically invalid and that one or all of the last four popes

---

denounce as evil any book which supports it ... The faithful layman can do all that and has always done so, to the Church's applause. This is not making himself the shepherd of the flock, nor even its humble servant ... What would be the use of the rule of faith and morals if the simple layman were unable to make immediate application of it himself in any particular case? ... The general rule of faith, which is the infallible authority of the Church, agrees – and *must* agree – that everyone apply it in the concrete by his particular judgment.

(including the present Pontiff) were either not popes at all or lost their office through heresy. I would be very interested to learn of a single theologian of repute anywhere in the English-speaking world who would uphold either of these propositions.

Before commenting on this paragraph, let us remind ourselves that a little earlier in the same review Davies protested as follows:

> Even more incredible than the spectacle of priests, without theological competence, pontificating upon topics which would have taxed the erudition of St. Thomas Aquinas, is that of laymen without formal theological training making '*ex cathedra*' pronouncements in this field.

These two extracts provide two clear instances of double standards. Davies condemns those who disagree with his opinions for doing something which those who support him are just as "guilty" of, and he brands others with the stigma of crimes of which he is himself a notorious and inveterate perpetrator. These double standards can best be highlighted by asking two simple questions:

(i) If the validity of the Novus Ordo and of John-Paul II's pontificate are subjects which would tax the erudition of St. Thomas, why is it only those who *oppose* their validity that are censured, and not those who *favour* it? (If the subject is too deep and demanding, surely one should leave it as uncertain: it cannot be any more temerarious to take one side than the other of a complex issue.)

(ii) Where shall we find a clearer example of "pontificating" by someone "without any theological competence" and of "'*ex cathedra*' pronouncements" by a "layman without formal theological training" than in Davies's forthright assertion that the two theological positions he mentions are "the two most pernicious errors prevailing within the traditionalist movement today"?

Further double standards sully the same page of Davies's review:

> I would ... submit that a theological thesis which does not have the support of some theologians of repute cannot be taken seriously.

This submission is self-contradictory, for it is *itself* a "theological thesis", yet Davies has adopted it without being able to mention a single theologian of repute who holds it. It is also quite false. Even if it has some validity in normal times, there is no Divine promise that during great crises the learned world will always retain some orthodox representatives. Nowhere did Our Lord promise that the gates of Hell would not prevail against "theologians of repute". Nor could He have, since the "reputable theologians" of His own day rejected to a man His Divinity and Messianic claims. Moreover, when Davies is not looking for a stick with which to beat those who reject the Conciliar Church, he does not believe in his own assertion; witness the fact that he gives his allegiance to the "traditionalist movement" *despite his insistence that it has no "reputable theologian" among its ranks.*

After three pages of this self-contradictory, magisterially expressed nonsense, Davies finally touches upon Dr. Coomaraswamy's book. He points out that Coomaraswamy includes a quotation purportedly from *Apostolicæ Curæ* only part of which is authentic and the remainder of which is clearly from a commentary and was included in the text by oversight; that he commits a similar mistake in relation to the *General Instruction on the Roman Missal*; that he gives a misleading account of the provenance of the "Ottaviani Intervention";[21] and

---

[21] The justly renowned critique of the 1967 *Missa Normativa* prepared by certain Roman theologians (chief among whom was the late Fr. Michel-Louis Guérard des Lauriers O.P. who was later explicitly to deny that Paul VI and his successors were legitimate successors of Peter) and approved by Cardinals Ottaviani and Bacci.

that he says that the Anglicans at the time of the Reformation forbad kneeling to receive "Communion", which they did not.

It is the role of a reviewer to identify such errors as these, and Davies has astutely found several. Of these, the historical error is inconsequential; the error about the Ottaviani critique is still fairly minor; the error about *Apostolicæ Curæ* is quite serious, though not necessarily the fault of the author, as it is the kind of error for which a printer could have been responsible; and the mis-attribution of a paragraph to the *General Instruction* is thus the only serious error which must be blamed upon the author. It should not be there. It is deplorable. But, that said, surely Davies's conclusion is an excessively harsh one to draw from the evidence he has furnished.

> This type of factual error, and I could cite others,[22] makes it impossible to accept the book as a serious work of scholarship, and will provide useful ammunition for those wishing to discredit the traditionalist movement.

Of course, such harshness is certainly a permissible view. It is a sustainable opinion that Coomaraswamy's errors are such as to render his book unworthy of consideration as a serious work of scholarship. *But this view has an inescapable corollary.* It is written: "With what judgement you judge, you shall be judged: and with what measure you mete, it shall be measured to you again." (Matthew 7:2) So it is clear that Davies is inviting us to judge his own works by the same standard. If the errors highlighted in this *Evaluation* (and there are hundreds of them) are as grave as, or graver than, Coomaraswamy's, then Davies stands condemned from his own mouth. If they are not, we may anticipate a satisfactory answer from Davies to the *Open Letter* constituting the epilogue to this *Evaluation* and challenging him to substantiate certain propositions which, if they are false, as

---

[22] It is fair and safe to presume that the "others" would not be more serious than the peccadillo about kneeling for Communion, as Davies would obviously have selected the most serious errors for analysis.

the present writer maintains they are, are evidently much more serious errors than those of which Davies convicts Dr. Coomaraswamy. Only those of an exceedingly sanguine disposition will wish to start ticking off the days on a calendar as they wait.

Most of the rest of Davies's review is absorbed by an attempt to show, not that Coomaraswamy's theses are false, but that they are incompatible with the position of Archbishop Lefebvre, a circumstance which, though true, is irrelevant. There is one more highlight worthy of note, however. It consists in the following words:

> Dr. Coomaraswamy argues that a pope can lose his office through heresy. This is correct, but if it happened it would have to be so manifest as to be beyond any possibility of doubt, and would need to be made known to the Church through the 'declaratory' sentence of a general council.

This claim will be refuted elsewhere in this *Evaluation*, so it will suffice here to draw attention to the obscurity of Davies's reasoning by addressing to him a few pertinent questions:

(i) Mr. Davies, upon what *authority* do you assert that for a pope to lose his office by heresy his heresy would need to be "so manifest as to be beyond any possibility of doubt"?

(ii) Supposing you to be correct on this point, however, you must be aware that Dr. Coomaraswamy, ourselves, and many others, maintain that there are manifest heresies in decrees of Vatican II, signed by John-Paul II and which he continues to defend in full awareness of the Church's prior contrary teaching . If a signature on a widely-circulated heretical decree is not manifest enough for you, what would be?

(iii) Do you really mean "beyond any *possibility* of doubt", or do you mean "beyond any possibility of *reasonable* doubt"?

(iv) Are you aware of any theologian of higher status than St. Robert Bellarmine, a Doctor of the Church, who has considered the topic of loss of office by a heretical pope as deeply as St. Robert does in his *De Romano Pontifice*?

(v) Assuming – from your failure ever to have mentioned any – that you are not, how is it that St. Robert makes no mention of the alleged need for the heresy to be "so manifest as to be beyond any possibility of doubt," but instead insists that a manifest heretic cannot be pope?

(vi) In the interval between the pope's falling into public heresy and the declaration of this fact by a general council, would the pope, or would he not, be the Vicar of Christ?

(vii) If he would, are you not asserting that a public heretic (who is not even a Catholic) can be pope?

(viii) If not, may Catholics who are aware of the pope's heresy reject his pontificate, or must they treat the non-pope as pope pending a hypothetical future declaration?

(ix) Who would summon the general council, given that according to Canon Law only the pope can do so?

(x) Can you name any approved pre-Vatican II theologian who taught as *certain* this position that such a declaration is necessary before one may treat the heretical "pope" as a usurper?

(xi) Do *you* regard it as certain?

Even in the absence of any attempt by Davies to answer them – and there are good grounds, mentioned later in the *Evaluation*, for doubting whether he ever will attempt to answer them – the questions themselves are enough to attest Davies's utterly unscholarly approach to controversy, whereby he deems it necessary to cite authorities only on what is undisputed, and quite inappropriate to do so on a matter of crucial importance to Catholics and which is currently a matter of widespread and fierce disagreement.

Davies's parting shot as he ends his review is that:

Dr. Coomaraswamy writes page after page attempting to prove his bizarre theses, but does no more than display his terrifying ignorance upon the subject of sacramental theology.

As has been made clear, the present writer is by no means in full agreement with Dr. Coomaraswamy's theological stance, considered as a *whole*; but he wishes to register that, having had the privilege of meeting and talking to Dr. Coomaraswamy at length on several occasions, the prospect of Michael Davies accusing him of "total confusion" and "terrifying ignorance" is almost comical. Dr. Coomaraswamy's erudition, theological and otherwise,[23] is simply in a different league from that of his assailant. It is enough to say that errors as gross as Davies's pretentious nonsense about "humanism" or ignorance of the meaning of "speculative theology" would not conceivably slip out in his victim's after-dinner conversation, let alone in his serious writings.

---

[23] Not to mention his courtesy and general culture.

CHAPTER THREE
THE VACANCY OF THE HOLY SEE

"Though we, or an angel from heaven, preach a gospel to you besides that which we have preached to you, let him be anathema." (Galatians 1:8)

Introduction

It is axiomatic that an enemy of the truth, no matter how skilfully and unflaggingly he succeeds in passing himself off in more favourable circumstances as being on the side of the angels, will inevitably show his true colours when faced with a clear statement of the very facts which he is engaged in denying, suppressing or distorting. Davies is no exception to this rule – witness his hysterical reaction to the suggestion of the vacancy of the Holy See, whenever it crops up, from no matter what source. On some subjects – even the validity of the new rite of Ordination (examined in chapter 9 of this *Evaluation*) – Davies has been prepared to debate his opponents, dealing at least in some measure with what they actually say. On what he calls "sedevacantism" he is not: his opponents are instead to be misinterpreted, ridiculed, abused and reviled, libelled and finally forgotten. On no account are they to be allowed to present their case even in order for Davies to refute it. On no account will a letter written to Davies on this subject receive a courteous and reasonable reply dealing with its contents. On no account will Davies ever mention, or have anything to do with, anyone who, to use his own extremely comprehensive clause, "*suggests* that Pope John Paul II *might* not be a true Pope."[1] (Emphasis added.)

---

[1] "The danger to the Faith of those attending Tridentine Masses is far more

(See his article in *The Remnant* for 15th August 1985.) Davies dedicated one of his new books to Fr. Oswald Baker and held him up as a model of how priests should have reacted to the introduction of the Novus Ordo. He visited and spent several days with Colorado's remarkable Fr. Dan Jones.[2] He even extended his friendship to the present writer. You will not, however, find these three or any other "sedevacantists" referred to with approval – or, indeed, referred to at all – in Davies's writings after the date that he was apprised of their holding the position that the Holy See is vacant. They are now all definitely classified as "unpersons".

In 1982 Davies devoted an article to the claim that the Holy See is vacant. This article,[3] and one or two other comments made *en passant* elsewhere in his writings, until late 1986 represented Davies's position and the totality of his argument against the sedevacantist position and must therefore be subjected to analysis.

Misrepresentation

The first objection that must be made to it does not in fact relate to the article itself, but to its introduction as printed in *Christian Order*. While this introduction was not written by Davies himself but by Fr. Paul Crane S.J., the editor of the periodical in question, it is quite in keeping with the spirit of the article itself and Davies has never dissociated himself from it, although it goes so far as to give a completely false picture of the nature of "Sedevacantism",[4] which it does by giving the

---

likely to be present in certain so-called traditionalist ... chapels where the priests *suggest that Pope John Paul II might not be a true Pope ...*"

[2] Frs. Baker and Jones, whatever their other convictions may be, both recognize that the Holy See is vacant, and both have become victims of Davies's "silent" treatment purely as a result of holding this position.

[3] The article, entitled "The Sedevacantists" was published in *Christian Order* for November 1982 and in *The Remnant* for 15th June 1982

[4] The word is Davies's, not mine, but I have no objection to the word "sedevacantist". Although invented by those who deny that the Holy See is

impression that "sedevacantism" is not a theological position, but an *organized sect*. Here is what it says:

> In this incisive and exceedingly useful article, Michael Davies explains the sedevacantists [just as a scientist might 'explain' radiowaves or a dentist might 'explain' toothaches!]. The recent illicit Consecration of three bishops, to say nothing of the attempt a little earlier of one of their number to assassinate the Pope, has highlighted this group. An outline of its origins and activities is called for. Michael Davies gives both.

The reader ignorant of the subject will inevitably form from these words the conclusion that "sedevacantists" are a "group", led by three illicitly consecrated "bishops" who have despatched "one of their number" (presumably a fully paid-up member) "to assassinate the 'Pope'." This is not just libellous, it is sordid. It is reminiscent of the tactics used by the most blatant and extreme heretics of the Conciliar Church against all traditional Catholics. Such are the tactics which Fr. Crane considers called for in order to neutralize the effects of the manifestation of a theological position hostile to his own – a position that has been arrived at, independently of one another, by many who are well able to rival his own or Michael Davies's theological competence, has been defended by writers endowed with at least as much erudition as those who commonly write in *Christian Order*, and is firmly believed by many (alas not all equally orthodox on other points!) throughout the world. And though Davies did not write the words, he made no protest at this deliberate misrepresentation, and indeed, to all appearances, set out to rival his editor's dishonesty in the ensuing article – as the remainder of this chapter will abundantly show.

---

vacant, this is no more reason for rejecting it than for rejecting such words as "Christians", "Jesuits", "Gothic", and many others which, like the ones just mentioned, were originally coined as terms of opprobrium by the Church's enemies. What is clear is that if those who do not recognize the Vatican II papal claimants may be called "sedevacantists", those who *do* recognize them may by the same token be termed "sedeplenists".

God Will Forgive Thuc Followers

The observations with which Davies opens his article, as it is their tone rather than their theology which is objectionable, will be treated in Chapter 4, devoted to Davies's "Dishonesty, Inconsistency and Arrogance". As far as the present chapter is concerned, the first part of the article that calls for examination is Davies's assertion, in relation to those involved in the illicit episcopal Consecrations by Archbishop Thuc, that, "if this is their honest belief, if they have searched their hearts and sincerely believe that, like Luther, they cannot act otherwise (*'ich kann nicht anders'*) – then God will forgive them." Passing over the fact that Luther never said these words,[5] look for a moment at Davies's bland assurance, "if this is their honest belief ... then God will forgive them." May God forgive *him*. It is surely not for an unqualified layman to take upon himself in a casual, almost offhand way, to declare patronisingly to his readers the terms upon which Almighty God is or is not prepared to forgive those who have broken His laws. This is not to say that the subject should not be discussed; it should. But when it *is* discussed, it should be discussed thoroughly, to avoid giving any false impressions; that it should be discussed with delicacy, in view of the fact that the salvation of souls may be dependent upon what is said; and, above all, especially in the case of an untrained lay writer such as Michael Davies or the present writer, that it should be discussed in the light of *authorities*, who should be *quoted*.

Davies complies with none of this. Instead he gives his reader a one-sentence summary of what is necessary to obtain God's forgiveness as casually as he might tell a visitor where to catch a bus home. And what he says is *not true*. Exemplifying the truth of Alexander Pope's maxim that "fools rush in where angels

---

[5] I.e. his alleged declaration at the Diet of Worms "Here I stand. I cannot do otherwise," now recognized as apocryphal even by Protestant historians. (See, for instance, *The Catholic Encyclopædia* (1913), Vol. IX, p. 446)

fear to tread," Davies, in abject ignorance of the subject which he is discussing, suggests that the mere belief or opinion that what one is doing is correct is all that matters, and that God will condemn no one who had such a conviction at the time of his sinful actions. Indeed he seems to imply even that Luther himself may have been in invincible ignorance of the truth of the Catholic Church! The truth he overlooks is that "there is a way which seemeth just to a man, but the ends thereof lead to death." (Proverbs 14:12) Or, to put the same thought in theological instead of Scriptural terms, whereas an *invincibly* erroneous conscience excuses from guilt, a *culpably* erroneous conscience does not – a truth Davies could have learnt from any approved moral theologian.[6]

When is a Schismatic not a Schismatic?

Now let us move on to the theological arguments contained in the article.

It is noteworthy that Davies begins his refutation of the thesis that the Holy See is vacant by borrowing an explanation of what is meant by the term "schismatic" from Fr. Donald Sanborn – a priest whom Davies no doubt selected as reliable on account of his membership of the Society of St. Pius X, but who has ironically since been expelled from the Society for maintaining that the Holy See is, at least probably, vacant. The extract from Fr. Sanborn[7] which Davies quotes is as follows:

> Schism in Canon Law is defined thus: 'If, finally, anyone denies that he is subject to the Supreme Pontiff, or if he refuses communion with those members of the Church who are subject to him, he is schismatic.' That is a literal translation of Canon 1325 par. 2. I invite all and everyone to check my reference and to check my translation.

---

[6] As an example, I refer him and any readers who wish to pursue the topic to St. Alphonsus Liguori's *Theologia Moralis*, lib. 2, "Treatise on Sin", n. 4.
[7] It originally appeared in Fr. Sanborn's *Open Letter to Priests* of 1978.

Evidently Davies did not take Fr. Sanborn up on his invitation, since anyone who checked Fr. Sanborn's "literal translation" of Canon 1325§2 would have discovered that Canon 1325§2 in fact refers to "one who *refuses* [*renuit*] to be subject to the Supreme Pontiff ..."; and there is a world of difference between defining a schismatic as one who "*denies* that he is subject to the Supreme Pontiff" and one who "*refuses* to be subject to the Supreme Pontiff." The translation provided by Sanborn and adopted by Davies suggests that anyone who *claims* to be subject to the Roman Pontiff, however untrue his claim may in reality be, cannot be regarded as schismatic; whereas, according to the Church's own definition, whether or not a person is a schismatic does not depend on his *personal opinion* of whether or not he is subject to the Roman Pontiff, but upon the *reality* of the matter. However much a person may admit the duty of submission to the pope, if he in fact refuses to be subject to a validly reigning pope, he is classified as a schismatic.

A Convenient Digression

In fact this error, although important in itself, is not especially material to Davies's argument. What *is* material is the *use* that Davies makes of the definition. This use, which does not depend on the substitution of "denies" for "refuses", is to proceed directly from it to the purportedly inevitable conclusion that those who reject the pontificate of John-Paul II are schismatics.

And, of course, that is a complete begging of the question. That is to say, Davies has taken for granted, in order to reach his conclusion, what has yet to be proved – namely, that John-Paul II *is* the Roman Pontiff. After perpetrating this fallacy, Davies suddenly wakes up to the fact that it is just too blatant for him to get away with it, and points out:

> The Vietnamese Archbishop and the priests he has consecrated would probably claim that they wholeheartedly accept the teaching expounded by Fr. Sanborn, but they would claim nevertheless that

they are *not* schismatic as the Holy See is vacant at present, and therefore, as there is no Sovereign Pontiff, they cannot be accused of refusing communion with him.

So far so good. Now we await the demonstration that the claim that the Holy See is vacant is incorrect. Indeed, since it is obviously the central point of this article, many of his readers will surely expect it to follow at once, now that it has been introduced in this way. But those who allow their hopes to be thus raised are immediately subjected to disappointment, for now Davies seems to leave his fallacy on ice for the time being in order to digress. This is how he proceeds:

> Archbishop Ngo-Dinh-Thuc has in fact issued a public statement proclaiming that the Holy See is vacant. There are indications that illicitly consecrated bishops may meet together and elect one of their number as 'Pope'. Those who claim that the Holy See is vacant are known as 'sedevacantists' (from the Latin *'sede vacante'*, 'vacant see'). Archbishop Lefebvre has always repudiated this theory.

Notice that these four successive sentences, which are all part of the same paragraph, have no logical connection with one another. Davies scatters his fire at random, unable to arrange one thought logically after another in order to construct an argument. So what, if a retired Vietnamese prelate has proclaimed the See vacant? So what, if some pseudo-bishops plan to elect a pseudo-pope? So what, if "sedevacantist" is derived from the Latin? So what, if a retired French prelate who retains the traditional Mass does not accept this position? Let us allow the theoretical possibility that all these points are of the utmost relevance. The fact remains that Davies makes not the slightest attempt to tell us *what* relevance they have. His usually pellucid prose is markedly absent.

Post Hoc Propter Hoc

Next, Davies quotes Archbishop Lefebvre to confirm what his position on the matter is, as if this had some relevance. This passage includes the following gem:

> They will soon be disposed to choose a 'pope' from among themselves, which demonstrates that logically this position leads to schism.

Of course, this is the same fallacy again. One might as well say that those who oppose abortion will eventually be led to assassinate abortionists, which demonstrates that opposition to abortion logically leads to murder. In reality there is nothing logical about such reasoning at all, whether in Archbishop Lefebvre's use of it or in the parallel offered. The position that the Holy See is vacant is certainly not refuted by the possibility that some of those who hold it may be driven to a precipitate, uncanonical and invalid "papal election". The Archbishop's words also clearly imply the view that "sedevacantists" are *not* schismatics prior to such an election, which is in stark contrast with Davies's previously expressed view that they are schismatics already. And as a matter of fact Archbishop Lefebvre has never excluded lay sedevacantists from the Mass centres of his Society and has been happy for his priests to collaborate with some sedevacantist clergy[8] which he would hardly have done had he believed them to be outside the Catholic Church.

Davies then draws attention once more to the attempt of Fr. Juan Fernandez Krohn to assassinate John-Paul II, whom he refers to as "the Pope", although, as he is presumably conscious, whether Wojtyła has a right to this title is the very point under dispute and he has yet to prove it. Davies laments that:

---

[8] E.g. Frs. Vinson, Mouraux, Siegel, Raffali, Schoonbroodt, Vérité, Katzer, Hatswell, Buckley, Donohue and Baker.

... the enemies of the Society of St. Pius X will no doubt capitalize on the fact that the priest concerned had been a member of the Society implying that the Archbishop has some sympathy for the sedevacantist theory – which is ironic when he is coming under so much fire for refuting it.

Well, "refutation"[9] is one word to use to describe the contorted and fallacious reasoning found in the passage quoted above. To borrow a catch-phrase often used by Davies, *it's a point of view*. What, however, is much more than a point of view, and indeed quite certain, is that, whatever use the enemies of "the Society" may make of it, Davies himself is determined, in a very subtle way, to "capitalize" on Krohn's assassination attempt by drawing attention to the fact that this lunatic, who ought never to have been ordained, but *was* ordained at Écône, happens to hold the view that the Holy See is vacant. Note too that Fr. Krohn was still a member of the SSPX at the time of the assassination attempt; only afterwards did the Society deem it politic to disown him.

Audi Alteram Partem!

Davies then quotes an extract from the newsletter of the Orthodox Roman Catholic Movement[10] saying that:

> Although priests of the O.R.C.M. have preferred to say as little about the Vatican II popes as possible and to give them the benefit of the doubt as regards their election and legitimacy, we have not denied that there are grounds for doubt and that those who deny their legitimacy have the authority of weighty theologians on their side.[11] It may be that John-Paul II and his three predecessors (or two) lost the papacy as these new Bishops believe by falling into heresy.

---

[9] Owing to the increasingly frequent misuse of this word, readers are reminded that to "refute" means to *prove* to be *false*, not merely to reject or argue against.

[10] An American traditionalist organization.

[11] Archbishop Lefebvre several times recognized the same point. (J.S.D.)

Davies now considers that he has allowed the opposition to state their case, and he spends the rest of his article attempting to pull it to pieces for the benefit of his readers.

First, he takes the question of whether a heretical pope would automatically forfeit his office. On this, his opening assertion is that "the Church has never made a definitive pronouncement upon this subject, and so we must take the consensus of theological opinion as our guide."

As many readers will know that this is simply untrue, since Paul IV's bull *Cum Ex Apostolatus* is undoubtedly "a definitive pronouncement upon this subject"[12] as it deals expressly with the case of heretics elected to the papacy, and, by implication, with a pope who might fall into heresy after his election – if such a thing be possible. But although he suppresses this information, Davies does nevertheless go on to give the correct answer:

> The answer is that a pope who pertinaciously embraced formal heresy would by the very fact be deprived of his office, as it is

---

[12] Regrettably it is not possible in this *Evaluation* to devote as much space to this important Apostolic Constitution as it deserves. At this point it must suffice to cite the part of it which is most relevant to Davies's extraordinary claim. This is taken from paragraph 6:
By this Our Constitution *which is to remain valid in perpetuity* ... We enact, determine, decree and *define* ... that if ever at any time it shall appear that ... the Roman Pontiff, prior to his ... elevation as Roman Pontiff, has deviated from the Catholic Faith or fallen into some heresy: the promotion or elevation, *even if it shall have been uncontested and by the unanimous consent of all the cardinals*, shall be null, void and worthless; it shall not be possible for it to acquire validity ... through the acceptance of office ... nor *through the putative enthronement of a Roman Pontiff* ... nor through the *lapse of any period of time* ... it shall not be held as *partially legitimate* in any way.
The Constitution goes on, in paragraph 7, to authorize anyone, even "the laity", no matter how universally such an illegitimate pontiff might otherwise be accepted, "at any time to withdraw with impunity from obedience and devotion to those thus promoted or elevated and to avoid them as warlocks, heathens, publicans, and heresiarchs."

impossible to be a Catholic and a heretic at the same time, and the pope must be a Catholic.

This is clear enough, but Davies is not prepared to leave it at that.

Beware of Private Judgement

But the Church would need to know of this. The pope could hardly be said to have lost his office simply because one layman, one priest, one bishop, or even one Cardinal, declared that he had lost his office. (...) If other bishops stated that the Pope was not a heretic and not deposed, how could we judge between the two parties except by making our own private judgement the ultimate criterion of who is and who is not the Vicar of Christ?

Of course the pope could not be said to have lost his office *because* some individual said so; he would have lost his office *because* he had fallen into heresy. Was that not already established? Davies's ambiguous use of the word "because" affords him a foothold from which to use his "private judgement" argument which was analysed in the previous chapter. He is suggesting, in effect, that one can be certain of no fact, even in the natural order, unless it is taught by the Church. Thus, if the Church teaches that a heretic cannot be pope, Davies regards it nonetheless as a "private judgement", and not permissible, for a layman to say to himself: "Therefore, *this particular* heretic cannot be the pope."

As has been shown, this view is founded on a misunderstanding of what is meant by "private judgement" and is a travesty of the Church's teaching. The reason that the Church gives *general* rules and *general* teachings is *precisely* so that we may all use our God-given reason to apply these rules and teachings to *particular* situations as they arise. (See footnote 20 on p. 85 for Fr. Felix Sarda y Salvany's explanation of this point.) Those who say "a heretic cannot be pope, and this man is a heretic, but, of course, we must await the judgement of the Church before coming to the conclusion that he is not pope," are certainly not showing humble obedience to the teaching of the Church. On the contrary, they are showing contempt for her by refusing to apply her directives. The fact that the onus could even be placed on an uneducated layman to establish to his own satisfaction the invalidity of a particular putative pontificate is evident from Pope Paul IV's bull mentioned above.

The Judgement of a General Council

Davies then continues:

> The theological consensus is that there is one certain way by which we could know that a pope has been deposed: a general council of the Church would have to declare that this was the case. Please note carefully – and this is a rather complex point – the general council would not be deposing him. It has no such authority and we are forbidden by Vatican I to appeal from the authority of a pope to a general council. The sentence of the Council would not be judicial but declaratory, simply informing the faithful that the man occupying the see of Peter had ceased to be Pope due to obdurate heresy.

Really? Once again, we have only Davies's word for this; and, once again, Davies's word cannot be relied on. It is true that theologians have hypothesized about how the entire Church might be informed of the vacancy of the Holy See in the event of a vacancy owing to heresy; but there has certainly never been a consensus that no one could know of the vacancy of the See until some official declaration had been made. For a start, those involved in making such a declaration or in summoning a council to discuss the matter would obviously have to know in advance that the See was vacant, for they would certainly have no power to summon and participate in a council over the head of a validly reigning pope. But in fact, though less obvious, it is equally certain that they would be no better off if it had already been established that the See was vacant because, as the 1917 *Code of Canon Law* clearly states, it is impossible to have a general council without a pope.[13] Canon 222 reads as follows:

(i) There can be no general council unless it is convoked by the Roman pontiff.

(ii) It is the right of the same Roman pontiff to preside, either in person or through others, over a general council, to determine and designate the matter to be discussed and in what order, to transfer, suspend or dissolve the Council and to confirm its decrees.

Davies goes on to tell us that the general council would not be deposing the "pope" since it has no such authority and "we are forbidden by Vatican I to appeal from the authority of a pope to a general council." In reality, an appeal from the authority of a pope to a general council was forbidden as long ago as 1460 by Pope Pius II in his bull *Execrabilis*; but anyhow it is difficult to see the relevance of this, since the man in question, as Davies has already accepted, would not be the pope at all, as his loss of office would have taken place *automatically*.

Davies continues as follows:

> The sentence of the Council would not be judicial but declaratory, simply informing the faithful that the man occupying the See of Peter had ceased to be Pope due to obdurate heresy. But no such sentence has been passed upon any Pope subsequent to Pope Pius XII, and we have no right to regard them as anything but validly elected Popes who reigned lawfully, or are reigning lawfully.

The Duty of Submission to a Non-Pope

Davies seems unaware of the enormity of what he is suggesting. He admits that the sentence of a council would not depose the heretical "pope" since, by virtue of his heresy, he would already have ceased to be pope; but he insists that, prior to the sentence of a council, the faithful "have no right to regard" heretical claimants to the papacy "as anything but

---

[13] In fact this has been the case for much longer than this, because, as Pope St. Gregory VII declared in the year 1076, "No council may be called general without the instruction of the pope" – see Ven. Cardinal Baronius: *Annales*, Vol. XI (p. 424 in the Venetian 1705 edition). Evidently this rule was not new in the eleventh century and there is every reason to presume that it is either apostolic or Divine in origin.

validly elected Popes." In other words, if a man has been elected to the Holy See by the cardinals, Davies will never admit that he is not a lawfully elected and reigning pope until he is informed of this fact by a general council, even if in the meantime the "pope" in question is pouring out the most blatant heresies every time he opens his mouth. Of course, since the individual is, as Davies admits, *not* in fact the pope, he could meanwhile be wrecking the Church, changing all the rites, destroying the faith of hundreds of millions, performing invalid canonizations, and much else; but Davies requires all the faithful, by a pious fiction, to submit to regarding a man as pope even if he is not pope. In other words, he is telling us that the Church not only permits but actually requires the faithful to accept as true something which is quite definitely not true. And if Davies were consistent with his own principles, this would mean that he would be obliged provisionally to acknowledge as valid the election of a heretic, no matter how blatant, to the papacy – even if the Protestant Archbishop of Canterbury himself were elected, which, given the hyper-Ecumenism of most of those whom Davies accepts as cardinals of the Catholic Church, is perhaps not so far-fetched as it sounds.

Practical Consequences

Davies proceeds as follows:

> Let us now examine some of the practical consequences of the sedevacantist theory. These are enormous, and Archbishop Lefebvre has rightly drawn attention to their serious nature on several occasions .... Clearly, if Pope Paul VI and his two successors were not popes, then the Cardinals they created are not cardinals, and no real cardinals have been created since the pontificate of Pope Pius XII (presuming that he was a true pope).

This part of Davies's article is full of abrupt changes of direction and digressions which destroy the unity and sequence of the argument. Immediately after the passage just quoted, Davies goes on to describe the election process of a pope which we may pass over since it is already obvious where his argument is leading. Then he resumes his consideration of the consequences that flow from accepting the invalidity of promotions to the cardinalate since 1958:

> Now, if there have been no cardinals appointed since the pontificate of Pope Pius XII (or Pope John XXIII), then the only men who can lawfully elect a true Bishop of Rome, and hence a true pope, would be the cardinals appointed by Pope Pius XII who are now a declining minority within the college of cardinals. There is also no doubt at all that these cardinals all recognize the legitimacy of the last Pontiffs and have no intention whatsoever of electing a single 'true pope' in opposition to Pope John-Paul II. Therefore, when these cardinals die, it means that there will be no one left to elect a pope ....

"If John-Paul II is not Pope, Jesus Christ is not God"

Here Davies assumes that in the absence of validly appointed cardinals the Church is left powerless to provide herself with a new visible head on earth, a view supported by no theologian I am aware of and contradicted by many.[14] However in what follows he parts company not only with theology but also with logic, thus setting the tone for the remainder of the article.

> ... and the papacy will have come to an end – which would mean, in fact, that the Divine promises of Our Lord had failed, which would mean that He could not have been Divine, and there never would have been a Catholic Church. Archbishop Lefebvre has indeed been wise to point out the grave consequences of the sedevacantist theory.

---

[14] Notably by Louis Cardinal Billot : *De Ecclesia Christi*: Quæstio XIV, thesis XXIX; Jean-Baptiste Cardinal Franzelin: *De Ecclesia*, Thesis XIII, scholion; Giacomo Tommaso Cardinal Cajetan: *De Potestate Papæ et Concilii*, cap. XV; St Robert Bellarmine (Doctor of the Church): *De Romano Pontifice* and *De Clericis* lib. I, cap. VII, prop. V and cap. X, prop. VIII); Dom Adrien Gréa: *De l'Église et de sa Divine Constitution*); Fr. E. J. O'Reilly S.J. *The Relations of the Church to Society*, (London, John Hodges, 1892); Lorenzo Spinelli: *La Vacanza della Sede Apostolica*, Milan, 1955.

The truth is that the Church is *not* absolutely dependent on the official electors to provide herself with a new visible head, for this power devolves in case of necessity to the next representatives of the Roman Church. But even aside from this it is crucial to note that the papacy continues to exist even between the reigns of individual popes and the Catholic Church will always be founded upon the papacy, no matter how long she may continue to exist without a legitimate actually reigning pope.[15]

Secondly, Davies does not explain how he comes to the conclusion that the prolonged absence of a pope means that "the Divine promises of Our Lord" have failed. To accept his conclusion we should need to know which Divine promises he is referring to. When exactly did Our Lord promise that there would always be a pope or that papal interregna could only be short? Davies does not bother to tell us, but what seems most likely is that he has in mind Matthew 16:18, "Thou art Peter; and upon this rock I will build My Church and the gates of Hell shall not prevail against it," and has been led astray by a woolly recollection, on his part, of those words of Our Lord. The obvious meaning of them, confirmed by many Fathers of the Church, is that Our Lord founded His Church upon the first pope and promised that the *Church* would never be conquered by Satan. He definitely did *not* promise that the "gates of Hell" would never succeed in securing the invalid election of a heretic to the Holy See, or that there would always be a reigning pope

---

[15] "It is necessary to distinguish between the See and its occupants ... in considering the subject of its 'perpetuity'," says the leading Jesuit theologian of the nineteenth century, Cardinal Franzelin. "The See ... is a perpetual right of primacy ... and never ceases to conserve ... the power which was established by God for the individual successors of Peter ...; but the individual occupants of the Apostolic See are mortal men, and for this reason, though the See can never fail, it *can* be vacant, and indeed often *is* vacant. At such times the ... institution of perpetuity certainly remains ... but ... actually belongs to no one." (Franzelin: *De Ecclesia*; "Thesis on the Perpetuity of the Papacy.")

to lead the Church; nor has any pope, Father, or Doctor of the Church ever suggested that he did.

It is conceivable, one must suppose, that Davies has in mind, not Matthew 16:18, but the only other promise made by Our Lord which might be considered relevant, i.e. the promise of papal infallibility. But this means only that a true pope can never fall into heresy *in his official teaching*. As is evident from the decree *Cum Ex Apostolatus*, promulgated by Pope Paul IV and confirmed in every detail by Pope St. Pius V, it does *not* mean that the cardinals will never elect to the highest office in the Church a man who is ineligible to that office by virtue of prior heresy.

Diabolically-Inspired Madness

Davies then comments on the possibility that "sedevacantists" will "come together and elect a pope", as *some*, indeed, certainly may. By another extraordinary leap of logic he infers from the fact that some may disregard the laws of the Church that a theological position which they happen to share with many others who respect these laws is necessarily false. In fact, he uses a stronger expression than "false": here are his exact words.

> There is by no means complete harmony among the sedevacantists, and it is far from impossible that we shall eventually see several rival sedevacantist 'popes' anathematizing each other from different parts of the world .... Could any true Catholic, any one with a sense of what it means to be a Catholic, give any consideration, let alone serious consideration to such madness? I have no doubt that it is diabolically-inspired madness.

Because some of those who hold the belief that the Holy See is vacant might conduct an obviously invalid "papal election", with the result that the collection of heretical non-popes, consisting today of John-Paul II in Rome, Gregory XVII in Spain, Emmanuel I in Italy and another pretender in Canada, may be joined by one or several more, Davies concludes that all those who hold the view that the Holy See is vacant are guilty of "diabolically-inspired madness". Such a blatant piece of fallacious reasoning would certainly not have escaped Davies's attention if it had been used *against* him by a representative of the Modernist wing of the Conciliar Church. It amounts to saying that it is possible to reject a position without even considering the arguments supporting it, because some of those who hold it may at some stage in the future be tempted to hold a different, obviously untenable, position.

Evidently this is no more logical than the chimera of a "sedevacantist pope" with which Davies contradictorily menaces us. But the reason for such a superabundance of slipshod argument and fallacious reasoning may well be that it is not really on the basis of his logic that Davies is expecting his readers to agree with him: certainly he appears to think that his own authority is sufficient for this purpose even when unsupported by any effort at argument, for he says "*I* have no doubt that it is diabolically-inspired madness" and "*I* have no doubt at all that at present Satan is concentrating his efforts upon the traditionalist movement with very great success." Many of us will agree with the last sentiment quoted, but the fact that this is Davies's opinion is obviously not in the slightest degree relevant to his case and no one but a megalomaniac would have included among the "evidence" in an article on controverted theological questions, his own *opinions* on the subject in question.

A Dearth of Weighty Theologians

Further on in his article Davies writes:

I would like to make two further comments concerning the O.R.C.M. article. Firstly, I have not heard of any 'weighty theologians' who uphold the sedevacantist theory, just as I do not know of a single weighty theologian who thinks that the New Mass is invalid *per se* in either its Latin or English version. Nor do I know of any instance which could justify accusing one of the four popes subsequent to Pope Pius XII of formal heresy.

It may well be true that the number of *weighty theologians* who hold the view that the Holy See is currently vacant is exactly the same as the number of contemporary *weighty theologians* who recognized the Divinity of Our Lord two thousand years ago – namely, none. However, Davies does not tell us what significance he attaches to this fact. For it to have any significance it would be necessary to establish that weighty theologians are always right or that no theological opinion can be correct which is not supported by at least one weighty theologian. If Davies is really defending either of these views, he should say so and prove his case. Meanwhile, suffice it to note that, as we shall shortly see, there is no dearth of genuinely weighty theologians of the *past* who have held that any purported pope who taught heresy would be manifesting the fact that he was not validly occupying the papal office, and that there are also countless theologians and several popes who have branded as heretical, doctrines unequivocally espoused and officially taught by John-Paul II who cannot fail to be aware of these facts. Surely the only reason that Divine Providence has not furnished us with weighty theologians today to show us how to put these two facts together and draw the logical conclusion from them is simply that weighty theologians are quite unnecessary to draw an inference that would be obvious to a small child.

As for the absence of a weighty theologian who thinks that the New Mass is invalid *per se* in either its Latin or English version, one is lost for words. Surely before assessing the opinions of "weighty theologians" on this subject, it would be necessary to establish whether the "weighty theologians" had committed themselves to the New Mass by celebrating it. Of what value is the view of a "weighty theologian" that the "Mass" which he celebrates daily is valid? Could one expect him to hold the contrary view? And anyhow, *is* there such a creature as a "weighty theologian" alive today? Certainly there are a handful of those who have a competent grasp of textbook theology and are able to apply it and express it reliably, but they could scarcely be called "weighty theologians" in their own right. There are undoubtedly some aging Dominicans and Jesuits who have studied their St. Thomas well in their youth and still remember it. But even those of them who may have been lecturers or professors in seminaries at some stage would scarcely dream of considering themselves to be "weighty theologians". Theologians they may be, but *weighty* theologians they certainly are not. Such a distinction could have been granted to a number of writers in the last century and the early part of this century, but, this writer knows of no one living who merits it, and no piece of writing connected with the Catholic religion that has emerged in the last twenty years could be termed a "weighty theological treatise".[16] Indeed no one, whatever his theological standpoint, who was familiar with the writings of the weighty theologians of the past, would contemplate including among their number any author of the second half of the twentieth century,[17] whether orthodox, modernistic or frankly heretical, except possibly the Protestant Barth and the Modernist "Catholic" Rahner – neither of whose failure to denounce John-Paul II and the New Mass will cut much ice with Catholics who are acquainted with their credentials. And lest it be suggested that this is merely a question of John S. Daly's opinion against Davies's, we invite anyone who doubts the reality of the picture just painted of the theological desert in which we live to find out from Davies himself which theologians alive today he regards as weighty (he might ask for the names of a few non-weighty ones also to

---

[16] Perhaps an exception should be made for Arnaldo Vidigal Xavier da Silveira's study on *The Theological and Moral Implications of the New Rite of Mass* or for Fr. Bernard Lucien's *Études sur la Liberté Religieuse*.

[17] The nearest approach is of course Fr. Réginald Garrigou-Lagrange O.P. (1877-1964).

contrast them with) and to check directly with the individuals in question what genuine claim they have to be considered even *"auctores probati"* (*approved* authors) let alone *"auctores gravis nominis"* (*weighty* authors). Relevant to this question is the fact that no theological author not expressly recognized as such by the Church can be considered even merely "approved" unless he enjoys "common reputation ... to this effect." (Fr. F.S. Miaskiewicz J.C.D.: *Supplied Jurisdiction*, p. 201, Catholic University of America, 1940)

Affected Ignorance?

In reality, the assertion that Davies does not know "of any instances which could justify accusing one of the four Popes [sic] subsequent to Pope Pius XII of formal heresy" is simply dishonest. As we shall be seeing in a later chapter, Davies himself has drawn attention to some of their heresies and made it clear that they contradict previous teaching of the Church, but has carefully shied away from considering the question of whether they are (a) merely erroneous or (b) actually heretical. In other words, if he was ignorant of such instances of heresy at the time that he wrote this article, his ignorance was certainly not invincible.

But deeper insight into the standards of scholarly integrity and objectivity which Davies observes is gained from the fact that, *since he wrote the article, such heresies have been pointed out to him from countless different sources and have been thoroughly documented in writings which have been widely available*, and of which Davies could have avoided taking notice only if he was determined to bury his head in the sand.

Indeed, the present writer was one of those who adduced some instances of heresy for him, in a letter dated April 1983.

To quote those parts of the letter in which the recent claimants to the papacy were convicted of heresy would involve duplication of evidence produced elsewhere in this chapter, but the letter reproduced two passages of heretical import contained in the decree on religious liberty and, by contrasting them with previous papal teachings, argued them to be heretical: "The doctrine of freedom of conscience and religious liberty is condemned heresy," was its conclusion.

And Davies's reaction to this letter was ... – complete silence; silence which exposes more eloquently than any commentary the utter mendacity of his assertion that "if anyone knows of a case where one of these popes has formally and pertinaciously contradicted the defined teaching of the Church, I would be interested to know of it."

The Ordinary Magisterium: Divinely Guaranteed Source of Falsehood

It is not the least remarkable feature of this veritable catalogue of outrageous offences committed against truth and logic, that the greatest outrage of all is reserved for the very end of his article. There we read as follows:

> The case of the Vatican II Religious Liberty Declaration is one of the key-arguments of the sedevacantists. They claim that it is heretical and that any Pope endorsing it must '*ipso facto*' forfeit his office. It must be remembered that the Declaration is a document of the Ordinary Magisterium of the Church, and that the possibility of error occurs or can occur in such documents where it is a matter of some *novel teaching*. The Magisterium can eventually correct such an error without compromising itself.

It is so difficult to bring oneself to believe that anyone can, without quoting a single authority, so blatantly invent theology for the purpose of deceiving, and leading astray, his readers, that, lest any readers be carried by the sheer brazenness with which Davies exposes himself, it must be emphasized, in the clearest and most unambiguous terms, that the assertion that the Ordinary Magisterium can teach error, whether in a "novel teaching" or otherwise, is completely unfounded. And what is even less credible is that the Ordinary Magisterium could teach an error *previously condemned* by the Church in a document recognized as infallible by all serious theologians, as is *Quanta Cura*. In fact, the assertion that "the Magisterium can eventually correct such an error without compromising itself" is obviously absurd. The word "Magisterium" means "teaching authority" and how can it be suggested that *any* teaching authority could admit that it had taught a glaring error and retract it without diminishing the status of its authority?

An Apparent Incompatibility

Yet what follows immediately afterwards in Davies's article manages to be even worse:

> Nor has it been proved conclusively that this document does indeed contain error. What many traditionalists, myself included, maintain is that a passage included in the Declaration appears incompatible with previous teaching of the Magisterium. Some of the theologians most directly responsible for drafting this Declaration have admitted that they are as yet unable to demonstrate how the teaching of the Declaration can be reconciled with previous teaching. It will, therefore, be the eventual task of the Magisterium to evaluate the objections made to the Declaration and then to explain how it is compatible with previous teaching, or, to admit that it is not compatible and proceed to correct it.

Notice that Davies denies that the presence of error in the Declaration on Religious Liberty has been "proved conclusively". He insists that his own position is merely that part of the Declaration *appears* incompatible with previous teaching. The reality of the matter, as can be verified by anyone who cares to compare the key passage from *Quanta Cura* with the relevant passage in the Vatican II declaration concerning religious liberty (*Dignitatis Humanæ*), is that the two documents contradict one another as definitely as black is the opposite of white. Davies's fantasy, by contrast to the reality, is that it has not yet been "proved conclusively" that black is the opposite of white; instead that, in his opinion, black "appears incompatible" with white. And this is no particularly serious problem. It simply means that the Magisterium will eventually – what do the confused faithful do in the meantime? one wonders – have either to explain how black is the same as white, or else admit that black is not white. At the moment, of course, the Vatican's policy is to avoid comparisons between black and white (*Quanta Cura* and *Dignitatis Humanæ*) at any cost. But in the unlikely event of its ever making a declaration on the subject, the declaration would either have to maintain the self-evidently false proposition that the two documents are compatible (i.e. that black is white) or would have to admit having previously taught error; for it would have to discard *either Quanta Cura* or *Dignitatis Humanæ* – a course which would obviously inspire no confidence that the decision then made would not itself be reversed at some future point.

A More Than Apparent Incompatibility

However, one is forced to suspect that Davies has adopted this position merely in order to justify the stance in relation to the Holy See which he is maintaining in his article; for it was certainly not his position two years earlier in 1980 when he wrote his pamphlet *Archbishop Lefebvre and Religious Liberty*. There, on p. 9, he wrote thus:

> It [the most blatantly un-Catholic section of the Declaration on Religious Liberty] could certainly be considered the most important article in any document of the Council as, until it is corrected by the Magisterium [!], *it represents not simply a contradiction of consistently re-iterated and possibly [!] infallible, papal teaching but an implicit repudiation of the kingship of Christ.*

And on p. 10 he wrote, in connection with the heretical sentence of the Declaration:

> The sentence just cited is, then, neither in harmony with the revealed word of God nor reason.

It seems, therefore, that:

(a) When the occupancy of the Holy See is not at stake, Davies is prepared to face reality and admit that the controversial passage in the *Declaration on Religious Liberty* is *definitely* erroneous and in conflict with Divine revelation (i.e. heretical); but

(b) When he realizes that recognition of this fact may lead to the conclusion that the Holy See is vacant, he at once exercises what George Orwell calls "protective stupidity"[18] and denies the clear evidence of his own reason by saying that the error is not "proved conclusively," and that the passage merely "*appears* incompatible with previous teaching."

All of which, to the present writer at least, "appears incompatible" with even the most minimal standards of scholarship or honesty.

Prevarication

It is no less staggering that Davies has the effrontery to tell his readers that "some of the theologians [sic] most directly responsible for drafting this Declaration have admitted that they are as yet *unable to demonstrate* [emphasis added] how the teaching of the Declaration can be reconciled with previous teaching." Can *anyone* who is prepared to take on the task of teaching about the Catholic Faith not know that, when a heretical "theologian" who is engaged in overturning the Church's teaching says, "I am not yet able to show how this new doctrine is compatible with the old doctrine," what he knows that his fellow-subversives will understand by those words is that the new doctrine quite evidently neither is nor can be compatible with the old doctrine, but that he is hoping that, by implying that a reconciliation may "one day" be discovered, people will be prepared to give him and his heresy the benefit of the doubt in the interim?

---

[18] *Nineteen Eighty-Four* (p. 170 in the Penguin edition).

With regard to Davies's suggestion that the Magisterium can teach error and then acknowledge and retract its mistake, the facts have already been made clear. In the passage just quoted, he conveys the impression that such a course on the part of the Magisterium is not only a theological possibility, but even a relatively routine affair, of which the mechanics may be taken for granted. Nonchalantly he informs us of the supposed procedure by which the Magisterium will "evaluate the objections made to the Declaration and ... if necessary ... admit that it is not compatible and proceed to correct it;" and from what he says, those who do not know better could hardly fail to infer that it is a regular and automatic procedure for a pope on issuing a formal declaration teaching Catholics what they must believe on some subject, then to await "objections" from the faithful, to "evaluate" these when they arrive, and if necessary to alter his teaching in the light of them.

Needless to say this is not and never has been and never could be the procedure of the Catholic Church, *which holds that the papal Ordinary Magisterium is protected by a special Providence from ever leading the faithful into error*. In fact it is nothing but a thinly disguised version of the theory of Hans Küng and others that popes ought to amend the teachings of the Church in the light of what the "faithful" want to believe.[19] On reading such passages in Davies's writings it is necessary forcibly to remind oneself that the author is almost everywhere recognized, not as a neo-Modernist of the Karl Rahner school, but as – in the words of one of the reviews quoted on the cover

---

[19] If, strictly for the sake of argument, the possibility (which is in fact no possibility at all) be allowed that Davies is right, and the Ordinary Magisterium is liable to fall into error which can subsequently be corrected, it is hard to see how he can be *certain*, for instance, that artificial birth control, which, in the opinion of most Catholic theologians has not been condemned by the Extraordinary Magisterium either, is truly immoral. Why could not the Magisterium "evaluate" the "conscientious dissent" of the liberals and change its infallible mind on this topic as well as on that of religious liberty?

of *Cranmer's Godly Order* – "the most brilliant polemicist of the right."

Further Titbits

This concludes the consideration of Davies's article on "The Sedevacantists", and before proceeding to consider his other major article on the occupancy or otherwise of the Holy See it seems appropriate at this point to comment on one or two extracts from his other writings which touch on the same subject.

Let us turn to the first volume of Davies's *Apologia Pro Marcel Lefebvre*. On p. 188 he writes:

> Many episcopates, which declare themselves to be in communion with the Pope, and whom the Pope does not reject from his communion, are objectively outside the Catholic communion.

Then he goes on to mention specifically the episcopate of Holland and the episcopate of France as having departed from Catholic communion as a result of heresy, and comments:

> There is no question here of some handful of marginal dissidents as the Pope [Paul VI] insinuates in his allocution. There is the question of the greater part of the actual holders of the Apostolic succession. Legitimate holders? Yes, but prevaricators, deserters, impostors.

Within the space of a few lines, therefore, Davies has asserted:

(a) that the majority of contemporary bishops are "objectively outside the Catholic communion;" but, in the same breath,

(b) that they are at the same time "legitimate;" and, as if this were not enough, in the next breath,

(c) that while not ceasing to be legitimate holders of the episcopal office, they are also "deserters" and "impostors."

It seems that Davies's only consistent feature is his inconsistency.

On pages 416 and 417 of the same work, Davies devotes a short consideration to the hypothesis of a heretical pope. He reaches no definite conclusion on the subject himself, but he does mention the correct doctrine, namely that a heretical pope would automatically cease to be pope at the same time as he would automatically cease to be a member of the Church, attributing this doctrine to "one school of thought, represented by St. Robert Bellarmine." What, interestingly, he does not do, in this passage, is to go as far as some writers have done, and assert that, no matter how blatant the heresies of a claimant to the papacy may be, he will continue to occupy the office validly since he will not be a heretic till he has received a canonical warning, which, as he is the supreme authority in the Church and there is no authority competent to issue such a warning to him, can never happen. He simply lays down that the heretical "pope" in question probably is *not* a true pope, but nevertheless must be treated as if he is one. Which of these positions is the more ludicrous? Strong arguments could be mounted for either of them deserving the prize.

On p. 599 of *Pope Paul's New Mass*, Davies quotes an important extract from the famous Counter-Reformation Jesuit theologian Suarez which is worth reproducing:

> The pope can be a schismatic if he does not want to have union and bond with the whole body of the Church as he should, if he attempts to excommunicate the whole Church, or if he wants to abolish all ecclesiastical ceremonies which are confirmed by Apostolic tradition, as Cajetan remarks.

Davies comments on this as follows:

> It is an indisputable fact that never in the history of the Church has any pope presided over so wholesale an abolition of traditional customs and ceremonies as Pope Paul VI.

Davies could have gone further, and pointed out that there is *no* liturgical ceremony of the Church which he did *not* abolish or alter. And of course, this means that, in the opinion of Suarez, Paul VI was a schismatic and therefore outside the Church.

And, having quoted such a crucial passage from such a distinguished theologian, what use does Davies then make of it? Almost unbelievably, he *completely passes over* the question of whether Paul VI *was* in fact a schismatic, and simply uses the extract to support his claim that a true pope can give a command which is morally illicit.

By this stage it is obvious that all of Davies's comments which are remotely related to the vacancy of the Holy See amount to no more than wishful thinking; and that they flow automatically from an attitude which he states explicitly in an article in *The Remnant* for 15th August 1985. Not only, he says, does he object to priests who *hold* that John-Paul II is not a true pope; he objects also to all priests who even go so far as to "*suggest* that Pope John-Paul II *might* not be a true pope."[20]

What this means is that Davies is basically classifying the idea that the Holy See might be vacant as a bad thought which should never be entertained but should be driven from the mind as soon as it enters. And excellent advice this is in relation to temptations against faith or chastity; but *not* in relation to the "temptation" to use one's God-given reason to work out how Catholic doctrine and law apply to the present situation in the Church. Far from being sinful, this last is surely the *duty* of all conscientious Catholics; and those who follow Davies's example and advice by rejecting a reasonable theory out of hand

---

[20] A category which certainly includes Archbishop Lefebvre: "While we are certain that the faith the Church has taught for 20 centuries cannot contain error, we are much further from absolute certitude that the pope is truly pope." (*Le Figaro*, 4th August, 1976) 2. "It is possible we may be obliged to believe this pope is not pope. " (Talk, March 30 and April 18, 1986, published in *The Angelus*, July 1986) "I don't know if the time has come to say that the pope is a heretic (...) Perhaps after this famous meeting of Assisi, perhaps we must say that the pope is a heretic, is apostate. Now I don't wish yet to say it formally and solemnly, but it seems at first sight that it is impossible for a pope to be formally and publicly heretical. (...) So it is possible we may be obliged to believe this pope is not pope." (Talks, 30th March and 18th April, 1986, text as published in *The Angelus*, July 1986)

and shrinking from serious examination of the evidence for it will certainly not be able to plead on the Day of Judgement that their ignorance was invincible.

Communist Tactics

Writing in *The Remnant* on 15th June 1986, Davies informed his readers that those who reject John-Paul II as the legitimate pope

> ... are men who are to be pitied and prayed for rather than answered.

Certainly there exists a "nut-case" category of souls so impervious to reason that the attempt to persuade them by logic to abandon their errors is a forlorn one and not worth embarking on, but it is not immediately clear why all those who consider John-Paul II to be a heretic and ineligible to be pope must necessarily be classified along with them. There is, after all, at the very least a *"prima facie"* case for accusing Wojtyła of heresy (whether the Vatican II religious liberty doctrine falls into this category is, after all, mentioned[21] in Davies's own writings, and there are countless other examples), and there is a law in the *Code of Canon Law* (Canon 188§4) and a weighty papal bull (*Cum Ex Apostolatus*) confirming the common opinion of theologians that a pope cannot retain his office if he should fall into heresy.

Readers are invited to reflect on the unmistakably sneering tone of Davies's sentence just quoted – it cannot even be argued that he is charitably touting for pity and prayers for those who reject John-Paul II, for *"are* to be pitied and prayed for rather than ..." is a description rather than a request. And it should not be forgotten that one of the favourite Communist methods for silencing criticism is publicly to brand its opponents with the stigma of insanity or similar, a tactic the use of which by the Conciliar Church has on more than one occasion been

---

[21] Albeit very inadequately treated!

documented. It might be added that St. Thomas Aquinas quotes thousands upon thousands of erroneous "objections" to his various teachings in his massive *Summa Theologiæ*, but to not a single such objection, however absurd, is the Angelic Doctor's reply, "those who hold this opinion are not worthy of an answer and deserve only pity and prayer," or anything remotely resembling that reply.

V

It seems, moreover, that Davies himself did not sincerely believe what he had said, for in 1986 there was an about-face and he decided once more to "answer" the "sedevacantist" case.

Discussion of how he did so will involve us in a certain amount of historical background concerning correspondence between, on the one hand, N.M. Gwynne and John S. Daly of Britons Catholic Library, and on the other, the late Mr. Hamish Fraser, editor of *Approaches*[22] and Michael Davies. For convenience initials will sometimes be used instead of the full names of those involved. This background is as follows.

In April 1986, John-Paul II, as few readers of this *Evaluation* will be unaware, visited the synagogue in Rome and, while there, declared that the Jews were not responsible for the crucifixion of Our Lord. Shortly afterwards, N.M.G. happened to be writing to Hamish Fraser[23] on another subject, and he made use of the opportunity thus presented to ask Fraser

---

[22] A traditional Catholic periodical which has now been replaced by a similar but less impressive one called *À Propos* edited by Hamish Fraser's son Anthony.

[23] Hamish Fraser (1913-1986) was a convert from Marxism and had been a volunteer to fight against Catholicism in the Spanish Civil War where he was a political commissar and ultimately a lieutenant of the Secret Police (SIM), fighting with the 15th International Brigade. His review *Approaches,* founded in 1965, was always worth reading and his understanding of the subversive action of the organized anti-Christian forces in the political and religious domains was far superior to Davies's.

whether he considered John-Paul's statement to be heretical. N.M.G.'s reason for putting this question was not in order to find out the answer – which, given that Holy Scripture, as unanimously understood by the Fathers, teaches that the Jews *were* responsible, is surely affirmative. Rather it was:

(a) to try to persuade Fraser to commit himself on the subject of whether John-Paul II had actually uttered heresy (this being, of course, half-way to convincing him of the vacancy of the Holy See); and

(b) to see if Fraser might furnish any useful authorities affirming the collective responsibility of the Jews for the horrendous crime of deicide – which was not unlikely in view of the subject's falling more within Fraser's sphere of competence than our own.

Though amicable enough, Fraser's response, dated 19th April, evaded the question. Instead of answering it pointed out the extraordinary disposition of Divine Providence according to which the "First Reading" of the Novus Ordo, on the very day that John-Paul exculpated the Jews, constituted a clear refutation of his words, including as it did the statement of St. Peter to the Jews that (to quote the version Fraser quoted) "it was *you* who had Him executed by hanging on a tree."[24] (Acts 5:30)

Undeterred, N.M.G. sent back a reply which included the following paragraph:

> You didn't answer my question on whether that particular statement of John-Paul II was technically heretical. I really would like to know your view on this ....

Here is the relevant part of Fraser's response, which was dated 29th April:

> Re the statement by JP II alleged to be heretical, alas! having by now mislaid your letter in the sea of paper which afflicts me for my

---

[24] The translation is taken directly from a Novus Ordo "missalette" and is from the Jerusalem Bible.

sins I cannot now recall which statement you had referred to. In any case my reply would be essentially that of the late Père Joseph de Sainte Marie O. Carm ....

And at the foot of the page, Fraser quoted in French a statement by this contemporary French theologian (1931-85), of which the following is an English translation:

> Some people think that they can justify their indiscriminate attitude by convincing themselves that the bishops – and the pope, the Abbé de Nantes adds – are heretics, and have consequently cut themselves off from communion with the Church. They must be reminded that only the formal sin of heresy or schism has the effect of excommunication, and not error in good faith. And in order for the sin of heresy or schism to be formal, the person who is materially in error must have been admonished by the hierarchy and called upon to retract his error or disobedience. As the hierarchy has today given up complying with this duty, the sin of schism or heresy is not consummated, nor, consequently, is communion with the Church broken. (*Lettre à un Ami*, Nº 16, 24th March 1975)

Now this is all very well; or at least it *would* be if it were true. But it is not. **It just is not**. As some readers will know and others will not, the theory that formal heresy is not verified unless canonical warnings are given *was invented by certain unscrupulous "traditionalists" in the post-Vatican II era to justify their continued allegiance to Paul VI and John-Paul II.* In reality the *Code of Canon Law* itself makes clear that the only essential features of the crime of heresy are error in the intellect (either doubt or denial concerning one or more dogmas) and pertinacity in the will – i.e. obstinacy in this position despite *awareness* that it is contrary to the teaching of the Church. Canonical warnings are called for only when someone is "*suspect* of heresy". When there is *no doubt* that he is a heretic, the warning would be superfluous. Moreover, even when the person is only *suspected* of heresy, the necessary warnings can be administered by *anyone at all* – there is no need for the hierarchy to be involved.

The obvious next step for N.M.G. to take, therefore, was to write again to Fraser asking him to supply authority for Père Joseph's assertion. Here is the full text of N.M.G.'s letter dated 2nd May 1986:

> Dear Hamish,
>
> Many thanks for your letter incorporating a photocopy of the passage by the late Père Joseph.
>
> If he is right in asserting that one does not become a formal heretic, and subject to the penalties applicable to formal heretics, unless and until one has received canonical warning(s), those who believe that the Holy See is vacant do not have a leg to stand on. However, *is* he right? His assertion is not new to me, of course, and I and others have searched diligently and for some time for authority supporting his assertion; but have found none. On the contrary, all my searches, which include all the recognized commentaries on Canon Law, papal statements, Fathers and Doctors of the Church, other recognized theologians, etc. (pre-Vatican II, of course) have indicated that the very opposite is the case, and that no canonical warning, or warning of any kind, is necessary.
>
> Naturally, if there were such an authority, I for one would accept John-Paul II as pope forthwith. Perhaps you could dig one up or find someone who can. On the other hand, if there is no such authority, and indeed all the authorities are on the other side, people like Père Joseph have no business inventing such a doctrine.
>
> Would it be a good idea to raise this whole question in a future *Approaches*?
>
> I look forward to hearing from you.
>
> (...)

Hamish Fraser's undated reply to N.M.G.'s request for some authority supporting his position was as follows:

> I make no claim whatever to expertise whether in theology or Canon Law. However, given the definition of a heretic in Canon Law (1917)† and since one can no more live outwith[25] the law of the Church than jump over one's own head, I can't see what is your problem ....

---

[25] Fraser, a Scot, uses the Scottish form "outwith" meaning "outside".

†Cf. Michael Davies's article in *Approaches* Nº 77 enclosed.

And attached to the letter was a copy of Davies's first article on the validity of Archbishop Lefebvre's Orders which will be examined in Chapter 9(A) of this *Evaluation*. In this article the following words had been marked with a "highlighter":

> ... since 1918 we have had the *Code of Canon Law* and Pope Benedict XV's constitution *Providentissima Mater Ecclesia*. This has become the law of the Church and defines what it means to be a heretic. A heretic, according to the *Code of Canon Law*, is one who, having said, written or given a teaching contrary to Catholic truth, refuses to admit and retract his error after having been warned canonically that he must do so. (*loc. cit.*, p. 11)

In summary, Hamish Fraser, a retired teacher turned Catholic writer, makes an assertion in 1986 about what is contained in Canon Law; as evidence for this he cites the same assertion made by a priest of the Conciliar Church in a small circulation French periodical in 1975; and when he is asked for *real* authority, he produces the same assertion made in 1980 by Mr. Michael Davies, a teacher and part-time writer. Thus, when it comes to it, the only available authority in support of the word of a member of the teaching profession who is at least partially deceived by the Conciliar Church is the word of another member of the teaching profession who is at least partially deceived by the Conciliar Church, neither of whom, to the best of my knowledge, is endowed with infallibility. And Fraser accused *others* of trying to jump over their own heads!

N.M.G.'s next effort to pin Fraser down was dated 27th May:

> Dear Hamish,
> Many thanks for your letter. In the second sentence you said: 'Given the definition of a heretic in Canon Law (1917) and since one can no more live outwith [which I presume is Scots for 'outside'] the law of the Church than jump over one's own head, I can't see your problem.'

I fully agree that it is impossible to live outwith or outside the Catholic Church.

However, you referred me to Michael Davies's article which contained the astounding words: 'A heretic according to the *Code of Canon Law* is one who, having said, written or given a teaching contrary to Catholic truth, refuses to admit and retract his error after he has been warned canonically that he must do so.' I do not know where Michael Davies gets this 'Canon Law definition' of a heretic from, but it was certainly not in the 1917 *Code* itself nor in any commentary on the Code. The facts are quite otherwise.

I enclose a copy of Canon 1325 in Latin, together with Fr. Augustine's commentary on it which is one of the fullest commentaries to have been written in English, and I invite you to find any reference to refusal to retract or to canonical warnings, either in this canon or in any canon in the *Code*, which could conceivably be applicable (...) That paragraph by Michael Davies is quite simply an invention, and moreover an invention of an extremely serious matter. He says it is 'proof' of his assertion that 'thus no prelate is a formal heretic within the terms of the Code of Canon Law.'

(Both quotations from Michael Davies are from p. 11 of the *Approaches* N° 71 that you enclosed.)

I hope for your comments on the above.

(...)

The correspondence continued with the following note to N.M.G. from Fraser, in which the latter "passes the buck" to Davies:

Many thanks for your letter and enclosures, copies of which I have forwarded to Michael Davies.

Every good wish,

(...)

N.M.G.'s reply (7th July) is self-explanatory:

Many thanks for your note of 3rd June. I have been abroad and have only just received it.

I note that you have sent copies of my letter and its enclosures to Michael Davies. What will you do if he makes no answer, which from my experience is how he usually deals with questions on this subject?

Best wishes,

(...)

On July 10th Fraser wrote as follows:

As it happened I had sent on your letter etc. to Michael Davies just as he was doing a piece, *The Divine Constitution and Indefectibility of the Church*, which he amended to deal with the points you had made. It will be included in *Approaches* 93-4, now in course of preparation. Therefore, when you get it you'll be able to see what *in effect* is his reply.

On 14th July N.M.G. wrote to Fraser asking if he would be kind enough to let him have an advance copy of the Davies article, and on 19th July a copy duly arrived. One of the most noteworthy features of this essay by Davies, and a feature which was immediately apparent to N.M.G. and to the present writer in reading this advance copy, was that, in addition to including, as one could have safely expected, many examples of the slapdash scholarship and faulty theology that permeate all of Davies's writings, it was even defective in the very areas in which Davies's writings are generally admirable – namely prose style and clarity of thought. Previously we had always been happy to say that, no matter how strongly one might disagree with Davies, at least he had the virtues that one always saw exactly what point he was making and that one never found his writing onerous to read. But there is no sign of such virtues in *The Divine Constitution and Indefectibility of the Church* (which, despite this drawback, is currently in print under the title *I Am With You Always* and has enjoyed a wide circulation – doubtless because it argues, however ineptly, in favour of what a large number of people *wish* to believe). It is a very shoddy piece: theology aside, the writing is turgid, difficult to follow and generally laborious, while the argument throughout is extremely loose, not only where he is defending the indefensible, but even where the point he is making is perfectly true. Although I shall shortly be examining it in some detail, the only part which is relevant for present purposes is a passage which concerns the extent to which admonitions (i.e. formal warnings), etc., are necessary before the canonical effects of heresy (excommunication, loss of office, etc.) take place. We quote this passage in full:

> Once the crime of heresy becomes public, even though it incurs *ipso facto* excommunication, the censure incurred must be made public. A judicial examination of the crime takes place, and a formal declaration (declaratory sentence) is made that the delinquent has incurred censure. This involves the question as to whether the crime of heresy requires an admonition from the competent authority within the Church before the penalty of excommunication is pronounced. The old[26] *Code of Canon Law* does not state this specifically, but an eminent theologian has assured me that this was the case in practice. It is evident that if a sentence was to be pronounced the person involved would be informed, and that if he then abjured his heresy he would escape censure.

Aha! The truth has been allowed to creep out. After blithely telling his readers for years (e.g. in *Approaches* N° 77 quoted above) that the *Code of Canon Law* defines a heretic as one who has received "canonical warnings" and resisted them, at last Davies admits the truth that "the old *Code of Canon Law* does not state this specifically," though he did not take the obvious next step of acknowledging that he had misled his readers in former pronouncements he had made on the subject. Nor, for that matter, did he make a further sacrifice of pride to truthfulness and inform his readers that the *Code* not only "does not state this 'specifically'", but does not say it *non*-specifically either. But what he *does* do is give us at least what we have so

---

[26] I.e. the 1917 *Code of Canon Law* as opposed to the revised *Code* promulgated by John-Paul II in 1983 and described by Archbishop Lefebvre and Bishop de Castro Mayer in their joint letter of 21ˢᵗ November 1983 as containing "errors...not to say heresies".

long been waiting and asking for, namely an authority – to wit, "an eminent theologian"! Thus the words of Hamish Fraser are vouched for by Père Joseph, and the words of Père Joseph are vouched for by Michael Davies, and the words of Michael Davies are vouched for by an anonymous theologian, whose credentials are, in turn, vouched for by Michael Davies.

But Davies's readers are not permitted to know *who* the anonymous theologian *is*, and consequently are prevented from independently examining the theologian's credentials to establish whether or not Davies's esteem for him is well-founded. So, at bottom, the fact is that Hamish Fraser is standing on the shoulders of Père Joseph, and Père Joseph is standing on the shoulders of Michael Davies, and Michael Davies is standing on *his own* shoulders – but since it is no more possible to stand on one's own shoulders than it is, in Hamish Fraser's vivid metaphor, "to jump over one's own head," the entire column of mutually dependent warriors collapses to the ground in confusion.

N.M.G. thought it more prudent not to point out the absurdity of the whole affair to Fraser at this stage, for he was hoping against hope that Fraser might publish a letter from him, together with a (doubtless inadequate) rejoinder from Michael Davies, thus making the truth available to a more extensive readership than would otherwise have been the case. Consequently, N.M.G. replied (8th August) in the following terms:

> Dear Hamish,
> I am so sorry for my delay in answering your letter of 19th July, in which you very kindly enclosed an advance copy of Michael Davies's piece with his comments on the vacancy or otherwise of the Holy See.
> My comments on what Michael Davies says in that article, relevant to the issue, are as follows:
> His argument seems to be that no one can be excommunicated through public heresy under the 1917 *Code of Canon Law* unless

and until he has received a canonical admonition from a competent authority. Michael Davies's authority for this is an 'eminent theologian' who has told him that the Church never officially declared a heretic excommunicated until he had been admonished and given the opportunity to repent.

Contrary to what Davies says, the facts on this point of Canon Law *are* explicitly covered in the 1917 *Code*. And what the *Code* indicates is that what Davies says is undoubtedly correct in respect of an *occult* heretic, for Canon 2314 makes it clear that, while all heretics are excommunicated '*ipso facto*', an occult heretic would not lose his offices until the competent authority imposed this penalty on him. But *public* heretics, aside from the provisions of this canon, fall under Canon 188§4, which expressly says, of those "who *publicly* defect from the Faith", that they lose all their offices '*ipso facto*' and '*without any declaration*'.

By way of authority for this assertion, Jone's *Commentary on the Code of Canon Law*, paraphrasing Canon 188§4, says that public heresy leads to all offices becoming vacant automatically, while 'on account of defection [from the Faith] which is *not* public, loss of office is indeed imposed but *must be inflicted by a judgement.*' In other words what Michael Davies claims to be universal is only *particular*, to occult heretics.

The distinction is completely clearly drawn.

In view of this, I don't think that Michael Davies has got to grips with the problem.† I look forward to your thoughts.

(…)

†I.e. because of course no one has ever suggested that John-Paul II is an *occult* heretic.

This letter received no reply from Fraser, but in late September a letter arrived from Davies himself, the body of which was as follows:

Hamish sent me a copy of your letter of 8 August. I was in the U.S.A. from the end of July to the beginning of September, and I had to return to school within a few days of getting back. I am only now able to start dealing with the correspondence which accumulated in my absence.

The article in *APPROACHES* was, to a large extent, a draft of a booklet which will be printed in the U.S.A. this month. This version will contain a number of corrections and improvements, but nothing of any great significance.

I am well aware of Canon 188§4, but did not include it in the study as I understand it does not refer to heresy, the rejection of an article of the Faith, but to apostasy, defection from the Faith. An apostate who has totally abandoned the Catholic Faith is deemed to have resigned. As one of the canon lawyers I consulted remarked concerning this Canon: 'If a bishop joins the Baptists he ceases to be bishop of the diocese.'

I would be very interested in seeing a photocopy of the relevant passage from Jone's Commentary which, you say, interprets Canon 188§4 as referring not to complete apostasy but to heresy. I would then submit it to the same canonist for his opinion. Should it transpire that you are correct, I will ensure that my booklet is amended in subsequent editions and that a correction is published in *Approaches*.

Needless to say, the whole question is to some extent merely academic, as the old Code is no longer in force, and, of course, no one has to the best of my knowledge, been able to cite an instance of the pertinacious denial of a *de fide* doctrine on the part of the Pope.

All good wishes,

(...)

The following reply, composed by N.M.G. and J.S.D. together, was sent on 8th October 1986:

Dear Michael,

Many thanks for your letter of 19th September on the subject of Canon 188§4 of the 1917 *Code of Canon Law*. I too was away at the time that your letter arrived, so I hope that you will forgive the delay in responding to it. I was very pleased to be able to discuss the topic with you because one thing I am sure of is that, whether my position in respect of John-Paul II is right or wrong, I am certainly not alone in holding it, and I do not think that the argument based on Canon 188§4 has really been given satisfactory treatment by any defender of the validity of John-Paul II's pontificate.

Before I address the key question of whether the words '*a catholica fide publice defecerit*'[27] refer to heretics or only to apostates, may I clear up what I believe to be a slight confusion in your letter on the meaning of the term 'apostate'?

You wrote:

'I understand it [Canon 188§4] does not refer to heresy, the rejection of an article of the Faith, but to apostasy, defection from the Faith. An apostate who has totally abandoned the Catholic Faith is deemed to have resigned. As one of the canon lawyers I consulted remarked concerning this canon: 'If a bishop joins the Baptists he ceases to be the bishop of the diocese.'

It appears from this paragraph that you understand the word 'apostate' to apply, for instance, to someone who leaves the Catholic Church and becomes a Baptist, and that you are restricting the connotation of the term 'heretic' to those who reject one article of the Faith while not admitting that they have left the Church or become members of another religion.

In fact the terms are somewhat differently defined in Canon 1325§2 of the 1917 *Code* itself, and it is obviously those definitions which should be followed. According to this canon, a heretic is anyone who 'pertinaciously denies or doubts any of the truths which must be believed with Divine and Catholic faith, while continuing to call himself a Christian;' and the same source defines an apostate as one who has 'totally withdrawn from the Christian Faith.'

Thus a Catholic who became a Baptist would be a *heretic* just as much as one who denied the Assumption while continuing to call himself a Catholic. He would not be an *apostate* according to the Canon Law definition of the term. An apostate would be someone who became a Hindu or an atheist.[28]

---

[27] These words are part of Canon 188§4, which states, as readers will recall, that "if a cleric publicly defects from the Catholic Faith, all his offices become vacant by tacit resignation accepted by the law itself, *automatically and without any declaration.*" (This footnote was not part of the original letter sent to Davies, but has been added subsequently for the benefit of readers of this *Evaluation*.)

[28] Fr. Augustine's *Commentary* (Vol. VI, p. 335) says that "an apostate ... is

I realise that outside the *Code* the term 'apostasy' is [sometimes] more broadly defined (including, for instance, even religious who abandon their Orders without sullying their faith at all), but the canonists use the term only as it is defined in the *Code*, and this is obviously the best way of avoiding confusion.

(Naturally we have to use the Canon Law definition rather than the wider usage for this discussion, because what is at issue is a matter of Canon Law.)

So, having established that, the question is whether the automatic loss of office referred to in Canon 188§4 is visited only upon apostates as you have suggested or, as I maintain, upon all those comprehended by the terms 'apostate' *and* 'heretic' according to Canon 1325§2. Obviously if I can demonstrate from authority that my interpretation is correct, it will follow that Canon 188§4 is not restricted to apostates either in the sense of those who completely abandon Christianity or in the sense of those who forsake Catholicism to join a 'Christian' sect.

I think that the enclosed photocopies[29] show that there is really no doubt about the matter. All the authors agree with Jone who writes, under Canon 188§4, that 'defection from the Faith is contained in apostasy and *heresy*.' The only disputed question is whether pure schism (without the almost inevitably concomitant heresy) constitutes 'defection from the Catholic Faith', on which subject the more common opinion is in the negative.

I don't suppose that there is any dispute between us about the fact that heresy is committed by denial (or positive doubt) of any truth-to-be-believed-with-Divine-and-Catholic-faith, and not only by joining a non-Catholic sect; but I thought it worth noting that Mgr. Sipos, on p. 608 of his *Enchiridion Juris Canonici*, of which I enclose a copy, states this explicitly. 'But it is not required that a heretic join any heretic sect.' You will notice that, in the case of Fr. Jone and several other authors, it is necessary to refer to what they

---

one who rejects the whole deposit of faith and becomes an unbeliever," which evidently is *not* true of a Baptist. (This footnote *was* part of the original letter.)

[29] Photocopies from about ten different Canon Law commentaries were enclosed, showing that Canon 188§4 applies to *all* heretics. (Footnote added in this *Evaluation*, not in the original.)

write about Canon 2314 as well as Canon 188§4 to obtain a clear picture of their doctrine.

As I expect you already realise, I do not agree with your statement that 'the whole question is to some extent merely academic as the old Code is no longer in force,' as I believe that it can be demonstrated that John-Paul II most certainly had tacitly renounced his ecclesiastical offices at a time when there was no doubt at all as to which *Code* was in force, and that therefore, not possessing the papal office, he had no power to enact any legislation. I shall not attempt to tackle that topic in this letter, but I hope that we will be able to discuss that point in the future. Obviously there is no need to do so until we are agreed as to what effects would necessarily follow if such pertinacious heresy can be demonstrated.

I should of course be very interested in any opinion you obtain from canon lawyers on the basis of the photocopied material which I am enclosing, and I hope that you will let me know what they say. Obviously if they try to explain away what is taught in the Canon Law manuals to which I have referred, I should want to produce further evidence, but I do not expect that this will be needed.

Incidentally, it may be worth pointing out that in the footnotes to the [...] 1917 *Code*, Pope Paul IV's bull *Cum Ex Apostolatus* is cited as a source for Canon 188§4, and since this bull makes no reference to apostasy but only to heresy, and was particularly aimed against those who held heretical beliefs while continuing to call themselves Catholics and without joining any non-Catholic sect, it is clear that it could not validly have been quoted as a source for Canon 188§4 if that Canon referred only to apostates. (You will appreciate that this point holds good irrespective of whether or not *Cum Ex Apostolatus* is still in force.)

I very much look forward to hearing from you.

(...)

P.S. By the way, I don't know whether you know that John Daly (whom I think you know) and I work together on a number of projects. He and I are jointly responsible for this letter.

On the 9th October N.M.G. sent a copy of this letter to Hamish Fraser to keep him up to date. A week later, Fraser suddenly died. He was a first-rate journalist and a formidable opponent in the eyes of those at the vanguard of the Conciliar "Renewal". He was also an exceedingly likeable and good man. But, tragically, he died still to a considerable extent deluded by the fundamental imposture of the Conciliar Church, and his delusion was in large measure due to his unmerited respect for Michael Davies in matters of theology and Canon Law.

On 25th October Davies wrote a short note explaining that he had been unable to do more than glance at our letter and enclosures as he was busy completing a lecture which he was due to deliver in India the following week. He added: "You can rest assured that, just as was the case with your *per saltem* [sic; he means "salt*u*m" – J.S.D.] query, you will hear from me eventually." N.M.G. answered this note on 17th November:

> Dear Michael,
> Many thanks for your 'holding' letter of 25th October, letting me know that your Indian lecture tour was temporarily interrupting your dealing with my letter and enclosures.
> I hope you return safely from India in due course, and much look forward to hearing from you.
> Best wishes,
>
> (…)
>
> P.S. I have just come across what I think is the most explicit authority I have encountered on the subject of our disagreement, so I am taking the opportunity of enclosing it with this letter in the hope that when you reply to my last letter you will include this evidence in your consideration also. It consists of a quotation from the theologian de Lugo, who is frequently quoted by other authors as having considerable authority.

The enclosure referred to in the P.S. was as follows:

> Neither is it always demanded in the external forum that there be a warning and reprimand, as described above, for somebody to be punished as heretical and pertinacious, and such a requirement is by no means always admitted in practice by the Holy Office. For if it could be established in some other way, given that the doctrine is

well known, given the kind of person involved and given the other circumstances, that the accused could not have been unaware that his thesis was opposed to the Church, he would be considered as a heretic from this fact .... The reason for this is clear, because the exterior warning can serve only to ensure that someone who has erred understands the opposition which exists between his error and the teaching of the Church. If he knew the subject through books and conciliar definitions much better than he could know it by the declarations of someone admonishing him, then there would be no reason to insist on a further warning for him to become pertinacious against the Church. (Cardinal de Lugo, disp. XX, sect. IV, N°s 157-158).

By 24th March 1987, not having heard a word from Davies N.M.G. was finding it increasingly difficult to comply with his advice to "rest assured" that he would hear from him. He was also perturbed by the fact that his *Approaches* article on the indefectibility of the Church had appeared in other places *without* the correction he had promised to incorporate if we proved our case. So N.M.G. addressed the following "chaser" to Davies:

Dear Michael,
I thought that I had better write to you again because I am rather concerned by the length of time during which I have not heard from you on the subject of the application of Canon 188§4 and automatic resignation to heretics as defined in Canon 1325§2 of the 1917 *Code*.
In your letter of 19th September 1986 you said that you would submit the evidence I offered in support of my position to a canon lawyer, and you promised: 'Should it transpire that you are correct, I will ensure that my booklet is amended in subsequent editions and that a correction is published in *Approaches*.'
However since that time I have observed that the article in question has been through several editions without any amendment in the light of the evidence with which I presented you.
Naturally this surprised me, because the evidence I sent you included photocopies from several canonical commentators of the highest authority who explicitly considered the question at issue,

and all took the view which I am maintaining and which you deny in your article/booklet on indefectibility of the Church. May I ask what your present position is on the subject in dispute between us and, if it is unchanged, how you answer the very clear interpretations of Jone, Sipos, Fr. Augustine etc.?

(...)

This letter elicited a prompt reply from Davies dated 27th March:

I am sorry not to have been in touch with you before.
As you are probably aware, I have many commitments in addition to my work as a full time teacher, and I have to impose an order of priorities upon the demands upon my free time. At the moment completing the *Apologia III* and my Religious Liberty book are the top of the list, plus trying to supply as many articles as I can manage to *The Remnant* and various other journals.
In my, admittedly fallible opinion, the possibility that the Holy See is vacant is so unlikely that, together with the Bayside 'revelations' or Palmar de Troya, it is not one which comes remotely near the top of the list. Writing the article for Hamish took up a great deal of my time.
Nonetheless, I did keep my promise and sent all the material which you sent me to a canon lawyer who assured me that it provided no reason whatsoever for changing anything in my article, and that what I had written was perfectly correct. You may or may not be aware that a slightly revised version has now been published in book form with the title 'I am with you always'. It can be obtained from Carmel of Plymouth.
I can assure you that I intended, and still intend to write to you at some time concerning the material you sent me, mainly as a gesture of courtesy. I may do so during my Easter holiday, but if I cannot manage it then I will do so in my summer holiday.
All good wishes,

(...)

It is difficult to know for sure which feature of this extraordinary letter is the most remarkable. Is it the fact that writing about such things as fig biscuits, rugby football and Al Jolson films in *The Remnant*[30] is a priority over getting to the bottom of a serious theological dispute? Is it the admission that his opinion is fallible (one would certainly not get that impression from his often-made boast that no one has been able to point out a theological error in any of his books)? Is it the unprecedented concession that the vacancy of the Holy See is merely "unlikely" rather than *impossible* as he has maintained elsewhere? Is it the typical bullying tactic of sneering at an argument which he has signally failed to answer? (If N.M.G. and J.S.D. are being so dense, why does it take so long to expose them? If the ten canonists they quoted do not say what they claim they say, could this not have been shown in the same space that Davies devoted to proffering his excuses?) Perhaps worse still is the staggering implication that Davies's pet canon lawyer is to be considered infallible even when he gives not the slightest justification for his position.

Nor should that unbelievable final paragraph be overlooked as a contender. To call it complacent would be an understatement. The tone can only be described as *regal*: Davies will

---

[30] Here are a few examples which could be multiplied almost indefinitely if the point were not already made:

(i) "I am unable to devote all the time I would like to making sense of it [a Conciliar Church publication] as I am trying to keep up with a diet of two Jolson films a day to commemorate his centenary." (*The Remnant*, 31st May 1986)

(ii) "I was somewhat surprised at the extent of the response evoked by my article on South Africa... It was the largest response to anything I've written for some time, with the exception of my reflections on the subject of Fig Newtons and my refusal to believe in the existence of Kalamazoo." (*Ibid.*)

(iii) "...While I was in the U.S.A. enjoying sunshine in most places except Boston, England had the worst August on record for many years. The only bright spot was the Bears versus Cowboys match in London climaxed by a William Perry T.D. Thanks to the thoughtfulness of Howard Walsh of 'Keep the Faith' I was able to watch it in San Francisco on a Video, but that's another story." (*The Remnant*, 15th October 1986)

condescend to write to us "at some time" and "mainly as a gesture of courtesy". Beneath the studiedly affable language, what he is in fact telling us is that our letter and arguments are so blatantly ludicrous that they do not deserve to be treated as part of a serious debate which actually calls for reply, but that, notwithstanding this, he will, out of the goodness of his tender heart, snatch five minutes from his valuable time, when it is convenient to him, in order to correct the foolish errors of this pair of half-wits "as a gesture of courtesy".

God help him! As though it were compatible with courtesy to point out that such condescensions are made only for courtesy's sake!

All in all, both for its content and for its supercilious, sneering tone, Davies's letter can be fairly described as utterly disgusting.

The following reply was despatched on 1st April 1987:

Dear Michael,

Thank you for your letter of 27th March explaining that you have not been able to reply to my letters and evidence owing to your many other commitments.

As you will remember, this latest exchange of correspondence was occasioned when I asked Hamish for an authority demonstrating that no one is a formal heretic until he has received a canonical warning and he quoted to me your statement to that effect in *Approaches* N° 71, p. 11.

One half of our disagreement arose when I pointed out that your statement was explicitly contradicted by the definition of a heretic found in the 1917 *Code of Canon Law* itself (Canon 1325§2). As we pursued that one, a second disagreement came to light when you maintained that the provisions of Canon 188§4 – automatic loss of office for clerics who publicly defected from the Catholic Faith – applied only to those who join a false religion, not to those who simply deny a Divinely revealed doctrine.

In response to this, I sent you a batch of photocopies from reputable canonical commentators stating or directly implying the opposite, including for instance, the following extract from Mgr. Sipos: 'It is not required that a heretic join any heretical sect'. (*Enchiridion*

Juris Canonici, p. 608) I followed that up by sending you an extract from the noted theologian de Lugo relating to the first part of our disagreement. 'Neither is it always demanded in the external forum that there be a warning and a reprimand as described above for somebody to be punished as heretical and pertinacious ....' (dis. XX, sect. iv, n. 157-8.)

In other words, in respect of both halves of our dispute I submitted for your consideration statements of Catholic authorities who explicitly deny the very point which you maintain.

In your latest letter you tell me: 'I did keep my promise and sent all the material which you sent me to a canon lawyer who assured me that it provided no reason whatsoever for changing anything in my article.'

While I make no claim to a similar degree of learning to that of a canon lawyer, I think that I can be forgiven for being unable to see how he can be right. When you say 'black' and Catholic authorities firmly say 'white' I cannot see how anyone loyal to Catholic principles can be entitled to continue saying 'black' without answering the authorities who hold the contrary.

I do assure you that I earnestly wish to resolve this issue. Obviously you are the person whose comments on the above I am most anxious for, because it is you who are publicly promoting what, as far as I can see, the authorities deny. But if other priorities prevent you from replying in the immediate future, I wonder if you would be kind enough to put me in touch with your canon lawyer friend so that I can discuss the issue with him?

Best wishes,

(...)

This letter has never received a reply. Nor has the promised treatment of the objections presented in it ever been received although at the time of going to press the Easter and Summer holidays not only of 1987, but even of 1988 and 1989 are, to say the least, long gone. And Davies's undertaking to correct future editions of his work (see p. 128 of this *Evaluation*) if our objections turned out to be justified, has not been honoured, despite the fact that he has supplied not one jot of evidence, logic or authority to counter the wad of extracts from highly-reputed canonical text-books that N.M.G. and J.S.D. sent him to prove their point. In fact, he has not even done the barest minimum that would be considered normal scholarly practice even in non-Catholic circles – namely to make *reference*, in subsequent editions, to the fact that a serious challenge, which he has yet to refute, has been made against part of his essay.

Having thus explained how Davies's pamphlet *The Divine Constitution and Indefectibility of the Church* came into the writer's life, it is obviously necessary to devote a little space to a refutation of its principal thesis, which is that for the Holy See to be vacant – as I and many others hold it to be – is impossible, being contrary to the teaching of the Church that this could happen.

Davies's argument is a straightforward one:

(a) The constitution of the Church was bestowed upon her by Our Lord.

(b) It is a dogma of the Faith that this constitution is indefectible – i.e. can never undergo substantial change.

(c) But the papacy and the hierarchy are essential components of this Divine constitution.

(d) Consequently those who affirm that the Church is currently bereft of pope and bishops are implicitly denying the dogma of the indefectibility of the Church's Divine constitution.

I think that Davies would agree that this is an accurate summary of his argument, but to make sure I am being completely fair, I quote a representative passage of his exact words below:

> The word 'indefectible' means unable to fail. When used with reference to the Catholic Church it means that the Church will persist until the end of time, and that she will preserve unimpaired her essential characteristics. The constitution received from her Divine Founder must, as Pope Pius XII explained, remain firm. The Church will always remain faithful to it, particularly in the two aspects specifically mentioned by the Pope, the transmission of

truth and grace. We can be absolutely certain of this because the constitution of the Catholic Church has a Divine origin. Our Lord Jesus Christ Himself founded His Church, and He imparted to her the Divine constitution which He has solemnly guaranteed will remain essentially immutable until the end of time. The Church can never undergo any change which would make her, as a social organism, something different from what she was constituted by Our Lord. If any essential change took place in her constitution she would cease to be the Church which He had founded. It would mean that Our Lord had made promises which He could not fulfil, which would mean that He was not Divine. This would make the entire Christian religion meaningless. (P. 12)

Davies bases this on many Catholic authorities, to whom he furnishes references (some of which, unfortunately, seem to be wrong) in his footnotes. Among the essential characteristics of the Church he includes the papacy, the bishops and her visible external structure.

The most important truth to be understood if one is to make a correct assessment of Davies's case is the definition of the word *essential*. Davies is certainly right that the Church must always possess whatever is *essential* to her constitution, but to establish exactly which features are essential to her, we must know what that word 'essential' means, according to scholastic philosophy from which it is borrowed. This Davies himself tells us on p. 13:

> In scholastic philosophy the essence, substance or nature of anything is its innermost reality. It is that which makes it what it is and not something else.

Hence the normal Latin definition of the word "essence" is "*id quo ens est id quod est*" – "that by which a thing is what it is". Accordingly, a feature is essential to something if without that feature it would cease to be itself. For instance, a soul is essential to human nature. A man with no soul is a contradiction in terms. By contrast, an *arm* is not *essential* to human nature because a man with no arm would remain a man.

So far so good. But what at this point is also important to realize, as Davies does not, is that a feature which is *not* essential is *not* thereby necessarily relegated to a position of being *inconsequential*. Legs, arms, nose and ears are none of them *essential* to a man, but they are all important parts of a properly functioning human being. A man with none of them would be severely handicapped, but, because he would still be a *man* without them, they are not *essential*. Philosophically they are termed "proper" or "integral" to human nature.

Now by the same token, we may know with complete certainty that an *actually reigning* pope is *not* essential to the Church. For on each of the two hundred and sixty occasions when a pope has died (or in one or two cases – such as that of Pope St. Celestine V – resigned) there has been *no pope* for an interval. If a pope were *essential* to the Church, the Church would cease to exist whenever the Holy See fell vacant, which of course is not the case. The truth is that a pope is *"proper"* to the Church – just as an arm is "proper" to the human body – and that without a pope the Church is, so to speak, handicapped. *But she retains her identity*.

From this it inevitably follows that the vacancy of the Holy See presents *no contradiction whatsoever* to the dogma of the indefectibility of the Church's divine constitution. Davies himself is aware of this difficulty with his thesis and makes the following comments:

> What of the interregnum between pontificates when the Chair of St Peter is vacant? Some of these interregna have been extremely long. In such cases a legitimate authority takes charge of the Holy See and supervises its affairs until a new pontiff is elected. This authority is known as such to the faithful, and the visible hierarchical nature of the Church is not interrupted in any way. (P. 19)

I have no idea what he means by saying that when the Holy See is vacant "a legitimate authority takes charge ... and supervises its affairs .... This authority is known as such to the faithful." What is this authority? It is certainly not known to this writer. The truth is that during the *"sede vacante"* period there is an authority (the college of cardinals) the competence of which extends to whatever is necessary to elect a new pope, *and no further*. But there is *no authority whatsoever* which can "supervise the affairs" of the unoccupied Holy See. Indeed, in his constitution *Vacantis Apostolicæ Sedis*, Pope Pius XII expressly rules that:

> While the Apostolic See is vacant, the Sacred College of Cardinals has absolutely no power or jurisdiction in those matters which, while he was alive, the pope was responsible for – whether to offer a favour or simply to do justice by someone – nor even to put into effect such an action undertaken by the deceased pope. All these things it is bound to reserve for the future pope. (Chapter I, paragraph 1.)

Anyhow, cutting through the irrelevancies with which Davies clutters his case, the fact is that, as he himself admits, even an "extremely long" interregnum does *not* contradict the dogma of the indefectibility of the Church. And once that is admitted, there is no reason whatsoever to affirm that the Holy See cannot be vacant for a period of many years. The Catholic maxim has it that *"plus aut minus non mutant speciem"* – a change of *degree* cannot affect *principle*.

No one is suggesting or implying that the *papacy* is not essential to the Church's constitution, for it certainly is. But the papacy continues to exist even when there is no actually reigning pope, as Cardinal Franzelin explains in the passage quoted in footnote 15 on p. 105 above.

At one point in his essay Davies suggests that the *"sede vacante"* thesis conflicts with the dogma of the visibility of the Church. There are no grounds for holding that the Church is invisible when forsaken by the great mass of her prelates, however.[31] Nor is the Church invisible if her members are

---

[31] Mgr. J. Hagan: *A Compendium of Catechetical Instruction*, Instruction 332

drastically reduced in number: indeed there was a time when the whole Catholic Church was gathered in a single room. (Acts 1:15 and Acts 2:1)

No matter how lyrical Davies may wax over the indefectibility of the Church's Divine constitution, therefore, it is all to no avail; for, true though it is that the indefectibility of the Church's constitution is a dogma, it is equally true that there is no incompatibility between that dogma and the present situation in which the papal and practically all episcopal offices are unoccupied.

V

The correspondence that has just been quoted shows more than sufficiently that there is not the slightest substance in Davies's claim, on p. 24 of his *Divine Constitution* essay, that the canonical effects of heresy – exclusion from the Catholic Church and immediate loss of all offices held in the Church – are not deemed to apply until the Church has pronounced on the matter, a suggestion which, moreover, as we have seen, is expressly denied by Canon 188§4. Discussion of most of the other errors in the same essay, of which there are the usual smattering, may conveniently be deferred until we come to those

---

writes:
> The Church is a visible society.
> When we say that a society is visible we do not merely mean to say that it is composed of visible human beings; but we mean that there is something in its constitution that characterizes it, identifies it, and enables us to distinguish it from all other societies with which it may come into contact
> ...
> In fact, even a secret society must be a visible society, since even a secret society must have its own constitution and organization ... In the same way, in times of persecution, the Church was often in hiding, and might under the circumstances be regarded as a secret society; but even then it had its own constitution and organization just as much as in its palmiest days of prosperity, and hence was always a visible society.

chapters of this *Evaluation* which are specifically appropriate to each individual item; but there remain one or two passages which can best be looked at straight away.

"Prima Sedes a Nemine Judicatur"

On p. 27 Davies writes as follows:

Anyone in the Church who possessed the temerity to pass judgement on the Pope and declare him a heretic, would be acting beyond the limits of his authority, '*ultra vires*', and would himself become liable to canonical censure.

In this passage and elsewhere Davies persistently misapplies the axiom *"prima sedes a nemine judicatur"* – "the first see is judged by no one."[32]

What the axiom forbids, and *all* that it forbids, is that anyone or any class of people should act as superior to the pope and pretend to possess any authority over him. It has no application whatsoever to the question of a "heretical pope" precisely because a heretical pope is an impossibility. In the event of a "pope" pertinaciously maintaining heresy, there would be no question of judging the *pope*; merely of making the practical judgement (for which no authority whatsoever is required) that a given individual, *purporting* to be the successor of St. Peter, cannot in fact be so because he does not profess the faith of Peter.

Davies's position amounts, in fact, to saying that there is no distinction between judging *whether* a particular person *is* the pope and judging the pope. But by forbidding us to judge whether a particular person is the pope or not, Davies in effect requires us to accept uncritically the validity of anyone's claim to be pope. After all, if John-Paul II's claim may not even be questioned, why should one be allowed to question the claim of some other pretender to the papacy, such as Clemente Domínguez Gómez of Palmar de Troya, who, since 1978, has

---

[32] Canon 1556.

styled himself "Pope Gregory XVII"? If one is "judging the pope" by examining Karol Wojtyła's credentials, one must be "judging the pope" by examining Dominguez's. But of course in reality one is doing no such thing in either case. Davies's point involves a crass begging of the question: it presumes the very point that is disputed – John-Paul II's legitimacy – as its grounds for forbidding us to question it.

Moreover, the principle that it is permitted to all Catholics to make proper use of their reason to form a judgement on whether a pope, or purported pope, has fallen into heresy and is therefore not pope is clearly confirmed by history. Particularly prior to the 1870 Vatican Council, the belief that a pope, as a private individual, could fall into heresy – and consequently lose his papal office – was widespread; and – as we shall see – Catholic authority certainly did not hold that there was anything inappropriate about a private individual applying his intellect in order to recognize that such a thing had factually taken place.

From a number of examples which could be given to demonstrate this, I restrict myself to a single one, the case of Pope Pascal II. This pope had strenuously opposed the practice of "lay investitures" by which civil rulers appointed whom they chose to ecclesiastical offices, but, in the year 1111 he was imprisoned by the uncrowned Holy Roman Emperor, Henry V – who was demanding that the pope yield to him (Henry) the right of lay investiture – and during his imprisonment he consented to allow Henry this right, though it scarcely appears compatible with Catholic doctrine. Up to this point there was no question of formal heresy, because a man acting under great fear is not considered necessarily to be declaring his true belief; but *after* his release Pascal was extremely dilatory about annulling these privileges – to such an extent that the question of whether he might actually be a heretic was mooted.

At the forefront of those pressing the pope to manifest his orthodoxy was St. Bruno of Segni. He informed the pope bluntly in a letter that his actions were contrary to Catholic doctrine and that if he was obstinate in them he would be a heretic; and Pope Pascal knew exactly what was at stake for he tried to deprive Bruno of his authority as abbot of Monte Cassino, and, as the famous Church historian the Venerable Cardinal Baronius records, he accompanied his attempt with the following significant words:

> If I do not remove his authority over the monastery, he will, by his arguments, remove the government of the Church from me.[33]

Many other prominent ecclesiastics joined Bruno in denouncing the pope's position as at least materially heretical, and, in fact, the pope eventually retracted his concession so that St. Bruno was able to exclaim: "God be praised, for it is the pope himself who has condemned this heretical so-called privilege."[34] And the implication was and is clear: if he had *failed* to condemn it, he would *not* have been the pope. Indeed an entire synod also threatened to detach itself from Pascal (i.e. cease to recognize him as pope) if he did not ratify its condemnation of the privileges; and among those responsible for this threat were St. Hugh of Grenoble and St. Godfrey of Amiens.[35]

But according to Davies's doctrine, all these saints who "possessed the temerity to pass judgement on the Pope" were abusing their authority to such an extent that they made themselves liable to canonical censure. Well, to use for a second time one of Davies's own expressions, "it's a point of view."

Heresy: Is There Such a Thing?

On p. 29 of *The Divine Constitution...* Davies repeats the same nonsense that he included in his original "Sedevacantists" article, according to which, on the one hand "there is no case whatsoever for alleging that any of the Conciliar popes have

---

[33] Ven. Card. Baronius, *Annales*, ad ann. 1111, n. 32.
[34] Hefele-Leclerq, Vol. V, pt. 1, p. 555.
[35] *Loc. cit.*, et seq.

been suspect of heresy in the very restricted meaning of the term in the old Code of Canon Law," while on the other hand, when it comes to the subject of pre-and post-Conciliar doctrine on religious liberty, "it has yet to be shown how they can be reconciled." In other words, according to Davies, the apparently stark contradiction between Pope Pius IX's infallible *Quanta Cura* and Paul VI's exceedingly fallible *Dignitatis Humanæ* does not even constitute a *case* for *alleging suspicion* of heresy. His justification of this is not that he can show how the two documents are not contradictory after all, but that *someone – one day – may* be able to shed some light on the matter.[36]

But if it is possible blatantly to contradict the dogmatic teaching of the sovereign pontiff without there even being a *case* for *alleging* a mere *suspicion* of heresy, what would one have to do to commit heresy? I am at a loss to answer the question and must therefore presume that for Mr. Davies formal heresy is something completely hypothetical and the Church's legislation on the subject so much useless, inapplicable baggage.

How to Detect Orthodoxy

On p. 30 of the same booklet he writes:

Pope John Paul II has issued a good number of very orthodox documents, such as Holy Thursday Letters on the Eucharist and the priesthood. It is only fair that we judge the orthodoxy of any Catholic by the totality of his published opinions, and not solely by particular actions or statements which appear suspect or ambiguous.

We can readily believe that many of Davies's readers took enthusiastically to heart this assertion as to what a fair and Catholic attitude ought to be, regarding it as wise, broad-minded, suitably respectful, typically charitable, and thoroughly

---

[36] Davies himself has consistently rejected as unsatisfactory the valiant efforts of Dr. Brian Harrison and others to achieve a reconciliation of the two contradictory doctrines, and surely he is right. Neither have the occupants of the Vatican shown any inclination to accept their strained interpretation of their *Dignitatis Humanæ* flagship!

Catholic; but unfortunately there are a few problems attached to it: first, it is simply untrue; secondly, it is utterly illogical; thirdly, it is diametrically opposed to Catholic tradition; and fourthly, it is a complete invention. What Davies is telling us, in effect, is that we must judge wolves, at least in part, by their sheep's clothing. And what follows inescapably from his remarkable doctrine is that a person can pronounce *any number* of heresies without convicting himself of being unorthodox, provided merely that, with the typically forked tongue of a prelate of the Conciliar Church, he every so often expresses true doctrine as a counterbalance. And how vulnerable the Church would be to heresy if it were so, given that according to St. Pius X (*Pascendi Dominici Gregis*) this sort of dissimulation is a prominent characteristic of those heretics who today are most afflicting the Church!

> It is one of the cleverest devices of the Modernists ... to present their doctrines without order and systematic arrangement, in a scattered and disjointed manner, so as to make it appear as if their minds were in doubt or hesitation, whereas in reality they are quite fixed and steadfast.

But of course Davies's doctrine is *not* correct. By contrast, the Catholic maxim is "*bonum ex integra causa; malum ex quocumque defectu*".[37] This means that, whereas a man is properly said to be good (or, *mutatis mutandis*, orthodox) only if he is *completely* good, he can be said to be bad on the basis of *any* defect whatsoever. Not only is this Catholic teaching; it is a matter of plain common sense. No one would say that a man is a good singer because he sings *some* notes in tune. *All* the notes must be in tune; otherwise he is a *bad* singer. Equally, it would be nonsensical to say: "Mendax is a very honest chap – he tells

---

[37] "Goodness can be predicated only of what is *completely* good, whereas badness can be predicated of anything which is *in any way* bad." This principle is enunciated, in slightly different terms, by St. Thomas Aquinas (*Summa Theologiæ*, I, II, Q. 18, A. 4); the version quoted is the one commonly used in Catholic philosophy text-books.

the truth about 75% of the time." Unless Mendax tells the truth 100% of the time, he has no claim at all to be honest. Indeed, it is worth noting that, if Davies's fantastic assertion were well founded, it would mean that, in assessing whether Henry VIII was entitled to be considered a Catholic rather than the founder of a new schismatic Church of which he made himself the head, we should have to take into account his having once written an excellent defence of the seven sacraments in refutation of Luther's revolutionary theology.

The New Mass and Indefectibility

The above heading, appearing on p. 32 of Davies's essay, introduces the final section of that work, and may conveniently be borrowed for the final section of this chapter. Under that heading, Davies writes as follows:

> The indefectibility of the Church extends only to what is mandated or authorised by the Roman Pontiff as a universal law or practice.

Davies italicizes these words throughout, which gives the impression that they are a quotation, and he even adds a footnote referring them to the *Dictionnaire de Théologie Catholique*, Vol. IV, coll. 2182, 3, 2185, 2194, 2197 or 2205.[38] But on referring to these columns in the original work, *it turns out that they nowhere contain the italicized words*, nor, indeed, any other words expressing the same meaning, and that in fact the doctrine they convey concerning the extent of the Church's indefectibility in its application to her discipline and praxis, as opposed to her formal teaching, is much broader than that which Davies dishonestly attributes to them. Thus we learn, for instance, that the infallible Ordinary and Universal Magisterium of the Church extends in scope to any teaching, even implicit, manifestly contained ...

---

[38] Davies's reference includes several column numbers as it applies also to other quotations he has taken from this work.

... in the discipline and general practice of the Church, at least in respect of everything truly mandated, approved or authorized by the universal Church. (Col. 2194)

How is it, I enquire, that in Davies's statement of the doctrine, allegedly based on this authority, the word "approved" has dropped out, and "mandated or authorized" appears in place of "mandated, *approved* or authorized"? And how is it that "discipline and *general* practice" of the original has turned into "universal law or practice"?

The answer to these questions is not hard to find. Davies goes on to assure us on the basis of this dishonestly twisted statement of Catholic doctrine that:

It [the indefectibility of the Church] guarantees no more than that the pope will not *command us* to adopt a practice that is intrinsically bad or harmful to the Faith.

And on p. 3 he remarks gloatingly:

The fact that the Latin Missal of Pope Paul VI is free from doctrinal error and mandates no intrinsically harmful practices will not surprise any Catholic acquainted with the indefectible nature of the Church.

And, of course, if Davies had not taken note of the overwhelming probability that none of his readers would get round to checking a reference in a French work, and had not decided that this probability made it sufficiently certain that if he falsified a quotation he would not be detected, but had instead told us what the *Dictionnaire de Théologie Catholique* **really** says, he would not be able to get away with this distortion; for it is not true to say that "indefectibility ... extends *only* to what is mandated or authorized" by the pope if it applies *also* to what he "*approves*". And if the Church's prerogative of infallibility extends not only to what is *universally mandated* but also to what is *generally approved*, the Latin Novus Ordo becomes irrelevant, for general approval must include all the vernacular versions as well, replete with heresy as they are. In short, the Michael Davies distorted version of the dogma of indefectibility can be made to fit the Conciliar Church, whereas the version of the same doctrine found in the Catholic reference work on which he purports to rely is utterly inapplicable to the Conciliar Church because it shows that the protection of the Holy Ghost over the *Catholic* Church would prevent her from acting in the way that the *Conciliar* Church manifestly *does* act.

Let us close this chapter with a question: if Davies will not stop at falsifying references to authorities in order to justify his untenable case, just where *will* he stop?

APPENDIX

THE OPINION OF SUAREZ ON THE QUESTION OF A HERETICAL POPE

Writing in *The Remnant* on 15th February 1987, Davies summarized his position on the consequences of a pope's falling into heresy as follows:

> And what of the Pope himself? Does what I have written imply that the Pope could never be a heretic and forfeit his office? Of course it does not. Such a possibility exists, but it would have to be manifest and so notorious a heresy that no doubt of its existence could remain in the minds of the faithful. Reputable canonists and theologians also teach that high authorities in the Church would have to make [sic] a declaratory sentence that the Pope had lost his office through heresy. The Pope would not be deposed as a result of this sentence. No one in the Church has the right to judge or depose the Pope. They [i.e., presumably, the "high authorities"] would simply be declaring what had been manifest through his own actions.

Davies gives the impression, perhaps accidentally, that the doctrine he is putting forward is held by *all* "reputable canonists and theologians", which is very far from being the case. He neither gives references to any of the canonists and theologians in question, nor lets his readers into the secret that in every era of the Church there has been a much stronger contrary opinion holding that by formal public heresy a pope would lose his office *ipso facto* (automatically), prior to and irrespective of any declarations to this effect which might or might not be made by "high authorities in the Church". As readers will be aware, the different schools of theological opinion on this subject (of which St. Robert Bellarmine enumerated five) are no longer of practical interest, because ecclesiastical authority has decided the entire question by the terms of Pope Paul IV's definition on the subject contained in his bull *Cum Ex Apostolatus* (1559) and by Canon 188§4 of the 1917 *Code of Canon Law*.[39] However, it is true that there have been theologians and canonists (including several not without eminence) who have at some point in history maintained a position similar to that outlined by Davies in the quotation above, and to do his case justice it seems appropriate to examine this position briefly.

As representative of this opinion, I have chosen the theologian whom I believe to have been its most illustrious and competent defender, the Spanish Jesuit Francisco Suarez (1548-1617)[40] who came from a converted Jewish family and was praised by Pope Paul V as "a pious and eminent theologian". His consideration of this topic is found in his work *De Fide, Spe et Charitate*, tr. 1, disp. x, sect. vi, and covers about five closely printed and argued pages of Latin of folio size.

Does it appear rash, it is worth asking before going any further, to embark upon what amounts to an attempt by a layman without formal theological training to refute the teaching of a holy and extremely erudite theologian? There are, in fact, two solid reasons why no apology is due on this score:

(i) The opinions of a theologian are not, and cannot be, of any greater weight, as such, than the arguments which he adduces in their favour, and such opinions may *always* be disputed by anyone sufficiently informed on the topic in question to understand the theology involved.

(ii) Those of us who decline to accept Suarez's opinion have a number of very distinguished predecessors. To mention but

---

[39] While the pope is nto directly subject to penal law, it is notable that Canon 188§4 is *not* a penal Canon. It does not deprive clerics of their offices for heresy; it interprets public defection from the faith as an act of tacit resignation from those offices, to which it gives immediate effect. In practice the theological debate about the loss of the papacy following pubic heresy closely parallels the debate (now closed) as to the loss of lesser ecclesiastical offices under the same circumstances.

[40] The fact that he wrote after the promulgation of *Cum Ex Apostolatus* in no way contradicts my assertion that this bull makes his position untenable, for, as will be shown later in this appendix, he was clearly not aware of the Bull's contents.

one, St. Robert Bellarmine characterizes it as an opinion which in his judgement "cannot be defended". (*De Romano Pontifice*, Cap. XXX)

I turn now to what Fr. Suarez has to say.

To begin with, it must be made clear that he is not in agreement with Davies on everything. In fact he does not accept at all that a pope *can* fall into heresy, whereas Davies maintains that this is possible. Suarez considers the question only because his opinion that the eventuality is inconceivable was, though "more pious and more probable" and even "to be held", not *absolutely* certain. As I also subscribe to the view that a true pope cannot fall into heresy even in his private acts, it is evidently a part of my position that all of the Conciliar "popes" forfeited their offices by falling into heresy long *before* their putative elections – making these elections null and void (a possibility which Suarez expressly recognizes). Nonetheless, it is obviously logical that the consequences of a pope's falling into heresy after election (if that be possible) should be the same as if he had been a heretic prior to his election, for either it is possible for a public heretic validly to occupy the office of pope or it is not. Hence this question has at least indirect relevance to the situation existing today.

Another difference between Suarez and Davies is that, while Davies appears to hold the position that a manifestly heretical claimant to the Holy See would cease *ipso facto* to be pope, but that the faithful could not be allowed to act on this fact by withdrawing their allegiance from him until a general council had notified them of it, Suarez apparently opines that the public heretic actually remains pope until the general council takes official cognizance of his heresy, at which point he ceases to be pope.[41] Where they are in agreement, however, is on the

---

[41] To both views, however, the words of St. Robert Bellarmine are equally apposite: "The condition of the Church would be most wretched if it were obliged to recognize a manifestly ravening wolf for its pastor."

principal point that one is not entitled to withdraw one's allegiance from a Roman pontiff until he has been *officially declared* a heretic.

Suarez recognizes that the main position conflicting with his is that of the school which holds that a heretical pope would be deposed *ipso facto* without need of any declaration. Considering, for reasons which I shall shortly examine, that the opinion of this school is untenable, he adopts the view which I have outlined above as his, but he did not adopt it, it must be emphasized, because there is any direct authority for it. His reason was simply that "it cannot be believed that Christ left the Church without any remedy in such a great danger [i.e. the danger arising from a heretical pope]," and that his own explanation is the only reasonable alternative to the *ipso facto* deposition, which he believes to be impossible.

Not surprisingly, Suarez recognizes that there are considerable difficulties associated with his position, and he does his best to resolve them as follows:

To the difficulty of who would be competent to declare the pope a formal heretic, he replies, persuasively, that nobody except a general council of all the bishops could be competent to do this, but he is forced to admit that there is no express warrant in Divine or human law authorizing even a general council to make such a declaration.

He then continues as follows:

> Next, however, a second problem arises, namely how such a council could legitimately be assembled; for only the pope can legitimately summon one.

Once again he has no authority to answer this query, but reasons that there are two available solutions:

(a) That a series of provincial councils throughout the world all agreeing in the same conclusion would be tantamount to a general council without the difficulty involved in summoning all the bishops to one place. This theory, however, is evidently:

(i) impractical, since the organisation of such a series of provincial councils would probably be exceedingly difficult if not impossible;

(ii) false, because a series of provincial councils is *not* tantamount to a general council, since at the latter all the bishops can hear one another's views, and this does not apply to the former;

(iii) unreasonable, since it would leave the path open to countless disagreements, e.g. about what percentage of the bishops need to be agreed before the pope could be condemned; and

(iv) of no value, because, as it is no more than a conjecture, it would be impossible to know that the theory was correct and constituted sufficient grounds for the faithful to withdraw their allegiance from the pontiff.

(b) That "perhaps ... for this business specially concerning the pontiff himself, which is, in a sense, in opposition to him, a general council might be legitimately assembled either by the college of cardinals or by the consent of the bishops; and if the pontiff attempted to prevent such assembly he would have to be disobeyed because he would be abusing the supreme power contrary to justice and the common good." This is once again quite useless, because, being only a hypothesis, the deliberations of such a questionable council could never have binding force. Moreover, the hypothesis has been officially rejected by the Church since 1917; the *Code of Canon Law* declares that "An Ecumenical Council not summoned by the Roman pontiff is an impossibility ['*dari nequit*']," (Canon 222§1) and that "the decrees of a council do not have definitive obligatory force unless they have been confirmed by the Roman pontiff and promulgated by his command." (Canon 227)

The third difficulty which Suarez tries to solve is this:

> By what right can a pope be judged by an assembly of which he is the superior?

Let us first remind ourselves of Davies's solution to this obvious and grave question. He simply maintains that the maxim *"prima sedes a nemine judicatur"* ("the first see is judged by no one") does not apply. Because the pope has already forfeited his office automatically when his heresy was made public, the council is not deposing its superior, but declaring that he who seems to be its superior is in fact not so because he is bereft of all authority. This solution, of course, concedes that the pope actually forfeits his office *ipso facto* on being publicly guilty of heresy, and therefore leaves no grounds whatever for Davies's insistence that those who are aware of this fact prior to its being officially declared are obliged to continue to submit to a non-pope as if he were the Vicar of Christ.

Now let us turn back to Fr. Suarez. As I have indicated, he differs from Davies on this point, holding that it is only as a result of the council's condemnatory sentence that the pope loses his office.

He too addresses himself to the problem of how a council could condemn its own superior who "can be judged by none", and in doing so he refutes a specious argument which has been used by the theologian Cajetan to cope with this difficulty.

Cajetan's argument was that the council would not be condemning the pope *as pope* but as a private individual. But this theory, as Suarez convincingly points out, cannot be accepted. If it *were* accepted, it would be possible for anyone presumptuous enough to judge a pope simply to claim that he was judging him in his private rather than his public capacity, an interpretation which would negate the very principle which the maxim is intended to safeguard: that the pope is not to be judged. The solution which Suarez proposes, and which he considers to be, unlike Cajetan's, not only sufficient to account for the deposition of a heretical pope, but also reconcilable with the principle that the pope must not be judged, is as follows:

> So should the Church depose a heretical pope, she would not do this as a superior, but by the consent of Christ the Lord she would juridically declare him to be a heretic and hence utterly unworthy of the pontifical dignity; thereupon he would be deposed immediately by Christ and, having been deposed, would then be inferior and could be punished as such.

But I fear that in reality he comes no closer to solving the difficulty than Cajetan did. If the judgement of a general council that the pope is a heretic were to be considered binding even against the pope's own judgement that he was *not* a heretic, this could only be on the bases:

(a) that appeal is made from the pope's judgement to a council, an action which incurs automatic excommunication under Canon 2332, and

(b) that a council can be the pope's superior, at least for some purposes – a proposition which is heretical.

Anyhow, once again the hypothesis is of no value precisely because, being hypothetical, there could be no certainty that it is correct, and indeed, as I have shown, since 1917 at the latest it has been certain that it is *not* correct.

Thus, Suarez's opinion that a heretical pope would forfeit his office, not automatically, but only by virtue of condemnation by a council, involved its author in insoluble doctrinal difficulties, owing to its incompatibility with other doctrines. This incompatibility alone would compel us to reject Suarez's opinion concerning heretical popes, but perhaps more important still is the fact that Suarez makes it clear that he has adopted his theory, not because of its intrinsic merit, but because it is the most reasonable alternative he can see to the rival view that offices are lost automatically by virtue of public heresy, a view which he found unacceptable. Hence, if it is possible to show that Suarez's reasons for rejecting this latter opinion are definitely mistaken, because they have been denied by the Church's authorities, we may conclude that Suarez lends no support at all to Davies's thesis. Indeed we may be certain that its author would himself have rejected it had he been alive today, owing to the fact that his only reasons for not accepting the doctrines of Bellarmine and others have been repudiated by the Church whose docile son he was.

But to establish this bold claim that Suarez is really a negative witness *against* Davies, the objections which Suarez makes to the theory that a heretical pope would lose his office automatically must be carefully examined. This theory, which Davies rejects but which I maintain is today inescapably certain for all Catholics, was evidently well known to Suarez, for he devotes careful attention to it. After outlining his own theory of how to cope with a heretical pope, he refers to the view of others that such a pope "is immediately deposed by God Himself without regard to any human judgement." He then sets out what he considers to be the four best arguments used by the defenders of this view and gives, in each case, his reasons for not being convinced by them. First he shows – to his own satisfaction, if to no one else's – that the thesis in question is not compellingly true; then he adds further reasons for thinking that it is not only doubtful but in fact *definitely wrong*.

My next task is therefore to examine Suarez's stated reasons for rejecting the position I am defending.

I shall begin my examination by considering his refutation of the arguments in favour of my position and I shall do this with a view to showing (a) that they are of no force, and (b) that they are no longer opinions that a Catholic is entitled to maintain.

(i) The first of his four best arguments *against* his own thesis (and in favour of that of writers like his contemporary and confrère St. Robert Bellarmine) is stated by Suarez as follows:

'All the jurisdiction of the Church is founded upon faith,' so those who have no faith cannot have jurisdiction.

In answer to this reasoning Suarez denies the fact, pointing out that the power of Order is superior to that of jurisdiction but that it is a dogma that Holy Orders are not lost if faith is lost and that, moreover, faith can be lost without exterior indication whereas the opinion that even occult heretics[42] forfeit their offices has not "a shadow of probability".

My response to this refutation is that it would lose its force entirely if he had stated the argument more correctly, and had said instead that *external profession* of the true faith is a necessary foundation of ordinary jurisdiction. Suarez's comparison with the power of Order is inconclusive because, although Order is admittedly a *greater* power than jurisdiction, it is also a different *kind* of power, and there is thus no reason for thinking that what applies to one will necessarily apply to the other.

(ii) Moving on to the second argument against him which he tackles, Suarez admits that: "The Fathers often indicate that no one who lacks faith can have jurisdiction in the Church [he then gives references to SS. Cyprian, Ambrose, Augustine, Thomas Aquinas and Popes Gelasius and Alexander II]." But his only response to this is that there are (also) "Fathers who.. consider that a heretic *deserves* to be deprived of all dignity and jurisdiction," thus implying that such heretics are not already *ipso facto* deprived thereof.

On this subject Suarez's credibility is open to serious question, for his contemporary St. Robert Bellarmine, who was thoroughly familiar with the whole of patristic literature, assures us in his own consideration of this subject[43] that "the Fathers are *unanimous* in teaching, not only that heretics are outside the Church, but also that they are '*ipso facto*' deprived of all

---

[42] I.e. those who fall into heresy but give no exterior indication of having done so.

[43] *De Romano Pontifice*, a part of his famous *Controversies*.

jurisdiction and ecclesiastical rank." Certainly, the single instance adduced by Suarez in support of his statement shortly after the words quoted above does nothing to weaken St. Robert's assurance, for Suarez's claim that some Fathers differed from the view he rightly attributes to SS. Cyprian, Ambrose, Augustine, etc., is, he says, gathered from the first epistle of Clement I [the fourth pope, writing to the Corinthians in the closing years of the first century] which says, according to Suarez, that St. Peter taught that a heretical pope is *to be deposed* (rather than *automatically deposed*). And yet the fact is that St. Clement *nowhere* represents St. Peter as having said anything of the kind, as readers can confirm by reference to any of the translations of this epistle available in good libraries. The nearest St. Clement approaches to the subject is his statement that "our Apostles", i.e. SS. Peter and Paul, "knew that there would be contention concerning the name of the episcopacy" and consequently left instructions "in what manner, when they [bishops and deacons] should die, other approved men should succeed them in their ministry (Chapter 44)." It is of little consequence whether Suarez was trusting an unreliable secondary source, or a corrupt primary text, or whether he has just made a mistake; what cannot be denied is that his position is based on a misrepresentation of the teaching of the Fathers.

In passing, it should perhaps also be mentioned that, if any of the Fathers did assert that heretics *deserve* to be deprived of their dignity, this would not necessarily imply that they had *not* forfeited their office *ipso facto*, because it could equally refer to their *de facto* possession of the external trappings of the office.[44]

---

[44] This would appear to be supported by the nearest instance I know to a statement by a Father of the Church that heretics *deserve* to be deprived of their dignity. Pope St. Celestine I (422-432) in his letter to John of Antioch preserved in the Acts of the Council of Ephesus (Vol. 1, cap. 19), says:

> If anyone has been excommunicated or deprived either of episcopal or clerical dignity by bishop Nestorius and his followers since the time that they began to preach those things, it is manifest that he has persevered and continues to persevere in communion with us; nor do we judge him to have

(iii) In his examination of the third argument against him, Suarez says that the position against which he is arguing

> ... is reinforced by a popular ['*vulgari*'] argument to the effect that a heretic is not a member of the Church and cannot therefore be its head.

His response to this argument involves a subtle distinction, so I cite it in full:

> It is replied [i.e. Suarez himself replies] that a heretical pope is not a member of the Church as to the substance and form by which the members of the Church are made such, but that he is nonetheless its head as to office and influence ['*influxum*']; which should cause no surprise as he is not the first and main head acting by his own power, but, as it were, the instrumental head and vicar of the first head who is able to convey His spiritual influence to His members through any secondary head whatsoever; for in a similar way He sometimes baptizes and on occasion even absolves through heretics.

This distinction seems exaggerated, for the pope is evidently more than a merely passive instrument of Christ. Certainly a heretic can validly baptize and in some circumstances even validly absolve, for he is then truly a "mere" instrument through whom Christ acts. But the manner in which the popes govern the Church and exercise jurisdiction is quite different, for it is their own intellects which they use to make the numerous decisions that have to be made, and a pope is therefore visible head of the Church in a much more than instrumental sense. It is one thing

---

been removed, because one who has already shown that he ought himself to be removed ['*se iam præbuerat ipse removendum*'] cannot by his own judgement remove another.

Here it is evident that in referring to Nestorius and his supporters as "*removendi*" – "those who *ought* to be removed" – St. Celestine does *not* mean that they retain their offices until deposed. That is precluded by the fact that he expressly judges their authoritative acts to have been null *even prior to their deposition*. His meaning is evidently that they ought to be removed *physically* from the accoutrements of the office which they had already *ipso facto* forfeited. See also the same pontiff's letter to the clergy of Constantinople.

for Our Lord in rare cases to use enemies of the Church for the specific purpose of validly administering certain sacraments; it is quite another for Him unconditionally to delegate His Divine authority to such an enemy for the purpose of governing the Church. Hence Suarez's distinction seems quite unjustified and a wholly inadequate response to his opponents.

(iv) The last argument against himself that he puts forward is:

> Likewise a heretic must not be greeted, but entirely avoided, as is taught by Paul in Titus 3 and by John in his second epistle; so much less must he be obeyed.

To this objection Suarez answers that "heretics are to be avoided *as much as possible* ['*quoad fieri potest*']" and that this does not contradict his theory but merely makes it imperative to proceed to depose the pontiff at the earliest opportunity.

I would suggest that it certainly *does* contradict both his theory and Davies's. If they are right, it means that in the inevitable interim period before a heretical pope could be deposed – a period which might be long in duration – the faithful would be subject to, and required to obey, a man whom they are Divinely commanded to shun. And here we do not need to rely solely on logic, clear though the position is, for St. Robert Bellarmine, Doctor of the Church, has given short shrift to Suarez's opinion, enquiring:

> How can we be asked to avoid our own head? How could we separate ourselves from a member who is attached to us?[45]

These four arguments, as I have said, constitute Suarez's response to his opponents' position. Next, he gives his grounds for thinking that the view he offers as an alternative to that of his opponents is the correct one, and these grounds must now be considered. I shall allow Suarez to state his case before assessing its validity, and I shall do my best to allow him to do so in his own words, although the length of the original text and

---

[45] *De Romano Pontifice*, XXX.

its desultoriness make it impossible to achieve this except by placing in sequence extracts which do not occur consecutively in the original – a method which I believe to be justified in the circumstances, as it in no way misrepresents or weakens its author's case:

> The main question is whether he [a pope] can be deprived against his own will .... There does not seem to be anyone by whom he can be deprived.
>
> In the case of heresy [some] say that he is deposed immediately by God himself.
>
> Against this opinion I say that ... in no case, even of heresy, is the pontiff deprived of his dignity and power by God without the previous judgement and sentence of men .... *And later in considering the other punishments of heretics ... we show that no one at all is deprived by Divine law of ecclesiastical dignity and jurisdiction because he is guilty of heresy.* (Emphasis added)
>
> Because it is a very grave punishment, for it to be incurred '*ipso facto*' it would have to be expressed in the Divine law; but no such law is found laying down this rule about all heretics in general or about bishops in particular or with special reference to the pope; nor is there a certain tradition on the matter.
>
> Nor can the pope fall from his dignity '*ipso facto*' because of a human law, because this would have been passed either by his inferior [i.e. someone below the rank of pope] ... or by his equal [i.e. some previous pope] – ... but neither a previous pope nor anyone inferior to the pope is ... able to punish the pope actually reigning, given that the reigning pope will be equal to the latter and superior to the former.

So the nub of Suarez's argument is that neither Holy Writ nor sacred tradition contains any Divine law according to which heretics are *ipso facto* deprived of their offices, and indeed it is his view they are *not* deprived of their offices except by the legitimate intervention of ecclesiastical authority; that there is no human law on the subject either, but that even if there were, this would not bind a pope because he is necessarily superior to all human law.

Suarez goes on to consider the objection that a human law on the subject *could* bind the pope if it were interpretative of a Divine law. This he rejects as an idle hypothesis ("*commentitium*") because no such Divine law exists, nor any human law interpreting it.

He also asserts that the absence of such a Divine law "is confirmed by the fact that such a law would be pernicious to the Church," a view which he supports by the consideration that, if *occult* heretics were automatically deprived of their offices, no one could be certain that a jurisdictional act was valid, whereas if only *manifest* heretics were thus deprived *ipso facto*, "greater troubles would follow, as we should be doubtful about how notorious the fact had to be for it to be considered that [the pope] had fallen from his dignity, so schisms would arise in consequence and everything would become perplexed ...."

Now these last two confirmatory objections can be dismissed at once, because the exact meaning of the terms "occult", "public" and "notorious" have now been determined authoritatively for us by the Church in Canon 2197 and there is no doubt that it is only of *public* heretics that anyone seriously maintains the automatic loss of office. Moreover, it is not apparent that a theory can legitimately be rejected on the grounds that it could give rise to disputes and perplexities, because there is no Divine guarantee that the Church will be free of disputes and perplexities, as indeed is solidly proven by the fact that her history is full of them. Nor is there any basis for thinking that the doctrine according to which a general council or a series of provincial ones could indirectly depose the pope by judging him to be a heretic would be any less fecund in troubles, schisms and perplexities.

So we are left with Suarez's argument that popes, like other clerics, retain their office in case of heresy until a judicial declaration of their heresy is made for the reason that there is no Divine law to the contrary. *And this one remaining base on which Suarez's position stands is totally annihilated by the fact that, notwithstanding the dignity it once had of being a respected though minority opinion, it is today known to be certainly false.* I quote from *De Processu Criminali Ecclesiastico* by Dr. Francis Heiner[46] (Emphasis added):

> Ancient authors disputed whether the penalty of privation of benefices [incurred by heretics] is incurred '*ipso facto*' or after judicial sentence. *But owing to the provisions of subsequent laws the matter is no longer doubtful.* In the constitution *Noverit Universitas* of Pope Nicholas III dated 5th March 1280, for instance, it is said: 'But heretics ... are to be admitted to no ecclesiastical benefice or office; and if the contrary should have occurred, We decree that it is null and void; for, from now, We deprive the aforesaid of their benefices, wishing them to have none perpetually and in no wise to be admitted to the like in the future.' Now the words 'from now We deprive' are equivalent to the words '*ipso iure*' [by the law itself], as is taught by Suarez [*De Legibus*, Bk. 5, c. 7, n. 7][47] and other canonists. Pope Paul IV says the same thing even more clearly in his constitution *Cum Ex Apostolatus* dated 15th February 1559, in which, after confirming the penalties established by his predecessors against heretics, he says in express words: 'Of those who in any way knowingly shall have presumed to receive, defend, favour or believe those so apprehended, confessed or convicted [i.e. heretics] or to teach their doctrines, ... each and every cleric ... is *by that very fact* deprived ... of all ecclesiastical office and benefices.' Hence it cannot be doubted that clerics are deprived of their benefices *ipso facto* for the crime of heresy.

It will doubtless already have occurred to readers that Suarez's position is anyhow untenable, because it conflicts with *Cum Ex Apostolatus* which expressly extends its provisions to the case of heretics elected to the Holy See. The fact is that, as I

---

[46] The author of this work, published at Rome in 1862, was an auditor of the Holy Roman Rota.

[47] Heiner is not suggesting that Suarez agrees with him as to the *ipso facto* deprivation of heretics, but only to the equivalence of certain phrases to *ipso iure* or *ipso facto*, which is the subject of the chapter of Suarez to which he refers.

have already mentioned and as is clear beyond any doubt from the reasoning from his *De Fide, Spe et Charitate* that I have quoted, Suarez must have been unaware of that bull. And this of course destroys any possible credibility that his hypothesis could ever have had. One cannot possibly even begin to have a case if one is not in a position to deal with one of the most authoritative and compelling argument against it.

And since Suarez's time there has been an additional decree on the subject from the Holy See: Canon 188§4 of the 1917 *Code of Canon Law*, which provides that:

> If any cleric ... publicly defects from the Catholic Faith ... all of his offices become vacant '*ipso facto*' and without any declaration, by tacit resignation accepted by the law itself.

It is interesting to note that the last words of this canon effectively introduce a nicety which had evidently not occurred to Suarez in his argument that human law cannot deprive one who is equal or superior in authority to its promulgator – namely that the automatic loss of office incurred by heretics is not, strictly a *privation*, which is the act of a *superior*, but an act of resignation on the part of the heretics themselves. This is so even if they do not directly wish to resign, because by choosing a role radically incompatible with holding office in the Church (i.e. the role of heretic) they have externally expressed, at least interpretatively, the will to resign; and so the law itself interprets their action, and their office automatically falls vacant.

Finally, it should be noted that Suarez's contention that there is no Divine law whereby heretics are automatically deprived of their offices is not correct. The words of St. Paul and St. John forbidding communication between the faithful and heretics (as quoted by Suarez himself) constitute just such a law,[48] as the

---

[48] Although the law is implicit rather than explicit in the Apostles' words, it is nonetheless inescapable, as it would certainly not be compatible with these apostolic injunctions to recognize a heretic as having authority in the Catholic Church. Many other laws recognized to be Divine in origin – such as that prescribing the seal of confession – are deduced from passages of

unanimous teaching of the Fathers to the same effect, vouched for by St. Robert Bellarmine, proves beyond question. Consequently the automatic exclusion of even uncondemned heretics from all ecclesiastical offices pronounced by *Cum Ex Apostolatus* and in recent times by Canon 188§4 do indeed "bind the pope", because although promulgated by his equal, they are *interpretative* of Divine law.

It is thus certain that the premises upon which Suarez bases his hypothesis – namely the absence of any Divine law or human law applicable to a pope who falls into heresy, as well as the view that even non-papal heretics retain their offices until officially deposed – are entirely unfounded and in conflict with explicit judgements of the Church's highest authority. The corollary of this fact is that it is not open to Catholics today to recognize Suarez's view even as a legitimate opinion. The opposite opinion, taught by St. Robert Bellarmine, St. Alphonsus Liguori and countless others, is the official view of the Church herself. All heretics, including a heretic elected to the Holy See or a pope who, if such a catastrophe be possible, became a heretic after being validly elected, lose their offices *ipso facto*, and that both by Divine and by human law.

Important Note

At the time of going to press (1989) the first serious moves seem to be afoot, among those who recognize the current vacancy of the Holy See, to organize a makeshift papal election, and it appears probable that some sort of an election will take place during 1990. It should be noted that those involved in this undertaking are clearly acting rashly, as they are preparing for the election without having given any satisfactory demonstration that an election such as they envisage will be valid. For instance, they invoke the election of Pope Martin V by the Council of Constance as a precedent for an extra-canonical election,

---

Scripture in which they are even more implicit, but nonetheless certain.

without even considering Cardinal Franzelin's case demonstrating that the election in question *did not in any way depart from the Church's laws then in force*. And similarly they have signally failed to establish *who*, in the absence of cardinals, diocesan bishops or Roman clergy, are the competent electors and in what numbers they would need to be convened. And unless the answers to these questions can be established *with certainty* from Catholic authority, it is clear that any such election will succeed only in creating a "doubtful pope" whom all faithful Catholics, in accordance with the axiom that "a doubtful pope is no pope" (Wernz-Vidal: *Jus Canonicum*, lib. 2, n. 454), will be bound to reject.

No attempt will be made in this *Evaluation* to discuss any further the question of whether a valid papal election can still take place today, and, if so, how. But it is emphasised that the conclusion that the Holy See is today vacant by no means *necessitates* any sort of irregular papal election, as no Catholic doctrine would be incompatible with continuation of the current vacancy for some years to come.

CHAPTER FOUR
DISHONESTY, INCONSISTENCY AND ARROGANCE

"A lie is a foul blot in a man, and yet it will be continually in the mouth of men without discipline."

(Ecclesiasticus 20:26)

"All my writing is governed by one criterion only, the truth."

(Michael Davies: *The Remnant*, 30th November 1988)

The attentive reader of the works of Mr. Michael Davies cannot fail to be struck by certain extremely unpleasant symptoms. Although the superficial student may overlook them or dismiss them as defects of style rather than of character, it emerges on any more profound investigation as outside the realm of doubt that he is arrogant, dishonest and unscrupulous, and that he frequently descends to a level of absurdity which, given the gravity of the topics he writes on, cannot fail to leave an extremely unsavoury taste.

As these allegations are grave, they must be substantiated, once again by examining and analysing a series of examples taken from Davies's works.

"It's the Mass that Matters"

Let us begin by looking at a case in which Davies exposes the truth to apparent refutation by defending a true and correct position with an invalid argument. He does this on p. 140 of *Cranmer's Godly Order*, where he writes:

> But this despised remnant [i.e. the recusants of the English Reformation] had a treasure denied to those who treated them with such contempt, the Mass of St. Pius V, 'the most beautiful thing this

side of heaven'. This was the pearl of great price for which they were prepared to pay all that they had – and pay it they did, priest and layman, butcher's wife and schoolmaster. The victors had the churches and cathedrals built for the celebration of the traditional Latin Mass, the vanquished had the Mass, and it was the Mass that mattered.

So it was for the *Mass* that the martyrs laid down their lives – the Mass of St. Pius V! This is the argument which Davies uses to defend the True Mass – and it is quite without foundation. Let us overlook the fact that a great many of the English martyrs had never even attended "the Mass of St. Pius V", since the Mass in use in this country until the "Reformation" was for the most part in the "Sarum" rite. Even if they *had* been devoted to the specific rite of Mass which Davies is defending, the fact remains that to suggest that they died *for* this particular rite is sheer invention. It would be equally arbitrary and false to suggest that they died for the traditional rite of Confirmation or Extreme Unction. Moreover, had they died for a particular liturgical ceremony, they would not have been martyrs at all, since they would not have died for the Catholic Faith, death in this cause being the very definition of martyrdom.[1] What the martyrs died for was "the Faith once delivered to the saints" (Jude v. 3)

---

[1] "The one and only true cause of martyrdom is *faith* in those things which are to be believed or done." (Pope Benedict XIV: *De Servorum Dei Beatificatione et Beatorum Canonizatione*, book III, chapter XIX, n. 3) The learned pope goes on to explain the meaning of "faith in those things which are to be *done*," observing that "if anyone dies for the exercise of some virtue which faith commands or commends, this can be called a profession of faith *by actions* and such a one would be a martyr ..." (*Ibid.*). Hence, a priest who risks death to *say* Mass, or a layman who risks death to *attend* it, could certainly be a martyr if apprehended and executed for this "offence"; but the reason for his being a martyr would not be his preference for a particular liturgical *form* – for this is not an object of faith at all – nor even his eucharistic *piety*. It would be his *faith* manifested by his witnessing to the Catholic doctrine that celebration of, or attendance at, Mass, *in any rite whatsoever that the Church approves of* is a salutary action which no tyrant can lawfully forbid.

taught by the Church outside of which there is no salvation. It is true that they loved the True Mass and that they would never have attended any perversion of it, whether the Anglican service or the Novus Ordo, but it was not for this that they laid down their lives. They laid down their lives rather than apostatize from the Church.

Moreover, that this was so the martyrs themselves made very clear. Let us quote some of the testimonies they gave as to the cause for which they died:

(i) Father John Kemble, shortly before his death, spoke as follows:

> I die only for professing the old Roman Catholic religion, which was the religion that first made this kingdom Christian, and whoever intends to be saved must die in that religion.

(ii) Blessed Henry Morse said, immediately before he was hanged:

> I am come hither to die for my religion, for that religion which is professed by the Catholic Roman Church, founded by Christ ... out of which ... there can be no hopes of salvation.

(iii) Venerable John Baptist Bullaker, while kneeling at the scaffold before his martyrdom, responded as follows to the enquiries of the sheriff:

> I am greatly indebted to you and to my country for the very singular and unexpected favour I have received ... a favour of which I deem myself most unworthy, a favour for which I always yearned, but never dared to hope; to wit, to die in defence of the Catholic, Apostolic and Roman faith.

(iv) Blessed John Southworth began his final speech before death as follows:

> This is the third time I have been apprehended, and now being to die, I would gladly witness and profess openly my faith for which I suffer .... My faith is my crime, the performance of my duty the occasion of my condemnation.

(v) Blessed Mark Barkworth, when his time came to face death, declared:

> For this Faith I now desire to die more than I ever desired to live. No death can be more precious than that which is undergone for this Faith, which faith Christ taught and a hundred thousand martyrs have sealed it with their blood.

(vi) Fr. Edward Morgan, shortly before being hanged, drawn and quartered, told the crowd assembled to witness the gruesome event:

> There is but one God, one Faith, one Baptism, one true Church, in which is found true hope of salvation, out of which there can be none; and for this true Church of Christ I willingly die.

(vii) Finally, Fr. Hugh Green, who was executed in 1642, declared plainly:

> I am here condemned to die for my religion and for being a priest.

All of the above extracts are taken from either *Martyrs of the Catholic Faith in England* by the Venerable Richard Challoner or *Franciscans and the Protestant Revolution in England* by Francis Borgia Steck. It is notable that neither in these two works nor in any other on the English martyrs of that period that I have examined is there any instance to be found of a martyr who claimed to be dying for the Mass, still less for a particular rite of Mass. Davies has simply invented his assertion because it is convenient for his argument, hoping to intimidate his readers, by means of the confidence with which he makes the assertion, into believing it without his having to engage in the impossible task of proving it with true evidence.

Inconsistency

This *Evaluation* has already provided sufficient evidence that inconsistencies abound in Davies's writings and inconsistency is generally due to dishonesty, either conscious or unconscious. Hence it is unsurprising that Davies's dishonesty is most direct, and his inconsistency most noticeable – almost brazen – on the subject of the claimants to the papacy since the death of Pope Pius XII.

For instance, in a 1982 lecture, the text of which was published in the issue of *The Remnant* dated 31st October 1983, Davies gave a description of an occasion on which a bishop of the Conciliar Church made his cathedral available for the ceremony of conferring episcopal Consecration on a member of the Episcopalian sect in that sect's own invalid ritual. The Conciliar bishop attended the ceremony, hugged the pseudo-bishop, and, in Davies's words, "congratulated him on receiving an office which he had not received." To this, very properly, Davies commented: "I ask you – when a Catholic bishop allows this, is there any point at all in calling him a Catholic?"

Is there any point indeed? However in that same year, 1982, a confrère of this bishop, during a visit to England, acted in an entirely comparable way. This of course was John-Paul II. During that massively publicized visit he too engaged in joint worship with heretics; he too hugged a heretical pseudo-bishop – Dr. Runcie; he too acknowledged this impostor as validly possessing the office to which he lays claim by calling him "Archbishop of Canterbury"[2] and allowing him to be referred to as the "Successor of St. Augustine".

---

[2] The last Archbishop of Canterbury was Reginald Cardinal Pole who died on the same day as Queen Mary in May 1554. Since then a series of heretical married laymen have masqueraded as his successors, possessing neither valid Orders nor apostolically conferred jurisdiction, and indeed possessing no claim at all to the office in question apart from the "authorization" of the secular power, which has no competence whatever in the ecclesiastical sphere. When the English hierarchy was restored by Pope Pius IX in 1850, the British Parliament insisted, as a condition of "permitting" this, that different sees be chosen from those usurped by the Anglicans. To avoid fruitless conflict the new Primate of England was thus named by the Holy See the Archbishop of *Westminster*, this see replacing Canterbury. Thus the next successor of St. Augustine after Cardinal Pole's death was Cardinal Nicholas Wiseman, who was appointed in 1850 to the newly established primatial see of Westminster. Cardinal William Godfrey was the legitimate successor of Wiseman, Pole and Augustine at the time of the Second Vatican Council, in the course of which, *felix opportunitate mortis*, he died.

But although Davies devoted at least one article to this outrage, in vain did any of its readers look for the pertinent question, "When a 'pope' allows this, is there any point at all in calling him a Catholic?" And certainly one can see that the answer which such a question would have not merely invited, but positively demanded, would have given Davies a measure of discomfort.[3]

The blunt fact is that the episode with Dr. Runcie seems hardly to have affected Davies's astonishing position, expressed in November 1981:

> And what of the Pope? Let us thank God that he has recovered from the foul attack upon his life. Let us thank God that he is so evidently Catholic.

Certainly as recently as 13th December 1984 Davies was assuring those readers of *The Remnant* who had not cancelled their subscriptions in disgust in 1981 after reading the words quoted above, that:

> One of the greatest signs of hope for the Church at present is the open animosity now being displayed towards Pope John-Paul II by liberals throughout the world.
>
> (...)
>
> I am very happy to say that, whatever reservations traditionalists might have concerning Pope John-Paul II, he is certainly hated by the world.

By reading what newspapers, I wonder, could one receive the impression that the attitude of "liberals throughout the world" to John-Paul II is one of "open animosity" and that a man who is undoubtedly a more popular "star" than any politician, monarch, actor or musician of our day is "certainly hated by the world?" Unless Mr. Davies takes a newspaper I am not acquainted with, I can only assume that to produce such an illusion he must read whatever paper he *does* take through spectacles tinted such a

---

[3] I am grateful to Fr. Vida Elmer's *Monograph N° 72* for highlighting this inconsistency.

deep shade of rose that they not only distort reality, but make it appear the very *opposite* of what it is.

Distorting the Statements of Archbishop Lefebvre

Let us look at some more of Davies's misrepresentations. In the *Apologia Pro Marcel Lefebvre*, Vol. 1, pages 103-104, he quotes the following extract from Archbishop Lefebvre's letter to Paul VI dated 31st May 1975:

> Prostrate at the feet of Your Holiness, I assure you of my entire and filial submission to the decisions communicated to me by the Commission of Cardinals in what concerns the Fraternity of St. Pius X and its seminary.
> However, Your Holiness will be able to judge by the enclosed account if in the procedure, Natural and Canon Law have been observed.

This letter of course concerns the instruction to close the seminary. To this unambiguous letter, Davies adds a footnote in which he says:

> Non-observance of Natural and Canon Law which evidently annuls the preceding paragraph.

In other words, Davies is saying that when Archbishop Lefebvre assures Montini of his "entire and filial submission to the decisions communicated to" him by Montini's Commission he should be understood to mean that he is in fact *refusing* his submission to the decisions in question!

This is simply dishonest. There is no possible way that such a meaning can be extracted from Archbishop Lefebvre's words. The meaning of the letter is quite clearly that Archbishop Lefebvre is promising to obey the decisions communicated to him while at the same time protesting at the way in which the proceedings against him have been conducted. It is immaterial whether or not at the time he wrote the letter it was *really* Archbishop Lefebvre's intention to submit to Montini's instruction. What is at issue is the fact that Michael Davies, in order to rescue his hero from an apparent inconsistency, is prepared calmly to tell his readers that black means white and expects them to believe him.

And, almost incredibly, his gall seems to have paid off; for I have never heard of a single protest against this ludicrous misrepresentation.

He plays the same trick again on p. 328 of the same book, immediately after finding himself forced, by a letter from Montini to Archbishop Lefebvre which he has quoted, to refer to the occasion when Archbishop Lefebvre publicly and clearly adopted the position that the Conciliar Church is not the Catholic Church. For readers who are not familiar with Archbishop Lefebvre's famous words on that occasion, this is what he declared in a document carefully drafted for public circulation on 29th July 1976:

> This Conciliar Church is schismatic, since she has taken as her own base principles opposed to those of the Catholic Church, such as the new concept of the Mass ... as well as that of the natural right (pretending it is of Divine origin) of each person and each group of persons to religious freedom. The Church which states such errors is at the same time schismatic and heretical.[4]

I wonder whether Davies had sufficient conscience left to gulp as he wrote the following commentary:

> Mgr. Lefebvre has indeed referred to the 'Conciliar Church' being in schism, but in a lighthearted manner. He has a highly developed sense of humour and can be provocative at times.

Once again, what can one say? What, what, *what* is there in those words of Archbishop Lefebvre that is remotely comical? Possibly Davies will claim that he himself laughed uproariously when he first read them, but I find it difficult to imagine the same passage provoking even a smile in anyone else who read it. *Possibly* humorous, I should have thought, is the suggestion

---

[4] *Quelques réflexions à propos de la "suspens a divinis".*

that there is something amusing in a bishop solemnly stating his opinion on the current position in the Church in his first official statement on the subject after his clash with the Vatican, and making the clear assertion, without any indication that he does not mean it literally, that the Conciliar Church is schismatic and heretical – an assertion, moreover, which was being seriously advanced also by other writers in France at that time, and in respect of which he would have therefore given a disastrously false impression of his stand if he had not meant what he said.

In fact, as scarcely needs saying, Davies's explanation, expressed in his characteristic fashion with the confidence applicable to something which admits no doubt, is exactly the opposite of the truth. And this truth does not cease to be true merely because the Archbishop has often made statements incompatible with this one.

The Infallibility of Archbishop Lefebvre

Davies in fact seems quite unable to think straight in connection with Archbishop Lefebvre. On page XV of his introduction to the Volume I of his *Apologia Pro Marcel Lefebvre*, for instance, he says:

> Archbishop Lefebvre has stated on many occasions that all he is doing is to uphold the faith as he received it. Those who condemn him condemn the Faith of their Fathers.

For those sentences to be worth uttering at all, there must have been intended to be some logical connection between them; but what this logical connection may be is not the easiest thing in the world to discern. The reasoning that Davies seems to be presenting to us is that, because Archbishop Lefebvre has said that he is doing nothing but upholding the Faith as he received it, those who condemn him are therefore condemning that Faith. What of the possibility that Archbishop Lefebvre's assertion that "all he is doing is to uphold the faith as he received it" is not true? It does not seem to have occurred to him. He does not even consider it necessary to offer any justification or support for his statement. Archbishop Lefebvre has made the claim — therefore, it *must* be true. Archbishop Lefebvre has said that he is right — it therefore follows, as night follows day, that those who disagree with him *must* be wrong.

In short, those two sentences suggest that Archbishop Lefebvre has become in Davies's eyes an oracle of Divine Revelation. The authority he enjoys in Davies's eyes is certainly, from what we shall be seeing in the next chapter of this *Evaluation*, much higher than that which Davies attributes to the *Ordinary* Magisterium, for what other men have to argue and prove, Archbishop Lefebvre needs only to assert and he must be believed.

This supine suspension of Davies's critical faculties is even more apparent on p. 213 of the same book where, without the smallest indication that he recognizes the absurdity of what Archbishop Lefebvre is saying, he quotes the following extract which I invite readers to examine with their own critical faculties fully alert:

> Well, I appeal to St. Pius V — St. Pius V, who in his bull said that, in perpetuity, no priest could incur a censure, whatever it might be, in perpetuity, for saying this Mass. And consequently, this censure, this excommunication, if there was one, these censures, if there are any, are absolutely *invalid*, contrary to that which St. Pius V established in perpetuity in his bull: that *never* in any age could one inflict a censure on a priest who says this Holy Mass.
> Why? Because this Mass is canonized. He canonized it definitively. Now a Pope cannot remove a canonization. The Pope can make a new rite, but he cannot remove a canonization. He cannot forbid a Mass that is canonized. Thus, if he has canonized a Saint, another Pope cannot come and say that this Saint is no longer canonized. That is not possible. Now this Holy Mass was canonized by Pope St. Pius V. And that is why we can say it in all tranquillity, in all security ....

Each of the above quoted paragraphs contains an argument, somewhat loosely expressed; and in each case the argument is wholly invalid. I am not, of course, disputing Archbishop Lefebvre's statement that priests are still entitled to say Mass according to the liturgy codified by St. Pius. I am merely pointing out that *the arguments which he uses to defend this position are invalid* – blatantly invalid – and that Davies himself is so far subjugated by his subject as apparently not to notice any problem and to relay the fallacies to his readers without adverting to the slightest problem of logic or theology.

It is easy to verify the logical validity of an argument by re-expressing it *formally*. In other words, just as the informal mental arithmetic by which we check our bills can be re-expressed in set *mathematical* form, so too the proofs we use to support our convictions on any topic can be re-expressed in set *logical* form. And just as the formalized system of mathematical computation enables us to confirm the correctness of our informal mental calculation or to expose any errors therein, so too, formal logical expression enables us to test the validity of our arguments.

The usual formal expression of an argument is the syllogism. It consists of two statements accepted as true and a third statement which undeniably flows from the first two; for instance:

All spirits are immortal.
The soul of man is a spirit.
Therefore, the soul of man is immortal.

When we re-express an argument as a syllogism it is stripped of rhetorical techniques and any other support it might be lent by its context, and reduced to its bare essentials, so that any fallacy in it can at once be perceived; and, by the same token, if the argument is valid, this too will be apparent; so that anyone who acknowledges the two initial statements ("premises") must either acknowledge the conclusion also or bid farewell to intellectual integrity.

With this background, let us now return to Archbishop Lefebvre's arguments and subject them to the simple test of re-expression as syllogisms.

If the argument contained in Archbishop Lefebvre's first paragraph is restated in this way, it can be set out as follows:

    i.   The first statement or proposition is that St. Pius V made a ruling that no priest could incur a censure for saying the Tridentine Mass.

    ii.   The second statement was understood by Archbishop Lefebvre rather than directly expressed, and is, obviously, that Archbishop Lefebvre's priests *do* say this Mass.

    iii.   The conclusion inferred is that any censure brought against them by Montini – even on the assumption, of course, that he is a true Pope – is invalid.

To ensure complete clarity let us now restate this syllogism as succinctly as possible:

    i.   No priest can be censured for saying the Tridentine Mass.

    ii.   Archbishop Lefebvre's priests say the Tridentine Mass.

    iii.   Therefore, Archbishop Lefebvre's priests cannot be censured.

And viewed as nakedly as this, the argument is of course patently spurious. It would be just as sensible to assert: "No one can be arrested for carrying a walking stick; therefore no one who carries a walking stick can be arrested." Naturally a person who carries a walking stick *can* be arrested for doing something *else* which *is* criminal; and, in the same way, a priest who says the Tridentine Mass cannot be censured for *that*, but can certainly be censured for any number of *other* activities which *are* subject to censure.

Moreover nobody had ever claimed to be censuring Archbishop Lefebvre or his clergy for saying the Tridentine Mass; the purported censure was inflicted for the crime of illicit Ordination – which certainly *is* a crime in canon law (although, for other reasons, Paul VI and his henchmen had no right to censure anyone for it or anything else).

Now let us turn to the argument in the second paragraph, and restate that too as a syllogism. In this form it runs like this:

    i.   Whatever is canonized is irreversibly fixed.
    ii. The Tridentine Mass is canonized.
    iii. Therefore, the Tridentine Mass is definitively fixed.

Here the fallacy which invalidates the argument is a more subtle one. At first sight no flaw is apparent, because the argument depends upon an equivocal or ambiguous term. It is as if one were to argue:

    i.   That bird is a crane.
    ii. A crane would be useful on a construction site.
    iii. Therefore that bird would be useful on a construction site.

Obviously, the key word which gives the above syllogism its deceptive appearance of validity is "crane". Having, as it does, more than one meaning, it is used with a different meaning in the second premise from that which it bears in the first, and this makes the syllogism as invalid as it would obviously be if the bird referred to had in fact been a heron.

And exactly the same deception is perpetrated by means of the word "canonized" in Archbishop Lefebvre's second argument. We are all well aware that once a saint has been canonized the process is irreversible, and that no one can un-canonize the saint. But when a liturgical rite is spoken of as having been canonized, the word is used with a different sense. The *canonization* of a saint, on the one hand, is a process protected by the divine guarantee of infallibility. The *canonization* of a rite, on the other, is a purely legislative act: certainly it cannot contradict the Faith, but it is not guaranteed to be a wise or prudent action and therefore may well be open to alteration by another pope.

It must be borne in mind that the point at issue is *not* whether a legitimate pope has or has not the right to change the Tridentine Mass after its canonization by Pope St. Pius V's bull *Quo Primum*; it is whether Archbishop Lefebvre's *argument* that he has no such right is logically sustainable. And clearly it is not, for a very good reason: although it is an indisputable fact that canonization in the first sense of the word that we have looked at is unchangeable, this by no means proves that canonization in the *second* sense of the word is unchangeable, any more than whatever is true of the first sense of *any* word proves *anything* about that word in some other sense it may bear. This is not an abstruse theological point. *The Concise Oxford Dictionary*, for instance, clearly records the first meaning of "canonize" – "declare officially to be a saint" – and adds a secondary, different meaning: "sanction by church authority". For a bishop to argue from one meaning to the other, and for a theological writer to quote him doing so without disclaimer, indicates, on the part of both, a cavalier attitude to simple logic and on the part of the latter a degree of hero-worship which ill becomes any writer claiming to be objective.[5]

Moreover, Davies's recent independent stance, mildly critical of Archbishop Lefebvre's unlawful Consecration of four bishops in mid-1988,[6] does not improve, but aggravates this aspect of his writings, for it means that, whereas previously Davies had himself been treating Archbishop Lefebvre as infallible as well as requiring others to do so, now it seems that he, Davies, is entitled to doubt Archbishop Lefebvre's inerrancy on one isolated point, and that on this one point others also are entitled to disagree with Archbishop Lefebvre and support Davies – who

---

[5] In fact Archbishop Lefebvre, in his sermon delivered at the 1976 ordinations, was probably speaking extempore and is to that extent more excusable than Davies.

[6] See, for instance, *The Remnant* 30th November 1988 for a statement of Davies's attitude to the Society of St. Pius X and its founder since the Consecrations.

would thus seem to have inherited some of Archbishop Lefebvre's forfeited status – and yet this "grave error of judgement"[7] made by Archbishop Lefebvre does *not*, in Davies's views, give any ground for re-opening and examining anew other controversial questions concerning the present situation of the Church about which he has in the past encouraged his readers to accept Archbishop Lefebvre's opinions as definitions.

Disneyland Theology

Probably the most fantastic piece of Davies's dishonesty in connection with Archbishop Lefebvre, occurred in an article which he wrote in *The Remnant* for 31st July 1983. It is worth quoting the whole extract since it is a good illustration of how the combination of Davies's style, the esteem in which he is held, and the supineness of a sufficiently large number of his readers,[8] allow him mercilessly to bully his readers into believing whatever he wishes them to believe without his having to supply the smallest particle of evidence.

First it is necessary to recount the main events which precipitated the article from which I shall shortly be quoting. The story began when priests of the Society of St. Pius X established Mass-centres in the United States during the 1970s. Archbishop Lefebvre divided the country into two "districts", the Northeast[9] and the Southwest, each to be served by a separate group of priests. The Southwest group has a college at

---

[7] Letter to *The Daily Telegraph* by Davies, published 6th June 1988.

[8] It is important to note that, provided that there are sufficient uncritical and admiring readers of his works, Davies can afford to ignore people who consider his writings to be pernicious, even though they too are considerable in number; for the latter are denied a forum which would reach the former. Publications such as *The Remnant*, *Christian Order* and *Approaches/ÀPropos*, for instance, would never print articles or even letters severely critical of Davies.

[9] The spellings of "North East" and "South West" as one word are those used by the SSPX itself and for the purposes of this chapter I shall follow this usage.

St. Mary's, Kansas, produces the periodical called *The Angelus* and in those days had the notorious Fr. Hector Bolduc[10] as its superior. The Northeast District, under Fr. Clarence Kelly, was based at Oyster Bay, New York, had a seminary at Ridgefield, Connecticut, and produced *The Roman Catholic*.

Even leaving aside consideration of the errors with which it was infested, *The Angelus* has never been a serious periodical. This was not always true of *The Roman Catholic*, however. In the early 1980s its editors were showing themselves to be, unlike the regular contributors to *The Angelus*, perfectly capable of writing articles of such competent scholarship and accurate reasoning that only occasionally did their writings go astray. But this relatively high standard was not maintained. About five years ago, a deliberate decision was taken to downgrade the contents of the magazine in order to try to interest a wider range of readers, and it is a fair indication of the extent to which *The Roman Catholic* immediately degenerated to say that since then it has been every bit as trivial as *The Angelus* and arguably more so. It is not that *The Roman Catholic* has new editors; it is that its existing editors have chosen to prostitute their talents to popular lightweight journalism.

Even before 1983 the clergy of the two districts differed considerably in character, the Northeast being considerably more "hard line" than the Southwest. Articles in their respective

---

[10] Fr. Bolduc is notorious as a compulsive liar of the kind ready to regale gullible listeners with mendacious accounts of his friendship with Elvis Presley and his work in military intelligence. More seriously his dishonest claims to have graduated from the Catholic University of America and to have accomplished a significant part of the normal priestly formation before his acceptance at Écône beguiled Archbishop Lefebvre into ordaining him after a mere nine months of seminary training. On one occasion, under interrogation in a court of law, Fr. Bolduc went so far as to declare that "you could not be a priest in good standing at the present time without being a member of the Society of St. Pius X". On another, the *Kansas City Star* newspaper reported that he had scandalized a children's catechism class by claiming that "there is no pain or suffering or fire associated with Purgatory". (Cf. Dz. 570s.)

periodicals, differences of pastoral practice, and private conversation ensured that the differences between the two groups became publicly known, and it became clear that, generally speaking, though it was the Southwest group which departed further from the standards Catholic clergy ought to observe, it was the Northeast group which was "out of step" with the bulk of Archbishop Lefebvre's Society of St. Pius X.

Particular points of friction between the priests of the Northeast District and Archbishop Lefebvre were:

(i) The Archbishop's insistence (as of early 1983) that the liturgy as reformed by John XXIII be used throughout the Society, despite the facts

　(a) that the liturgical changes it incorporated, presided over, as they were, by the notorious Freemason Annibale Bugnini, were evidently a prelude to the Novus Ordo, and

　(b) that the Society's 1976 General Chapter had authorized the use of the *totally* unreformed liturgy.

(ii) The fact that Archbishop Lefebvre allowed "priests" ordained in the 1968 rite to function in the Society despite the strong grounds for regarding this rite as of doubtful validity.

(iii) Archbishop Lefebvre's insistence that the marriage annulments which the Conciliar Church hands out at the drop of a hat to separated spouses be regarded as valid.

(iv) Archbishop Lefebvre's refusal to allow members of the Society to dissent from his present convictions concerning the validity of the Novus Ordo, the occupancy of the Holy See, etc. (The Northeast clergy for the most part held the See to be vacant and the new sacramental rites to be doubtful, but they were demanding *not* that the Society officially adopt these convictions but that it should simply *permit* its priests to hold them.)

(v) Archbishop Lefebvre's policy of expelling from the Society without following the due canonical procedure members who clashed with him on these and other issues.

For a while the dispute simmered quietly without leading to open breach; but on 25th March 1983 nine priests of the Northeast Section wrote a firm but respectful letter to Archbishop Lefebvre concerning their anxieties on the subjects mentioned above. Then things moved fast. All nine signatories to the letter were purportedly dismissed from the Society, and one of them (Fr. Dolan) was also dismissed as rector of the seminary. Archbishop Lefebvre wrote to as many of the Society's supporters in the Northeast District as he could, denouncing the nine priests who had offended him and not only presenting a misleading version of the facts surrounding the dispute, but even going so far as to quote St. Thomas as saying something which he does not say.[11] The nine priests were prompt to point out these misrepresentations and to note that the expulsions and dismissals were in flagrant defiance of Canon Law. (And indeed they *were* in defiance of Canon Law, though it is difficult to feel any sympathy for their victims in view of the fact that the St. Pius X Society has, from its inception, scarcely ever been known to take the slightest notice of any canon law whatsoever.)

Thereafter the nine priests effectively became a separate organization from the Society of St. Pius X. When Archbishop Lefebvre went to the U.S.A. in 1984, three of the four seminarians he then ordained to the priesthood left him

---

[11] "The basic principle of the Society's thinking and action in the painful crisis the Church is going through is the principle taught by St. Thomas Aquinas in the *Summa Theologiæ* (II-II, Q. 33, A. 4) that one may not oppose the authority of the Church except in the case of imminent danger to the Faith." This was the assurance given by Archbishop Lefebvre to his society's "Friends and Benefactors" in a letter to them dated 28th April 1983. But in fact St. Thomas says no such thing. The only sentence in the article in question which remotely resembles the words attributed to him by Archbishop Lefebvre is as follows: " ... where danger threatens the Faith, prelates should be rebuked by their subjects even publicly." As the nine dissident priests considered themselves to be subject to Archbishop Lefebvre as their prelate, it was understandable that they should retort, as they did, that this was precisely the point they had been trying to make!

immediately after Ordination – relying on a strained interpretation of the vow of obedience they had just taken to their superiors in the Society – to join the breakaway nine who thus became twelve. A legal battle has been waged, at great length and cost to the supporters of both groups, over the ownership of the Society's property in the Northeast District, and the Society of St. Pius X has formed a skeleton network of priests who remain loyal to Archbishop Lefebvre to compete with the twelve dissidents in offering their priestly services.

And it is worth noting that since the split a great deal of ink has been spilt by both sides in the efforts of each to justify its position at the expense of the other, and in the course of the paper war much that is scarcely edifying in the conduct or positions of *both* sides has been brought to light. The dissidents have certainly had much the stronger case and have presented it much more persuasively, but neither has succeeded in fully justifying its own position, for the excellent reason that neither position takes full account of the present vacancy of the Holy See and the gravity of recognizing it and making it known.

Now, with this background in place, here is the comment which Davies thought the episode merited:

> This brings me to the subject of recent upheavals in the Society of St. Pius X. I promised to make some comment upon this in my last letter. My comment will be brief, surprisingly brief some readers may consider. The reason is that all that needs to be said upon this topic has appeared in the June and July issues of *The Angelus*, the official English-language journal of the Society of St. Pius X .... Those who require the facts about what has happened can do no better than obtain these two issues. All I will add is that I support the Archbishop totally in the action he has taken, my one regret is that he did not expel the ringleaders of what must be termed the Oyster Bay sect two years ago. [The punctuation anomaly is as in the original. – J.S.D.] If he had done so, only four priests rather than nine might be lost to the Society. While these priests retained their status as official members of the Society it could not be considered a credible traditional Catholic organisation, at least in

the North East district. It is now up to the priests who have remained loyal to the Archbishop to give the Society a credible image. It will not be an easy task as there is a lot to live down. As to the propaganda being sent out from Oyster Bay in favour of the new sect, it has about as much relevance to Catholic theology as the literature distributed by Jehovah's Witnesses. It can only be termed a Disneyland theology, with Goofy as the principal author. But, as I have just remarked, the Devil can appear as an angel of light, and for some years at least thousands of traditional Catholics will assist at the masses of priests of the new Oyster Bay sect, just as they do at masses of the Diem Sect,[12] or the Old Roman Catholics, and come out feeling all warm and tingly because they have been present at the traditional Mass, and deluding themselves that they are staunch upholders of tradition.

Here Davies is using against this group the very tactics which are used by the Modernist revolutionaries against him and anyone else who opposes in any degree the revolution.

As support for this last accusation, readers are invited to notice in particular that Davies does not condescend to employ a single argument! Relying on his own status and "authority" in the eyes of his readers, trusting that they will accept whatever he says, he simply declares:

> As to the propaganda being sent out from Oyster Bay in favour of the new sect, it has about as much relevance to Catholic theology as the literature distributed by Jehovah's Witnesses. It can only be termed Disneyland theology, with Goofy as the principal author.

Strong language! And of course as soon as one examines what he is saying at all attentively, it is obvious that he has adopted – sunk to – the customary technique of propagandists of using violent words to drive home his point without needing to proffer any evidence for it. Anyone who has read the 1983-4 issues of the Oyster Bay periodical *The Roman Catholic*, in which the dissident priests made their case and wrote on many other theological topics, knows that, it bore a much closer

---

[12] *Sic*. A misrecollection of the name of Archbishop Ngô *Dinh* Thuc?

resemblance to Catholicism than does the bulk of what is published in *The Remnant* or *The Angelus*.

And what makes it even worse is that times without number Davies has complained during his writing career that his arguments are not taken seriously by the Conciliar Church; that, instead of facing up to his justifications for his position, Novus Ordo priests simply dismiss him as a schismatic or a crank.[13] Now he adopts *exactly* the same course in his response to the Oyster Bay controversy. *Disneyland theology written by Goofy*, he sneers; the former members of the Society of St. Pius X based at Oyster Bay should have been dismissed from the Society a long time ago; Archbishop Lefebvre is right in what he is doing – and anyone who wants this to be proved to him need only read the propaganda on this subject put out by Archbishop Lefebvre's side.[14] Thus in the light of Davies's own

---

[13] Cf., for instance, his "Open Letter to the Editor of the Universe" (*Christian Order*, May 1982), a piece of sustained invective which for its literary merits deserves comparison with the diatribes of Swift and Pope, but the cogency of which is seriously undermined by the fact that its accusations are no less applicable to its author than to its addressee.

[14] Of course, *if* Davies's claim were legitimate that "all that needs to be said upon this topic has appeared in ... *The Angelus*," then, although his observations would still be distasteful and of no value except as a record of the private and unsubstantiated opinions of an English schoolmaster on a theological dispute, the absence of any attempt on Davies's part to support his claims would be unobjectionable except to the extent that his claims go beyond those made by and supported in *The Angelus*. But, in the first place, his claims certainly *do* go beyond those of *The Angelus*, for *The Angelus* did not, for instance, make any attempt to demonstrate the charge of schism against the dissidents – hence Davies's characterization of them as a non-Catholic sect amounts to no more than yet another attempt at browbeating his readers to accept his assertions in the absence of any evidence, whether furnished by himself *or* by *The Angelus*. And secondly, even to the extent that *The Angelus*, in the issues to which Davies refers his readers, attempts to answer the case made by the dissident Oyster Bay priests, its response is so weak as to be quite incapable of satisfying anyone who had not already made up his mind that he was on Archbishop Lefebvre's side. For instance, on the central question of the vacancy of the Holy See, *The Angelus* nowhere attempted to answer the evidence showing John-Paul to be ineligible to the

protests when others treat him as he treats others his dishonesty is aggravated by hypocrisy.

The Credibility of the Society of St. Pius X

Before leaving this episode, let us also note what is perhaps the most interesting sentence of all in Davies's article in *The Remnant*. About half-way through, the following words will be found:

> While these priests retained their status as official members of the Society it could not be considered a credible traditional Catholic organisation, at least in the North East district.

Now if Davies had been an honest man, rather than a time-server, he would not have waited until after the priests had been expelled to declare publicly that until their expulsion the Society had not been a "credible traditional Catholic organisation". He would have said *at the time*: "the Society of St. Pius X is not a credible traditional Catholic organisation." The only reason that he did not say this is that he found it inconvenient.

Is there a Modernist Conspiracy?

Another of the subjects which induce Davies to mislead his readers with the assistance of his well practised mental gymnastics is that of conspiratorial infiltration into the Church for the purpose of destroying her. Any temptation that any of his readers may have to believe that the collapse of the institutional side of the Catholic Church in the last three decades has been

---

papacy, and simply assumed the very point under dispute – i.e. his legitimacy – accusing the nine dissidents of "moving ... too far away from the Pope." (July 1983, p. 2). And on the subject of the use in the Society of "priests" ordained in the new rite, the dubious validity of which, one of the nine – Fr. Jenkins – had so triumphantly shown (see p. 360 *et seq.* of this *Evaluation*), Fr. Williamson writing against the nine conceded that the new form of Ordination was not definitely valid but insisted that he had "no *serious* doubt" about it – a fact which is irrelevant, as the Canon 732§2 of the 1917 *Code* requires *not* a *serious* doubt, but merely a *prudent* doubt, to make conditional re-Ordination necessary.

DISHONESTY, INCONSISTENCY AND ARROGANCE

deliberately brought about by conscious agents of Satan is emphatically one which they must resist. On p. 45 of *Pope John's Council,* for instance, he says:

> With the evidence that is available, it would be an exaggeration to claim to be able to prove that, as a body, these men [i.e. the liberals] are motivated by a conscious and malicious desire to destroy the Church.

And although on p. 117 he goes as far as to admit the existence of a Masonic conspiracy against the Church, he immediately afterwards negates the effect of that admission: his readers are *not* to let themselves suspect that what has taken place in the Church in recent years is the direct result of the machinations of these conspirators. This is what he solemnly tells them:

> The great danger here is to begin with a theory and then find the facts to prove it while ignoring evidence that points in another direction. St. Pius X warned us that the Church is under attack from internal enemies determined to destroy her from within ....

Is Davies going to draw from this the lesson that, since the destruction has now taken place, the "internal enemies" in question were responsible? Far from it.

> ... but we would be foolish to presume that most or even many of the leading progressives are deliberately conspiring to destroy the Church.

Why Davies is so enthusiastic to rule out any interpretation of the Vatican II revolution as the effects of conspiratorial forces within the Church, I do not pretend to know, though certainly an inconvenient consequence of such an interpretation is that it would strongly suggest that those who have led the revolution – i.e. Roncalli, Montini, Luciani and Wojtyła – were also conscious conspirators.

What is especially deplorable in this case is that Davies ignores and conceals from his readers not only evidence but the very existence of a vast body of literature on the subject.

Moreover, it is subtly done. He is happy to quote from Graber's inadequate little book *Athanasius and the Church of our Time*, which puts some blame for the revolution on Masonic infiltration; but not a hint appears in his works of the existence of major works of scholarship produced by such authors as Count Léon de Poncins[15] and Maurice Pinay[16] giving strong grounds for belief that the revolution was controlled by conspirators down to its finest details throughout.

One of the most relevant pieces of source material of all in connection with the conspiracy against the Church is the *Permanent Instruction of the Alta Vendita*, a lodge of anti-Catholic revolutionary Freemasons known as the Carbonari, who were very active in nineteenth century Italy. This instruction came into the hands of the Church in 1846 and was communicated by Pope Gregory XVI to a French historian and anti-Judæo-Masonic writer Jacques Crétineau-Joly (1803-1875) who, in a book called *L'Église Romaine en face de la Révolution*, later published it with the approval of Pope Pius IX. It is worth giving some extracts:

> Our ultimate end is ... the final destruction of Catholicism, and even of the Christian idea. The work which we have undertaken is not the work of a day, nor of a month, nor of a year. It may last years, a century, perhaps .... Catholicism has a vitality which survives such attacks with ease .... We may therefore allow our brethren in those countries to work off their frenzy of anti-Catholic zeal, allow them to ridicule our Madonnas and our apparent devotion. Under this cloak we may conspire at our convenience, and arrive, little by little, at our ultimate aim .... The pope [meaning, of course, a true pope – J.S.D.], whoever he may be, will never enter the secret societies. It then becomes the duty of the secret societies to make the first advances to the Church, and to the pope, with the object of conquering both. That which we should seek, that which we should

---

[15] His works relevant to the subject include *Freemasonry and the Vatican*, *Judaism and the Vatican*, and *Secret Powers behind Revolution*.
[16] *The Plot Against the Church*.

await, as the Jews await a Messiah, is a pope [i.e. clearly a *usurper* of that office – J.S.D.] according to our wants .... In order to secure to us a pope in the manner required, it is necessary to shape for that pope a generation worthy of the reign of which we dream .... In a few years, the young clergy will have invaded all the functions and will govern, administer and judge. They will form the council of the Sovereign and will be called upon to choose the pontiff who will reign. That pontiff, like the greater part of his contemporaries, will be necessarily imbued with the Italian and humanitarian principles which we are about to put into circulation .... Seek out the pope of whom we give the portrait. You wish to establish the reign of the elect upon the throne of the whore of Babylon? Let the clergy march under your banner in the belief always that they march under the banner of the Apostolic Keys ....

Lay your nets like Simon Bar-Jonah. Lay them in the depths of sacristies, seminaries and convents, rather than in the depths of the sea .... You will fish up a revolution in tiara and cope, marching with cross and banner.

Such was the blueprint of the enemies of the Church by which to destroy her, which they had conceived a hundred and fifty years ago. In the last thirty years we have seen exactly what they plotted come to pass – not the visible destruction of the Church by the violence of external enemies, for that was not Satan's intention at this point, but as close to the complete destruction of her as is possible without her ceasing to exist entirely, accomplished by invisible enemies who finally procured the invalid election into her highest offices of men imbued by the errors of liberalism and other heresies; of men who, while doing their best to direct attention from what they were doing, have apparently[17] succeeded in "reforming" the Church from within, and in changing her into a wholly different organization, engaged in the work of Satan rather than of God.

---

[17] "[A]pparently" because the reformers have long since ceased to be members of the Church, leaving her smaller, of course, but just as pure in her doctrine and practice as she was before.

Yet Mr. Davies would have his readers believe that there is no connection between the plan of 1846 and the actuality of 1989. Such a position can be based upon nothing but a prodigious degree of self-deception.

Further Remarkable Observations of Mr. Michael Davies

The following quotations, also taken from Davies's works, require less comment than the foregoing and for the most part will be allowed to stand for themselves.

First comes this surprising sentence from p. 19 of *Pope John's Council*:

> There was a definite need for a widespread liturgical renewal in the pre-Conciliar Church.

So Davies is not really a defender of the Tridentine Mass at all. He is opposed to the Novus Ordo, but he is also opposed to the Mass of Pope St. Pius V. What he favours is the as yet unwritten Davies Ordo Missæ, which lies somewhere between the two.

And that sentence was certainly no mere slip of his typewriter, for in an article in *The Remnant* for 31st May 1979 he again made it clear that this was his position. Although he was opposed to the present "New Mass", he said there, he was by no means opposed to all possible "New Masses"; and if the Novus Ordo were adapted to make it resemble the traditional Mass more,

> ... a refusal of traditionalists to revise their attitude in any way would constitute immobilism and it would be hard to justify it with a convincing defence.

V

In *The Remnant* of 30th November 1981 Davies's readers were invited to join him in the following sentiments:

> Let us thank God that he [John-Paul II] is so evidently Catholic.

Let us rather hope that no comment is necessary.

Examples of Arrogance

Another of the characteristics manifested in Davies's writings is arrogance. Readers tending to accept Davies as a trustworthy authority appear on the whole scarcely to have noticed this, but, especially once attention is drawn to it, to an eye which has retained any sort of power of critical judgement, it could hardly be more obvious. Here are two instances, both of them interesting because, while on the surface they appear by no means unacceptable, in fact they could not have been written except by someone with a grossly inflated concept of his own self-importance.

The first is on p. 623 of *Pope Paul's New Mass*, where he refers to "Professor J.P. van der Ploeg O.P., a theologian for whom I have the greatest respect."

Now there is of course nothing, as such, wrong with having great respect for a theologian, but that does not prevent Davies's words from being something that no one with even an ounce of Catholic humility would ever say, even if he had the learning and judgement of a Doctor of the Church. For what is objectionable about them is that he considers it to be of some significance to his readers that he holds this particular professor in high regard. The implication is that since he, Davies, holds van der Ploeg in great esteem, his readers should do the same. And whereas this might not matter if van der Ploeg's theological eminence or lack of it were something upon which little depended, it certainly *does* matter when it is a major factor in support of Davies's case.

Other writers, when quoting an authority, might say something like: "Professor Smith, a theologian who is widely respected in Catholic circles ..." or "Mgr. Bloggs, whom the *Catholic Encyclopædia* describes as a weighty authority on this subject ...". Davies, however, feels that his *own* judgement is of such weight that it is not only worthy of being given but – and this is the real point – it is also sufficient to obviate the need to cite further testimonials in Professor van der Ploeg's favour. In effect he is saying: "You can safely accept that he is an eminent theologian because *I* am telling you that this is what *I* believe. There is no need for you to look for any further evidence in confirmation of my judgement."

Exactly the same attitude is apparent on p. 335 of the same work where he writes:

> I concur with Dr. Francis Clark that the term 'intention of a rite' should be avoided.

Whether Davies is right in his contention is discussed later in this *Evaluation*; but what is of interest in the present context are the words "*I concur* with Dr. Francis Clark". Of what relevance is it that Davies is in agreement with Clark? Rightly or wrongly Clark is held in some esteem as a competent scholar in his restricted field of research and his opinion on the subject will be listened to with respect, but who is Michael Davies that we should be interested in his opinion of Clark's contention?

Let there be no misunderstanding. The non-specialist may certainly express his view. But he cannot expect his readers to attach any weight to it unless he says why he holds it, so that they may weigh up his case for themselves. If Davies had given his *reasons* for agreeing with Clark the sentence would be unobjectionable. But in the world of scholarship, and in any civilized circles, even in the non-Catholic world, only a man of the very highest authority and learning in a specific field would consider the weight of his judgement to be such that his opinion on a controversial subject would be of interest even in the absence of any argumentation. Thus, for instance, a professor who had devoted twenty years of life to studying the works of Tacitus might fittingly say: "I agree with Dr. Blogg's theory as to the probable completion of Tacitus's *Annals*." But even someone who had achieved considerable general reputation as a classical historian without, however, having made a special study of the subject at issue, would not make such an assertion without stating his evidence, because the assertion would simply be dismissed as the unsupported opinion of someone with no special competence or reputation on the matter being discussed.

Likewise it is no crime to state a fact about the status of an authority cited – such as that a particular author is considered to be the leading scholar in his field, or that his treatment is excellent, very learned or whatever – provided that such assertions are *accurate* and would be *generally recognized as such*. If they are controversial or immoderate assessments, clearly they are quite out of place unless substantiated by reference to evidence justifying them. And it is by trotting out immoderate qualifications of his selected authorities, supported by nothing save his own, often painfully unqualified opinion, that Davies falls foul of accepted scholarly and literary courtesy and exposes his not inconsiderable conceit.

It is not surprising that Davies, whose works have been applauded without restraint by traditional Catholics throughout the world since they first appeared, should have succumbed to pride and conceit, but it is a facet of his character which all those who ever read him, or recommend his writings to others, should be aware of.

Others Also Notice

Now although Davies's most fervent admirers have apparently remained blind to this particular feature of their hero, it *has* in fact been noted by others. Here are two examples:

In his parish bulletin of 12th December 1982, Fr. Oswald Baker, parish priest of St. Dominic's, Downham Market, England, wrote with delicate irony:

> The November issue of *Christian Order* carried a bitter attack on the Archbishop [Thuc]. His lay critic, in a sadly uncharacteristic manner, (the article contains 'I' some thirty times), begins the attack with a somewhat imperious admonition, concerning both 'the U.S.A. and Europe'. 'I have warned from time to time of an

increasingly schismatic mentality ....' Such an opening, on such a subject, is unusual from anyone below the rank of pope.

And in the February 1982 issue of *The Roman Catholic*, Fr. Anthony Cekada wrote the following comment, under the heading "By What Authority?"

> Michael Davies has recently written an article in *The Remnant* in which he says that 'some traditional Catholics, both priests and laymen,' are headed in a 'schismatic direction' on the question of the new sacramental rites. Further, he states that 'I do not have the least hesitation in recognizing the members of C.U.F. [Catholics United for the Faith] as my fellow Catholics – though I can no longer extend this recognition to some priests and laymen claiming to be traditional Catholics.' The argumentation by which he attempts to justify his first statement leaves one with the impression that he defines 'schism' as 'disagreement with the theories of Mr. Davies'. As regards his second statement, the best possible response to such insufferable pretension is a chorus of raucous laughter. Are those who disagree with the theories of Mr. Davies on the new sacraments now supposed to recant and submit themselves to his quasi-pontifical authority in the hope of receiving his 'recognition'? Mr. Davies, I believe, has acquired a rather inflated idea of his own importance. Those who regularly follow his columns are urged to recall that he is a school-teacher and part-time journalist – and, as such, he has no authority to 'extend recognition' to anyone.

It is questionable whether Davies would even be prepared to "extend" to this admirable summary his "recognition" of it as "a point of view"!

CHAPTER FIVE
WHICH SIDE IS MICHAEL DAVIES ON?

"He that justifieth the wicked and he that condemneth the just, both are abominable before God." (Proverbs 17:15)

The Blunt Truth

The purpose of this chapter is to establish where Davies stands in the theological spectrum and, insofar as the proponents of rival theological positions (each thought by its supporters to be correct and Catholic) can be thought of as opposing armies (surely not an inappropriate image), on what side Davies is fighting. By reference to many pertinent quotations from his writings, it will be shown:

(a)   that in the most fundamental division that exists among those who call themselves Catholics today – namely, whether or not one acknowledges the religion of which Karol Wojtyła (John-Paul II) is head (with all its new rites, new catechisms, "lay ministers," charismatics, ecumenism, religious liberty and episcopal collegiality) as the Church founded by Jesus Christ upon the rock of St. Peter – Michael Davies is firmly with the "Conciliar Church", and therefore opposed to the *Catholic* Church which – as is extensively demonstrated for the benefit of those not already aware of the fact throughout this *Evaluation*, and especially in Chapter 3 – is most certainly *not* the organization led by John-Paul II, but rather a "sect of perdition" (2 Peter 2:1); and

(b) perhaps more surprisingly to those who have read his works superficially, that if a division be made between, on the one hand, those who attack and oppose the aspects of the Conciliar Church in which it differs from pre-Conciliar doctrine and practice, and denounce the men responsible for introducing them, and, on the other hand, those who defend the novelties in question and go out of their way to vindicate their perpetrators and protect them from attack and exposure, Michael Davies definitely belongs to the *latter* group.

The fact recorded in paragraph (a) above will surprise no one who is familiar with Davies's writings, for his recognition of the Conciliar Church is openly avowed. The fact recorded in paragraph (b) is much less well known, for Davies is often thought of as an *opponent*, rather than a *defender*, of the leading revolutionaries of the Conciliar Church. But some readers may be tempted to wonder what relevance it has, even if it can be shown to be true. Whether or not one acknowledges John-Paul II as pope, all will concede to be a matter of the highest importance, but exactly how a particular member of the Conciliar Church views the "ravening wolves" (Acts 20:29) responsible for all that Catholics rightly find objectionable in that sect might seem to be of slight moment. And if the individual in question were just a rank-and-file Novus Ordo attender, I should be inclined to agree. But the extraordinary favour Davies shows, despite his vaunted "traditionalism", for the chief innovators is certainly not without significance, I submit; for, even if we allow that he may have a "blind spot" on the subject of the recent apparent occupants of the Holy See, this ought not to prevent a writer who professes to adhere to the traditional teaching of the Church, and is undertaking to expose the machinations of the Conciliar Church, from calling a spade a spade and apportioning responsibility where it lies. And yet this is certainly not what Davies does. On the contrary, he consistently refuses to go beyond a certain point in his criticisms of the Conciliar Church and its senior prelates, and no less consistently makes exceptional efforts to defend these monsters and minimize their evident complicity in, and responsibility for, the post-Conciliar debacle.

Take, for instance, Angelo Roncalli, known, though the title is debatable, as Pope John XXIII ....

"Good Pope John"?

Readers of *Pope John's Council* will find that this book contains copious evidence that John XXIII was a liar and a liberal who compromised with Communism, and, on the basis of an alleged "inspiration" (contrary to all the rules of Catholic theology for the "discernment of spirits"), opened a council which set about the subversion of the Church on a massive scale. They would consequently be forgiven for raising an eyebrow at Davies's assertion on p. 2 that, "there is no doubt that he ["Pope John", *sic*] was a good and holy pope who may possibly be canonized ...."[1]

Unorthodox Interpretations

Eyebrows would be likely to raise somewhat further on reaching p. 9 of the same work, where we find Davies quoting and agreeing with "Pope Paul" as to the fact that Vatican II did not authorize any changes of traditional doctrine. To cap this, lower down on the same page Davies writes: "No one has been able to misuse Pope Paul's *Mysterium Fidei* (his encyclical on the Eucharist) or his *Credo of the People of God* as instruments for undermining traditional teaching, because these documents are not open to unorthodox interpretation."

The first point to be made about this remark of Davies's, whereby he attempts to defend the orthodoxy of Paul VI, is that

---

[1] This remarkable prediction is capped in Davies's pamphlet *The Church 2000: Recipe for Ruin* where he refers to "the wholly orthodox and traditional Pope John" (the pages are not numbered; the pamphlet is a run-off from *Christian Order* for April 1974).

it is simply not true. Putting aside *Mysterium Fidei* and restricting ourselves to the *Credo of the People of God* to save space, we find that the document Davies commends to us as not susceptible of heterodox interpretation in fact *invites* and *encourages* heterodoxy. It does this:

(i) By its frequent use of insufficiently accurate language – for instance, the statement that God "*reveals Himself* as Father, Son and Holy Ghost" (paragraph 9), which achieves studied compatibility with the heretical view that the Trinity is a mere guise assumed by God for His dealings with men, rather than intrinsically real and eternally immutable. Another example of the same vagueness is the reference in paragraph 28 to "the souls of those who die in the grace of Christ – whether they are still to make expiation in the fire of Purgatory or are received into Paradise ... at once upon separation from the body" – words which could be used in good conscience even by someone who doubted the existence of Purgatory.

(ii) By its omissions and neglect to condemn prevalent errors. As the promulgation of new creeds or statements of faith, such as took place at the Council of Nicæa and again under Pope Pius IV, has previously been ordered only to clarify Catholic doctrine on points where it has been subject to attack, the failure of Paul VI's "Credo" to condemn the errors which were evidently most prevalent at the time of its appearance – for instance, neo-Modernism, the denial of the social rights of the Church, the denial of the objective moral order and belief in the evolution and indefinite re-interpretation and updating of revealed doctrine – inevitably appears to tolerate and sanction these heresies. This impression is reinforced by the absence of any clear criterion governing which doctrines are included in the "Credo" and which are not. The doctrines taught are neither the principal ones of the Faith (the Divinity of the Holy Ghost and His procession from Father and Son are pointedly omitted) nor those which are most subject to attack. Hence the impression that whatever is *not* included in the "Credo" need not be believed as "of faith" is evidently given.

(iii) By more direct offences against Catholic doctrine, such as the unqualified application to non-Catholics of terms such as "Christians", "Disciples of Christ" and "believers" ("*credentes*") which in their strict sense belong only to Catholics.

But even aside from these facts, which I admit could have eluded a careless reader of this disgraceful document, there remains a far more serious objection to Davies's defence of Montini; one, indeed, so glaring that it can only be its very enormity that has caused it to be overlooked by so many Davies readers. It is the grotesqueness and absurdity of the prospect of a "pope" whose "orthodoxy" is such that it can only be traced by scholars who have hunted through the many thousands of pages of ecclesiastical documents promulgated by him and have found *two* (*Mysterium Fidei* and *The Credo...*) which they consider sufficiently innocuous to put them forward as evidence in his favour. Any reader who has yet to appreciate that the very fact that Davies can seriously offer such evidence in favour of Montini's orthodoxy is the best proof of his *lack* of orthodoxy, is invited to consider how he would have reacted to a statement by a purportedly Catholic writer that Pope St. Pius X, or for that matter, Pope Pius XII were definitely Catholic in their belief, and his production, to attest the truth of this contention, of *two* documents which were claimed not to be open to heretical interpretations!

Vatican II – a Classic

Even allowing that Davies might have skimmed through *The Credo of the People of God* so quickly that he did not notice any of its betrayals of Catholic doctrine, it is scarcely excusable that in a book devoted to exposing Vatican II he quotes with approval Bishop Rudolph Graber to the effect that the documents of Vatican II, "are formulated orthodoxly, in places nothing short of classically"!! (p. 9)[2]

Where Fact Must Yield to Expediency

However, it seems that Davies bases this position not so much on what the documents *actually* say as on what they *must* say. Thus, on p. 56 of *Pope John's Council*, he writes:

> When a Protestant praises some aspect of a Vatican II document as a step towards Protestantism it can be argued that he is in error *as this cannot be the case* .... (Emphasis added.)

In other words, Davies knows in advance by a special enlightenment that the Conciliar documents *cannot* contain any tendencies towards Protestantism, and as a consequence of this he need waste no time actually reading the documents to see whether such tendencies *are* there. It is interesting to note that a review quoted on the back cover of Davies's book says that it is "based not on conjecture but on *fact*" – an assertion easily rectified by inverting the two nouns: "Davies's book is based not on fact but on conjecture."

On p. 63 Davies continues to rely on the same fallacy of "a priorism" – i.e. the rejection of a valid demonstration on the grounds that its conclusion is unacceptable, no matter how strong the evidence supporting it may be. He is discussing the question of whether the Conciliar Decree on Ecumenism

(a) denies the need for Protestants to be converted to the Catholic Church, and
(b) instead suggests that Catholics and Protestants are together moving towards Christ.

Here is what Davies says:

---

[2] Just to drive the point home, on p. 211 of the same work Davies repeats himself: "The doctrinal and moral teaching of the Council is ... usually stated orthodoxly and even classically."

Is such an interpretation consistent with the Decree itself? Technically the answer must be that it is not. As Fr. Holloway[3] rightly insists, Conciliar documents must be interpreted in a sense that conforms to tradition. But this does not alter the fact that '*periti*' [theological experts – J.S.D.] have worded it in such a way that Protestants, whose sincerity we have no right to question, believe that it is consistent with the Decree.

Cutting away the bluff, it appears that Davies admits that, when it comes to the actual *words* (which he blames on the "periti" instead of on the Bishops and "Pope" who accepted them and who alone claim to occupy the office of competent judges in matters of faith), the Decree does indeed convey the heretical sense. But since he starts from the unproven assumption that the council was Catholic and orthodox, he declares, on the "authority" of a little-known Novus Ordo priest, that the document "must be interpreted" in a traditional sense, even if this means "interpreting" black as white. Thus, rather than face the fact that Vatican II was heretical – a fact which, on his own admission, is evident even to Protestants – Davies is forced into ostrich-like refusal to look reality in the eye.

Going Against the Whole Tradition of the Church

A few pages later, Davies records the fact that, during the debate at the council on the constitution *Gaudium et Spes*, Cardinal Browne, Master General of the Dominicans, declared:

---

[3] Fr. Edward Holloway is, Davies informs us on p. 53 of *Pope John's Council*, "far from having Modernist sympathies". Those for whom Holloway's acceptance of the Novus Ordo does not constitute a sufficient refutation of this assertion are referred to Holloway's book *Catholicism: A New Synthesis* (the title surely is already disquieting), in which he attempts to reconcile Catholic dogma with Darwinian evolution, of men as well as animals, declaring, in stark contradiction to Pope Pius XII's *Humani Generis*, that "evolution of all matter, including life and mankind" has been "proven" by "factual proof" and is "*right*". (*op. cit.*, p. 37) In fact, Fr. Holloway's book is based on private revelations allegedly received by his mother in 1929, including a "Master-Key" whereby to reconcile Catholicism with what today passes for "science".

"If we accept this definition we are going against the whole tradition of the Church and we shall pervert the whole meaning of marriage." Of course, the Fathers *did* accept the definition without substantial change, but even then Davies refuses to accept that Cardinal Browne's words were literally true, amounting, as they do, to a charge of heresy against the council.

Moreover, although I have been unable to locate in the *Acta* of the council the precise words Davies (following Archbishop Lefebvre, *A Bishop Speaks*, p. 105) attributes to Cardinal Browne, I did note that Browne certainly protested more than once about the unorthodoxy of the section concerning matrimony in *Gaudium et Spes* (see *Acta*, Vol. 4, 3, pp. 67-9; Vol. 3, 6, pp. 86-88) as well as against other decrees (*Acta* Vol. 4, 1, pp. 605-7 on religious liberty, for instance) and that other Fathers of the council were also constantly accusing of heterodoxy decrees which were subsequently accepted. Thus on the same controverted passage about the ends of matrimony, Cardinal Ottaviani protested at the implication that the Church had erred in past centuries (*Acta*, Vol. 3, 6, p. 85) and Italian Bishop Carli regarded the declaration concerning the Jews as so un-Catholic that he even circularized letters to all the Fathers about it and protested against it in his diocesan pastoral letter. In connection with the Vatican II-invented doctrine of episcopal collegiality, Cardinal Browne, who was probably the finest theologian of all the council Fathers and "periti" together, went so far as to declare that the council's doctrine was incompatible with the infallible dogmatic constitution *Pastor Æternus* of the 1870 Vatican Council. Here, and perhaps elsewhere too, he closed his speech with the resounding and emphatic admonition "Venerabiles Patres, *caveamus!*" ("Let us beware!") (*Acta*, Vol. 2, 4, p. 627), but the Fathers voted for collegiality with cheerful unconcern, and the only notice they took of Browne's words was contemptuously to substitute the nickname of "*Caveamus* Browne" for his Latin title of "*Cardinalis*".

Upon This Rock

On p. 78 of the same book, we learn to our amazement that the Council had such a damaging effect on the Church that "the fact that she has not collapsed completely is an impressive testimony to the fact that she is built upon a rock."

What, one asks, would be necessary before Davies would consider that a complete collapse *had* taken place?

Davies is so adamant in his refusal to admit heresy in the council documents that he is prepared to clutch at any straws to avoid this admission. Thus, on p. 96 of *Pope John's Council*, in a valiant attempt to vindicate the orthodoxy of the decrees, he writes: "The true Catholic position can usually be found by those who look hard enough ...." He seems quite unaware of the folly of what he is saying – that a Catholic, looking through the documents of a general council of the Church, will, if he really racks his brains, generally speaking find *some* way of reconciling most of what the council teaches with the defined doctrines of the Church! Thus a general council, instead of being the *source* to which a Catholic turns to *learn* his Faith, becomes instead the object of a party game by which Catholics have to foist some wholly improbable interpretation on obviously heretical texts in order to "save the appearances" of the Conciliar Church.

Recommended Reading

On p. 137, Davies goes further and says that the chapter on Our Lady in the council documents "has emerged as a very fine if far from perfect exposition ... and every Catholic could benefit from reading it." What is ludicrous in this comment is that we should learn our Marian doctrine from a source which Davies himself acknowledges to be "far from perfect." Assuming that Davies does not consider the many pre-Vatican II papal encyclicals about Our Lady to be "far from perfect," and is satisfied with the orthodoxy of the writings of (for instance) St. Bernard, St. Alphonsus and St. Louis de Montfort about the

Mother of God, one is bound to wonder why he commends his readers to inflict upon themselves the perusal of a Vatican II document, with all its errors, defects and turgid prose, in preference to the works of authors who are above all criticism.

Archbishop Lefebvre's personal theologian during a substantial part of the Council, the admirable Fr. Victor-Alain Berto (1900-1968), took a very different view. In his judgement, the fate of the Council itself was determined by its attitude to Our Blessed Lady. It had been intended that the Council should devote a separate document to her honour, but this was vigorously opposed by the ecumenical cohort. For Fr. Berto, when, under the influence of Protestants and Protestantisers, the Council voted, 29th October 1963, by 1114 votes to 1097, to downgrade the intended schema *On the Most Blessed Virgin Mary, Mother of the Church*, to a simple chapter in the schema on the Church, it delivered a calculated insult to the Mother of God, dismissing her without recall, and succeeding in banishing all her good influence from the Council hall.

> The fate of the Session was settled that day in Heaven, whose King is a Son who will not suffer his Mother to be outraged. ... The vengeance fell swiftly ... .
>
> Those who comprise an ecumenical council ought to know that the expulsion of the Blessed Virgin is an act liable to have consequences, and may not be ratified by Someone who opened the gates of heaven to her. It ought to be evident that the intervention of the Holy Ghost is not a *right*, to be switched on by the bare fact of being a council.
>
> *Qui habitat in cælis irridebit eos, et Dominus subsannabit eos*.[4] The Holy Ghost, who overshadowed Mary[5] is the same Spirit that broodeth over the waters[6]. That is why this Second Session[7] was not only sterile but a *bog*, owing to the just withdrawal of God. ...

---

[4] "He that dwelleth in heaven shall laugh at them: and the Lord shall deride them."

[5] Luke 1:35.

[6] Genesis 1:2.

[7] Writing shortly after the events he describes, Fr. Berto is unable to

Meanwhile the Holy Ghost, who descends from the Father's side only if He is sent by the Son (*"quem ego mittam vobis a Patre"* ["whom I shall send you from the Father"]) remains in Paradise. What is He waiting for ? simply for the Council to choose to take place as in the Cenacle *"cum Maria Matre Jesu"* ["with Mary the Mother of Jesus"].

Such is the history of the Second Session – its only true history.[8]

No Evidence of Heresy

On p. 214, Davies seems to have forgotten the indictment which he quoted earlier from Cardinal Browne, and writes the following striking paragraph:

> What, then, must our attitude be to the documents of Vatican II? It must, above all, be a Catholic attitude and as such must exclude such simplistic responses as a 'rejection' or 'refusal' of the council – whatever such terms mean [as if he didn't know! – J.S.D.]. Do those who use them mean that the Council was not convoked regularly, that its documents were not passed by the necessary majority, that they were not validly promulgated by the Pope, that they contained formal heresy? I have yet to see one word of solid evidence produced to substantiate such allegations. It has been a characteristic of Protestant sects to decide which general councils they will or will not accept and it is a cause for very deep regret to find some Catholics who claim to be traditionalists adopting a similar position.

---

anticipate what the remaining two Sessions of the Council had in store.

[8] Letter of 30th November 1963.

[9] Moreover Archbishop Lefebvre himself was certainly one of those who "rejected" or "refused" the Council. For instance in an interview published in *Le Figaro*, 4th August 1976, he said:

"This Council, both in our eyes and in those of the Roman authorities, represents a new Church, which they call the Conciliar Church. We believe we can state, in the light of internal and external criticism of Vatican II, i.e. by analysing this Council's texts and studying all its ins and outs, that by turning its back on tradition and breaking with the Church of the past, it is a schismatic Council."

Of course, the majority of Davies's readers will not have been conscious of the documentation available which demonstrates plentiful instances of heresy and other theological errors in the documents of the council, and will consequently presume that, when Davies says that he has not seen a word of solid evidence produced to substantiate such allegations, he means that the assertions are made gratuitously and that no evidence has been adduced to support them. In reality, Davies is simply refusing to recognize as "solid evidence" arguments which he finds inconvenient.[9] Indeed he himself quotes from, and comments at some considerable length in more than one of his books on, the council's erroneous teaching on religious liberty, and he quotes the Brief *Post Tam Diuturnas* of Pope Pius VII (1814) in which that pope brands religious liberty as a *heresy* – but he *still* refuses even seriously to discuss the possibility that the Council does indeed contain heresy!

Davies compares those Catholics who reject Vatican II with Protestants who "decide which general councils they will or will not accept." Of course this begs the question, since it presumes to begin with that Vatican II *was* a general council. There is nothing Protestant about following the laws and teachings of the Church in order to determine whether a given assembly of bishops was or was not a general council of the Catholic Church. For instance, of the two councils of Ephesus, the first was an orthodox general council of the Catholic Church, while the second was a heretical anti-council. In exactly the same way, the first council of the Vatican was a genuine general council, while the second was heretical and non-Catholic. There is nothing Protestant about recognizing this.

Montini and Communism

On p. 182 of *Pope John's Council*, Davies quotes the late Hamish Fraser asserting that "like Maritain, Pope Paul has the faith of Peter." This is the position which Davies is determined to defend even at the cost of complete defiance of common sense, indeed in defiance of evidence to the contrary which he himself produces and sees the significance of. As obvious an illustration of this as any is to be seen in his treatment of Montini's attitude to Communism, a creed which, of course, is certainly not compatible with "the faith of Peter."

On p. 184 of the same book, he writes that "the Pope is certainly not pro-Communist." That would appear straightforward enough, or at least consistent with the supposition that "Pope" Paul had "the faith of Peter," were it not for the fact that on p. 182, a mere seven pages earlier, he has been forced to admit that "there are a number of instances in which Pope Paul's policies in the international field have been *far from neutral*." (Emphasis added.) Well, we should not *expect* neutral policies from someone who had the faith of Peter and was not a Communist; but Davies's clarification is not what we should expect either. His next sentence reads: "His attitude to the Communist aggressors in Vietnam was, to put it mildly, hardly calculated to advance the causes of Christianity or freedom."

And in fact Davies has no difficulty whatever in recognizing clear pieces of evidence of Paul VI's blatantly pro-Communist position[10] for what they are. If we turn to another of his books, *Apologia Pro Marcel Lefebvre*, Vol. 2, we find on p. 214 a reproduction of a poster (translated into English on p. 225 of the same book) which was published and circulated by "The Communists of Rome and its province" on the death of Paul VI. The contents of the poster, which was plastered over the walls of Rome, included the following:

---

[10] Moreover it is an established fact that the Conciliar Church in 1962 entered an agreement with Soviet Moscow by which it undertook not to condemn Communism by name an undertaking in which Montini, later Paul VI, was closely involved and which he continued to respect until his death in 1978. See, for instance, *The 1962 Rome-Moscow Agreement Definitively Confirmed*, a supplement to the review *Approaches*, N° 86.

> The Communists of Rome and of its province express their sorrow and condolences for the death of Paul VI, Bishop of Rome ... remembering him ... for his passionate involvement and the great humanity with which he worked for peace and the progress of peoples ....

Moreover, without any apparent trace of embarrassment at implicitly, but nonetheless blatantly, contradicting his dogmatic pronouncement that "the Pope is *certainly not* pro-Communist" (emphasis added), Davies introduced the text of the poster with the following commentary (p. 224):

> The Italian Communist Party has good cause to be grateful to Pope Paul VI, not to mention Pope John XXIII. *As a direct result* of the modification of Vatican hostility towards Communism, the Communist Party is now poised to take over in Italy. (Emphasis added.)

One might be able at a stretch to grant that it would be an interesting exercise to search for and set out a few arguments which would make some sort of a case that, notwithstanding evidence to the contrary produced by Davies, Paul VI was not *necessarily* pro-Communist – though it must be added that Davies nowhere does this, and in one sense he can hardly be blamed for I should not know where to start myself if I were faced with this task. But even with that done, we should still be asking ourselves: what is it that Davies has seen – and which he forbears to share with his readers – that makes Paul VI's lack of pro-Communist sympathies so "*certain*"?

In the hope of some illumination, let us examine another passage in which Davies further develops and elaborates on the same theme and also gives us some insight into his manner of using evidence in making deductions. (See the Scriptural verse with which this chapter is introduced.)

Turning a Blind Eye

On p. 196 of *Pope John's Council*, he once again refuses to face evident reality. In this case the reality which he shies away from is the existence of malice as a motive influencing the destructive activities of the Church's enemies. It is evident that Davies's reason for refusing to admit even the possibility of such malice is a misunderstanding of the nature of charity – a misunderstanding which originated in Protestantism and remains characteristic of English Protestantism even today; namely, the notion that it is somehow uncharitable to call a bad man bad. Davies writes as follows:

> Just as it would be wrong to suggest that the Pope is pro-Communist in any way, although his policies have served the purposes of Communism, it would be equally wrong to suggest that his theological views are *in any way* tainted by the Protestant heresy. Should this be the case, in view of such encyclicals as *Mysterium Fidei* and *Humanæ Vitæ*, in view of his *Credo* and of the innumerable totally orthodox discourses which he never ceases delivering [!], it would mean that he was *deliberately* using his position to deceive the faithful and destroy the Church. There is no need to resort to so improbable an hypothesis.... (Emphasis added.)

In summary, Davies is saying that, because Montini uses a little sheep's clothing instead of revealing himself as a wolf in every word and deed, there is no need for us to accept the "improbable hypothesis" that he is *deliberately* doing what he is *actually* doing. Of course, the fact that Montini was "deliberately using his position to deceive the faithful and destroy the Church" is not a hypothesis at all. It is what he *visibly did* throughout his fifteen-year "pontificate". His was the authority by which were passed all the directives which reduced what had been the institution of the Catholic Church to the rubble which remained at his death in 1978. However, Davies's "charity" is such that, had he observed Montini careering through St. Peter's wielding a sledgehammer, desecrating the altars and smashing the statues with the hysterical abandon of a Cranmer or a Ridley, he would still have refused to entertain the "improbable hypothesis" that "the pope" was *deliberately* destroying the sacred edifice.

An Extravagant Gesture

On the next page, Davies writes:

Thus, in presenting Dr. Ramsey with an episcopal ring and inviting him to bless the crowds the clear impression was given, not least to Dr. Ramsey, that he really was an Archbishop and the Primate of all England, successor of St. Augustine. Unfortunately, the Pope has a definite predilection for such impulsive and rather extravagant gestures, kissing the feet of the Metropolitan Meliton at the end of 1975, for example. Doubtless, he considers them examples of fraternal charity without realising the harm they do to the integrity of the Faith. More seriously, he has referred to the Church of England as a 'sister Church' ....

It is remarkable that Davies has the effrontery to accuse others of resorting to an "improbable hypothesis" when he can write such a passage himself. Are we really to consider his supposition that Montini did not realise the harmful effect of his cavorting with heretics as anything other than an "improbable hypothesis"?

Just What the Council Ordered

Another wholly unjustifiable exoneration of the Conciliar Church occurs on p. 300 of *Pope John's Council*. There Davies declares that:

While the council did not order any of the liturgical abuses which now so distress faithful Catholics, it opened the door to them ....

It is important not to be deluded by the fact that this sentence seems critical of Vatican II into overlooking the fact that in reality it absolves the council of *direct* responsibility for the outrages which are now perpetrated in what were once temples of Catholic worship. Davies assures us that "the Council did not order any of the liturgical abuses which now so distress faithful Catholics," and the fact that this statement occurs in a subordinate clause and is offset by a mild criticism does not alter its impact in the slightest.

Thus we learn that, although to be distressed by abuses which were *not* ordered by Vatican II is compatible with being "a faithful Catholic," those of us who *are* distressed by the council's liturgical changes automatically cease to qualify as "faithful Catholics" for the simple reason that, in Davies's view, no liturgical abuses *were* ordered by the council. Let us therefore consider whether this view is justified, presuming that, for the purposes of Davies's statement, the fact that the council's calls for liturgical innovations were sometimes couched in the form of "recommendations" does not prevent them from being considered "orders", since, in the first place, such recommendations certainly had the *force* of orders and were carried out as such, and, in the second place, if Davies had intended such a distinction, he would have written that, while the Council did not *order* the liturgical abuses, it did in many cases specifically *recommend* them. But Davies concedes no such thing and insists that it did no more than "open the door to them."

The fact is that, if Davies's point is valid, he is apparently excluding from being regarded as "faithful Catholics" all those who were "distressed" by the encouragement of "full, conscious, and active participation in liturgical celebration" by "all the faithful;" by encouragement of the laity "to take part by means of acclamations, responses, psalms, antiphons, hymns, as well as by actions, gestures and bodily attitudes;" by the wider use of the vernacular "especially in readings, directives ... prayers and chants;" the encouragement of "Bible services;" concelebration; revision of Mass and sacramental rites; the abolition of the hour of Prime from the Divine Office and revision of the entire Breviary; the revision of the calendar, etc. – all of which were specifically recommended (and, in some cases, *ordered*) by the council's constitution on the Sacred Liturgy entitled *Sacrosanctum Concilium*. The fact that Davies does not regard any of these disgraceful innovations as a cause for distress on the part of "faithful Catholics" is a clear indication of his true position.

Credit Where Credit is Due

While taking every opportunity to criticize any traditionalist, whatever his stance, who dares to allege that there might be heresy in the documents of Vatican II, or to make personal criticisms of the papal claimants of the Conciliar Church, Davies takes every opportunity to shower praise upon those who say the Novus Ordo and have been actively involved in the attempt to destroy the Church.

In Vol. II of *Apologia Pro Marcel Lefebvre*, we are assured, on p. 102, that "the members of the Sacred Congregation for the Doctrine of the Faith are theologians of the highest competence" ... although not, it would appear, sufficiently competent to recognize any of the defects of the Conciliar Church, even those which are so glaring that Davies himself is forced to recognize them. As is pointed out elsewhere in this *Evaluation*, Davies also more than once represents Karl Rahner as a sound Catholic theologian and quotes, as if they were trustworthy authorities, a number of priests who say the Novus Ordo – including Fr. Edward Holloway, Fr. Paul Crane, Cardinal Heenan, and, remarkably, even Cardinal Ciappi, whom he describes, on p. 56 of the same book, as "one of the finest theologians in the Church, having been theologian to Pope Pius XII, Pope John XXIII and to Pope Paul VI." Is it not staggering that Davies can laud in this manner a man who has been prepared to have his implicit sanction given to all of the heresies and errors which emanated from Montini during his "pontificate" without dissociating himself *in the slightest* from any of them? What, we must ask ourselves, would any of Davies's "finest theologians" have to do in order to lose this exalted status in his eyes? – apart, that is, from suddenly declaring that the Holy See was vacant.

Given that the Conciliar Church is an institution in which the wholesale propagation of heresy from the pulpit, in the classroom, in books and periodicals, by priests and bishops, not only takes place without restraint, but is *acknowledged* to do so even by Davies himself as indeed is plain to anyone familiar with the elementary doctrines of the catechism, one would not think it unreasonable to conclude that the Prefect of a "Sacred Congregation for the Doctrine of the Faith" had a very great deal to answer for, being personally responsible for ensuring that what manifestly and universally *is* happening, should *not* happen. Davies will have none of it, however. For him, the late Cardinal Šeper was "not only ... totally orthodox and traditional, but ... an outstanding theologian."[11] How can anyone who is "totally orthodox" survey, unprotestingly, the destruction of the Catholic Faith? Davies does not tell us, but let us suppose for a moment that the paradox is not an insoluble one. Surely, then, we might anticipate that a "totally orthodox and traditional" prelate such as Šeper would have detected at least some of the theological objections to the New Mass – if not its heresies and blasphemies, at least the tendentious and Protestant-inclined spirit that informs it all. But Šeper did not. "He recognized that there was a liturgical problem, but believed that it could be solved simply by faithful adherence to the missal of Pope Paul VI," Davies informs us (*loc. cit.*), falling over himself to excuse the "Cardinal's" appalling blindness to the evident. Nor am I exaggerating in the claim that he was falling over himself, for the excuse he produced was so preposterous that surely no one in full possession of himself could even have thought it, let alone written it and left it in the proofs for publication. The excuse he offers us is that for Slavonic Catholics the Mass is of less central significance than it is for those of us in the English-speaking world – as though the Mass were an optional and regional devotion like membership of the Sodality of Our Lady!

---

[11] *Apologia Pro Marcel Lefebvre*, Vol. III, p. 153.

As Catholic Slavs are very properly sensitive of their honour, and regard their Catholic orthodoxy as its crown, readers of Slavonic extraction may well not be able to believe the gratuitous insult that Davies pays them unless his exact words are reproduced; so here, without further comment, in all their extravagant incredibleness, they are:

> His [Šeper's] lack of concern where the New Mass is concerned is probably the result of being brought up in a country where there was no large Protestant minority. The same may be true of Pope John Paul II. Slavonic[12] Catholics come into contact with members of the Orthodox Church far more frequently than they do with Protestants. The Eucharistic teaching of the Orthodox Church is very close to that of the Catholic Church. There has never been the saying: "It is the Mass that matters," among Slavonic Catholics. Thus, the changes made in the Mass following the Second Vatican Council do not have the same significance for them as they do in countries such as England where similar changes were made by the Protestant Reformers.

Most Bishops Orthodox

Moreover, Davies's eagerness to exonerate the perpetrators and abettors of what he calls "the liturgical revolution", of which many instances have been and will be adduced in this *Evaluation*, at times leads him into actual dishonesty. For instance, on p. 220 of *Pope Paul's New Mass* he writes:

> At this point, in order to avoid misunderstanding, I must make it clear that I have no wish to condemn all the bishops in Britain, the United States, or any other country. In Britain, for example, most are still orthodox in their personal belief .... I know that there are bishops in Britain, Australia and the U.S.A. who have made at least an effort to uphold orthodoxy and have been pilloried by the liberal media for doing so .... The role of a bishop in the post-Conciliar period has been hard.

---

[12] Franjo Šeper was Croatian, as is Davies's wife.

All this is, of course, fantastic nonsense. Davies knew perfectly well that every one of the bishops of Britain at the time he wrote was using and approving the vernacular Novus Ordo, and he has himself implicitly admitted that it contains heresy. For instance on p. 44 of *Pope Paul's New Mass* he makes the following reference to the I.C.E.L.[13] translation of the Roman Canon which is still (substantially unaltered) in use and has been used by all the bishops whom he describes as orthodox:

> I well remember by own parish priest, Fr. Desmond Coffey, announcing from the pulpit that he refused to use this translation of the Canon as, after a careful examination, he had found at least a hundred serious mistranslations, omissions and even *heresies* ....

On p. 93 of the same book, Davies inadvertently duplicates the same information in slightly different terms:

> I well remember my own parish priest, the late Fr. Desmond Coffey, listing its serious omissions, mistranslations, distortions, and outright *heresies*.

Now Davies is clearly quoting the words of Fr. Coffey approvingly, and thus admitting the presence of "outright heresies" in the liturgy used by all the bishops of Britain whom he describes as "still orthodox in their personal belief." Unless he has the clairvoyant ability to perceive that the British bishops do not in fact believe these "outright heresies" which, week after week, they utter solemnly from the sanctuaries of their cathedrals, it is evident that his defence of their orthodoxy is no more than wishful thinking.

Of course it should not be thought that the heresies of the Novus Ordo are restricted to the official English mistranslation of the Canon (now called the "First Eucharistic Prayer"), and Davies himself shows that this is not so. On p. 621 of *Pope*

---

[13] I.C.E.L., the International Committee on English in the Liturgy, is the subject of a detailed footnote on p. 362 of this *Evaluation* to which readers who want more information are referred.

Paul's New Mass he points out the following about another of the "Eucharistic Prayers":

> The preface to Eucharistic Prayer IV contains a straight-forward affirmation not of semi-Arianism but of Arianism: 'Father in Heaven, it is right that we should give you thanks and glory: you *alone* are God, living and true.' This could be a stanza from one of the hymns which Arius used to propagate his heresy.

Now this heresy – one of the *very* few instances of the countless heresies of the Conciliar Church which Davies is prepared to acknowledge as such – is *not* a mere mistranslation in the English version. It existed in the original Latin also as promulgated from Rome on the authority of Paul VI. *And Davies knows this*: during a telephone conversation with the present writer in the summer of 1983, he expressly confirmed his awareness that this heresy occurs in the Latin of the Novus Ordo as promulgated by Paul VI in 1969.[14] Readers may form their own conclusions as to why Davies does not point out in his books that the heresy occurred in the original Latin, although he was prepared to admit privately to the writer of the present article that he even possessed a photocopy of the heresy as promulgated in Rome.

---

[14] The Latin *today* reads "*Vere iustum est te glorificare, Pater sancte, quia unus es Deus vivus et verus, qui es ante sæcula et permanes in æternum*", which is ambiguous; but Davies himself – he stated in the telephone conversation referred to above – has a photocopy of the original, unambiguously heretical wording, "*solus es Deus.*"
Having touched on this point, I should explain that, although the currently used Latin version of the Novus Ordo can be translated "Thou art the one God," which is *not* heretical, it is *not* true to say that the heresy appears only in the vernacular version, because, as *originally* published in Rome and circulated from there throughout the world, the Latin read "*solus* es Deus" which can mean only "You *alone* are God." And this certainly *is* heretical. For the original Latin text, copyright by the Libreria Editrice Vaticana, see *The New Eucharistic Prayers* by Peter Coughlan (foreword by Annibale Bugnini, the Masonic originator of the Novus Ordo), published 1968 by Geoffrey Chapman.

Yet Davies is also prepared to assert that "there is no formal heresy in the New Missal." He said these words in an article in *The Angelus* for December 1984. This was evidently another piece of wishful thinking, since it became extremely convenient for Davies to defend this position when John-Paul II graciously permitted the use of a vandalised version of the True Mass *on the condition that those who took advantage of this "indult" did not regard the New Mass as heretical.* Here is the text of the condition as expressed in the indult:

> There must be unequivocal, even public evidence, that the priests and faithful petitioning have no ties with those who impugn the lawfulness and doctrinal rectitude of the Roman Missal promulgated in 1970 by Pope Paul VI.[15]

Davies insists that he has no ties with such individuals and certainly is not one of them himself and is thus entitled to take advantage of the indult. And it is quite true that Davies does not *directly* "impugn the lawfulness and doctrinal rectitude of" the New Mass, but the evidence which he quotes in his works – never mind the even more abundant evidence which he *omits* to quote – is more than sufficient to demonstrate to anyone who is not completely impervious to conclusive proof, that the New Mass is in fact the very reverse of doctrinally sound.

Hence even the Society of St. Pius X, despite its state of compromise with the Conciliar Church's authorities, refuses to countenance Davies's position by which he goes so far as to maintain that the Novus Ordo is doctrinally sound. An editorial comment next to an article by Davies in *The Angelus* (December 1984, p. 18) defending the orthodoxy and lawfulness of the Novus Ordo dissociated the Society from his comments, observing that "the official position of the Society of St. Pius X

---

[15] The original Latin reads: "*Sine ambiguitate etiam publice constet talem sacerdotem et tales fideles nullam partem habere cum iis qui legitimam vim doctrinalemque rectitudinem Missalis Romani, anno 1970 a Paulo VI Romano Pontifice promulgati, in dubium vocant.*"

is that it cannot accept some of the conditions imposed by the Indult; especially acceptance of the doctrinal soundness of the New Mass." Unperturbed, Davies declared in *The Remnant* for 14th August 1986 that the New Mass "is definitely valid, contains no heresy, *and nothing that is intrinsically bad or harmful to the faithful*," which must have left a number of readers wondering why they bother to go to the Tridentine Mass instead. In fact the only criticisms Davies was prepared to make of the Latin Novus Ordo were that it is "without splendour, flattened and undifferentiated." The present writer, to be honest, has no idea how a differentiated liturgy differs from an undifferentiated one or why it is preferable for a liturgy to be differentiated; but what appears quite clear from Davies's words is that his only objections to the New Mass *per se* are *æsthetic*. It is true that when Dr. Rama Coomaraswamy made this very charge against Davies (in the *Roman Catholic*, Summer 1982), the latter, stung, retorted: "When have I said that I upheld the Tridentine Mass only because it is more 'æsthetically pleasing'?"[16] But whether or not Davies had said such a thing in 1982, he certainly did say it, by implication, in *The Remnant* article referred to above.

And while we are on the subject, it should be observed that Davies *does not in fact defend the Tridentine Mass at all*. That Mass was codified in 1570 by Pope St. Pius V. The Mass Davies defends is the updated 1962 Mass of John XXIII. In his "Letter from London" published in *The Remnant* for 15th January 1978, he declared that:

> The only ideal solution for the question of the Mass must be the reinstatement in [*sic*] its 1962 version, as the only Mass of the Roman rite.

Even this, however, is an improvement on the position he took in his article in *The Remnant* for 31st May 1979, where he expressed himself quite open to a revised version of the *New*

---

[16] In his unpublished reply dated 26th June 1982.

Mass, incorporating three prayers from the Tridentine Mass and with a correct translation – " ... although we would be faced with a New Mass, it would not be *the* New Mass we have rightly opposed.[17]

Error or Heresy

In order to maintain his position that the "popes" of Vatican II have not been guilty of heresy, one of the techniques to which Davies resorts is that of criticizing their heresies as "errors", while refusing even to admit the possibility that they are heretical. A typical example of this occurs on pages 285-293 of *Pope Paul's New Mass*, which Davies devotes to analysing the famous heresy promulgated by Paul VI in Article 7 of the *Institutio Generalis* (1969) of the New Roman Missal. The

---

[17] Relative to the question, "Which side is Michael Davies on?", it is not inappropriate to point out that in the same article Davies also said that he had always, until 1979, voted for the Labour Party and had been on a picket-line on behalf of his union (the National Association of Schoolmasters) only the previous month – a fact which he capped by declaring that most British Trades Unions still perform "a just and valuable function." Given that the Labour Party has from its Communist-sponsored inception had an overtly Socialist policy and that the Church has ruled that even the most mild and mitigated form of Socialism "cannot be brought into harmony with the dogmas of the Catholic Church" (Pius XI, *Quadragesimo Anno*), one is certainly left wondering whether Davies can really be as naive as he seems. By the 1960s, indeed, the Labour Party had degenerated into a blatant Communist front-organisation, but Davies seems not to have noticed this. I wholeheartedly sympathise, however, with his assertion that the truly diabolical British teachers' unions continue to "perform a just and valuable function." The function in question is, of course, to call frequent, blatantly unjustified strikes which have the praiseworthy result of minimising, for the duration of the strikes, the systematic subversion of the youth of our nation normally practised in the classroom when the teachers are *not* on strike. Alas, I fear that this is not the function Davies had in mind and even if it were, it would not justify giving public support to the principal teachers' unions, if only because the scandal given by the sight of comfortably-off adults in responsible positions abandoning their duties to demand more money is more than enough to offset whatever good effects may accrue to their students from a temporary interruption in the organized intellectual rape currently known as education.

original version of this article, which purported to be a definition of the Mass, was as follows:

> The Lord's Supper or Mass is the sacred assembly or meeting of the People of God met together with a priest presiding, to celebrate the memorial of the Lord. For this reason the promise of Christ is particularly true of a local congregation of the Church: 'Where two or three are gathered in my name, there am I in their midst.' (Matthew 18:20)

This is a clear instance of heresy by defect. Indeed it was so blatant that, in a unique concession to the outcry it caused, Montini was forced to issue an emended version of the article in 1970.

The definition as it is given above invites the view that the Mass is a meeting at which Catholics celebrate a commemoration of the Last Supper. No mention is made of transubstantiation, of the unity of the Mass with the Sacrifice of Calvary, of the propitiatory value of the Mass, or of the fact that the Mass, as such, is celebrated by the priest, with the laity merely being present. Davies devotes eight pages to considering the defects of this article and the significance of its eventual retraction, but at no stage does he even question whether it might be heretical.

This is surely a classic manifestation of what George Orwell called "crimestop". Let us look at that author's definition of the term he coined in his famous novel *Nineteen Eighty-Four*:

> The first and simplest stage in the acquired inner discipline ... is called, in Newspeak, *Crimestop*. *Crimestop* means the faculty of stopping short, as though by instinct, at the threshold of any dangerous thought. It includes the power of ... being bored or repelled by any train of thought which is capable of leading in a heretical direction. *Crimestop*, in short, means protective stupidity. But stupidity is not enough. On the contrary, orthodoxy in the full sense demands control over one's own mental processes as complete as that of a contortionist over his body.

In outlining the protective stupidity which the forces of subversion were, and are, planning to foist on the whole of mankind in order to ensure their success in establishing the kingdom of Satan upon earth, Orwell (who, as one of the minions of those forces – he was a member of the Fabian Society – was in a position to know) has surely given a very vivid description of Davies's syndrome. Davies can attack the scandals, abuses and errors of the Conciliar Church, and does so even quite violently and often with great perceptiveness; but whenever he finds himself being carried by the force of his argument in a direction which might lead to his having to put a question mark over the validity either of recent pontificates or of the identification of the Conciliar Church with the historic Catholic Church, invariably he shies away.

The process has by now very probably become wholly unconscious and he may well earnestly believe that he is expounding the whole truth on the present situation in the Church. Mental contortion can become so easy as to be automatic, just as can physical contortion; but in both cases arduous practice is necessary, which is by no means unconscious.

Dignitatis Humanæ

Most ambivalent of all is Davies's position on gravity of the error of religious liberty as stated in the Vatican II decree *Dignitatis Humanæ*. Here, Davies acknowledges that the decree contradicts previous teachings but once again shies away from the question of whether or not the teaching which it contradicts is proposed by the Church as Divinely revealed. If it is Divinely revealed, anything which contradicts it is of course heretical. On the other hand, the Church has some teachings which are not Divinely revealed and which it is not therefore technically heretical to deny.[18]

---

[18] See Note on p. 235.

In his pamphlet *Archbishop Lefebvre and Religious Liberty*, Davies writes of *Dignitatis Humanæ*:

> The declaration contains a number of statements which it is not easy to reconcile with traditional papal teaching and in Article 2 there are two words, 'or publicly', which appear to be a direct contradiction of previous teaching.

On pages 9-10 of the same pamphlet he goes further, commenting:

> It could certainly be considered the most important article in any document of the Council as, until it is corrected by the Magisterium [!], it represents not simply a contradiction of consistently re-iterated and possibly infallible papal teaching but an implicit repudiation of the Kingship of Christ.

The suggestion that a genuine general council of the Catholic Church can contradict previous infallible papal teaching and later be "corrected by the Magisterium" is perhaps Davies's most flabbergasting departure from Catholic doctrine. So far as I am aware he entitled to full credit for originality in inventing it, for it is an idea quite unheard of in the annals of purportedly Catholic theology. Indeed it should be obvious to anyone that there would be no purpose whatsoever in *having* a Magisterium if it could teach heresy and later retract it and replace it with orthodoxy. When would one ever know whether the doctrines being taught by it were true, false, heretical or anything else? And if a subsequent "correction" was made by the Magisterium, how would one know whether the "correction" itself was true, false, heretical or anything else? Davies's doctrine is not only a novelty, not only a complete departure from any previous Catholic teaching, not only an attack at the very roots of the Church's teaching Magisterium, but utter madness. And I lay down a formal challenge to Davies or anyone else who would seek to defend his orthodoxy to produce *a single text* from any Catholic theologian prior to Vatican II which suggests that it is remotely possible for a declaration of the Church, be it through the medium of the Extraordinary Pontifical Magisterium or through the medium of the Ordinary Pontifical Magisterium, to contradict previously defined teaching.

But the point being made here is that Davies, having admitted the fact that there is a contradiction between Vatican II and previous – "possibly" infallible – teaching, then refuses even to entertain the possibility that the passage may be heretical. He does not even consider this possibility worth mentioning in order to deny it.

Let us now consider the question of whether Davies is right in terming the Church's condemnation of religious liberty as only "*possibly* infallible."

In order to do this, I must begin by undertaking the vitally important task of establishing exactly when it is, and in what circumstances, that the Church speaks infallibly. This will require a lengthy digression, for it is impossible briefly to convey an accurate understanding of the Church's complex teaching about infallibility. But I assure readers that it is well worthwhile making the effort to comprehend what follows, and not just for the sake of following the argument refuting Davies's position vis-à-vis religious liberty, but also because it is crucial to a correct interpretation of recent events in the Catholic Church.

Nor, in fact, shall we ever be very far from our subject; for the topic of infallibility, heresy and Ordinary and Extraordinary Magisterial acts is one on which Davies has perpetrated many catastrophic errors, and some of these will be highlighted as the correct doctrines which he has contradicted are explained.

Infallibility

Surely an urgent need exists for a clear explanation concerning the meaning of the terms "heresy", "infallibility", "*ex cathedra*", etc. This is because there are strong grounds for suspecting that prior to Vatican II, not merely a few Catholics, but the *average* Catholic-in-the-pew would have replied roughly as follows if asked when the teachings of the Church were protected from error:

> The Pope is infallible if he speaks '*ex cathedra*', i.e. uses his supreme authority to define a matter of faith and morals to be believed by the whole Church; and the same applies to a general council. And anyone who denies the infallible teachings of popes or councils is a heretic. *But* whenever these conditions are *not* fulfilled in papal teaching, the pope is *not* infallible, though we are nonetheless generally bound to accept his teaching and to comply with it.

Since Vatican II, most "traditionalists" – i.e. those who reject "the changes" but acknowledge the legitimacy of the Conciliar "popes" – have been caught on the horns of a dilemma by the question of the Ordinary Magisterium; for, on the one hand, their fidelity to Catholicism as practised in the 1940s and 1950s has made them staunch defenders of the Church's doctrine forbidding artificial birth control and other doctrines taught only by the Ordinary Magisterium, but, on the other hand, they generally claim that they are *not* bound to accept the teachings of Vatican II notwithstanding the fact that, on their assumption that this council was a genuine Catholic council, its teachings are, at the very minimum, *exceedingly* weighty pronouncements of the Ordinary Magisterium. How do traditionalists solve this difficulty? Many of them do so by saying that the teachings of the Ordinary Magisterium *are liable to error, and not binding on the Catholic conscience, unless they are completely traditional and have been repeated frequently by the highest Church authorities.*

Perhaps some readers find these sentiments in approximate accord with their own beliefs. But the truth is that the explanations given above, however widespread they may be, or may have been before Vatican II, are a travesty of the correct Catholic doctrine on the subject, and every Catholic ought to know the correct doctrine on such a matter. Indeed even from a purely practical point of view, those who cannot distinguish the true doctrine from the false surely lack knowledge which is necessary in order to negotiate the minefields of error which every Catholic must today cross and recross in the course of his daily life.

Correct Terminology

Let us now endeavour to set the record straight.

First, an important clarification of the relevant terminology.

Doctrines are classified by theologians in three different ways, according to:

(a) the kind of magisterial act by which they are taught,
(b) the degree of protection from error entailed,
(c) the nature of the consequent obligation of belief

Thus, for instance:

(a) Some theologians speak of doctrines as *"ex cathedra"*. When they do this, they have under consideration the *manner* in which a pope has taught these doctrines.
(b) And other authors might call the identical doctrines *"infallibly taught"* or *"protected by infallibility"*.[19]
(c) Other theologians might, equally accurately, categorize the same doctrines as *"binding under pain of heresy"*. What

---

[19] Strictly speaking the expression "infallible teachings" is incorrect because "infallible" means "unable to err", and the capacity to make or avoid making mistakes cannot relate to a *teaching*. It is only the *person pronouncing the teaching* who can possess the supernatural protection from error correctly known as infallibility. Hence, when Bishop Thomas Connolly of Halifax suggested during the 1870 Vatican Council that the term "infallible" be applied in the council's decrees to the doctrine taught, the spokesman of the deputation responsible for drafting the decrees rejected this suggestion as ungrammatical and it was for this reason that the decree on papal infallibility (*Pastor Æternus*) eventually taught that the pope was *infallible* in defining, but referred to the doctrines defined by him not as "infallible" but as "irreformable". (See Mansi: *Sacrorum Conciliorum Nona et Amplissima Collectio*, Vol. LII, col. 762c and Denzinger 1839.) However in popular writing the use of the expression "infallible teaching" as shorthand for "teaching protected by infallibility" is so well-established that it would be pedantic to hope to exclude it altogether.

would be under consideration in this case would be the *censure attached* to contradiction of the teachings in question.

In order to conform to the system used by the Church herself and her most illustrious theologians, I propose to categorize the different kinds of Catholic beliefs according to the *kind or degree of faith or submission* owed to them, but when appropriate I shall indicate where the categories overlap.

Divine and Catholic Faith

The highest category of Catholic belief comprises those doctrines which are to be believed *"de fide divina et Catholica"*.[20] Canon 1323§1 states clearly which doctrines are included in this category:

> All those things are to be believed with Divine and Catholic Faith which are contained in the word of God, whether written or handed down, and which are proposed by the Church, either by a solemn judgement or by the Ordinary and Universal Magisterium, to be believed as having been Divinely revealed.[21]

Two conditions, therefore, are necessary before we may judge that a particular doctrine is to be believed *"de fide divina et Catholica"*.

The first is that the doctrine in question must have been revealed by Almighty God as part of His public revelation to mankind. This applies exclusively to doctrines contained in Holy Scripture or passed down from Apostolic times by Sacred Tradition, for one of the doctrines which must be believed *"de fide divina et Catholica"* is that there has been no new public revelation since the time of the last Apostle (St. John).

The second condition is that the doctrine in question must be *proposed by the Church* for the belief of the faithful *as having*

---

[20] "by (or with) divine and Catholic Faith".
[21] The wording of this Canon is taken from the Dogmatic Constitution on the Catholic Faith of the 1870 Vatican Council. (Denzinger 1792)

been Divinely revealed. For it to fit into the category we are at present considering, it is not enough that the doctrine in question be proposed by the Church and that she require all the faithful to assent to it – even though, as we shall see shortly, a doctrine taught in this manner would definitely be *true* – unless it is also clearly indicated that the doctrine was revealed by God Himself. This could be indicated by a direct statement to that effect as in Pope Pius IX's definition of the Immaculate Conception,[22] or by the statement that the doctrine is taught in Holy Scripture, the entire contents of which were revealed by God – a fact which is itself to be believed "*de fide divina et Catholica*".[23]

Moreover, as the canon quoted makes clear, the Church may propose a truth as Divinely revealed *either* by a solemn judgement (i.e. a definition of the Extraordinary Magisterium) *or*, equally well, by the Ordinary Magisterium, which can be exercised in various ways as will shortly be explained.

What is Heresy?

The term "heretic" is applied in its strict sense *only* to one who doubts or denies a doctrine to be believed "*de fide divina et Catholica*". This is stated in Canon 1325§2, where a heretic is defined as "one who after Baptism, while continuing to call himself a Christian, pertinaciously denies or doubts any of the truths which are to be believed with Divine and Catholic faith ('*de fide divina et Catholica*')."[24] Hence it is *not* true, as is

---

[22] "We declare, pronounce and define that the doctrine ... was revealed by God." (Denzinger 1641.)

[23] For instance, in his encyclical *Diuturnum Illud* Pope Leo XIII taught that the Divine origin of the civil power is evidently attested by Holy Scripture, as a consequence of which encyclical theologians recognize this as a truth to be believed "*de fide divina et Catholica*" (e.g. Sixtus Cartechini S.J. in *De Valore Notarum Theologarum*, p. 34 (Rome, 1931)).

[24] Cf. also the following definition furnished by Fr. Cartechini (*op. cit.:* p. 19): "A heretical proposition is one which is certainly opposed, contrarily or contradictorily, to a truth which is certainly known to have been sufficiently proposed in the Church as revealed." (The distinction between "contrarily" and "contradictorily" is that the *contrary* of "black" is "white", whereas the

widely believed, that to deny *any* truth taught "*ex cathedra*" by the popes or defined by an ecumenical council is sufficient to convict oneself of heresy, because the Church can teach theological truths concerning faith or morals by such solemn judgements even when they have *not* been directly revealed by God, and the denial of such truths, as we have seen, is not technically heresy.[25]

This point is made by Fr. Cartechini (*op. cit.*: pp. 41-3) as follows:

> The popes can condemn propositions, even '*ex cathedra*', as being not necessarily heretical, but even as merely false or scandalous .... The popes have sometimes defined some points of doctrine to be held, but not to be held '*de fide divina et Catholica*'.
>
> ... From these examples it is apparent that an '*ex cathedra*' statement is not always a dogma.[26] Likewise the popes sometimes oblige the Church to admit certain factual truths as 'dogmatic facts'[27] ... such as the nullity of Anglican Orders ....
>
> *Even in defining such things the pope and councils are infallible* ....
> Something can be defined as '*de fide*' without being necessarily '*de fide divina et Catholica*' [i.e. if it is infallibly taught but not Divinely revealed], in which case ... it should be termed '*de fide ecclesiastica*'.

Fr. Cartechini also explains in the same place that it was for this reason that the 1870 Vatican Council phrased its definition of papal infallibility so that the object of this infallibility was

---

contradiction of "black" is "not black".)

[25] Some theologians (St. Alphonsus Liguori, Fr. Marín-Sola, O.P., and others) hold that as God has made the Magisterium infallible even with regard to truths that are not directly revealed, the rejection of any truth so taught by the Magisterium equivalently entails denial of God's revelation and therefore contains essentially the same malice as heresy. But until the Church herself formally recognizes this equivalence the censure "heretical" is not at present applied to such denial.

[26] The term "dogma" is synonymous with "a truth proposed by the Church as divinely revealed".

[27] The term "dogmatic fact" is defined later in this section.

said to be "truths to be *held*" rather than "truths to be *believed* with Divine faith".

The same point is made by Cardinal Billot[28] in Thesis XVII of his *De Ecclesia Christi* in the following words:

> The infallible power of the Magisterium has for its primary object those matters of faith and morals which are contained ... in the deposit of Catholic revelation. But secondly, it is extended also to truths not revealed in themselves but which are required to safeguard the deposit of revelation ....

So, to summarize what has been said so far, not everything taught by the Extraordinary Magisterium is to be believed "*de fide divina et Catholica*", and it is possible to deny some teachings of the Extraordinary Magisterium without being a heretic, depending on whether or not the doctrines in question are proposed as *Divinely* revealed.

The Role of the Ordinary Magisterium

Having established this fact, the other principal truth on this subject, this one not nearly so well known but just as important, must not be overlooked. It is that *it **is** possible to become a heretic by denying a truth **not** taught by the Extraordinary Magisterium* (i.e. the solemn definition of pope or council) *at all*. This is a consequence of the following facts:

(a) that one is a heretic who doubts or denies *any* Divinely revealed truth proposed as such by the Church, and
(b) that the Church can sufficiently propose a belief as Divinely revealed even through her *Ordinary* Magisterium.

---

[28] Perhaps the greatest theologian of our century, Billot was hailed by Cardinal Merry del Val as "the honour of the Church and of France" and dubbed a "living Thomas Aquinas" by Cardinal Parocchi. His theological works were used by Pope St. Pius X who raised Billot to the cardinalate and in the reign of Pope Pius XII were still employed as direct sources for pronouncements of the Magisterium. (Information taken from *Tres Maestros* by Professor Gustavo Daniel Corbi.)

Readers are reminded that according to Canon 1323, quoted earlier, the Church can propose a Divinely revealed truth for the belief of the faithful "either by a solemn judgement *or by the Ordinary and Universal Magisterium*." Nonetheless, it is not always easy to discern which doctrines are taught by the Ordinary Magisterium so as to bind under pain of heresy, so we need criteria whereby we may know *with certainty* when the Ordinary Magisterium proposes a truth in this way.

Emphasis must be placed on the need for certainty, because, in a case where there is objective doubt as to whether the Church proposes a belief as Divinely revealed, the censure of heresy is not applicable. According to Canon 1323§3: "Nothing is to be understood as dogmatically declared or defined unless this is manifestly certain." Also, as the Ordinary Magisterium comprises all the authoritative teaching of the popes and bishops in union with them, it is necessary to establish by exactly what means particular doctrines taught by the Ordinary Magisterium can be recognized as possessing that exceptional authority whereby propositions contradictory to them must be branded heretical.

In order to explain this, it is first necessary further to clarify the use of the word "infallible". As has been said, this word means "unable to err", but this definition can be misleading because the different kinds of authoritative Catholic teaching can be immune from error in different ways and although not all of these are commonly called "infallible" there is a sense in which all of them may be so.

With reference to doctrinal declarations made by the Holy See in which the conditions necessary for infallibility in its strictest sense are absent, Cardinal Franzelin notes that "in such declarations, though the doctrine is not infallibly *true* ... it is nevertheless infallibly *safe*." He notes that Catholics are not only bound to accept such declarations by refraining from external denial of them, but that they must bring their *opinions* also into line with those of the Church – "*ita non solum loquendum sed etiam sentiendum est*" – and this intellectual acceptance of doctrines taught without strict infallibility is due, he says, "*not* to the motive of Divine faith (on account of the authority of God revealing) ..., but to the motive of sacred authority," for the Divine assistance protecting the Church from teaching error is not restricted to the charism of infallibility in respect of the Extraordinary Magisterium or in respect of a multiplicity of mutually corroborative acts of the Ordinary Magisterium. There is also, he declares, a "*universal* ecclesiastical or doctrinal providence" protecting *every* statement of the Church which impinges on doctrine. "The sacred authority of this universal doctrinal providence is," according to the learned cardinal, "an abundantly sufficient motive, enabling and obliging the dutiful will to command the religious or theological assent of the intellect." (*De Divina Traditione et Scriptura*, 1875, pages 129-131)

In other words, a supernatural protection from error governs every act of the Holy See which affects doctrine, so that all such acts are *in a sense* infallible. But the word "infallibility" is applied by conventional usage to that extraordinary and direct Divine protection which is due only to *certain* of these acts. Readers are asked to bear in mind, therefore, in reading what follows, that, owing to this specially adopted theological sense of the word "infallibility", some Catholic writers who will be quoted exclude certain doctrines from the realm of "infallibility" without by any means wishing to imply by this exclusion that the doctrines in question are therefore liable to error.[29]

We have already seen from Canon 1323§2 that the Ordinary Magisterium can propose a doctrine as Divinely revealed and to be believed "*de fide divina et Catholica*". But, as such proposal

---

[29] The consequences of misapprehension in this area could easily become very serious. If the teaching is not "infallible" (protected from error), it could – understandably but fallaciously – be argued that it must be liable to error; and if it is liable to error, it may be false and we cannot be required to believe that which may be false.

could not bind the faithful unless it were genuinely infallible in the sense described above, it is clear that this infallibility can in certain circumstances protect the teaching of the Ordinary Magisterium.[30] Hence Fr. Cartechini (*op. cit.*, p. 33) explains that

> Those things which are taught infallibly by the Ordinary Magisterium concerning faith and morals, as having been Divinely revealed, can and must be said to require acceptance 'with Divine [and] Catholic faith', even if in fact many people do not recognize this.

But evidently, although *all* the official doctrinal teaching of pope and bishops, as contained in encyclicals, allocutions, pastoral letters, etc., pertains to the Ordinary Magisterium, it is *not* all protected by infallibility, so it is necessary to establish criteria by which to discern exactly which doctrines taught by the Ordinary Magisterium have the same "infallible" status as if they had been taught by the Extraordinary Magisterium. As any *formal definition* of pope or council on a point of doctrine will constitute an act of the Extraordinary Magisterium, it is evident that the Ordinary Magisterium embraces all authoritative exposition of Catholic doctrine which is *not* expressed in the form of a solemn definition. Such expositions may be made by the pope or by bishops; they may be explicit or implicit; may be expressed in the liturgy, in Canon Law, in the rules of approved religious orders, or in the teaching of theologians sanctioned by the Church. A comprehensive list of potential sources is given by Fr. Cartechini (*op. cit.*, pp. 33-40). And to determine whether any particular doctrine taught by any of these means is *infallibly* proposed by the Ordinary Magisterium, the question that must

---

[30] This is illustrated by the fact that Pope Pius XII's "*ex cathedra*" Bull *Munificentissimus Deus* invokes the agreement of the Ordinary and Universal Magisterium of the Church (i.e. as expressed by the teaching of the bishops) that the Assumption of Our Blessed Lady is a Divinely revealed truth as a certain argument that it must be so, and can therefore be defined as such by a solemn judgement of the Extraordinary Magisterium. (Denzinger 1792)

be asked is simply whether the Church has, at least implicitly, claimed the assent of all the faithful to the doctrine in question.

To establish this, it must be remembered that the Ordinary Magisterium, like the Extraordinary Magisterium, can be exercised by the pope alone, or by the pope and the other bishops acting in unison. With this background let us invite Dom Paul Nau to explain to us how the pope and the bishops are known to demand the assent of all the faithful to some doctrine which they teach otherwise than through the Extraordinary Magisterium. What follows is cited from his essay *Le Magistère Pontifical Ordinaire au Premier Concile du Vatican*,[31] which appeared in the *Revue Thomiste*, Vol. LXII, 1962, pages 341-397:

> In pronouncing a solemn judgement, the supreme judge affirms, by his sentence, that a doctrine does or does not belong to the revealed deposit. This sentence binds the whole Church. It cannot be subject to error, lest it mislead the Church. It must be guaranteed by Divine assistance: by virtue of this Divine assistance, the affirmation which comprises it will necessarily be *true*.
>
> In the teaching and preaching which constitute the Ordinary Magisterium, on the other hand, the teacher of the Faith does not pronounce on whether or not the doctrine belongs to the deposit. His role is to *teach* the doctrine and make it known. He cannot do this by a single, isolated act. Only a *body* of acts will be able to reach the *body* of the faithful and to enable them to grasp the meaning of the doctrine: a solitary episcopal instruction, no, but the concordant teaching of the body of Catholic bishops, yes; a solitary pontifical discourse, no, but the constant teaching of the successor

---

[31] Complementary to this essay, and available in English, is Dom Paul Nau's 1956 (50 page) study *The Ordinary Magisterium of the Church Theologically Considered*. In it Dom Paul specifies three variable factors by which it is possible to gauge when the papal Ordinary Magisterium engages infallibility:
   (i) the will of the sovereign pontiff to commit his authority behind the enunciation of a doctrine;
   (ii) the impact ... of his teaching on the Church;
   (iii) the continuity and coherence of the various affirmations. (*op. cit.*, p. 20)

of Peter, yes. No episcopal instruction is guaranteed infallible, nor does any pontifical discourse, taken on its own, – unless it proclaims a definition '*ex cathedra*' – enjoy this privilege ....

A doctrine universally taught as revealed, even when no definition has intervened, necessarily expresses, thanks to this [Divine] assistance, the revelation entrusted by Christ to the Apostles. It is certainly faithful to this revelation and it is therefore an obligatory rule of faith ....

A doctrine is likewise assured of the same fidelity and similarly constitutes a rule of faith, from the sole fact that it has been constantly taught as revealed, by the successor of Peter.

It is worth noting, before closing this brief summary of Catholic doctrine about the Ordinary Magisterium, that some theologians, including Fr. Cartechini, have held that even isolated acts of the Pontifical Ordinary Magisterium can be truly infallible. The present writer follows Dom Paul Nau, who denies this, arguing that the instances adduced from certain papal encyclicals are in fact acts of the *Extraordinary* Magisterium. And indeed it is hard to see what real distinction could be made to show that an isolated papal act, definitely protected by infallibility, would *not* be an act of the Extraordinary Magisterium.

Summary of Doctrine on Divine and Catholic Faith

So, in summary:

(i) A doctrine must be believed "*de fide divina et Catholica*" if it is proposed by the Church as Divinely revealed, either in a solemn judgement or by the Ordinary Magisterium, whether expressly or implicitly in the practice of the Church.

(ii) What the crime of heresy essentially consists in is *the deliberate doubt or denial* of such a doctrine.

(iii) It will also be remembered that the pitfalls to be avoided are:

(a) the assumption that all judgements of the Extraordinary Magisterium on matters of faith and morals necessarily propose the doctrine in question as Divinely revealed – this cannot be presumed, and is proved only if the judgement, at least implicitly, states that the doctrine was revealed by God;

(b) the assumption that *only* acts of the Extraordinary Magisterium – solemn judgements of popes or councils – are sufficient to propose a doctrine for belief "*de fide divina et Catholica*".[32]

Holy Scripture

In a discussion about what constitutes heresy, special mention needs to be made of the contents of Holy Scripture, because it is

---

[32] Michael Davies adopts *both* these common misapprehensions on pages 9 and 10 of his pamphlet *The Divine Constitution*. Referring indiscriminately to definitions of the Extraordinary Magisterium, he writes:
> Teaching which must be accepted with this degree of certainty is referred to as of divine and Catholic faith ('*de fide divina et Catholica*') ... its pertinacious rejection is called 'heresy'.

This is false, because the Extraordinary Magisterium can define a point of Catholic belief infallibly, *which is not part of Divine revelation at all* (such as the existence of the minor Orders, defined at Trent), in which case it will be termed "*de fide ecclesiastica*" and its denial will *not* be heresy, strictly speaking.

In the same place he says that:
> Teaching is infallible only when the special assistance of the Holy Ghost which guarantees this is invoked. *Pastor Æternus* restricts this assistance to definitions ...

The error here is proved by the fact that infallibility also pertains to teaching of the Ordinary Magisterium, i.e. to doctrinal instruction addressed to the entire Church, *not* by an isolated definition of pope or council, but by a multitude of acts, either of all the bishops, including the pope, or of the pope alone. Unbelievably Davies contradicts himself *on the very next page*, where he writes, correctly: "Infallible teaching is *not* confined to pronouncements of the Extraordinary Magisterium." It seems in fact that he is under the impression that the infallible teaching of the Ordinary Magisterium consists only in the teaching of all the bishops, whereas the teaching of the papal Ordinary Magisterium can in reality be infallible alone. (See the two studies of Dom Paul Nau referred to earlier.)

a dogma, as has been said, that the whole contents of Holy Scripture are Divinely revealed and it might be presumed from this that the denial of any part of Holy Scripture constitutes heresy, strictly so called. This is substantially true, but is subject to some important qualifications.

The most important of these qualifications is based upon the fact that, as the words of Canon 1323§1 make clear, for a doctrine to be believed[33] "*de fide divina et Catholica*", proposal by the Church is necessary *in addition* to the fact of its being contained in the Word of God, either written or handed down. Nor will it suffice to argue that the Church proposes the whole contents of the Holy Scripture for belief "*de fide divina et Catholica*", because if this general proposal were sufficient for the purpose in question, the phrasing of Canon 1323§1 would be inane, which is impossible. It is clear that *specific* proposal as Divinely revealed is called for.

But having said this, it is also a fact that, although many of the truths contained in Holy Scripture have *not* been specifically proposed for the belief of the faithful as Divinely revealed, one truth which certainly *has* been proposed as Divinely revealed is the inerrancy of Holy Scripture. Consequently to contradict that which is *certainly* found in Holy Scripture amounts to a denial of the dogma of Scriptural inerrancy and is heretical on that count.

The renowned Jesuit theologian Fr. Augustine Lehmkuhl explains this point as follows:

> ... if anyone reading a fact related in Holy Scripture which ... pertains to faith, denies that fact, by that very denial he denies also the canonicity and Divine inspiration of the book in question or a part of it, whereas the Catholic Church has defined this inspiration to be '*de fide*'. So one who seeks to excuse himself on the pretext that the particular truth has not been defined by the Church in any canon or inserted in a Creed is grossly mistaken ['*turpiter errat*']. It is enough that I should deny any truth which I clearly understand to

---

[33] Or, at least, for it to be *obligatory* to believe a doctrine in this way.

be taught in an inspired book for me to commit heresy. (*Casus Conscientiæ*, Vol. I, n. 1009)

Finally, it must be understood that:

(a) Heresy is not definitely committed by someone who argues that a particular verse of Holy Scripture is a scribal interpolation and hence erroneous, unless the Church has specifically taught the contrary, for this in itself would contradict no dogma.

(b) Likewise, if the meaning of the passage in question is open to doubt, he cannot be condemned as a heretic, even if the interpretation favoured by the objector is highly implausible, unless his interpretation *definitely* contradicts the Scriptural meaning or unless the Church has authoritatively interpreted the passage.

"De Fide Divina"

After "*de fide divina et Catholica*" comes the category "*de fide divina*". This includes whatever truths have been revealed by God but *not* proposed by the Church as Divinely revealed. Divine faith is that by which we believe any truth which we know to have been revealed by God. Normally we know such truths through their having been proposed as such by the Church, but we *may* certainly have Divine faith in doctrines not proposed by the Church when it is nonetheless certain that they are Divinely revealed.

And in fact it is quite normal for converts to acquire *Divine* faith before they yet have Divine *and Catholic* faith, if they attain supernatural certainty of the Christian revelation before they have been convinced of the infallibility of the Catholic Church as the divinely appointed vehicle of the doctrines it contains.

All the clear teachings of Holy Scripture not specifically proposed by the Church are also to be believed "*de fide divina*". An error contrary to one of these truths is described as "*error in fide*" – an error in faith – and is, according to Fr. Cartechini, "a mortal sin directly against faith", but not directly subject to any ecclesiastical censure.

Other Doctrines Taught with Infallibility

The next category of Catholic beliefs contains all those truths *not* directly revealed by God, but nonetheless infallibly taught by the Church either by the Extraordinary or the Ordinary Magisterium. These truths include, for instance, the invalidity of Anglican Orders, taught by Pope Leo XIII in *Apostolicæ Curæ* (Ordinary Magisterium), and the existence in the Catholic Church of the minor Orders, taught by the Council of Trent (Extraordinary Magisterium). These truths bind every Catholic conscience and must be believed "*de fide ecclesiastica*", i.e. with ecclesiastical faith, because they are certain, not as having been directly revealed by God (they were not), but through being indirectly included in the infallibility of the Church.

Fr. Cartechini ventures the opinion that a proposition contrary to such teaching may be termed "heretical against ecclesiastical faith," – the word *heretical* being used here "not … in its strict meaning but in a looser sense …." (*op. cit.* p. 43)

He also explains that one who denies such a doctrine commits "a mortal sin directly against faith" and may incur an ecclesiastical censure.

Other Theological Notes

There are five more categories of definite Catholic truths before we descend to the level of mere opinions. A belief can be:

(i) "Proximate to faith" – if it is almost unanimously considered to be Divinely revealed.[34]

(ii) "Theologically certain" – if it is the direct and inevitable logical conclusion of two premises, one revealed and the other certain in some other way.[35]

---

[34] E.g. That Our Lord claimed throughout his life to be the Messias.

[35] E.g. the legitimacy of the Council of Trent. Such truths are sometimes

(iii) "A Catholic doctrine" (another term which is often used in a looser sense but is here defined strictly) – if it is taught as definite by the Church but without engaging infallibility.[36] It is important to register the fact that, by virtue of belonging to this category, *whatever* is taught as definite in papal encyclicals, etc., pertains to "Catholic doctrine" and must be believed by Catholics. It is consequently quite impossible for the pope to lead us astray by any such official teaching.

(iv) "Certain" – if it is agreed among all theological schools but not closely bound up with any revealed truth, in which case to deny it would (at least almost invariably) be a mortal sin of temerity.

(v) "Safe" – if it is contained in the doctrinal decrees of the Roman Congregations, in which case to deny it publicly would be a mortal sin of disobedience.

These last categories have been briefly summarised because once one has correctly understood the distinction between *"de fide divina"*, *"de fide divina et Catholica"* and *"de fide ecclesiastica"*, it is more important to remember that true internal and external assent is owed also to all the other categories than it is to be able to differentiate between them, as is clear from the following three authoritative statements:

(i) "Nor must it be thought that that which is expounded in encyclical letters does not of itself demand consent, on the basis that in writing such letters the popes do not exercise the supreme power of their teaching authority. For these matters are taught with the ordinary teaching authority of which it is true to say 'He who heareth you, heareth me;' (Luke 10:16) and generally what is expounded and inculcated in encyclical Letters already for other reasons

---

known as dogmatic facts.

[36] E.g. The fact that the use of periodic continence without a weighty reason is mortally sinful.

appertains to Catholic doctrine. But if the supreme pontiffs in their official documents properly pass judgement on a matter which up to that time has been under dispute, it is obvious that this matter, according to the mind and will of the same pontiffs, cannot be any longer considered a question open to discussion among theologians." (Pope Pius XII: *Humani Generis*)

(ii) "It is not enough to avoid heretical perversity, but it is also necessary diligently to flee from those errors which, to a greater or lesser extent, come close to it; wherefore everyone is obliged also to observe the constitutions and decrees by which such perverse opinions are proscribed and prohibited by the Holy See." (Canon 1324)

(iii) "When we speak of the Vicar of Christ, our place is to obey, not to question. We must not seek to limit our obedience to the pope's commands by restricting the scope of their application. We must not quibble over his clear instructions, distort their meaning, misinterpret them in the light of our own prejudices and destroy their obvious substance. We must not assert any other rights against the pope's right to teach and command us. We must not debate the validity of his decisions or argue about his commands; to do so would be to offer a direct insult to Jesus Christ Himself ...." (Extract from an allocution delivered by Pope St. Pius X when he was Patriarch of Venice: see *Pie X, le Saint* by Hary Mitchell, p. 73)

And Now Back to Religious Liberty

After this exceedingly long digression, which was necessary to establish what Catholic doctrine is on the subject of infallibility, we can at last return to Mr. Michael Davies and his claim that the Church's condemnation of religious liberty is only *possibly* infallible.

First, let us state what is meant by religious liberty insofar as it has been consistently condemned by the Church. It is the principle that a man is entitled to profess whatever religion he chooses, publicly and privately, without interference from the civil authority unless his religious actions are in direct conflict with public order. This right, Vatican II unequivocally asserts, belongs to every man. That it is in contradiction to previous papal declarations[37] Mr. Davies cannot deny, so instead he casts doubt on the infallibility of those declarations with which it is in conflict, whether individually or collectively.

It will be remembered from pages 153 and 159 that the teaching of encyclical letters can constitute infallible expressions of the Ordinary Magisterium in accordance with their relative solemnity, impact and continuity. If we judge the papal teaching on religious liberty by these standards, it is evident that *few doctrines of the Ordinary Magisterium have a more certain claim to infallibility*. It would be excessively lengthy to quote all the declarations of the Holy See, and in fact this is unnecessary; for Mr. Davies will surely accept the testimony of Archbishop Lefebvre, delivered in one of his interventions at Vatican II itself. Here are Archbishop Lefebvre's words:

> This conception of religious liberty, which in his encyclical *Immortale Dei* Leo XIII calls a 'new law', was *solemnly condemned* by that Pontiff as contrary to sound philosophy and against Holy Scripture and Tradition.
> This same conception, this 'new law' *so many times condemned* by the Church, the Conciliar Commission is now putting before us, the Fathers of 'Vatican II', for us to subscribe to and countersign. (September 1965, recorded in the *Acta Synodalia* and in Archbishop Lefebvre's *I Accuse the Council!*, Angelus Press 1982 – emphases added)

The Archbishop's statement is historically and theologically accurate. It is therefore that the Church has condemned the

---

[37] For instance the teaching of Pope Pius IX's *Syllabus* that it is *wrong* for a Catholic country to allow non-Catholic immigrants the right to worship publicly. (Condemned proposition 78; Denzinger 1778)

doctrine of religious liberty *repeatedly and emphatically*, which proves, by the standards stated by Dom Paul Nau and of Fr. Cartechini, that this teaching is protected by infallibility even if it pertains only to the Ordinary Magisterium. The matter is simply not open to doubt.

The Status of Quanta Cura

However, Davies's doubts of its infallibility[38] are even more flagrantly unjustifiable than this, for in reality this notion of religious liberty has been condemned by the *Extraordinary* Magisterium too. This condemnation was made in Pope Pius IX's encyclical letter *Quanta Cura* (1864), where the pope writes as follows:

> Contrary to the teachings of the Holy Scriptures, of the Church, and of the Holy Fathers, these persons do not hesitate to make the following assertion: 'The best condition of human society is that wherein no duty is recognized by the government of correcting, by enacted penalties, the violators of the Catholic religion except where the maintenance of the public peace requires it.' From this totally false notion of social government, they fear not to uphold that erroneous opinion, most pernicious to the Catholic Church and to the salvation of souls, which was called by Our above-quoted Predecessor, Gregory XVI, insanity ('*deliramentum*')[39] namely, 'that liberty of conscience and of worship is the peculiar (or inalienable) right of every man, which should be proclaimed by law.' (Denzinger 1684-90)

It should be understood that "violators of the Catholic religion" does not mean those who persecute the Church with violence or physical means, for "the maintenance of public peace" already requires that such men be punished. What Pope Pius IX is teaching[40] is that the civil authority ought to impose

---

[38] It will be recalled that Davies thinks the Church's condemnation of religious liberty no more than "*possibly* infallible."

[39] In the encyclical *Mirari Vos*, 15 August 1832.

[40] I.e. the contradictory of the proposition which he is condemning.

sanctions on those who attack the Church or promote false religions by pen or by word of mouth, *even if this constitutes no direct threat to public peace and order*. The basis for these sanctions is not, therefore, the protection of public order, but the principle that the state has the duty (*per se*) to protect its citizens from error.[41] Vatican II maintains the contrary, repeatedly, in its declaration *Dignitatis Humanæ* on religious liberty, for instance by its teaching, in paragraph 3, that a man's right to posit religious acts without interference springs, not from the objective rectitude of such acts, but from his subjective conviction that they are right – so that the State can make no distinction between external religious manifestations on the basis of their conformity with, or opposition to, objective truth, and must treat all religions equally in respect of their "right" to propagate their beliefs. In its seventh paragraph *Dignitatis Humanæ* also teaches in very explicit terms that the civil authorities may interfere with the exercise of religious liberty only for the sake of "public peace" – *the very error condemned by Pope Pius IX.*

To prove, then, that *Quanta Cura*'s direct condemnation of *Dignitatis Humanæ* is "*ex cathedra*", we need look no further

---

[41] See, for instance, *Immortale Dei*:

"If the mind assents to false opinions, and the will chooses and follows after evil, ... both fall from their native dignity into an abyss of corruption. Whatever, therefore, is opposed to virtue and truth, may not rightly be brought temptingly before the eye of man, much less sanctioned by the favour and protection of the law. ... for which reason the State is unfaithful to the rule and prescription of nature if it allows licence of opinions and evil deeds to run wild, leaving unpunished the alienation minds from truth and souls from virtue."

Thus, for instance, it would be appropriate to restrain a mathematics teacher who taught his pupils that $2 + 2 = 5$, it would be appropriate to prohibit propaganda in favour of contraception and it would be supremely appropriate for the State to prevent its citizens from being disquieted in their faith by the proselytism of Jehovah's Witnesses, Protestants, Modernists or the members of any other sect hostile to the truth which God has revealed and entrusted to the Church of whose credibility He has made himself the public Guarantor.

than the paragraph in which Pope Pius IX imposes his teaching on the faithful. Here are his words:

> So, amid such great perversity of depraved opinions, thoroughly mindful of Our Apostolic office and of our most holy religion, of sound doctrine and of the salvation of the souls entrusted to us by God, and in our very great concern for the good of human society itself, We have determined once more to raise Our Apostolic voice. Hence, by Our Apostolic authority We reprove, proscribe and condemn each and every one of the perverse opinions and doctrines individually mentioned in this document, and We will and command that they be held absolutely as reproved, proscribed and condemned by all the sons of the Catholic Church. (Denzinger 1699)

It will be remembered that the 1870 Vatican Council defined that the pope speaks *"ex cathedra"* – and thus infallibly – when, "exercising the office of shepherd and teacher of all Christians by his supreme Apostolic authority, he defines a doctrine concerning faith or morals to be held by the whole Church." (Denzinger 1839) It can readily be seen that all these conditions are undeniably fulfilled in *Quanta Cura*, and that the Church's condemnation of the doctrine of religious liberty espoused at Vatican II thus derives its infallibility even from the Extraordinary Magisterium.

And, for the benefit of anyone who might deny that the foregoing *can* be readily seen, the *"ex cathedra"* status of *Quanta Cura* is *also* confirmed by the illustrious theologians who consider its status. For instance, Canon J.M. Hervé S.T.D., in his *Manuale Theologiæ Dogmaticæ* (Vol. I, n. 485), says of *Quanta Cura*: "It is evident from the very words of its conclusion that the encyclical has full and *infallible authority*" (emphasis in the original). And the renowned Cardinal Billot uses *Quanta Cura* to refute those who argue that it is difficult to know when a doctrine is taught *"ex cathedra"*. With reference to the passage from it quoted above, he rhetorically asks whether "it could by any chance be said" that its *"ex cathedra"* status "is doubtful, uncertain or in any way obscure?" (*De Ecclesia Christi*, thesis XXXI)

No, it certainly cannot be regarded as doubtful, let us fervently reply, except by those who think that they know better than the dogmatic teaching of the 1870 Vatican Council interpreted by theologians of the calibre of Cardinal Billot. But alas, it seems that Davies is one of those who think that they do know better than such authorities, for, as we have seen, in his pamphlet *Archbishop Lefebvre and Religious Liberty* (p. 10) he describes the whole of the Church's doctrine condemning religious liberty as only "possibly infallible", including *Quanta Cura* and the countless other constitutions, encyclicals and briefs in which it is condemned. Moreover, he states openly in *Apologia Pro Marcel Lefebvre* (Volume I, p. 322) that he regards *Quanta Cura* itself as only "possibly infallible".

NOTE TO THE 2015 EDITION

While I continue to have not the slightest doubt that the doctrine of religious liberty taught by Vatican II's *Dignitatis Humanæ* is in direct conflict with the infallible teaching of *Quanta Cura* and numerous other magisterial teachings, I would hesitate today to claim that it is certainly *heretical*, as opposed to falling under a somewhat lesser censure. I think that doubt might be cast on the part of my argumentation purporting to demonstrate that the precise doctrine denied by Vatican II has been sufficiently proposed by the Magisterium as *divinely revealed*. Precisely because I would today regard this question as a matter of legitimate debate I have decided to leave my 1989 arguments in place in this revised edition, subject only to the present disclaimer.

The issue in my view makes little difference to the practical conclusions to be reached, because:

- **the Vatican II decree on Ecumenism, *Unitatis Redintegratio*, is certainly and explicitly heretical on a subject which no one doubts is an object of divine revelation;**
- **the true Church, under the guidance of a true pope, not only cannot teach the faithful heresy, but cannot teach them condemned error falling under a lesser censure either.**

Is Religious Liberty Heretical?

In any consideration of the religious liberty controversy stirred up by the Vatican II declaration, there is one question which ought to be settled at once. That is the question of whether the Vatican II doctrine of religious liberty, infallibly condemned both in *Quanta Cura* and by repeated acts of the Ordinary Magisterium, is in fact *heretical* in the strict sense of that term.

Referring back for a moment to the quotation from *Quanta Cura*, let us note in particular the statement that the false doctrine of religious liberty condemned therein is "contrary to the teachings of the Holy Scriptures". By this statement the pope is affirming, indirectly but unmistakably, that the false doctrine is heretical; for the contrary[42] doctrine, he says, is Divinely revealed, since all the contents of Holy Scripture are revealed by God.

Nor is it possible to evade this conclusion on the pretext that the doctrine condemning religious liberty may be simply "*de fide divina*" rather than "*de fide divina et Catholica*" if the latter has not been proposed by the Church. Even if it had not been adequately proposed elsewhere, this statement of the pope binds the Catholic conscience to admit that the falsity of the doctrine

---

[42] Or, strictly, the contradictory.

of religious liberty *is Divinely revealed*, and *Quanta Cura*, therefore, constitutes a sufficient proposal in itself. This would be so even if a non-"*ex cathedra*" encyclical had declared a particular doctrine to be contrary to Divine revelation, and is all the more certainly true in the case of a document with the additional solemnity and authority of the Extraordinary Magisterium.

This conclusion is corroborated by the fact that Catholic theologians recognize certain truths as having been proposed by the Church for belief "*de fide divina et Catholica*" merely by the assurance contained in a conventional encyclical that the belief in question is contained in the Bible or otherwise revealed by Almighty God. Here are two examples:

(i) Fr. Cartechini[43] explains that the truth of the Divine origin of the civil authority must be believed "*de fide divina et Catholica*" by virtue of the following passage from Pope Leo XIII's encyclical *Diuturnum Illud*:[44]

But as regards political power, the Church rightly teaches that it comes from God, for it finds this clearly testified in the Sacred Scriptures and in the monuments of antiquity .... In truth, it is clearly established by the books of the Old Testament in very many places that the source of human power is God ... [the pope goes on to give Scriptural quotations confirming this fact]. (*Acta Sanctæ Sedis*, Vol. XIV, p. 3 et seq.)

(ii) Another instance of the same thing, furnished by the same theologian (*loc. cit.*), is the proposal of the dogma of the Divine origin of matrimony in Pope Leo XIII's encyclical *Arcanum Divinæ*. This is simply affirmed in the words:

From the Gospel we see clearly that this doctrine [i.e. the Divine origin of matrimony] was declared and openly confirmed by the Divine authority of Jesus Christ. (*Acta Sanctæ Sedis*, Vol. XII, p. 385 et seq.)

---

[43] *Op. cit.*, pp. 33 *et seq.*
[44] Not to be confused with **Divinum** *Illud* of the same pontiff.

In each case the statement in any encyclical that a particular truth is taught in Holy Writ is sufficient to constitute its proposal to the faithful as Divinely revealed and to brand any contradictory proposition as heretical in the strictest sense. *A fortiori* the same must be true of the statement in *Quanta Cura* that religious liberty is contrary to Holy Writ. The conclusion that it is heretical is consequently inescapable.

Although it is true that Davies does not directly discuss this point of whether the teaching of the Church on religious liberty is "*de fide*" and whether it would consequently be heretical to deny it, the very fact that that he does *not* discuss the question of its "*de fide*" status it is itself a strong point against him. For if he is a scholar of integrity, *why* did he not discuss it? Why is it that, despite considering the subject of religious liberty at some length in many of his works and pointing out the contradiction between Vatican II's *Dignitatis Humanæ* and papal teaching contained in *Quanta Cura* and elsewhere, Davies never goes on to consider exactly what theological note is to be attached to the Vatican II error? Can this glaring failure to consider the question, which cannot but immediately spring to the mind of anyone who recognizes the contradiction between the traditional doctrine and the new, be explained except as a studious avoidance of a dangerous topic?

Moreover, even without discussing it directly, it is quite clear what Davies's view of the subject is – or, at least, what the impression he wants to give to his readers is. Again and again, notably in the two long essays in which he purports to address and refute the thesis that the Holy See is vacant, he tells us that the "pope" cannot possibly be accused of heresy despite his having signed *Dignitatis Humanæ*.

For instance, in *The Divine Constitution and Indefectibility of the Catholic Church*, Davies writes as follows:

> ... there is no case whatsoever for claiming that any of the Conciliar popes have lost their office as a result of heresy. Anyone wishing to dispute this assertion would need to state the doctrines

'*de fide divina et Catholica*' which one or more of these popes are alleged to have rejected pertinaciously. There is not one instance which comes remotely within [*sic*] this category. (p. 29)

Again, in *The Remnant* for 15th February 1987 he assures those gullible enough to believe his unsupported words that "by no possible stretch of the imagination can the present Pope be accused of denying pertinaciously any '*de fide*' doctrine ...." Note that in both of these passages Davies is at pains to convince us that the thesis accusing John-Paul II of heresy is not only wrong but a non-starter – "not ... remotely" ... "by no possible stretch of the imagination ...." I am prepared to acknowledge that someone acquainted with the facts might yet sincerely believe that my case convicting *Dignitatis Humanæ* of containing heretical propositions is open to refutation, *but surely no honest person could maintain that there is not even the appearance of a case to be answered.*

More on Religious Liberty

It will already be apparent from the comments made above that the subject of religious liberty is one on which Davies is definitely not at his best. And it must now be added that, while this would be serious enough had he only had occasion to touch on the topic once and at no great length in his writings, it is made a very great deal worse by the fact that he has written so much about it – a circumstance partly brought about by Archbishop Lefebvre's having made it the main plank of his case in his correspondence with the "Sacred Congregation for the Doctrine of the Faith", thus causing Davies to devote a large part of Vol. II of his *Apologia Pro Marcel Lefebvre* to it. Fortunately there is no need to undertake the daunting task of analysing in depth all that Davies has written on the subject, including the material in the *Apologia*, because he has published a small pamphlet entitled *Archbishop Lefebvre and Religious Liberty* (1980) in which his position is concisely set out;[45] and it is to this pamphlet that we shall now turn our attention.

On p. 2 Davies is attempting to justify the Church's doctrine according to which the ideal state is a Catholic state – that is, a state (a) the constitution of which explicitly recognizes the truth of the Catholic Church, (b) the laws of which are in accordance with the Catholic Church's teachings, (c) the state functions of which are marked by the solemnities of the Catholic Church,[46] (d) any official education supplied by which is Catholic, and (e) which, under normal circumstances, as a matter of policy forbids all attempts to spread or publicize false religions opinions hostile to that of the Church, while ruthlessly extirpating the hidden enemies of both Church and state.

Davies quotes the teaching of Pope Leo XIII in *Libertas Humana* that reason itself forbids the state "to adopt a line of action which would end in godlessness – namely to treat the various religions (as they call them) alike and to bestow upon them promiscuously equal rights and privileges;" and he then comments as follows: "Thus, a state in which Catholicism was the religion of the overwhelming majority of the inhabitants should be a Catholic state."

Now the corollary of Davies's statement is that in states in which Catholicism is *not* the religion of the overwhelming majority of the inhabitants, these rules should need not apply and the state should need *not* be a Catholic state. Indeed, since there is no country today in which the overwhelming majority of the inhabitants is Catholic, Davies implies that it is quite correct for there to be *no* Catholic state in the world today. Moreover, this is effectively the case even if, for the sake of the argument, we acknowledge as Catholics all those whom Davies himself would regard as Catholics – that is, all those who choose to call themselves by that name, regardless of their beliefs – for even

---

[45] Davies's long-promised book *The Second Vatican Council and Religious Liberty* finally appeared in 1992, three years after the original publication of this *Evaluation*. (2015 footnote.)

[46] Cf. Pope Pius XII, *Mediator Dei*: "Divine worship is a duty for human society as such and not only for individuals."

on these terms the only country in the world in which "Catholicism" is the religion of the overwhelming majority of the inhabitants is a tiny and isolated French dependency called the Wallis and Futuna Islands.

Well, of course, *if* it is the teaching of the Church that in 1989 no country ought to be a Catholic state, we must accept it. But what is Davies's authority? Upon what does he base this assertion? Such a teaching is certainly *not* an implication of the passage which he quotes from Pope Leo XIII, although his word "thus" directly implies this. Nor, in fact, is it an implication of any other papal teaching that Davies will ever be able to find, since, far from being a correct statement of the position of the Catholic Church on this topic, it is a travesty of her teaching. The Church's teaching is that *every state without exception* has the *absolute* duty to be a Catholic state *in the fullest sense of those words*, regardless of the proportion of its citizens who are members of the Catholic Church. It is certainly *more likely* that this absolute moral duty will be complied with by a state in which the majority of the citizens are Catholics, but the duty is not in the slightest diminished even in the case of a state which numbers not a single Catholic among its inhabitants.

The reason for this is that for all moral purposes the state is nothing more than a collection of individuals acting in concert and, as such, *is bound by exactly the same moral rules as bind individuals*. And, needless to say, one of the primary moral rules which binds every individual possessing the use of reason is the duty of joining the Catholic Church. This is clearly stated in Canon 1322 of the 1917 *Code of Canon Law*, which reads as follows:

> The Church has independently of any civil power the right and the duty to teach all nations the evangelical doctrine; and all are bound by Divine law to learn this doctrine, and to embrace the true Church of God.

And the doctrine that this principle applies just as much to the state as to the individual is clearly taught by Cardinal Gasparri in the following passage from his *Catholic Catechism*:

> This distinction between the two societies does not mean that the state can, as though wholly separate from the Church, behave as though there were no God and repudiate all responsibility for religion as being something alien to itself and of no importance. Nor, out of the various forms of religion, can it choose any one it likes. For *the state no less than individual citizens is bound to worship God according to that form of religion which He has Himself commanded*, and the truth of which He has established by proofs that are certain and leave no room for doubt; that form of religion is the only true Church of Christ.[47] (1932 edition, p. 109, footnote 162, emphasis added.)

This of course explains why the Church has consistently opposed the constitutional dechristianization of the nations of what was once Christendom and has never for an instant thought it necessary to take a census of the religious faith of the citizens to discover whether national apostasy is a legitimate choice in any particular case.

The Church and Democracy

A related subject on which Davies habitually gives a distorted impression of the Catholic position is *democracy* among the various available forms of government. I refer in particular of course to democracy as it is understood and practised in our day throughout the world by the nations in which secular humanism is the prevailing philosophy.

On p. 3 page of the same pamphlet (*Archbishop Lefebvre and Religious Liberty*). Here Davies writes:

---

[47] Cf. also the following teaching of Pope Leo XIII: "It is a sin for the state not to have a care for religion ... or out of many forms of religion to adopt that one which chimes in with its fancy; for we are bound absolutely to worship God in the way which He has shown to be His Will." (*Immortale Dei*, 1885)

The Church is not opposed to democracy in the sense that the people choose those who govern them by means of a vote based on national suffrage. The Church is not committed to any particular form of government.

In *Pope John's Council*, on p. 278, he indicates even more strongly that the Church's position is one of indifference

The Church is *equally* prepared to accept a monarchy or a government chosen by free elections, as in the Western democracies.

And on 15th October 1984 in his *Letter from London* column in *The Remnant*, Davies censured Communists for being "subverters of democracy". What he is seeking to convey was the fact that Communism was something unmistakably evil, but he does not brand the Communists as partisans of a system condemned by the Church as "intrinsically evil",[48] or as subverters of the Church, or as subverters of the Divinely ordained institution of private property, or as members of an institution which has murdered one hundred million people in the twentieth century. No, to ensure that he strikes the foes as hard as he can Davies rebukes them for being *undemocratic*.

It is clear enough that Davies himself is an admirer of modern democracy as a polity and believes that the Church is quite as content to see the nations governed by it as by any other. Far different, however, is the truly Catholic perspective.

Now it is true that the Church does not regard any particular form of government as *mandatory* and that she has recognized many different kinds of government as *legitimate*. This is because a state is entitled to establish whatever form of government it chooses, provided that this government does not conflict with the objective moral order established by God, and, consequently, the Church shrinks from restricting the liberty of her children in the form of government that they choose, especially as in most cases the form of government is already in

---

[48] Pope Pius XI: *Divini Redemptoris*.

existence and attempts to change it may be attended by greater evils than any advantage to be gained. But this by no means implies *indifference* for the Church in fact makes it very clear that some forms of government much wiser than others and more propitious to the temporal and spiritual good of citizens.

This is why Davies and the many writers who express the same sentiments are guilty of misrepresentation when they imply that the Church has no *preference* in the matter of government. The truth is not so much that "the Church is not opposed to democracy." as that her opposition to does not attain outright condemnation of democracy in itself. And when we examine the Church's attitude to democracy *not* in itself but *as currently practised*, we find that her hostility is greater still.

Although the Church is not committed *absolutely* to any particular form of government as the one and only form which she finds morally *tolerable*, she is certainly committed to a particular form of government *relatively*: that is to say, in that there is one which she favours especially, fosters in every way, cherishes, praises and is, of course, governed by herself – the system of *monarchy*. And by contrast the form of government consisting in a system of unhesitating acceptance of the manipulated will of 51% of the population is one she can only view with the deepest disquiet.

It is important not to be misled, in studying this subject, by the semantic confusion which may arise when Catholic authorities often use terms such as "democracy" or "Christian democracy" in a sense quite different from the popular understanding of these terms. For instance, the Holy See has declared that its use of these terms does not refer to a political system at all, but to a philanthropic movement:

> It would be a crime to distort this name of *Christian democracy* to politics, for although democracy implies popular government, yet in its present acceptation it is so employed that, removing from it all political significance, it is to mean nothing else than a benevolent

and Christian movement on behalf of the people .... (Leo XIII: *Graves de Communi*)

That the Church condemns no form of government which is not intrinsically evil was specifically stated by Pope Leo XIII in his encyclical *Immortale Dei* when the pontiff was also at pains to clarify that limited popular involvement in the government is certainly not intrinsically evil:

> This then is the teaching of the Catholic Church concerning the constitution and government of the State. No one of the several forms of government is in itself condemned, insofar as none of them contains anything contrary to Catholic doctrine, and all of them are capable, if wisely and justly managed, of ensuring the welfare of the State. Neither is it blameworthy in itself, in any manner, for the people to have a share, greater or less, in the government.

So democracy, when limited to a system whereby the people share in the government – for instance by electing those who actually govern – is not intrinsically evil or condemned by the Church. But is this what democracy means to the modern mind (which, after all, is the mind which Michael Davies is addressing)? Is it not a fact that democracy, as the term is commonly used to day, means a system of government according to which all citizens are equal and elect their leaders on a principle of "one man one vote" so that rulers are thought to receive the power to govern by virtue of the popular consent? And if this is what democracy has come to mean, is it true today, as Davies says, that the Church regards this system with indifference?

In examining this last question, the first point to be noted is the teaching of the Church as to the equality of all citizens. Here are two papal pronouncements on the subject:

> 1. "It is utterly untrue, and mere empty talk, to say that all citizens have equal rights." (Pius XI: *Divini Redemptoris*)

2. "Christian democracy must preserve the diversity of classes." (Pope Leo XIII, reiterated by Pope St. Pius X in *Notre Charge Apostolique*)

Evidently the egalitarian aspect of modern democracy is not a matter of indifference to the Church. What, then, of the principle of "one man one vote"? Those Catholics who consider such a system laudable, or even acceptable, are recommended to read with attention the following observation of Pope Pius XII:

> The life of the nations is now disintegrating through blind worship of the force of numbers. Every citizen is now a voter, but ... as such, he is only a unit of a number making up the majority. His position, his place in the family or in the professions are not taken into account. (Allocution *Très Sensible* of 6th April 1951, the text of which appeared on pages 278 *et seq.* of the *Acta Apostolicæ Sedis*, Vol. 43)

So the Church considers that, where the people are involved in government by voting, *at the very least* it is necessary that the "worship of numbers" be avoided by grading the weight attached to an individual's vote according to his status and by respecting the existence of the family as the intermediate society linking the individual to the State. And in addition to the factors mentioned by the pope, there are of course others to be considered. In mid-nineteenth-century England fewer than one fifth of adult males had the right to vote while some persons had two votes or more at the same time; indeed plurality of voting in the United Kingdom did not end until the abolition of the University Seats in 1948 and it persists to this day in favour of university graduates in elections to the Irish Senate (*Seanad Éireann*).

Another difficulty in those countries where the government is elected by a national poll is the extension of the franchise to women, whose Divinely appointed competence does not extend in the slightest into the realm of government, and whose involvement therein, whenever and wherever it occurs, has invariably been a major factor in the destruction of the family.

Hence the Church has always opposed granting the vote to women. (See Dr. Orestes Brownson: "The Woman Question", *Catholic World*, May 1869, and a second article with the same title which appeared in *Brownson's Quarterly Review*, October 1873. Both appear in Volume XVIII of his collected works.)[49]

In the light of these facts, is there, it may be enquired, a single country left on earth which practises "democracy" in a fashion which meets with the Church's approval?

The next "democratic" principle which we must examine in the light of Church teaching is that according to which the populace, by its vote, gives power to its leaders and can consequently withdraw that power at will.

On this subject, St. Pius X wrote in *Notre Charge Apostolique*:

> ... those who preside over the government of public affairs may indeed, in certain cases, be chosen by the will and judgement of the multitude .... But while this choice marks out the ruler, it does not delegate the power; it designates the person who will be invested with it.

This point is crucial, because, given that the right of governing comes not from the people but from God, as the Church teaches, it is quite impossible for any expression of the popular will to revoke this Divine authority once it has been given, except in accordance with the constitution of the country in question; whereas if, in the words of the Masonically-inspired American Declaration of Independence, "governments are instituted among men, deriving their just powers from the

---

[49] It is not intrinsically evil for women to have the vote, in countries whose constitution contains an element of democracy, any more than it is intrinsically evil for a woman to wear the crown in a hereditary monarchy. But such a situation is *abnormal*, opposed to the normal relations between the sexes and to the normal role of the Christian wife and mother. It is one thing to extend exceptional toleration to such abnormalities where they are inevitable in our post-lapsarian world, but it is quite another deliberately to multiply them.

consent of the governed," [50] the governed evidently remain free to change their government, in whole or in part, at will – a truly diabolical recipe for continual revolution, utterly condemned by the Church.

Needless to say, what is taught by modern democrats, in practice and in theory, is the very opposite of St. Pius X's doctrine, nor is this the least of all their errors. All insist that in a democracy, in the modern sense of the term, the people be fundamentally self-governing and sovereign. Thus to the modern democrat the concentration of the power of government in the hands of elected individuals is a regrettable concession to practicality but must not obscure the fact that it is the people who govern themselves and that those whom they elect are no more than representatives of the popular will.

Again, in his perspicacious denunciation of the democratic "Sillon", *Notre Charge Apostolique*, St. Pius X makes clear the gulf between the modern view and what the Church can accept.

> ... if the people retain the power, what becomes of authority? A shadow, a myth; there is no more law properly so-called – no more obedience.
> Our predecessor stigmatized a certain *democracy* which goes to such lengths in its perversity as to attribute sovereignty in society to the people ....

Likewise Pope Leo XIII taught in *Immortale Dei* that "every civilised community must have a ruling authority." It is contradictory that this authority be identical to those subject to it.

Another feature of democracy as understood today is that in *true* democracy – it is asserted – it is the sanction of the people (even if expressed through their elected representatives) which

---

[50] The false political philosophy of Rousseau and Paine is of course entirely incompatible with Catholic doctrine on the origin of political power as taught in Pope Leo XIII's 1897 encyclical *Divinum Illud*.

gives laws their force. In contradiction, however, to this view, Pope Leo XIII insists that:

> In political affairs and in all matters civil, the laws aim at securing the common good, and are not framed according to the delusive caprices and opinions of the mass of the people. (*Immortale Dei*)

That such a doctrine should be condemned is no cause for surprise; for, if it be once conceded that no law can bind the people to which they have not given their consent, only one more step is needed to make the popular will sovereign over Divine as well as human law, by proclaiming that whatever the people (or rather the *majority* thereof) has sanctioned cannot be condemned by comparison with any objective standard.

And is it not this very principle which constitutes the distinguishing mark of electoral democracy as practised in Europe, the U.S.A. and elsewhere – the absolute sovereignty of the majority of the populace expressing its will by poll? Surely it is, for where this tenet is not recognized, it is considered that true democracy does not exist.

On what other basis, for instance, is it possible to explain how British Prime Minister, Mrs. Denis Thatcher, was able to describe the 1982 victory in the Falklands War as "a victory for *democracy*". Evidently she did not mean by those words that the rights of the inhabitants of the Falkland Islands to vote in British parliamentary elections had been vindicated, especially as they have no such right. She meant that a blow had been struck towards the destruction of a régime not elected by a national poll and headed, therefore, by a president answerable not to an abstraction ("the majority of the populace") but to individuals, to the law and to God. In blunt reality the problem was that the president in question had not yet capitulated to the unrestrained depravity of the rabble by authorising the wholesale slaughter of unborn children in the name of popular sovereignty.[51] Mrs.

---

[51] The legalisation of abortion throughout the Western world, beginning with the British 1967 Abortion Act which set the ball rolling, surely shows that the

Thatcher was hailing the downfall of a régime which had not yet surrendered unconditionally to the infallibility and omnipotence of 51% of its subjects over the Ten Commandments.

This species of democracy, which "disregards any criterion other than the popular will expressed at the polls and in parliamentary majorities," is, as the Rev. Dr. Don Felix Sarda y Salvany expresses it, "in the order of ideas ... an absolute error and in the order of facts ... an absolute disorder." (*Le Libéralisme est un Péché*, 1886, pp. 6 and 11; English edition, *What is Liberalism?*, pp. 19 and 27.)

We think that modern democracy has been accurately described and its radical incompatibility with Catholic principles duly shown. It remains to be shown that democracy, even when in full accord with Catholic principles (as it never is today), is nonetheless attended by dangers intrinsic to it and is consequently an inferior form of government.

The principal dangers of democracy – allowing the masses to take part in government – are two.

The first is simply that the masses are the least equipped to make serious judgements on matters calling for knowledge, thoughtfulness, and other qualities by no means universally possessed. Pope Pius XII highlights this danger when he informs us that:

> He who would have the star of peace to shine permanently over society, must ... set his face ... against their [the people's] excessive reliance upon instinct and emotion, and against their fickleness of mood. (1942, Christmas Message)

The second danger, which is derived from the first, is that demagogic manipulation (now a highly developed science) can easily bring the masses to assent to *any* proposition presented to

---

expression of the popular will in a nationwide poll is now taken as sovereign even over the Divine and natural law. If this is so, a system which treats the people as a higher authority than their Creator, is itself a greater evil than any of the individual iniquities perpetrated in its name, being the cause of all of them.

them by the media, etc., in an attractive way. Hence, in his Christmas Message for 1944, Pope Pius XII points out that:

> The masses ... can be used by the state to impose its whims on the better part of the real people.

Indeed it is impossible for a Catholic to deny this, given the clear testimony of Holy Scripture according to which, as the great Cardinal Pie notes,[52] the first attempt at universal suffrage after the Incarnation resulted in the release of Barabbas and the condemnation of Christ.

As to which is the *best* form of government, St. Thomas Aquinas follows Aristotle in teaching that:

> The best form of government is in a state or kingdom wherein *one* is given the power to preside over all, while under him are others having governing powers. (*Summa Theologiæ*, I– II, Q. 105, A. 1)

After St. Thomas, probably the best known Catholic exponent of political theory is another Doctor of the Church, St. Robert Bellarmine, who is often hailed as an early democrat. However, the following is a straightforward statement of St. Robert's position by his biographer Fr. James Broderick S.J.:

> Democracy he considered to be a perfectly legitimate form of government, but he resolutely denied that it was the only or best form. Like his masters, the scholastics, he is a convinced monarchist, and goes out of his way to justify and exalt the monarchical régime. His first argument is based on the agreement of all ancient writers, Hebrew, Greek and Latin. From among them he quotes Philo, Homer, Herodotus, Plato, Isocrates, Aristotle, Plutarch, Seneca, St. Justin, St. Cyprian, St. Jerome and St. Thomas. Then he turns to the Scriptures and makes capital out of the fact that God had not created several heads and fathers of the human race, but only one. The very constitution of nature points in the same direction, he urges:

---

[52] Address delivered on the occasion of the blessing of the Catholic Circle of Parthenay, *Œuvres du Cardinal Pie, tom.* IX, pp. 226-227.

> God has implanted a natural tendency to the monarchical form of government not only in the hearts of men but in practically all things .... In every family the government of mother, sons, servants and everything else, belongs naturally to the father of the family .... Even living things, which are devoid of reason, seem to desire and strive after the rule of one. 'One queen to the bees, one leader to the flock, one ruler to the herd,' says St. Cyprian, and St. Jerome adds that cranes fly wedge-wise after one leader.

The history of the Chosen Race provides another argument: for their government, constituted by God Himself, was always monarchical whether the supreme head was called a patriarch, a judge, or a king. Finally, reason showed the plain advantages of monarchy. (*The Life and Work of Blessed Robert Cardinal Bellarmine S.J.*: Vol. I, p. 230)

And yet, despite the fact that the Church has indicated her full approval of what St. Robert Bellarmine says by giving him the exalted status of Doctor of the Church, she has not been able to say that it is the duty of a society to prescribe for itself a monarchical form of government and to refrain from prescribing for herself a democratic one. How are St. Robert Bellarmine's approved teaching and this last-mentioned fact to be reconciled?

The answer is that the Church cannot say that government according to the rules of God – that is, government dedicated to the promotion of the true interests and true liberty of the individual and the family unit – is impossible under the democratic system. Not only in theory, but, however rarely, in practice too, it *is* possible. For instance, the democratic system of government of fifth century B.C. Athens, although, being pagan, far from perfect, could certainly have been satisfactorily "Christianized" without difficulty; and a modern historical example in which the reign of Christ the King was, though only for a short period, not frustrated by a democratic régime is furnished by Ecuador, under the presidency of Gabriel García Moreno, in the second half of the nineteenth century.[53]

---

[53] It should be noted, however, that Garcia Moreno himself was far from satisfied by the constitution under which he was elected and that his efforts

Moreover, Pope Leo XIII, when stressing the intrinsic acceptability of the democratic form of government, would not even have wanted to bring into the discussion the question of whether other forms of government were preferred to that of democracy, because underestimation of the excellence of monarchical government was the very reverse of the error he was trying to extirpate and the evil he was trying to prevent. The error he was opposing was that democracy in no circumstances could be a permissible form of government and the evil which threatened was the overturning of democratic government, and its replacement with monarchical government, *by means of revolution*. And revolution, rebellion against a legitimate, non-tyrannical government, however undesirable the form of that government may be, is *never* permissible. That genuinely *is* something which is intrinsically evil.

Once this background is in place, it is clear that there is no conflict between the teaching of Pope Leo XIII and that of St. Robert Bellarmine: for having said that democratic government is not intrinsically evil, one has said a very large part of what can be said in favour of it. We are still left with the fact that *all* introductions of it over the last few centuries have been anti-Christian in origin and in effect. *Never* during our era has the purpose of replacing traditional monarchical government, whether with a "constitutional" puppet-monarchy, or a republic, or a democracy, been for the purpose of increasing the liberties and rights in the country concerned of the Catholic Church or of the family or the individual; and *never*, other than for the very briefest of spells, has anything but the opposite happened in practice.[54]

---

on behalf of his country were constantly frustrated under that régime owing to the vulnerability of the masses to manipulation. (See R.P. Auguste Berthe C. SS.R.: *Vie de García Moreno*.)

[54] Not even the emancipation of Catholics in nineteenth century England provides an exception to this generalization; for this was not a gratuitous act, but was granted only subject to the conditions which the enemies of the

No sane person can regard it as desirable that a country be governed by men for the most part quite unfitted for government, exceedingly prone to manipulation, capricious, never vindicated in historical experiment, and from whose decisions no recourse is possible; but that, in its essence, is democracy. Certainly it is false, as we have seen, to represent the Church as having no preference for that form of government by which she is herself governed. Still worse is it to suggest that

---

Church wanted and which they well knew would ultimately do the Church more harm than good – as indeed many Catholics at the time realized, and vociferously pointed out. The reason that the enemies of the Church wanted emancipation in England was so that they could impose on her in England also some equivalent of Gallicanism, Josephism, Americanism or, to use the non-local and most appropriate term for this particular and (in the long term though not always in the short term) very deadly form of attack on the Church, Cæsarism; that is, put her most important areas of influence – such as education, the most crucial one of all – *under the control of the civil government*. And effective Cæsarism, further and further tightened up by subsequent legislation, was exactly what was achieved by Catholic emancipation in nineteenth century England. Nor, incidentally, should it be thought that democracy is in any sense immune to the vice of Cæsarism. What is implied by Cæsarism is possible under *any* form of government, as Cardinal Manning shows very clearly in this excellent passage from his *Cæsarism and Ultramontanism* (pp. 19, 20):

The sovereignty of Cæsarism is absolute and dependent on no conditions; it is also exclusive, because it does not tolerate any jurisdiction above and within its own. It does not recognize any laws except of its own making.

Now this supreme power need not be held in the hand of one man. It may be a People or a Senate, or a King or an Emperor. Its essence is the claim to absolute and exclusive sovereignty. It by necessity excludes God, His sovereignty and His laws. The sole fountain of law is the human will, individual or collective. Cæsar finds the law in himself, and creates right and wrong, the just and the unjust, the sacred and the profane. He has no Statute-book but human nature, and he is the sole and supreme interpreter and expositor of that natural law. Therefore law, morals, politics and religion all come from him, and all depend upon him. The Sovereign Prince or State legislates, judges, executes by its own will and hand. This sovereign power creates everything; it fashions the political constitution; it delegates jurisdiction, revocable at its word; it suspends or measures out personal liberty; it controls domestic life; it claims the children as its own; it educates them at its will, and after models and theories of its own device.

democracy, as practised in the "civilized" world today, could be regarded by the Church as anything but a diabolical tyranny in conflict with natural and Divine law.

Religious Liberty Again

Returning to the pamphlet *Archbishop Lefebvre and Religious Liberty*, a further clear error occurs on. This time Davies writes:

> To sum up, the consensus of papal teaching is that a Catholic state has the right but not the obligation to restrict the public expression of heresy.

Is that clear? Although the state has the *right* to restrict the public expression of heresy, it does not have an *obligation* to do this. If this is so, how is it to be reconciled with the fact that Pope Pius IX's *Syllabus of Errors* (Proposition 78) condemns the assertion that "it was praiseworthily determined that in certain regions known to be Catholic, immigrants were entitled each to the public exercise of their own religion?" If the state has no *obligation* to restrict the public expression of heresy, how is it that Pope Pius IX has commanded all Catholics to *reject* the view that a particular state acted correctly in failing to restrict the public expression of heresy within its confines?

Indeed, on the very next page of his pamphlet Davies quotes from the same pope's *Quanta Cura* (1864) the condemnation of those who, "contrary to the teaching of Holy Scripture and the Fathers, deliberately affirm that the best form of government is that in which no *obligation* is recognized in the civil power to punish ... the violators of the Catholic religion ...." Thus, the pope on the one hand teaches that there is an *obligation* to punish the violators of the Catholic religion (i.e. not only *violent persecutors* of the Church, but also those who attempt by the spoken or written word to subvert Catholics), while Davies on the other hand assures us that no such obligation exists. The truth is that the state *has indeed* an *obligation*, *per se*, to restrict the public expression of heresy, but that this obligation sometimes ceases to bind when complying with it would be liable to bring about worse evils, or because a greater good can be achieved by tolerating the public expression of heresy in particular circumstances as a provisional measure.

CHAPTER SIX
MISCELLANEOUS DOCTRINAL ERRORS

"Doctrine to a fool is as fetters on the feet, and like manacles on the right hand." (Ecclesiasticus 21:22)

I have endeavoured as far as possible in this *Evaluation* to divide the objectionable features of Davies's writings into orderly categories and to consider each category separately. There were, however, a large number of errors against the Catholic Faith, sometimes even deserving the qualification "heretical" in the strict sense, which did not fit readily into any of the obvious specific categories which comprise the subjects of the other chapters of this *Evaluation*, and I have therefore decided to assemble some of them in a single chapter. Here I propose to analyse these errors more or less at random and without undertaking the more detailed kind of treatment which the collective examination of many inter-related errors, inevitably calls for.

In one respect this chapter will be less valuable than the others, in that it will not present the correct doctrines except to the minimum extent necessary to refute Davies's errors. But in another respect it may prove just as useful inasmuch as, by exposing Davies's unreliability – to use no stronger word – on a wide range of topics, it will serve to demonstrate that on no topic whatsoever can Davies be trusted.

Of these errors, some, doubtless, arise from carelessness and inadvertence; some, quite evidently, from plain ignorance and lack of due study; some from a misplaced reliance on other

Catholic writers with undeserved reputations; and some, very regrettably but demonstrably nevertheless, from a conscious, or at least half-conscious and certainly blameworthy, twisting of facts, suppression of truth and misrepresentation of the Church herself. What the cause of each particular error is, there is in fact no purpose in spending any time trying to identify, because, tragically, the *effect* of an error remains the same whatever the cause; and even if all of the errors had been made in good faith, they would constitute a scarcely less formidable indictment of their author than if they had been perpetrated as a result of demonstrable malice. In one who takes upon himself the awesome responsibility of writing Catholic polemics such ignorance is crass indeed, at least in the popular sense and as a rule in the theological sense. [1]

---

[1] When a person commits a sin which is in itself exceedingly grave but which he does not realise to be so when he does it, the imputability of the sin will depend upon the kind of ignorance under which he is labouring. If he could not possibly have known that his action was wrong, his ignorance is termed "invincible" and the sin is not imputed at all. If his ignorance arose because he was *slightly* careless in ascertaining the necessary moral theology before acting, it is called "light" ignorance and he will be held guilty of venial, but not mortal, sin. If he genuinely endeavoured to work out what he ought to have done in the circumstances but was gravely negligent in these efforts, his ignorance is termed "grave" and the sin will be imputed as mortal, though by no means as grave a mortal sin as if it had been done in full consciousness of its unlawfulness. Next, if his only efforts to find out the necessary facts were so pathetic and negligent – in proportion to the evident gravity of the question – that they could not have been expected to be sufficient, his ignorance will be called "crass" or "supine": in this case the ignorance will scarcely palliate the intrinsic gravity of the crime at all, and the sin will be imputed almost as if it had been done in full consciousness. Finally, for the sake of completeness, the one remaining species of ignorance should be mentioned, namely "affected" ignorance which is verified when a person deliberately avoids any effort whatsoever to find out whether his intended action is lawful or not lest by discovering that it is *un*lawful he be prevented from doing it. This kind of ignorance, which adds the malice of hypocrisy to the crime, actually makes the person guiltier than if he had committed the crime in full knowledge of its sinfulness.

These species of ignorance are considered by canonists in their treatments of

Moreover I and many others have drawn Michael Davies's attention to some of his grosser errors, and if he has ever publicly corrected a single one I have never noticed it. This is why the present forthright denunciation has become necessary.

The "Catholic Duty" to "Oppose Papal Teaching"!

On p. 417 of Vol. I of his *Apologia Pro Marcel Lefebvre*, Davies writes that "a Catholic has the right and sometimes the duty to oppose papal teaching or legislation which is manifestly unjust, contrary to the Faith, or harmful to the Church."

In Chapter 8 of this *Evaluation*, which concerns Davies's contempt for the law, it will be shown that the assertion that a pope can pass legislation (as opposed to private commands) which is contrary to the Faith or harmful to the Church is emphatically denied by all Catholic theologians who treat of the subject, their unanimous teaching being that in promulgating laws the pope is protected from offending against Faith or the good of souls. Now admittedly that particular error might be excusable in, say, a schoolboy whose religious education did not extend beyond the last question of the *Penny Catechism*, and who – thank God – would not be flooding the world with polemical works purporting to defend the Catholic religion; but surely the suggestion that a Catholic can sometimes have the duty to *oppose* papal *teaching* and that such teaching is liable, on occasion, to be "contrary to the Faith", would be recognized as an undisguised heresy even by children who had scarcely passed the age of reason if they had received the bare minimum of Catholic instruction!

What is more fundamental or well known among the doctrines of the Church than that the teaching of the pope is protected from error by the Holy Ghost? To Catholics the words "papal teaching" can mean nothing except doctrinal instruction given

---

Canon 229, by moralists in their considerations of human acts (cf. Noldin-Schmitt, *Summa Theologiæ Moralis*, Vol. I, n. 49), and by St. Thomas: *Summa Theologiæ* I-II, Q. 76.

by the pope in the exercise of his office, for they certainly do not embrace private commands, legislation or the expression, even on theological matters, of the personal opinions of a pope. And doctrinal instruction publicly given by the pope in the exercise of his office is *exactly* what every Catholic, even the most minimally instructed, knows to be immune from error. Moreover readers will scarcely need to be reminded that what even the most minimally instructed Catholic knows, in turn, about inerrant Catholic doctrine is that anyone who "opposes" it or claims that it is "contrary to the Faith", far from being an orthodox Catholic fulfilling an acknowledged "Catholic duty", is either already a heretic or is one on his way to becoming one.[2]

Of course, it is true that not all of the teaching of a pope is uttered in the exercise of the Extraordinary Magisterium, but the fact remains *that the papal Ordinary Magisterium is also protected from error* and most specifically from *previously condemned* error. The pope, when instructing the members of the Church as to what they should believe on points of Catholic doctrine, is not permitted by the Holy Ghost to lead them into harmful error. In case any readers have been so infected by Davies's pernicious influence as to doubt this, here, once again, is what Pope Pius XII wrote on the subject in his encyclical *Humani Generis*:

> Nor must it be thought that what is expounded in encyclical Letters does not of itself demand consent, on the grounds that, in writing such Letters, the popes do not exercise the supreme power of their Teaching Authority. For these matters are taught with *the ordinary teaching authority, of which it is true to say: 'he who heareth you, heareth Me'*.

---

[2] It would not necessarily be heretical to *deny* a doctrine authoritatively taught by the pope unless it were taught *as Divinely revealed*, but to "oppose" such teaching would implicitly deny the pope's undoubted right to teach and claim our submission in the whole field of doctrine and using whatever medium he may choose to communicate his teaching to the faithful.

In his classic study *The Ordinary Magisterium of the Church Theologically Considered*, which has already been referred to several times, Dom Paul Nau writes:

> The Ordinary Magisterium, like the solemn judgement, equally demands belief in the doctrine put forward. Therefore they both convey assurance against error. If this certainty were lacking, in effect no one would be bound to give it his loyal assent, that is to say, to adhere to it on the authority of the supreme truth.

Moreover, as long ago as 1682, nearly two centuries before the definition of the infallibility of the Extraordinary Papal Magisterium, the Faculty of the University of Paris gave a warning which shows that, even prescinding from the theological facts, Davies's attitude is not Catholic in terms of elementary courtesy and reverence: "Whatever opinion one may profess on the infallibility of the pope, it is just as disrespectful to proclaim publicly that he can be wrong as to say to children: 'Your parents may be lying to you.'" The same point is made by Dr. W.G. Ward (*Dublin Review*, October 1878) in the following terms:

> All Catholics are of one accord in believing that the Roman Pontiff should be listened to with obedience when, alone or with his particular council, he settles anything in doubtful matters, no matter whether, in the case, it is or is not possible for him to err. This doctrine of obedience, or intellectual submission, requires the authority of no theologian or of any host of theologians to defend it and prove its truth. Its influence permeates the whole framework of the Church; it rules her outward action, is the living bond of her social life; and it holds uncontrolled sway over her interior unseen actions, over the mighty tide of supernatural life that ebbs and flows within her vast ocean-like soul.

Revision of Papal Teaching

On p. 284 of *Pope Paul's New Mass*, Davies again broaches the topic of papal infallibility – this time during a discussion of Paul VI's famous retraction of the heretical article 7 of the

General Instruction on the Roman Missal. Many readers will no doubt be familiar with the circumstances surrounding the event, but for the benefit of those who are not, the facts may be summarized by saying that the *General Instruction* which served as an introduction and rubrical guide to the Novus Ordo Missæ, included in its seventh article a definition of the Mass which, by its pointed failure to mention the sacrificial aspect of the ceremony, or the essential role of the priest, was clearly heretical. What was unusual about this particular heresy, however, among the myriads promulgated in the Conciliar Church, was that the rank-and-file laity at that time still retained sufficient vestige of Catholicity to recognize it as such and sufficient gumption to protest, though – alas! – few enough drew the appropriate conclusions concerning the status of the usurper who had been responsible for it. At any rate, the protest was vociferous enough to ensure the prompt appearance of a second edition of the *General Instruction*, in which the seventh article had been revised to bring it more into line with Catholic doctrine.

This retraction is of course without parallel, and is of the utmost significance in that it constitutes the sole instance of recognition by the highest authorities of the Conciliar Church of their own heterodoxy.

After relating the facts summarized above, Davies makes the following observation on the episode:

> What precedent is there in modern times for a pope having to revise even his personal teaching in response to a charge of unorthodoxy (as did Pope John XXII) let alone officially promulgated doctrinal teaching?

Typically, while appearing to protest at Montini's behaviour and to contrast it unfavourably with Catholic praxis, Davies is subtly undermining the case which he ought to be defending. To see how this is so, it is enough to contrast with Davies's observation the conclusions which a solidly *Catholic* writer would have drawn from the same facts. The latter would have spotted at once that the key point to be made is that retraction of his officially promulgated doctrinal teaching by a true Roman pontiff is not only something entirely unknown to history, but something which Catholic theology teaches to be *impossible*.[3] The next step of the argument – that Montini could not, therefore, have been a true Roman pontiff – is obvious.

But Davies is *not* a solidly Catholic writer, and far from saying this, or anything like this, he goes out of his way to concede the key point to those who would want to defend the Conciliar Church.

He does this by asking "What precedent is there *in modern times* for a pope having to revise his teaching ...?", a question which implies that it is only *in modern times* that popes have been accustomed to adhere to their original doctrines rather than to revise them *ad lib*. If Davies had been prepared to enquire what precedent can be found *in the whole of the Church's history* for a pope revising his officially promulgated teaching, the question would have had a point, but even then it would have been *weak* because few readers would want to wade through the histories of the Church to answer it. Most telling – and completely correct – would have been simply to state the fact that there is *no* such precedent. As it is, his question is the

---

[3] Thus in his encyclical *Immortale Dei* Pope Leo XIII writes:
   Whatever the Roman pontiffs have hitherto taught, or shall hereafter teach, must be held with a firm grasp of mind, and as often as the occasion requires, must be openly professed.

Needless to say, the duty of believing and professing whatever the popes have taught also binds subsequent popes, and for one pope to retract the teaching of a previous pope would amount to a public declaration that the Magisterium had erred. And for the infallible Vicar of Jesus Christ to declare that either he himself or some previous infallible Vicar of Jesus Christ had taught error which had to be corrected would be contrary to the nature of the papal Magisterium. It is important that it be appreciated that the principle applies to teachings of popes in the Ordinary Magisterium as well as to the Extraordinary Magisterium. This is clear enough from these words of Pope Leo XIII, but it has also been extensively demonstrated in Chapter 5, pages 221 *et seq*.

soggiest of damp squibs, for if Montini's heterodoxy has parallels in the earlier centuries and looks odd to us simply because "in modern times" popes have developed a custom of not tampering with previous pronouncements of the Magisterium, it is evidently not much to be concerned about. And, of course, if Davies is right in implying that early Catholic history might conceivably be peppered with cases of doctrinal revision by those accepted to have been legitimate popes, no question-mark can possibly hang over Montini's legitimacy by virtue of his having done nothing worse than to revert from the high standards of his immediate "predecessors" to the lower standards of earlier popes.

Hence I would summarize Davies's offence by saying that, when he could easily have demonstrated that Paul VI had violated the Catholic Faith in a way that no true pope ever had (and, by virtue of his public retraction, had even tacitly admitted to having done so), he not only failed to hint at the real extent and significance of what had taken place, but gratuitously implied that "other" (i.e. genuine) popes had been guilty of identical behaviour. In other words, when he should have seized the opportunity to attack Montini without mercy and to strip the sheep's clothing from him, exposing him for what he was (and more particularly for what he was *not*), instead he rounded on the popes of earlier centuries, most of them illustrious for sanctity, and shamelessly directed his fire at them, besmirching their well-deserved reputations for doctrinal orthodoxy, and thereby flying in the face of history and of theology. Nor should we minimize the extent of the theological implications of Davies's words; for if Catholic theology could admit that popes had occasionally erred in their doctrinal teaching and had to correct it in the light of protests elicited by their errors, it is evident to everyone that the duty incumbent on all Catholics of unconditional assent to papal teaching would be a duty to assent to propositions that only *might* be true but also might quite possibly be heretical: a duty under which any correctly formed conscience would justifiably find it difficult to rest easy.

While reading the foregoing criticisms the reader may himself have begun to feel uneasy; for at first glance it looks as though an instance of a pope who provided a precedent for Montini's volte-face on the Mass by teaching error and subsequently recanting it – John XXII (1316-34) – has actually been cited by Davies.

And it must immediately be pointed out that this is in appearance only, for even Davies himself is not suggesting that John XXII did what Montini did. He is stating that John XXII did something much less spectacular than what Montini did, and that even John XXII's offence has no parallel "in modern times", let alone Montini's.

But even this aspect of Davies's sentence is unsatisfactory; for the structural obscurity is not the sentence's only defective feature, nor indeed its *most* defective feature. Much worse is its nebulous language, and this, I fear, is *not* an innocent mistake, for it occurs all too frequently when Davies is trying to mislead his readers.

I am referring to the words "personal teaching".

Now it is impossible to *deny* that Pope John XXII revised his "personal teaching", because in *one* possible sense of those words he did just that. But any Catholic must be loath to concede the truth of such an allegation in words which admit more than one meaning, because it would inevitably be taken to mean something quite different from what actually occurred – a fact of which Davies cannot be unaware. So let us abandon Davies's woolly terminology altogether, and describe in plain English what really happened.

The facts are that this pope, in writings published before his election as pope, and in at least one *privately-delivered sermon* after his election, had expressed the view that the souls of the just do not see God until after the General Judgement. *At no stage did he represent this as a teaching of the Church or himself purport to teach it to the Church.* He put it forward as his private belief, and the subject was one on which the Church had not up to that time defined. When his support for this opinion – which, it is perhaps not irrelevant to note, he shared with a number of other theologians – gave rise to considerable disturbances, he appointed theological commissions to examine the matter, and before his death professed himself satisfied that his opinion had been erroneous.

So at no stage did the pope deliver a doctrinal judgement in support of his error nor come near to addressing that error to the Catholic faithful even as an exercise of the Ordinary Magisterium; and *not even in the expression of his personal opinion* did he contradict any doctrine which had been defined up to that point. (The doctrine under dispute was in fact defined by his immediate successor.)

And the final point to be made under this heading is that not only did Pope John XXII not abuse papal teaching authority in any of these ways; but – if Catholic doctrine is to be believed – neither he nor any other pope *could* have done so.

In the light of this clarification, readers will see why I objected to Davies's term "personal teaching" as misleading.

Thus, in summary, far from being an attack on Montini and a defence of Catholic doctrine, Davies's commentary on the revision of article 7 of the *General Instruction undermines* Catholic doctrine, lets Montini entirely off the hook, and instead gratuitously attacks a *true* pope for a crime of which he was not guilty.

Infallibility of the Ordinary Magisterium

Davies falls into another error on the authority of the Ordinary Magisterium on p. 213 of *Pope John's Council*, quoting, with unqualified approval, the following extract from Archbishop Lefebvre's book *A Bishop Speaks* (p. 170 of the French edition):

> What is the criterion to judge whether the Ordinary Magisterium is infallible or not? It is fidelity to the whole of tradition. In the event

of its not conforming to tradition we are not even bound to submit to the decrees of the Holy Father himself.

The second sentence here is not true. As is made clear in Dom Paul Nau's 1956 study quoted earlier, there are in fact *three* criteria for discerning the weight of authority behind a particular exercise of the papal Ordinary Magisterium and, in particular, for distinguishing those exercises of it which are truly infallible from those which are not. On p. 20 of *The Ordinary Magisterium of the Church Theologically Considered*, Dom Nau writes:

> As the Ordinary Magisterium is made up of a whole complex of expressions of unequal authority, its use in terms of theology supposes the existence of criteria allowing us to distinguish the relative value of each of these expressions. These criteria can apparently be reduced to three:
> - the will of the sovereign pontiff to commit his authority behind the enunciation of a doctrine;
> - the impact, more or less extended, of his teaching on the Church;
> - the continuity and coherence of the various affirmations.

Archbishop Lefebvre, followed by Davies, chooses only one of these three relevant criteria. And even that criterion he then distorts and misapplies. To show that this is so, let us spell out in full what Catholic doctrine concedes with regard to papal pronouncements that do *not* fulfil Dom Paul's requirements.

Briefly, a decree of a pope which (a) was relatively limited in its extent and effect on the Church, (b) manifested no intention to teach definitively, and (c) expressed a theological judgement which had not previously been taught by the popes, would indeed not be infallible, and thus far Archbishop Lefebvre is right. But this is a far cry from suggesting that even such a decree could teach *doctrinal error in actual contradiction to the voice of tradition*. It is one thing not to be infallible, but it is quite another to fall into error that is contrary to Catholic doctrine as authentically conveyed by sacred tradition; and these two things Archbishop Lefebvre, followed by Davies, confounds. In other words, the fact that not all papal teachings are of equal authority and bind the consciences of the faithful in the same way, is being twisted to make it appear that some teachings of the pope may actually contradict Catholic doctrine. If this were so, it would mean that Catholics, who in reality at the very least are obliged to show a respectful silence to *every* papal teaching[4] on religious matters, might actually be bound in conscience to *reject* and *denounce* the teaching of the pope! At this juncture it seems fitting to draw to the attention of readers that Davies maintains that if the Holy See were vacant it would mean "that the Divine promises of Our Lord had failed!"[5] Not only is this not so, as was shown in Chapter 3, but the theory on which Davies relies to defend John-Paul II's legitimacy suffers from the very weakness he wrongly charges "sedevacantists" with; for if Catholics were obliged to condemn and denounce the teachings of the legitimate successors of St. Peter on faith and morals, Our Lord's promise that "he who heareth you, heareth Me" (Luke 10:16) would indeed have failed.

An Exorbitant Demand

Another remarkable error on the same subject occurs on pages 169-70 of *Apologia Pro Marcel Lefebvre*, Vol. I. First of all, Davies quotes a letter written by Archbishop Benelli on 21st April 1976 to Archbishop Lefebvre in which the former demands from the latter a letter affirming his "full attachment to the person of His Holiness Pope Paul VI and to the totality of his teaching ...";[6] then Davies comments:

---

[4] And, except where the pope makes it plain that his teaching is not authoritative, almost invariably true internal assent as well as respectful silence is obligatory.

[5] See Davies's article *The Sedevacantists* in *The Remnant*, 15th June 1982, cited in Chapter 3 of this *Evaluation*.

[6] Letter of 9th June 1873. The full text in Latin and French is cited by Mgr. Gaston de Ségur in his *Les Francs-Maçons: Ce qu'ils sont - Ce qu'ils font - Ce qu'ils veulent.*

A pope who thus wishes to impose a *full* attachment to the *totality* of his *own* teaching – that makes a double[7] difficulty .... As is known, or should be known, the totality of the teaching of a Pope (especially of a modern Pope, speaking much and often) does not involve papal authority in the same degree in all its parts; it can often happen that the authority is not involved at all, when he speaks as a private doctor. *Full* attachment to the *totality* of the teaching is an exorbitant demand; it is a form of unconditional submission.

The words emphasized by Davies indicate that he would find it, perhaps, acceptable if Archbishop Lefebvre had been asked to show only *partial* assent to the totality of Montini's teaching, or that he would prefer it if he had been asked to show *full* assent to a *part* of his teaching, or at least that he would find one of these alternatives acceptable. But what he does *not* find acceptable, his words indicate no less clearly, is that a pope should demand *full* attachment to the *totality* of his teaching. Perish such an extravagant thought on the part of a pope! Indeed Davies goes further and emphasizes the fact that the assent was demanded to the totality of *his own* (i.e. Montini's) teaching, as though it would have been more acceptable if Archbishop Lefebvre had been asked to assent to the totality of someone else's teaching.

The fact is, however, that, notwithstanding Davies's objections, had Montini been a true pope, as Archbishop Lefebvre and Davies both believed him to be, the request would have been a perfectly reasonable one. In fact it is not very far different from what had been said by true popes about their teaching. Pope Pius IX, for instance, indicated the correct Catholic attitude to be one of "entire and absolute submission to the Holy See" and that sound Catholics "do not ... diverge in any way from its doctrine and its teaching." (Letter to the Bishop of

---

[7] The second "difficulty" which Davies refers to after the words quoted is, he says, that Montini requires assent to his own teaching "by itself" without reference to the teachings of his "predecessors".

Quimper, 28th July 1873) And a month earlier, writing to the Viscount de Morogues, he had called for "a perfect adhesion to the spirit and doctrines of this Chair of Peter." To the extent that there is any significance between these demands and that which Montini (through Benelli) addressed to Archbishop Lefebvre, it lies only in the fact that Pope Pius IX was much *more* demanding, calling, as he did, for adhesion, not only to his own teaching, but also to that of all other popes – and adhesion, come to that, not only to their teaching but even to their "spirit".

While, therefore, it is, of course, perfectly legitimate and indeed a duty to refuse adherence to Montini's teaching on the grounds that he was not a pope and that his teaching was very often *false*, it is quite unjustified for those who, like Davies and Archbishop Lefebvre, acknowledged him as a true pope, to protest at his demanding from them the adherence which is in fact due to every pope and which the popes have traditionally insisted on from their subjects.

Finally, it is certainly impossible to accept Davies's objection that the word "teaching" is too general because some papal teaching is not authoritative. Not only is "teaching" the very word that Pope Pius IX used, but *all* papal teaching – if the term be properly understood – demands our adhesion. Evidently when reference is made to the "teaching" of a pope in such a context, this is not intended to include opinions expressed by him as a private theologian or statements on matters of natural fact (history or science, for instance) with no direct connection with the Faith, and this is taken for granted. Hence, any Catholic who was told that he must accept the totality of the teaching of a pope would reasonably understand this to mean the doctrines taught by the pope in his authoritative documents and pronouncements.[8] And since such authoritative pronouncements will never contradict the Faith and are uttered by the voice of

---

[8] Thus Pope Pius IX demanded, without any qualification, that the minds of Catholics be penetrated "with all that the Holy See has *taught* against certain culpable doctrines." – Letter to the editors of *La Croix*, 21st May 1874.

him to whom Our Lord said, "He who heareth you, heareth Me," (Luke 10:16) the demand is certainly not exorbitant. Indeed it is a simple statement of Catholic doctrine so well known that very likely the first intimation of the authority of the Church given to a child at the age of three or four years would be the parents' explanation that "we have to believe everything that the pope teaches."

It is almost as though Davies wanted to display not only as many *errors* as possible against Catholic doctrine, but as many *species* of error against as well. On this occasion he seizes the opportunity provided by one of the rare occasions when a representative of the Conciliar Church actually made a statement compatible with Catholic doctrine to go out of his way to brand it as presenting "a double difficulty" and as representing "an exorbitant demand." As to his plaintive protest, "it is a form of unconditional submission," one can only say, yes, Mr. Davies, it *is* a form of unconditional submission; exactly the same form which Pope Pius IX demanded by the words "entire and absolute submission to the Holy See." Unconditional submission is *exactly* what is required of every Catholic, and it is something with which you ought to have come to terms before seeking admission to the Church.

In view of Davies's denial that Catholics are bound to accept the totality of papal teaching and his assertion that Catholics are not bound to submit to papal decrees if they are not in conformity with tradition, one naturally infers that he shows proportionately less respect still for the decrees of the Sacred Congregations in Rome – which would mean, if I correctly assess his respect for the pontifical Ordinary Magisterium as little more than lip-service, that he would probably pay more attention to Dietrich von Hildebrand than to the Holy Office. In this connection it seems appropriate to draw attention to the following papal expositions of Catholic doctrine on the submission owed to such lesser authorities. Readers may be surprised to learn that in fact the assent owed to Roman

Congregations is higher than the assent which Davies claims is owed to the pope himself!

Here is the teaching of Pope Pius IX in *Tuas Libenter* (1863):

> ... it is not sufficient for learned Catholics to accept and revere the ... dogmas of the Church, but ... it is also necessary that they subject themselves to the decisions pertaining to doctrine which are issued by the Pontifical Congregations .... (Denzinger 1864)

And this is the same doctrine expressed by Pope St. Pius X in *Præstantia Scripturæ* (1907):

> We declare and expressly command that all men without exception are bound in conscience to submit themselves to the judgements of the Pontifical Biblical Commission ... and also to the decrees of the Sacred Congregations pertaining to doctrine and approved by the pontiff. Nor can those who impugn these decisions in word or in writing escape the charge of disobedience and temerity and on this account be free of grave sin. (Denzinger 2113)

And Davies, despite the foregoing, is so anxious to accept Vatican II as a valid, Catholic Council that he tells us unblushingly that Catholics are free, without incurring any guilt, to reject the doctrinal teaching of an Ecumenical Council!

The True Author of Catholic Dogma

In his article entitled *Further Reflections on the New Ordination Rite*, which appeared in *The Roman Catholic*[9] in 1981, Davies commits a serious error on the subject of the authority of the Magisterium. In the course of a discussion on infallibility, he wrote: "But in no sense is God the author of dogmatic pronouncements ...." He was not denying that dogmatic pronouncements are necessarily true, which indeed he explicitly accepted; but he was indubitably asserting that such pronouncements, being drawn up by men, are *exclusively* the work of men, and it is here that what he says is misleading. His

---

[9] To their credit, the editors of this periodical pointed this error out to their readers.

error does not lie in the inference that dogmatic decrees are truly the personal work of the pope responsible for drafting them and are not as a rule directly inspired by the Holy Ghost as is the case with the books of Holy Scripture. That much is true. But what is quite unacceptable is to say that God is *"in no sense"* the author of such decrees, for this amounts to an implicit denial that God is even *indirectly* their author by virtue of His having revealed the contents of them. This is unacceptable because dogmatic decrees invariably treat of or relate to Divinely revealed teachings on the subjects of faith and morals. What the pope teaches will simply be a reiteration of what has always been believed by the Church, having been passed down by the Apostles who first heard the doctrines in question from the Divine lips of Our Blessed Lord. And in *that* sense, which is undoubtedly a *real* sense, God most certainly *is* the author of the contents of dogmatic decrees, for it was He who revealed the contents of the deposit of revelation in the elaboration of which, alone, is the pope enabled to pronounce infallibly.[10] This is made clear in the following extract from the decree *Pastor Æternus* of the 1870 Vatican Council:

> For the Holy Spirit was not promised to the successors of Peter that by His revelation they might disclose new doctrine, but that by His help they might guard sacredly and faithfully set forth the revelation transmitted through the Apostles or deposit of faith. (Dz. 1836)

Davies as an Indifferentist

A letter by Davies was published in the correspondence columns of *The Tablet*[11] on 9th November 1985. He was

---

[10] As just mentioned, a pope certainly *can* teach infallibly on matters which are not directly revealed by God; but in such cases his teaching will still amount to an elaboration of matters directly revealed, since he will be applying the Divinely revealed doctrines to particular situations later arising.

[11] *The Tablet* is the "highbrow" English Conciliar "Catholic" weekly. It is renowned as *extremely* "progressive" and has published nothing remotely resembling Catholic doctrine since the late Mr. Douglas Woodruff (1897-

protesting at certain inaccuracies in a report of Archbishop Lefebvre's latest visit to England which had appeared in the previous week's issue. His letter contained the following paragraph:

> The alleged anti-semitism in the archbishop's lecture is equally non-existent. His criticisms were not directed against the Jews as such, but against the Vatican for what he considers is the indifferentism pervading a recent document on Catholic-Jewish relations. I have not yet read the document, and so I cannot say whether the archbishop's criticisms are justified or not. If they are not he could be criticised for making an accusation which he cannot substantiate, but this is a far cry from accusing him of anti-semitism. I consider that the documents of the Anglican-Roman Catholic International Commission manifest an attitude of indifferentism, but I am by no means anti-Protestant.

Yes, he really wrote it: "I am by no means anti-Protestant."

On one of the rare occasions when the Modernist "mafia" permitted the publication in one of their official organs of a letter hostile to their position, the letter in question is vitiated by a statement just as redolent of indifferentism as many of those to be found in the documents on "Catholic-Jewish relations" or in the A.R.C.I.C. reports! The statement is clear and unequivocal: Michael Davies is not opposed to Protestants. Is he then quite content for men to spurn the true Church of Christ and set up in His name a host of false religions, perverting the Gospel and leading others to eternal perdition? Is he not then opposed to heresy and blasphemy? Do insults to the dignity of the Mother of God leave him unmoved?

Nor is it possible to object that Mr. Davies means no more than that he is not hostile to Protestants considered *as individuals*. The only reasonable interpretation that his words can bear is that he is not hostile to Protestants *as Protestants*. In

---

1978) resigned from the editorship in 1967. Its circulation is now a pitiful 10,000 and production is made possible only by extensive subsidies from Lord Forte, who is a director, and others.

other words, he is not hostile to Protestantism. In the first place, this is what is commonly understood by being "anti-" a particular group. For instance, no one ever supposed that Mgr. Jouin, with his Anti-Judeo-Masonic League wished ill to Jews and Masons *as individuals* – on the contrary, he ardently desired their conversion. His hostility was in respect of their affiliation to the evils of Judaism and Freemasonry. But the title of his league avowed that he *was* anti-Judeo-Masons as such.

Secondly, if Davies meant that he is anti-Protestant*ism*, although having no personal animosity towards individual "separated brethren", he is sufficiently literate to make his meaning clear, and sufficiently intelligent to recognize the impression which his words would obviously give, especially to a readership almost exclusively inebriated with the wonders of ecumenism.

If anyone is still inclined to put a favourable construction on Davies's words, let him ask himself in all honesty whether Davies would have been prepared to write in one of his articles, without a word of qualification: "I am by no means anti-Sedevacantist."

An Insult to Our Blessed Lady

The following passage occurs on p. 128 of *Pope John's Council*:

> There had been legitimate differences of opinion among Catholic theologians before the Council, not on the fact that Mary had co-operated with Our Lord, but on the nature and extent of that co-operation. An important school of thought, favoured by Pope Pius XII, had come to see Our Lady as co-operating in the acquisition of our salvation and wished to see the Magisterium define her as Co-Redemptrix and Mediatrix of all graces. Another school favoured an approach emphasizing her position as a member of the Church like ourselves, differing from us not in the essence but in the degree of her perfection.

Note that Davies represents the doctrines of Our Lady's Co-Redemptrix-ship and Mediatrix-ship of all graces as no more than the opinions of a school, and considers the opinions of those who deny these doctrines, and who think the Mother of God to be no more than "a member of the Church like ourselves" (though holier) to be legitimate. It would be possible to fill many pages with the clear testimonies of the Fathers, Doctors, saints and popes refuting this and showing that the opinion minimising Our Blessed Lady's special privileges and denying her the titles of Mediatrix of all graces and Co-Redemptrix of the human race are very far from legitimate, but let us be content with the mere minimum citation of authorities necessary conclusively to vindicate Our Blessed Lady's unassailable right to these titles.

As to Our Lady's being Mediatrix of all graces, this truth was officially recognized by Popes Pius IX, Leo XIII, St. Pius X, Pius XI and Pius XII. The Church has approved a feast and special Mass of Mary, Mediatrix of all Graces, and in consequence the eminent and learned Mariologist Canon Gregorio Alastruey explains that "Mary is truly mediatrix of the human race *and this doctrine pertains to the deposit of faith*". (*The Blessed Virgin Mary*, Vol. 2, p. 133, emphasis added)

Although there is no feast in honour of Our Lady as Co-Redemptrix, Pope St. Pius X explained this doctrine and taught it as quite certain (*not* the opinion of a school) at considerable length in his encyclical *Ad Diem Illum*. The doctrine and title have also been approved by at least three other popes and by three decrees of the Sacred Congregation. Canon Alastruey affirmed in 1952 that "it is safe to say that theologians throughout the world now *unanimously* accept the title of co-redemptrix as properly belonging to Mary." (*op. cit.*, Vol. II, p. 142, emphasis added)

CHAPTER SEVEN
THE SOCIETY OF ST. PIUS X

"He that entereth not by the door into the sheepfold, but climbeth up another way, the same is a thief and robber." (John 10:1)

Was the Society of St. Pius X Canonically Erected and Does it Have the Right to Confer Holy Orders on those not Incardinated into Particular Dioceses?

A considerable proportion of Vol. I of *Apologia Pro Marcel Lefebvre* is taken up with consideration of the legal status of Archbishop Lefebvre's "Society of St. Pius X" and in attempting to provide answers to such questions as the following:

(i) Was the Society canonically erected in the first place?
(ii) Was it canonically suppressed by Rome?
(iii) Did it, and does it, have the right to ordain priests who are not incardinated into (i.e. registered as belonging to) a particular diocese?

Readers will by now probably not be wholly surprised to learn that Davies's treatment of the subject is slovenly and contains a number of clear errors and several instances of the suppression of obviously pertinent facts.

In order to expose these errors it will be necessary to:

(i) summarize the principles of Canon Law involved; then
(ii) state Davies's case for defending the lawfulness of the erection and practices of the Society; finally
(iii) show why certain aspects of both the facts and the laws involved, to which Davies makes no reference, demonstrate that the canonical basis for the erection of the Society is

extremely shaky and that its practice of Ordination without incardination has no canonical foundation whatsoever.

Given that the Society of St. Pius X was erected was 1970 it is clear that, to the extent that the Society has any legal existence whatever, it is as an institution within the *Conciliar* Church. But the object of this examination, is to demonstrate that, *even if* Davies and Archbishop Lefebvre were right in believing the Holy See to be occupied, it would *still* be impossible to maintain that the erection and conduct of the Society have been in conformity with Canon Law. In other words, the fact that the Society of St. Pius X has no legal status does not depend on the answer given to the questions hanging over the status of recent purported occupants of the Holy See – crucial and far-reaching in its effects though this issue is – but also follows from facts which cannot be denied even within Davies's and Archbishop Lefebvre's own terms of reference: in short, the Society of St. Pius X – with its hundreds of members and thousands of followers, its seminaries and other religious houses throughout the world, the vast sums of money it has accumulated, and its enormous influence – has no claim whatever to canonical existence and Davies's attempt to argue the contrary is founded on fraud.

On 7th October 1970 Archbishop Lefebvre opened his seminary at Écône with a small group of students to be trained for the priesthood. On 1st November 1970 the ordinary[1] of the Diocese of Fribourg, the part of Switzerland in which Écône is located, issued the decree by which the Society of St. Pius X was canonically established as an association of which Archbishop Lefebvre himself was the superior. The idea behind this was for the seminarians to join the Society and remain in it after Ordination. In the seminary's early years the "authorities"

---

[1] An ordinary is the person – almost invariably a bishop – who is in charge of a diocese or quasi-diocese. A bishop who is not in charge of a diocese is not an ordinary.

in Rome tolerated, and in some cases approved, its activities. Naturally, few priests were ordained to begin with; but even so, many more were than ought to have been by any remotely Catholic standards, for the seminary course was often absurdly short: a period of two or three years training was apparently the norm to begin with, and at least one student was ordained after as little as nine months.

Canon Law (Canon 111§1) requires that before a man be admitted to the clerical state (the first step towards the priesthood), either he be incardinated into a diocese so that the bishop of that diocese will take responsibility for appointing him to a position upon his Ordination, or he be ascribed to (enlisted as a member of) a religious order or congregation which will fulfil the same role.[2] Prior to 1975 most of those ordained at Écône (very few though they were) were incardinated regularly into various dioceses, if anything that takes place under the auspices of the Conciliar Church can be described as regular,

---

[2] Incardination is the formal admission of a cleric to membership of the clergy of a particular diocese. Canon Law has wisely provided throughout the history of the Church that all clerics, without exception, be either incardinated into a diocese or "ascribed" as members of a religious order or congregation. The purpose of this is, in the words of Canon 111§1, "so that unattached clerics be in no wise admitted," which is a rule which looks both to the good of the clergy and of the whole Church by ensuring the following:
(a) that every cleric has a bishop or religious superior who is responsible for him, will not let him starve in the event of illness, and will ensure that he has an office of some suitable kind;
(b) that someone is responsible for overseeing the morals, etc., of every cleric and for administering counsel and, if necessary, punishment; and
(c) that the Church's clergy is prudently deployed to obtain maximum spiritual benefit for the faithful.
But more essentially still it ensures that priests receive proper mission to exercise their sacramental powers.
Obviously, in the event that one's bishop or superior falls into heresy when there is no one to replace him, one becomes in a sense an "unattached cleric" and one may continue to minister in one's diocese; but the presence of unattached clerics in dioceses which still have bishops is not countenanced by the Church.

principally by conservative bishops. Archbishop Lefebvre, however, says that he applied to the Sacred Congregation for Religious and received permission to ascribe into the Society of St. Pius X itself three of those whom he wished to ordain thus avoiding the need for their incardination into a diocese.[3]

A new factor emerged on 6th May 1975, when, on instruction from Cardinal Tabera, the new (Conciliar) ordinary of the diocese of Fribourg, Bishop Mamie,[4] notified Archbishop Lefebvre that he was withdrawing his canonical approval from the Society of St. Pius X. Canonically such a notification might appear to be of no effect, however, since Canon 493 says: "Any *'religio'* [religious order or society] even of diocesan right only [i.e. established only in a particular diocese], having been once legitimately established, even if it consists in but a single house, cannot be suppressed except by the Holy See ...." However, as we shall see, the Society of St. Pius X had not in fact been established as a *"religio"* at all.

Archbishop Lefebvre then appealed to Rome against this decision, but was informed by a commission of "cardinals" that it had been approved and authorised by the "pope" (Paul VI) and was not therefore subject to appeal. Naturally, whatever is ruled by a true pope, as Archbishop Lefebvre recognized Paul VI to be, is definitive in respect of such matters as the erection or suppression of religious organisations. Thus, canonically speaking, the Society of St. Pius X ceased to exist: it had been suppressed by the authorities *which its own superiors recognized as legitimate* – the very authorities, indeed, which had established it in the first place. There could therefore be no

---

[3] The Church requires (Canons 979§1 and 982§1) that anyone being ordained priest be subject either to a diocesan bishop (as a secular priest) or to a religious superior (as a regular). As we shall see later, the Archbishop was not on any terms a religious superior and the three authorisations to ascribe into the Society belong to the realm of myth.

[4] Consecrated 6th October 1968, presumably in the new and very doubtfully valid rite. He was certainly a modernist and for that reason opposed to the Society's foundation in the diocese.

question thereafter of ordaining priests to be ascribed into the Society, since canonically the Society did not exist and would certainly not have received the permission from the Sacred Congregation for Religious which it is falsely claimed that it had received three times before; and there was, equally, no possibility any longer that any diocesan ordinary would agree to have priests from Écône incardinated into his diocese. Thus the Ordination of any priest would be unlawful under Canon 111§1.

Nonetheless, on 29th June 1975 Archbishop Lefebvre went ahead and performed a number of Ordinations at Écône. He did so despite the fact that Canon 2373 imposes automatic suspension on any bishop who ordains a man who is not duly incardinated or ascribed by solemn religious profession. The Archbishop Lefebvre saw fit to ignore this law and the censure attached to it.

Moreover, he has, of course, has continued to ordain priests up to the present day, all of them being purportedly ascribed into the Society of St. Pius X and distributed in dioceses throughout the world without reference to those whom he recognize and they recognize as the legitimate ordinaries of these dioceses; and the rest of the story is well known.

Davies's defence of Archbishop Lefebvre's conduct in this matter can be summarised as follows:

(a) The Society of St. Pius X was canonically erected as a society of priests living the common life but without taking the special vows necessary to make it a religious order, and, having been erected in one diocese, could not lawfully be suppressed except by the Holy See.

(b) The seminary was also lawfully erected, approved by Rome; and the Sacred Congregation for Religious three times gave permission for members of the Society to be ascribed directly into the Society instead of being incardinated into a diocese.

(c) In 1974 Rome sent a deputation to assess the seminary and some members of the deputation made scandalous comments to the seminarians which were incompatible with Catholic doctrine.

(d) As a result of this, Archbishop Lefebvre made a precipitate public declaration in which he made his disapproval of the conduct of Paul VI and his revision of the liturgy, etc., painfully clear.

(e) By way of reaction to this declaration, the bishop of the diocese in which the seminary was located withdrew his approval of the Society of St. Pius X; but this action was invalid since only the Holy See can suppress a legitimately established religious order even if it exists in only one diocese.

(f) Archbishop Lefebvre appealed to Rome "suspensively" against the decree of suppression of the Society – i.e. he appealed against it to the Holy See in such a way that he was permitted to continue to function pending the declaration of the Holy See.

(g) The Holy See then made it clear that the suppression of the Society was a personal act of the "Holy Father" and therefore subject to no appeal, but this action is to be rejected as an immoral attempt to give retroactive legitimacy to an unlawful and invalid action which is not binding since it was based upon misinformation and was opposed to the rules of natural justice.

(h) Archbishop Lefebvre had therefore the moral and legal right to keep the seminary and Society in existence and, faced with the difficulty of finding dioceses in which to incardinate those whom he wished to ordain, he was entitled to ascribe them into the Society itself. Why? Because permission to do this had been given on three distinct occasions by Rome, which, in the opinion of some canonists, was sufficient to establish a custom by which the same could take place thereafter without specific authorisation on each occasion.

(i) Hence Archbishop Lefebvre's position is, in Davies's eyes, canonically unassailable.

That is Davies's case for the defence. One must grant that it displays a certain amount of ingenuity. There is presumably *some* extrinsic reason for its having been swallowed unquestioningly by so many. But it does not wash. It none of it even begins to wash.

The first question to be answered is whether the Society was in fact canonically erected as Davies claims (p. 122: "The Society of St. Pius X was established according to all the requirements of Canon Law ...."). The answer to this is that, if we accept, for the sake of argument, the position of Archbishop Lefebvre and Davies concerning the occupancy of the Holy See, the Society *was* canonically erected, but *not* as a religious order or congregation, which is how Davies represents it, and *not* permanently and unconditionally, as he also gives us to believe. Here is a translation of the pertinent part of the decree of erection of the "International Priestly Fraternity of St. Pius X":

> We, Francois Charrière, Bishop of Lausanne, Geneva and Fribourg, having invoked the Holy Name of God, and observed all canonical prescriptions, decree the following:
> (1) The International Priestly Fraternity of St. Pius X is erected in our diocese *as a "Pia Unio"* ["Pious Union"].
> (2) The seat of the Fraternity is established at the Maison Saint Pie X, 50 Route de la Vignettaz, in the episcopal town of Fribourg.
> (3) We approve and confirm the attached statutes of the Fraternity for a period of six years '*ad experimentum*', a period which will be able to be followed by an equal period by tacit extension, after which the Fraternity will be able to be definitively erected in our diocese or by the competent Roman Congregation.
> (...)
> Done at Fribourg in our diocese on the 1st November 1970, the Feast of All Saints.
> (Signed: Francois Charrière, Bishop of Lausanne, Geneva and Fribourg.)

From the foregoing it can be clearly seen that the Society was not erected as what Canon Law calls a *"religio"* (a religious order or society). It was erected as a *"pia unio"*. Furthermore, it was not given an existence which automatically continued indefinitely until lawfully suppressed, whether by the Holy See or by any other body. On the contrary, its statutes were approved *for a period of six years only*, on the understanding that they could continue thereafter *provided that the ordinary raised no objection in the interim*, and that, anyhow, after twelve years (which expired on 1st November 1982) the Society would need to be re-authorized. Finally, the bishop makes it clear that it is only after the expiry of this twelve year period that the Society will be able to be "definitely erected", from which it follows that at the date of the decree in 1970 the Society had certainly *not* been "definitely erected", and could not have been until 1982, by which period it was scarcely likely that any member of the Conciliar Church in a position to erect religious societies or even *"piæ uniones"* would have been prepared to confer this status on the Society of St. Pius X.

The plain facts are that: (a) if the Society of St. Pius X was intended to be a *"religio"*, then the decree of its erection was invalid, since it was not erected as a *"religio"* but as a *"pia unio"*; and (b) even if we regard it merely as a *"pia unio"*, it was erected only on a temporary and experimental basis for a period of six years, which would have been extended to a maximum of twelve years if the Ordinary had not objected in the meanwhile. However, as is admitted by all concerned, the Ordinary *did* object to the Society before the expiry of the first experimental six years and the second period of six years did not therefore follow. And anyhow, even if it *had* followed, this would have allowed the Society to exist only until 1982.

Upon no basis whatsoever, therefore, not even as a mere *"pia unio"*, can it be claimed that the Society has any canonical basis for its existence after the year 1982.

But let us suppose, just for the sake of argument, that the Society had been and remained to this day a legitimate Catholic *"pia unio"*. How would this help Archbishop Lefebvre's doughty apologist? The answer is that it would not help at all. What is crucial to Davies's defence of the legality of ordaining priests without incardination is not whether the Society has any legal existence as a *"pia unio"* but whether the Society can be, or could ever have been, classified as a *"religio"*; for Canon 111§1 permits a man to be admitted as a cleric only if he has been either incardinated in a *diocese* or – and this is the *only* exception – if he has been ascribed to a *"religio"*. The Society of St. Pius X is, of course, *not* a diocese and its members are ordained (apart from a few whom Archbishop Lefebvre has ordained to become members of traditionalist houses of various religious orders such as Benedictines and Dominicans) only on the basis that they are ascribed into the Society itself; and this, if the Society is not a *"religio"*, is impossible; and as we have just seen, the Society (or, to be accurate, "Fraternity") was officially erected not as a *"religio"* but as a *"pia unio"*. Moreover, as we shall shortly see, while Davies does not go so far as to admit that the Society is merely a *"pia unio"*, as the documentation which established it unambiguously states, he does indicate that it is a "society of the common life"; and canonically speaking "a society of the common life" is not a *"religio"* either.

It is now necessary to define the terms that we have just met, in order to ensure that we have a clear picture of the issue under examination. A tabular presentation is appropriate.

(a) A *"religio"* is defined in Canon 488§1 as a "society approved by the legitimate ecclesiastical authority in which the members, according to the laws of the society itself, emit public vows, perpetual or temporary, but to be renewed at regular intervals, and thus strive after evangelical perfection."

(b) Of "societies of the common life", Canon 673§1 says: "A society of men or women in which the members imitate the manner of life of religious living in community under the rule of their superiors according to approved constitutions, but are not bound by the three customary public vows, *is not, properly speaking, a 'religio'*, nor can its members be properly called religious." Thus this canon not only defines for us what such a society *is*, but also carefully distinguishes it from what it is *not*.

(c) Finally, Canon 707§1 apprises us that "associations of the faithful which are erected for the exercise of any work of piety or charity are called *'piæ uniones'* ('pious unions')." From this it is clear that a pious union is an organization which may even be open to lay folk without restriction. For instance, the Society of St. Vincent de Paul, which flourished in many Catholic parishes before Vatican II and consisted simply of organised bodies of layfolk, with occasional clerical members, for the relief of the poor and suffering in their parishes, was a "pious union".

So was the Society of St. Pius X really no more than a "pious union"? On this subject Davies adopts as his own the views expressed by Fr. Boyd Cathey (who, subsequently to writing the article in question, left the Society of St. Pius X under a malodorous cloud and ceased to function as a priest), and reproduces an entire article by Fr. Cathey as an appendix to Vol. I of *Apologia Pro Marcel Lefebvre*. In this appendix Cathey admits that the Society was a "priestly" society "of common life without vows, in the tradition of the Foreign Missionaries of Paris" and attributes this to the first article of the statutes of the Society. I have not seen independent confirmation of this particular authority that he cites, but I have no reason to think that he has not represented accurately the content of the statutes; and of course Canon 673§1 has just told us that a society of the common life without vows is *not* a "*religio*".

Cathey is perhaps not unaware that he has set himself a problem; for, when quoting the decree of erection of the Society (quoted a little earlier), he adds an asterisk after the words "pious union" and provides a footnote which reads as follows:

> The bishop's use of the expression '*pia unio*' here is a little confusing. A '*pia unio*', as Canons 707-708 make clear, is not normally a moral person. It means a lay association. A religious 'society of the common life', as the approved Statutes of the Society of St. Pius X specify it is, described in Canon 673, is really very like a religious institute but without public vows. It is possible that Bishop Charrière intended here '*pia domus*' as the first step towards a new religious institution.

I shall be returning shortly to the question of whether Cathey's grounds for escaping from the bishop's definition of the Society as a pious union are valid; but before doing so it is necessary to observe that *if* what he says is valid he has opened up a *new* can of worms. It would follow that the Society *may never have been canonically erected at all*; for if the Society defined itself in its statutes as a priestly society of the common life without vows, a decree of erection which refers to it as a "pious union" would surely be invalid. In the same way, an understanding between buyer and seller of a property that the property in question was a large family house would be of no force if the deed of sale referred to it as a dog kennel; and even if the disappointed purchaser could demonstrate that the dog kennel did not exist, far from entitling him to the house, this would merely demonstrate that he was not entitled either to the house (since it was not mentioned in the deed) or to the kennel (since it did not exist). Certainly it is difficult to reconcile this strange inconsistency with Davies's assertion, made without hesitation or qualification, that the Society "was established according to all the requirements of Canon Law."

But anyhow, *is* Fr. Cathey right in suggesting that the bishop referred to the Society as a "pious union" only by a slip of the pen? The only evidence in favour of his assertion is (a) the fact that it has widely been presumed that the Society was much more than a "pious union", and (b) the fact that such a definition apparently conflicts with the Society's statutes which, however, remarkably – or perhaps, in the circumstances, not remarkably – seem neither to be available for inspection nor to be reproduced in any of the works, in French or English, defending Archbishop Lefebvre and his organisation.

Against such an interpretation, the most obvious argument is the intrinsic unlikelihood of such a slip. Why should a bishop, in a formal document, refer to a religious society as a "pious union" when he would obviously know the difference (which is a vast one) between the two terms; and anyhow, why should such an error go unrecognized by those to whom the decree of erection related?

Nor is this the only argument against Fr. Cathey. Further evidence is furnished by a letter dated 27th October 1975 written by Cardinal Villot to the Presidents of Episcopal Conferences. In this letter, which relates entirely to the events surrounding Archbishop Lefebvre and his organisation, Villot makes an important assertion, and, while in general *creditworthy* is far from being the epithet that best describes arch-Modernist Villot, in this case there is no reason to doubt his word, since it is evident that he does not realise the significance of what he is saying. Here is what he says:

> The Priestly Fraternity of St. Pius X was instituted on 1st November 1970 by Mgr. Francois Charrière, the then Bishop of Lausanne, Geneva and Fribourg. *A diocesan pious union, it was destined in the mind of Mgr. Marcel Lefebvre to be subsequently transformed into a religious Community without vows.* Until its recognition as such – which recognition moreover was not given – it consequently continued to be subject to the jurisdiction of the Bishop of Fribourg and to the vigilance of the dioceses in which it carried on its activities. Such is the position according to law.

As has been said, the mere fact of Cardinal Villot's having made this statement does not by any means prove that it is true. But surely it has the ring of truth, independently of the source from which it comes; for it reconciles the disparate pieces of evidence so far collected. In summary, it appears that the Society was erected in 1970 as a pious union, as stated in the decree of erection; that Archbishop Lefebvre had the *intention* at some stage in the future, when he could obtain the due approval, to turn this "pious union" into a society of the common life without vows; but that this transformation was overtaken by events and never took place.

I am convinced that this is the correct account of what happened; but even if Fr. Cathey's version of events is preferred, this still leaves the Society as no more than a community without vows. In neither case is there any pretext for claiming that it is a *"religio"* (which, by definition, *does* have vows); and since it is not a *"religio"*, it certainly cannot ascribe its members into itself in order to give them the right to adopt the clerical state. To this it may be objected that on three occasions Rome gave permission for the Society to ascribe members to itself in place of incardination. But *did* Rome in fact grant this permission? The only evidence we are offered appears in the appendix to Davies's work which consists of an article by Fr. Cathey, referred to above, in which it is stated that: "As early as 1971 Archbishop Lefebvre had been assured by Cardinal Wright that within a short time the Society of St. Pius X would enjoy the privilege of ascription into the Society." A footnote (which is presumably Cathey's but may be Davies's) quotes as authority for this assertion "a letter to Archbishop Lefebvre, 15th May 1971." It is noticeable, however, that nowhere in Davies's book, which gives copious documentation for almost every assertion, is there any further reference to this letter; still less is there a photographic reproduction of it as is the case with Cardinal Wright's letter to Archbishop Lefebvre of 18th February 1971 on a different subject. Moreover, the letter is neither mentioned nor figures in any way in the work called *L'Évêque Suspens* by Yves Montaigne, the French work which collects together almost all the documentation relevant to the

Archbishop Lefebvre case. Such an omission must definitely be regarded as suspicious.[5]

Nor is that the only reason for suspicion concerning this alleged right of the Society to ascribe members into itself instead of incardinating them into dioceses or into regular religious orders or societies. It seems highly unlikely that even in the Conciliar Church the "Sacred Congregation for Religious" would grant permission for clerics to be ascribed into a *pious union* as opposed to a religious order or congregation.

This is not because there is anything implausible in the Conciliar Church's overturning longstanding and sensible Catholic laws and traditions, but because this particular law is just as important to the Conciliar Church as it has been to the Catholic Church; for one main purpose of the law, it will be remembered, is to enable the authorities to "keep tabs" on the clergy and ensure that they are doing what the authorities deem best. Not that the motives for wanting this control are the same in each case, of course. Under the Catholic Church, it was required so that the authorities could see to it that each priest was using his talents to save souls, while in the Conciliar Church it means that priests must be used to corrupt souls, that every priest must go on enough "renewal" courses to re-educate him, and that any signs of lingering Catholicity must be ruthlessly exterminated. But, irrespective of the use made of their control, both the Catholic Church and the Conciliar Church have needed and used tight control over their clergy, and if the Conciliar Church were to allow its clerics to be "ordained"

---

[5] 2015 footnote. In fact, following the publication in 2002 of Bishop Tissier de Mallerais's on the whole objective and serious biography of the Archbishop, it is now possible to dismiss the whole allegation as unfounded. It emerges from the book that Archbishop Lefebvre addressed repeated requests to the Sacred Congregation for the Clergy for the privilege of incardinating his clergy into the Society itself, but always without success. And in fact, until 1976, all priests ordained in the Society had been incardinated into an existing diocese or religious order, with the single exception, in 1975, of Fr. Sanborn.

without being incardinated into a diocese or having made solemn vows in a full and permanent religious order, it would be gratuitously abandoning this control. To allow temporary vows in a "pious union" to take the place of solemn vows in a religious order would be absurd, if only because after a limited period (two years in the case of the Society of St. Pius X) the priests could freely leave the organization and would then be without any direct superior to govern them. To appreciate the absurdity of the suggestion that temporary vows in a "pious union" could have such an effect, it is only necessary to imagine a priest being excused from incardination because he happened to be a member of the Society of St. Vincent de Paul.[6]

So Davies's claim that three students had been ascribed into the Society itself with the approval of the Conciliar Church's authorities in Rome is not only supported by no evidence but also seems to be intrinsically unlikely. And there is one other piece of evidence against the claim: Davies *himself* denies it! On p. 140 of the same work he asserts unequivocally that "up to this point [1975] the priests ordained at Écône had all been regularly incardinated into dioceses in accordance with the requirements of Canon Law." How, one asks oneself bemusedly, is this compatible with the assertion that at least three priests had not been incardinated at all but had been ascribed into the Society itself instead?

More serious still would seem to be Davies's position that, notwithstanding Paul VI's unequivocal suppression of the Society, it nonetheless continued to exist, providing Archbishop Lefebvre with a canonically erected framework in which to pursue his resistance. Davies does not deny that a legitimate pope – which he takes Montini to be – has the right to suppress a religious order, or a society of the common life, or even a "pious union". But his position seems to be that if the suppression is

---

[6] Readers who wish to research this point more fully are referred especially to *Ordination in Societies of the Common Life*, Catholic University of America, 1958, by the Rev. John G. Nugent, C.M., J.C.L.

unjust, or based on false information, it is therefore null, so that the Society continues to exist notwithstanding the contrary will of the Vicar of Christ (by which I mean, of course, the man whom he *thinks* to be the Vicar of Christ).

On this subject there is no need to repeat the theological arguments already provided elsewhere. Instead I draw attention to an exact historical parallel which clearly shows the *Catholic* reaction to the suppression – even the *unjust* suppression – of a religious order: the suppression of the Society of Jesus (the Jesuits) by Pope Clement XIV in 1773.

Now it could scarcely be claimed that the Jesuits at that time were less significant than the Society of St. Pius X. Furthermore, they included among their countless thousands of members theologians and canonists at least as competent, it will be generally agreed, as those who guide Archbishop Lefebvre and the anonymous priests who approve of Michael Davies's writings. And, needless to say, the members of the Society of Jesus were no more anxious for their religious order to be suppressed than were Archbishop Lefebvre and his priests for their *religious order/society of the common life/pious union* to be suppressed; they would have been happy to avail themselves of any escape, compatible with the Faith, from obedience to the papal command. Nonetheless, with one accord, the Jesuits forsook their houses – some of which had been sanctified by the labours of martyrs and saints and had a tradition of two centuries behind them – in most cases to subject themselves to the diocesan authorities and to function as secular priests, and in some cases to join other religious orders or congregations. Other than in one or two exceptional countries where the Holy See authorised it, the Society simply ceased to exist. *And no one claimed otherwise.* No recalcitrant group of Jesuits continued to take in novices or claimed that Pope Clement's act was null through injustice – his decree, however much deplored and lamented, was universally obeyed.

To make the parallel complete, it remains for me to establish that the suppression of the Jesuits was *indeed* an unjust act and one causing great harm to the Church, because that is the presumption *mutatis mutandis* regarding the Society of St. Pius X which Archbishop Lefebvre and Davies use to justify the former's actions. For this purpose it is sufficient to quote the words of Pope Pius VII,[7] the pope who was to restore the Jesuits in 1814. The following is a reproduction, taken from the source mentioned, of a conversation between Pope Pius VII and a French priest, the abbé Proyart, who, in a biography of the French king, Louis XVI, had sharply criticised the action of Clement XIV in suppressing the Jesuits.

Proyart: "People have given me a scruple for speaking as I have one of Clement XIV, most Holy Father, yet God knows that it was not in the bad sense of philosophers who have calumniated every pope except the destroyer of the Jesuits."

Pius: "What you say of him is unfortunately only too true. I heard the minutest details of the business from a prelate who was in Clement XIV's service, and then entered mine. He was the very prelate who offered Pope Clement the bull of suppression to sign. As soon as he had signed it, he threw his pen on one side, the paper on the other, and seemed beside himself."

Proyart: "It seems to me, most Holy Father, that if the Powers [i.e. the kings and other national rulers] forced him to suppress their own staunchest ally [i.e. the Society of Jesus], the pope should at least have avoided blaming those whom he was compelled to use unjustly [in the bull of suppression, Clement had listed a string of charges against the Jesuits, most of them calumniatory and unsubstantiated]. Still less should he have treated them as if they were criminals."

---

[7] These words are taken from a standard collection of historical source material – *Clément XII et Clément XIV, Pièces Justificatives*, N° 17.

Pius: "Most certainly. Even supposing that the Church had been threatened by far greater evils than the suppression of this important Order, at the dictates of kings misled by their advisers, a bull of three lines should have given this unhappy sentence: 'yielding regretfully to the force of things, etc., etc.'"

Thus there is no escape from the conclusion that the suppression of the Jesuits by Pope Clement XIV was, and was accepted by at least one later pope to have been, extremely unjust and damaging to the Church. Hence, whatever theological principles Davies and others use to defend Archbishop Lefebvre's resistance – and fundamental principles are all that they can rely on, for as we have seen the law does not help them – these principles were evidently unknown in 1773, and consequently, like every other religious principle which was heard of for the first time less than two hundred years ago, they were not revealed by God, but invented and propagated by the Father of Lies.

Let us now summarize. The following are the inescapable facts:

(a) Archbishop Lefebvre is wrong in acknowledging the legitimacy of the Conciliar "popes".

(b) But even if we admit for the sake of argument that he is *right* to acknowledge the Conciliar "popes", he is still wrong in holding that his society is validly erected.

(c) But even if he were *right* in holding that his society was validly erected – which he is not – he is wrong in holding that it could ascribe clerics into itself.

(d) But – finally – even if he were *right* in holding that it *could* ascribe clerics into itself, he is wrong in thinking that its suppression by Montini was invalid – *unless* he is prepared to accept that Montini was not pope.

In other words, the Davies-Archbishop Lefebvre defence of the Society of St. Pius X is a chain of arguments *every* link of which is entirely without validity.

CHAPTER EIGHT
DAVIES AS AN ANARCHIST

"He that turneth away his ears from hearing the law, his prayer shall be an abomination." (Proverbs 28:9)

Anarchy

Even readers who were well aware before reading this *Evaluation* of the enormity of Davies's departure from Catholic orthodoxy, may be taken aback by the assertion that he is an anarchist. Nonetheless it is true, for an anarchist, by definition, is someone who rejects law and authority and advocates the principle that human behaviour should be regulated by no external control but only by personal inclination. The word "anarchist" therefore fits very well a great many of those who identify themselves as traditional Catholics and it can be used to describe Michael Davies even more appropriately than most others, since, by his writings, he has made it explicit that he *believes and defends* the anarchist theory which most others espouse only implicitly by their actions.

Anarchy in the Church

Ecclesiastical anarchism is a more serious error than purely civil anarchism, as the need for law and authority in the Church is, if anything, greater than that in civil society, owing to the fact that the Church is a society belonging to the *supernatural* order, whose immediate end is the sanctification and salvation of souls – the supreme end for which mankind was created – and therefore has a more exalted dignity that any merely secular society could have.[1]

Very seldom in the history of the Church have those who claim to be her members denied her right to make laws and to give commands that bind all her subjects in conscience; but today this is exactly the claim widely made by traditional Catholics. Surely no writer of fiction could have invented such a situation.

For while the vast majority of those who claim to be Catholics have been completely swept along by the Conciliar revolution, so that their beliefs bear hardly any resemblance to Catholic doctrine any longer, of those who have recognized the perversity of the revolution which has been imposed in the name of the Church throughout the world, the vast majority, even if they remain orthodox on most points of Catholic doctrine, have been deceived and seduced into polluting their orthodoxy with a number of errors and heresies, probably the most obvious of which lies in their attitude to the Church's juridical authority.

The cause of this calamity is not hard to find. It lies simply in the fact that, when the revolution took place (between 1958 and, say, 1970), those Catholics who wished to remain orthodox were faced with a dilemma: whereas they had previously always associated orthodoxy with obedience to ecclesiastical authority, they now found that to obey those whom they mistakenly thought to be their pastors was a path which evidently led to heresy and apostasy, while to retain orthodoxy in the Faith of their childhood necessitated disobedience. Why more of them did not recognize that the solution to this dilemma lay in the fact that those apparently in authority had lost all authority by virtue of having publicly lost the Faith is difficult to say. There are several possible reasons, all of which probably contributed in some measure. One major factor must have been the emergence of Archbishop Lefebvre as the *de facto* leader of the traditionalist resistance to the revolution, and the fact that he insisted on at least nominal recognition of the "pope" and other

---

[1] Pope Leo XIII, *Satis Cognitum* ; Pope Pius XII, *Mystici Corporis*.

Conciliar bishops as legitimate. Another factor must have been the loss of any sense of the enormity and utter hatefulness of heresy,[2] caused by the gradual onset of liberalism during this century. Also there was the natural fear of the enormous and irrevocable[3] step of contesting the legitimacy of the heretical usurpers – a step which is especially daunting for timid souls in view of the fact that these usurpers sometimes have realistic, if superficial, sheep's clothing, consisting of sporadic orthodox utterances and concessions to tradition.

But whatever the reasons, what happened is well known. The theory that the papacy, had fallen vacant through the heresy of its apparent occupants was put forward and believed by a few even from the earliest days of the revolution, but it received comparatively little publicity. The majority of those who came across it rejected it, and there must have been many to whom the possibility had simply never occurred. Both groups faced the predicament of a choice between, on the one hand, retaining, substantially, the doctrines contained in their catechism and the devotional practices that had been dear to them throughout their lives, and, on the other hand, continuing to obey their pastors. Many adopted the "obedience" option and remained in their parishes, speedily becoming a large and, in some circles, well-publicized category of people forever bewailing "the changes" but forever petrified at the suggestion that they might do anything but suffer in silence in the same pew they occupied

---

[2] Cf. Fr. F.W. Faber in *Spiritual Conferences* (chapter, "Heaven and Hell"), p. 351: "I beg of God in His infinite compassion to keep alive in me to the last hour of my life the intense hatred of heresy, with which he has inspired me, and which I recognize as His gift." Also Fr. H.A. Rawes in *Cui Bono?* (London, 1864): " ... as we love God with a strong, undying love, so let us hate heresy with a strong, undying hatred. If we ever begin to slacken in our hatred of heresy, we may be sure there is something amiss with our souls."

[3] "Irrevocable" at least in the sense that rejecting the Conciliar Church requires a radical change of a kind incompatible with the inconsistencies and frequent tergiversations often found among conservative members of the Conciliar Church.

before Vatican II. Many others, however, refused to submit to this torture and the resolution which they found to this dilemma is summarised in the title of a book written by one such[4] – "Faith is Greater than Obedience."

Of course, there is no doubt that the statement that faith is greater than obedience is true in itself; for faith, being one of the three theological virtues, is superior to every virtue except hope and charity. But the implication of the statement is that, faced with a choice between orthodox belief and due obedience, the correct path is to abandon the virtue of obedience entirely. It is reminiscent of the answer given by the deceitful harlot to King Solomon in III Kings 3:26. "Let it be neither mine nor thine, but divide it," it may be remembered, was how she indicated contentment with the King's proposal that, since both she and the other harlot claimed to be the mother of the disputed baby, it be cut in two with a sword and they each take a half. The truth is that, just as half a baby is of no use to anyone, in the same way, faith without obedience is of no avail to salvation. This is because obedience to ecclesiastical authority is a definite requirement for salvation and has been defined to be such by Pope Boniface VIII in his famous bull *Unam Sanctam*. (Dz. 469)

In fact faith is normally *impossible* for those who do not accept the duty of obedience, since, by denying the duty of obedience to ecclesiastical authority, *one thereby denies an article of faith* and loses the theological virtue of faith entirely; and this fact holds good even if one retains a purely *human* assent to most of the other articles of the Faith.

When is Disobedience Legitimate?

Now it is true that there *can* be occasions which justify a Catholic in disobeying instructions given by legitimately constituted ecclesiastical authority concerning even those

---

[4] Fr. Albert Drexel (1889-1977) an alleged beneficiary of private revelations.

matters which fall within its competence; it is true that such disobedience can be morally permissible and indeed of moral obligation. But these occasions fall into but a single category, namely when the authority in question gives an instruction which it is impossible to obey without committing definite sin. Then disobedience to the ecclesiastical superior is no more than an accidental effect of an act of obedience to a higher authority. To suggest that, outside that one exceptional category already envisaged and recognized by the Church, there are further categories in which, in order to retain the Faith, it is necessary for us to disobey legitimate authority, or, as is often claimed in traditionalist circles, that one is entitled to disobey any command coming from a legitimate authority which is, despite its legitimacy, engaged in actions harmful to the Church, is to postulate an impossibility. There is simply no Catholic answer to the question of whether one should choose the virtue of faith without obedience, or the virtue of obedience without faith; for the true Catholic knows that he must have both together and that any apparent need to sacrifice one to the other must result from a misreading of the situation. Faced with such a dilemma, he re-examines the circumstances which appear to present such a dilemma for as long as it takes him to ascertain what factor he is overlooking; knowing, by faith, that such a factor there must *definitely* be. And in the case we are considering, the solution he must eventually arrive at – a solution which is seen to be more than fully supported by independent evidence as soon as he starts looking in the right direction – is of course that the authorities of the Conciliar Church are not lawfully constituted Catholic authorities at all, and are therefore entitled to no obedience whatsoever, even in respect of commands and laws which would have been binding had they been imposed by *legitimate* pastors.

In short, when we examine the position of Michael Davies on the subject of the obedience owed by Catholics to ecclesiastical authority, we encounter the tragic result of a refusal to re-examine the assumptions which had produced an impossible dilemma – a refusal which in turn leads to the abandonment of obedience in a vain attempt to preserve the Faith.

Before proceeding to analyse Davies's position on the obligation of obedience to the laws and commands of Catholic authority, it must be made clear that, for the purposes of this examination, we shall once again have to assume as valid Davies's false premise that the members of the Conciliar Church's hierarchy hold legitimate authority in the Catholic Church. This is, obviously, because Davies himself believes they are legitimate and argues that Catholics may disobey them *despite* this presumed legitimacy. Normally it would be sufficient for a Catholic to reply to that they are *not* legitimate, and that they therefore have no entitlement to the obedience of anyone who wishes to be a Catholic. But for the purpose of analysing Davies's *doctrinal* errors, it must be shown that *even if* the authorities of the Conciliar Church *were*, as he considers them, Catholic authorities, *retaining* their offices and jurisdiction but *abusing* them by issuing inexpedient commands and promulgating undesirable laws, his conclusion that one is entitled to disobey them at whim[5] and with impunity is certainly not a conclusion which is compatible with Catholic teaching.

Let us begin by establishing what Catholic doctrine on this subject is, an exercise which need not take us long. A good summary of the attitude of Catholics to the laws of the Church is presented by St. Robert Bellarmine in his *De Romano Pontifice*, lib. IV, cap. 15:

---

[5] The words "at whim" are not a gratuitous rhetorical flourish. On p. 6 of this *Evaluation* a statement by Dietrich von Hildebrand, quoted and approved by Davies, was analysed, to the effect that prelates who are guilty of certain misdemeanours "lose the right to claim obedience in disciplinary matters." If they have entirely lost the right to be obeyed, in Davies's view, evidently it is no injustice to say that he holds that they may be disobeyed at whim, for there can be no reason for granting or refusing obedience to those who have no right to it except personal preference.

In the Catholic Church it has always been believed that bishops in their dioceses and the Roman Pontiff in the whole Church are the ecclesiastical rulers ['*principes*'] who can, by their own authority and without the consent of the people or advice of the priests, pass laws which bind in conscience, give judgements in ecclesiastical trials after the manner of other judges, and, finally, impose punishment.

That is clear enough, and the principle should be almost instinctive to all Catholics. But of course, as has already been indicated, while this is what every Catholic should know from his Catechism-learning days, and is a truth which there can be no excuse for ignorance of, it is nevertheless true that the matter *is* more complicated than this. It is equally true that – as St. Robert himself makes clear in the same chapter – there *are* times when Catholics are entitled, *and even obliged*, to disobey the commands and conceivably even the laws of legitimate authority.

In the case of *laws* only a brief summary is necessary, for the possibility of a law (i.e. a universal and permanent command) conflicting with a Catholic doctrine or requiring Catholics to perform some action which is not conducive to their spiritual welfare could only exist at local level. The Holy Ghost protects the supreme authority of the Church from promulgating such a law.

This is what one famous nineteenth century theologian, Fr. H. Hürter, has to say on this subject – and his teaching is confirmed by every Catholic theologian who addresses the same point. In his *Compendium of Dogmatic Theology*, Vol. I, p. 277, he informs us that "the Church *cannot* approve a general and universally obligatory discipline which is contrary to faith or morals or which causes grave harm to religion."

Thus the only three occasions when it is permissible to disobey a universal law of the Church which has not been revoked are:

(i) When the law is *physically or morally impossible* to comply with. Moral impossibility, in this case, would mean that obedience to the ecclesiastical law would require disobedience to a higher law, as, for instance, if, to comply with the law requiring assistance at Mass on Sunday, one had to abandon a sick person in need of continual attention.

(ii) *Automatic cessation* of the law. This occurs whenever supervening circumstances make it impossible for a law to achieve *any* of the good ends for which the legislator instituted it. (It may also occur by virtue of a contrary custom *where this custom is known and approved of by the legislator*.)

(iii) *Epikeia*. This is the principle according to which a law which remains *generally* in force may cease to bind a *particular individual* in a *particular case* because wholly extraordinary circumstances render the law either harmful or excessively burdensome to *that* individual in *that* case. Since epikeia may never be invoked when recourse to the legislative authority is possible, it is evident that epikeia cannot be a sufficient pretext to justify traditionalists in withholding obedience from those whom they (erroneously) consider to be the legitimate authorities of the Catholic Church.

In the case of *commands* – that is, instructions given by ecclesiastical authority to *particular* groups or to individuals *on particular occasions*, as opposed to *laws*, which are *general and permanent* instructions – evidently epikeia and automatic cessation cannot apply, since the one giving the command will be aware of the circumstances at the time of giving it. Moral and physical impossibility, however, will continue to excuse, and there is in addition one other occasion when disobedience becomes permissible and indeed mandatory, an occasion which, it must be emphasized, does not affect ecclesiastical *laws* but *only* commands. This is when the authority gives a command compliance with which would involve a definite sin on the part of the person obeying.

Let us examine this exception in a little more depth. It is expressed succinctly in the *Penny Catechism*, question-and-answer number 197, where we read:

> By the fourth Commandment we are commanded to love, reverence, and obey our parents *in all that is not sin* .... We are commanded to obey, not only our parents, but also our bishops and pastors, the civil authorities and our lawful superiors. (Emphasis added)

Similarly, Fr. Patrick Murray in his *De Ecclesia*, Disputatio XVII, Sectio IV, n. 90, teaches that "one is always bound to obey the (Roman) pontiff when he gives an absolute command, whether he does so infallibly or not, *in everything which does not involve manifest sin*."

And of course what must be particularly noticed for our present purposes is that the duty of obeying our parents and lawful superiors, whether ecclesiastical or secular, is a binding obligation except where such obedience would be sinful *for us*. Thus it follows that if a case were to arise in which a lawful superior gave a command which it was sinful *for him to command*, but which involved no sin in obeying it, one would be bound to comply with it.[6] When, for instance, King David arranged for the command to be given to Urias the Hethite to stand in front of the battle line, mortal sin was undoubtedly committed *by King David*, since his purpose was to ensure that Urias would be killed in order that he, David, might continue his unlawful relationship with Urias's wife. But *on the part of Urias* no sin whatever was involved in his complying with the sinfully *given* command, because it is the duty of a soldier – obliged like

---

[6] Cf. the following extract from Pope Leo XIII's encyclical *Diuturnum Illud*: "The only reason which men have for not obeying is when anything is demanded *of them* which is openly repugnant to the natural or Divine law, for it is equally unlawful to command to do anything in which the law of nature or the will of God is violated." (*Acta Sanctæ Sedis*, XIV, 3 *et seq.*)

everyone else to obey, not only his parents, "but also his bishops and pastors, the civil authorities and," as in this case, "his lawful superiors" – to take whatever position in battle his commanders assign to him. On the contrary, therefore, his obedience to the instruction was correct and virtuous and indeed it would have been sinful for him not to have obeyed.

In considering the subject of when it is permissible to disobey ecclesiastical authorities, it is of the highest importance to bear in mind this distinction: if one would sin by obeying a command, one may and must *disobey* it; but if the superior sinned by *commanding* something that the subject can nonetheless *obey* without sinning himself, obedience remains obligatory.

One other fine point needs to be considered before this summary of relevant Catholic doctrine will be complete, namely the question of how a Catholic should conduct himself if he is *in doubt* as to whether obedience to the instruction of a lawful superior is or is not sinful. The answer of the Church on this point is clear and definite – one is obliged to obey. The reason for this is that the presumption is in favour of the superior, so that any doubt as to whether compliance with his command is sinful or not should be resolved by presuming that it is not sinful. Moreover, this, it must be stressed, applies even when compliance with a command appears to be *probably* sinful. Only when *definite* sin is involved is one entitled, and obliged, to disobey, as is clearly stated by St. Ignatius Loyola when he writes:

> When, in my opinion and judgement, the Superior bids me to do something which is against my conscience, or sinful, and the Superior thinks the contrary, *I ought to believe him* unless he is *manifestly* wrong. (*Monumenta Ignatiana*, series 1ª, XII, 660)

And the same doctrine is taught by St. Bernard, St. Bonaventure, St. Benedict, and especially by St. Augustine, who makes it clear that it applies even in relation to the obedience due to temporal rulers – "to obey them [temporal rulers] with a good conscience, it is not necessary to have evidence that their commands are lawful, but it is sufficient that the contrary is not recognized *with certainty.*" (*Contra Faustum Manichæum*, book 22, chapter 75) This teaching of St. Augustine's, St. Thomas Aquinas explains, is based on the fact that "it does not belong to the subject to decide whether a thing is possible or not, but to the Superior alone ...." (*Summa Theologiæ*, I, II, Q. 13, A. 5)

Finally, although there is no need to consider the case of immoral or unjust laws promulgated by the pope to be of *general* application in the Church, this does not necessarily apply to ecclesiastical laws of more restricted scope, such as diocesan laws. It is *not* impossible that a bishop might promulgate a law for his diocese which manifestly required a sinful act, such as would be the case if he demanded that priests take less than fifteen minutes in the celebration of Mass.[7] In such a case he should evidently be disobeyed. Nor is it impossible that he should promulgate a law which could be obeyed without sin but which was manifestly contrary to justice, for instance by forbidding priests of the Dominican order to write in public on theological matters, or by making clerics born in the month of April ineligible for certain ecclesiastical offices. In such a case, St. Robert Bellarmine teaches that the law would be invalid and not strictly binding in conscience, but he adds that it ought nevertheless to be obeyed if scandal would arise from disobedience to it. (*De Romano Pontifice*, lib. IV, cap. 15)[8]

---

[7] Moral theologians agree that to say Mass in less than fifteen minutes is impossible without gravely sinful irreverence.

[8] "For if the Pope were to order the Lenten fast to be observed alike by children and adults, by weak and strong, by the sick and the healthy, the law would be unjust [and therefore, as has been pointed out two paragraphs earlier, no law at all]. The same would apply if he ordered that only rich men and nobles might be admitted to the episcopate, excluding the poor and commoners even if they were more learned and virtuous. This would be unjust absolutely speaking, even though it might be just in some particular place and time on account of some special circumstance. And although an unjust law is no law at all and hence does not of itself bind in conscience, yet

The proper course for the victim of such an injustice is, of course, if necessary, to appeal to the Holy See, but meanwhile to follow Our Lord's counsel: " ... if a man will contend with thee in judgement and take away thy coat, let go thy cloak also unto him." (Matthew 5:40) What must never be forgotten is that the permission to disobey an unjust but not sinful instruction does not apply to general laws of the Church, for they are protected from such abuses; does not apply to particular commands given to individuals by popes or bishops, for here the only question is whether the person commanding has authority over the person being commanded in the matter of the command (a law must, by its nature, be just and useful, which is not so, however, of a command, which looks to the individual rather than to the community); and does not apply to cases where the instruction *seems* unjust, but only where it is *manifestly* and undeniably so, for it is the business of the superior to assess the justice of his commands, not of the inferior.

The Davies Doctrine of Obedience

Having established this background, we may now turn to the sharply contrasting doctrines of Mr. Michael Davies on the same subject.

On page XV of his Introduction to *Pope John's Council*, Davies writes as follows:

> Some readers may wonder why this book has no '*imprimatur*' and whether one was asked for but refused. The answer is that, as I was refused an '*imprimatur*' for *Cranmer's Godly Order* solely on the grounds that both the Censor and Bishop concerned disapproved of the priest[9] to whom it was dedicated, there was clearly no point in

---

a distinction must be made according to the kind of law involved. For when a law is unjust by its subject matter, i.e. it is contrary to divine law (whether natural or positive), not only does it not oblige but it must on no account be observed, in accordance with the words of Acts V 'We ought to obey God rather than men.' (...) But when a law is unjust by virtue of its end, its author, or its form, it ought to be obeyed whenever scandal would follow if it were not."

subjecting myself to such a farcical procedure for a second time .... However, the typescript was vetted by a number of well-qualified priests who assured me that it is free from any doctrinal or moral error. I would like to express my gratitude for their help but will not name them as it would be a poor return for their kindness to bring the pursuivants down upon them.

Let us mention in passing that the value of the assurance of the anonymous "well-qualified priests" may be gauged both from the fact that they lack the courage to face up to the authorities of the Conciliar Church without the cover of anonymity, and from the numerous errors contained in the book they have approved which are exposed in this *Evaluation*. Not least of these errors is Davies's attitude to the Church's law concerning ecclesiastical censorship of religious books. This law, as found in the 1917 *Code of Canon Law*, which even on Davies's own terms was the law in force at the time he wrote the above quoted extract, is straightforward in its requirements. Canon 1385§1, 2° says:

> Without prior Church censorship even laymen are not allowed to publish ... books concerning the Bible, theology, Church history, Canon Law, natural theology, ethics, or other religious and moral sciences; books or pamphlets of prayers or devotions, or of religious, moral, ascetic, or mystical doctrine, and instructions, and other works of a similar nature, even though they are intended to foster piety; or other writings, in general, which contain anything having a special bearing on religion or morality.

Needless to say, almost all of Davies's writings[10] fall under the provisions of this canon and certainly *Pope John's Council*

---

[9] This priest was Fr. Oswald Baker. – J.S.D.

[10] With the obvious exceptions of his frivolous discussions of Al Jolson, Fig Newtons, Kalamazoo, cocktails, space travel and rugby football, etc., all of which topics, incredibly, he has considered worthy of the attention both of himself and of the readers of his *Letter from London* column in *The Remnant*. Cf. footnote 30 on p. 134.

is no exception. For the benefit of any readers who may not be fully acquainted with the correct procedure, it is as follows:

(a) The author must submit the proofs of his work either to the bishop of his diocese or to the bishop of the diocese in which publication is proposed.

(b) On receiving the manuscript, the bishop assigns a censor (who should be a learned theologian) to examine the book and give a statement as to whether or not it contains anything objectionable from the Catholic point of view, such as an error against faith or morals.

(c) If the bishop receives a favourable verdict from the censor, he gives his *"imprimatur"* (the Latin for "let it be printed"), and publication can proceed.

(d) In the event that either the censor or the ordinary refuse permission to publish on unreasonable grounds (and there is no obligation upon them to state their grounds for refusal), the author is entitled to refer the matter to other bishops who might authorise publication in their own dioceses, *provided that he informs them that another ordinary has refused his application,*[11] or to the Holy See. *On no account*, however, is he permitted to publish without an *"imprimatur"* on the grounds that he has been assured by "a number of well-qualified priests" that his manuscript is "free from any doctrinal or moral error."

Davies states correctly that the application of the law of censorship in the Conciliar Church, as he had learned by experience in the attempt to have his first full-length book approved, is a "farcical procedure." The conclusion which he draws from this, however, is entirely gratuitous – namely that, rather than subject himself to a "farcical procedure", he is automatically entitled to publish *without* ecclesiastical approval.

And of course the fact that the diocesan censors of the Conciliar Church are unreliable – which, it need hardly be said,

---

[11] Canon 1385§2.

the present writer would be the very last to dispute – is no guarantee that Davies's handpicked "well-qualified" priests are any *more* reliable. Indeed, any reader who has persevered with me thus far and has seen the number of serious errors concerning the Catholic religion that these priests have allowed him to include in his published writings is in a position to know that reliable they most certainly are not!

But in a sense this is not the point, which is simply that, whatever the quality of the alternatives an author might believe to be available, (a) he cannot simply *presume* that a work is orthodox because he cannot obtain a fair hearing from an ecclesiastical authority to settle the point, and (b) the law forbidding publication without an *imprimatur* does not simply cease to exist merely because one bishop, or even several, apply it unjustly.

I am not, of course, denying that *in some circumstances* it may be permissible to publish without ecclesiastical approval. For instance, when it is likely to be of considerable benefit to souls that a particular truth be publicized *and recourse to ecclesiastical authority is impossible*, a writer who had taken sufficient steps to ensure the orthodoxy of his writings might prudently publish by virtue of epikeia. And indeed if it were to become wholly impossible to obtain an *imprimatur* by legitimate means it is probable that *cessatio legis* – the automatic cessation of the law – would indeed take place.

My point is that Davies makes no claim to invoke such a justification (and would have difficulty in formulating his case, for he *has* access to those whom he recognizes as having authority), but suggests that the abuse of the authority which he mistakenly attributes to his diocesan bishop and censor[12] justifies him automatically in publishing with no approval

---

[12] I.e. it is the *authority* which Davies mistakenly attributes to these gentlemen, not the abuse thereof.

whatsoever, in the face of the refusal to sanction his work of the authorities he recognizes.

I opened this examination with the justification given by Davies in *Pope John's Council*, because to the best of my knowledge it was there that he used it for the first time. But in fact that treatment of his was comparatively brief and did not directly treat the legal position; and it is elsewhere in his writings, particularly in treating of Archbishop Lefebvre and the Society of St. Pius X, that he devotes space to attempting a complete clarification of his position. And, as readers are by now possibly expecting even before I say it, the clearer Davies's position becomes, the less Catholic it evidently is.

In a thirteen page appendix to *Pope Paul's New Mass*, Davies analyses what he calls "the right to resist an abuse of power". This analysis is a slovenly and inadequate treatment of a complex subject, but even as far as it goes it is vitiated by a careless – though far from inconvenient – error which strikes at the very heart of the matter. This error is made clear in the following extract:

> However, if – which God forbid – a pope did revoke the right of every priest to celebrate the Tridentine Mass, employing a form which left no doubt as to the strict legality of his action, would this mean that traditionalist priests would have no alternative but to celebrate the Novus Ordo Missæ? This conclusion is by no means certain. Simply because an action is legal it does not follow that it is right. It is possible for a person in authority, even a pope, to act '*ultra vires*', to abuse his authority. In such a case the faithful would have the right to resist.

Davies seems not to realise the true meaning of the term "*ultra vires*", but his meaning is clear nonetheless. He is saying that whenever a person in authority abuses his authority by giving a command which, in the eyes of God, he ought not to have given, his subjects are entitled to refuse to comply with his order. And the same assertion recurs throughout the appendix and elsewhere in Davies's writings (e.g. his article entitled "Obedience" in *The Angelus* of December 1986).

It is completely untrue. It contrasts sharply with the doctrine of the *Penny Catechism*, St. Robert Bellarmine and Fr. Murray (which is also the doctrine of St. Thomas and every other Catholic authority) as set out at the beginning of this section, since Davies holds that the subject is entitled to disobey whenever *the superior sins in giving the command*. Catholic doctrine, by contrast, is that the subject is entitled (and obliged) to disobey only when *he* (the subject) *would sin by obedience*. Evidently if a true pope were to command Catholic priests to say the Novus Ordo Missæ they would indeed have to refuse to obey, since obedience would involve the commission of a mortal sin (in fact several). But if a pope rashly introduced unwise liturgical changes that did not undermine faith or reverence,[13] priests would *per se* have no alternative but to obey, since, although the pope might very well be sinning by giving the command, no sin would be involved on their part in complying with it.

On p. 596 in the same book (*Pope Paul's New Mass*), Davies reminds us of his rendering of this point of doctrine. Here he writes: "Cardinal Newman stresses that if a man is sincerely convinced that what his superior commands is displeasing to God, he is bound not to obey." We must hope for Newman's sake that what he meant, when he used this ambiguous assertion, was that a man is bound not to obey when he is convinced that *obedience to* what his superior commands would be displeasing to God, but we can have no such hope as to what Davies means in the interpretation of the passage, which is that whenever a superior displeases God by giving a command, the command is robbed of all force and rendered null.[14]

---

[13] As some think that St. Pius X did with regard to the Roman Breviary and as many think that Pope Pius XII did in 1955 with regard to the cereonies of Holy Week.

[14] He repeats the same error in his pamphlet *The Divine Constitution* ... (p.

Once again, it must categorically be said, *it is completely untrue*. Moreover, it is just as well that it is; for if it were true, it would lead to chaos. It would mean, for instance, that if there were evidence that even the most sacrosanct laws of the Church had been originally promulgated by a pope for some sinful ulterior motive, we should be entitled to disobey them with impunity – an absurdity unsupported, of course, by any Catholic authority.

On the basis of this ambiguous quotation from the anyhow unreliable Cardinal Newman and of a handful of other quotations from Catholic sources which in reality touch only on the question of commands (and not of laws) which it would be sinful to *obey*, Davies argues that Archbishop Lefebvre is justified, not only in resisting the flagrant sacrilege of the Novus Ordo, but also in acting in all respects as if the authorities of the Church at Roman and diocesan level had ceased to exist while nevertheless insisting that they remain in place! Indeed the Archbishop has gone so far as to authorize some of his priests to administer Confirmation although a papal indult is absolutely necessary for the sacrament to be validly administered by one who is not a bishop, and he has in some cases relieved those he has ordained to the major Orders of the obligations thereby incurred (clerical dress, recitation of the Divine Office, celibacy, etc.) for which he has not the slightest power. And of course, as we have seen in Chapter Seven, he has refused to close his

---

31) where he asserts that the faithful "have the right to refuse to obey him [the pope] if they are convinced in conscience that a particular command will harm rather than build up the Mystical Body." The error is twofold. First, Davies turns the subject into the superior by constituting him judge of what ought to be done (imagine practising such "obedience" in any army at war!), whereas Catholic doctrine forbids the subject to judge a command unless the facts are manifest. Secondly, he makes *an error of judgement by the superior* a sufficient reason for disobedience, whereas the Church permits disobedience only when to obey would be a *sin* (against natural or Divine law or against a human law from which the superior has no power to dispense) *for the subject.*

seminary and wind up the society of priests which he founded, when called upon to do so by those whom he recognized as his ecclesiastical superiors, including the man he took to be Pope.

The Case of Robert Grosseteste, Bishop of Lincoln

As a supposed historical precedent for behaviour such as that of Archbishop Lefebvre in his wholesale disobedience to (purportedly) papal laws and commands, Davies has more than once invoked the memory of England's great scholar-bishop, Robert Grosseteste (1170?-1253), for instance, in Appendix III of *Pope Paul's New Mass*, and in Appendix II to *Apologia Pro Marcel Lefebvre*, Vol. I. Although "probably the most fervent and thorough-going papalist among mediæval English writers,"[15] nevertheless, when Pope Innocent IV attempted to command him to appoint unworthy candidates to ecclesiastical offices, Grosseteste defied him outspokenly:

> In 1250, when he was at least eighty years of age, he went to the Papal Court to make his protest. He stood up alone, attended by nobody but his official .... Pope Innocent IV sat there with his cardinals and members of his household to hear the most thorough and vehement attack that any great pope can ever have had to hear at the height of his power.[16]

But with typical lack of the attention to detailed reasoning which is always necessary in theological controversy, Davies has never demonstrated that the two cases are truly parallel. Nor, in fact, could he have succeeded in doing so if he had tried, for they are not. What is fundamentally objectionable in Archbishop Lefebvre's position (given his wrong-headed acceptance of John-Paul II), and completely incompatible with Catholic doctrine, is *not* his refusal to obey an intrinsically immoral command – for instance, to say the Novus Ordo Missæ – but his

---

[15] *Grosseteste's Relations with the Papacy and the Crown* by William Abel Pantin, M.A., F.B.A., in *Robert Grosseteste, Scholar and Bishop*, edited by D.A. Callus, 1953, p. 183.

[16] Sir Maurice Powicke, introduction to Callus's collection of essays, p. xxiii.

refusal to obey commands which, though they may appear to him to threaten harm to the Church and to be most ill-advised, are by no stretch of imagination intrinsically immoral – such as the command to wind up the Society of St. Pius X; coupled with his open disobedience to long-standing ecclesiastical laws (touching on the rights of ordinaries, for instance, and the requirements for lawful Ordination). And although Grosseteste provides an excellent instance of a historical Catholic figure who defied a pope who issued a command which he (Grosseteste) considered it would have been patently immoral to obey, he certainly does not provide any precedent for opposing any command which it would *not* be intrinsically immoral to comply with; still less can it be claimed that he ever infringed any ecclesiastical *law* on any pretext whatsoever.

His position is accurately stated by Pantin (*loc. cit.*, p. 191):

> The problem of an unlawful command might seem to many a hypothetical or academic one; to Grosseteste, *with his conviction that any unworthy appointment to a cure of souls was a mortal sin*, it appeared very real. (Emphasis added)

This crucial distinction, between a command which one is convinced it would be a mortal sin – "contrary to Christ's precepts," to use Grosseteste's own words taken from his memorandum to the pope at Lyons in 1250 – to comply with, and a command which one deems a sin on the part of the authority issuing it but which it is not intrinsically immoral to heed, is what either eludes Davies or is deliberately suppressed by him.

The Defence of the Ambrosian Rite

Another historical episode invoked by Davies as a precedent for the disobedience of contemporary traditionalists to those whom they recognize as the lawfully appointed successors of St. Peter, is the refusal of the Catholics of Milan to abandon their ancient liturgy, known as the Ambrosian Rite, in favour of the Roman Rite. On p. 601 of *Pope Paul's New Mass*, he informs us that "a number of popes, including Nicholas II, St. Gregory VII and Eugenius IV, attempted to impose the Roman Rite on the people of Milan. The Milanese even went to the extent of taking up arms in defence of their traditional liturgy, the Ambrosian Rite, and they eventually prevailed." What Davies *fails* to tell us, however, makes this information irrelevant and destroys the intended parallel with the present situation; for although the popes named by Davies – or rather, I believe, their legates – *wished* the Milanese to switch to the Roman Rite, they never issued a command or a law requiring them to. It is worth noting that Popes Nicholas II and St. Gregory VII, who both reigned in the late eleventh century found the Milanese rebellious on matters much more serious than their liturgical preferences. The Milanese clergy were guilty of simony and concubinage almost to a man and at one point determined to embark on a schismatic rebellion against Rome. It was in their endeavours to reinforce proper ecclesiastical order in Milan that several popes wished to see the Roman Liturgy used there, and if the Milanese rejected the idea, this had as much to do with their general spirit of insubordination as with fidelity to local tradition. Certainly no writer approved by the Church has ever held up the behaviour of the Milanese in this dispute as a model for the imitation of subsequent generations.

When the Milanese took up arms – if the riot in question is appropriately so described – it was not in response to a papal initiative at all, but to an imprudent manoeuvre of Pope Eugene IV's legate, Cardinal Branda de Castiglione, who was promptly dismissed; so the Milanese situation provides no example whatever of resistance to papal jurisdiction except insofar as the Milanese flirted with schism rather than abide by Catholic morality concerning their simony and concubinage – hardly an example that can be put forward by a Catholic writer for his readers to follow.

What is a Law?

In the same appendix in *Pope Paul's New Mass*, on p. 541, Davies makes another error on the subject of obedience due to laws of the Church. Purporting to summarize the teaching of St. Thomas Aquinas, he says:

> A law can cease to bind without revocation on the part of the legislator when it is clearly harmful, impossible, or irrational. This is particularly true if a prelate commands anything contrary to Divine precept. ... St. Thomas ... teaches that not only would the prelate err in giving such an order but that anyone obeying him would sin ....

The first sentence quoted directly implies that the supreme authority in the Church might impose a law which is "clearly harmful, impossible, or irrational." By contrast, the authorities quoted at the beginning of this chapter demonstrate that according to Catholic doctrine the Holy Ghost protects the Church from ever promulgating a law which is incompatible with the Faith, or harmful to souls. Indeed its denial of this truth was one of the grounds on which Pope Pius VI condemned the Synod of Pistoia (see Denzinger 1578). Later in the passage quoted, Davies refers to an "order" as though this were the subject under discussion whereas what he mentioned previously was a "law". Now it is of course perfectly compatible with the Catholic Faith that a prelate, and even a pope, might give a *command*, or *order*, with which it would be sinful to comply – and the teaching of St. Thomas goes no further than this – but it seems that Davies is either so careless or so ignorant of his subject that he writes as though a law and a command were the same thing, whereas the former is a universal and permanent instruction, and the latter no more than a particular and temporary one.

On p. 203 of Vol. I of *Apologia Pro Marcel Lefebvre*, Davies writes as follows:

> ... even if it is conceded, for the sake of argument, that the Vatican had the law upon its side, it does not follow that the Archbishop was necessarily in the wrong. There are many orthodox Catholics who evade the necessity of considering the Archbishop's case on its merits by reducing the entire question to one of legality. 'Archbishop Lefebvre is in breach of Canon Law,' they argue, 'therefore he is wrong.

It is disingenuous for Davies to suggest – "even if it is conceded, for the sake of argument" – that there is any question over whether or not Archbishop Lefebvre is in breach of Canon Law. For anyone who acknowledges the validity of the pontificate of Paul VI, the Society (a) was founded for a trial period only in a single diocese, and (b) was suppressed by the supreme authority, whose power to suppress a religious order, congregation, society or house is unquestionable; and, as we have already seen, even in the famous case of the suppression of the Society of Jesus, which is generally recognized to have been a grossly misguided action, it was never, and has never been, suggested that the action was invalid and that the Society of Jesus continued to exist legally all along. Hence Archbishop Lefebvre's practice of "incardinating" those whom he ordains into his non-existent Society, in order to avoid the need for dimissorial letters required by Canon Law, is without the smallest canonical foundation, and in some cases – such as the erection of seminaries in Italy, Germany, the United States and Argentina – he does not himself deny that he is in breach of the law.

But let us proceed to Davies's answer to the "many orthodox Catholics who ... reduce the entire question to one of legality – 'Archbishop Lefebvre is in breach of Canon Law, therefore he is wrong.'" This is how Davies continues:

> At the risk of labouring a point which has probably been made sufficiently clear already, the law is at the service of the Faith. It is intended to uphold the Faith and not to undermine it. Given that the

manner in which the case against the Archbishop was conducted constituted an abuse of power, then he was entitled to resist.

Of course, this is not an argument at all. It contains no vestige of a reasoning process. The law is indeed intended to uphold the Faith, but this can scarcely be taken to imply that anyone who has a bright idea which in his view would advance the cause of the Faith is entitled to pursue it without regard to the prescriptions of the law. The law is necessary precisely because, without it, countless individual initiatives on behalf of the Faith would lead to nothing but a barren chaos. By contrast, the Church, like every well-ordered society, greatly prefers the evil, such as it is, that some particular initiative which might have borne fruit should perish without ever seeing the light of day, to the much greater evil that disorder should be introduced into her mission. Once again Davies is making an assertion for which the only justification is his fundamental error on the doctrine of obedience to legitimate authority. Archbishop Lefebvre was entitled to resist the man whom he publicly recognized as pope because the action against him constituted an abuse of power, Davies tells his readers. Disobedience is permissible whenever the superior sins in giving his command, is necessarily the underlying presumption. Emphatically, neither the assertion nor the assumption is true. And it is worth mentioning that, not surprisingly, Davies generally avoids stating this doctrine expressly and succeeds in giving the impression that it is authoritatively approved by confounding it with the wholly separate case in which the subject would sin if he were to obey.

Later on the same page, Davies writes:

> His [Archbishop Lefebvre's] position is based upon one fundamental axiom [sic]: the action taken against him violates either Ecclesiastical or Natural Law, possibly both. If he is correct then his subsequent actions can be justified and the legality or illegality of subsequent Vatican decisions is irrelevant.

The reasoning is rather elliptic in this passage, but it seems that what Davies is trying to indicate is this:

During the period when Archbishop Lefebvre's seminary and religious society were recognized by the Vatican, he was, on his own premises, entitled to ordain priests from dioceses throughout the world sent to Écône by bishops who were ready to accept any priest emanating from a seminary approved by the Vatican. However, various actions were taken against him by those in Rome and by the ordinary of the diocese in which his seminary was located, some of which actions appeared to breach ecclesiastical or natural law. These actions culminated in the suppression of the seminary and the society, and the suspension of Archbishop Lefebvre himself from all clerical functions by the man whom he recognized as pope. Archbishop Lefebvre then found himself in a position where diocesan bishops were no longer prepared to accept for the ministry in their dioceses priests trained and ordained at his seminary since he no longer had the approval of the Vatican. He therefore considered himself justified in continuing to ordain priests to be attached to no diocese at all in the face of the plain law of the Church.

An analogous piece of reasoning in connection with civil instead of canon law might be as follows:

> A man was running an efficient business, and making a satisfactory living for himself and his family. Then the government instituted proceedings against him on a trumped up breach of office fire-regulations and convicted him. Thereupon they forcibly closed his office and evicted him leaving him destitute.

So far, on Davies's premises, the case parallels Archbishop Lefebvre's exactly. The conclusion, if we are to pursue the same reasoning, is that the man in question, since he is the victim of an illegal and immoral process, is therefore entitled flagrantly to disregard all laws in the attempt to restore himself to the position which he has unjustly forfeited since, evidently, once one person disobeys the law, the laws cease to have all relevance and validity!

I have no intention of denying that a great many of the Archbishop's current initiatives *could* be justified, once they were placed in the context of an accurate assessment of the nature of the crisis. The point here is that the only justification we are given for Archbishop Lefebvre's infractions of Canon Law is that he is no longer bound by the law because he is himself the victim of its unjust application.

Legal Minutiæ

Davies has not yet quite completed his case against the position of his "many orthodox Catholics." On p. 204 he offers a final tactical suggestion as follows:

> Those who condemn the Archbishop invariably ignore this fundamental axiom[17] and concentrate upon the legal minutiæ of the subsequent sanctions. Those who support the Archbishop will do so most effectively by continually redirecting attention to this axiom rather than allowing themselves to be diverted into futile and endless discussion on these legal minutiæ.

Well, there is no doubt that Davies is right in saying that the most *effective* tactic for those who support Archbishop Lefebvre, would be the refusal to discuss the relevant details of Canon Law and to pontificate instead in very general terms about how Archbishop Lefebvre himself is the victim of an illegal process and how the law does not apply in extreme situations. What he does not devote any space in his book, or anywhere else, to considering, however, is whether this tactic is honest or compatible with Catholic principles, and he would land himself in terrible difficulties if he did this in any serious manner.

As far as what he *does* say is concerned, perhaps the only direct comment it calls for is that once a man begins to sneer at

---

[17] It is impossible to introduce this quotation by quoting the axiom referred to, because, strangely, Davies has not, in fact, mentioned an axiom at all in what comes before. What he represents as an axiom is the allegation that "the action taken against [Archbishop Lefebvre] violates either ecclesiastical or natural law, possibly both."

"legal minutiæ" and to insist that the *only* points relevant to discussion are those of morality – Divine law, not human law – his orthodoxy is already in a precarious state; for, as we have seen, it is an article of faith that the Church has the right and power to supplement the Divine law and natural law by her own ecclesiastical laws, thereby rendering unlawful certain actions which would otherwise be lawful[18] – as indeed she has done, for instance, by forbidding healthy Catholics over the age of seven to eat meat on Fridays.

When Davies finds that Canon Law obstructs what he considers to be the correct course for traditional Catholics to follow, he will casually invoke the "higher law" of "faith". And since such an attitude makes each individual his own judge of when he may disobey the laws and legitimate commands of (those whom he recognizes as) ecclesiastical authority, it is of no consequence whatever if one who takes this line would never explicitly deny – indeed even explicitly admits – the existence of objective ecclesiastical law. In practice he is no more bound by his theoretical recognition of ecclesiastical authority than a Protestant is bound to believe the contents of the Bible. And if the chaos to which private judgement has reduced Protestantism in its interpretation of Scripture can correctly be called anarchy – as it surely can – the term is no less appropriately applied to those who subject the laws of the Church to a simultaneous process of "private interpretation" and "higher criticism."

---

[18] "If anyone say that the baptized are free from the *precepts of the Church*, whether written or handed down, so that they are not *bound* to observe them unless they voluntarily subject themselves thereto, let him be anathema." (Council of Trent, Canon 8 on Baptism, Denzinger 864)

CHAPTER NINE
ERRORS CONCERNING
SACRAMENTAL THEOLOGY

"Beware lest any man cheat you by philosophy and vain deceit."
(Colossians 2:8)

Introduction

The vast bulk of Davies's writings on Catholic subjects either documents the worst "abuses" of the Conciliar Church or analyses the theological questions raised by the "reforms" introduced in the wake of Vatican II. Since the changes in the rituals of the seven sacraments are the most evident and inescapable features of the Conciliar Church, the majority of Davies's theological analyses have been devoted to sacramental theology and as a result he has acquired a certain amount of knowledge about that subject, some of it derived from reliable sources and some of it from sources which are much less reliable. And unfortunately, while the sources which are unreliable lead him into catastrophic errors, one thing which they do not do is prevent an *appearance* of confident erudition, an appearance which characterizes all Davies's writings on this subject; and the resulting combination of error dressed up with specious scholarship is pernicious to an extent which it would be hard to exaggerate.

It would be a desperately laborious task to assess everything that Davies has written about sacramental theology, and rather than attempt it, so the following considerations will be limited to a sample of four major topics. The examination of these four topics will be more than enough to expose gross deficiencies in

Davies's knowledge of sacramental theology which are entirely representative of his incompetence throughout the field of sacramental theology.

The four topics which I have selected, each of them of the utmost gravity, are these:

(A) The validity of the Orders of Archbishop Marcel Lefebvre
(B) The validity of the 1968 new rite of Ordination
(C) The theory of sacramental validity, with particular reference to the principle known as *"significatio ex adjunctis"*
(D) The validity of the Novus Ordo Missæ
(E) Odds and Ends.

The title "Odds and Ends" has been given to Section (E) because it will treat of a few less momentous, but nonetheless serious, errors which cannot be passed over and which do not fall into any of the other categories.

CHAPTER NINE SECTION (A)
THE VALIDITY OF THE ORDERS OF ARCHBISHOP LEFEBVRE

For some years an argument has been in circulation among traditional Catholics to the effect that Archbishop Lefebvre does not have valid Orders and that priests emanating from his seminaries are not therefore validly ordained. Some, such as the late Dr. H.M. Kellner, take the view that this is completely definite and that Archbishop Lefebvre's Orders, and all Orders emanating from him, are certainly invalid. Others regard Archbishop Lefebvre's Orders and those emanating from him as *doubtful*. A much larger third group, needless to mention, has maintained that these opinions are quite unfounded and that the Orders of Archbishop Lefebvre himself and of those ordained by him are indubitably as valid as those of the Apostles themselves.

Before embarking on my own assessment of this dispute, and especially of the efforts of Michael Davies towards resolving it, I should emphasize that the subject being treated at the moment is not *lawfulness*; it is *validity*. The argument leading to the conclusion that Archbishop Lefebvre's Orders are doubtful or invalid is based upon the fact that Archbishop Lefebvre was ordained a priest by the man who was later to become Cardinal Achille Liénart and who was also to be the principal bishop of the three who took part in Lefebvre's episcopal Consecration in 1947. Liénart was a high-ranking Freemason, the argument proceeds, and this makes it unlikely, in the view of some, or impossible, in the view of others, that he should have had the intention of doing as the Church does, and at the very least probable that he would have had a positive contrary intention thus invalidating the sacrament, even if he had used the correct matter and form.

And I complete this very brief summary of the argument by noting that the original allegation of Liénart's affiliation to Freemasonry was made by the Marquis de la Franquerie in his book *L'Infaillibilite Pontificale*, in which he asserts that Liénart was initiated in 1912 and had risen to the thirtieth degree by 1924.

To avoid any risk of misunderstanding, I wish to declare expressly at the outset that I am entirely satisfied that the Orders of Archbishop Lefebvre and of those derived from him via the traditional rite of ordination are valid.

Now it so happens that this is exactly the position held by Michael Davies, who maintains, no less firmly than the present writer, that Archbishop Lefebvre has validly received all four Minor Orders and all four Major Orders, culminating in his valid episcopal Consecration in 1947. And this being the case, readers may well wonder why I should choose, as my first example of Davies's theological ineptitude, his writing on a question to which I believe he has got the answer 100% right. The reason is simply that, although Davies gets the *answer* to the question right, he gets nothing else whatever right about it. In particular, he uses a series of invalid arguments; he tells outright lies both about theology and about matters of easily ascertainable non-theological fact, such as whether a particular author holds a particular opinion or not; he invents facts to suit his case and browbeats his readers by his usual tactics of sneering at the opposing case instead of substantiating his own position; and, in short, his defence of Archbishop Lefebvre's Orders is so appalling from every point of view that it not only does not validly prove the conclusion he reaches, but makes it almost a psychological impossibility for anyone who is aware of the extent of its feebleness and dishonesty to believe that the conclusion it defends could nevertheless be true *despite* Davies's defence of it. In fact the present writer knows of people who might never have questioned Archbishop Lefebvre's Orders if Davies had remained silent but who have gone to their graves in doubt of them as a result of studying Davies's articles arguing in favour of their validity.

Nor should this give the slightest cause for surprise, for it is axiomatic that the cause of truth can suffer more from false arguments used to defend it than from any direct attack. If an innocent man is apprehended by chance in circumstances which strongly suggest his involvement in a serious crime, he will sin not only against honesty but also against ordinary human prudence if he lies to make his defence appear more plausible, for should his lie be exposed as such, who *then* will believe him to be innocent? In the same way, when Michael Davies is so determined to defend the validity of his hero's Orders that, being unable to discover a valid argument by which to do so, he strings together a case for the defence in which inaccuracies and misrepresentations of theological sources rub shoulders with shamelessly invalid arguments, it is evident that in the long run he is doing no service whatever to the cause of truth.

But this is something of an anticipation. For the time being no mention will be made of the arguments which do *not* appear in Davies's case and which would have substantiated his conclusion had he used them. These considerations will be deferred until after Davies's arguments have been analysed, and readers have been able to ask themselves, after the dénouement of this theological farce, what conclusion a person of integrity would tend towards after reading them.

It was at the beginning of the eighties that Davies embarked on his attempt to defend the validity of the Orders of Archbishop Lefebvre, which he did in two articles printed, on this side of the Atlantic, in *Approaches*, N⁰ˢ 71 and 72. In the first of these articles he opens by claiming that the allegations that the founder of the Society of St. Pius X was neither priest nor bishop had emanated from a "malicious campaign to discredit Archbishop Lefebvre," and declares that Liénart's supposed Masonic affiliation "is based totally on hearsay and that there is no supporting evidence which will be acceptable in a court of law."

This is how he summarizes his position on this point:

I had therefore concluded that the case against the Cardinal [Liénart] was no more than a gratuitous allegation some time before the question of Archbishop Lefebvre's Orders had been raised. Thus the whole case against the validity of the Archbishop's Orders is based upon an unproven basic premise. As there is no concrete evidence that Cardinal Liénart was ever a Mason, there is clearly no reason for questioning the validity of his Ordination.

Reasonable though this summary may appear at first sight, Davies, while not saying a single thing which is actually false, is nevertheless engaging in "*suppressio veri*" (i.e. the suppression of pertinent truths) on a heroic scale. Here are some of the truths which he shamelessly conceals:

(i) Archbishop Lefebvre himself, who had most reason to deny it, on more than one occasion explicitly admitted his unqualified acceptance of de la Franquerie's assertion that Cardinal Liénart was affiliated to Freemasonry.

(ii) Liénart's behaviour throughout his episcopal and cardinalatial career gave copious circumstantial evidence supporting the allegation, notably the vital role he played in the hijacking of Vatican II almost from the start by the liberal camp of which he was one of the most notable representatives. Given, therefore, that the Masonic plot to humiliate and destroy the Church is an established historical fact and that Liénart's actions were perfectly calculated to further these aims, the view that the case against the cardinal was "no more than a gratuitous allegation" shows more generosity to the miscreant than Davies ever showed to a sedevacantist.

(iii) The Marquis de la Franquerie is arguably the greatest living expert on the Judæo-Masonic conspiracy against the Church, being now in his late eighties and having been, in his youth, one of the right-hand men of the late Mgr. Jouin, founder and director of the Anti-Judæo-Masonic League and editor of its periodical the *Revue Internationale des Sociétés Secrètes*. He has thus been aware of Freemasonry's inroads into the senior hierarchical positions in the Church from the time when they were just beginning and when, incidentally, there still remained in elevated positions in the Church men who were well aware of what was happening and determined to oppose it by every means at their disposal.[1]

(iv) Moreover, in assessing the credibility of de la Franquerie's allegation that Liénart was a Mason, Archbishop Lefebvre would also have been able to draw on the evidence of his close acquaintance with Liénart, who not only had ordained him, consecrated him and been his ordinary for some time, but even hailed originally from the same part of the world as Archbishop Lefebvre – the diocese of Lille in France. And the fact that his personal knowledge of Liénart in no way inhibited his acceptance of the accuracy of de la Franquerie's allegation certainly provides negative evidence in its favour.

Thus Davies's suggestion that there is no concrete evidence is shown to be unfounded. Much more realistic is his claim that the evidence of Liénart's affiliation would not be enough to secure a conviction in a court of law. But surely this is irrelevant, for Catholics are not trying to secure the criminal conviction of Liénart, who died in 1973, but to satisfy themselves of the validity of the orders derived from him, which happen to include all orders deriving from Archbishop Lefebvre himself. The evidence, such as it is, has sufficed to convince many prudent Catholics that Liénart was at least probably a conscious infiltrator of the Church, enrolled in the ranks of her sworn enemies; and that likelihood certainly justifies us in examining with great care the possible effects of this on the validity of the

---

[1] The significance of this, of course, is that the prelates who actively supported Mgr. Jouin's labours against the organized forces of subversion, including a number of cardinals, would have given him and his close associate de la Franquerie access to whatever information they had at their disposal which they thought could be helpful. Hence de la Franquerie had available to him in the 1920s and 30s a much more fertile source of information than was available to writers who entered the fray in the 1950s, by which time the hierarchy, in so far as it had not been infiltrated, consisted almost entirely of temporizers.

Orders of those whom he ordained, for sacramental validity is certainly not something with which risks may be taken.

Thus far it has been shown that Davies conceals pertinent facts from his readers and makes invalid inferences on the basis of the few facts which he considers his readers adult enough to be exposed to.

Would a Freemason Ordain Validly

Continuing his article, Davies then asserts that, even if it were accepted "for the sake of argument" that there have been some Masonic bishops,[2] this does not supply sufficient reason to doubt the validity of Orders conferred by them. That Ordination or episcopal Consecration conferred by a Mason would be *unlawful* he acknowledges; but that they would be anything other than definitely *valid* he denies. Even, therefore, if Liénart had been a Freemason – which Davies regards as a gratuitous suggestion – this would not have prevented him from conferring valid Orders; so there is no reason to doubt the validity of Archbishop Lefebvre's Orders. I now quote Davies directly:

> The standard theological manuals state that for the Sacrament of Order the ordaining bishop must have the habitual intention of doing what the Church does and the ordinand [person being ordained] must have a least the habitual intention of receiving the sacrament. An *actual* intention of the will takes place when there is an actual advertence of the mind to what is being done, but for sacramental validity a *habitual* or *virtual* intention is normally adequate .... In order to administer a sacrament validly the minister requires neither faith nor the state of grace nor holiness of life. He need not believe that the Catholic Church is the true Church; nor

---

[2] Davies's claim that this presumption is made only "for the sake of argument" is ludicrous. It is completely established that there have been Masonic bishops in the Catholic Church, Talleyrand being a notable example, and it is doubtful whether any historian, Catholic or secular, who has considered the matter has ever dreamt of denying this. Indeed Davies himself (*Pope Paul's New Mass*, pp. 497 *et seq.*) supplies completely conclusive evidence of "Archbishop" Annibale Bugnini's affiliation to the Craft.

that what the Church teaches concerning a particular sacrament is true; nor that the sacrament will effect what the Church teaches it will effect; he need not even believe in God or that the administration of the sacrament will have any effect at all. Furthermore, even if the minister is a heretic and intends to act not as the Catholic Church acts but as his own denomination does, believing his own denomination to be the true Church, his intention is sufficient providing that he does not specifically exclude what is essential in the sacrament.

... Thus, for a sacrament to be invalid the minister must have what is termed 'a positive contrary intention', i.e. he would have to make a clear and deliberate resolution *not* to do what the Church does in the sacrament.

Up to this point Davies is representing Catholic sacramental theology reasonably accurately. His only substantial error is his statement that "for sacramental validity a *habitual* or virtual intention is normally adequate," for although a *virtual* intention is *usually* adequate, the same is most certainly *not* true of an *habitual* intention: indeed Frs. McHugh and Callan explain in their discussion of "Requirements ... for Valid Performance of a Sacrament" that " ... an habitual intention is *not* sufficient ...." (*Moral Theology*, n. 2666). But apart from this manifestation of his inveterate carelessness, the substance of what Davies has said is unquestionably true, and one of the implications that follow from what he has told us is that, whatever a man's beliefs may be, they need not prevent him from validly administering a Catholic sacrament. Thus a bishop who loses his faith is not thereby rendered unable to confer valid Orders. The Orders which he confers will, as Davies says, be invalid only if he forms a "positive contrary intention" by making up his mind that he *wants* the sacrament to be invalid or is determined to exclude that which the Church wishes to effect by, and believes is effected by, the sacrament of Order.

Now it should be fairly admitted that what Davies has said is quite sufficient to refute the allegations of such writers as the late Dr. Hugo Kellner, who, it may be remembered, maintained that a Freemason is *incapable* of validly conferring Orders.

But Davies's theology, although perfectly correct on this specific point, is not *relevant* to the mainstream case against him, which contends not that a Freemasonic bishop *cannot* validly ordain or consecrate, but that he *may well* choose not to do so. Davies is overlooking the fact that a bishop who is a Freemason is a totally different kettle of fish from one who lives in concubinage or even has lost his faith. This is because one who sins through weakness has no reason to sin further by deliberately framing his intention to nullify his sacraments, and still less motive has an unbeliever for doing the same because he does not believe in the sacramental effect anyhow, or that his intention will make any difference to it. But Freemasonry is an organization which conspires maliciously to harm the Church: why then would it not *wish* to invalidate sacraments in order to deprive the Church of grace? Certainly a Masonic *bishop* could not be compared with a businessman who joins his local Lodge in unsuspecting good faith, for no cleric could be unaware of the Church's teaching and laws concerning Freemasonry. So a man who was simultaneously a high degree Freemason and a high-ranking prelate of the Catholic Church might well be an exceptionally malicious and conscious servant of Satan. It is credible, therefore, that he might *believe* Catholic sacramental theology and use its doctrine of positive contrary intentions to harm the Church as much as he could.

Next in his article Davies introduces an argument with which this writer has no quarrel. It is based on an extract from Pope Leo XIII's encyclical *Apostolicæ Curæ* and I shall return to it at the end of this section when considering the *valid* arguments in favour of the validity of Archbishop Lefebvre's Orders. For the time being I omit it, as I omit also his introduction of the analogy of Archbishop Cranmer, who performed ordinations in the Catholic rite while harbouring heretical disbelief in the Catholic theology of the priesthood. It has already been noted that the Church's acceptance of these Orders as valid is not relevant to the case of a Freemason who is not a *disbeliever* in the priesthood, but an *enemy* of the priesthood.

Passing over these topics, we come directly to that part of Davies's article in which he simultaneously, finally and entirely parts company with both honesty and with orthodox doctrine. Here is how he introduces it:

> However, let us adopt the extreme position. Let us assume that a Masonic bishop has infiltrated the Church with the avowed intention of harming Her by introducing a positive contrary intention into Ordination ceremonies, and hence afflicting the Church with invalidly ordained priests and bishops. There is a possibility that by forming such an intention he could invalidate the Ordination of a priest. But this would not be the case in the Consecration of a bishop since Pope Pius XII promulgated his Apostolic constitution *Episcopalis Consecrationis* on November 30th 1944.
>
> Up to that time, although a single bishop could perform a Consecration validly he was normally required to be assisted by two other bishops, but it was not clear whether or not they were co-consecrators. However Pope Pius declared that 'in the fullness of Our Apostolic Authority ... the two Bishops who by ancient disposition, according to the prescriptions of the Roman Pontifical, assist at the Consecration, must also "consider" themselves consecrating Bishops with the same Consecrator and from now on must be called "co-consecrators.'
>
> THIS MEANS THAT FOR AN EPISCOPAL CONSECRATION PERFORMED SINCE 30TH NOVEMBER 1944 TO BE INVALID ALL THREE BISHOPS MUST HAVE FORMED A POSITIVE CONTRARY INTENTION *NOT* TO DO WHAT THE CHURCH DOES IN THE SACRAMENT OF ORDER. TO PUT IT MILDLY, THE CHANCES OF THIS HAPPENING ARE SOMEWHAT REMOTE. [*Davies's emphasis throughout*]

Consecration "Per Saltum"

The above argument – notwithstanding the screaming capitals it concludes with - is a completely valid one...if it is considered in isolation from the circumstances to which Davies intends it to apply. Indeed it must be promptly conceded that it would clinch Davies's case if the only point at issue was whether *Fr.* Lefebvre had been validly consecrated *bishop*. But there is in fact a much more fundamental question which must first be established: namely whether *Mr.* Lefebvre was ever validly ordained *priest* in the first place. For if his priestly Ordination is questionable, his episcopal Consecration will be no less so unless it can be established that a layman can be validly consecrated bishop without having first received the priesthood as a necessary intermediate step. It would evidently be of no avail for Marcel Lefebvre to have been consecrated by ten or a hundred bishops, all of them with a correct intention, if he lacked a necessary pre-condition to the validity of episcopal Consecration by never having been validly made a priest.

This raises two questions:

(a) Is there any reason to doubt the validity of Marcel Lefebvre's Ordination as a priest?

(b) Can a person who is not a priest validly receive episcopal Consecration?

To the first question the answer is straightforward, for, as already mentioned, the bishop responsible for ordaining him a priest was Achille Liénart, the same individual who was later to consecrate him and whose intentions in conferring orders is the very subject doubt has been cast on. Hence, there certainly *is* a question to be answered as to the validity of Archbishop Lefebvre's Ordination, for if we cannot be sure that he was ever a priest, we certainly cannot be sure that he was ever a bishop, except perhaps by demonstrating that the priesthood is *not* a necessary stepping-stone to the episcopate.

But here Davies has anticipated us, and he answers this objection as follows:

> A question could arise here as to whether a man who had not received valid priestly Ordination could be validly consecrated as a

bishop. The answer is that under the present *Code of Canon Law* it is forbidden to receive a higher Order without those which precede it, i.e. Ordination *per saltum*.[3] This law is not invalidating; but one who has maliciously, i.e. *mala fide* [in bad faith], received an Order *per saltum* is *ipso facto* suspended from the exercise of the Order received (Canon 2374). Obviously there would be no question of *mala fide*[*s*] in an ordinand who had honestly believed himself to be receiving valid priestly Ordination from a man who had formed a secret positive contrary intention not to ordain him. There is only one Sacrament of Order and episcopal Consecration has the effect of giving it to the bishop in its fullness.

Indeed in the early centuries those chosen as bishops were sometimes consecrated without previous priestly Ordination.

It is this argument which leads Davies to his conclusion:

THERE IS THEREFORE NOT THE SLIGHTEST ROOM FOR DOUBT REGARDING THE VALIDITY OF ARCHBISHOP LEFEBVRE'S OWN ORDERS OR THOSE CONFERRED BY HIM.

What Davies has just said may well appear to be well argued and reasonable notwithstanding the intemperate capitalisation. Indeed, if readers did not know Davies as well as I hope they are beginning to, they could be forgiven for thinking that it is conclusive.

But for those who are no longer so naïve, a question remains to be asked: *is it true?* Is what Davies has told us about the validity of the Consecration of bishops *"per saltum"*, and about the practice of such Consecrations in the early centuries, reality or invention?

On 31st December 1980, shortly after he had first read the article which has just been quoted, Mr. N.M. Gwynne wrote to Davies. Drawing attention to the assertion, at the end of Davies's piece on Archbishop Lefebvre's Orders, that "there is

---

[3] *"Per saltum"* is the Latin for "by a jump" and is the theological jargon used to designate the reception of an order by one who has not received the order that would normally precede it.

not the slightest room for doubt" regarding their validity, he pointed out that this assertion depended on the premise that episcopal Consecration received *"per saltum"* is definitely valid, whereas this crucial leg of the argument was in fact the only assertion in Davies's article for which he adduced no evidence. At the same time, N.M.G. drew Davies's attention to what is recorded in the Divine Office for the feast of St. Ambrose. This saint was consecrated bishop of Milan, after having been elected to this office while still a layman; but although this happened as early as the fourth century, he nevertheless had to receive *all the minor Orders and all major Orders in sequence before his episcopal Consecration*. N.M.G. closed his letter as follows:

> The point is that, on the face of what I have found, the evidence contradicts you rather than supports you; and it seems to me that for there to be, as you claim, 'not the slightest room for doubt,' you must have some evidence which very clearly and unmistakably overrides what I have come up with.
> I wonder, therefore, if you could very kindly give it to me. Obviously a list of the bishops so consecrated [i.e. without previous priestly Ordination] together with proof that it happened, or a quotation by one of the early Church Fathers that it was a common or occasional practice, would be very adequate.

To this letter Davies replied on 12th January 1981 promising to write a clarification on the subject of Ordination *"per saltum"* in the next number of *Approaches*. He also added a few comments on the evidence for Liénart's membership of Freemasonry and the difficulty of eliciting a formal ruling from the Holy See on the subject of episcopal Consecration *"per saltum"* and several other subjects. But, what he did *not* do in his letter was to *offer any evidence that episcopal Consecration "per saltum" is definitely valid* – notwithstanding the fact that this was the sole subject of the enquiry which N.M.G. had made to him.

N.M.G. then wrote to him again on 14th January 1981, first thanking him for his letter, and then returning to the main subject of his earlier letter, as follows:

> You state in your essay that, even in ... [the case that Liénart had a positive contrary intention during Lefebvre's Ordination as a priest], 'there is not the slightest doubt regarding the validity of the Archbishop's own Orders, etc ...' because episcopal Consecration has the effect of conferring the priesthood (if it is lacking) as well as the episcopacy and 'indeed in the early centuries those chosen as bishops were sometimes consecrated without previous priestly Ordination.'
> Do you agree that I have fairly summarized (and accurately quoted where appropriate) the position you took?
> If so, I ask you to support what you have stated to be a fact with evidence. You say that there is no formal definition on the matter, so that your statement of certainty must rest on the evidence of Consecration without previous Ordination having definitely happened, such evidence either being of a specific individual to whom it clearly and to everyone's agreement did happen, or perhaps a statement by one of the Fathers that it was a customary, or infrequent, or whatever, occurrence.
> If you have such evidence, could you please let me know where I can find it? If you do not have such evidence, could you please, in the interests of truth, withdraw the unsupported statement?

Anyone who has read in Chapter 3 of this *Evaluation* how Davies often deals with unwelcome correspondence will surely not be astounded to learn that this letter received no reply.

On 6th February N.M.G. wrote to Davies once more to check that he had received the letter and offering to send him another copy if it had gone astray. This letter *did* elicit a reply. Dated 13th February, it was of some length, opening with an apology for the delay in replying, which Davies blamed on his backlog of letters, and continuing with a number of other points. He then repeated the argument which he had produced in his original article in *Approaches* – to the effect that the contrary intention is never presumed when the correct matter and form are used – and followed this by asserting, with self-important sarcasm, that:

> As far as I am concerned, I am not prepared to take the possibility that Mgr. Lefebvre's Orders are invalid any more seriously than I am the claim of Clemente of Palmar de Troya that he is the Pope, or that Paul VI was kidnapped and replaced by a man with a rubber face mask.

Once again, Davies had made no attempt to address the only subject about which he had been questioned. In other words, when questioned as to the basis on which he had publicly stated that "there was not the slightest room for doubt," he repeatedly and consistently offered not the smallest scrap of evidence that the Church had even once at *any* time – let alone "sometimes", as he stated – recognized the validity of the Consecration of a bishop who had not previously been ordained priest.

At this point N.M.G. gave up the attempt in despair until, after the passage of some weeks, issue number 72 of Hamish Fraser's *Approaches* appeared, carrying another article by Davies, five A5 pages long, with the heading *Ordination "per saltum"*. In order to give Davies a fair hearing this article will be reproduced in its entirety (except the Introduction), with comments interposed as called for. What follows starts on p. 60 of that issue of *Approaches*:

> The subject of Ordination *per saltum* was raised during the controversy concerning Anglican Orders which was settled by the bull *Apostolicæ Curæ* in 1896. In a lecture delivered before the bull, but first published in 1896, a celebrated Anglican liturgist, F.E. Brightman, referred to the matter (S.P.C.K. edition, 1958, p. 38).[4] Brightman is one of the greatest liturgical authorities in the English-speaking world and his research into early liturgies is admired by both Catholic and Protestant historians. Brightman noted that if, for the sake of argument, it was conceded that the form for the priesthood in the Anglican Ordinal was inadequate, the same could

---

[4] Davies inadvertently omits the title of Brightman's work: it is *What Objections Have Been Made to English Orders?*

not be said of the form for Ordination as a bishop. Catholic theologians accepted that it could be an adequate form. He wrote: 'It is clear that for something like ten centuries it was not uncommon for deacons to be consecrated directly to the episcopate .... Therefore, even if the English Church did not ordain true presbyters, it would not follow that it has no priests or otherwise affect the Order of the Episcopate.'

So one of the main "authorities" that Davies relies on to support his belief about "Ordination *per saltum*" is not even a member of the Catholic Church at all: he is a Protestant! Davies expects his readers to give credence on a complex theological issue to the view of F.E. Brightman whose qualifications entitling him to our intellectual submission are that, a life-long member of the Church of England, his mind was at all relevant times darkened both by ignorance of a large part of Divine revelation and by the gross errors in which his sect had enmeshed him from his youth. And, for Heaven's sake, Brightman's utterly false general religious position is not the only factor demanding that his testimony be dismissed from consideration. He was also himself a clergyman – a "priest", as he would have put it – of the Church of England, and the very words of his that Davies quotes were written in the context of a defence of the absurd thesis that the Church of England possesses a valid sacramental priesthood. As a High Churchman Brightman was unlikely to be impartial in defending his own "priesthood" and this is yet another reason for us to be sceptical of what he says in the cause of maintaining an opinion that the Catholic Church has ruled to be false; and his contention that it was for ten centuries not uncommon for deacons to be consecrated directly to the episcopate is a central plank of his case.

But of course facts are facts whatever the source from which they reach us, and we should certainly be obliged, and therefore unhesitatingly prepared, to give due weight to any *evidence* which Brightman might produce in support of his assertion. But we are not put to this trouble, for Brightman does not cite a single authority for what he alleges or mention a single verifiable instance of Ordination "*per saltum*" in history.

This lack of evidence might dismay a reasonably conscientious Catholic, but it does not dismay Davies, who without shame or apology simply adopts the unsupported statement of a *biased heretic* as an authority to which respect should be given and attention paid in a dispute over *Catholic* theology. And in doing so, while he has certainly shed light on his own character, he has not advanced his readers' knowledge on the subject of episcopal Consecration *per saltum* in even the smallest degree.

Let us return to his article:

> Pope Leo XIII referred to this possibility in *Apostolicæ Curæ*, but stated that the possibility of Anglican bishops being ordained *per saltum* was not *relevant* as their rite for the Consecration of a bishop was just as invalid as that for Ordination to the priesthood.

Pope Leo did indeed refer in his bull to the argument that the Church of England could possess valid episcopal Orders if their form for episcopal Consecration were valid. This argument depends both on the validity of the Anglican formula of Consecration and on the belief that "*per saltum*" Ordination is valid; and Pope Leo dismissed it on the basis that, notwithstanding Brightman's breezy confidence on the subject, their Consecration formula is *not* valid. But he certainly did not concede that "*per saltum*" Ordination is valid, for he did not suggest at all that Anglican episcopal Orders *would* be valid if their Consecration formula was adequate. He simply abstained from addressing this question at all. Nor should this come as any surprise, for the truth of the matter,[5] despite Davies's vaunted certainty, is that the point is a matter of dispute even among very learned theologians. As Pope Leo XIII had a *definite* argument

---

[5] I.e. of whether one who is not a priest can validly be consecrated bishop without first having received priestly Orders.

to refute the pretences of the Protestants on this topic, he would naturally have had no purpose in weakening the argument agreed on by *all* Catholic theologians, by adding that *per saltum* episcopal Consecration *may* be invalid.

So his silence cannot be construed as altering in the slightest degree what had been the Church's position long before he wrote, and has remained so ever since – namely, that the validity of episcopal Consecration conferred upon those who have not been validly ordained to the priesthood is *doubtful*, and is thus not a matter on which any Catholic may lay down the law to another. Against this background, let us now take up Davies's article which is devoted to vindicating his claim that, in this matter, on which the most learned theologians are happy to admit their doubt, there is in fact no room for doubt whatsoever.

> Clearly, as is so commonly the case in matters relating to sacramental theology, there has been no *de fide* pronouncement on the question of Ordination *per saltum*. It is permissible to hold the opinion that such Ordinations are valid, or that they are invalid.

Is it now? One stares in amazed bewilderment at this admission, wondering what flight of fantasy could make it compatible with the assurance he gave, only a single issue of *Approaches* previously, that 'there is only one Sacrament of Order, and episcopal Consecration has the effect of giving it to the bishop in its fullness .... THERE IS *THEREFORE NOT THE SLIGHTEST ROOM FOR DOUBT* REGARDING THE VALIDITY OF ARCHBISHOP LEFEBVRE'S ORDERS ....'

Resuming the article:

> At one time many or most theologians would have denied the possibility [that Consecration *per saltum* can be valid], basing their opinion primarily on the current practice of the Church ....

The present writer has researched the opinions of numerous Catholic theologians of the past on this topic and has found many who are opposed to the validity of *per saltum*

Consecration; but *none* who bases his opinion "primarily on the current practice of the Church." Back to Davies:

> In his classic work *Anglican Orders and Defect of Intention*, Dr. Francis Clark comments (p. 174): 'That episcopal Orders can be validly conferred on a subject who is not a priest has come to be more and more accepted. Lennerz (*De Sacramento Ordinis*, Rome 1953, n. 235) considers that the opinion which denies the validity of Ordination *per saltum* can no longer be sustained.'

It should be noted that in no sense could Fr. Heinrich Lennerz S. J (1880-1961) be considered a theological authority of any weight. He is simply a mid-twentieth-century Jesuit who wrote a few short theological textbooks which do not even *purport* to get involved in any depth in theological argument. And in the manual to which Davies refers, he devotes only a very short space to the treatment of the question of episcopal Consecration *per saltum*. There he does indeed assert that such a Consecration is definitely valid, but he attempts to prove his position by but a single argument which genuinely learned theologians have not regarded themselves as justified in adopting as conclusive – that, in his view, it can be shown to be historically certain that there have been occasions when the Church has recognized such Consecrations as valid.

Now it is perfectly true that, *if* it could be shown that the Church *had* recognized such Consecrations as valid, Fr. Lennerz would have fully established his case. But, as will be shown at the end of this treatment of Davies's article, in considering the actual instances adduced by Fr. Lennerz, and as a number of theologians who have analysed the cases in depth concur, *all* of the instances adduced by him can be dismissed as unproven. Moreover, even if – as has certainly not yet been done – one *could* prove that one or two episcopal Consecrations without prior priestly Ordination had actually taken place, this in itself would not be sufficient to prove that the Church had recognized them as valid. In default of some authoritative pronouncement, they would not necessarily indicate that the procedure was anything more than an irregularity, unapproved by the Church and of questionable validity.

Let us return to Davies's article. At this point he quotes a couple of assertions from Addis and Arnold's[6] *Catholic Dictionary* (9th edition, p. 629). The first of these is:

> St Cyprian was made priest and bishop without passing through the lower grades (*Vita Pontii*, cap. 3 ed. Hertel [*sic*: this should read 'Hartel' – J.S.D.] p. xciii).

Does that appear decisive in Davies's favour? Those who think so have failed to notice that Davies, here as elsewhere, has subtly confused the issue by speaking in *general* terms of Ordination *"per saltum"*, his implication being that exactly the same principles apply to the *Ordination for the priesthood* of a man who is *not yet a deacon* as apply to the *Consecration* to the *episcopate* of a man who is *not yet a priest. But the same principles do not apply*. As we shall see later on, virtually all authorities are in agreement that it is possible validly to ordain a man to the major orders (subdeacon, deacon, priest and bishop) who has not yet received minor orders (doorkeeper, lector, exorcist and acolyte) and to ordain a man a deacon who has not been ordained a subdeacon, and even to ordain a man a priest who has not yet been ordained a deacon; but the same unanimity is *far* from existing in relation to the question of whether it is possible to consecrate a man a *bishop* who is not yet a priest. Hence the fact is that, in adducing the example of St. Cyprian, Davies has adduced something which is of no relevance at all. Since there is no suggestion that St. Cyprian was consecrated *bishop* without having previously been ordained *priest*, he is simply not a parallel.

Here now is the second assertion which Davies quotes from the *Catholic Dictionary*:

---

[6] Once again it may not be irrelevant to note that Fr. William Addis, the author of the article cited by Davies, was to abandon the priesthood and the Catholic Faith not long after compiling the Dictionary in question.

> Morinus, a very high authority, denies that antiquity furnishes any instance of a person who was not already a priest being consecrated bishop. But clear cases are produced by Chardon (812), and Martène (*De Antiq. Eccles.* [the full title of this work is *De Antiquis Ecclesiæ Ritibus* – J.S.D.] Lib. I; Rit. cap. 8, a. 3. The lower order is contained in the higher, and Church history records sudden elevations justified by extra-ordinary merit and emergency.

This assertion is at least relevant, but unfortunately Davies does not conduct his own investigations of the "clear cases" allegedly produced by Chardon and Martène and is content to trust the judgement of Addis and Arnold. In fact it is very doubtful whether Davies *could* have verified these examples, for it is not easy to obtain the works cited by Addis and Arnold are hard to obtain and are written in densely printed Latin not always easy to follow and nowhere in his writings does Davies indicate that he reads Latin easily.

However, having made the effort to study the cases adduced by Martène under the reference given, I note that the learned Benedictine treats in the same section all cases of *per saltum* ordination, irrespective of which Orders were involved, and the theologically quite distinct topic of the *interstices* or intervals to be observed between the reception of each successive Order and the next. In many of the examples adduced from antiquity it is unclear whether the brief and obscure citations given in fact refer to actual omission of any particular Order or only to omission of the canonical interval.

Very often what is clear is that a man was *appointed* directly from one Order to another, omitting any appointment to or exercise of the intervening Order, but without asserting that he never received the relevant ceremony of ordination. And most of Martène's cases do not refer to the episcopate anyway.

In fact I see only two which clearly do and one of them is remarkable in another respect. For, as was mentioned a little earlier, those theologians who oppose the opinion that "*per saltum*" Ordination is definitely valid justifiably point out that, even if a clear historical case *were* one day produced, it would still be necessary to take the further step of showing also that the highest authority in the Church had been aware of what took place *and had recognized the Consecration as valid.* But in the case of Constantine (†c. 769), apparently consecrated bishop *per saltum* by George Bishop of Præneste, a Council held by Pope Stephen III to judge his case not only degraded him from every ecclesiastical Order but forbad all those who had purportedly received Orders from him to exercise the Orders so received.

This leaves us with only one alleged case: that of John, disciple of St. Gall, who, from being a deacon, became bishop of Constance, without receiving ordination to the priesthood. At least, Martène thinks that this is "clear enough" from Strabo's life of St. Gall, Chapter 25.[7] But Strabo's elegant Latin is no substitute for first-hand knowledge. He is writing two centuries after the event, adapting an already adapted version of an older text (now extant only in fragments) which was itself committed to writing long after the events it recounts. This is a tenuous basis on which to overturn the received theology of St. Thomas and the formal statement of Pope Nicolas the Great!

Davies now continues as follows:

> *The Catholic Encyclopædia* (1913), Vol. XI, p. 282, notes that the majority of theologians and canonists consider that episcopal Consecration requires the previous reception of priest's Orders for validity. It continues:
>
>> 'Others, however, maintain that episcopal power includes full priestly power, which is thus conferred by episcopal Consecration. They appeal to history and bring forward cases of bishops who were consecrated without having previously received priest's Orders, and although most of the cases are somewhat doubtful and can be explained on other grounds, it seems impossible to reject them all. It is further to be remembered that scholastic theologians mostly required the previous reception of priest's Orders for valid episcopal Consecration because

---

[7] He mistakenly writes Chapter 23.

they did not consider episcopacy an Order, a view which is now generally abandoned.'

Sufficient comment on this short extract is surely given by the fact that Davies admits that the author of the article in *The Catholic Encyclopædia* notes that "the majority of theologians and canonists consider that episcopal Consecration requires the previous reception of priests Orders for its validity." In other words on his admission most competent experts formally disagree with the thesis he is defending as certain! And does he wish us to believe that the *majority* of theologians and canonists have expressed their opinions without reading the allegations made by those who hold the opposite position concerning supposed historical cases of episcopal Consecration without priestly Ordination? Or does he want us to reject the teaching of the *majority* of theologians and canonists because Fr. Hans, the author of this article in *The Catholic Encyclopædia*, instructs us to do so? It is not that the teaching of a majority of learned theologians is of itself infallible and may never in any circumstances be rejected. But, to say the very least, it would be rash indeed to dismiss the teaching of the majority of theologians and canonists as *definitely wrong*, as Davies does, without having studied the matter in *great* depth and *personally* assessed how much weight can be put on the assertion – which in any case is somewhat tentatively worded – that "it *seems* impossible to reject them *all*" (i.e. all the cases brought forward – emphasis added).

As will become apparent, I have done my best to examine the evidence with appropriate care. And while it cannot be denied that the *number* of bishops of the past alleged by some scholar or other never to have been ordained priest might be sufficient to persuade compilers of encyclopædias, and others who lack the time for detailed research, *numbers* of alleged cases as such have no greater authority than the *individual* cases of which they are made up; and I have not succeeded in finding a single individual case which appears at all conclusive. Nor clearly has such an instance been discovered by the many learned theologians and canonists who have also made their investigations and have rejected the conclusion reached by Lennerz and others, and so enthusiastically adopted by Davies. And there is no shame in having much greater trust in the majority of theologians and canonists in this matter than it *suits* Davies to have.

Comment must now be made on the assertion, made in the extract from *The Catholic Encyclopædia* quoted by Davies, that "scholastic theologians mostly required the previous reception of priest's Orders for valid episcopal Consecration because they did not consider episcopacy an Order." The *Catholic Encyclopædia* is a useful work of reference if used judiciously, but it is very far from being entirely reliable,[8] and this particular assertion is certainly mistaken. On this point the scholastics followed St. Thomas Aquinas, for whose doctrine readers are referred to his *Summa Theologiæ*, Supplement, Q. 40, A. 5 (*"Sed Contra..."*). There they will see that, while it is true that St. Thomas teaches that a man cannot validly be consecrated bishop unless he has first received priestly Ordination, and while it is also true that he teaches that the episcopate is not an Order in its own right, it is *not* true that, as *The Catholic Encyclopædia* states, *he bases the former on the latter*. Absolutely on the contrary, he attempts to prove the *latter* from the *former!* In other words, he argues that the episcopate cannot be a separate Order from the priesthood because:

> One Order does not depend on a preceding Order as regards the validity of the sacrament, but the episcopal power depends on the priestly power *since no one can receive the episcopal power unless he already has the priestly power*.

---

[8] Inspection of its articles concerning the Holy House of Loretto and the Holy Shroud of Turin will cure any temptation to excessive trust in the judgements expressed in its pages without careful assessment of the author responsible for each article.

St. Thomas obviously regarded it as so definite that one who is not a priest cannot validly be consecrated bishop that it was unnecessary to prove it, for he certainly would not have been guilty of the fallacy of using an unproved and debatable premise to argue that the episcopate is not an Order. Moreover, while theologians today widely recognize the episcopate as a distinct Order from the priesthood, their difference with St. Thomas is, generally speaking, terminological rather than theological, since most theologians even in the twentieth century have continued to hold the Thomistic doctrine that the priesthood and the episcopate are more closely related to one another and interdependent than are the other Orders. And the fact that the Council of Trent, an authority which no Catholic may question, groups them both together under the general term *"sacerdotium"* conclusively corroborates the position of those who have maintained that the relationship between the priesthood and the episcopate is different from, and closer than, that between the other Orders (major and minor).

Next Davies refers to the statements on the subject of episcopal Consecration *"per saltum"* in the famous and exhaustively erudite fifteen-volume French theological dictionary, the *Dictionnaire de Théologie Catholique*:

> The *Dictionnaire de Théologie Catholique* also accepts that the position taken against episcopal Ordination [sic] *per saltum* by so many theologians is because they follow St. Thomas. It is interesting to note here that the position of St. Thomas regarding the matter and form of priestly Ordination which has been endorsed by the Council of Florence and incorporated in the *Catechism of the Council of Trent* was superseded by the Apostolic constitution *Sacramentum Ordinis* in 1947. (See Appendix I to my book *The Order of Melchisedech*.)

The relevance of Davies's reference to St. Thomas's teaching on the matter and form of priestly Ordination is not at first sight apparent, but presumably he wishes to demonstrate by it that St. Thomas, a very weighty authority in explicit opposition to his opinion, is not infallible. While it is surely inconceivable that any Catholic would not know this – one of the most important and fundamental items of Catholic instruction is that of when the Church speaks infallibly, after all – it is perhaps worth observing that it would not in fact be possible to deduce it validly from the evidence Davies offers. For the fact is that Pope Pius XII's constitution *Sacramentum Ordinis* did *not* contradict St. Thomas. It merely taught that, *from the date of that particular decree* – that is, 1947 – the tradition (formal handing over) of the instruments was not to be held as part of the matter of the sacraments; as to what might have been the case *prior* to 1947, it gave no decision or ruling at all.

Davies here quotes from the *Dictionnaire de Théologie Catholique*, the extract (in Davies's stilted translation) coming from Vol. XI, column 1388:

> Once one admits that the episcopate is an order adequately distinct from the simple priesthood, one can conceive it as including eminently within itself all the powers of the priesthood. Were not the Apostles ordained as bishops without passing through the priesthood? (See *Acts*, XIII, 3.) In the Apostolic Church there were only priest-bishops and deacons: see in particular Philippians 1:1 and Clement of Rome's Letter to the Corinthians, 42. Many of the popes, principally in the first centuries, were elevated immediately from the diaconate to the sovereign pontificate without receiving any other Ordination but that of episcopal Consecration! One recalls also the Ordination of the antipope Constantine. See the *Liber Pontificalis*, Nos 227, 257, 292, 427, 455, 579, 264-265.

Readers of Davies's article, confronted with this extract taken out of context, cannot fail to presume that it indicates the mind of the author of the article in the *Dictionnaire de Théologie Catholique* concerning the validity of episcopal Consecration received *"per saltum"*. Or rather, they cannot fail to *if they still trust Davies*. If they check the article in question for themselves, however, they will find that the extract certainly does *not* indicate the mind of the author. It has been selectively edited by

Davies to give the *impression* that it does, but the full article contains strong arguments *against* Davies's position with which Davies does not deem it safe to confront his readers, and it concludes, *not* by affirming that episcopal Consecration received "*per saltum*" is *definitely* valid, but only that it *may* be valid.

Let us now rectify Davies's omission by drawing attention to certain *other* parts of the *Dictionnaire de Théologie Catholique* article which he has been content to pass over in silence.

The first thing which Davies carefully omits to tell us is that the article he is using as an apparent authority for his position actually opens by annihilating his earlier argument based on St. Cyprian. It will be recalled that he chose St. Cyprian, from Addis and Arnold's *Catholic Dictionary*, as an illustration of Ordination "*per saltum*" recognized as valid by the Church, on the basis that this saint was apparently ordained to the priesthood without passing through the lower ranks such as the diaconate. Having encouraged his readers to believe that this was a satisfactory parallel to the case of a non-priest being consecrated bishop,[9] the fact that he wished to quote from the *Dictionnaire de Théologie Catholique* shortly after pulling this trick on them may have posed for him a moral problem of considerable delicacy. For what the very article from which he wished to quote makes clear is that, while on the one hand virtually all theologians now admit the validity of the reception of Orders up to and including the priesthood without passing through the lower ones, nevertheless on the other hand there is still fierce dispute about whether this *also* applies to reception of the episcopate by non-priests.

At this point I translate directly from the *Dictionnaire de Théologie Catholique*:

---

[9] Indeed he did not even make it clear that this was not what had happened to St. Cyprian.

It must be recognized that the *almost unanimous* response of modern theologians is affirmative: 'All authors consider the Consecration of a bishop to be *invalid* unless it is preceded by the priesthood.' [Emphases added, and the article goes on to quote various authorities for this assertion, including St. Alphonsus Liguori, Book 6, n. 793 of his *Theologia Moralis*].

Davies's solution to his difficulty was simply to suppress this passage entirely, leaving his readers the wholly erroneous impression that its author was *adopting*, rather than merely *citing*, the arguments in favour of Davies's own view and that he sees no solid arguments in favour of the opposing view. In the interests of carrying his readers to the conclusion he "needs", Michael Davies has entirely parted company with the minimum standards of scholarly integrity.

The article from the *Dictionnaire de Théologie Catholique* then goes on to point out that it is by no means necessary for those who accept that the episcopate is a distinct Order from the priesthood to acknowledge that episcopal Consecration "*per saltum*" can be valid.

> The partisans of the adequate distinction do not all accept this conclusion. God could have established the priestly character as a necessary pre-condition for the episcopate, just as he demands the baptismal character before priestly Ordination.

This, the article informs us, was in fact the teaching of St. Alphonsus (*Theologia* Moralis, Book 6, n. 738). The article next raises the all-important question of historical fact:

> A question of fact must dominate the discussion – whether the Church has ever considered as valid the episcopal Consecration of a simple deacon. Nicholas I protested against such an allegation when it was made by the supporters of Photius.

The article goes on to cite various historical authorities who are in agreement with Pope St. Nicholas the Great in denying that the Church has ever considered such an episcopal Consecration as valid; and the names of these authorities carry no little weight, including among their number, as they do, Von Hefele and Hergenröther.

Then the following important statements follow:

> The handful of probable facts related by Martène [it will be remembered that Martène is the chief authority adduced by Davies's extract from Addis and Arnold earlier in favour of the validity of *per saltum* Consecration – J.S.D.] in his *De Antiquis Ecclesiæ Ritibus*, book 1, chapter 8, article 2, are of slight importance, either because they are not well-known and therefore not sufficiently established as historically certain, or because they can be explained on the basis of the ignorance of those involved .... *They must have been abuses which did not engage the authority of the Church.*

Regrettably, one can well see why Davies preferred his readers not to know about this passage.

Next the article says that, according to Pope Benedict XIV, it is permitted, notwithstanding the weight of the earlier arguments against the validity of Consecration *"per saltum"*, to hold the contrary view. In other words, the view which Davies tries to foist on his readers as *certain* is so far from being so that the great scholar-pope Benedict XIV found it necessary to consider whether it was even permitted for Catholics to hold it at all! Next in the article comes the passage which Davies has quoted; but readers are again reminded that what is said in it is put forward, *not* as the definite view of the author of the article, *but as **one** of the positions which **some** theologians have maintained and which the article therefore records in order to represent honestly the actual state of theological debate.*

Indeed, immediately after the passage quoted, the author of the article – as we do *not* learn from Davies – actually points out that such arguments are by no means conclusive. This is what he writes:

> Undoubtedly rejoinder could be made [to these arguments] by recourse to the hypothesis formulated in the past by St. Robert Bellarmine that, in a single Ordination [ceremony], it was possible

to communicate at the same time both the diaconate and the priesthood ... and that the brief indications in the *Liber Pontificalis* take priestly Ordination for granted rather than distinctly indicating it .... Whatever the right answer may be ... there are no peremptory arguments for one side or the other.

This is the *true* position of the *Dictionnaire de Théologie Catholique* which Davies pretends is in agreement with his own position!

Let us now say plainly what must be said. When a writer who sets out to teach Catholics quotes a passage in support of his standpoint from a highly respected authority, and omits to mention or give the slightest hint that the authority *itself* does not regard the opinion expressed therein as definitive, but merely cites it as one opinion among many, he has become a deadly danger to all who love truth. He has forfeited all right to credibility and must be publicly exposed for the same reasons that habitual perpetrators of other grave crimes must be denounced.

I now return to Davies's article to follow his argument a little further:

> Fr. Lécuyer explains that the accepted view in the West is that the bishops receive 'the fullness of the priesthood'.[10]

There is a remarkable lack of agreement among the authorities on whom Davies relies. On the one hand he has put forward the *Dictionnaire de Théologie Catholique* which, as we have seen (though without any help from Davies), assures us that the notion that one who is not a priest can validly be consecrated bishop is denied by modern theologians "almost unanimously". On the other hand, he introduces Fr. Lécuyer, who, writing two or three years before Vatican II, tells us that "the accepted view of the West" is exactly the contrary. Now here what is at issue is not the opinion of one author against that of an another about a point of doctrine, but a matter of straightforward historical fact.

---

[10] J. Lécuyer, *What is a Priest?* (Burns and Oates, 1959), p. 31.

So what is the reason for the discrepancy? The straightforward answer is that Lécuyer not only has no reputation of any sort as a learned theologian, but that there are the gravest grounds for doubting his claims. For in fact Fr. Joseph Lécuyer (1912-1983) was a notorious modernist who collaborated with Fr Yves Conger at Vatican II, contributed substantially to drafting the new Protestantised post-Vatican II ordination rites, and was selected in 1968 as suitably progressive to replace Archbishop Lefebvre who was ousted by a coup as Superior-General of the Holy Ghost Fathers. In other words, Lécuyer's credentials are, in the eyes of traditional Catholics, entirely negative, but Davies fails to mention this.

Nor does Davies quote a shred of evidence adduced by Fr Lécuyer in support of his assertion; and what he says can be summarily dismissed as the nonsense, either incompetent or deceitful, which it undoubtedly is. One thing which *all* reputable authorities admit, whatever their view on the validity of "*per saltum*" Consecration may be, is that a considerable majority of theologians[11] hold that such Consecrations are invalid, and anyone who is either unaware of this fact or deliberately lies about it is evidently disqualified from himself expressing an opinion on the theological issue, since even if he is honest he is certainly no scholar. However, Davies continues, for his present purposes, to treat Fr. Lécuyer as if he were infallible and his view decisive:

> He [Lécuyer] refers to studies by Mgr. Andrieu among the liturgical documents of the Middle Ages which reveal that on several occasions:
> 'Episcopal Consecration was conferred on candidates who were not yet priests, but merely deacons, readers [lectors], or even laymen.'

---

[11] Including such great names as Pope St. Nicholas I (the Great), Pope Benedict XIV, St. Thomas Aquinas, St. Alphonsus Liguori, St. Robert Bellarmine and Cardinal Hergenröther.

Let us remind ourselves that, as the author of the article in the *Dictionnaire de Théologie Catholique* pointed out, (a) the various instances adduced by certain historians prove nothing at all, since they are almost invariably doubtful, and (b) even if the instances had not been doubtful, they would still not qualify as relevant, because none of the historians brings forward any evidence to show that if *per saltum* consecration ever did take place it was anything other than an irregularity – and of course the fact that an irregularity took place does not prove that the sacrament was validly conferred.

The passage which Davies is quoting from Lécuyer continues with the following illuminating assertion:

> 'The practice appeared so normal in the 8th and 9th centuries that it is officially provided for by a Roman Ordo of the 8th century which, during the Consecration of a bishop, includes the following short dialogue between the consecrator and the candidate.
> 'What is your status?'
> 'I am a deacon' [or a priest, or any other degree).'

Here Lécuyer has completely given himself away, for his assertion is not merely false but utterly preposterous. We have already seen the extract from the *Dictionnaire de Théologie Catholique* which pointed out that Pope St. Nicholas the Great (858-867) *protested* against the allegation that the Catholic Church had *ever* permitted the episcopal Consecration of a simple deacon when this allegation was made by followers of the schismatic Photius.[12] And Pope St. Nicholas himself reigned

---

[12] In his Letter 152, to Hincmar and the other bishops in the "Kingdom of Charles" (Migne: *Patrologia Latina*, tom. 119, coll. 1152-61), Pope St. Nicholas I observes that the Eastern schismatics accuse the Western Church of allowing a deacon to be consecrated bishop "without receiving the office of a priest" ["*non suscepto presbyteratus officio*"], while their own leader, Photius (who had usurped the See of Constantinople from its legitimate occupant Ignatius), had been raised to the episcopate by the intervention of the emperor out of the blue from having been a layman.
Photius had in fact been raised on successive days to the ranks of monk, reader, subdeacon, deacon, priest and bishop in defiance of Canon 5 of the

in the ninth century, the very time when the practice which he denies had ever happened was, according to Fr. Lécuyer, in fact "normal"! Moreover, Fr. Lécuyer assures us that this practice is provided for in the Roman Ordo, which Pope St. Nicholas must himself have used when consecrating bishops!

And given that another of Davies's chosen authorities, Addis and Arnold, points out the historically certain fact that "the Church has *always* disapproved such Ordinations ...", what is there left to say other than that anyone who tries to represent any abuses that may have occurred in the early centuries as "normal" and "officially provided for" is simply making up the facts? The obvious truth is that, if such a dialogue really did occur in an official Roman Ordo, as is alleged, this is because the bishop would interrupt the proceedings when the candidate declared himself not yet ordained priest, and insert the Ordination ceremony for a priest before proceeding to his episcopal Consecration, which would almost certainly have been deferred in order to observe the canonical interstice (i.e. the prescribed interval between reception of the different Orders).

With the following short paragraph, Davies brings his article to a close:

> Probably, the most detailed examination of the question of episcopal Consecration *per saltum* is found in Gasparri's *De Sacra Ordinatione*. The author concludes that such Ordinations are valid.

Second Council of Nicæa, from which it can be seen that, far from ordaining deacons directly to the episcopate, the Western Church by the eighth century also insisted on the observance of a *due interval between the reception of each Order*. It is conceivable that this canonical interval may not always have been observed in the case of deacons being raised to the episcopate, but what is quite inconceivable of course is that Pope St. Nicholas I should have considered the Consecration of Photius as uncanonical merely because he was ordained to each Order successively without a sufficient interval having been observed if, in the Roman Church, it was customary not only to omit intervals between the different Orders, but even to omit some of the Orders – such as the priesthood – altogether.

"The author concludes that such Ordinations are valid." Those are Davies's exact words, and they are *a brazen lie*. Any readers who care to check for themselves in *De Sacra Ordinatione* will find out that what Cardinal Gasparri does there is first to put forward a strong case in favour of *both* positions and finally to summarize without reaching *any* absolute conclusion either way on the validity of *per saltum*. Some of his closing words have already been quoted in the extract taken from the *Dictionnaire de Théologie Catholique*; but they are worth repeating here:

> There are no peremptory arguments for either opinion. We therefore consider that the second opinion [that one who is not a priest can validly be consecrated as a bishop] is truly *probable*, both intrinsically and extrinsically on account of the authority of so many and such great men of learning. [Emphasis added – J.S.D.]

Although there would not be any escape from the fact that Davies has told his readers a bare-faced lie, no matter what the exact force of the word "probable" is, it should be pointed out that the term "probable" in the sense in which it is invariably used in Catholic theology, and in which Cardinal Gasparri is using it there, is very much weaker than it is in its everyday sense; so that while it could not in *any* conceivable sense mean "definitely true", it is in fact even further away from such a meaning than might at first sight appear. For the benefit of any who are not aware of the fact, all that "probable" in its technical theological sense means is that the opinion thus described is sufficiently well-grounded to be justifiably defensible as an opinion. It by no means indicates, as it does in the everyday sense, that the opinion is *more* likely than a contradictory opinion; in fact it can equally apply to an opinion which, though justifiable, is the *least likely* of all the various justifiable opinions on the subject, each one of which also, of course, is in the category of "probable"; and it might even be very unlikely indeed; and Cardinal Gasparri gives no indication that he personally considers the case in favour of the validity of *"per saltum*" Consecration to be more likely or less likely than the case against it.

What *is* certain, however, is that Cardinal Gasparri regards the validity of such Consecration as *no more* than probable; and what is equally certain is that, in matters where sacramental validity is at stake, the Church *categorically forbids* Catholics to trust to opinions which are *merely* probable. Hence Gasparri observes that if a practical case were to arise in which episcopal Consecration had been conferred upon a deacon who was not yet a priest, the deacon in question would first need to be ordained priest, "and then the episcopal Consecration *would have to be repeated*, but on account of the probability of the second opinion it would be repeated *conditionally*." And he goes on to indicate that the same would apply to any Confirmations and Ordinations which had been performed by the doubtfully consecrated bishop prior to the conditional re-Consecration.

All these facts Davies, in his representation of Cardinal Gasparri's doctrine, has suppressed. And given that, in order to prove his point, he must establish that episcopal Consecration "*per saltum*" is not only *probably* – no matter how probably – but *definitely* valid, and that he has called forward Gasparri as an authority to help him establish this, it has only to be said that his suppression is evidently, thoroughly and sickeningly dishonest.

V

This discussion cannot be closed until I have kept my promise to examine in greater detail the alleged historical cases of bishops who have been consecrated without having previously been ordained priest. A number of such instances, most of them taken from the notoriously unreliable *Liber Pontificalis*, are cited by Lennerz and Gasparri, the former claiming that they are conclusive, the latter, however, indicating that they certainly are not.

Here are a few samples of the instances adduced as conclusive evidence by Lennerz:

(i) "According to his epitaph, Pope [St.] Liberius was a reader, deacon and [then] *'summus sacerdos'* ['high priest' – a term taken to mean bishop]."

(ii) "[St.] Gregory Nazianzen tells of someone who was baptized and created bishop immediately after Baptism."

(iii) "Pope [St.] Innocent I ruled that bishops should always be raised from the ranks of the 'clergy'." [This is taken to imply that there was no necessity for them to be priests rather than among the lower ranks of the clergy such as mere deacons or sub-deacons.]

Needless to say, such evidence is not merely inconclusive; it is actually difficult to see how an intelligent man can call it evidence at all. It is highly unlikely that an epitaph, even of a pope, will include a detailed account of his career, and there is no reason to suppose that the writer of this one wished to indicate anything more than that Liberius had fulfilled the office of lector, then the office of deacon, and finally the office of bishop, while never fulfilling *as a separate office* such functions as acolyte or simple priest. There is no sign that any implication is intended that he did not receive those *Orders* distinctly. A much more likely sense would be that whereas he was known as "Liberius the lector" or "Liberius the deacon", he was never known as "Liberius the priest" because, having been *chosen* a bishop while he was still a mere deacon, he would have been a simple priest only for a day or two as a necessary step prior to his Consecration.

Even more ambiguous is the extract from St. Gregory Nazianzen's writings. The statement that a newly baptized person was immediately afterwards created bishop does not necessarily indicate episcopal Consecration at all. It could mean no more than he was nominated to the episcopal *office* at that stage (in the same way that St. Ambrose was elected bishop *even before* his Baptism) and that he then received all the necessary Orders in due sequence. Equally, the word "immediately" ("*statim*") can have a variety of meanings, and certainly in such a statement need not mean that the episcopal Consecration took place so soon after Baptism that there was no interval in which to receive the other Orders.

Thirdly, the decree of Pope St. Innocent I (401-417) simply means that a layman or a catechumen should not be *chosen* as bishop whereas a cleric of any rank may. It does not mean that a cleric in one of the lower ranks would not have to receive all of the intervening Orders before his episcopal Consecration.

Obviously Pope St. Innocent's decree must be read in the light of other evidence as to the rules for eligibility to the episcopate in the early Church; and such evidence is fatal to Lennerz's theory. Included in it are two statements of Pope St. Cornelius who reigned in the middle of the third century; one insists that a man "does not suddenly arrive at the episcopate, but only by means of other ecclesiastical offices," and the other that he "rises through all the ranks of religion." (See St. Cyprian, Letter 52 [*alias* 55] and St. Gregory Nazianzen, *Orat.* XX of St. Basil.) Furthermore, the same rule was made a canon at the Council of Sardis in 347 A.D. (Canon X) and by a number of subsequent provincial councils; and St. Leo the Great, and others, make it clear that a man could be *elected* to the episcopate while still only a deacon (Letter 84; c. 6) *without this affecting in any way the duty of receiving the intermediate Order of the priesthood*, as indeed took place in the famous case of St. Athanasius. (See St. Gregory Nazianzen, *Orat.* XXL.)

In the context of these and many other more or less contemporary statements, it is clear that the words of Pope St. Innocent can be construed as permitting Consecration "*per saltum*" only by someone determined to ignore the context and find a "proof text" at any cost.

It is perhaps worth observing that, particularly in the very early centuries of the Church (and more especially in Holy Scripture), it not infrequently seems from documentary records as if deacons are being raised immediately to the episcopate without having received the priesthood previously. The reason for this, as is evident from Gasparri (*op. cit.*), is that the episcopate and the simple priesthood have always been regarded as more closely united than the other Orders, so that, while all the other Orders are distinct from one another, the priesthood and episcopate comprise, as it were, two parts of the same whole; and consequently it was some time before the priesthood emerged clearly as a separate order *frequently* possessed by those not yet raised to the episcopate. As St. Robert Bellarmine remarks (see *Dictionnaire de Théologie Catholique*, Vol. XI, col. 1388), it was undoubtedly common for some time for a deacon to be ordained priest and consecrated bishop *at the same time*; but this by no means indicates that the two were not regarded as distinct Orders or that the rite of priestly ordination was omitted. What happened was simply that the two often went together; so that it would be quite usual to refer to the senior clergy as "deacons and bishops" since all of the priests would *also* be bishops.

And of course, contrary to Davies's interpretation, this militates rather *in favour* of the invalidity of *"per saltum"* Consecration than against it; for it stresses that the relationship between the episcopate and the priesthood is unlike the relationship between the other Orders, any of which can be validly (though, it must be stressed, unlawfully) received by one who has not received the lower ones. And if the episcopate and the priesthood are two parts of the same thing (to use the terminology which Cardinal Gasparri coins), it is evident that the episcopate cannot *include* the priesthood; for while the whole of anything can, and of course certainly does, contain its parts, a part, by very definition, cannot contain the whole.

V

In the course of this lengthy examination of the validity of Archbishop Lefebvre's Orders, I believe that I have established, in opposition to Davies's assertions in each case, the following:

(i) there are considerable grounds for supposing that the prelate who ordained Archbishop Lefebvre priest and was principal consecrator of him as a bishop was an active and malicious enemy of the Church;

(ii) as such it would have been possible for him to nullify the validity of the priestly Ordination of Marcel Lefebvre by forming a positive contrary intention;

(iii) if Archbishop Lefebvre's priestly Ordination were invalid, a possibility which Davies is prepared to entertain, this would have rendered his episcopal Consecration of *doubtful validity* regardless of the presumably correct intentions of the two co-consecrators (Bishops Ancel and Fauret), because it is *entirely uncertain* whether episcopal Consecration can validly be conferred upon a subject who is not yet ordained priest.

With this background I ask readers in all earnest whether, weighing the question purely on the basis of their familiarity with Davies's presentation of the case, and putting aside for a moment any personal preferences they may have or any other factors which might influence them, they do not consider it contrary to every inclination of human nature and to every rule of ordinary prudence to suppose that a proposition which merited such a defence as that which has just been analysed might nevertheless be true? My own view is that the cause of doctrinal orthodoxy in this instance would have been much better served if Mr. Davies had *not* been numbered among its defenders.

What is the truth as to the Validity of the Orders of Archbishop Lefebvre?

It is beyond all question that there is no theological consideration according to which a man *cannot* employ an intrinsically valid rite while nullifying it by his intention, for the Holy See has on numerous occasions declared the sacrament of Matrimony to have been invalid owing to the defective intention of one or both parties, the parties to marriage being themselves its ministers. And there is no reason to think that, if the minister of one sacrament can have a defective intention despite valid use of the Church's ritual, the minister of another sacrament cannot. Moreover the Holy Office in 1690 condemned the proposition of Farvacques that "Baptism is valid, even if conferred by a minister who observes the full and external form of baptizing, but in his heart makes the resolve: I do not intend to do what the Church does."[13] Evidently, then, a Freemason *could* simulate Baptism by following the ritual correctly while deliberately withholding his consent, and no less evidently the same would apply equally to any other sacrament.

But all that has been said above leads to no conclusion beyond that there is no *absolute* certainty as to the validity of any particular sacrament in any particular case. The apparent, or even quite indubitable, sanctity of a priest does not prove him validly ordained. The beneficial effects apparently resulting from the reception of the sacrament at the hand of a priest do not prove him validly ordained. Sensible spiritual consolations associated with his sacraments do not prove it. Wonders and prodigies do not prove it. We can never be *sure* that any sacrament is valid with the same certainty that we have in respect of the truth of the Catholic Faith or even of the truth of the multiplication tables. We can be sure only with what is – by analogy with true certainty – called "moral certainty": a sufficient sureness to act on in practice.

Let us now enquire under what circumstances the validity of a particular sacrament administered according to the correct rite, seriously used, may be considered doubtful. Where the Church instructs us, either by her direct teaching, or by her practice, or

---

[13] H. Denzinger *et al.*, *Enchiridion Symbolorum*, N° 1318.

by the teaching of her approved authors and theologians, human wisdom must fall silent, and bow before the superior wisdom of the Church, the Spouse of Eternal Wisdom. And on the subject of the validity of Orders, and of other sacraments, conferred according to the Catholic rite, seriously used, the Church *does* instruct us: they are to be presumed valid unless the contrary is *certain*, and certain as a result of exterior manifestation.

> Concerning the mind or intention, insofar as it is in itself something interior, the Church does not pass judgement; but insofar as it is externally manifested, she is bound to judge of it. Now if, in order to effect and confer a sacrament, a person has seriously and correctly used the due matter and form, he is for that very reason presumed to have intended to do what the Church does.

Thus wrote Pope Leo XIII in his letter *Apostolicæ Curæ* condemning Anglican Orders. He does not deny the abstract possibility that a minister *may* have a contrary intention when administering a sacrament in due form; but he teaches that, if no such a defect of intention is manifested *during* the performance of the rite,[14] the Church *presumes* it not to exist.[15]

And there is no room for doubt that Pope Leo's doctrine (that validity must be presumed) is *universally* applicable, and even *specifically* applicable to the case of Masonic prelates. I call to witness Cardinal John de Lugo (1583-1660), one of the foremost moral and dogmatic theologians of the seventeenth century. "The Church judges to be truly baptized," he writes (*Disputationes Scholasticæ et Morales, Tractatus de Sacramentis, Disputatio VIII:, De Ministro Sacramentorum,*

---

[14] for instance by making unauthorized changes in the ritual, or by evident signs of lack of seriousness.

[15] Cf. St. Thomas Aquinas, *Summa Theologiæ*, III, Q. 64, A. 8:
"Hence the opinion is preferable that the minister of the sacrament acts in the person of the whole Church, whose minister he is, so that as the intention of the Church is expressed in the words uttered, this suffices for the validity of the sacrament unless the contrary be expressed outwardly ...."

Section III), "him whom she sees baptized exteriorly in due form." And he adds that, if a priest pronounced the formula of absolution without intending truly to absolve, "the absolution would be invalid although exteriorly it would falsely be thought valid." Moreover, he informs us that an action of which the invalidity depended on an occult (i.e. secret, not manifested outwardly) defect of intention "would be externally presumed valid for as long as the defect of intention was not certain" ("*quamdiu non constaret de defectu intentionis*").

The same doctrine is taught by Cardinal Billot (1846-1931) whose credentials as a theologian, outlined in footnote 28 on p. 221 of this *Evaluation* are such that it is hard to think of anyone who has approached his stature since his death. "As often as there is no appearance of simulation on the part of the minister," he declares, "the validity of the sacrament is sufficiently certain with moral and human certainty." (*De Sacramentis*, Vol. I, ed. 6, p. 201)

Readers will surely agree that there is no ambiguity in the position of these authorities that when the rites of the Church are correctly used as far as can be externally judged, the sacrament must be presumed valid unless it is *proved* invalid. And notwithstanding the delirious claims of the Kellners,[16] Baisiers[17] Dictioneris[18] and the survivors of the Schuckardt shipwreck known as the C.M.R.I.,[19] there is no credible case for saying that membership of Freemasonry renders it *certain* that a man has a positive contrary intention.

---

[16] Dr. Hugo Maria Kellner wrote several theologically inept papers denying that a Freemason can validly confer any sacrament.

[17] Monsieur W. Baisier of Antwerp has maintained the same thesis, mistakenly insisting that the intention required for sacramental validity must be "a **good** intention" (*Sti. Pii V Sodalitas Information*, N[os] 42 and 43).

[18] Philip Q. Dictioneri, alias Richard Morton, attacked the possibility that Archbishop Lefebvre's Orders are valid in several articles, most of them being incoherent and incomprehensible.

[19] See numerous articles in their periodical *The Reign of Mary*.

Indeed there is even specific evidence that the Church applies this principle in practice to Masonic clerics, for in her *Code of Canon Law* (1917) she takes express juridical cognizance of the existence of Masonic clerics by making them liable to other penalties in addition to the excommunication visited automatically on all Catholics who join the Lodge. But her legislation does not include the faintest hint of any *a priori* doubt as to the validity of the ministrations of Masonic prelates. It would have been quite easy to make their excommunication "most specially reserved to the Holy See", so that Rome would learn of all such clerics who were apprehended or who confessed, and could prudently investigate the validity of their ministrations before absolving them; but as this was not done the only explanation of the neglect of this and other possible safeguards lies in the principle we have already seen: that the Church presumes even the sacraments of Freemasons to be valid – in fact even the sacraments of Satanists – unless the existence of a contrary intention, belying the intention expressed in the ritual itself, has been conclusively demonstrated.

This evidence is all the more conclusive in the light of the fact that the Holy See certainly has been prepared to acknowledge an Ordination as invalid and forbid those ordained at it to use their Orders until they had been "re-ordained" when the existence of a positive contrary intention *has* been proved. A striking instance of this is furnished by the case of the South American Bishop Antonio González de Acuña, who, before an Ordination ceremony, declared and confirmed with an oath his intention *not* to ordain any candidate who was of mixed blood. Several such candidates presented themselves during the ceremony and thought themselves to be ordained, but when the case was referred to Rome, the Sacred Congregation of the Council (13th February 1682) pronounced the Orders to be invalid in the case of candidates of mixed blood.[20]

---

[20] Pope Benedict XIV: *De Sacrosancto Missæ Sacrificio*, 3, 10.

It is undeniable that a marked contrast to this decision is found in the case of the Masonic Bishop Charles-Maurice de Talleyrand-Perigord (1765-1838), whose membership of Freemasonry is certain. He had been validly consecrated bishop on 16th January 1789 and was lawfully appointed to the diocese of Autun. After the Revolution, when the Constitutional Committee attempted to create a national Church to replace the Catholic Church, it was to Talleyrand that they turned for the Consecration of the candidates whom they wished to make bishops to usurp the sees which were occupied by faithful Catholic prelates who had refused the oath to the Civil constitution; and consecrate them he did. (*Catholic Encyclopædia* [1913], article: "Talleyrand-Perigord") The relevance of this is that subsequently when France was reunited with the Holy See during the pontificate of Pope Pius VII, although the pope insisted that these "constitutional" bishops who had been unlawfully and indeed schismatically consecrated should publicly recant their errors and submit to the jurisdiction of the Holy See, in the case of those of them who did this, he cheerfully confirmed their episcopal status, without questioning in the slightest the validity of their Orders. Moreover Talleyrand himself recanted his errors on his death-bed and seems to have died sincerely penitent, in which case he would surely have admitted it if he had in fact consciously invalidated any Orders he had conferred.

This parallel to the Liénart-Archbishop Lefebvre situation was, I believe, first noted by Dr. Rama Coomaraswamy (further information about whom will be found on pp. 71 *et seq.* and 91 of this *Evaluation*), in his article *Cracks in the Masonry*, which appeared in *The Roman Catholic* for June 1982. Since its appearance this article has been criticized by a number of writers who have claimed to be able to refute the main plank of its case by pointing out that, as those whom Talleyrand consecrated had already been validly ordained to the priesthood by non-Masonic bishops, Talleyrand would have been unable to invalidate the episcopal Consecration, for he was assisted in it by two other bishops who were not known to be Freemasons. As this argument is at first sight convincing, it is regrettable that neither Dr. Coomaraswamy nor anyone else, to my knowledge, has pointed out the fact that it is entirely spurious. The reason for this is that, in accepting the validity of the Consecration of the constitutional bishops, Rome must have been relying on a *certain*, not a merely *probable*, theological opinion: otherwise the safer course would have been to insist on conditional re-Consecration. And not until Pope Pius XII's 1944 constitution *Episcopalis Consecrationis* was it *certain* that the bishops who assist the principal consecrating bishop in the ceremony of episcopal Consecration are also co-consecrators and therefore capable of supplying any defects in his intention.

CHAPTER NINE SECTION (B)
THE VALIDITY OF THE 1968 NEW RITE OF ORDINATION

Part 1: Michael Davies's Case in Favour of Validity

On 18th June 1968, by his constitution *Pontificalis Romani Recognitio*, Paul VI replaced the traditional rite of Ordination with a new rite which suppresses every prayer and ceremony that clearly suggests the intention of conferring the power of offering the Holy Sacrifice and of absolving sins – a rite which gives the clear impression that the community is appointing the ordinand to act as public minister of worship without having any supernatural privileges or powers denied to the laity. And one of Michael Davies's most serious errors of sacramental theology is to defend, as certain, the validity of this new rite, in both its Latin and English forms.

Moreover this particular error seems less excusable than most of his other errors, for:

(a) he once held the correct view on this subject, namely that the new rite is invalid in both Latin and English; and,

(b) after he abandoned the correct view and became a supporter of the validity of the new rite, his error was very capably exposed in a written debate, published in *The Roman Catholic*, between Davies and Fr. William Jenkins.

My analysis of Davies's error on this subject, for which I shall be drawing heavily on the material published in *The Roman Catholic* and on Davies's book on the subject, *The Order of Melchisedech*, will necessarily centre around the wording of the essential formula of Ordination,[1] which is almost, but not quite, identical in both the new (Latin version) and the old rites of Ordination. And for this reason I begin by quoting both versions in their entirety with a literal English translation of each.

---

[1] I.e. that central part of the rite of Ordination by which the sacrament is actually conferred and which, to that extent, corresponds to the Consecration of the Mass.

Continual reference to these formulæ will be necessary while reading what follows in this section. Here they are:

The Traditional Form in Latin	*The New Form in Latin*
Da, quæsumus, omnipotens Pater, in hos famulos tuos, Presbyterii dignitatem. Innova in visceribus eorum Spiritum sanctitatis *UT*² acceptum a te, Deus, secundi meriti munus obtineant; censuramque morum exemplo suæ conversationis insinuent.	Da, quæsumus, omnipotens Pater, his famulis tuis, Presbyterii dignitatem. Innova in visceribus eorum Spiritum sanctitatis; acceptum a te, Deus, secundi meriti munus obtineant; censuramque morum exemplo suæ conversationis insinuent.
Literal English Translation	*Literal English Translation*
Grant, we beseech Thee, Almighty Father, *into* these Thy servants, the dignity of the Priesthood; renew the Spirit of holiness within them *SO THAT* they may hold the office of second rank from Thee, O God, and may by the example of their conduct inculcate strict morality.	Grant, we beseech Thee, Almighty Father, to these Thy servants, the dignity of the Priesthood; renew the Spirit of holiness within them; may they hold office of second rank received from Thee, O God, and by the example of their conduct inculcate strict morality.

Davies's book *The Order of Melchisedech*, which was published in 1979, is devoted to consideration of the new rite of Ordination of priests, rather than of any of the other Orders.[3]

---

[2] Emphasis added to draw attention to the key word present in the traditional rite but omitted in the New Rite.

[3] In fact *The Order of Melchisedech* also discusses the new rite of Ordination of deacons. It does not, however, touch on the rite of consecrating bishops, as might have been expected, because, at the time he wrote this work, Davies was unable to see any way in which the new rite of episcopal consecration

Most of it is taken up with a perceptive and justified comparison of the defects of this new rite with those of the ritual of Ordination used in the Church of England which led Pope Leo XIII, in his encyclical *Apostolicæ Curæ* of 1896, to declare the Orders conferred by that ritual "absolutely null and utterly void". Among the things Davies points out are:

(i) The Protestant Reformers stripped away from the Catholic rite everything which suggested Eucharistic sacrifice – a doctrine which they denied.

(ii) They mutilated or expunged all the parts of the ceremony which were theologically explicit, leaving the prayers either, on the one hand, vague and indeterminate, or, on the other hand, suggestive that the minister had no special power but rather a mandate from the people whom he served and represented.

(iii) Nonetheless, the Anglican rite contained, and still contains, a prayer which, *were it found in the context of a Catholic rite*, might be sufficient to confer valid Ordination.

(iv) But in the context of the rest of the Anglican rite, this prayer was judged by a binding and irreversible declaration of the supreme Magisterium incapable of validly conferring the sacrament, owing to the fact that the other prayers and actions of the rite in no way indicated that a Catholic interpretation of this in itself vague and insufficiently determinate prayer was called for. On the contrary, the historical fact of the deliberate stripping away of whatever recalled Catholic doctrine on the subject of the Mass and the priesthood demanded that the ambivalent prayer should be interpreted in a heretical sense, making it incapable of validly conferring the sacrament.

---

could possibly be valid! Nonetheless, in 1983, Davies told the present writer on the telephone, that he no longer had the slightest doubt of the validity of the new rites, even that of episcopal "Ordination."

Davies then goes on to point out that exactly the same can be said of the 1968 "Catholic" rite. He asserts (erroneously, as we shall see) that there is *no difference* in the actual formula of Ordination between the new rite and the old, but points out that the formula in itself does not explicitly convey Catholic doctrine on the subject of Ordination, and, owing to its being open to a variety of interpretations, could be used without qualm of conscience by a Protestant, if this were done in a different context from the traditional Catholic rite. And on this basis he points out:

(a) that the more explicit prayers of the traditional Catholic rite, by virtue of the principle known as *significatio ex adjunctis* (signification from adjuncts or circumstances), give the character to the formula of Ordination itself in order to make it a valid form for conferring the sacrament; and

(b) that the same formula, even though open to a Catholic interpretation in itself, would by no means necessarily be valid if it were used in a rite deliberately denuded of every indication of Catholic doctrine.

Part 2. Valid or Invalid? The Debate

The Order of Melchisedech has many remarkable features, but far from the least remarkable of these is that the reader comes to the end of it still unsure whether Davies holds that the new rite is valid or invalid,[4] for the text appears to contradict itself. Here, for instance, are some passages which appear to suggest that Davies doubts its validity:

(i) "The most impressive argument for the validity of the new rite is based on the contention that the Holy Ghost would

---

[4] My word does not have to be taken for this: the reviewer in *The Remnant*, for instance, took the book to be "an implicit case for the invalidity of the New rite of ordination" (17th September 1979), whereas the priest who contributed the book's foreword clearly thought that it was an attack on the theological vagueness of a rite of which the validity was not in question.

not permit the supreme authority in the Church to promulgate an invalid sacramental rite. It is claimed that no matter what the intentions of those who actually devised the rite, once it had been accepted by the Pope and promulgated with his authority, it must, *ipso facto*, be valid. In addition to this it is also argued that the acceptance of a sacramental rite by virtually the entire Church also constitutes irrefutable proof of its validity. Given the truth of this argument as a general principle, *it does seem reasonable to express some reservation with regard to the new Ordination rite*. It was imposed upon the Church without any consultation with national hierarchies and, as has been shown, some bishops have expressed considerable reservations." (p. 99)

(ii) "As a final comment on the new Catholic Ordinal, I would like to quote a passage from *Apostolicæ Curæ* and to ask any reader to demonstrate to me how the words which Pope Leo XIII wrote of Cranmer's rite cannot be said to apply to the new Catholic Ordinal, at least where mandatory prayers are concerned. Pope Leo wrote of the authors of the Ordinal and ... 'the abettors whom they associated with themselves from the heterodox sects ... [that] ... being fully cognisant of the necessary connection between faith and worship ... under a pretext of returning to the primitive form they corrupted the liturgical order in many ways to suit the errors of the reformers. For this reason, in the whole ordinal not only is there no clear mention of the sacrifice of Consecration, of the '*sacerdotium*' and of the power of consecrating and offering sacrifice, but ... every trace of these things which have been in such prayers of the Catholic rite as they had not entirely rejected was deliberately removed and struck out. In this way, the native character or spirit of the *Ordinal*, as it is called, clearly manifests itself....'"

(iii) "I have also been reliably informed of a recent case in which one British bishop agreed to the request of some ordinands to be ordained in the old rite as they had *grave doubts concerning the validity of the new one*." (Emphasis added)

(iv) "If the new Catholic rite is considered satisfactory, then the entire case put by *Apostolicæ Curæ* is undermined .... If the new Catholic rite, shorn of any mandatory prayer signifying the essential powers of the priesthood, is valid, then there seems no reason why the 1662 Anglican rite should not be valid too ...." (p.97)

That all seems clear enough. Or, rather, it *would* seem clear enough if there were not other indications that Davies in fact holds the new rite to be valid. For instance, he sees fit to include a foreword in his book by Professor J.P.M. van der Ploeg O.P. in which the latter says:

> There can be no doubt of the validity of the New Rite but there are certain features which the author deplores.

And in his own "Author's Introduction", Davies himself writes:

> My complaint against the new Catholic rite of Ordination is not that it is invalid, but that it lends itself to the ambiguous interpretation to which ... the Anglican rite is open.

In February 1981 Fr. William Jenkins, who subsequently became one of the nine Oyster Bay fugitives from the Society of St. Pius X, wrote an article in *The Roman Catholic* entitled "Purging the Priesthood in the Conciliar Church". Taking Davies's equivocal position with regard to the validity of the 1968 rite as his starting point, this article was a scholarly and effective demolition of such arguments as have been adduced in favour of the validity of the new rite, and argued cogently that the new rite is of doubtful validity.

Although hostile to Davies's opinion, Jenkins treated him with respect and his article elicited a reply from Davies which was published in a subsequent issue of *The Roman Catholic*. This in turn was capped by a further article by Fr. Jenkins, and in the course of this debate Davies's paltry grasp of the principles of Catholic theology was made painfully clear.

Here, to begin with, are some extracts from Fr. Jenkins's article:

> This essay proposes: (i) to identify and assess what appears to be Mr. Davies's main point about the new Ordination rite, (ii) to show that the validity of the new rite is doubtful, and (iii) to explain the practical consequences of this doubt.
>
> (...)
>
> Throughout his book, Mr. Davies contends that the new form of priestly Ordination is exactly the same as the traditional form. Speaking of the new rite, he says: 'Where the rite for ordaining a priest is concerned, the first point to make is that the matter and the essential form designated by Pius XII in *Sacramentum Ordinis* remain unchanged. This is a point in favour of the new rite. It is the only point in its favour.' (p. 74)
>
> Mr Davies repeats this assertion three more times in the course of *The Order of Melchisedech*.[5] His final mention of this occurs on p. 126 of the book, where he comments on it using the words of Fr. Francis Clark S.J.,[6] who wrote in his study *Anglican Orders and Defect of Intention* that, 'Since the constitution Sacramentum Ordinis of Pius XII, it would seem that no priestly Ordination in which the minister uses exactly the words described in that document ... could be impugned on the grounds of defective form, whatever defects there might be in the other elements of the rite.' (p. 183)

---

[5] Pp. 79, 88, 126.

[6] Dr. Francis Clark is a learned former Jesuit who has written two books and a number of articles on the theological technicalities of Anglican orders and the effect of a defective intention in invalidating the ordination rite. He was laicized (i.e. reduced from the priesthood to the lay state) by the Conciliar Church, although this was apparently for more respectable reasons than those commonly invoked by those priests who abandon the Conciliar Church to "marry", and it appears that his position on the subject of sacramental theology is almost completely sound, even if occasionally misleading (see p. 403 *et seq.* of this *Evaluation*) – J.S.D.

Because he believes that the form of the Sacrament has not been changed, Mr. Davies implies that the new rite of priestly Ordination must be valid, regardless of its defects.

Although later in the book, Mr. Davies admits some reasonable reservations regarding the validity of the new rite, he nonetheless makes his point exceedingly clear in his writings which have followed the book.

And Fr. Jenkins then goes on to cite places in which Davies has made clear his current firm belief that the validity of the new rite of Ordination is unassailable.[7]

Jenkins is about to point out that Davies is guilty of a crucial error in stating that the form of the sacrament of Order is the same in the 1968 rite as in the traditional Roman rite; but before quoting his words on that subject, it is worth drawing attention to a footnote which he includes in commenting on the extract quoted above from Dr. Clark's work. It should be understood that Davies's argument, based on Clark, is that the 1968 rite *must* be valid, because it contains the same essential matter and form as were found in the traditional rite; the prayer and action specified by Pope Pius XII as essential to, and effecting, validity. On this argument Jenkins comments:

> This argument favouring the validity of the new Ordinal is not conclusive, because Fr. Clark's opinion is just that – an opinion – and is not theologically certain. The Jesuit priest appears to recognize this himself, when he uses the words 'it would seem that' to introduce his thesis. There are, in fact, equally noted theologians who would disagree with Fr. Clark, or at least qualify his statement. For example, another Jesuit theologian, Fr. Felix Cappello, maintains that the bare words of the form are not enough; the words of the formula must also be presented in a 'consecratory manner'. He says: 'For validity there is required, besides no substantial change ... that the words of this formula be presented in a consecratory manner, and not just in a historical, instructional or promissory way.' [Evidently these words of Fr. Cappello apply

---

[7] Which, of course, remains Davies's position to this day.

specifically to the Mass rather than to Ordination, but the same principle applies: in view of the opinion of Fr. Cappello and other like-minded theologians, it cannot be maintained that the *mere* use of the essential formula–for *any* sacrament–automatically guarantees its validity, if it is not used in the context of the Church's ritual insofar as the ritual itself impinges on the form and affects its signification. – J.S.D.] *Tractatus Canonico-moralis de Sacramentis*, Turin, Italy, 1962) Vol. I, bk.1, cap.1, art. II.

But, as we are about to learn, the fact that Clark's opinion is not a certain one is not the only reason for holding that the 1968 rite of Ordination is of doubtful validity. A second is that Davies's statement that the 1968 form of Ordination[8] is the same as that of the traditional rite, is not true. Jenkins writes:

> However, there is a grave error at the root of Mr. Davies's reasoning. While he does give the text for the *traditional* Latin form of Ordination, nowhere in *The Order of Melchisedech* does he give the Latin form for the *new* rite of Ordination. Had he compared the traditional and new liturgical books, he could have easily seen that the two forms are *not the same*. In the new rite, the form for ordaining a priest has suffered a change which – however insignificant it may appear at first glance – has very grave implications.

Jenkins then goes on to quote the exact wording of the two forms. First he gives both of them in Latin, as quoted previously on p. 356. Then, of the traditional form he gives his own English translation, and of the 1968 form the provisional I.C.E.L.[9]

---

[8] The *form* of a sacrament is the name given to the particular words of the rite which actually confer the sacrament. In the Mass this would be the words of Consecration, and in the sacrament of Ordination it has been certain, since 1947, that the form consists of the words found in the Preface and quoted at the beginning of this section in Latin and English on the left hand side of the page.

[9] For readers who are not familiar with the institutions of the Conciliar Church, it should be explained that I.C.E.L. is the *International Committee on English in the Liturgy*, a multi-million-pound international profit-making organisation, incorporated in the U.S.A., to which the hierarchies of the Conciliar Church in English-speaking countries have entrusted the task of

English translation and the current I.C.E.L. English translation, the latter of which is a looser rendering, but the former of which is a faithful version, with the exception of its intolerable use of the word "presbyterate" instead of "priesthood".

Fr. Jenkins comments on the significance of the slight difference between the two Latin forms as follows:

> Close examination of the two Latin formulæ reveals that the traditional form contains the word '*ut*' which the new form deletes. Despite its small size, the Latin word '*ut*' carries a weight of significance – which significance the Church wishes to convey by placing it in the traditional formula of Ordination. The word '*ut*' establishes a relationship between that which precedes it in the sentence and that which follows it in the sentence. When it is used with a verb in the subjunctive mood (the verb '*obtineant*' is used in the formula in the subjunctive mood), then it shows that what comes before it somehow 'causes' or is done 'for the sake of' what follows it.

---

translating the blasphemous and heretical new sacramental rites of their religion, with the well-known results – loose, ugly translations which take every opportunity of departing from the Latin in order to become even more heretical than the original versions promulgated by Montini. I.C.E.L. has copyrighted its translations, which are the only ones approved for liturgical use by the Conciliar Church, and charges a heavy fee to all those who wish to reproduce their texts in missals, missalettes, or whatever. The nine-man advisory committee of I.C.E.L. included such individuals as Fr. Gerald Sigler of the U.S., who was suspended for promoting unnatural practices within marriage, Fr. Harold Winston (recently deceased) of England, who, in his pamphlet welcoming the Novus Ordo, appeared to deny the validity of the Tridentine Mass, and minor academic Professor H.P.R. Finberg (1900-1974), often a lone dissenter as the committee adopted its ignoble betrayals of the Latin originals. Cardinal Gray, chairman of the I.C.E.L. episcopal committee, justified the copyrighting and royalty fees of the translation of the Novus Ordo on the grounds that it was necessary "to prevent local modifications of texts," (*The Universe*, 7th March 1969) but Edward Fiske, religious editor of the *N.Y. Times* declared the real reason to be that I.C.E.L. had borrowed huge sums of money from the hierarchy of the Conciliar Church which they could not repay by any other means (*Catholic Currents*, 10th December 1969). Considerations of space preclude any attempt to mention the countless other scandals perpetrated by the I.C.E.L.

This explanation by Fr. Jenkins is perhaps a little clumsy; but what he says will become completely clear if it is realized that – as he should have told his readers – the primary dictionary meaning of the word "*ut*" is "so that" or "in order that". Continuing his article:

> For example, the Latin sentence 'veniunt *ut* te videant' means 'they are coming *for the purpose* of seeing you' or '*for the sake* of seeing you' [or '*in order* to see you' – J.S.D.], and shows that their seeing you is the purpose and result of their coming. When one removes the '*ut*' (as in the new form), then the Latin reads 'veniunt; te videant'. The English sense is 'they are coming; may they see you!' The '*ut*' in the first example shows purpose. Its omission in the second example *replaces* the idea of *purpose* with a mere *exhortation* [or *wish* – J.S.D.]. (Emphases added – J.S.D.)

By way of further commentary, another traditional Catholic priest (the late Fr. Philip Shelmerdine M.B., B.S.) succinctly summarized the point which Fr. Jenkins is making here by observing that there is a big difference between the sentence "I have a gun; you may die" (no "*ut*") and the sentence "I have a gun *in order that* you may die."

Resuming Fr. Jenkins's article:

> With this in mind, we look at the two Latin Ordination forms, the traditional and the new. Both forms call upon God the Father to renew in the hearts of the candidates the Spirit of sanctity, who is the Holy Ghost. Both forms ask that they obtain the 'office of second rank' ('*secundi meriti munus*').
>
> However, the traditional form clearly conveys the understanding that the new infusion of the Holy Ghost is the *cause* of their obtaining the office of second rank in becoming priests, and that their elevation to the office of second rank is the *purpose and the result* of this renewal of the Holy Ghost within them. By the deletion of the one word '*ut*' the new Latin form has destroyed any such causal relationship between the two supernatural events.

The point is surely clear enough: the omission of the word *"ut" effects a real change in the meaning* of the essential formula itself upon which sacramental validity depends.

Passing over the section of his article in which Jenkins goes on to examine the new I.C.E.L. translation of this defective form – a translation which introduces further errors and makes the formula even more blatantly defective and incapable of conferring valid Orders – we come to the following important remarks:

> The Catholic bishops of England noted in *A Vindication of the Bull 'Apostolicæ Curæ'* that ... the Church ... has guarded the prayers and ceremonies which have come down to her from the earliest ages, careful *not to omit* anything; for 'in adhering rigidly to the rite handed down to us, we can always feel secure; whereas if we omit or change *anything*, we may perhaps be abandoning *just that element which is essential.*'
>
> (...)
>
> Fr. Clark himself holds that the only guarantee of validity rests on using 'the exact words prescribed' by Pius XII's Apostolic constitution *Sacramentum Ordinis*. Perhaps the exact words of the traditional Latin form guarantee validity, and cannot be nullified in any context, no matter how heterodox [although a *respectable* opinion, this is in fact debatable – J.S.D.]; but this new form of Ordination, *precisely* because it does *not* use 'the exact words prescribed', must be interpreted according to the same standards as the Anglican formula in the context of the rite which surrounds it [a context which is plainly intended to avoid any suggestion of a sacrificing priesthood – J.S.D.]. (Emphases added – J.S.D.)

Jenkins then goes on to consider the "two extrinsic[10] arguments urging the validity of the new ceremony." He quotes these two arguments from Davies as follows:

---

[10] I.e. arguments for the validity of the 1968 rite which do not appeal to the rite itself to demonstrate its validity but appeal instead to some outside circumstance or authority which is alleged to prove the validity of the rite irrespective of its intrinsic qualities.

(i) "The first argument 'is based on the contention that the Holy Ghost would not permit the supreme authority in the Church to promulgate an invalid sacramental rite.'

(ii) "The second argument is counterpart to the first: 'The acceptance of a sacramental rite by virtually the entire Church also constitutes an irrefutable proof of its validity.'"

In this writer's view Fr. Jenkins does not make a very effective job of answering these arguments. How could he have done so? Whatever his private opinions on the matter may have been at the time – and they have since been somewhat crystallized by his subsequent expulsion from the Society of St. Pius X – he was hampered by the necessity, if he was not to expose his own sedevacantist convictions, of *not* drawing attention to the fact that the "authority" which imposed the 1968 rite was not a valid Catholic authority at all.

As readers will be aware, neither of Davies's arguments is of the slightest force since the 1968 rite was imposed by an authority which is no more Catholic than is the Dalai Lama or the Sanhedrin, so that, *far* from being accepted by the Catholic Church as a whole, the new rite has been rejected entirely by the *Catholic* Church, and accepted, to the extent that it has been accepted at all, only by the *Conciliar* Church.

Despite this self-imposed handicap, one thing in relation to this matter that Fr. Jenkins *is* able to point out is that Davies, in his book, *refutes his own arguments*, even on the basis that it be supposed that the Conciliar Church is the Catholic Church. For Davies correctly informs his readers that the text of the new Ordination and ritual *has not been made generally available to the Catholic (or rather, the Conciliar) faithful*. And "it is hard to see," he validly adds, "how it can be claimed that a rite has been accepted by the entire Church when it is definitely withheld from 99.9% of the faithful." (*The Order of Melchisedech*, p. 100)

Later in his article Fr. Jenkins writes as follows:

> While it is true that a defective intention can invalidate a form sufficient in itself, nevertheless, neither a sufficient intention nor any external authority can make valid a form and a rite which is of itself defective.

This point made by Fr. Jenkins is crucially important, and it is an argument which Davies has never made any attempt to answer. Catholic theology requires that a sacramental formula, in order to *effect* the sacrament, should also *signify* it; and it is part of the definition of a sacrament that it effects what it signifies by virtue of signifying what it is intended to effect. Thus, a formula which *failed* to signify the nature of the sacrament which it was intended to effect could never be capable of effecting it, and not even a papal decree could make it do so. Often Davies's arguments depend on the unfounded supposition that the blatant, intrinsic invalidity of many of the new sacramental formulæ of the Conciliar Church can be countered merely by asserting that they have been promulgated by legitimate authority, as though no answer were necessary to the objection that they contain hardly any suggestion of the Catholic doctrine concerning the sacrament in question. In other words, he argues as if the Church had the power, by virtue of an authoritative pronouncement, to make the words "The weather is fine today," or "Two lumps of sugar please!" into a valid sacramental formula; and the plain fact is that she cannot. Our Lord gave his Church many powers and prerogatives, even over sacramental formulæ, but the power to change the meaning of language was not among them, as the Council of Trent made clear when, in defining the extent of the Church's right to change sacramental rituals, it declared that this right was a *qualified* one which did not permit any change in those parts which are substantial. (Denzinger 931) Nor is it any answer to this criticism to object that the formulæ Davies defends are closer to the valid traditional ones than would be a remark about the weather or an order in a restaurant. Indeed such an objection would entirely miss the point, which is that *if* the alleged authorization of the Church in itself constituted sufficient evidence of validity and made it unnecessary to explain *how* the formula *could* be valid, the same argument would necessarily also suffice to render indisputably valid any formula whatsoever, no matter how far removed from the signification of the sacrament. In any dispute the actual wording of a formula simply would not come into the discussion. And since no reasonable person would acknowledge such a defence as sufficient in the case of a formula such as "Roses are red and violets are blue," anyone who invokes it as sole sufficient defence of less radically modified formulæ like the one under consideration is applying double standards.

Let us now turn to Davies's reply to Fr. Jenkins' article, which, it may be remembered, was published in a subsequent issue of *The Roman Catholic*. Again the most notable passages will be reproduced and relevant explanations and comments interspersed.

> I must begin by congratulating Fr. Jenkins on his perceptive reading of my book. He remarked correctly that within its text I appear to entertain doubts as to the validity of the new rite of Ordination, in contrast with the position I have taken in subsequent articles, and the opinion of Professor van der Ploeg, stated in his Foreword, that there could be no doubt about the validity of the new rite.
> As a result of the research involved in writing *The Order of Melchisedech* I had come to the same conclusion that Fr. Jenkins reached in his February article, i.e. that a positive doubt existed as to the validity of the new rite. Fr. Jenkins remarked, giving his judgement of the position I had taken in my book: 'He appears to conclude that if *Apostolicæ Curæ* is correct, then the new rite of Ordination must be invalid; and if the new right of Ordination is valid, then *Apostolicæ Curæ* – a professedly definitive papal decision – is wrong.' *This was precisely the conclusion I had reached after completing the research for the book.*
>
> (...)
>
> Furthermore, in his article, Father Jenkins has brought forward a new reason for anxiety which I had not detected before my book

was published, i.e. the removal of the word '*ut*' from the Latin form of the traditional rite. Another member of the Society of St. Pius X had alerted me to the removal of this word before I had read Father Jenkins' article, and I had already obtained theological advice on the significance of this omission before reading his comments .... While I very much regret having failed to notice the missing '*ut*' I have been somewhat consoled by learning from Archbishop Lefebvre that he hadn't spotted it either.

Hmm! As the Archbishop, unlike Davies, had not taken it upon himself to write an entire book on the subject, it is difficult to see why Davies should be "consoled" to learn that an error which in himself could be attributed only to crass carelessness should, have ensnared others also through what in them could have been no more than a venial oversight.

I return to the article:

On the basis of his examination of the new rite Father Jenkins has concluded that a positive doubt exists as to its validity. I accept that this is a perfectly reasonable conclusion based on a study of the rite itself. I am also in complete agreement with Father Jenkins in his conclusions as to the duty of a Catholic when a legitimate doubt concerning the validity of a sacrament exists .... However, what remains to be proved is that a legitimate doubt exists ....

This incredible sentence makes it look as though Fr. Jenkins's article consisted of nothing but unsupported assertions!

... Competent theologians have presented me with reasons which I found so convincing that they left me with no alternative but to conclude that I must accept the new Ordination rite, in its Latin and vernacular forms, as certainly valid.

Davies goes on to say that, after he had published *The Order of Melchisedech*, the theological advisers to whom he submitted it, while telling him that his book was completely orthodox, nevertheless "assured [him] that it was not possible for a pope to promulgate an invalid sacrament. He would be protected from such an enormity by the indefectibility of the Church."

And he then proceeds:

I had thus come to the conclusion that there could be a doubt concerning the new Ordination rite because I had considered that rite in itself, in *isolation* from the doctrine of the Church. Seen within the context of the Church's indefectibility, as a rite of the Catholic Church promulgated by the Sovereign Pontiff, it could not be otherwise than valid. Thus, given that Pope Paul VI was indeed the validly elected pontiff who had not lost his office through public heresy, I now consider that Catholics have an obligation to accept at least the Latin versions of all the new sacramental rites as certainly valid.

This paragraph contains a glaring fallacy. It is Davies's open admission that he is grounding his entire position concerning the validity of the new rite on the wholly unproven premise that Paul VI had not lost his office through public heresy. This, in summary, is how Davies builds up his argument:

First, he says in effect, the 1968 rite of Ordination *appears* to be invalid, but must be deemed valid as having been promulgated by a valid pope.

Then he remembers that the "valid pope" in question also *appears* to have been a public heretic (" ... given that Pope Paul VI ... had not lost his office through public heresy ....").

Finally, he administers the "coup de grace". That is, instead of getting himself bogged down in attempting to show why Paul VI was not a public heretic and why, in consequence, his rites must be accepted as valid notwithstanding the fact that they are quite evidently not so, he ... just ... glides ... on, trying to give the impression that he has answered the objection, but in fact leaving it entire.

Next in the article comes a considerable amount of irrelevant discussion of the indefectibility of the Church, and then Davies returns to the question of the validity of the 1968 rite of Ordination. He is now arguing against his own position as put forward in *The Order of Melchisedech*. There he had pointed out that Anglican Orders were deemed invalid because the form, although it could conceivably be valid in the context of a

Catholic rite, was in fact located in a rite which had been deliberately stripped of Catholic significance and therefore could not be said to be determined towards a Catholic meaning by the *adjuncts*[11] of the sacrament. And he had suggested that the adjuncts surrounding the 1968 rite were very similar to those surrounding the Cranmer rite of Anglican Ordination, so that both were subject to the same criticisms. In this article, however, he now argues that the adjuncts are *different*. The 1968 rite, he says, does in fact have a Catholic significance, by virtue of *"significatio ex adjunctis"*. This follows, he assures us, from the fact that the historical adjuncts surrounding the 1968 rite of Ordination include ... the teaching of Vatican II! Not that he actually *likes* the products of Vatican II ....

> ... I am not an admirer of the acts of the Second Vatican Council. But if they are examined carefully it will be found that all the essential teaching on the priesthood is contained in them.

And he adds:

> Pope Paul VI re-stated Catholic teaching on the priesthood and the Mass quite clearly in such documents as his *Credo* and *Mysterium Fidei*, which appeared in the year immediately preceding the imposition of the new Ordination rite. Another *ex adjunctis* point in favour of the new rite, pointed out to me by a professor at Écône, is

---

[11] These *adjuncts* are all those factors and circumstances which are associated with a sacramental form and can therefore give extrinsic determination to such parts of the form as are intrinsically indeterminate. The *primary adjuncts* are other prayers and actions contained in the sacramental ceremony, while *secondary adjuncts* can include the known beliefs of the minister or of the authors of the rite and conceivably the contemporary historical situation. It should be noted, however, that the entire theory of "*significatio* (or '*determinatio*') *ex adjunctis*" is no more than theologically probable (see Section (A) of this chapter for the technical meaning of "probable"), and that the inclusion among the sacramental *adjuncts* of circumstances as remote from the actual ceremonies as contemporary beliefs of persons other than the minister of the ritual has such scant theological support that it is doubtful whether it is even probable.

that the immediate context for the Ordination rite was the Tridentine Mass. He [the Écône professor] wrote:

'The new Catholic [sic] rite, despite its defects, did not come in with the New Mass but several months earlier. The context of the Ordination for those first months would therefore have been the Tridentine Mass, substantially, and no reasonable doubt can be raised, it seems, about such Ordinations done according to the official Latin text.'

In fact, by 1968, the preliminary texts of the Novus Ordo had already been issued by the Vatican and little was left of the traditional Mass in the parishes, but anyhow this is of course immaterial. The essential form of the sacrament of Order had been changed and so the rite had been rendered *intrinsically* doubtful. And this could not be remedied by secondary or even primary adjuncts; for whereas adjuncts certainly *can* lend sufficient determination to an indeterminate formula to make it valid, and in some rituals approved by the Church they do exactly this, nevertheless when an indeterminate formula occurs in a rite that is guaranteed neither by the Church's sanction nor by tradition, the question of whether the relevant adjuncts suffice to make it valid is a matter of theological opinion which can never be conclusively settled by private individuals. Or, if Michael Davies believes that privately evaluated secondary or tertiary "*significatio ex adjunctis*" can suffice to make a rite certainly valid when its essential formula is not definitely sufficient in itself, let him produce some Catholic authority to support his contention.

What comment could adequately convey the irony, and even poignancy, which pervade these last few extracts? "To the best of my knowledge no one has been able to point out a theological error in any of my books," Davies has written. Now, uniquely – I defy readers to locate another instance – he admits that he *has* erred; but – and it is here that the irony and poignancy lie – it is his *original* position that was *correct*, and his *new* position which is wrong.

Davies moves on to the subject of the word "*ut*" which was omitted from the traditional formula as reproduced in the 1968 rite. He comments:

> All the authorities I consulted on this point replied without the least hesitation that the removal of '*ut*' does not affect the validity of the Latin form. They further agree that the English form provides an adequate if not a perfect translation.

Davies does not name his authorities in the article itself; but it is possible to work out who a number of them are, for elsewhere in the article he says that he consulted, in its preparation, "the three theologians who helped [him] with *The Order of Melchisedech*" – and in the Introduction to that work these are named as Fr. William Lawson S.J., [the late] Mgr. Philip Flanagan and Professor J.P.M. van der Ploeg. And anyone who knew a little bit more about these purported theologians than Davies sees fit to pass on to his readers would not find it very surprising that they defended the validity of the new rite of Ordination. Mgr. Flanagan, now deceased, used to say the Novus Ordo and was in good standing as a parish priest ("pastor" for American readers) of the Conciliar Church; and Fr. Lawson, while he himself says the Tridentine Mass (though with the Canon and other secret prayers for some reason said aloud, in defiance of the rubrics), is quite prepared to encourage others to assist at the New Mass, even if said by a priest ordained in the new rites. As for Professor van der Ploeg, well, when Davies himself asserted formally that traditional Catholics "do not have the good fortune to possess a theologian of repute among our ranks" (see p. 77), why did he consider van der Ploeg excluded? Was it because the Dominican is in fact more of a Scripture scholar than a theologian ? Or because, although himself using the traditional Dominican rite, he was hardly what is normally understood by a *traditionalist*?

Another authority by whom Davies says he was assisted is stated by him to be "a canonist", and this must almost certainly be his friend the Rev. Thomas Glover J.C.D., who was professor of Canon Law at Écône,[12] and who it is known that Davies does consult from time to time. To put *any* use by Davies of this "authority" in context, let alone the use of him as a judge of the validity of the new Ordination rite, it is surely not wholly irrelevant that Glover was *himself* ordained according to this rite! In this circumstance – his readers might have asked themselves, had Davies given them this information – might not Dr. Glover's theological judgement on the validity of the rite be open to more than a suspicion of prejudice? And is not the fact of Glover's Ordination in the 1968 rite – his readers might want to ask themselves now – one which Davies really ought to have told his readers who otherwise would have trusted him to choose as his advisers authorities who were not only competent but also without suspicion of bias?

There is one unusual feature in this particular example of Davies's tactics in controversy, which is that for once he cannot get away with his usual practice of doing no more than citing the "authority" of his anonymous theologian friends. As Davies of course realizes, readers of Fr. Jenkins's article in *The Roman Catholic* have all been informed – correctly – that since 1968 the form of the sacrament of Ordination as employed in the Conciliar Church has ceased to include the word "*ut*" and has therefore contained a definite change of meaning by comparison with the changed rite; and because they have been so informed – unless it is without motive and purely coincidence – he on this occasion evidently feels it necessary for him to give some show of logical support for his opinion and to explain how it is that the omission of this word leaves the validity of the sacrament definitely unassailable.

---

[12] Dr. Glover was relieved of position at Écône as a result of pointing out to Archbishop Lefebvre that his expulsion of the Oyster Bay priests was grossly uncanonical and that the seminaries could not be expected to acknowledge the validity of John-Paul II's pontificate while simultaneously rejecting the 1983 *Code of Canon Law*. (His own position was that the new *Code* should be recognized.)

Clever and complex is perhaps the best description of the case Davies puts forward. For this reason careful attention will be required on the part of the reader in order to follow the summary of it that I shall now give, but his attention will be handsomely repaid by the clear understanding that will follow of Davies's capacity, which perhaps falls not far short of genius, to invent arguments of genuine brilliance, arguments which often appear to be so obviously correct as to be not even worth questioning – unless and until they are compared with the teaching of genuine Catholic theologians, at which point they dissolve completely, exposed as radically incompatible with Catholic orthodoxy.

The relevant section of Davies's article is entitled "The Missing '*Ut*'", and in it he proceeds as follows:

He opens by making a correct distinction between the two parts of the sacrament of Order, pointing out that:

> the sacrament confers in the first place "the priestly character itself, the '*gratia gratis data*' [freely given grace];
>
> but, in addition to this,
>
> the sacrament of Order confers also the '*gratia status*' [grace of status], enabling and prompting the recipient to fulfil his office worthily ....

Davies then argues that the form of the sacrament of Ordination, as reproduced above, is divided into two parts, the *first* of which confers the sacramental character of the priesthood, and the *second* of which confers the "grace of status", i.e. a special increase of sanctifying grace enabling the recipient of the sacrament to acquit himself faithfully of his sacred ministry. Here are Davies's own words:

> The Latin form is in two parts. The first part refers directly to the conferring of the priestly character itself .... This part is in itself an adequate form for conferring the priesthood and consists of the words:

"Da, quæsumus, omnipotens Pater, in hos famulos tuos, Presbyterii dignitatem.' ['Grant, we beseech Thee, Almighty Father to these thy servants, the dignity of the priesthood.']"

(...)

The second part of the form [i.e. all the remaining words of the formula above] asks God to sanctify the new priest in such a way that, having received the priesthood, he will set a good example by his life (...). Having invoked from the Almighty Father the essential grace of the priestly character to be conferred upon the ordinand, the bishop then goes on to invoke the conferring of the sanctifying grace which should normally accompany the priestly character. But the two requests of the Church are distinct, i.e. that he may receive the priesthood and that he may be made holy. The first does not depend upon the second.

In short, what Davies is saying is that, as soon as the word "dignitatem" has been uttered, *the essential character of the priesthood has already been conferred*; and the remaining part of the form is intended merely to petition the necessary graces for the recipient of the sacrament, who has, in fact, already been ordained by the time they are uttered.

Perhaps the reader is tempted to suggest that such a division of the sacramental form is no more than an arbitrary suggestion of Davies and that, since it is not certain, it therefore cannot be used as the basis of a purportedly certain argument[13] defending the validity of the 1968 rite. But Davies is not to be underestimated. He does not flinch from facing up to such a retort, and replies by setting out to demonstrate that the second part of the formula is not concerned with the conferring of the priestly character itself, and is therefore irrelevant to it.

---

[13] Readers are reminded that the point which Davies had taken it upon himself to prove is *not* that the 1968 rite of ordination *may* be valid, but that it is *certainly* valid. Even if he succeeded in showing it to be *almost* certainly valid (which he does not), the remaining doubt would mean that new-rite *priests* – even in the event of their adopting the correct Catholic position – could no more be approached for the sacraments than if their Orders, like those of the Church of England, were *definitely* null.

The suggestion that the second part of the formula (after the word "*dignitatem*") has no reference to conferring the priestly character itself is not without immediate difficulties. Indeed it might even seem a positively surprising one, because the second part of the formula includes the words "*secundi meriti munus obtineant*", the obvious translation of which is "[so that] they may obtain the office of the second rank ", and this is surely on the face of it a definite indication that – unless these words are entirely redundant – they are necessary to the obtaining by the ordinands of the office in question, namely the priesthood. Once again Davies does not flinch, and answers as follows:

> The meaning of this second part is obscured by the translation of '*obtineant*' as 'they may obtain' in the traditional form in English, and in the provisional I.C.E.L. version, cited by Father Jenkins on p. 9 [of his article referred to previously – J.S.D.]. The Latin verb '*obtinere*' does not mean 'obtain' in our ordinary English sense, but rather 'lay hold', 'maintain', or, as the second I.C.E.L. translation expresses it: 'to be faithful to'. Thus, the translation of the second part of the traditional form would express the Latin exactly if it read: 'Renew in their hearts (or within them) the Spirit of holiness, so that they may *be faithful* to the office of the second rank received from thee, O God, and may, by the pattern of their lives, inculcate the pattern [sic] of holy living.'
>
> (...)
>
> The important passage here is the one which reads in Latin '*ut acceptum a te Deus, secundi meriti munus obtineant*.' The anomaly caused by translating '*obtinere*' as 'to obtain' is made clear in the translation of this passage cited by Father Jenkins: 'so that they may obtain the office of the second rank received from Thee, O God.' *A request is made that the ordinands may receive something which they have already received*, but this anomaly is removed when '*obtinere*' is correctly translated as 'be faithful to'. In other words, the second invocation is for the grace, not to obtain the priesthood *that they have already obtained* ('*acceptum*').

And it is difficult to doubt that those readers of *The Roman Catholic*, presumably the vast majority, who have studied neither the niceties of sacramental theology nor the finer points of meaning of liturgical Latin, will have found themselves unable to resist Davies's apparently cogent argument. The "office of the second rank", Davies argues, is referred to as "*acceptum*" meaning "received", and this past participle must surely indicate that the office has *already* been received by the stage that these words are uttered in the second half of the formula; and therefore, to avoid a chronological anomaly in the prayer, it is necessary to have recourse to his rendering of "obtineant" as "that they may be faithful to" rather than "that they may obtain". And if that is the correct translation, then indeed the second half of the formula is no more than a prayer for grace; and then indeed the minor change in it, which is all that omitting the word "*ut*" would amount to, will not affect the validity of the conferring of the sacramental character, which has already taken place during the first half of the form. Moreover, his readers will have been strongly encouraged in this opinion by Davies's assurance that such a rendering of the word "*obtineant*" is in fact the only one available, especially as they have learnt from an earlier part of the article that his insights into Latin are not all the fruit of his own erudition as he had "obtained the advice of a leading authority on Christian Latin."[14]

Although we can safely leave it to Fr. Jenkins, in his follow-up article in *The Roman Catholic* shortly to be quoted, to show that Davies's tortuous reasoning has brought him into direct conflict with the teachings of the Magisterium on the subject

---

[14] In the course of a telephone conversation in August 1983, Davies informed the present writer that the authority he was referring to was Dr. Christine Mohrmann who has been professor at the universities of Nijmegen and Amsterdam. Whether Dr. Mohrmann in fact told Davies that "*obtinere*" in ecclesiastical Latin can only mean "be faithful to", I do not know. But it is certainly not true, as can be verified, for instance, by reference to the Secret of the Votive Mass for the King. This Mass includes the words "*ut ... proficiant ... regi nostro ad obtinendam animæ ... salutem*", and their only possible meaning is "so that they may be of assistance to our king in *obtaining* the salvation of his soul."

under discussion, attention must first be drawn to one or two details which Fr. Jenkins neglects to address. These concern the translation of the word "*obtineant*".

The first thing to be pointed out is that, whatever else is to be said of the translation of "*obtineant*" as "may they be faithful to", one of Davies's arguments in support of it is quite worthless. This is the one which he bases upon his allegation that the translation of the word as "to obtain" leads to the anomaly that the minister of the sacrament would be requesting "that the ordinands may receive something which they have already received." The argument goes as follows:

(i) In the second half of the traditional Latin formula the prayer is made that the ordinands (adjusting the syntax to clarify the point) "*obtineant secundi meriti munus acceptum a te.*"

(ii) Those words mean either "may they obtain ..." or "may they be faithful to ... the office received from Thee."

(iii) Since it is illogical to ask for someone to obtain what they have already "received", the alternative translation of "be faithful to" is inescapable.

However plausible this may sound, the argument falls apart on inspection; for although it is true that the word "*acceptum*" is a past participle, this does not necessarily mean that it is past tense *in relation to the verb "obtineant"* and therefore carries no implication that the "*munus*" or office has already been received at the time that these words are uttered. This is because Latin participles sometimes have the force of subordinate relative clauses, and as there is no present participle passive in Latin the past participle is sometimes used – probably in imitation of the corresponding Greek participle – with a present, or even future sense.[15] Readers to whom this last sentence means little should

---

[15] Cf. O. Riemann: *Syntaxe Latine*, N°. 261, Paris, 1935, in which one of the examples selected by the author to illustrate this usage consists of the strikingly comparable phrase, "*munus assignatum a Deo.*"

not despair. In language comprehensible to all this means simply that the words "the second rank received from Thee" need not mean "the second rank which *has already been* received from Thee at the time this sentence is being spoken". It may mean "the second rank which *has been, is being,* or *will be* received from Thee".

This is a question concerning which philologists could debate indefinitely and it is neither necessary nor fair on readers to attempt to solve it here, especially as, even if Davies is correct in assuming that the word "*acceptum*" is intended to be past in relation to "*obtineant*", this by no means forces us to acknowledge his extremely loose rendering of the latter term as "to be faithful to". In fact this rendering is probably the least justifiable of those which could be found in a standard Latin dictionary, and the reason that Davies has chosen it is obviously that it favours his claim that the second half of the formula is no more than a prayer for Divine grace.

The evidence showing this is all too clear. One need only consider the primary meaning of "*obtinere*", which is "to hold", and to ask, first, why Davies felt he had to pass over it and, secondly, why he felt he had to withhold from his readers this most elementary of the various possible translations. For, after all, "to hold" is a translation which makes perfect sense in the context of the formula. Indeed, in the formula it could well have the sense of "receive and retain", and if this were the correct rendering of the passage it would mean that the prayer in the second half might be asking not only for sanctifying grace but also still for the character of the priesthood itself.

It is also worth pointing out that even if the latter part of the formula of Ordination did indeed refer to the sacrament *as if* it had already been received, this would not show that it *had* already been received, because, as the ceremony is considered as a whole from a liturgical point of view, its wording need not always accord with the theological reality of *when* the sacrament is conferred. Analogously in a *later* prayer of the Ordination ceremony the bishop says to the ordinands, "Receive the power to offer ...", even though they have certainly *already* received this power. Similarly, in the liturgy of St. John Chrysostom, God is called upon, *after* the Consecration, to change the bread and wine into the Body and Blood of Our Lord. The wording of liturgical prayers, therefore, though full of theological instruction, cannot be relied on to inform us of the *precise moment* at which each sacrament is conferred.

But useful though these linguistic and liturgiological complexities are for illustrating Davies's polemical techniques, consideration of them is not necessary in order to refute his position. Fr. Jenkins's answer to Davies, elegantly entitled, "The New Ordination Rite: An Indelible Question Mark", competently presents the definitive answer of the Church herself to Davies's disingenuous defence of the 1968 Ordination rite, and the time has now come for me to quote the most important part of it.

> Mr. Davies contends that the latter part of the sacramental form of priestly Ordination is not essential, and thus not required for validity. Therefore, the new rite of priestly Ordination must be valid [since the omission of the word 'ut' occurs in the latter part of the formula].
>
> Response. With this argument, Mr. Davies directly contradicts the teaching of Pope Pius XII's Apostolic constitution *Sacramentum Ordinis*. In the constitution, the Pope declared with his Supreme Apostolic Authority that the form of the Sacrament of Order must UNIVOCALLY SIGNIFY THE SACRAMENTAL EFFECTS – THE POWER OF ORDER *AND* THE GRACE OF THE HOLY GHOST. The Jesuit moral theologian, Fr. Felix Cappello – an authority of considerable importance – holds that the Pope thereby 'declared' a truth which concerns the very nature of the sacrament ....
>
> After so declaring the necessary elements of all such forms, the Pontiff then said the following concerning the Latin Rite form of Ordination to the Catholic priesthood:

'The form consists of the words of the preface, of which these are ESSENTIAL AND THUS REQUIRED FOR VALIDITY.'

And for the sake of brevity I interrupt Fr. Jenkins here to note that the pope then quoted *the whole* of the traditional Latin form (which I omit here as I have already quoted it at the beginning of this chapter) including the part which Davies claims to be *in*essential and *not* required for validity!

Taking up Fr. Jenkins's article again:

Why did the Pope include these latter words as 'essential and thus required for validity'? Because the first part of the form alone does not univocally express the two essential elements needed: the power of priestly order, *and* the grace of the Holy Ghost.

(...)

The first part of the formula containing the equivocal word 'priesthood' is further specified by the second half of the formula which contains the expression 'office of the second rank'. Furthermore, while the first part of the formula signifies the power of the priestly Order (as Mr. Davies's theologians agree), the latter part specifies the grace of the Holy Ghost accompanying the order. Both of these are essential and required for validity.

Indisputably, Fr. Jenkins has vindicated his position and proved that the 1968 rite of Ordination is, at the very best, of doubtful validity. Pope Pius XII expressly teaches to be essential the *whole* formula, including the words that have been changed. But the debate between Fr. Jenkins and Michael Davies also shed frightening light on the credibility of the latter as a purportedly learned and honest defender of the Catholic Faith. For it showed him contradicting the authoritative pronouncement of a pope *which happened to be inconvenient to the thesis he was defending.*[16]

---

[16] Whether Davies actually *adverted*, at the time he wrote it, to the fact that his thesis had been condemned in advance by Pope Pius XII, of course I do not know, not having been blessed with the ability to read souls. But what cannot be questioned is that the fact of its condemnation was perfectly familiar to him and could only have failed to occur to him as a result of his

It should be recalled that Davies makes it clear in the very article in which he denies its teaching *that he is familiar with Pope Pius's constitution referred to by Fr. Jenkins*, the constitution which devastates Davies's theory as to the non-essential-ness of the second half of the formula of Ordination. Let us look at these words again:

> By our supreme Apostolic authority we decree and establish ... that in the Ordination of priests ... the form consists of the words of the 'preface', *of which the following are essential and thus required for validity*:
> 'Grant, we beseech Thee, Almighty Father, to these Thy servants, the dignity of the priesthood; renew the spirit of holiness within them *so that* they may hold the office of the second rank received from Thee, O God, and may by the example of their conduct inculcate strict morality.'

Such are the words of the sovereign pontiff, the Vicar of Jesus Christ upon earth, to whom, in the person of Peter, were uttered the words "he who hears you hears Me". A writer on sacramental authority who, whether consciously or through felicitous inattention, announces that half of the words in question are not essential at all, has surely forfeited any claim to his readers' trust.

---

considering only what supported his case and ignoring whatever might contradict it.

Part 3: Is the New Rite of Priestly Ordination Valid?

Although most of this study has related to the question of the validity of the new rite of priestly Ordination, the spotlight has so frequently been turned on Mr. Davies his errors that the theological question may not have been treated clearly enough for all readers to follow. This third Part is therefore devoted to the consideration of the single question posed by its title: is the new rite of priestly Ordination in fact valid? Although the important subject of the 1968 Ordination rite was originally addressed in the context of a general evaluation of Mr. Davies's credibility, it is surely a duty now to settle it as definitely as possible before passing on.

Since all the authorities that are necessary to support the position here maintained have already been quoted, it is necessary only to summarize the facts.

Pope Pius XII's constitution *Sacramentum Ordinis* taught that the following words constitute the essential form of the rite of priestly Ordination:

> Grant, we beseech Thee, Almighty Father, into these Thy servants, the dignity of the priesthood; renew the Spirit of holiness within them *so that* they may hold the office of the second rank received from Thee, O God, and may by the example of their conduct inculcate strict morality.

As most readers are probably aware, the pope did not, in decreeing those words to be essential, make them the *only* form which was valid for conferring the sacrament. Our Lord Himself, of course, instituted the substance of all the sacraments, but in respect of some of them, including Holy Orders, He left the Church free to use any words which adequately convey the essential nature of the sacrament, and different words are used, for instance, in the Pontificals of the Catholic Eastern Rites which the Church recognizes as valid and lawful. What the pope *did* rule, however, was that in the *Latin* rite the words quoted *were* essential; hence any substantial change in them would be enough to make the validity of the sacrament doubtful. Secondly, it should be noted that he did not teach anything about what the essential formula of the sacrament of Order *had been* prior to his 1947 constitution. He taught only what it should be from then on. Moreover, while making it clear that *in the context of the ritual* of the *Roman Pontifical* the words quoted are those by which the priesthood is conferred, he did *not* teach that the same words would necessarily be capable of validly conferring the sacrament in any other context, such as if they were pronounced in a non-sacred setting or set in the context of an entirely different ritual. It is, in fact, a disputed point among Catholic theologians whether the formulæ defined by the Church as essential will necessarily be valid outside the full context of the Church's ritual. A sizeable proportion of theologians deny this. (See, for instance, Duns Scotus: dist. 8, quæst. 2, in 4 Sent., and many others cited by Fr. Maurice de la Taille S.J. in *thesis* XXXV of his *Mysterium Fidei*.) This makes the contrary opinion doubtful and unsafe to follow in practice, for which reason the validity of any factitious Ordination ceremony would be highly questionable if it *either* lacked the essential formula as defined by Pope Pius XII *or* put the essential formula in a new and different context. So to what extent does either of these factors apply to the new rite of priestly Ordination used in the Conciliar Church?

The straightforward answer is that *both* factors that could cast doubt on its validity *definitely* apply. In the first place, the rite has been drastically revised and, by omission, alteration, or, in a few cases, by being made optional, all those parts which unambiguously express the Catholic doctrine of the priesthood – the power of offering the sacrifice of the Mass and of absolving sins – have been neutralized. And secondly, though most of the words which Pope Pius XII declared to be "the essential form" of the sacrament have been retained, omitted, as we have seen, is the word "*ut*", meaning "so that"; the result of this omission being that the causal connection between the two halves of the prayer is no longer apparent. Thus a substantial[1] change of meaning has been introduced into the Latin version of the new rite which is emphatically *not* merely a matter of the use of a slightly different wording to say the same thing: even as to basic substance the essential form of the sacrament is not retained. And what is true of the *Latin* form of the new rite is even truer of the loose vernacular translations of the Latin which have been made all over the world and are the ones used in the vast majority of Conciliar-Church "Ordinations". These translations are as – deliberately – incompetent as all the other vernacularisations instituted and used by the Conciliar Church.

From the obvious conclusion flowing from the above facts, there are three apparent avenues of escape available to defenders of the new rite. These are as follows:

(i)   They can claim that the omission of the word "*ut*" is not a substantial change in the essential form.

(ii) Or they can claim that the form of the new rite, although indeterminate in itself, must be interpreted in the light of other parts of the ceremony, etc., and that the principle of

---

[1] In common parlance a change of wording would be called "substantial" only if it affected a relatively large part of the whole in which the change occurred, but in theological usage (and the word "substantial" in fact *belongs* to scholastic philosophy and theology and has been appropriated and distorted in everyday speech) its meaning is different and more exact. A change in the wording of a sacramental form is called "substantial" if it affects the "substance" of the sacrament, i.e. that which is so necessary to it that it cannot be altered without – at least potentially – affecting the sacrament's validity. In the Rubrics to the Roman Missal the Church prescribes as the touchstone for whether a change will invalidate the form or not the simple question whether "the words ... signify the same thing." (*De Defectibus Formæ*) Thus any altered formula the words of which signify something *different* from the correct formula – even if the difference affects only one small part of what is essential – will be sufficient to nullify the sacrament; for its difference from the Church's approved formula, however slight it may appear, means that it does not have the guarantee of validity which properly belongs only to those formulæ actually approved by the Church or to words which at least convey *the same meaning*.

"*significatio ex adjunctis*" thus gives the form a Catholic sense and makes it valid.

(iii) Or they can claim that the priesthood has already been conferred by the words "Grant, we beseech Thee, Almighty Father, to those Thy servants, the dignity of the priesthood", so that the subsequent omission of the word "*ut*" can have no effect on what has already taken place.

Now even if one or other of these claims were acceptable, none of them is sufficient to prove the new rite *definitely* valid, because, as we have seen, some Catholic theologians hold the opinion that even the *essential* formula prescribed by the Catholic Church may not be enough to confer the sacrament validly if stripped from the context of the Catholic rite and placed in a different context. Therefore, even if there had been no change in the *essential* form, the fact of the radical changes in the *in*essential rites and ceremonies alone is enough to cast doubt on its validity. And since I am asserting *not* that the rite is *certainly* invalid, but only that it is *highly doubtful*, this point is conclusive.

But even aside from this conclusive point, each of the three escape routes mentioned above can be shown to lead in fact to a dead-end. Let us now examine them one by one.

(i) For the first-mentioned avenue of escape to succeed, it must be *proved*, not merely supposed, that the word "*ut*" is of such slight significance that the change of meaning which it introduces cannot conceivably be more than a trifling irrelevancy; for in order to exclude *doubt* as to the validity of the new rite, nothing short of this can suffice. But how is this to be done?

The answer is that in only two ways could this conceivably be proved, if it can be proved at all. They are these:

(a) *Hermeneutically*,[2] by showing that the omission of "*ut*" makes no alteration to the overall significance of the sentence in which it occurs; or

(b) *Historically*, by showing that the Church has at some time in the past sanctioned the use of the essential formula of priestly Ordination as found in Pope Pius XII's decree but with the word "*ut*" omitted.

However,

(a) *Hermeneutically*. Any attempt to prove the point by this means is doomed to failure: the word "*ut*" ("so that"), as we have seen, establishes a causal connection between the two halves of the formula which is not apparent if this word is omitted; and therefore the meaning of the whole formula would be affected by the omission, because the purpose of the first half, and the cause of the second half, would no longer be made clear.

(b) *Historically*. The claim has been made that historical instances exist of the Latin formula minus the "*ut*", notably by the late SSPX priest Fr. Denis Marchal in the November 1984 issue of the *Catholic Crusader*, where he boldly asserted that the word "*ut*" was added in the thirteenth century. No less certainly, there is no truth in Fr. Marchal's claim, however, for the earliest text of the *Gelasian Sacramentary* (of which the Manuscript Reginæ 316 in the Vatican Library[3] is currently dated to around 750 A.D. and the liturgical contents are certainly earlier) contains exactly the same words defined by Pope Pius XII to be essential, *not* excluding the "*ut*".

But it would be a mistake to conclude from this – as some have – that the word "*ut*" has appeared at that point in every rite of Ordination historically used in the Catholic Church. In one or two manuscripts it is replaced by "*et*" (which may be a scribal error) and in others it is absent. It did not, for instance, appear in the pre-eighth century Gregorian Sacramentary partially preserved in the Montecassino palimpsest N° 271[4]. But it by no means

---

[2] Hermeneutics is the science of the interpretation of language and texts.

[3] See critical edition by the Protestant scholar H.A. Watson M.A., Oxford, 1894 (p. 23).

[4] See Dom Jean Deshusses, *Le Sacramentaire Grégorien: ses principales*

follows, because the word "*ut*" is omitted at that part of certain texts of an obviously valid ancient Sacramentary, that any other ritual which omits it at the same point must also be valid. This is because at the time that the Gregorian Sacramentary was in use Pope Pius XII had not yet defined what was the essential form of the Sacrament of Order, and when he eventually did so, his constitution was not retroactive. (As the form of the Sacrament of Order was not instituted "*in specie*" by Our Lord, the Church can designate any appropriate words for this role, and, within due limits, can modify the essential form.) Hence there is no certainty as to *where* the essential form of the Sacrament of Order lay in the marginally variant forms of the rite of Ordination in use in or before the eighth century. We know that the essential form occurred *somewhere* in each ritual approved by the Church, but that is *all* we know; it may not have been in the same place in each case. Hence it is perfectly plausible that, in those rituals which omitted the word "*ut*" in the second sentence of the two which comprise Pope Pius XII's essential form, other parts, and notably the following sentence, also at that time pertained to the essential form.

And the following sentence, in the rites which omit *our* "*ut*" contained a different but closely parallel "*ut*":

> "*Sit probus cooperator ordinis nostri, eluceat in eum totius forma justitiæ, UT bonam rationem dispensationis sibi creditæ redditurus, æternæ beatitudinis præmia consequatur.*" ("May he be an upright co-operator with our order; may the appearance of all justice shine forth in him SO THAT he may render a good account of the dispensation entrusted to him and may obtain the rewards of everlasting happiness.")

---

formes d'après les plus anciens manuscrits, Spicilegium Friburgense, Fribourg, 1988.

If the truly essential point is that the rite should make explicit the causal connection between the sacramental grace and its stated effects, this requirement would be adequately fulfilled by this second "*ut*" found in the Sacramentaries which lack ours, so that the phrase containing it would have been essential *at that time and in that particular sacramentary* (when it was the only relevant conjunction of causality), although it would have been *in*essential in the Gelasian form of the Roman rite of priestly Ordination as found in the pre-Vatican II *Pontificale Romanum*, which contained *both* the "*ut*" designated by Pius XII as essential in his day *and* the second "*ut*" in the above words which it also retained.

By contrast the 1968 rite of Ordination used in the Conciliar Church, although it could claim to be inspired by one or two early manuscripts of the Gregorian Sacramentary in omitting the word "*ut*", does *not* follow the same Sacramentaries in the following sentence. Indeed at that precise point the text of the new rite abandons any pretence to follow any specific ancient rite and hence any possibility of establishing its validity on the basis of historical precedent evaporates altogether. So although historical proof of the validity of the 1968 rite *would* be provided if the relevant part of the 1968 rite were in fact *globally identical* to some rite previously approved by the Church, this is not in fact the case.

In other words, the attempt to prove on historical grounds that the word "*ut*" is not essential in the sentence from which the 1968 rite omits it, though it proves this particular "*ut*" to be not *always* and in *every* context essential, totally fails to prove it to be inessential in the context of the 1968 rite, precisely because that rite had no historical existence, as an integral unit, before 1968, and what Paul VI identified as its essential form[5] is not identical to the known essential form of any historical rite

---

[5] By the "Apostolic Constitution" *Pontificalis Romani Recognitio*, 18th June 1968.

recognized by the Church as valid. And so the historical escape route for Davies and other defenders of the Conciliar Church is as blind as the hermeneutical one.

(ii) The second avenue of escape, it may be remembered, was that the formula of the new rite might derive a Catholic signification by virtue of "*significatio ex adjunctis*" – in other words from the full context in which they are uttered.

Once again, what is maintained by those who hold this position is simply an opinion which cannot be proved. And once again, therefore, the principle that an opinion which cannot be proved cannot make a rite of doubtful validity definitely valid is sufficient by itself to close off this particular escape route.

Moreover, as far as any question of "*significatio ex adjunctis*" from other parts of the ceremony is concerned, dispassionate consideration of the context in which the sacramental form appears serves only to confirm that the rite which confronts us is *not* constructed to ordain sacrificing priests and therefore cannot do so. Indeed on p. 97 of his *The Order of Melchisedech* even Davies admits – and who could possibly deny it? – that the new rite is "shorn of any mandatory prayer signifying the essential powers of the priesthood." And the most notable consequence of that act of shearing is that certain vital words used by Pope Leo XIII in his encyclical *Apostolicæ Curæ* of the Anglican Ordinal[6] apply equally to the new rite of the Conciliar Church. These are the words in question:

> In the whole Ordinal not only is there no clear mention of the sacrifice of Consecration, of the '*sacerdotium*' [priesthood], and of the power of consecrating and offering sacrifice, but ... every trace of these things which had been in such prayers of the Catholic rite as they had

---

[6] Ordinal means "ritual of Ordination".

not entirely rejected, was deliberately removed and struck out. (paragraph 30)

And the relevance of this is that Pope Leo XIII used this fact – which, I repeat, is equally applicable to the new rite – to *prove* his case that no indeterminate form found in the Anglican Rite could be sufficient to confer the sacramental validity, *"even on the hypothesis that it might be held sufficient in a Catholic rite approved by the Church."* He pointed out that, in view of the wholesale removal of all parts of the ritual indicative of Catholic doctrine touching on the priesthood, "any words [in the part of the ritual remaining] which lend themselves to ambiguity, cannot be taken in the same sense as they possess in the Catholic rite." (paragraph 31) And, as is well known, the pontiff went on to conclude that Anglican Orders "have been, and are, absolutely null and utterly void."

If there is anything clearer than the obvious fact that the rite of the Conciliar Church cannot be defended from the identical charge of nullity on grounds already dismissed in respect of Anglican orders by the supreme authority in the Church, this writer for one cannot think of it.

Before leaving this particular topic, there is one other matter connected with it which is worth mentioning if only as an illustration of the remarkable lengths some people will go to in order to avoid facing up to the obvious but uncomfortable. When Dr. Francis Clark, the author of *Eucharistic Sacrifice and the Reformation*, reviewed Davies's book *The Order of Melchisedech* in *Christian Order* for June 1979, he recognized that the validity of the new rite could be demonstrated neither by the claim that it retains the essential form (which it does not, and which would not be conclusive even if it did) nor by the claim that the indeterminate formula derives orthodox signification from unequivocal statements of correct Catholic doctrine elsewhere in the rite (for such statements are not to be found). He was not troubled by this, however. On the contrary: he found a remarkable defence on which to fall back. The new rite, he informed the readers of *Christian Order*, could derive Catholic signification from "*the religious context of the age.*" (p. 380) Thus what was to be taken into account, for instance, was the orthodox doctrine contained in some of Paul VI's encyclicals from roughly the same period.

Well, the admission that other defences of the validity of the new rite are inadequate is welcome, of course, but really! The suggestion that in 1968 or thereabouts – well after the conclusion of Vatican II – the Conciliar Church's doctrine on the priesthood was clearly and universally orthodox is so ludicrous as to be unworthy of refutation.[7] And of course even if the suggestion were soundly based on reality, the new rite could not thereby be proved to be valid. The notion that "*significatio ex adjunctis*" can include the content of contemporary papal encyclicals, etc., is – er ... – highly questionable. Far from being a notion that is recognized by Catholic theologians as certain, it is a mere novelty, and it is doubtful whether it rates even the very limited status of being considered theologically "probable".

No more need be said on the second possible avenue of escape.

(iii) The third and final one is Davies's own position. This, it will be recalled, is that the words, "Grant, we beseech Thee, Almighty Father, to these Thy servants, the dignity of the priesthood," are sufficient *by themselves* to confer the sacrament of priestly Ordination, so that whether or not the following part of the formula includes the word "*ut*" is immaterial. To this the only answer that is needed is the following solemn declaration of Pope Pius XII in his constitution *Sacramentum Ordinis* (1947):

---

[7] Though it is perhaps worth observing that it was only three years later that Hans Küng published his book *Why Priests?* while not ceasing to be considered by the Conciliar Church as an accredited teacher of Catholic doctrine.

"The form [of priestly Ordination] consists of the words of the 'Preface', *of which the following are essential and thus required for validity*:

"'Grant, we beseech Thee, Almighty Father, to these Thy servants, the dignity of the priesthood; renew the spirit of holiness within them so that they may hold the office of the second rank received from Thee, O God, and may by the example of their conduct inculcate strict morality.'"

In short, anyone who, like Davies, denies that the latter part of the form, *including the word "ut"*, is required for validity, is in conflict with the definitive teaching of the Magisterium on this point.

V

I believe it has now been satisfactorily demonstrated in this Part 3 of Chapter 9 that the new rite of Ordination is of doubtful validity for the following reasons:

(a) The word "*ut*" has been omitted from the essential form, which constitutes a substantial change of meaning.

(b) The remainder of the rite has been denuded of all clear references to the Catholic doctrine of the priesthood particularly insofar as this doctrine differs from Protestant beliefs about the ministry.

Validity is therefore guaranteed *neither* by the use of a form already recognized as valid by the Church *nor* by the use of any form of words univocally expressing the Catholic notion of the Order to be received. Either of these two defects *alone* would be sufficient to eliminate the possibility of certainty concerning the validity of the rite, and the occurrence of *both* of them can only reinforce the point.

All this having been established, there is one final consideration to which the pointed omission of the simple word "*ut*" from the essential formula gives rise. The rite has been proved to be doubtful, but the question remains as to *how* doubtful it is; in other words, that is, how *unlikely* is it that it is invalid? The opinion of the present writer is that the *invalidity* of the new rite is so likely as to be almost certain. And, ironically, the principle upon which this conclusion is based is one which is stated by Davies himself, on p. 40 of *The Order of Melchisedech*:

> There is far more significance attached *to the removal of a word from an existing form* than to its failure to appear in an ancient one.

The same point was made in even more striking terms by the Archbishop and Bishops of the province of Westminster in their *Vindication of the Bull 'Apostolicæ Curæ'* (1898)

> ... in adhering rigidly to the rite handed down to us, we can always feel secure; whereas if we omit or change *anything*, we may perhaps be abandoning *just that element which is essential.*

Part 4: Archbishop Lefebvre and the New Rite of Ordination

As Michael Davies has made himself the biographer and apologist of Archbishop Lefebvre, a short note on the Archbishop's own ambivalent attitude to the validity of the new rite of Ordination will not take us too far from our subject.

There may be some who are under the impression that Archbishop Lefebvre does not acknowledge the validity of the new rite; and if so they could surely be forgiven if they had formed their impression as a result of having heard or read the now famous sermon he delivered at Lille in 1976 when he first ordained men to the priesthood without the approval of the Conciliar Church. That sermon included the following thunderous denunciation:

> The union desired by these liberal Catholics, a union between the Church and the Revolution and subversion, is, for the Church, an adulterous union – adulterous. And that adulterous union can produce only bastards. And what are those bastards? They are our rites ... the sacraments are bastard sacraments – we no longer know if they are sacraments which give grace or do not give grace.

And since Archbishop Lefebvre then goes on to relate these comments *specifically* to the priesthood, he certainly appears to be indicating that it is doubtful whether the Conciliar Church's "bastard" Ordination rite validly communicates the sacramental grace and character of the priesthood. And where doubt exists as to the validity of a sacrament ... readers will by now be able to finish the sentence for themselves!

But had the same people a few years later read the June 1983 issue of *The Angelus*, they would have been startled by a strong contrast between the 1976 text and the same prelate's subsequent *practical* policy when confronted by priests who have been ordained in the "bastard rite". This is what *The Angelus*, published of course by the Society of St. Pius X, said in its editorial:

His Grace's policy is, and always has been, that if a priest [ordained in the 1968 rite] feels that he has not been properly ordained and approaches him and requests conditional Ordination, he will confer such conditional Ordination. The Archbishop has never insisted or forced a priest to accept conditional Ordination.

The clear implication – and lest there be any doubt, it is made explicit later in the same editorial – is that, if the "priest" in question "feels" that he *has* been properly ordained, albeit by a "bastard rite", Archbishop Lefebvre is quite happy to commend him to those who attend the Mass-centres of the Society of St. Pius X. And this was indeed the policy of the Society in respect of Dr. Thomas Glover, who was employed to teach Canon Law at Écône and served Society of St. Pius X Mass centres in England despite having been ordained in the new rite – a fact which gave rise to such a rift at the Society's London Mass Centre when Dr. Glover was transferred there that he was hastily despatched to the backwater of Yorkshire where he was later to abandon the clerical state altogether.

It is clear, therefore, that while the Archbishop has given conditional re-Ordination to *some* new rite "priests",[8] he has been quite happy to allow *others*[9] to continue to function without such re-ordination.

Unfortunately this inconsistency is such as to take the breath away. As others have pointed out already, the implication of Archbishop Lefebvre's policy as stated in *The Angelus* is that, if two twin brothers were both ordained in the new rite by the same bishop during the same ceremony, and both offered their services to the Society of St. Pius X, and one "felt" that he had been "properly ordained" while the other "felt" that he had not,

---

[8] For instance Frs. Sullivan, Ringrose, Bedingfeld, Hopkins and Michael-Mary Sim C.SS.R.

[9] For instance *Frs.* Thomas Glover, Philippe Tournyol du Clos and Philip Stark S.J. (Throughout this *Evaluation* I have adopted the course of generally using whatever titles clerics are commonly known by, irrespective of whether I believe that their ordination or appointment to office is valid.)

His Grace would be content to accept the services of the first twin at once, but would defer accepting the services of the second until he had (conditionally) re-ordained him.

Evidently the reality is that either both are valid priests or neither is, and whatever objective evidence there is applies equally to both of them. But the objective evidence simply does not play a part in Lefebvre's decision. What he takes account of is the "feelings" of those concerned; and these, of course, have no value whatsoever as evidence of whether or not they are truly priests, since the character of the priesthood is not something which can be detected by the senses, the imagination, or the emotions.

Finally, lest any readers should imagine that the inconsistency that we have just pointed out represents the full amplitude of Archbishop Lefebvre's oscillations on the subject of the new rite of Ordination, it should be pointed out that this is not the case. Fr. François Egregyi, a priest who studied at Écône and is well placed to know, revealed in his *Bulletin de Notre Dame du Très Saint Rosaire* Nº 13: (a) that in the early 1970s Lefebvre privately opined more than once that the new rite was intrinsically invalid owing to a defect of form,[10] and (b) that, notwithstanding this, Archbishop Lefebvre himself actually *used* the new rite for the Ordination of one Jean-Yves Cottard at the Abbey of Fautgombault in 1973. A fact so astounding could hardly be believed but for the confirmatory testimony produced by Fr. Egregyi for which readers are referred to the periodical mentioned above and the fact that Fr. Cottard himself, still with the SSPX, has admitted it. It is alleged by various sources that Archbishop Lefebvre afterwards, in private, supplied some parts of the Catholic ordination ceremony, an assurance so vague and

---

[10] Fr. Cekada has also put on public record that in 1975 the Archbishop considered the new rite of episcopal consecration to be invalid though he later changed his mind on the mistaken grounds that the new rite follows ancient forms recognized as valid. (*Journal de la France Courtoise*, Nº 379).

unverifiable as to offer little comfort, especially as others declare that Fr. Cottard refused these additions.

CHAPTER NINE SECTION (C)
THE THEORY OF SACRAMENTAL VALIDITY AND "SIGNIFICATIO EX ADJUNCTIS"

Introduction

In discussing the validity both of the New Rite of Mass and of the 1968 rite of Ordination, Davies covers in some depth the doctrine of sacramental intention and the principle known as *"significatio ex adjunctis"*. On this subject he makes several errors to which attention should be drawn.

I begin with the following statement from Davies's *Cranmer's Godly Order*, Appendix I, p. 139:

> The sacraments themselves are the source of the grace they convey providing they are administered by an authorized minister who intends to do what the Church intends and observes the correct ritual.

Succinct and short though this statement of the requirements for the validity of a sacrament is, Davies has managed to include in it no fewer than two theological errors.

An Authorized Minister

The first of these errors is the slipshod statement that the minister must be "authorized" as a condition of validity. The truth is that there are only two sacraments for the validity of which it is required that the minister be "authorized": Penance and (if we allow the inaccurate reference to the priest as "minister" of this sacrament) Matrimony. Of the other sacraments, the sacrament of Baptism, as is well known, can validly be administered by anyone at all; Holy Eucharist and Extreme Unction must be administered by a priest who has been *validly ordained*, but, although illicit, are certainly valid even if the priest is *not* "authorized" and has received his Ordination illicitly; and Confirmation and Holy Orders must be administered by a validly consecrated bishop if they are to be valid[1] – though once again it is immaterial to the *validity* of the sacrament whether the bishop is "authorized". It is unfortunate that there is no short way of expressing what is required on the part of the minister of each sacrament by way of Ordination, Consecration, or authorization, but this does not excuse Davies from making a statement which is without foundation. If an adequate statement cannot be made in as few words as might be hoped, a greater number of words must be used, and that is all there is to it.

Intention

The second error consists in asserting that the minister of a sacrament must "intend to do what the Church intends" – a mistake which Davies repeated in *Pope Paul's New Mass* on p. 336 where he writes of a "minister ... who intends to do what the Church intends" and on p. 132 of *The Order of Melchisedech* ("...the minister must intend what the Church intends...") The distinction which must be made here is a subtle one, but the issue is not one that can be avoided, for if what Davies has written were true it would undermine the Church's teaching that Baptism can validly be administered even by an atheist.

Here are the true facts relating to intention in connection with the administration of sacraments:

(i) A man may be said to intend to do what the Church *intends* only if he can honestly say, "I intend what the Church *intends*."

(ii) A man can truthfully say, "I intend what the Church *intends*," only if he *knows* the mind of the Church in relation to the effects of a sacrament and has the *intention* of producing those effects at the time that he is conferring the sacrament.

(iii) But of course in most cases neither a heretic, nor a member of any of the religions not derived from Christianity at all,

---

[1] Exceptionally a priest can administer Confirmation by special mandate of the Holy See, but without such a mandate the sacrament will be certainly invalid no matter how great the apparent need.

nor an atheist, *does* know the mind of the Church in relation to the effects of a sacrament, and such individuals therefore do not, and cannot, have the intention of producing those effects at such times as they may confer sacraments.

(iv) Nevertheless, Pope Leo XIII does not hesitate to give the status of *doctrine* to the belief that "a sacrament is truly conferred by the ministry of one who is a heretic or unbaptized, provided that the Catholic rite be employed."[2] And to express what is required on the part of the minister of the sacrament in order not to obstruct its validity, he quotes directly from St. Thomas Aquinas, who writes that the minister of a sacrament is, as it were, "a living instrument" of Christ and the Church, and that for the validity of the sacrament it is necessary that he should have an intention by which "he subjects himself to the principal agent [Christ and the Church], namely that he should intend to do what ... the Church does." (*Summa Theologiæ*, III, Q.64, A.8 *responsio ad primum*)

Does it seem a trivial difference that Davies said "intends to do what the Church *intends* while St. Thomas says "intends to do what the Church *does*"? In fact the difference is crucial, for a man may honestly profess to intend to do what the Church *does* even if he neither accepts, nor knows, nor cares what that is. It is sufficient that he should by an act of will undertake to "fit into" the Church's action. Provided he was prepared seriously to act as an instrument of the Church by seriously employing her rite, he would *by that very token* be intending to do what the Church does and would thus be able to confer a sacrament validly; and this remains true even if, for instance, he is convinced that the Church *is doing nothing at all*, but simply acting out a fruitless and ridiculous ritual. According to what necessarily follows from Davies's doctrine, however, the sort of person just depicted would be incapable of validly conferring a sacrament. *And this*

---

[2] *Apostolicæ Curæ*.

is contrary to Catholic doctrine. The difference between Pope Leo XIII and St. Thomas, on the one hand, and Davies, on the other, is therefore far from trivial.

This particular error of Davies's, presented to his readers at least twice, as we have seen, had an interesting sequel. In about 1980 the present writer, attended a meeting organized by the Latin Mass Society[3] at which Davies delivered a short talk and answered questions. And remarkably, when one of the questioners at the meeting referred to the need for the minister to intend to do what the Church *intends*, Davies put him right! The true doctrine, Davies told us perfectly correctly, is that the minister must intend to do what the Church *does*.

The mystery was solved for the present writer when in 1982 a Cambridge-based traditional priest, Fr. Ronald Silk, informed him that he, Fr. Silk, had notified Davies of his erroneous statement in *The Order of Melchisedech*, as a result of which correction Davies had since desisted from repeating his error.

To find Davies ceasing to propagate error comes as a pleasant surprise, of course; but the surprise ought to be rather greater than the accompanying pleasure, the latter being considerably reduced by the fact that Davies now refuses to acknowledge that he ever held the error in the first place. Thus it is that, conveniently forgetful of the assistance and correction which he had received from Fr. Silk – and that which he had received from countless others on other subjects – he was able to summon up the gall to boast in *The Angelus* for March 1984:

---

[3] The Latin Mass Society is an English liturgical association affiliated with the international association *Una Voce*. It was founded in 1965 with the support of many distinguished Catholics, such as Evelyn Waugh and Sir Arnold Lunn, to oppose the encroachment of the vernacular in the liturgy. When the Novus Ordo was introduced, the Society chose to support the traditional Mass rather than the Latin Novus Ordo. Lunn resigned as chairman but the Society clung to this position which it still holds, exclusively under the auspices of the Conciliar Church.

To the best of my knowledge, no one has been able to point out a theological error in any of my books ....

Readers may draw their own conclusions as to what light these words, which Davies has repeated, with slight variation, several times since, shed on any claim he may have to possess even in a low degree the virtues of honesty and humility.

A Term to Avoid

On p. 355 of *Pope Paul's New Mass*, there is another discussion about sacramental intention. Davies writes as follows:

> This brings up the thorny question of 'intention' which I have discussed in great detail in *The Order of Melchisedech*. I concur with Dr. Francis Clark that the term 'intention of a rite' should be avoided.
> A rite can have no intention. What matters is whether the Catholic Church pronounces that a particular sacramental rite is an adequate vehicle for confecting the sacrament it is intended to confect. In this case the Church has said that Eucharistic Prayer II does confect the sacrament. Where intention is concerned the beliefs or intentions of those who drew up the rite are not relevant once the Church has pronounced judgement.

Davies's more attentive readers will surely have been more than a little shocked by Davies's profession of concurrence with Dr. Francis Clark that one should not refer to the "intention of a rite" on the basis that a rite can have no intention. Had not Davies, on p. 79 of *The Order of Melchisedech*, published in 1979, a year before *Pope Paul's New Mass*, written the following?

> As is made clear in Appendix I this is a case where *the intention of the rite* must be deduced from other prayers and ceremonies .... (Emphasis added)

It would be pointless to dwell on Davies's inconsistency on this point; nor on his failure, when in *Pope Paul's New Mass* he expresses his new position, held too by Dr. Clark, to make any reference whatever to his previously having held the view he now rejects. Much more important is that his new position is quite unsustainable, and indeed would rather appear to have been invented, without any authority, in order to support the claim to validity of certain of the heretical sacramental rituals of the Conciliar Church.

For the problem with what Clark and Davies say is not merely that the term "intention of a rite" is in fact a perfectly sound one. It is also that this term is even *necessary* to some extent for an adequate discussion of the validity of a sacramental formula, and that in demanding its exclusion from theological terminology, therefore, Clark and Davies are in effect rendering us unable to express one of the most powerful arguments against the validity of the new rites.

Such tactics are reminiscent of those used by the "Ministry of Truth" in George Orwell's novel *Nineteen Eighty-four* to stamp out beliefs considered to be objectionable (known as "thought crimes"). The technique was simply to create a language ("Newspeak") in which it was impossible to express "thought crime". As one character in the novel explains:

> The whole aim of Newspeak is to narrow the range of thought. In the end we shall make thought crime literally impossible because there will be no words in which to express it. (Penguin edition, p. 45).

Of course, Davies is correct in stating that a rite, being irrational, cannot have an intention in the sense of an act of will. But the intention of a verbal formula invariably means the intention expressed by those words. In fact, Davies's rejection of this usage is based on the same absurd argument which is used by defenders of the heresy of religious liberty when they argue that it is incorrect to assert that "error has no rights". Error, being an abstraction, they superciliously pontificate, is incapable of having *rights*. But in truth, as Davies himself points out in the context of religious liberty, no one is in any doubt as to what is *meant* by the assertion that error has no rights; and in the same way there is no doubt as to what is *meant* by reference to the intention of a rite. When we refer to the intention of a rite we mean the object towards which its words, by their very nature, are directed, and which those words are calculated to obtain.

Thus in the formula for the sacrament of penance, for instance, the words "I absolve you of your sins" *contain within themselves, irrespective of the inward and invisible intention of the minister who pronounces them,* the outward and verifiable *intention* of effecting the absolution of the penitent's sins. Only by dishonesty could a minister pronounce those words with some other intention in mind. By the same token, those words could not, of course, be used by the Church as a formula for the sacrament of Baptism or Matrimony, as the *intrinsic intention* expressed in the rite would not be appropriate to the ends of those sacraments.

By denying that a rite can have an intention, and by asserting that "what matters is whether the Catholic Church pronounces that a particular sacramental rite is an adequate vehicle for confecting the sacrament", Davies again insinuates the error which already looked at on p. 366: that the literal meaning of the words of the sacramental form are irrelevant, and should not be subject to consideration in assessing the validity of a sacramental form, as if the Church could, if she chose, validly decree that the words, "May I have two eggs for breakfast?" should be a valid formula for effecting the sacrament of Ordination. And that, of course – as for all I know Davies would agree if confronted with that question expressly – is not the case. The words, "May I have two eggs for breakfast?", even if pronounced by a validly consecrated bishop who sincerely intended by them to confer holy orders upon an eligible candidate, would be incapable of having that effect, not simply because the Church has not declared them a sacramental form, but, primordially, because they contain within themselves *an intention* which is wholly incompatible with the conferring of holy orders. Indeed, it is evident to everyone that the words quoted *have the intention* of obtaining a breakfast of two eggs. They are a "valid formula" for ordering breakfast, but not a valid formula for conferring the sacrament of Ordination. For this very reason the Church never could declare them to be an adequate vehicle for conferring that or any other sacrament.

By his rejection of the term "intention of a rite", *Davies frees himself from the obligation of assessing the validity of the sacramental forms of the Conciliar Church on their intrinsic merits*, and allows himself to have recourse to the specious and simplistic argument that, since they have been approved by what he considers to be the Church, they *must* be valid. The truth is that, had he considered the new sacramental formulæ *in themselves*, and had he done so honestly, he could not have escaped from the realization that more than one of them is incapable of effecting the sacrament which it is intended to confer, because of wording which utterly fails to express the effects which the Church teaches that the sacrament in question has;[4] and this in turn would have led to the inevitable conclusion that the authority which approved these formulæ *cannot be the authority of the Catholic Church.*

Although considerable space has now been devoted to this subject, it is necessary to pursue it just a little further. Let us first return to St. Thomas Aquinas. He makes it clear in two separate passages in the *Summa Theologiæ* that the words used in sacramental forms must be appropriate to achieve the effects of the sacrament:

(i) "A second point is to be considered concerning the actual meaning of the words [of a sacramental form]. For ... *the*

---

[4] "Everyone knows that the Sacraments of the New Law, as they sensibly signify and effect invisible grace, must both signify the grace that they effect and effect the grace that they signify... the form alone is those words ... by which the sacramental effects are unambiguously [*univoce*] signified." (Pius XII, *Sacramentum Ordinis*, 30th November, 1947.

words used in the sacraments produce their effect by virtue of the meaning which they convey ...." (III, Q.60, A.8, reply).

(ii) "There must not be any falsehood in sacramental signs and a sign is false when it does not correspond to the thing signified." (III, Q.68, A.4)

And for good measure, and indeed final confirmation, the same point is made by Pope Leo XIII in *Apostolicæ Curæ*, where he writes:

> That 'form' consequently cannot be considered apt or sufficient for the sacrament which omits what it ought essentially to signify. [5]

The relevance of this crucial point of sacramental theology is that, on pages 335 and 336 of *Pope Paul's New Mass*, Davies quotes what might appear to be a denial of it by Dr. Francis Clark. This is what Davies quotes from Clark's *Anglican Orders and the Defect of Intention*, p. 76:

> The Church requires nothing more for validity than a valid sacramental form and valid matter. She nowhere lays down that there must be an orthodox 'intention of the rite' in addition to those two essential elements. There may be question whether the form *is* valid, that is, whether it does definitely signify, in the sense required by the Church, the sacramental grace or power to be conferred, but there is no need at all for the liturgical rite to express some further intention distinct from the significance of a valid form ....

---

[5] The same point is made by Fr. Maurice de la Taille, in his famous work *The Mystery of Faith*, Vol. II (pp. 455-6 of the 1950 English edition published by Sheed and Ward): "One thing, however, the [ministerial] intention can never do: it can never confer on the form a signification the form in itself does not possess. In other words, should the signification of the form be in any way deficient, the intention [of the minister] will not supply this deficiency."
Davies quotes those very words on p. 39 of *The Order of Melchisedech* (though he gives the impression that the words in square brackets are part of Fr. de la Taille's text, which they are not).

Although Davies has given his mentor Clark a helping hand to ensure that these words are as misleading as possible by snatching them from their original context where Clark *admits* a permissible sense for the term "intention of a rite" (" ... it is only in an applied sense that a document can be said to have an 'intention' of its own." – *ibid.*, p.75), I think that even in their original context they are misleading. This is partly because Clark quotes no authority for what he says except, the silly sneer of a Protestant parson in a book called *Why I am not a Catholic*; but what is intrinsically objectionable in them is that they could easily to suggest to the unwary reader that the "intention of the rite," i.e. the purpose manifested by the wording of the ritual, cannot be a relevant factor in assessing sacramental validity, because if it were it would constitute an additional essential factor beyond the valid matter and form which Catholic theologians unanimously consider to be both necessary and sufficient for validity. The reality, by contrast, is that the "intention of the rite" is a major factor in determining whether or not a given form is in fact valid in the context in which it occurs. The need for the "intention of the rite" to be correct, therefore, is not a *third* pre-requisite in addition to valid matter and valid form: it is one of the factors determining whether or not the *form* is valid. That is why St. Thomas and Pope Leo XIII (and Fr. de la Taille) take pains to insist that the rite *must* be appropriate to the end which it is intended to effect.

It is important to be alert also to a further error into which anyone reading Clark's words taken out of the author's original context and thrust into Davies's un-Catholic context could easily fall. This is to suppose that, if the only element the Church requires for a valid sacrament beyond a capable minister with a sufficient intention is "a valid form", any rite which contained the *essential* form would therefore definitely be valid.

If this were so, it would be certain that the essential form of the sacrament was sufficient to effect the sacrament validly – sufficient, therefore, even in the context of a rite which in all its *other* parts flagrantly denied Catholic truth with regard to the very nature of the sacrament in question.

Now admittedly *in some cases* this would be so. Clark himself cites instances of Baptisms where the sacramental form taken from Holy Scripture and as used in the Catholic Church was used in the context of a rite which was clearly intended to deny the doctrine of sacramental regeneration; and these rites were declared by the Holy Office, in 1949, to be valid. But one would be wholly unjustified in inferring, as Davies appears to on p. 335 of *Pope Paul's New Mass*, that the same applies to all the *other* sacraments. The sacrament of Baptism was given its form *specifically* by Our Lord, and its words are entirely unambiguous, so that, provided they are seriously used, they will infallibly have their effect. But in some cases the form of the sacrament which is determined by the Church to be essential to validity is *not* entirely unambiguous. And in such cases it is perfectly possible that such a formula, although valid if it occurred in the context of a Catholic rite where the other parts of the rite gave it a Catholic significance, according to many theologians would be, or might be, *invalid* in the context of a heretical rite which could impart a heterodox meaning to words which, in the absence of such distorting circumstances, would be an intrinsically valid formula.

Protestant Communion Service a Valid Mass?

Yet another remarkable and wholly unacceptable suggestion by Davies is that the "Communion Services" of the Church of England could be valid Masses if used by validly ordained priests. On p. 337 of *Pope Paul's New Mass* he quotes the following extract from Canon E.E. Estcourt, M.A., F.A.S., Canon of S. Chad's Cathedral, Birmingham:

> There is no question here about the validity of the Sacrament. As the common and received opinion among Divines is that the reciting of Our Lord's words from the Gospel is sufficient for

validity, it is clear that Anglican clergymen, if they are truly priests, and have a right intention, do really say Mass.

It seems that, by the time he had reached p. 337 of his book, Davies had forgotten what he wrote on p. 198:

There is a difference of opinion among theologians as to the precise nature of the 'form' required to effect a valid Consecration. Some say that the words of Consecration in one of the versions found in Scripture will suffice; *others claim that it is necessary for these words to be spoken within the context of a liturgy approved by the Church.*

And – need I add? – the *Anglican Book of Common Prayer* is *not* "a liturgy approved by the Church."

Yes, it is true that there have been *some* Catholic theologians who have maintained that recitation of the formulæ of Consecration as quoted in the Gospels with no other liturgical context suffices for a valid Mass; but that is a long step from its being "the common and received opinion among Divines." The contrary opinion is expressly maintained by St. John Damascene (Homily for Holy Saturday); John Duns Scotus, the Church's "Doctor Subtilis" (*In Sent.* 4, dist. 8, qu. 2); Blessed Angelo of Clavasio (*Summa Angelica*, Eucharistia, 1, n. 24); Cardinal Capisucchius (*Controv.* 3, quæst. unica); the Salmanticenses (*Cursus Theologicus*, tract. 23, disp. 9, dub. 2. in tom. II, part 1); Jugie (*De Forma Eucharistiæ*); Dupasquier; and many others; while even of those who think the contrary opinion more correct, most admit, with St. Alphonsus, Tournely, Pope Benedict XIV and Frassen, that the opinion of the above listed saints and scholars is a probable one.

Moreover, there have been *some* Catholic theologians who not only were not content to qualify this position as merely probable, but went further even than others who defended it wholeheartedly, by branding the *contrary* opinion (of which Davies is so sure) as *worthy of condemnation*. Among the first, of course, to maintain the sufficiency for validity of Eucharistic formulæ snatched straight from the Scriptures without the liturgical context used by the Church, were the Protestants of the Reformation era who created ceremonies along these lines with which to replace the Mass. One such individual was Archbishop Hermann de Wied of Cologne who, in his *Consultatio quomodo reformatio aliqua ... sit instituenda* (1543),[6] devised a Eucharistic ceremony in which the "Consecration" did not occur in a proper liturgical context such as that provided by the Canon of the Roman Mass or by the prayer "Μετὰ τούτων" in the Liturgy of St. John Chrysostom. The Archbishop was declining into heresy. The Canons of the Chapter of Cologne remained orthodox and responded to their archbishop's novel opinions in terms which leave no room for illusion as to their view of Canon Estcourt's opinion of the validity of such ceremonies:

> Urgent need compels us to point out the *sheer insanity* of those who think that the sacrament of the Body and Blood of Christ can be consecrated without the Catholic prayer which we call the Canon ..., but merely by the recital or reading of the words of St. Paul to the Corinthians (I Corinthians 11): 'The Lord Jesus Christ on the same night on which He was betrayed, etc.' For there the Apostle simply narrates the actions of Christ historically; and not in such a way as to supply any form of Consecration, whereby the priest, the minister of the Church, with the invocation of the Divine name, blesses and sanctifies the gifts set on the altar ('*proposita*'), not indeed by his own words, but by the omnipotent words of Our Lord Jesus Christ .... It is not difficult to prove this in similar cases in reference to the other sacraments. Christ taught the Apostles to baptize, saying: 'Go and baptize all nations in the name of the Father and of the Son and of the Holy Ghost.' Now who could be stupid enough to say that a priest who merely recited or read these words of the Gospel on the institution of Baptism, and did not pronounce the words of the essential form of Baptism, 'I baptize thee in the name of the Father and of the Son and of the Holy Ghost,' would truly and duly baptize a child?.. In just the same way

---

[6] He was to be deposed and excommunicated just three years after its publication by Pope Paul III.

we must hold that, should any one simply recite, or merely read over, the story of the institution of this sacrament, as set down by St. Paul, and neither invoke, as minister of the Church, the name of God on the proffered gifts of bread and wine, nor likewise direct the words of Consecration to the host there present, such a one would not consecrate at all, nor effect the true sacrament according to the Catholic sense and tradition of the Church. Quite other was the teaching and practice of the holy Fathers, both of the East and of the West, and indeed of the Apostles too. For as ministers of the Church they invoked the name of God on the Victim, and consecrated It with solemn prayer. (foll. lxxiii-lxxiv, quoted by Fr. Maurice de la Taille S.J. in his *Mysterium Fidei*, Thesis XXXIV)

But the vast majority of theologians simply do not discuss the subject of whether the Anglican Communion Service or any similar heretical hotchpotch could, if said by a valid priest, be a valid Mass, so it seems likely that Estcourt (writing before *Apostolicæ Curæ*) has simply *assumed* that authors who regard as sufficient for validity in themselves the words of Consecration found in the Anglican rite, can be counted as holding it to be *per se* valid. But of course this overlooks the question of whether the heretical rite could impose an adverse "*significatio ex adjunctis*", invalidating the formula.

From all these considerations, it emerges that a brief examination of the *facts*, such as would have taken Davies no more than an hour in a well-equipped library, would have been more than enough to put him wise to the fact that the point he was making, far from being "beyond question", was in fact very questionable indeed to anyone who chooses to assess the weight of theological opinion by objective standards – rather than by hunting down authors who agree with what he wants to say or by accepting as gospel the opinion of whatever third-rate text book he may have to hand.

But no traditional Catholic can discuss the subject of valid and invalid Eucharistic formulæ without being reminded of the vexed question of the validity of the Novus Ordo Missæ; and as no evaluation of Michael Davies could be complete without a consideration of this topic, this seems as appropriate a place as any to examine it.

Chapter Nine Section (D)
The Validity of the Novus Ordo Missæ

The present writer is responsible for a 15 page essay[1] arguing on the basis of respected Catholic authorities:

(a) that in the vernacular translations which translate the words "*pro multis*" as "for all men" in the formula of Consecration the Novus Ordo is *certainly invalid*; and

(b) that even in the original Latin forms, where the words "*pro multis*" are retained, it is still *of doubtful validity*.

The contents of that essay will not be repeated here and many will prefer to go straight to the master on the topic: Mr. Patrick H. Omlor; but, since Davies has given the subject quite a lot of space in his published writings, and in the course of doing so has perpetrated a number of errors of fact, logic and theology which have been accepted as true by some, possibly many, of his readers, the subject cannot be passed over altogether.

Falsified Formula of Consecration

I begin by summarizing as briefly as possible the relevant facts:

(i) The Latin formula for the Consecration of the chalice found in the Novus Ordo is given below on the left, with an accurate English translation on the right. In the centre, below, is the officially authorized English mistranslation.

---

[1] John S. Daly: *Is the Novus Ordo Missæ Valid?*, Britons Catholic Library, 1983.

LATIN	OFFICIAL ENGLISH	ACCURATE ENGLISH
ACCIPITE ET BIBITE EX EO OMNES: HIC EST ENIM CALIX SANGUINIS MEI, NOVI ET ÆTERNI TESTAMENTI, QUI PRO VOBIS ET *PRO MULTIS* EFFUNDETUR IN REMISSIONEM PECCATORUM. HOC FACITE IN MEAM COMMEMORATIONEM.	TAKE THIS ALL OF YOU, AND DRINK FROM IT: THIS IS THE CUP OF MY BLOOD, THE BLOOD OF THE NEW AND EVERLASTING COVENANT. IT WILL BE SHED FOR YOU AND *FOR ALL MEN* SO THAT SINS MAY BE FORGIVEN. DO THIS IN MEMORY OF ME.	TAKE AND DRINK YE ALL OF THIS, FOR THIS IS THE CHALICE OF MY BLOOD, OF THE NEW AND EVERLASTING COVENANT, WHICH SHALL BE SHED FOR YOU AND FOR MANY UNTO THE REMISSION OF SINS. DO THIS IN REMEMBRANCE OF ME.

(ii) As is indicated in italics, and as few if any readers will be unaware, the words *"pro multis"* have been mistranslated into English, as well as almost every other language, as "for all men", an outrage which has only been aggravated by the change to the "non-sexist" substitute "for all" that is now *de rigueur* in most English-speaking lands.

(iii) There are two separate senses in which we may speak of the end for which Our Lord shed His Precious Blood. The first sense is with reference to the *aim and sufficiency* of His Sacrifice (the *objective* redemption); and the second is with reference to the *actual effects* of His Sacrifice (the *subjective* redemption). Otherwise expressed, *objectively* Our Lord died in order to make salvation *available* to *all* men; but *subjectively* only *some* ("many") will be saved. Hence, if we are speaking of the objective redemption, Our Lord *did* shed His Blood for *all*, whereas if the reference is to the subjective redemption, His Blood was shed for many but *not* for all.

(iv) It is certain that in the words of Consecration the reference is to the subjective redemption – those who are actually saved, and that the words "for all men" are therefore in context theologically false and indeed heretical. *The Catechism of the Council of Trent* teaches that:

> With reason ... were the words 'for all' not used, as in this place the fruits of the Passion are alone spoken of .... (Emphasis added.)

This teaching carries the full weight of the papal Ordinary Magisterium, and the same doctrine is taught by St. Thomas Aquinas (*Summa Theologiæ*, III, Q. 78, A. 3), St. Alphonsus Liguori (*Theologia Moralis*, Bk. 6, Treatise on the Holy Eucharist, Dubium 6) and Pope Benedict XIV in his *De Sacrosancto Missæ Sacrificio* (Bk. II, ch. XIV, para. 11) which he wrote as a private doctor.

Which Words Are Required for Validity?

Having shown that the renderings "for all men" and "for all" constitute a doctrinal, liturgical and historical falsification,[2] we must now consider whether the falsification is such as to cast doubt on the validity of the Mass. We can establish the answer with the help of a few more relevant and definite facts:

(i) The Council of Florence in its decree for the Armenians teaches, as the Church has always taught, that:

   (a) the form for the Consecration of the chalice consists in the words, "For this is the chalice of My Blood, of the new and eternal testament, the mystery of faith, which will be shed for you *and for many* unto the remission of sins"; and

   (b) not until all of these words have been enunciated does transubstantiation occur. (Denzinger 715)

However, since some theologians have argued that its words concerning essential sacramental formulæ were intended as instructions to be observed in practice rather

---

[2] Readers will doubtless be aware that the risible claim that the Aramaic language uses the same word for "many" and "all", still used by some apologists for the Conciliar Church, is a complete invention without the slightest factual basis.

than as dogmatic definitions identifying the essential sacramental formulæ,[3] it is necessary for us to turn aside from documents of the Extraordinary Magisterium, to assess the mind of the Church by reference to the lesser authorities which speak in her name – Fathers and Doctors, popes, saints and approved theologians. To undertake a sufficiently detailed study of doctrine derived from all these disparate sources would be not only exceedingly arduous, but also far beyond the scope of this *Evaluation*. Fortunately, however, there is no necessity for the writer to undertake such a study for the task has already been exhaustively carried out by Fr. Maurice de la Taille S.J. in his work *The Mystery of Faith*, and particularly in its thirty-fifth thesis. "Truly a monumental work," exclaimed the normally staid reviewer of the *American Catholic Quarterly Review* upon the appearance in 1922 of Fr. de la Taille's work. "In fact, the first really great theological work on the Mass .... The treatment of the subject is masterly ...."

Fr. de la Taille, relying to some extent on the theological exposition he has already given throughout his work, devotes thirty-three large pages of dense scholarship to the topic of what exactly is necessary, from the point of view of the words of the ceremony, to effect transubstantiation. In his exposition he remarks that every eucharistic form approved by the Church as certainly valid (a) contains the words "This is My Body" and "This is My Blood," (b) contains an extension of the predicate of the latter sentence referring to the sacrificial purpose of the transubstantiation – "which will be shed for you and for many unto the remission of sins" (or some equivalent words), (c) introduces these words by a prelude referring to the historical context of the Last Supper in which they were

---

[3] See Cardinal Franzelin, *De Divina Traditione et Scriptura*, p. 120, where he records, but does not support, this opinion.

first uttered (in the Roman rite, "Who, the day before He suffered ..."), and (d) sets the whole complex of these parts in the overall context of a prayer addressed to God the Father.

And after carefully assessing the weight of theological opinion on each point, and analysing also the logical considerations affecting them, he concludes with confidence that not only are (a), the words, "This is My Body" and "This is My Blood" necessary for validity, but that (b) and (c) are no less essential, while it cannot be concluded with any certainty that even factors (a), (b) and (c) together would suffice in the absence of (d).

Most directly relevant to the Novus Ordo Missæ, with its flabbergastingly blatant mistranslation of "*pro multis*" as "for all men" or "for all" instead of "for many", is Fr. de la Taille's treatment of the necessity of words equivalent in meaning to "which will be shed for you *and for many* unto the remission of sins."

With regard to these words, while conceding that "modern theologians, for the most part, following St. Bonaventure (IV Disp., 8, 2, 1, 2), deny that such words are essential," he is not disposed to attach much weight to the authority of their opinion, given the gravity of that which expressly supports the opposing view. For this opposing view, to which Fr. de la Taille himself subscribes, he cites St. Thomas (in two places), the Salmanticenses (theologians of Salamanca who compiled an unsurpassed compendium of theology), Suarez, Scotus, "all the earlier Thomists up to Cajetan (who rejected it) ... besides ... quite a number of later theologians," John of Freiburg, Jacobus de Graffis O.S.B., Henricus Henriquez S.J., Franciscus Amicus S.J., F. Macedo O.M., Cardinal Capisucco ("at great length"), St. Pius V and the *Catechism of the Council of Trent* (Part II, "De Eucharistiæ Sacramento", capp. 21-23,). (I have omitted most of the references to save space. Readers may find them in Fr. de la Taille's work, which is not difficult to obtain on the second-hand market.) Nor is this catalogue complete – the rubrics of the Missal and the teaching of the Council of Florence, for instance, are not referred to in this part of his work as they have already been mentioned elsewhere.

Moreover, it must not be forgotten that in addition to these authorities, who support in express terms the necessity of the full formula, there are many others who clearly and firmly hold the same view but teach it *implicitly*, among whom may be included all those who argue that *even more* is needed for validity, such as the preamble referring to the Last Super. When these theologians are added, the list will include: Thomas of Walden, Angelus, Relbartus de Temesvar, Salmeron, Archbishop Joannes de Rada, Philip Faber, Cardinal Laurentius Broncatus de Laurea, Pasqualigo, Arbiol, Florus of Lyons (died c. 860), Remigius of Auxerre (died 908), Gerloh of Reichersberg, St. Gregory the Great and Pope Innocent III. Indeed Fr. de la Taille, whose competence and painstaking efforts will not be questioned even by his opponents, declares: "I at least have found NO EXAMPLE OF THE CONTRARY TEACHING BEFORE THE THIRTEENTH CENTURY." (Fr. de la Taille's emphasis)

Nor, however, is this the limit of authoritative support for Fr. de la Taille's view; because, although during the early centuries of the Church few theologians discussed in detail which words were essential to a valid Consecration, very many expressed their view implicitly but unmistakably by maintaining that the Consecration was effected by a *prayer* – i.e. by factor (d) of the four listed earlier. And of course the prayer in question – the Canon or equivalent – includes the *whole* of the Consecration formula as well as the prelude. Hence all supporters of this view may also be listed in defence of the necessity of the full formula. And they are neither few in number nor slight in the weight of their authority, for Fr. de la Taille is able to assert that "every single one of the earliest Fathers affirmed that WE OFFER THE SACRIFICE BY PRAYER." And he substantiates this assertion by quoting the words to this effect of Saints Ignatius of Antioch, Clement of Alexandria, Cyprian, Firmilian, Serapion, Saints Athanasius, Gregory of Nyssa, Ambrose, Jerome, Augustine and Isidore, as well as Tertullian, Origen and Eusebius of Cæsarea.

On that note I trust I may cease to précis Fr. de la Taille and accept his thesis as substantiated as far as any thesis can be by the theological status of those who support it.

This much established, let us return to the subject of the Novus Ordo Missæ, especially its vernacular versions, to apply what we have learnt. Here, the main question is whether the change from "for many" to "for all" is sufficiently radical to invalidate the Consecration.

(vi) On this subject the rubrics of the traditional Missal, as promulgated by Pope St. Pius V in 1570, constitute a definitive statement on the part of the supreme authority of the Catholic Church. In the fifth section, entitled, "*De defectibus formæ*", the formula of consecration of the chalice is given as quoted above, and the following clear explanation is given of which changes will or will not affect validity:

> But if anyone were to diminish or change the form of the Consecration of the Body and Blood so that by this change the words did not signify the same thing, *he would not confect the sacrament* ['*non conficeret sacramentum*'].

(ii) As it cannot be maintained that the change from "for many" to "for all men" is one in which the words continue to signify the same thing, it is clear that, by this unambiguous ruling of the rubrics, the Novus Ordo as celebrated with the "for all men" mistranslation is definitely invalid.[4]

---

[4] It should be noted that the Church has *never* recognized the validity of a

(iii) This conclusion is substantiated by the explicit statement of Fr. Franciscus Amicus S.J. in his *De Sacramentis*, disp. 24, n. 46, as to the necessity of the words "*pro multis*". He wrote: "The objection may be put that at least the words 'for you, for many' are not necessary, seeing that the sacrificial character is sufficiently declared by the words 'shall be shed'. But I deny the consequence. For unless the *end* to which the blood-shedding is directed be expressed, the sacrificial character is *not* expressed, since the Blood could be shed without being shed sacrificially, as would be the case if, for example, it were not shed as an act of worship on the part of anyone, or for the benefit of anyone."

(iv) It is also my contention that, even in its *Latin* form, or in a vernacular correctly translated from the Latin, the Novus Ordo Missæ is of doubtful validity. But, although this is an important issue in itself, it is a secondary one in the present context; so for evidence of the doubtful validity of the Latin form readers are referred to the essay on the subject referred to in footnote 1 on p. 409.[5]

Davies's Defence of the Validity of the Novus Ordo Missæ

This concludes the summary of the facts, proved in every case from incontrovertible Catholic authorities. We are now ready to look at Mr. Michael Davies's defence of the validity of the Novus Ordo, which is energetically conducted by means of suppression of the statements of such opposing authorities as cannot be rejected, heavy reliance on lightweight modern "crammers", and appeal to the lame arguments, long since refuted, peddled by these pseudo-authorities.

---

form which does not include the words "for many".

[5] The intrinsic validity of the Novus Ordo Missæ is also becoming increasingly irrelevant in so far as the number of priests ordained in a certainly valid rite by a certainly consecrated bishop who continue to use the Novus Ordo is in constant decline.

To give him a fair hearing, I shall reproduce below extracts from his treatment of the subject in *Pope Paul's New Mass*, Appendix V, entitled "The ICEL Betrayal"; and once again I shall from time to time intercalate pertinent comments.

On p. 265 Davies begins as follows:

> The translation of *pro multis* as 'for all' is, then, according to Father van der Ploeg, 'deplorable'. But he does not accept that it can cast doubt upon the validity of the Consecration. Firstly, by the time these words are spoken the Consecration has already taken place. Some Catholics claim that the entire Consecration formula for the Chalice as found in the Missal of St. Pius V is necessary for Consecration. The consensus of theological opinion does not uphold this view. A distinction is made between the complete Consecration formula and the essential form of the sacrament. It was the common teaching of the theologians long before Vatican II that only the words 'This is My Body' and 'This is My Blood' are essential for validity.

Davies's first argument begs the entire question. It is that the Consecration has already taken place before the words "for many" are uttered or – in the case of the Novus Ordo – *not* uttered. Having stated this as a fact, he at once admits that it is *not* taught by the Church and that not all Catholics agree with him. "*Some Catholics*," he informs us, in the tone of one anxious to do justice to a view hardly worthy of consideration, "claim that the entire Consecration formula for the Chalice ... is necessary."

Misinformation

But how, readers will be asking themselves, in view of the summary of the theological state of the debate provided above, can Mr. Davies neglect to inform us that the "some Catholics" in question were not, as might be inferred, a group of theological semi-literates, but include the greatest theologians and highest authorities recognized by the Church? Would Pope Eugene IV and the other Fathers of the Council of Florence have thought it conceivable, as they solemnly taught which words are necessary for a valid Consecration, that five hundred years later a layman, claiming to be a Catholic, would represent their judgement as the view of "*some Catholics*" and clearly mistaken to boot? Would Davies's readers guess, if they did not know it, that this apparently inconsequential group referred to as "some Catholics" included St. Thomas Aquinas? And Pope St. Pius V? And the holy scholars to whom the drafting of the Church's official catechism was entrusted – scholars who included in their number St. Charles Borromeo?[6] And the strings of approved theologians, including popes, listed by Fr. de la Taille? And scholars of the calibre and expertise on the subject of Fr. de la Taille himself? And, by implication at least, "every one of the earliest Fathers"?[7]

The next thing that Davies has told us, in the extract quoted above, is that the opinion of these authorities, among which are some of the most illustrious names in the history of theology, is not upheld by "the consensus of theological opinion." To the question of who is responsible for gauging the consensus "of theological opinion" or who has established the weight of this consensus, we are given no answer. Nor, as we read the remainder of Davies's comments, shall we find saints and popes, councils, Doctors of the Church and men of world-renowned scholarship mentioned as supporting Davies's view. We are just told, by definite implication, to ignore the opinion of those scholars who oppose Davies – scholars unworthy even to be named – on the grounds that, so Davies assures us,

---

[6] Also relevant to the status of the doctrine of the *Catechism of the Council of Trent* on the necessity for validity of the words "*pro multis*" is the fact that its contents consist exclusively of *doctrine*, all *opinions* being excluded: "All those who had part in the work of the Catechism were instructed to avoid in its composition the particular opinions of individuals and schools, and to express the doctrine of the universal Church, keeping especially in mind the decrees of the Council of Trent." (Introduction to the English translation of the *Catechism of the Council of Trent* by McHugh and Callan, p. xxiii)

[7] Fr. de la Taille, *op. cit.*, 1950 English edition, Vol. II, p. 467.

(a)   "the consensus of theological opinion" is against them; and, two sentences later,

(b)   it was the common teaching of theologians long before Vatican II that the words "This is My Blood" would suffice to effect Consecration.

That is what we are told; but if the reader should think that we have been told everything relevant, he is under an illusion; for Davies has been less than frank with us. We are *not* told, for instance, that this common teaching, insofar as it had any existence, was found almost exclusively among manualists[8] who were not so much theologians, in the literal sense of that word (i.e. men who *study* and *contemplate* Divine things), as writers who summarized theology sketchily in text books designed for seminary use and multiplied their deficiencies by copying one another. Nor are we told that, before Cajetan in the sixteenth century, hardly a single theologian can be found to have expressed this opinion. Nor yet are we told that, when Cajetan *did* teach it, only as an opinion, St. Pius V promptly ordered the opinion (together with several other egregious errors) to be struck out from his works! Nor are we told that Fr. de la Taille, who vehemently disputed this allegedly "common teaching", had studied the topic more deeply than the manualists whose opinions comprised this consensus before Fr. de la Taille broke it had dreamed of.

And those omitted facts *are* of some relevance. They appear also, incredible though the thought may seem, to have been known to Davies, for elsewhere he quotes, in another context, from the very section of Fr. de la Taille's work in which he opposes the view of Mgr. Pohle and those who agree with him on this topic. (See *The Order of Melchisedech*, p. 39)

---

[8] The famous Jesuit theologian Lacroix defines a mere manualist ("*merus summista*") whose status lends no credibility to the opinions he relays, as "one who takes opinions from various sources without examining them himself, and simply copies them." (*Theologia Moralis*, lib. 1, n. 160)

Up the Pohle?

It is now time to return to the passage from the appendix to *Pope Paul's New Mass*. Davies's next move is to quote one of the theologians who support his view: Mgr. Joseph Pohle (*The Sacraments*, Vol. II, p. 209). Incredibly, this manualist, whom no one would seriously claim to be even in the second, let alone the first, rank of theological brilliance,[9] is the *only* authority Davies quotes to refute so many saints, popes and renowned theologians. Here is what Pohle says:

> All theologians agree that '*Hoc est Corpus meum – Hic est Sanguis meus*' are undoubtedly essential. The majority further hold that these words are sufficient to ensure the validity of the double Consecration, although to omit the other words prescribed by the Church, especially in the Consecration of the Chalice, would be a grievous sin. The principle upon which this opinion is based may be stated as follows: that, and that only, belongs to the essence of the

---

[9] Anyone who has gained a doctorate in theology from a Catholic educational institute or has made a genuine and deep study of theology may be called a "theologian". If he writes a theological work which the Church authorizes to be published, he will be classified as an "*auctor*" – a theological writer. But such a one will not be an "*auctor probatus*" (*approved* author), until he is acknowledged as such by the Church "by specific judgment or by some other sign." (Miaskiewicz: *Supplied Jurisdiction*, p. 201) Hence Merkelbach notes that not all authors who have secured an *imprimatur* can be considered "approved". (*Summa Theologiæ Moralis*, II, n. 108, note 4) However, before an author's status even begins to lend real weight to his views independently of the cogency of his reasoning, he must not only be an "*auctor probatus*", but also "*gravis nominis*" – of great name (the sort of writer whose opinions are respected by others who write after him and whose opinions are regularly referred to on disputed points by learned men). No one can belong to this category, also referred to as "*omni exceptione major*" ("beyond exception"), if he has taught "a significant number of *improbable* opinions, rejected by other theologians." (Lacroix, *loc. cit.*) If we classify those who have special status as Fathers or Doctors of the Church as being in "the first rank of theological brilliance", it will be these "*auctores gravis nominis*" who constitute the second rank. Pohle, as an "*auctor probatus*", but far from "*omni exceptione major*", would be in the *third* rank, and consequently a very poor opponent, in terms of status and reputation, to St. Thomas Aquinas and St. Pius V.

sacramental form, which precisely designates the effect of the sacrament. Now, the words: 'This is My Body, This is My Blood,' effect [a mistake for "signify? – J.S.D.] the real presence of the Body and Blood of Christ under the appearances of bread and wine. Therefore, these words effect the presence and constitute the essence of the sacramental form of the Eucharist.

Pohle has little to learn from Davies on the suppression of the evidence against his position. He tells his readers about "the majority" of theologians, without making it clear that he is talking only of modern *manualists* whose teaching, even if it were unanimous, would hardly outweigh that of the authorities noted above. Nor does Pohle let slip the somewhat important fact that the rubrics of the Missal – the Church's official instruction to her priests on the subject at issue – sternly inform the celebrant that if he does not say the *complete* formula, *including the words "for many"*, transubstantiation does not take place, which means that, after his efforts, the wine is still no different from that which he might drink with his dinner.

Mgr. Pohle can hardly be unaware of the rubrics of the Missal. They are the official instructions of the Church about how to say Mass, and for him or any other priest to have undertaken the solemn duty of offering the Holy Sacrifice without thorough familiarity with the rubrics would have been more absurd and unthinkable than for someone to pilot an aircraft or perform intricate micro-surgery without having carefully studied beforehand the technical manual pertaining to those skills. But he has discovered a principle which in his view overrides such evidence. For him, as he explains in the passage just quoted, the essential words are those which signify *the essence of the sacrament*, and since the essence of this sacrament is transubstantiation, the words "This is My Blood" are alone essential. Not only is this a fatuous argument in itself; not only, in addition, do the rubrics of the Roman Missal contradict it; but it had already been specifically answered seven hundred years ago by the Angelic Doctor, St. Thomas Aquinas.

The Consecration exists not only for the *Sacrament* but also for the *Sacrifice* from which the Sacrament is inseparable. Transubstantiation is *not* the *only* effect brought about by the words of Consecration, St. Thomas pointed out, and therefore transubstantiation is *not* the *only* effect which they must signify. Here are his exact words:

> We should conclude then that all these words [i.e. the entire formula] belong to the essence of the form; the opening words, 'This is the Chalice of My Blood', signify the actual change of the wine into the blood ... the words that follow signify the power of Christ's blood which was shed in his passion – which power is now at work in this sacrament. This power is productive of *three* effects. [Emphasis added – J.S.D.] The first and greatest effect is that it gains an eternal inheritance for us; as the text of *Hebrews* puts it, 'we have confidence to enter the sanctuary by the blood of Jesus.' The words of the form 'of the new and eternal testament' signify just this. The second effect is justification, which is ours through grace and which is brought about by faith; as the text of *Romans* puts it, 'whom God put forward as an expiation by His Blood, to be received by faith ... to prove that He Himself is righteous and that He justifies him who has faith in Jesus.' This is the reason for adding the words 'the mystery of faith'. The third effect is that it takes away our sins which come between us and the first two effects just mentioned; the text of *Hebrews* says, 'the Blood of Christ will purify your conscience from dead works,' that is, from sins. This is signified by the words, 'which for you *and for many* [others] will be poured out for the remission of sins'. (*Summa Theologiæ*, III, Q. 78, A. 3)

Returning now from Mgr. Pohle to Davies, we find that immediately after quoting him, he proceeds:

> The same author, Mgr. Joseph Pohle, points out that it is 'utterably untenable' to maintain that all the words of the form of the Consecration of the Chalice found in the Missal of St. Pius V are essential for validity. He notes the parity between the Consecration of the bread and that of the wine, the first sentence '*Hoc est Corpus meum*' being absolutely parallel to the second, '*Hic est Sanguis*

meus.' He also mentions the conclusive argument that not all the words found in the Roman Canon occur in the Eucharistic Prayer of Eastern liturgies which the Church recognizes as valid. For example, the words '*Mysterium Fidei*' do not occur in the Eastern liturgies and hence cannot be essential for validity.

And how is it that neither Davies nor Pohle sees fit to tell us that St. Thomas Aquinas not only *believed* this "utterly untenable" doctrine, which as we have seen was adopted by St. Pius V's Roman Missal, but also explained why it was correct? – an explanation which Davies and Pohle do not think worth mentioning even if only to refute. Here is what St. Thomas says in the article just quoted:

> Some people have thought that the only essential part of the form is the words, 'This is the chalice of my blood', and that what follows is not necessary. But this is seen not to be true because the words that follow give us further knowledge about the predicate, that is, the blood of Christ; and so they are part of the complete phrase ....

St. Thomas also anticipates and refutes in advance Pohle's main argument in defence of his position, namely the claim that the words "which will be shed for you and for many" cannot be necessary in the Consecration of the Precious Blood for, if they were, equivalent words would be necessary for the Consecration of the Body of Our Lord. St. Thomas points out that what is necessary for the Consecration of the chalice need by no means exactly parallel what is needed for the Consecration of the host, because "the separate Consecration of the Blood explicitly represents the actual passion of Christ" in a way that does not apply to that of His Divine Body.

Moreover, turning to Pohle's argument based on Eastern rite liturgies which Davies cited, it is "*utterly untenable*" to entertain for an instant that St. Thomas was ignorant of the fact that some of them have Consecration formulæ slightly different from that of the Latin rite. Certainly it is evident that substituting one of the Eastern rite formulæ for the one which belongs to the Roman Mass would not invalidate the Consecration in the Roman Mass;[10]

but this does not help Davies and his sole authority, because no formula of *any* rite recognized by the Church as valid even *omits* the words "for many", let alone replaces them with the heretical "for all".

"With a single bound he was free!"

In his next paragraph, Davies makes us rub our eyes in disbelief. Having misinformed his readers of the standpoint of "the consensus of theological opinion" and having made up their minds for them on the basis of the tenuous authority of Mgr. Pohle, he tosses in, as if as an afterthought, one of the weightiest of the authorities against him:

> The section '*De Defectibus*, V,' in the *Rubrics of the Roman Missal*, states that the form for the Consecration of the Chalice consists of the words: 'Hic est enim Calix Sanguinis mei, novi et æterni testamenti, mysterium fidei, qui pro vobis et *pro multis* effundetur in remissionem peccatorum.' This was the teaching of St. Thomas, the Council of Florence, and *The Catechism of the Council of Trent*.

And having tossed them in, he immediately tosses them out again – needing no more than a one-paragraph footnote to put them firmly in their place! – a footnote which is worthy of close attention:

> Many readers may conclude that the teaching of three such weighty authorities is conclusive and that all these words must belong to the essential form. However, the same three authorities were also united in teaching what constituted the matter and form of the Sacrament of Order, and yet Pope Pius XII ruled in 1947 that both the matter and form of this Sacrament were located in different parts of the rite. I have treated this matter in great detail in Appendix I to my book *The Order of Melchisedech*.

---

[10] Though it would of course be sinful for anyone but a pope to do so on his own authority.

Let us pass lightly over the fact that Davies has named not *three* but *four* authorities. And let us not dwell on the fact that not even he can claim that Pope Pius XII contradicted the fourth of these authorities – the rubrics of the Missal which he used each day. Far more fundamental is the fact that Davies is here shamelessly misleading his readers to support his case. The impression that Davies is determined to create is that Pope Pius XII taught in *Sacramentum Ordinis* (1947) that St. Thomas, the Council of Florence and *The Catechism of the Council of Trent* had all *got it wrong* as to the matter and form of the Sacrament of Order. But in fact he taught no such thing! He simply taught that, *as from the date of his decree*, the matter and form of the sacrament of Order would be what he declared them to be.[11] That he made no ruling on what the essential matter and form might have been at some stage in the past is perfectly clear in *Sacramentum Ordinis* itself, in the words, "*if it were ever legitimately disposed otherwise*, We ordain that the 'tradition of the instruments' *at least for the future* ['*saltem in posterum*'], is not necessary to the validity of the holy Orders of diaconate, priesthood and episcopate". (Denzinger 2301)

So there is not the slightest evidence that the authorities named were mistaken on the essential matter and form of Holy Orders and it is even less likely that they would collectively err about the essential form of the Mass. Although it is more offensive still to suggest that they might do so in the company of the Rubrics of the *Roman Missal*.

---

[11] In the sacrament of Order, the essential matter and form were not specifically determined by Our Lord as in the Mass, but were left to the Church to arrange; for which reason the Church can also alter them at will (through her supreme head), as Pope Pius XII taught in the same decree: "Everyone knows that what the Church has ordained, she can change and abolish." (Denzinger-Schoenmetzer, 3858)

Conscience Breaks Through

Before closing this analysis Davies's final statement should be submitted to inspection. In it he exhibits unusual temerity by distancing himself somewhat from Fr. van der Ploeg's absolute certainty of the validity of the vernacular Novus Ordo, admitting that he himself is *not* quite certain of the validity of the "for all men" form and that he must therefore regard it as doubtful. Here is Davies:

> As I do not wish to be accused of trying to evade the issue on so serious a matter, I will give my opinion. Where the Latin form of Consecration is used in the *Novus Ordo* I am *absolutely* certain that there is a valid Consecration. Where a vernacular form is used, employing the phrase 'for all men', I am *virtually* certain that there is a valid Consecration, particularly in view of the assurance given by a theologian of Father van der Ploeg's eminence. Thus, if I were a priest I would not feel able to use the 'for all men' formula as I would consider myself guilty of probabilism – virtual certainty is not absolute certainty. (*Ibid.*, p. 629)

" ... particularly in view of the assurance given by a theologian of Father van der Ploeg's eminence," says Davies. Eminent indeed must van der Ploeg be in the field of theology to be given such clear preference over St. Thomas Aquinas! But what stands out in this passage is that when Michael Davies puts himself on the spot and considers himself forced to state his belief on the Novus Ordo in the vernacular,[12] he admits that he is *not* certain that it is valid.

This admission is worth highlighting because *elsewhere* in his writings, Davies, presumably somehow contriving to forget that he once forced himself to look at the underlying evidence and, as a result, found himself unable to escape from a conclusion that defied even the weighty authority of van der Ploeg, *cheerfully reneges on his admission*, taking it completely for

---

[12] And it is in the vernacular that the Novus Ordo is almost invariably said.

granted – without offering, or even suggesting the need for, a shred of new evidence – that the Novus Ordo is *definitely valid*.

Here, for instance, is what he says on p. 39 of his pamphlet, *The Goldfish Bowl*:

> These people ['sedevacantists'] also tend to believe that the New Mass is not valid, that is to say, that when the priest says the words of Consecration nothing happens. Such a view is theologically untenable.

"The New Mass," he says, eschewing this time any distinction between Latin and vernacular versions – in any event the Latin version is so rarely used that, for practical purposes, it is not worth taking into account.

Moreover, Fr. Roy Randolph pointed out in an article in the March 1981 issue of the *Roman Catholic* that in at least two other places in his writings, both in traditional Catholic periodicals, Davies has repeated the same contradiction of the position he took in *Pope Paul's New Mass*. "In these two independent articles," writes Fr. Randolph,

> ... In these two independent articles Mr. Davies seems to close the issue [of the validity of the Novus Ordo] with full dogmatic certainty of his position.

Then, after pointing out the contrasting moderation of his position in *Pope Paul's New Mass*, where Davies admitted that he was *not certain* that the Novus Ordo is valid, Fr. Randolph makes the following unanswerable point:

> If he is only virtually certain of the validity of the Novus Ordo then he has no right at all to attack those who do not believe in its validity.

Overall Conclusion of the Chapter

Sacramental theology is perhaps the subject concerning which Mr. Michael Davies's readers would consider his expertise the greatest, yet the present chapter has exposed errors which show, by their number and gravity that he is in fact completely out of his depth when writing about it. In view of this it is surely not inappropriate to address to him the rebuke which he himself once addressed to a correspondent who had made but a single error. Writing in *The Remnant* for 31st January 1983 Davies advised her bluntly:

> Sacramental theology is a subject concerning which you would be more prudent to remain silent.

CHAPTER TEN
THE ALLEGED FALL OF POPE LIBERIUS, HIS ALLEGED EXCOMMUNICATION OF ST. ATHANASIUS, AND OTHER ANTI-PAPAL LIBELS

"Glory not in the dishonour of thy father: for his shame is no glory to thee." (Ecclesiasticus 3:12)

Davies's Comments on Liberius

The following extracts from Michael Davies's writings all concern the same subject. They all say much the same thing. Indeed some readers will find them unbearably repetitive. My aim in reproducing so many almost identical passages is precisely to highlight the almost unbelievable frequency with which Davies adverts to the alleged fall of Pope Liberius into heresy and his alleged excommunication of St. Athanasius. Even this lengthy series represents a mere sample selected at random from a far greater number available, for Davies never misses the opportunity to drum these allegations into his readers' minds.

(i) From *Pope John's Council*, page xiv:

"Athanasius made his stand not so much against the world, '*contra mundum*', as against the bishops of the world – even to the point of having his excommunication confirmed by Pope Liberius – but it was the Pope who subsequently retracted and repented."

(ii) From *Pope John's Council*, p. 174:

"Those who base their defence of the faith on the axiom that whatever the pope decides must be right would find themselves in a hopelessly indefensible position once they began to study the history of the papacy. They would have to maintain that St. Athanasius was orthodox until Pope Liberius confirmed his excommunication; that this excommunication made his views unorthodox; but that they became orthodox again when Liberius recanted."

(iii) From *Pope Paul's New Mass*, p. 280:

"This Instruction [*The General Instruction on the Roman Missal*, Paul VI's decree instituting the Novus Ordo in place of the Mass] must surely be one of the most deplorable documents ever approved by any Supreme Pontiff, not excluding the examples of Popes Liberius, Vigilius, and Honorius I."

(iv) From *Apologia Pro Marcel Lefebvre*, Vol. I, p. 118:

"There is, in fact, a very striking comparison between Archbishop Lefebvre and St. Athanasius. Pope Liberius subscribed to one of the ambiguous formulæ of Sirmium, which seriously compromised the traditional faith, and he confirmed the excommunication of St. Athanasius. It is true that Liberius acted under pressure and later repented – but it is equally true that it was Athanasius who upheld the faith and was canonized."

(v) From *Apologia Pro Marcel Lefebvre*, Vol. I, pages 369-371:

"On 17th May 352, Liberius was consecrated as pope. He immediately found himself involved in the Arian dispute.

> "'He appealed to Constantius [the Roman emperor] to do justice to Athanasius. The imperial reply was to summon the bishops of Gaul to a council at Arles in 353-354, where, under threat of exile, they agreed to a condemnation of Athanasius. Even Liberius's legates yielded. When the pope continued to press for a council more widely representative, it was assembled by Constantius at Milan in 355. It was threatened by a violent mob and the emperor's personal intimidation: "My will," he exclaimed "is canon law". He prevailed with all save three of the bishops. Athanasius was once more condemned and Arians admitted to communion. Once more papal legates surrendered and Liberius himself was ordered to sign. When he refused to do so, or even to accept the emperor's offerings, he was seized and carried off to the imperial presence; when he stood firm for

Athanasius' rehabilitation, he was exiled to Thrace (355) where he remained for two years. Meanwhile, a Roman deacon, Felix, was introduced into his see. The people refused to recognize the imperial anti-pope. Athanasius himself was driven into hiding and his flock abandoned to the persecution of an Arianizing intruder. When he visited Rome in 357, Constantius was besieged by clamorous demands for Liberius's restoration ....'[1]

"The opposition to the anti-pope Felix made it imperative for Constantius to restore Liberius to his see. But it was equally imperative that the pope should condemn Athanasius. The emperor used a combination of threats and flattery to obtain his objective. Then followed the tragic fall of Liberius. It is described in the sternest of terms in Butler's *Lives of the Saints*:

"'About this time Liberius began to sink under the hardships of his exile, and his resolution was shaken by the continual solicitations of Demophilus, the Arian Bishop of Beroea, and of Fortunatian, the temporizing Bishop of Aquileia. He was so far softened by listening to flatteries and suggestions to which he ought to have stopped his ears with horror, that he yielded to the snare laid for him, to the great scandal of the Church. He subscribed to the condemnation of St. Athanasius and a confession or creed which had been framed by the Arians at Sirmium, though their heresy was not expressed in it; and he wrote to the Arian bishops of the East that he had received the true Catholic faith which many bishops had approved at Sirmium. The fall of so great a prelate and so illustrious a confessor is a terrifying example of human weakness, which no one can call to mind without trembling for himself ....'[2]

---

[1] This is a sub-quotation from Davies, taken from *The Popes* edited by E. John, p. 70.

[2] This is Davies's quotation taken with approval from *The Lives of the Saints* by Fr. Alban Butler, Vol. II, p. 10. Fr. Butler's work is by far the best of its kind in English and, provided the revisions by Thurston and Attwater, and, more recently, by Walsh, are avoided, surely worthy of the very highest recommendation. But scholarly as Butler is, he *does* sometimes slip out errors which cannot easily be excused. Such at least is the view taken by Dom Gueranger in his *Life of St. Cecilia*, in which he is forced to take issue with Butler on a number of points. The French writings of Fr. Darras and

"According to *A Catholic Dictionary of Theology* (1971) [edited by Fr. J.H. Crehan – J.S.D.] 'this unjust excommunication [of St. Athanasius – M. Davies] was a moral and not a doctrinal fault.' Signing one of the 'creeds' of Sirmium was far more serious (there is some dispute as to which one Liberius signed, probably the first). *The New Catholic Encyclopædia* (1967) describes it as a 'document reprehensible from the point of view of the faith'. Some Catholic apologists have attempted to prove that Liberius neither confirmed the excommunication of Athanasius nor subscribed to one of the formulæ of Sirmium. But Cardinal Newman has no doubt that the fall of Liberius is a historical fact. This is also the case with the two modern works of reference just cited and the celebrated *Catholic Dictionary*, edited by Addis and Arnold. The last named points out that there is 'a fourfold cord of evidence not easily broken', i.e., the testimonies of St. Athanasius, St. Hilary, Sozomen, and St. Jerome. It also notes that 'all the accounts are at once independent of and consistent with each other.'

"The *New Catholic Encyclopædia* concludes that:

> 'Everything points to the fact that he [Liberius] accepted the first formula of Sirmium of 351 .... It failed gravely in deliberately avoiding the use of the most characteristic expression of the Nicene faith and in particular the homo-ousion. Thus while it cannot be said that Liberius taught false doctrine, it seems necessary to admit that, through weakness and fear, he did not do justice to the full truth.'

"It is quite nonsensical for Protestant polemicists to cite the case of Liberius as an argument against papal infallibility. The excommunication of Athanasius (or of anyone else) is not an act involving infallibility, and the formula he signed contains nothing directly heretical. Nor was it an *ex cathedra* pronouncement intended to bind the whole Church, and, if it had been, the fact that Liberius acted under duress would have rendered it null and void.

"However despite the pressure to which he was submitted, Liberius's fall reveals a weakness of character when compared with those such as Athanasius, who did remain firm."

(vi) From an article by Davies in the November 1985 issue of *The Angelus*, enthusiastically entitled "God Bless Archbishop Lefebvre!":

Archbishop Darboy concerning St. Dionysius the Areopagite show that Fr. Butler erred also in connection with this great saint and apostle of Gaul.

> "In the fourth century, Pope Liberius showed lamentable weakness in the face of the Arian heresy. He signed an ambiguous semi-Arian formula and excommunicated St. Athanasius, defender of Our Lord's divinity. ... Liberius was the first Roman Pontiff not to be canonized whereas St. Athanasius was raised to the honours of the altar."

(vii) From *The Divine Constitution and Indefectibility of the Catholic Church*, a supplement to N° 93 of the periodical *Approaches*:

> "During the Arian heresy the weak Pope Liberius capitulated under pressure, signed a formula of doubtful orthodoxy, and excommunicated the heroic Athanasius. But at no time did St. Athanasius claim either that Liberius had ceased to be Pope or that the hierarchy had ceased to exist, even though most of the bishops had either succumbed to the Arian heresy or had condoned it through cowardice."

(viii) Also from *The Divine Constitution and Indefectibility of the Catholic Church*, supplement to *Approaches* N° 93, p. 35:

> "In the days of the Arian persecution, when St. Athanasius was a hunted fugitive excommunicated by the Pope, who could have imagined that the day was drawing near when the true Catholics who had been forced to worship outside their parish churches would be able to return to them in triumph?"

(ix) From *Archbishop Lefebvre – The Truth*, p. 32:

> " ... it is clear that there has been no crisis comparable to the present one since the Arian heresy, and during that heresy St. Athanasius, who made an almost solitary stand for the traditional faith, had to undergo the anguish of having his excommunication confirmed by Pope Liberius. But it was the pope who recanted and Athanasius who was eventually canonized."

(x) And finally, from *The Goldfish Bowl: The Church Since Vatican II*, p. 4:

> "In the fourth century, Pope Liberius showed lamentable weakness in the face of the Arian heresy. He signed an ambiguous semi-Arian formula and excommunicated St. Athanasius, defender of Our Lord's divinity .... Liberius was the first Roman Pontiff not to be canonized whereas St. Athanasius was raised to the honours of the altar."

The inevitable tedium involved in these repetitive citations might have been worse, for readers have been spared further quotations from an article by Davies called "Arianism" in the January 1987 issue of *The Angelus* and numerous other sources too, in which all the points made so often in the passages just quoted are repeated yet again, and at length. But enough is enough. It is now time to embark on one last repetition by summarizing the conclusions which any reader of those passages cannot very well fail to have reached.

The Inevitable Conclusions

These conclusions are, it will be agreed, as follows:

1. At the time of the Arian heresy most of the Catholic bishops fell into error, leaving St. Athanasius as almost the sole defender of the true Faith.
2. At first St. Athanasius was defended, though inadequately, by Pope Liberius, who took his side against the Arianizing Roman emperor, Constantius.
3. Subsequently, however, Pope Liberius, having been subjected to threats and exile, capitulated, and at least implicitly denied the Faith,
    (a) by signing a formula designed to favour heresy; and
    (b) by excommunicating St. Athanasius.
4. Since that time, there has been a certain amount of scholarly dispute over exactly which formula was signed by Pope Liberius, but one thing about which there is no doubt is that all serious scholars – led by Cardinal Newman – have been and are in agreement that both the signing of a heterodox document and the excommunication of St. Athanasius are historically certain, notwithstanding arguments to the contrary which have been put forward by certain best-forgotten apologists for the papacy whose zeal exceeded their erudition.
5. Despite his fall into, or close to, heresy, Liberius continued to be recognized as the true pope, and eventually recanted

his errors and revoked the decree of excommunication against St. Athanasius. (Davies in fact refers to this recantation three times.)

Such, in summary, are the conclusions which are imposed on the reader of the above passages written by Michael Davies about Pope Liberius – unless ... unless ... *unless* the reader has learned by hard experience to be a little cynical about Davies's scholarship. For, as on so many other matters, the reader cynical enough to submit Davies's claims to independent verification will be rewarded by the discovery that the truth is very different from Davies's representation.

The exact history of the Liberius-Athanasius episode is not easy to get to the bottom of. Indeed it is fraught with many pitfalls for the unwary. But there can be no excuse for presenting even doubtful matters – let alone long-exploded myths – as certain facts, as Davies so often has. Nor can there be any excuse for selective choice of tendentious or out-dated sources,[3] or for the suppression of material evidence.

Unfortunately, it is not possible adequately to counter Davies's distortions and replace his self-serving misrepresentations of history with reality except by detailed analysis. But the subject is far too important for the truth to go undefended.

And of course it is also of great importance in Michael Davies's view, which is why he writes of it so often. Why this is so is shown most clearly in his pamphlet entitled *The True Voice of Tradition*, published by the Remnant Press as a reprint of an article by Davies in *The Remnant* of 30th April 1978. This pamphlet, although not among those quoted above, offers yet another treatment of the same subject – in fact Davies fills no fewer than fifteen pages of it with repetitions of his allegations

---

[3] Writers of the sixteenth, seventeenth and eighteenth centuries were more likely to err on the subject, owing to the primitive state of the science of textual criticism which had led to the acceptance as authentic of certain early documents which are in fact, as we shall shortly see, undeniably spurious.

that Pope Liberius subscribed to the Semi-Arian heresy and excommunicated St. Athanasius. Using as his main source Cardinal Newman's work *The Arians of the Fourth Century*, he first gives a history of that era, *and then uses this history as a parallel to our own situation today*, a parallel from which he can argue that, *even if the "popes" of Vatican II have fallen into heresy, they should not be rejected*, just as St. Athanasius did not reject Pope Liberius as a valid pope. Rather – he maintains – we should all take courage from the fact that a single bishop, standing alone against all his brother bishops and the pope, can nevertheless be vindicated and even canonized.

The intended parallel with Archbishop Lefebvre is of course obvious.

The Facts

It must now be shown that Davies's representation of history, unfortunately both for the arguments he seeks to base on it and for the cause of truth in itself, is very far from reality. First, I shall list a few very clear facts which are strongly suggestive – to say no more – that the story of a fall from orthodoxy on the part of Pope Liberius is no more than a myth. This done, it will be possible to examine in more detail the great mass of evidence which, taken collectively, raises this conclusion from probability to certainty .

The main facts are these:

1. Pope Liberius was in reality a staunch opponent, not only of the Arians, but also of the Semi-Arians.
2. He was sent into exile by the Semi-Arian Emperor Constantius *precisely* because of the *failure* of the attempts of that emperor and his toady bishops to influence him to excommunicate St. Athanasius and accept as orthodox a compromised Semi-Arian statement of Catholic doctrine concerning Our Lord's Divinity.[4]

---

[4] Reminiscent of today's "Agreed Statements" entered into by the Conciliar

3. Constantius appointed Felix to replace the absent Liberius in the See of Rome, but Felix was not at that time accepted as pope by the Romans.
4. Felix himself did not in fact subscribe to Arianism, but he *did* acknowledge ecclesiastical communion with arianisers, for which reason, the fifth century historian-bishop Theodoret informs us, "none of the citizens of Rome entered into the church while he was inside."[5] (*History of the Latin Church*, Bk. II, c. 17)
5. The people of Rome remained loyal to Liberius and protested to the emperor at his detention.
6. Eventually their peaceable protests gave way to rioting, and as a result Liberius was permitted by Constantius to return to Rome.
7. On his return he was received as a victor there by the populace.
8. His reign in Rome then continued for a few years more, during which time he remained entirely orthodox, refused to compromise in the slightest degree on the orthodox doctrine of the Council of Nicæa, and was in full communion and friendship with St. Athanasius.
9. Some extant historical texts apparently of that period assert that the immediate reason for his return to Rome was that

---

Church in England with the Protestant Church of England and other heretical bodies.

[5] It is to be regretted that today so few of those who consider themselves to be Catholics recognize that it is sinful and abhorrent for those who have the Faith to take part in worships and sacraments of priests and bishops who, even if themselves orthodox, nevertheless recognize the heterodox as their fellow-members of the Church. One who is in communion with heretics is, of course, a schismatic and therefore outside the Church even if his own doctrine is sound: to participate in religious activities with such a one is therefore forbidden by the Divine law (as was recognized by the Roman layfolk of Pope Liberius's day) and by the ecclesiastical law today enshrined in Canon 1258 of the 1917 *Code*.

he had subscribed to a Semi-Arian formula. But many others favour the contrary view.

10. The weight of subsequent scholarship is strongly in favour of Liberius's orthodoxy, and orthodox Catholic scholars in particular – and it is they who have studied the subject in greatest depth and are most reliable – are overwhelmingly of the view that Liberius never fell, remained orthodox throughout his exile, and always remained in full communion with St. Athanasius.

The Historical Evidence Concerning the Excommunication of St. Athanasius

Let us begin our analysis of the historical evidence by looking at the assertion, which Davies makes repeatedly and as though it were a matter of no doubt, that Pope Liberius *excommunicated* St. Athanasius. Since two works of St. Athanasius provide the most commonly used evidence that Liberius subscribed to a Semi-Arian formula, anyone coming fresh to the question would be bound to expect Athanasius also to have provided testimony to the fact of his own excommunication by Pope Liberius; for he refers to Liberius in many places in his writings, he had known him well, and, as all admit, for at least most of the time none of the other bishops had given him (Athanasius) more valiant support.

But St. Athanasius gives *no* testimony that Pope Liberius excommunicated him. Indeed, not only is such a thing nowhere hinted at in the writings of Athanasius; the assertion is not made in historical discussions by *any other writer* who was contemporary with the events either. The alleged excommunication of St. Athanasius found its way into subsequent history – which it entered only as a fact of doubtful authenticity – *purely* on the basis of two letters attributed to Liberius himself and which must now be examined.

The first of the two letters, beginning with the words "*Studens paci*", is addressed to the bishops of the Eastern Roman Empire and in it Liberius asserts that he maintains communion with them and with the universal Church, but that he has excluded Athanasius from this communion. The second, "*Pro deifico timore*", is also addressed to the Eastern bishops and in it the pope says that he is in communion with them, but that he has excluded Athanasius. He also says that he, Liberius, has subscribed to the [Semi-Arian] formula of faith drafted at Sirmium.

Scarcely any further discussion of these letters is needed, because both of them may be dismissed at once as palpable forgeries. On the first it is sufficient to quote the immensely scholarly Canon Bernard Jungmann who, in his *Dissertationes Selectæ in Historiam Ecclesiasticam* (6th dissertation, Vol. II, pages 69-70), tells us:

> All critics since Baronius have held that it was not written by Liberius, even those who hold the other letters as genuine .... It is obvious that the letter is the work of a forger.

As to the second letter, its authenticity is maintained only by certain non-Catholic scholars who are known to be animated by hostility to the Holy See; and the renowned von Hefele and Dom John Chapman, for instance, have comprehensively exploded any possibility that Liberius could have written it.

In fact it is clear to any honest enquirer that this second letter must be the work of an inept forger too. One of its most obvious contradictions is that in it the supposed Liberius openly and shamelessly admits to having accepted Arianism and having condemned Athanasius, while at the same time incongruously saying that he is still in exile – ignoring, in other words, the well-known fact that the whole point of his having been sent into exile by the emperor was his refusal to do these very things. There is no escaping from the fact that this is a contradiction, for all the writers who maintain that Liberius *did* subscribe to a heretical formula agree that it was immediately upon doing so, and as a result of this, that Constantius authorized his return to Rome.

Thus the only two pieces of evidence on which the allegation that Liberius excommunicated St. Athanasius are based are both entirely worthless. By contrast, on the other side of the scales there are the obviously significant facts that:

(a) not a single other contemporary writer refers to it, and
(b) Athanasius himself, even in one of the two passages where he[6] refers to Liberius as having yielded to the sufferings which he underwent through his banishment, *goes out of his way to praise Liberius for having remained faithful to communion with him.* (Apologia Against the Arians – Migne, *Patrologia Græca*, Vol. XXV, col. 409)

Such is the historical basis for this allegation, which Davies regards as sufficiently proven to be rammed down his readers' throats at every available opportunity in his writings.

The Historical Evidence Concerning Liberius' Subscription to Heresy

Distinct from this charge, however, is the twin allegation that Pope Liberius yielded to the emperor's pressure to the extent of putting his name to the Semi-Arian heresy. Certainly he *could* have done this without excommunicating St. Athanasius, but whether he *in fact* did so is what must now be considered. And once again I shall begin by setting down once more a few facts upon which all are agreed and concerning which there is no doubt. These undisputed facts are:

1. Pope Liberius was elected pope, as successor to Pope Julius, in the year 352, two years after Constantius had become sole emperor and had begun his campaign to unite all Christians – orthodox, Arian and Semi-Arian – in a compromised creed. The defect of this creed was that it

---

[6] Whether it was really Athanasius who wrote these passages will be considered later.

carefully excluded the word ὁμοούσιος ("*homoousios*")[7] which was the touchstone of orthodoxy in all the disputes arising from the Arian heresy. Meaning consubstantial or "of one substance", it had been included by the Council of Nicæa (325 A.D.) in that Council's profession of faith on the grounds that it was a clear and unambiguous word which could be accepted *only* by those who believed that God the Father and God the Son possess the same Divine nature, this being the truth which the Arians denied and the Semi-Arians fought shy of.

2. Pope Liberius began by taking a firm stand for strict orthodoxy. Thus:

   (a) He refused to countenance the Arian heresy when stated straightforwardly; that is, in the assertion that the Son is "of different substance" from the Father.

---

[7] The First Council of Nicæa (325 A.D.) defined that Our Lord is consubstantial (ὁμοούσιος, "*homoousios*") with the Father. Arius and his followers maintained that He was a created being and therefore *not* one substance ("homo-ousios") with, but rather different from, or dissimilar (ἀνόμοιος "an-omoios") to, the Father. A compromising school of Semi-Arians arose who abandoned the strict Arian term "an-omoios" and favoured the proposition that Our Lord is ὁμοιούσιος "homo*i*-ousios" or of *like* substance with the Father. This compromise was condemned by the Church because, although it is, in one specific sense, true that Our Lord *is* of like substance with the Father, and although this differs from the orthodox expression "homo-ousios" only by a single letter (the smallest in the Greek alphabet), the choice of this expression rather than the Nicene term was evidently tantamount to a denial of the consubstantiality of Son and Father. Thus the Church utterly refused to countenance any attempt to find a formula of compromise acceptable to all conflicting parties (the practice now in favour in the Conciliar Church), and insisted on acceptance of the term most calculated to be *un*acceptable to all but the rigidly orthodox. Indeed when one group of Arians persuaded themselves that it was possible to interpret even the word "homo-ousios" in a manner compatible with Our Lord's having been created in time by God the Father, the Church still refused to admit them to communion, despite strong pressure from the emperor, until they recanted all their errors, in terms admitting of not the slightest ambiguity.

- (b) He refused to accept the defective Semi-Arian compromise that the Son is "of *like* substance" to the Father.
- (c) He refused to accept any profession of faith which did not include the Nicene "homo-ousios".
- (d) He upheld the acquittal of Athanasius from charges of heterodoxy which had been brought before his predecessor Julius.
- (e) When the legates whom he sent to the Emperor Constantius in Gaul were bamboozled into condemning Athanasius, he wrote both to Bishop Hosius of Cordova and to St. Eusebius that he deplored the actions of his legates and would himself rather die than incur the imputation of having thus agreed to injustice and heterodoxy.

3. At the council which the emperor summoned at Milan, without the approval or attendance of Liberius, *all* of the Western bishops other than the pope (nearly three hundred) subscribed fully to the wishes of the emperor – the rejection of communion with St. Athanasius and the adoption of a formula of faith which did not include the word "homo-ousios".

4. Pope Liberius wrote a letter to the faithful bishops (in the East) in which he said:

Make mention of me to the Lord in your prayers with the intention that, overcoming the assaults, ... I may be able to withstand and that the Lord may deign to make me your equal, with inviolate faith and without prejudice to the well-being of the Catholic Church. (Jaffé, n. 216)

5. In 353 Pope Liberius wrote to the Emperor Constantius stating that it was impossible for him to condemn Athanasius, and refusing to enter into communion with Arians or with those who were themselves in communion with Arians. And in Athanasius's *Apologia Against the Arians*, he himself tells us that Pope Liberius was aware of the fact that various slanders were being spread about himself (Athanasius) in order to bring about his

condemnation so that Arianism might flourish the better without his opposition. These are his significant and unambiguous words:

He [Pope Liberius] knew the secret of the machination mounted against us. (Migne, *Patrologia Græca*, Vol. XXV, col. 409)

6. Eventually, in the year 355, Liberius was seized and taken to Milan, where, according to Theodoret, he refused to denounce Athanasius.

7. In the course of this confrontation between the supreme secular power – the emperor – and the supreme spiritual power – the pope – Constantius rebuked Liberius for standing up for Athanasius against the world – *pro Athanasio contra mundum*. Hence, ironically, the famous phrase "Athanasius against the world", so often quoted as indicating that Athanasius was not even supported by the pope, and which indeed is sometimes wrongly attributed to St. Athanasius himself, was in fact originated in a context which itself makes it clear that the pope was the very person – virtually the *only* person – by whom Athanasius *was* supported against the *rest* of the world.

8. At this time Liberius also refused to subscribe to a Semi-Arian formula and, as already mentioned earlier, was consequently exiled on the orders of the emperor, who attempted to impose Felix as bishop of Rome in place of him. We are informed both by St. Athanasius and the famous preface to the "*Liber Precum*" that Liberius's exile lasted two years, so that his return must have taken place in the year 357.

9. We have no first hand account of what took place during Pope Liberius's exile in Thrace during those two years, but we do know, thanks to St. Jerome, that it was as a hero that he was welcomed back to Rome by the citizens who had clamoured for his return (St. Jerome: *Chronicon* – Migne, *Patrologia Latina*, Vol. XXVII, col. 501), and we also know that his orthodoxy was certainly not subject to

10. We also know that after returning from his exile he annulled the acts of the Semi-Arian Council of Rimini on the very grounds that, although it had nowhere positively affirmed a theological error, *it had tendentiously avoided the use of the crucial word "homo-ousios"*. Concerning this omission, Liberius commented:

> The impious and sacrilegious Arians have succeeded in assembling the bishops of the West at Rimini [this council took place in 359 with the approval of the Emperor Constantius], with a view to deceive them by false discourses, and to force them, by means of the imperial authority, either to strike out or openly to condemn a term very wisely inserted in the profession of faith.

11. Although there were only eighty Arians among the four hundred bishops from the Western Roman Empire who had met at the Council of Rimini, the orthodox Fathers of that council had eventually been deceived by the heretics into accepting as orthodox a formula which excluded the word *"homo-ousios"*, and because of this they too – that is, even those who had remained inwardly orthodox in belief – were summoned by Pope Liberius to make a formal recantation of their error if they wished to be recognized as Catholics. A little later, the judgement of Liberius, confirmed by his successor Pope St. Damasus, was published in a synodal letter by a council of 90 bishops. Damasus insisted on outward reparation as well as inward orthodoxy. "We believe," he thundered,

> that those whose weakness prevents them taking this step must be separated as soon as possible from our communion and deprived of the episcopal dignity so that the people of their dioceses may find respite in safety from error.[8]

---

[8] See *Catholic Encyclopædia* (1913) Vol. IX, art. "Liberius", p. 220; Pope Pius VI, brief of 10th March 1791 to Cardinal de la Rochefoucault, the Archbishop of Aix and the other Archbishops and Bishops of the *Assemblée*

12. One final relevant fact is that in the year 366, shortly before his death, Pope Liberius received a deputation of Semi-Arians led by Eustathius, and treated them just as if they were full Arians, insisting on their adopting the Nicene Creed before he would receive them to communion.

Clearly, in the light of this last episode, certain conclusions force themselves on the investigator even before he has examined such character testimony as there may be in support of Pope Liberius. The most obvious, I suggest, are these:

1. It is simply beyond credence that the pope, had he been known to have accepted the Semi-Arian heresy himself, would have made no public recantation; and not even the most determined of his opponents suggest that such a recantation was made, *with the single exception of Davies himself*.[9]
2. It is also beyond credence that if he had accepted the Semi-Arian heresy he would, in his subsequent behaviour, have made no distinction between the Semi-Arians and the Arians.
3. Still more absurd is the notion that he subscribed to the Semi-Arian formula having regard to the fact that, subsequent to his supposed subscription, he issued a decree permitting the bishops who had lapsed into Semi-Arianism – the very crime of which he himself is charged – to be restored to their offices if they were especially zealous against the Arians, and in that decree made no mention of himself. Naturally, if the charge against him were true, it would have been necessary to include in that decree some reference to his own fall and subsequent repentance, and some indication that he too was exercising himself with energy against the Arians in order to atone for his fall. Not

---

Nationale de France, concerning the Civil Constitution of the Clergy, decreed by the Assemblée Nationale.)

[9] But see footnote 20, on p. 468.

even hypocrisy could account for such an omission if his fall was publicly known as is alleged by his opponents; for he could not possibly have got away with such treatment of those who had sinned no more gravely than himself. The decree would have been greeted by a howl of rage and execration which would scarcely have stopped reverberating today.

4. In addition to Liberius's own attitude to Semi-Arians after his return from exile, there is plentiful other evidence that is quite inexplicable if we accept the allegation that he had fallen into Semi-Arianism. For instance, there is the fact that there was at no time and in no context whatever any outcry about any such fall on the part of Liberius, whereas there was no shortage of outcry concerning the fall of Bishop Hosius, who was of course of far less significance than the pope. Why did the world fall silent when – or rather *if* – Pope Liberius also fell? And why did Emperor Constantius make no attempt to make capital out of the fall?

These internal contradictions in the allegations made against Liberius stand out immediately, and already suffice to render the two main charges against Liberius – namely, his having excommunicated St. Athanasius and his having subscribed to a Semi-Arian formula – highly improbable. In other words, the difficulty in reconciling the universally admitted facts about Liberius with the two disputed allegations against him is so great that only clear and inescapable evidence from contemporary historical sources would constrain us to admit the truth of these charges. However, as history does record occasional instances of behaviour by otherwise venerable figures that is highly improbable or even inexplicable, we cannot entirely dismiss these accusations, even against such a heroic and revered pope as Liberius, without considering the evidence of the historians who wrote close to his time. We shall do this by systematically considering the evidence furnished on the subject by each of these historical sources. That is to say, I shall look at all the historians of the period, and record whether they say anything to support the accusations against Liberius which Davies has so enthusiastically retailed to his readers, or whether they oppose it, either explicitly, by affirming Liberius' unsullied orthodoxy and unbroken communion with Athanasius, or implicitly, by omitting any mention of these alleged lapses on Liberius's part – lapses so grave that had they actually occurred it would have been impossible for any disinterested historian to overlook them.

I begin with the catalogue of those writers who favour Liberius's orthodoxy.

The Testimony of Socrates

The first of these is the ecclesiastical historian Socrates[10] (379-c. 445 A.D.) who, in his *Historia Ecclesiæ*, brought Eusebius's ecclesiastical history up to date and, of interest for our purposes, recounts the battle between orthodoxy and Arianism. Although he makes no direct reference in this account to the anti-Liberian allegations, of which he seems to know nothing, he includes some information which bears upon the incidents involved and is certainly incompatible with the version of events, popularized by anti-Catholic historians, which Michael Davies subscribes to. Let us look at the relevant sections of his work:

> But the emperor [Constantius] ... gave to Ursacius [and Valens] and their associates full authority to take any action they chose against the Churches. He had the profession of faith which had been read at Rimini sent to the Churches of Italy, commanding that anyone who did not subscribe to it be expelled from the Church and others substituted in their places. And first of these, Liberius, bishop of the Roman city, when he had refused to give his agreement to that Faith, was sent into exile; and the party of Ursacius put in his place

---

[10] Who must not, of course, be confused with the pre-Christian Athenian philosopher of the same name.

one Felix who had been deacon of the Roman Church until he embraced the Arian perfidy and was elevated to the episcopate – though some say that he did not accept the Arian view, and accepted Ordination only under force.

So at that time in the Western regions there was nothing but revolution and tumult, some of the clergy being thrust out and exiled, others being substituted for them. And all these things were taking place by the authority of imperial edicts which were also sent to the East. But not long afterwards, Liberius was recalled from exile and resumed his see; the Roman populace had revolted and driven Felix out of the Church so that the Emperor had grudgingly yielded to them. The party of Ursacius, however, left Italy and, moving East, came to a town of Thrace called Nike. (*Historia Ecclesiæ* 2, 37)

[…]

Now as those who held the '*homo-ousios*' [i.e. the orthodox belief concerning the nature of Christ] were at that time severely troubled and had been put to flight, the persecutors began afresh their efforts against the Macedonians, who, yielding to fear rather than to actual violence, sent envoys hither and thither through all their cities with their message that refuge must be sought from the emperor's brother and from Liberius, the bishop of the Roman city, and that they should embrace their faith rather than communicate with Eudoxios. So they sent Eustathius the bishop of Sebastia, who had already been very frequently deposed, together with Silvanus from Tarsus in Cilicia and Theophilus, from another Cilician town called Castabala, instructing them not to disagree with Liberius in faith, but to enter communion with the Roman Church and confirm by agreement their faith in [the word] 'consubstantial'. So those who had differed from Seleucia [Eudoxius] came to Rome with their letters; and though they were not able to approach the emperor himself, as he was detained under arms in Gaul owing to the war against the Sarmatians, they presented their letter to Liberius.

Liberius at first refused to admit them, saying that they belonged to the Arian party and could not be received by the Church, as they had forsaken the Nicene Faith. But they replied that they had long repented and recognized the truth and had long since abjured the doctrine of the Anomians and confessed the Son to be in all respects like to the Father, the word "like" being, as they understood it, in no way different from 'consubstantial'. When they had said this, Liberius insisted on having a written statement of what they professed and they presented him with a memorandum which included the very words of the Nicene Faith .... When the envoys had committed themselves to the memorandum by way of security, Liberius received them in communion, and giving them .... letters dismissed them. (*Historia Ecclesiæ* 4, 12)

These extracts can be found in Greek in Migne's *Patrologia Græca*, Vol. LXVII, and in Kirch's *Enchiridion Fontium Historiæ Ecclesiasticæ Antiquæ* in Greek with a Latin version. What they show is that a learned and respected Catholic writer, who was of an age to have been able to acquire his information from contemporaries and eye-witnesses of the events he recounts, and who had clearly conducted a close investigation of Liberius's role in the battle of the orthodox Catholic Church with Arianism favoured by the emperor, either (a) had never encountered a suggestion that Liberius ever fell, subscribed to heresy or excommunicated St. Athanasius, or (b) had utterly dismissed such suggestions if he had met them. They also show that an account of what took place which includes nothing not of the highest credit to Pope Liberius is completely plausible and was taken seriously by the learned Catholics of the capital of the Roman Empire.[11] Socrates reports Liberius's staunch refusal to countenance even *semi*-Arianism or to be bullied by the emperor, and makes it clear that his return from exile could not be construed as evidence of any compromise on his part because it is satisfactorily accounted for by the turbulence of the Romans at being deprived of their respected bishop.[12] Finally, he

---

[11] Socrates wrote in Constantinople, to which the seat of government of the empire had been moved in 330 A.D.

[12] Nor are we dependent on the testimony of Socrates for the fact that the Romans took this stand. Even the *opponents* of Liberius testify to it, the

presents to us a picture of Liberius after his return from exile, behaving not as temporizer, nor even as a chastened penitent, but with the confidence and firmness, in insisting on even the finer points of doctrinal orthodoxy, which could belong only to a heroic confessor of the true Faith.

The Historian Theodoret

Another witness of the highest value in favour of the orthodoxy of Liberius is the scholarly Theodoret (c. 393-458), of whom the 1913 *Catholic Encyclopædia* (Vol. IX, p. 222) says:

> To Theodoret, Liberius is a glorious athlete of the Faith; he tells us more of him than any other writer has done, and he tells it with enthusiasm.
>
> It is Theodoret who has preserved for us the minutes of the inspiring interview between Liberius and Constantius at Milan to which reference was made earlier; and he both refers to the seditions excited in Rome by the absence of the pope and affirms that it was owing to them that 'the admirable Liberius returned to his beloved city.'

But the feature of his treatment of the subject of Liberius which is most noteworthy from the point of view of the question we are looking at is that, although the treatment is a lengthy one, there is no reference in it whatever to the charge against Liberius, not even in order to refute or dismiss it, any more than there was in Socrates's accounts. For this there can be but one explanation: that the allegation either had not by then, nearly a century after the fall had allegedly occurred, been made at all, or, at the very least, had not received sufficient circulation to be taken seriously. And neither of these alternatives, it hardly needs saying, could be possibilities if Liberius in fact *had* fallen; for such a unique and dramatic event would have been widely known within a very short time, and Theodoret would have been

---

Arian writer Philostorgius, for instance, describing how eagerly the Romans were demanding the return of their pope. (*The Catholic Encyclopædia*, 1913, Vol. IX, p. 220)

forced, if not necessarily to accept the truth of the allegations, at least to refer to them. (*Historia Ecclesiastica*, II, XIV/XVI; Migne *Patrologia Græca*, Vol. LXXXII, coll. 1033-1040)

Sulpitius Severus

Another important witness is Sulpitius Severus; for he was a historian, his life overlapped with that of Pope Liberius, and his piety puts him beyond all suspicion of partisanship and dishonesty. His *Historia Sacra* was written soon after 400, and in it, although he was certainly aware of an allegation that Liberius had fallen into heresy that was to be found attributed to St. Jerome, in passages the meaning and authenticity of which will be examined shortly, he too makes no mention at all of any such fact, which he had obviously dismissed as unfounded.

And the reason he gives for the restoration of Pope Liberius to Rome from his Thracian exile?

> ... *ob seditiones Romanas* – on account of unrest in Rome. (Migne: *Patrologia Latina*, Vol. XX, col. 151; Vol. II, 39).

Rufinus

Of great interest are the words of the historian Rufinus. Let us turn to the four-volume *General History of the Catholic Church* of Fr. J.C. Darras, a work the publication of which in the middle of the nineteenth century was greeted by a chorus of authoritative praise, including a special commendation from Pope Pius IX.[13] On p. 461 in Vol. I, Fr. Darras writes:

> In the words of Rufinus written about fifty years after this period, we perhaps see the first dark spots on the horizon, foreboding the storm of calumny which was soon to break upon the head of Liberius. [Darras considers the oblique reference of Rufinus the

---

[13] The author (1825-1878) was later to write a much more complete Church history which finally appeared in 42 volumes after his death. Although of great value it has never been translated into English and the final volumes by his continuators, Frs. Bareille and Fèvre, display a less solid judgement than that of Darras himself.

first hint because he rightly, as we shall see, rejects the allegations found in some editions of the writings of Saints Athanasius and Jerome as certainly erroneous and very probably interpolated. – J.S.D.] He [Rufinus] says: 'Liberius, Bishop of Rome, had returned while Constantius was still alive; but I cannot positively state whether it was that he had consented to subscribe, or that the Emperor would please the Roman people who, at his departure, had begged this favour.' Rufinus was a priest of Aquileia; in his youth he may have known Liberius; he had certainly known Fortunatian, Bishop of Aquileia, to whom [responsibility for] the fall of Liberius is imputed. And yet Rufinus knows nothing of it, undoubtedly because the calumny was only beginning to spread abroad; for if Liberius had actually signed an Arian formula, had he actually penned the pitiful letters of defection ascribed to him, *the Arians, who were all-powerful, would have left no one in ignorance of the fact.* [Emphasis added – J.S.D.] It would have been impossible for Rufinus to retain any doubt upon the subject. (Darras: *General History of the Church*, following Rohrbacher: *Histoire Universelle de l'Église Catholique*, tom. XI, pp. 430-2. The extract from Rufinus is taken from his *Historia Ecclesiastica*, I, 28; Migne: *Patrologia Latina*, Vol. XX, col. 498.)

This was written in 402-5 A.D.

St. Ambrose

St. Ambrose, one of the four great Latin Doctors of the Church, is a witness for the defence of Pope Liberius of obviously very great weight and value. He had known Pope Liberius personally and remembered him as an exceedingly holy man, and, far from making reference to any lapse from orthodoxy, refers to him as being "of holy memory" and "of very venerable memory." (Migne: *Patrologia Latina* tom. XVI, coll. 219 et seq.)

The Greek Menology

The next authority to be quoted is the Greek *Menology* – the Eastern equivalent to the martyrologies of the Western Church. Although compiled (by Symeon Metaphrastes) in the tenth century, the information it contains is much older, being based on the earliest available records of the individuals it commemorates. Considerable light is shed on Liberius by the following brief life of him:

> The Blessed Liberius, defender of the Faith, was Bishop of Rome under the empire of Constantius. Burning with zeal for the orthodox Faith, he protected the great Athanasius, persecuted by the heretics for his bold defence of the truth, and driven from Alexandria. Whilst Constantine and Constantius lived, the Catholic Faith was supported; but when Constantius was left sole master, as he was an Arian, the heretics prevailed. Liberius, for his vigour in censuring their impiety, was banished to Beroea in Thrace. But the Romans, who always remained true to him, went to the emperor and besought his recall. He was therefore, on this account, sent back to Rome and there ended his life, after a holy administration of his pastoral charge.

This passage is quoted from Darras: *General History of the Church*, Vol. I, p. 462, where it is referenced to Rohrbacher: *Histoire Universelle de l'Église Catholique*, tom. XI, p. 374. It would be superfluous to point out that this account is entirely incompatible with any known dereliction of his duty on the part of Pope Liberius. "Burning with zeal for the orthodox Faith, he protected the great Athanasius ...." Such is the Liberius commemorated by the Greeks in their menology, which constitutes an official liturgical work. A starker contrast to the Liberius that Davies presents to his readers could hardly be imagined.

St. Hilary

St. Hilary, bishop of Poitiers, was another contemporary of Liberius who had known him and been united with him in defence of the true Faith against Arianism. He is sometimes claimed as a witness to the fall of Liberius, but the only passage from his undisputed works adduced by the opponents of Liberius to support their claim proves nothing of the kind, while, on the other hand, the writings attributed to him in which Liberius is stated to have fallen were patently not written by him. Hence it follows that St. Hilary is silent on the subject of any fall of Liberius and must therefore have known nothing of it, which makes him an important indirect witness in Liberius's favour, for he would certainly have known of the event if it had had any foundation in fact.

Here are the very words which some writers have deemed adequate evidence of St. Hilary's agreement with the tale of Liberius's collapse into heresy.

> Then thou [the Emperor Constantius] didst bring thy war to Rome, whence thou didst snatch the bishop [Liberius]: and, wretched man that thou art, I know not whether thy wickedness was greater in restoring him than in abducting him! (*Contra Constantium*, II, 5-8; Migne: *Patrologia Latina*, Vol. X, 588 *et seq.*.)

Evidently St. Hilary is indicating that the emperor may have been guilty of wickedness in restoring Liberius to Rome, just as he was in snatching him from Rome. But in the first place St. Hilary is not certain about the matter – "I know not ..." – and, secondly, the nature of the wickedness in question is by no means apparent. Conceivably a compromise on Liberius's part could have accounted for the words – though surely this wickedness would more properly be ascribed to Liberius than to Constantius – but countless other explanations are equally or more plausible. For instance, if Constantius, angry at having to yield to the demands of the Roman populace and return their unflinching pope to them to avoid a revolution, had spitefully inflicted some terrible indignity on Liberius on the occasion of his return to Rome, this would perfectly well account for Hilary's words. Such an action would be thoroughly consistent with the character of Constantius, for bullies often descend to vindictiveness when they are thwarted, and it would account for St. Hilary's words quite adequately without necessitating the assumption that St. Hilary is referring to the alleged fall of Liberius, which has already been shown to be in the highest degree improbable and to which nowhere else in his copious writings does he make any reference. The *Catholic Encyclopædia* (1913) concludes that it would be gratuitous to understand the words we have been considering to refer to a fall of Liberius – see Vol. IX, p. 220.

A few of the more virulent opponents of Liberius have even dared to attribute to St. Hilary certain other fragments attacking Liberius which, in the style of their Latinity, sensibility of feeling, dignity of expression and charity are not only unworthy of any Catholic (let alone a saint and a Doctor of the Church!), but even of any pagan with any pretence to education or self-respect.

Pope St. Anastasius I

Highly relevant to St. Hilary's attitude to Liberius is the fact that Pope St. Anastasius I, writing in the year 400, placed Pope Liberius in the same category as St. Hilary *among the three most valiant defenders of the Faith in the time of Arianism*, adding that he (Liberius) "would have preferred to be crucified rather than blaspheme Christ with the Arians." See his letter to Venerius, Bishop of Milan. It is worthy of note that this papal letter was regarded as sufficiently definitive and authoritative, in its denial of the fall of Liberius, to justify its inclusion in Denzinger's *Enchiridion Symbolorum* (§93) – the collection of "definitions and declarations concerning matters of faith and morals" widely used by Catholic theologians – and to be introduced therein by the title "Concerning the Orthodoxy of Pope Liberius".

Pope St. Siricius

Another early pope who wrote of Liberius was Pope St. Siricius, who reigned 384-398 A.D. He records the fact that Liberius annulled the decrees of the Council of Rimini-Seleucia because of their omission of the word "homo-ousios", and mentions that he forbade at the same time the re-Baptism of those who had been baptised by the Arians. He also refers to him as being "of venerable memory" and, like the others already cited, offers no hint of any lapse from orthodoxy or compromise with unorthodoxy. (Migne: *Patrologia Latina*, Vol. XIII, col. 1133)

Other Saints and Historical Writers

In the year 432 A.D., St. Prosper re-edited one of the few early historical sources to record a supposed fall into heresy on the part of St. Liberius, St. Jerome's *Chronicon* ("Chronicle"). Whether the Latin Doctor and great translator of the Vulgate Bible was genuinely responsible for this reference to the fall of Liberius – perhaps as a result of his notorious carelessness in historical matters or owing to his having been misinformed by others – or whether the true explanation of the reference to an event so utterly at odds with all the evidence in St. Jerome's work should rather be attributed to a corruption of the text by a later hand is a question we shall shortly be looking at, but at this stage it should be observed only that St. Prosper unhesitatingly omitted from his text of Jerome the passages which suggested that Liberius had subscribed to heresy. He at least, therefore, who was in a much better position to judge than any later scholar, had no doubt that they were inauthentic.

In the sixth century were compiled the *Gesta Liberii* ("Deeds of Liberius"), a historical account of the principal events of the pope's life. Its unknown Latin author descends to considerable detail and furnishes us with much useful information about Liberius and his times – information which, though not corroborated by any other early writers, is nonetheless in the highest degree credible because it dovetails so well with what has come down to us from other sources. Hence its author must have been a learned man with access to copious information about Liberius – *more* information than was available to those who accuse Liberius of consenting to heresy – and yet he too is pointedly silent about the alleged fall of Liberius. On the contrary, he eulogizes him as *"constantly* fixed on the Trinity, preaching the Father, the Son and the Holy Ghost, and praising the God from God and light from light, the whole from whole, entirety from entirety, not created but begotten, not out of nothing, but out of the Father, *being the same substance with the Father* ...."[14] In other words, the Liberius presented to us by this writer is "constant" in, and especially conspicuous for, his devotion to the very doctrine he is said to have temporized over and allowed to be distorted, obscured or neglected. (See Migne: *Patrologia Latina*, Vol. VIII, col. 1390b.)

Also worthy of mention are the great St. Basil (329-379), Doctor of the Church, who refers to Liberius as "ὁ μακαριώτατος ἐπίσκοπος" – "the most blessed bishop" – in his Epistle N° 363 (Migne: *Patrologia Græca*, Vol. XXXII, col. 980a), and St Epiphanius (315-403), who was such a stickler for orthodoxy that he suspected St. John Chrysostom of heresy (Origenism), but who has nothing but praise for the pope, whom he refers to as "Liberius of holy memory" (see Darras, *ibid.*, pp. 457, 501).

Other Tributes to the Holiness of Liberius

Another fact which Davies does not mention, even if only to try to explain it away, is that Pope Liberius is honoured as a saint in the ancient Latin Martyrology. Although Davies says repeatedly that Athanasius was canonized and Liberius was not, this is in fact quite false. *Neither* was formally canonized, as the formal procedure of canonization did not exist at the period that the Church began to revere them (which was immediately after their deaths); but *both* benefited from the Church's official

---

[14] The Latin word *"consubstantialis"*, corresponding to the Greek "ὁμοούσιος" ("homo-ousios") of the Nicene Creed, is often translated as "being *of* the same substance with" or "being *of* one substance with", but in 1825 the Vicars Apostolic of England and Wales unanimously determined to expunge such renderings from the Catechism used in their territory and to replace them with the formula "being the same substance with", which rules out more definitely any possibility of misinterpretation.

recognition as saints in the form which *did* then exist, by their inclusion in the martyrologies of West and East.

In fact evidence in further support of the testimonies already given could be multiplied almost indefinitely, for instance from the historians Cassiodorus (490-583) and Theophanes (IXth century). But after such conclusive testimonies to Pope Liberius's sanctity and unfailing orthodoxy, what can be the need?

Instead, let us move on to an examination of such early sources as can be adduced in favour of the allegation of his having subscribed to heresy. It need hardly be said that, even if these sources might appear to be conclusive, the testimony of the authors just cited would oblige us to pause long for thought and to make us in the highest degree reluctant to accept the conclusion they tend towards. But in fact no such dilemma would occur to anyone who looks at the evidence attentively, for the miserable clutch of references from which the opponents of Liberius and enemies of the Holy See attempt to construct an adamantine case against Liberius are no sooner scrutinized than they fall away as probably inauthentic and certainly erroneous – as will now be shown.

The Writings of St. Athanasius

The most important testimony in favour of the thesis espoused by Davies according to which Liberius subscribed to Semi-Arianism is, as all opponents of Liberius's orthodoxy recognize, found in two passages from works of St. Athanasius himself, and these I shall now quote. The first is found in his *Apologia Contra Arianos*, N°s 89, 90; Migne: *Patrologia Græca*, Vol. XXV, col. 409.)

> Now if those bishops worthy of the name ['ἐπίσκοποι οἱ ἀληθῶς'] had opposed only with words those scheming enemies of ours who were striving to subvert whatever efforts were made on our behalf, or if they had been mere common men and not the bishops of such outstanding cities and the heads of such great churches, there would

admittedly be grounds for suspicion that they might have taken our side under the influence of some gift or favour. Since, however, they not only defended my cause with words but even underwent exile, and since Liberius, the bishop of Rome, was of their number – for even if he did not tolerate the sufferings of exile until the end, nonetheless, because he was well aware of the conspiracy launched against us, he remained in the place of his banishment for two years – and since their number also included the great Hosius, with bishops of Italy, the Gauls and others from Spain, Egypt and all the bishops from Pentapolis in Libya – for although for a short time, terrified by the threats of Constantius, he [Hosius] appeared not to oppose them, nonetheless the great might and tyrannical power of Constantius, not to mention his verbal and physical assaults, make it clear that the reason for his [Hosius'] yielding for a time was not that he considered us guilty but that he was unable to stand such treatment on account of the infirmity of his age – it would indeed be just for everyone, as having been apprised thereby of the injustice and injury done to us, to hate it and shrink from it the more, and especially in this connection to recognize what is most evident: namely, that we suffered these ills for no reason except because of the wickedness of the Arians. Should anyone therefore wish to find out the true facts about us and the sycophancy of the Eusebians, let him read those things which have been written on our behalf and accept as witnesses not one or two or three, but so great a multitude of bishops. Again let him take as witnesses Liberius and Hosius and their companions, who, when they discovered the crimes being committed against us, preferred to suffer extremities than to betray either the truth or the judgement granted in our favour ....

Readers will doubtless have found this extract, with its long and awkward parentheses, exceeding laborious to follow. The reasons for this will shortly be referred to.

The second paragraph from St. Athanasius's writings that is invoked to prove the capitulation of Liberius is taken from his *Historia Arianorum ad Monachos*. Having in chapters 35 to 40 of this work recounted enthusiastically the courageous resistance made by Liberius to the Emperor Constantius, he then, in chapter 41 (Migne: *Patrologia Græca*, Vol. XXV, col. 741), writes as follows:

> Now Liberius was sent into exile, and after two years eventually he was broken, and being terrified by threats of death he subscribed.

In themselves these passages appear to present a strong case against Liberius, readers may be thinking at this point. Let us turn to the Abbé Rohrbacher's famous and excellent *Histoire Universelle de l'Église Catholique*, Vol. XI, pp. 431-2, where the case against those passages is succinctly put in the following terms:

> It may be objected that St. Athanasius refers to the fall of Liberius both in his *Apology Against the Arians* and in his *History of the Arians*, which latter work was addressed to the hermits; but it is universally granted that the *Apology Against the Arians* was written at the very latest in A.D. 350, *two years before Liberius became pope*. The passage which speaks of his fall is, then, evidently a subsequent addition made by a strange and unskilful hand; for, far from giving any force to the *Apology*, it only makes it pointless and ridiculous. *The History of the Arians* was also written at a period prior to that of the supposed fall of Pope Liberius. This unfavourable passage is, then, another interpolation, equally unconnected with what precedes and what follows. But by whom could these interpolations have been made? We know that even during the lifetime of St. Athanasius the Arians forged a letter, in his name, to Constantius. What they could do whilst he was still alive was certainly easier of accomplishment after his death. Did not the Donatists invent a similar account of a fall on the part of Pope St. Marcellinus which was long received, but which all critics now acknowledge as false? Besides, the Arians were not the only enemies of Liberius; the Luciferian schismatics[15] were quite as eager to defame him.

---

[15] The Luciferians were a group of schismatics who followed the bishop of Cagliari whose name, remarkably, was Lucifer. This bishop's breach with the Church was occasioned by a ruling of the Council of Alexandria, 362 A.D., presided over by St. Athanasius, that although bishops and priests who had spontaneously embraced heresy were deemed to have forfeited their offices

The Trustworthiness of the Excerpt from the *Apologia Contra Arianos*

Now let us go back to the first passage quoted, the extract from the *Apologia Contra Arianos*. It has for some time been accepted by all, Pope Liberius's calumniators as well as his defenders, that this work was completed by the year 352 at the latest, so, since neither the fall of Liberius nor that of Hosius was even supposed to have taken place until after that year,[16] the passage quoted referring to their falls could not then have formed part of the *Apologia*. There is of course only one hypothesis which could meet this objection, and some anti-Liberian scholars, determined to believe that this evidence that the pope fell is authentic, have recourse to it: St. Athanasius updated his works at a later date.[17] Although there is no trace of any other evidence to support this convenient hypothesis, that does not in itself prove that it is false, and indeed it is generally difficult to prove the negative in the case of such a hypothesis.

---

and could be received, upon their repentance, only to lay-communion, nonetheless those bishops who had merely temporized through fear might, by an act of clemency, be permitted to retain their episcopal rank upon making an open profession of orthodox Catholic faith upon all the disputed points. Although this ruling was, of course, quite correct, Lucifer insisted on being "more Catholic than the pope", obstinately maintaining that fear could not excuse from censures and that heretics could never be restored to office even upon their repentance. The Luciferians, with "bitter zeal" (James 3:14), launched violent attacks on St. Athanasius, Liberius and all those who, while retaining the Faith, were anxious to temper justice with mercy in their dealings with those who had fallen. For a balanced treatment of Lucifer and his followers, whose history is in many elements confused by discordant testimony, see the *Annales Ecclesiastici* of Ven. Cardinal Baronius, *ad annum* 362.

[16] By contrast with the fall of Liberius, the fall of Bishop Hosius of Cordoba (256-359) is an established historical fact. This illustrious centenarian confessor was beguiled into signing a heterodox formula. Soon after he confessed his fault and died penitent.

[17] Probably the most prominent of the scholars who have championed this hypothesis was the famous nineteenth century ecclesiastical historian von Hefele.

But there are nevertheless a number of arguments which militate against it very strongly, and these I now briefly summarize:

(i) Two of the leaders of the heretical Arian bishops attached to the court of the Emperor Constantius, Valens and Ursacius, had recanted their heresies and returned to the Catholic Faith at the time that it is accepted that the earliest edition of *Apologia Contra Arianos* had been completed. Now although shortly after this they "returned to their vomit"[18] and became Arians once more, every extant text of the *Apologia Contra Arianos* represents them as being still Catholics. And how can this be if the hypothesis that Athanasius updated his work in order to make special reference to the supposed fall of Liberius and the actual fall of Hosius is correct? Would St. Athanasius not have been obliged also to update his reference to the orthodoxy of these well-known bishops? Indeed would he not, in their case, have been if anything even *more* obliged? After all, Hosius returned permanently to the Faith immediately after his fall (which had taken place under great pressure and in extreme old age), and even the worst enemies of Liberius are forced to admit that he was vehemently orthodox between the years 358 and 366 when he died. Neither of them, therefore, could have led others into error, whereas Valens and Ursacius would certainly have constituted a great danger to souls if Athanasius's readers had supposed on the authority of the holy Patriarch that they were still orthodox.

(ii) Although St. Athanasius's *Apologia Contra Arianos* was frequently used as source material by the historians Socrates and Theodoret, neither of them makes any mention of the fall of Liberius, even as an allegation to be denied, which omission clearly indicates that neither of them was aware that such allegations had been made. Moreover,

---

[18] 2 Peter 2:22.

Sozomen also used this work as source material, and although this historian *does* refer to the fall of Liberius, his account is quite different from the account given in St. Athanasius. Had the text of Athanasius which Sozomen used contained any reference to the fall of Liberius he would have

(a) certainly used it as source material and made reference to it to support his allegations, and

(b) needed to justify the difference between his account and that of Athanasius.

In addition, the internal evidence is also strongly opposed to the passage quoted being the work of Athanasius.

(iii) For a start, the reference to the fall of Liberius is in no way coherent with its surrounding context and has all the characteristics of a later interpolation – for if it were omitted, far from there appearing to be missing something, the text would gain in coherence.

(iv) Secondly, in each case the reference to the fall of Liberius is included in a parenthetical aside which disturbs the continuity of the whole passage and makes it, as the reader will have noted, extremely difficult to follow.

(v) Stylistically, the whole passage quoted is extremely poor and does not bear comparison with those writings of Athanasius which are of undoubted authenticity. The Greek particles are clumsily used and the vocabulary appears in places to be deficient, neither of which weaknesses is by any stretch of the imagination likely to have marred the writing of a native Greek speaker who was also a scholar, both of which the great Patriarch of Alexandria was.

(vi) Most strikingly of all, the whole of the passage is quite illogical. For instance, Athanasius is made to use the "argument from numbers" – his position *must* be right because a large number of bishops support him. But St. Athanasius was the last man to overlook that the truth is in no way dependent on, or proved by, the number of people who happen to believe it. He knew very well – indeed this is one of the principles on which the entire edifice of the Catholic religion rests – that if the truth *did* so depend, those who voted for Our Lord's crucifixion on Good Friday must have taken overwhelmingly the right decision. Furthermore, in the year 360, which is when, on the hypothesis that the passage was included as a subsequent updating by St. Athanasius himself, it must have been written, it was *far from true* that a large number of bishops supported him. This was still the period when it was almost as difficult to find a truly orthodox bishop as it is today. Finally, the passage invokes as the most credible witnesses in favour of Athanasius's orthodoxy the testimony of Liberius and Hosius, both of whom, it asserts, had themselves subscribed to formulæ of doubtful orthodoxy, which would be as absurd as for John S. Daly to apply to John-Paul II for an *imprimatur* to confirm the orthodoxy of the statement that the said John-Paul II is neither pope nor even a member of the Catholic Church.

It is on these grounds that Stiltingus writes:

I cannot attribute these additions to Athanasius, but rather incline to the view that the whole of this fragment was written later by a man with an imperfect knowledge of Greek and a still less perfect knowledge of logic. (*Dissertatio de Liberio*, c. 8, n. 125).

The Trustworthiness of the Excerpt from The Historia Arianorum

The authenticity of the second passage quoted, which comes from St. Athanasius's *Historia Arianorum ad Monachos*, is subject to similar objections:

(i)   The completion of this work must be dated about Easter 357 at the latest, since:

       (a)   no part of the historical account which it contains goes beyond Lent of that year, and

(b) in one place there is a reference to Leontius, the bishop of Antioch, as alive; and he died early in the year 357. (See Socrates, *Historia Ecclesiastica*, II, 37)

Hence this work also was finished *before* the events which it purports to relate took place (if indeed they ever *did* take place), and those, such as von Hefele, who wish to maintain the authenticity of this passage, are forced to suggest that it too was updated by St. Athanasius at some stage before his death in 373.

(ii) This last suggestion is not credible in view of the fact that Athanasius was still in exile at the time that he must have written the questionable passage, if he did write it. In that circumstance he would scarcely have been in a position to know with certainty of the fall of Liberius even it if *had* taken place, particularly in view of the fact that this fall remained a matter of doubt to a scholar like Rufinus, and to many others, much later.

(iii) If Athanasius updated this work after the year 357, why did he also not update the reference to Leontius as being alive?

(iv) Once again, many other historians of this period used this work of St. Athanasius as source material, but give no indication in their writings of being aware of the charge that Liberius had capitulated to the Arians.

(v) At least one of the allegations contained in this passage is historically highly improbable since, although it is well known that Constantius used various methods to gain the consent to his plans of the orthodox bishops, it is nowhere else suggested that he threatened them with physical violence. Despite his Arianizing, he did not question standard Christian morality which forbad hands to be laid upon one consecrated to God, all of which makes it most unlikely that he would have dreamt of making a death threat to a venerable bishop as is alleged.

(vi) Finally – and this applies to both the passages we have been examining – if our texts are indeed both updated second editions, why did not Athanasius say so somewhere in them, as had been the practice of all authors throughout history in updating their works, to avoid confusion between one text and another? This would have been an even more obvious course in his day than today, for the attribution of forged works to authors who had had nothing to do with them and the alteration of existing works by unauthorized hands were both at that time commonplace.

All these considerations together – and most of them even individually – leave no doubt that both of the passages found in the writings of St. Athanasius which refer to the fall of Liberius must be dismissed as inept forgeries, included without the saint's knowledge after his death – doubtless the work of the enemies of Liberius and the Catholic Church: either the Arian heretics, who were notorious for their dishonest history and for distorting the works of orthodox writers, or the Luciferian schismatics, who distorted the writings of St. Hilary in this period and were especially hostile to Pope Liberius. And finally, for the benefit of anyone who remains unconvinced by these considerations and still thinks it possible that St. Athanasius did indeed write the passage in question, there is another awkward fact to get over. This is that St. Athanasius was in a very poor position at the time to ascertain what was happening at a considerable distance away from his place of exile, and in view of the other evidence of Pope Liberius's unfailing orthodoxy that we have seen, there is no alternative other than to conclude that, even if written by his own hand, the extracts are completely erroneous and were included on account of his having been deceived by Arian propaganda.

The Writings of St. Jerome

Next in importance after these extracts from Athanasius as historical testimony in favour of the fall of Liberius are two extracts from the writings of St. Jerome. Once again let us begin by quoting in full the two passages in question before analysing them.

In St. Jerome's *Chronicon*, which was written about the year 380, the following occurs:

> In the 282nd Olympiad[19] Liberius was ordained as the 34th bishop of the Roman Church, and when he had been thrust into exile on account of the Faith all the clerics swore that they would receive no other in his place. But when Felix had been substituted in his priestly office by the Arians, very many of them broke their oath, and a year later they were expelled with Felix because Liberius, being overcome by the weariness of exile, had subscribed to heretical perversity and entered Rome as a victor.

And in c. 97 of his *Catalogue of Writers*, in treating of the early Christian bishop and writer Fortunatianus, St. Jerome writes as follows:

> Fortunatianus, an African by nation, and bishop of Aquileia when Constantius was emperor, wrote commentaries on the Gospels in orderly sequence in a brief and rustic style. He is held as detestable on account of the fact that, when Liberius, the bishop of the city of Rome, was travelling into exile for the Faith, he [Fortunatianus] was the first to solicit him, break his will and impel him to subscribe to heresy.

Before beginning to analyse these intriguing excerpts, the following comment by Jungmann (*op. cit.*, p. 77) is worthy of inclusion in full:

> We begin by warning that in historical matters the assertions of St. Jerome when they are finding fault with others cannot always be considered as well-founded. This is because throughout his works Jerome tends to be somewhat carried away by his hatred for heretics and likewise by his naturally vehement character, so that he is too quick to judge or falls into some exaggeration. It was therefore possible that at the time that he wrote these works, while resident in the East, he also believed the rumours spread about the

---

[19] I.e. during the four years from 349-353 A.D.

fall of Liberius, especially if he had come across evidence of this which had been forged by the Arians. But it is of greater moment that the passages quoted are found in short works which it is known have been subject to interpolation throughout and that the texts in question bear all the hallmarks of such interpolation.

The Trustworthiness of the Excerpt from the "Chronicon"

First, the passage quoted from the *Chronicon*. The following points are relevant:

(i) The manuscripts of the *Chronicon* are extremely corrupt and have been subject to numerous additions and interpolations, as is readily admitted even by authors hostile to Liberius such as Tillemont.

(ii) The whole of this account as quoted is evidently a summarised version of the account found in the preface to the *Liber Precum*, to which reference will be made later, and it is evident that whoever was responsible for this passage, whether Jerome or some later interpolator, based what he wrote entirely on this source. And the *Liber Precum* is well-known to have been written by Luciferians, who were the enemies of Liberius and of other orthodox Catholics. Moreover, the very passage in which the alleged fall of Liberius is described also contains shocking libels against St. Damasus, who later became pope and at whose request Jerome translated the Vulgate Bible; and this is of special significance in that Damasus was a personal friend of Jerome's and it is in the highest degree unlikely that Jerome would have given any credence to allegations made about Liberius in a document which proved its own untrustworthiness by making such obviously false assertions concerning such a good friend of his.

(iii) It is worthy of note that St. Jerome was an especially conspicuous defender of the prerogative of the Holy See by which its incumbents, the Roman pontiffs, are preserved from every error against the Faith, as he maintains in his famous letters to Pope Damasus on the questions of faith. How could he have reconciled this position with a belief that Pope Liberius, Damasus's immediate predecessor, had subscribed to heresy, and how could he record this subscription as a historical fact which called for no explanation or justification?

(iv) The passage is quite unhistorical in suggesting that Liberius was in exile for a period of only *one* year, and appears very confused in what it says about the position of Felix. The credibility of what is said in the same passage concerning Liberius is therefore obviously open to the gravest reservations for this reason alone.

(v) The final sentence is absurd and paradoxical in its statement that Liberius was overcome by weariness in exile and subscribed to heresy and was thereupon received *as a victor* when he returned to Rome. Why should the Romans, about whose fervent faith St. Jerome so often and emphatically tells us, give a hero's welcome to a pope who had been able to return to them only by virtue of lapsing into heresy?

(vi) Hardly less paradoxical is the statement that the clergy who had compromised with Arianism were expelled from Rome when Liberius was allowed to return as a result of subscribing to heresy. Evidently, if Liberius was permitted to return only because he had capitulated to the Arian heresy, he would scarcely have expelled from Rome those who had shown no greater weakness than himself!

(vii) In the most ancient extant text of St. Jerome's *Chronicon*, the Codex Vaticanus, *the extract concerning the fall of Liberius is not to be found*.

(viii) In the text of the *Chronicon* edited by St. Prosper of Aquitaine (in the early fifth century) the following version is found instead of the words quoted above:

> Liberius was ordained, the 34th [bishop] of the Roman Church, and when he was thrust into exile for the Faith in the 9th year of his episcopate, all the clergy swore that they would receive no other in his

place. But when Felix was substituted in his priestly office by the Arians, very many of them broke their oath, and when Liberius returned to the city a year later, they were ejected with Felix.

Surely no disinterested scholar could argue that the version relied on by the anti-Liberians has a greater claim to authenticity than this version.

The Trustworthiness of the Excerpt from "De Viris Illustribus"

Let us now move on to the second passage attributed to St. Jerome and quoted above, the section about Fortunatianus in his *De Viris Illustribus* or *Catalogue of Writers*. The following objections to its authenticity present themselves:

(i) Most obviously, the statement that Liberius yielded and subscribed to heresy at the solicitation of Fortunatianus, bishop of Aquileia, does not even approach being plausible; for, of those authors who address the subject, not a single one, even among those who maintain that Pope Liberius eventually capitulated, hesitates to agree that he went into exile with no intention whatsoever of submission. Even the other passage attributed to St. Jerome, the one from the *Chronicon*, says that the pope yielded as a result of the *weariness of exile*, which could hardly be so if the cause of his fall was something said to him when he was *setting off* for exile. Indeed if he had capitulated to Arianism at the instance of Fortunatianus, while on his way to exile, there would have been no further cause for his exile and the two years of desolation which he spent in the East would have been inexplicable.

(ii) No other author refers to this meeting between Liberius and Fortunatianus, not even St. Jerome's contemporary, Rufinus, who, as we have seen, makes it clear that, although he is aware of the allegation that Liberius capitulated to Constantius, he does not accept that it is true, and indicates that he is unaware of any foundation for it. This would certainly be remarkable if the allegation *was* true; for Rufinus lived for a long time at Aquileia, the episcopal city of Fortunatianus, and it is of course there that his solicitation of Liberius must have taken place if it took place at all.

(iii) It is clear that the attribution of the blame for the fall of Liberius to Fortunatianus is based on letters attributed to Pope Liberius himself which are today universally acknowledged as spurious.

(iv) One important fact concerning the supposed fall of Pope Liberius which must now be mentioned is that those who believe it to have taken place allege that it occurred in the presence of the Emperor Constantius and of legates of the bishops of the East and the West, as well as of Africa. What follows from this is that, if the fall had really happened, there could be no possible doubt as to its having happened, and therefore the bare *existence* of doubt (and the testimony of Rufinus alone is sufficient for this) proves the fall to be utterly impossible.

Credibility of the "Liber Precum"

Mention has more than once been made in the foregoing pages of the *Liber Precum* or *The Book of Prayers of Faustinus and Marcellinus*, to give its full title translated into English. Written in 384-5 A.D. by devotees of the schismatic Luciferian faction, who, it may be remembered, were possessed by "bitter zeal" and were determined to be more "Catholic" than the Catholic Church, it contained libellous allegations against various popes and bishops, including even St. Hilary, who had also, they alleged, lent support to heretics. As a source of information on Pope Liberius its complete unreliability is immediately evident, for it asserts that his fall had taken place before Emperor Constantius ever came to Rome. And even if what it says were taken as true, it would be of fairly insignificant help to the detractors of Pope Liberius, for it says of him merely that he "gave his hands to perfidy" which, taken alone, cannot constitute an assertion that he subscribed to any heretical formula, still less that he excommunicated St. Athanasius. (More information about this Luciferian tract can be found in Jungmann's *Dissertationes*, Dis. 6, n. 88.)

Should We Trust Sozomen?

The final source alleged to make reference to Pope Liberius's fall which is worthy of attention is the *Historia Ecclesiastica* of Sozomen, written about 450 A.D. It is of some interest in that it presents an account which is markedly different from that of the other early historians to whom reference has been made, and the most convenient way of conveying to readers the information they need about the relevant passage in it is to reproduce here the summary of it and the assessment of what weight should be given to it which are to be found in the article on Pope Liberius by Dom John Chapman in *The Catholic Encyclopædia* (1913), Vol. IX, p. 220:

> Sozomen tells a story which finds no echo in any other writer. He makes Constantius, after his return from Rome, summon Liberius to Sirmium (357), and there the pope is forced by the semi-Arian leaders, Basil of Ancyra, Eustathius, and Eleusius, to condemn the "homo-ousion"; he is induced to sign a combination of three formulæ: that of the Catholic Council of Antioch of 267 against Paul of Samosata (in which "homo-ousios" was said to have been rejected as Sabellian in tendency), that of the Sirmium assembly which condemned Photinus in 351, and the creed of the Dedication Council of Antioch in 341. These formulæ were not precisely heretical, and Liberius is said to have exacted from Ursacius and Valens a confession that the Son is 'in all things similar to the Father.' Hence Sozomen's story has been very generally accepted as giving a moderate account of Liberius's fall, admitting it to be a fact, yet explaining why so many writers implicitly deny it. But the date soon after Constantius was at Rome is impossible, as the semi-Arians only united at the beginning of 358, and their short-lived influence over the emperor began in the middle of that year .... Further, the formula 'in all things like' was not the semi-Arian

badge in 358, but was forced upon them in 359, after which they adopted it, declaring that it included their special formula 'like in substance'. Now Sozomen is certainly following here the lost compilation of the Macedonian (i.e. semi-Arian) Sabinus, whom we know to have been untrustworthy wherever his sect was concerned. Sabinus seems simply to have had the Arian story before him, but regarded it, probably rightly, as an invention of the party of Eudoxius ....

In short, the account of Sozomen is incompatible with all other historical accounts, is evidently founded upon the writings of an untrustworthy heretic, errs grossly in its history concerning other matters taking place at the same time as the alleged fall of Liberius, and anyhow does not in fact assert either that Liberius subscribed to a heretical formula or that he excommunicated Athanasius.

Philostorgius

I referred to Sozomen as the final source worth bothering with, but there *is* one other – and only one other – historian adduced by the enemies of Pope Liberius as support for this position; and he must therefore receive a mention, though scarcely more. This is Philostorgius, who was writing between the years 425 and 433 A.D.

All that need be said about him is that he was a member of the Arian sect, which, as many readers are doubtless already well aware, was renowned both for misrepresenting history and for falsifying the writings of others. Anyone who is prepared to accept the unsupported assertion, of a writer with this background, that a Vicar of Christ, to whom, in the person of St. Peter, Incarnate Truth Himself said "I have prayed for thee that thy faith fail not" had subscribed to *the very heresy propounded by the writer's own sect*, brands himself as a member of the group of "historians" who study history, not to discover the truth, but to gather together, without regard for the strength of whatever evidence exists, as many allegations and rumours discreditable to the Catholic Church as they can. It is not in order to try to convince such people that this *Evaluation* has been written, and that is why what has been said here about Philostorgius is all that will be said.

Conclusions Concerning the Unsullied Orthodoxy of Pope Liberius

The time has come to summarize what has emerged from our examination of the allegations against Pope Liberius. This can fairly be done by simply reproducing the following passage from Jungmann's 6th dissertation, n. 109:

> Having weighed up everything, therefore, we reach the conclusion that the fall of Liberius is fictitious, and that Liberius neither fell into heresy nor lent his assistance to the perfidy of heretics; and that this pontiff in reality subscribed to no formula of Sirmium nor to any other document which shrank from the profession of the word '*homo-ousios*' consecrated by the fathers of Nicæa; nor did he condemn St. Athanasius or enter into communion with the Arians.

Conclusions Concerning the Gravely Sullied Scholarliness and Integrity of Michael Davies

Having established that Michael Davies has been purveying falsehood as truth and libels against the papacy in his purported defence of the Catholic Church, my task is not yet completed; for the question of his scholarly integrity cannot be evaded.

For instance it will be remembered that on three occasions when Davies makes reference to Pope Liberius's alleged fall and excommunication of St. Athanasius *he adds also that Pope Liberius subsequently made a recantation*. And a recantation by Pope Liberius is asserted *by no historian whomsoever*, be he contemporary with Liberius or of any subsequent period, be he pro-Liberius or anti-Liberian, be he Catholic or Protestant or even Arian. It is simply an invention on the part of Davies to add credibility to his tale.[20] And in his article in *The Angelus*,

---

[20] No, I am wrong. Since writing the above in my first draft, I have come

January 1987, Davies threw in three more whopping fabrications for good measure. There he declared, first, that "in the fourth century the simple fact of communion with the Pope did not guarantee orthodoxy as the Arian bishops were in communion with Liberius" (which they most certainly were *not*); secondly, that "it was, for a time, communion with Athanasius rather than communion with the Pope which signified a true Catholic" (again, neither true nor claimed by any serious historian); and thirdly, that faithful Catholics "had ... to worship outside the 'official' churches, the churches of bishops in communion with Liberius" – all flying in the face of the easily ascertainable fact that we have seen earlier: that not even St. Athanasius himself was stricter than Liberius in refusing even the *appearance* of being in communion with anyone of questionable orthodoxy.

So far so bad. But there is another area in which Davies displays even more blatant bad faith; that of the use he makes of references to scholarly authority on the matter under discussion. And this must be examined at somewhat greater length.

The Division of Scholarly Opinion

It would not be true to say that Davies never at all acknowledges that there *is* scholarly dissension on the question of the fall of Liberius and his excommunication of St. Athanasius; but such acknowledgements are very rare, and even when they are made they are formulated in terms which suggest

---

across new information. There is in fact a single historian who has fallen into the same egregious trap as Davies has, by referring to a "repentance" on Liberius's part. The author in question is the anti-Catholic Gibbon in his *Decline and Fall of the Roman Empire*, Vol. II, p. 345; but as this work is on the *Index of Forbidden Books* it is to be hoped that Davies was not using Gibbon as a source and that Davies and Gibbon each invented the same fictional episode independently. So whereas my statement that *no* historian agrees with Davies is not strictly *exact*, it dos not seem to be *unfair*. Writing in the *American Catholic Quarterly Review*, 1883, Fr. P.J. Harrold reproaches Gibbon with this falsification of history, remarking that "there is nowhere on record a 'seasonable repentance', nor anything approaching it in the career of Liberius." Davies himself clearly merits the same reproach.

that the dissenters are a small minority of over-zealous fanatics whose historical learning is unworthy of serious consideration. Here, for instance, is what he writes in both *Apologia Pro Marcel Lefebvre*, Vol. I, p. 371 and *The True Voice of Tradition*, p. 9:

> Some Catholic apologists have attempted to prove that Liberius neither confirmed the excommunication of Athanasius nor subscribed to one of the formulæ of Sirmium. But Cardinal Newman has no doubt that the fall of Liberius is an historical fact.

In other words, such is the measure of Davies's contempt for these "Catholic apologists", that he deems them worthy only of anonymous obscurity, and considers the weight of Cardinal Newman's opinion alone sufficient to justify his readers in dismissing them as unworthy of further attention.

And what is the truth on this matter? It can easily be seen simply by comparing a list of those serious scholars who hold the theory that Liberius capitulated to Constantius with a list of those who defend his orthodoxy.

Anti-Liberian Writers

Let us begin with those who may broadly be regarded as on Davies's side. They comprise Moeller, who was a Gallican; Barmby, who was a Protestant; Langen, who was an Old Catholic; Tillemont, whom Fr. W.H. Anderdon S.J. selects in his *Britain's Early Faith* (p. 39) as the archetypal sceptic; Döllinger, the famous scholar who left the Church at the time of the declaration of Papal Infallibility in 1870 and became an Old Catholic; Cardinal Newman, in his *Arians of the Fourth Century*, written in 1833, twelve years before his conversion in a work in which he accuses the papacy of having apostatized altogether at the Council of Trent;[21] Renouf; Schiktanz; Fr.

---

[21] Newman does not for a second consider the likelihood that some of the patristic texts have been interpolated. He does admit that the heterodox text signed [i.e. alleged to have been signed] by Liberius cannot be identified. For his anti-Roman bias even after his conversion, see Richard Sartino, *Another*

Alban Butler[22]; the infidel Gibbon, whose *Decline and Fall* is on the *Index* and who seems to have decided whether or not to accept allegations hostile to the papacy purely on the basis of whether they would be useful for bringing the Catholic Church into disrepute. I cannot bring myself to add the name of St. Robert Bellarmine to this list, for he was at best no more than a highly tentative anti-Liberian and appears to express contradictory views on the subject in two different places (*De Romano Pontifice* lib. IV, cap. 9 and lib. II, cap. 30, para. 2). Moreover he was writing at the dawn of critical historiography, before any question had been raised as to the authenticity of some of the patristic manuscripts he was using, and he emphasizes that any brief defection from his celebrated orthodoxy on the part of Liberius is a matter of doubt.

On the other hand I freely offer Michael Davies the support of E. Amman in the *Dictionnaire de Théologie Catholique*. Indeed special mention is called for in his case, because the *Dictionnaire de Théologie Catholique* is a justly famous work and generally reliable. What must never be forgotten, however, is that all encyclopædic works inevitably suffer from the defect that some of their contributors tend to be less reliable than others, for equality in this field, as in any other field, is simply not a characteristic of the human race – a fact which obstinately continues to apply no matter what rarefied levels of scholarship are reached, and a fact which no editor can overcome because no editor is competent to verify all his contributions. As regards Amann's article as an example of this phenomenon, it is sufficient to note that he quotes in inverted commas – yes, *quotes* – what purport to be the passages from the writings of St.

Look at John Henry Cardinal Newman.

[22] Butler insists that the Sirmian formula signed by Liberius cannot have been a heretical one, and emphasizes Liberius's valiant measures to defend orthodoxy both before and after the allaged "fall", but, the possibility that he was relying on interpolated texts never having occurred to him, he cannot see his way to exculpating Liberius entirely.

Athanasius in which the "capitulation" of Pope Liberius has been interpolated, and that in each case the true meaning is both grossly distorted and further corrupted with inventions of his own. In other words, not content with passing off, in defiance of the overwhelming evidence we have seen earlier, the contemporary pseudo-Athanasius as Athanasius, he falsifies even that corruption. A forgery is not sufficient for his purposes; he must embellish it with further forgeries of his own. (See *Dictionnaire de Théologie Catholique*, Vol. IX, column 638.)

Anyhow the foregoing writers are the most renowned historians of the anti-Liberian school.

Exceptions

There are also writers who hold the more moderate position, similar to that maintained by Sozomen among the ancients, that Liberius subscribed to a formula deliberately couched in ambiguous terminology, which, although it was in fact open to a heterodox interpretation, led him genuinely to believe that the formula was a statement of the Catholic Faith. These writers include Baronius,[23] von Hefele, who was a liberal, Funk, and Duchesne, a notorious Modernist, some of whose writings are on the *Index of Forbidden Books*.

---

[23] It should be noted that Baronius, writing in the 1580s, was the first Catholic historian to attempt the laborious task of piecing together the full facts about Liberius from the often conflicting details scattered throughout the writings of earlier historians, and that he often relied on texts transcribed for him by others, being therefore unable to verify their authenticity personally. It is not therefore very surprising that, on the strength of the letters of Liberius himself, now universally recognized as inauthentic, he was deceived into accepting the fact of Liberius's subscription to an ambiguous formula: certainly he does not regard Liberius as a heretic and no less certainly he is at pains to highlight the way in which his orthodox Catholic contemporaries eulogized Liberius even after the date of his supposed fall. The same applies to his close friend St. Robert Bellarmine who, however, holds that *if* Liberius subscribed to heresy, or was publicly believed to have done so, he thereby *forfeited the papacy.*

Pro-Liberian Writers

The very least that can be said of the list of writers who have defended the orthodoxy of Liberius is that it is no less impressive than what we have seen so far. It comprises the Mediæval Byzantine historian Georgio Cedrenos (c. 1100), faithful relayer of the traditions of Eastern Christendom; Stilting; Zaccaria; Palma; Dom Guéranger (*The Liturgical Year*: Feast of St Eusebius); Cardinal Hergenröther, the famous vindicator of Catholic orthodoxy against the attacks of Döllinger at the time of the 1870 Vatican Council; Jungmann, whose work on the subject covers eighty pages of close argument and is in this writer's opinion entirely conclusive alone;[24] Grisar; Freis; Flavio; Corgne; Rohrbacher, whose *Histoire Universelle de l'Église Catholique* has been justly hailed as "sublime" (Palme), "monumental" (*Catholic Encyclopædia*), and the finest history of the Church written since the sixteenth century and should be snapped up by anyone with the ability to read French[25] who comes across it; Dom John Chapman in his article in the 1913 *Catholic Encyclopædia*; Alzog in his *Universal Catholic History*, Vol. I, p. 542; Darras in his *General History of the Catholic Church*, p. 456 *et seq.*; Reinerding; Schneeman; Wouters; Barthélémy in his *Erreurs et Mensonges Historiques* which earned a papal accolade; Harrold in *The American Catholic Quarterly Review*, 1883; Fr. Luke Rivington in *The Primitive Church and the See of Peter*; Dumont; the renowned Scriptural exegete Menochius; the *very* learned historian and theologian Ballerini; Galland; the *Roman Breviary* itself (December 16th); and the famous Gallican bishop Bossuet, who

---

[24] For readers who understand Latin, there can be no substitute for the direct study of this work to understand the whole historical episode.

[25] The first volume is prefaced by a generous letter of approval from Pope Pius IX in which the pontiff declares that the work has "long been commended by the testimony and praise of wise men." The saintly President Gabriel García Moreno of Ecuador (1821-1875) read its fourteen hefty volumes three times!

originally argued in favour of the capitulation of Liberius but, according to his secretary, D. Ledieu, wished to have what he had written on this subject deleted from his works. Nor ought we to overlook the renowned *Enchiridion Symbolorum* first edited by Fr. Heinrich Denzinger and later appearing in more complete editions with various learned editors, for under N° 93 it lists the letter of St. Anastasius vindicating Pope Liberius (referred to earlier) under the heading "*De orthodoxia Liberii Papæ*" – "Concerning the orthodoxy of Pope Liberius".

According to What Criteria Does Davies Select His Sources?

Very revealing and instructive is the bibliography to Davies's booklet on Liberius and Athanasius, listing the six works which Davies has drawn on for the material used in the pamphlet. To offer a brief assessment of these works will not take long.

Two are "Catholic dictionaries", one of them published as late as the 1970s and therefore obviously unreliable. One is a small book called *A Handbook of Heresies* by M.L. Cozens, which, though sound, devotes only seven pages to the entire topic of Arianism and Semi-Arianism and nowhere even mentions Liberius. Another, the only full-length book, is *The Arians of the Fourth Century* by Davies's hero, Cardinal Newman. And the two remaining works are the 1913 *Catholic Encyclopædia* and the 1967 *New Catholic Encyclopædia*.

Bearing in mind how frequently and emphatically Davies has put forward his opinion on what is recognized by everyone else to be a very controversial subject, this bibliography is of course ludicrously short. But there is another feature of it which is of even greater interest. This, to which reference has already been made in this *Evaluation*, is that, whereas five of the works given in the bibliography are also cited in the text of the booklet – most of them more than once – the sixth, the 1913 *Catholic Encyclopædia*, does not feature in the text at all.

It is in fact difficult to see why the 1913 *Catholic Encyclopædia* rates a mention in the bibliography, unless it is simply that Davies, who uses it as a reference work for many *other* purposes, was simply embarrassed to cite only the 1967 *New Catholic Encyclopædia* and thus admit openly that he was ignoring everything in the more traditional and obviously more reliable work in favour of this inferior post-Vatican II substitute which itself stands under far heavier accusation of compromise with heresy than Pope Liberius ever did!. As for *why* he did the opposite of what any true Catholic would do who wanted to consult an encyclopædia, and turned single-mindedly to the post-Vatican II version published under the umbrella of the Conciliar Church – that admits no difficulty whatever of explanation. The 1913 *Catholic Encyclopædia*, which Davies frequently quotes in his works on subjects other than Pope Liberius, *contains an excellent and cogent article arguing that the various charges made against Liberius are entirely spurious*, and for Davies this is sufficient to make it, in Orwellian terms, an *un*-encyclopædia.

Needless to say, the dreadful *New Catholic Encyclopædia*, like all such works which have emanated from the Conciliar Church in order to "update" and outdate their pre-Conciliar counterparts, seizes every opportunity that presents itself to undermine the Church and diminish the esteem which Catholics should have for the Holy See, by invariably siding with the enemies of the Vicar of Christ in the allegations which they bring against him. Davies stands revealed as a man who is prepared to turn to such a source as this to bolster up his prejudices while dismissing traditional and trustworthy authorities who contradict the thesis which he finds it convenient to champion.

Davies's Other Papal Victims

Lamentably, Pope St. Liberius is not the only Vicar of Our Divine Redeemer whom Davies subjects to his odious calumnies. Far from it; he appears to *revel* in dredging up every scandal, true, false or doubtful, about the popes which he can locate.

Thus on p. 413 of *Apologia Pro Marcel Lefebvre*, Vol. I, he writes:

> Pope John XXII actually taught heresy in his capacity as a private doctor. (Many papal utterances express no more than the personal opinion of the Pope and do not involve the teaching authority of the Church.) Pope John XXII taught that there was no particular judgement; that the souls of the just do not enjoy the beatific vision immediately [after death]; that the wicked are not at once eternally damned; and that all await the judgement of God on the Last Day.

And the same allegation is made on p. 21 of *The Divine Constitution*, where again he assures us that "this opinion [i.e. the error that the just do not enjoy the beatific vision between death and the General Judgement] was condemned as heretical;" though on this occasion he also takes the opportunity to give yet another example of his incompetence in handling even simple elements of Catholic theology, "informing" us just a few lines later that:

> ... belief in the Particular Judgement is not a teaching which must be believed '*de fide divina et Catholica*' as it has not yet been promulgated as such.

How does this last question, taken in conjunction with its immediate predecessor, provide an example of Davies's incompetence? Let us ask him a few questions, make a few observations, and see what emerges.

(i) If Pope John XXII was expressing "no more than [his] personal opinion",[26] Mr. Davies, why do you use the word "taught" repeatedly, suggesting the contrary?

(ii) Where is the heresy in Pope John's doctrine? Is it his denial of the Particular Judgement or in his denial that the just enjoy the beatific vision before the General Judgement?

---

[26] Which is true, as Pope John specifically stated this to be the case.

(iii) At first sight, it appears that the denial of the Particular Judgement is where you see the crux of the heresy issue. But, of course, if, as you inform us, this doctrine is not "*de fide divina et Catholica*", its contradiction *cannot* be heretical. By definition, heresy is a proposition in contradiction to one which is proposed by the Church for belief "*de fide divina et Catholica*" – i.e. as Divinely revealed.

(iv) If, however, the alleged heresy lies in the denial that the beatific vision antedates the General Judgement, ought you not to have explained that the contrary proposition was not dogmatically defined until 1336, two years after Pope John XXII's death, in the bull *Benedictus Deus* (Denzinger 530) so that Pope John's opinion was *not* heretical at all *at the time he voiced it*?

(v) How is it, it must be *extremely* pertinent to ask, that you are so casual in branding the genuine popes of the authentic Catholic Church as heretics even when their errors were not contrary to a doctrine to be believed "*de fide divina et Catholica*",[27] but so fierce in your defence of the godless usurpers who call themselves popes in the Conciliar Church? What sort of treatment, by contrast, would you have meted out to any traditional Catholic who had dared to suggest that John-Paul II had taught heresy, if the error in question had not been defined (or otherwise proposed) as Divinely revealed prior to the contradiction's having been expressed?

(vi) Would not a serious theological writer, concerned with avoiding any possibility that his readers might be misled by him into error, have made it clear to them that, even though the Church does not teach that the Particular Judgement is Divinely revealed, she nevertheless *does* teach that it is *theologically certain*, and therefore to be believed by all

---

[27] At least at the time in question.

Catholics under pain of mortal sin? Let us, anyhow, remedy this defect, turning for authority to the Redemptorist theologian praised by St. Pius X, Fr. J. Herrmann. In his *Institutiones Theologiæ Dogmaticæ*, tr. XVI, n. 1936, he tells us:

> ... the proposition that the soul of every man is judged immediately after death, is not explicitly defined '*de fide*', but *is*, however, implicitly contained in [other] definitions....

More of the Same

It is now my unenviable duty to return to the same appendix to *Apologia Pro Marcel Lefebvre*, Vol. I, which contains this deplorable misrepresentation of Pope John XXII; for the passage that has just been examined is – alas! – only one example among many that it contains of the same feature of Davies's writing. In fact it is no exaggeration to say that in this appendix he indulges in a veritable orgy of anti-papalism. For six pages he does nothing but produce pope after pope, each of whom he accuses of various crimes until the reader receives the impression that the two hundred and sixty successors of St. Peter, far from being, as a group, more outstanding for holiness and wisdom than any comparable group of men in history – which is the reality – were in fact a collection of incarnate devils, specializing in every species of sin that can be thought of and defiling the highest dignity to which a man can be raised – the vicarship of Christ Himself – with their abominations.

But before looking at the catalogue of allegedly unworthy popes to assess its accuracy, let us remind ourselves of the principles applicable to the exposure of deplorable incidents in the lives of others, and in particular in the lives of the representatives of the Church. These principles[28] can be summarized as follows:

---

[28] See, for instance, McHugh and Callan, *Moral Theology*, N° 2072 "Revelations About Historical Personages".

(i) Everyone, the dead as much as the living, has the right to his good reputation except where he is (or was) *evidently* bad. Thus the "benefit of the doubt" must be accorded where it is due, and apparently unworthy actions must be construed as charitably as is reasonably possible.

(ii) Even where crimes are certain, it is wrong to draw attention to them without good reason.

(iii) Certain categories of individuals – our parents and our prelates especially – are entitled to our special allegiance, so that we should be very slow to believe evil of them and slower still to publicize it. Indeed, as a generality, our duty to our parents, our bishops and especially to the popes is to spread their honour and to *conceal* anything we may know that tends to their dishonour.

(iv) Nonetheless, where the interests of others would be seriously prejudiced by silence, it can be lawful and even obligatory to draw public attention to the misbehaviour even of popes, where this misbehaviour is definitely true.

(v) "The first law of history is not to dare to lie ; the second is not to fear to tell the truth."[29]

It will be apparent from them that whether Davies is guilty of grave offences against the Fourth and Eighth Commandments will depend on whether his allegations are *true* and whether there was proportionate reason for him to make them. If they are, or may well be, false, no necessity could justify publicizing them ; and similarly, if making them public is liable to do more harm than good, their truth (if they *are* true) is no defence either. These points will be considered shortly, but it is now time to introduce the victims of Davies's caustic attacks.

Among the spectres Davies raises are Pope Zosimus, who was, we learn, weak on discipline and too soft-hearted towards miscreant prelates ; Pope Boniface II, who tried to nominate an allegedly unworthy deacon as his successor but was persuaded

---

[29] Pope Leo XIII, *Sæpenumero considerantes*, 1883.

not to; Pope Vigilius (the allegedly unworthy deacon who eventually became pope nonetheless), who is said to have written heretical letters while pope – a charge long since exploded by the Church's most erudite historians, but cheerfully repeated by Davies notwithstanding this easily ascertainable fact; Pope Honorius, who (it is widely believed) unwittingly wrote letters open to heterodox interpretation[30] and according to some failed to oppose heresy with due vigour; Pope Sergius, who was, if we are to believe certain contemporary accounts, a notorious blackguard; Pope John XII, whose pontificate by all accounts was a disgrace from the point of view of his personal morality; Pope Saint Gregory VII – yes, you did correctly read *Saint* Gregory VII – who in Davies's judgement was wrong in his justly applauded crushing of the Emperor Henry IV;[31] Pope Gregory IX, who is said to have appointed an unworthy candidate as inquisitor in France; Pope Sixtus IV who was guilty of extravagant nepotism; and Pope Innocent VIII who "lacked the personality and intellectual capacity for the office of pope" and is said to have had illegitimate children (though in fact they were (a) legitimate and (b) begotten before he became a cleric).

Davies even throws in Pope Boniface IX, on the grounds that he apparently increased taxation and enriched the Church by offering indulgences to generous alms-givers. Try as he may, the

---

[30] St. Robert Bellarmine denies that the incriminated letters in fact contain any offence against orthodoxy, however accidental, and he makes a surprisingly powerful case for believing that the Acts of the Third Council of Constantinople have been interpolated where they condemn Honorius (*De Romano Pontifice*, lib. II, cap. XXX).

[31] This spectacular and egregious libel of a pope *who is also a canonized saint*, which Davies also included in an article in *The Angelus*, April 1979, moved French writer Jacques Tescelin, in an article entitled "Davies au pays des merveilles" ("Davies in Wonderland") in the wholly outstanding Belgian Catholic periodical *Didasco* (May-June 1980), to pose himself the question: "Is Michael Davies a serious author?" His conclusion was straightforward and surely justified: "After his articles of April 1979 and April 1980 it is impossible for us to reply in the affirmative."

present writer cannot see anything clearly reprehensible in Davies's charges here, and doubts whether the most exacting moral theologian could either. But why worry about such a detail if you are Michael Davies? Why not include Boniface willy-nilly with the other presumed miscreants just the same? Why hesitate to cast aspersions, founded or unfounded, on the reputation of long dead sovereign pontiffs? Of what importance is the honour of the Church and the Holy See, after all, and obeying, except where there is solid necessity to do otherwise, the Scriptural demand that we cover the nakedness of our fathers?[32]

The whole collection is both nauseating and pathetic, and can only leave readers wondering which of its many revolting features is to be most deplored. On the one hand there is the unapologetic enthusiasm with which Davies exposes to the common gaze the sins and weaknesses of those whom he should consider his spiritual fathers whose honour he is bound by the Fourth Commandment to preserve and defend rather than to attack. Then there is Davies's naiveté and gullibility in plastering his pages with these hideous allegations, scarcely ever making the slightest attempt to justify them, never at any point mentioning that there is often a credible defence made by Catholic historians of his victims, assiduously ignoring one of the best attested general facts of history, which is that popes are often slandered by their contemporaries, and ignoring equally the duty not to bear false witness against our neighbour, which continues even after our neighbour's death when he is longer able to defend his good name. Finally there is the fact that in this purported work of traditional Catholic scholarship Davies unblushingly admits that his source material for the whole filthy catalogue was not one of the recognized great histories of the papacy, such as that of von Pastor, or one of the great histories

---

[32] See Genesis 9:20-27; Ecclesiasticus 3:12 ("Glory not in the dishonour of thy father, for his shame is no glory to thee.").

of the Church, such as those of Baronius, Rohrbacher or Hergenröther, but ... well, let us allow Davies himself to tell us his source and to describe it as he sees fit:

> ... the very scholarly one-volume work on the same subject, *The Popes*, edited by Eric John and published by Burns and Oates in 1964. It is only necessary to glance through the brief lives of the popes in this book to find literally hundreds of examples of 'faults, stupidity, blunders, extravagances, and weaknesses' among [i.e. on the part of] the Popes.

The present writer has no difficulty in believing this claim. What, after all, should we expect from a popularizing history whose commercial success would bear a direct ratio to its raciness and spiciness? Is it not evident that Mr. John's book was not written, as were the *Annals* of the Venerable Cardinal Baronius, to vindicate the Holy See from the imputations of its enemies?[33] Given that there were several single-volume histories of the popes in English already, is it credible that Mr. John and the *soi-disant* scholars who contributed to the text he edited were making an urgently necessary contribution to historical scholarship?

I have not devoted much time to reading through Eric John's work, but in the time I *have* spent I not only noticed that Davies in no way understates its tendency to criticize the popes, even on the flimsiest of evidence, but also failed to notice a single expression indicating that its editor and contributors were Catholics, rather than free-thinkers!

But when all is said and done, surely the most appalling aspect of his enthusiastic disloyalty lies in the fact that it was so

---

[33] Although, as has been said earlier, the obligation of honesty can at times require the admission of sin on the part of popes by even the most devoted Catholic historians, and Baronius is both a devoted Catholic historian and a historian who faces squarely up to his obligations to truth, no one would claim that "glancing through" his pages would swiftly bring to light "hundreds of examples of 'faults, stupidity, blunders, extravagances and weaknesses'" on the part of the popes.

unnecessary. Let us look very briefly at the ostensible purpose of the appendix in which the passages synopsized above occur.

Its title is *The Right to Resist An Abuse of Power* and the thesis defended in it is that in certain circumstances – namely when obedience would be clearly sinful – it is lawful to disobey even the highest authorities in the Church. Now let us set aside the fact that Davies hopelessly mis-states the clear teaching of the Church on *when* one may disobey lawful authority, and let us set aside also the fact that the entire discussion is irrelevant to the conciliar "popes" because they are demonstrably not "lawful authority". Even so, why would it not have been fully sufficient to quote the teaching of the Church's great theologians (extracts from Aquinas, Bellarmine and Suarez would have covered the topic quite adequately), perhaps with the addition of one or two appropriate historical instances of popes who gave orders compliance with which would have been sinful? To what possible end was it necessary to catalogue every allegedly questionable episode in the history of the papacy? How did it assist Davies in providing his thesis about obedience to remind us that Pope Sixtus V produced a bad version of the Vulgate or that more than one pope appears to have begotten illegitimate children at some point in his life?

As to the details in Davies's catalogue, while some are true, many are exaggerated and others wholly fictitious. There can be no need to offer specific refutations of the allegations, because the time and space that would be required can be more usefully employed for other purposes.

Pope Leo XIII, that great friend of true historiography, has surely said what needs to be said, in the apostolic epistle *Sæpenumero considerantes*, 1883.

He notes, as if fresh from reading Davies's works, that

> (a)mong the greatest Pontiffs, even those eminent for virtue have been accused and defamed as ambitious, proud and imperious.

And when he seeks to identify "... the main stratagems by which those who strive to render the Church and the Papacy suspect and odious win confidence ..." he remarks that

... with great energy and duplicity they attack the history of the Christian centuries and especially the annals of the Roman Pontiffs.

Against this, he declares the simple truth:

The incorruptible records of history, when studied calmly and without prejudice, constitute a magnificent and spontaneous apology for the Church and the papacy ...

And he issues a warning that Davies would have done well to heed:

[I]t is both dangerous and unjust to sacrifice historical truth to hatred of the papacy ...

CHAPTER ELEVEN
SALVATION OUTSIDE THE CHURCH?

"O Timothy, keep that which is committed to thy trust, avoiding the profane novelties of words, and oppositions of knowledge falsely so called." (1 Timothy 6:20)

A Telephone Conversation between John S. Daly and Michael Davies

In August 1983 the present writer spoke to Davies at considerable length by telephone. The conversation centred on two main questions:

(i) Is John-Paul II a public pertinacious heretic?
(ii) Do public pertinacious heretics automatically forfeit all ecclesiastical offices they may possess and become ineligible to acquire any new ones, including the papacy?

Davies's tactic, witnessed by his then colleague Mr. N.M. Gwynne, was to deny *both* points, but if forced to retreat from one of them, to take refuge in the other – a process he was able to repeat indefinitely. Thus when Canon 188§4 was invoked to show that heretics forfeit all offices *ipso facto* and without need for any declaration, he would divert attention from that point by insisting that John-Paul II was *not* a heretic; and then, when religious liberty, salvation outside the Church and other heresies were adduced as examples of heresies to which Karol Wojtyła pertinaciously subscribed, he would resist this claim until he could sustain that position no longer, whereupon he rushed back to his original claim, that heretics do *not* automatically lose their offices anyway, as though the earlier conversation in which this claim was refuted had never taken place. Each claim was maintained in alternation, the cycle being repeated several times; and it was never possible to make him remember the arguments against both of them at the same time, with the result that he was invulnerable.

During the course of the argument an exchange took place which showed that Davies was highly unlikely to recognize as heretical the position of John-Paul II on salvation outside the Church as he appeared to share that position. This part of the conversation ran more or less as follows:

J.S.D. John-Paul II subscribed to heresy by endorsing the Vatican II Decree on Ecumenism, which teaches salvation outside the Catholic Church.

M.D. That is not heretical. Non-Catholics can certainly be saved.

J.S.D. But the Church has frequently and solemnly defined that there is absolutely *no* salvation outside the Church. For instance [reaching for copy of Denzinger], Pope Boniface VIII in *Unam Sanctam* said:

> We declare, say, define and pronounce that it is absolutely necessary for the salvation of every human creature to be subject to the Roman pontiff.

M.D. Yes, I know; but that doctrine has *developed*. It is perfectly orthodox Catholic belief that Protestants, Jews and pagans can all be saved despite their errors if they are sincere and obey their consciences. "No salvation outside the Church" is taken to mean no salvation for those *culpably* outside the Church.

J.S.D. Do you think that Pope Boniface VIII meant that in his "*ex cathedra*" definition?

M.D. Oh, no. *He* meant that non-Catholics could never go to Heaven at all. But that is where *doctrinal development* comes in. You see, Cardinal Newman explained that doctrines can develop provided that each change is compatible with what went before.

J.S.D. And you maintain that the doctrine that there *is* salvation outside the Church is "compatible" with the doctrine that there is *no* salvation outside the Church?

M.D. Yes. It's surprising just how much doctrines can develop. I am thinking of doing a doctorate with the Open University[1] on this subject, showing how Catholic beliefs can change dramatically but still remain the same Faith. Salvation outside the Church is the best example.

J.S.D. But don't you accept that supernatural faith[2] is necessary for salvation?

M.D. Non-Catholics have *implicit* faith. For instance, a Hindu woman who commits suttee[3] will go to Heaven because she believes in good faith that she is doing the right thing.

J.S.D. But surely *good* faith [sincerity in one's religious convictions, whatever they may be] is not the same thing as *supernatural* faith [the infused theological virtue by which we firmly believe what God has revealed as made known by His Church] ....

It would be superfluous to prolong this attempt to reconstruct the conversation, for its purpose has now been achieved. It is simply to highlight two positions which Davies maintains which can be accurately formulated as follows:

(i) It is possible for non-members of the Catholic Church, and even non-Christians who deny even her most fundamental doctrines, to be saved, if they

(a) earnestly consider that what they believe is right, and
(b) act in accordance with those beliefs.

---

[1] A non-residential academic institution founded by a recent British Socialist government to instruct and provide qualifications for mature students.

[2] Supernatural faith is the virtue whereby we believe all that God has revealed. Since this revelation is entrusted to and expounded by the Catholic Church, those who are refuse the Church's authority are cut off from the ordinary means of knowing what God has in fact revealed and of having this supernaturally firm belief in it.

[3] I.e. kills herself by jumping on her husband's funeral pyre as an act of homage to Brahma or other members of the Hindu pantheon.

(ii) It is possible for a doctrine to develop in such wise that what would once have been considered heretical may become orthodox (and conceivably vice versa), provided that the historical formulation of the original doctrine is not denied but is re-interpreted to mean something quite different from what Catholics in past centuries always took it to mean and considered to be the only available interpretation.

The reason that both of these heresies are here treated together is that they are mutually supporting and neither can be adequately refuted without refuting the other. It is impossible to show that there is genuinely no salvation outside the Catholic Church if it be possible for a dogma so to develop that it need no longer mean that which it once meant. Similarly it is impossible to refute this theory of doctrinal development convincingly without refuting the "new interpretation" of the maxim "no salvation outside the Church",[4] which to most Catholics not aware of the confidence trick which has been played upon them appears to furnish an irrefutable specimen of such doctrinal development.

At this point a somewhat demanding theological discussion becomes necessary. After allowing Davies to state his doctrines in his own words, I shall be forced to set out in full the possibility – or rather impossibility – of salvation outside the Church. The demands of the topic are such as to call for heavy reliance on the most competent authorities.

Davies States His Position

Let us first consider the question of salvation outside the Church. Davies must be allowed to state his own position in his own words or in the words of whichever authors he may have chosen to make his own. For instance, Davies borrows the

---

[4] "*Extra Ecclesiam nulla salus.*"

following statement from Canon Smith's *Teaching of the Catholic Church*:

> To some that [the Catholic] Church has not been made known, to others she has been made known, but inculpably they have not recognized her for what she is. In their case we may be sure that God will take account of their good faith, of their sincere desire to please God, and will make it so that they receive grace from the life-giving Head. He will take the will for the deed, and those who are in inculpable error will be united 'by desire', though not in fact, to the visible Church of Christ. (Quoted in *Pope John's Council*, p. 173)

And on p. 142 of *Cranmer's Godly Order*, Davies says in his own words that:

> ... God is not bound by the sacramental system even though He instituted it, and .... He can and does give grace in other ways to those who do not have access to the sacraments and who have never had the saving word of faith proclaimed to them.

This may seem unclear, for Catholic theology distinguishes two kinds of grace: *actual* grace, which is a supernatural assistance given by God to enable men to do supernaturally good actions, and *sanctifying* grace, which is supernatural life itself, a share in the life of God and the necessary condition for the salvation of a man's soul. *Actual* graces are given by God to sinners and unbelievers as well as to Catholics, but *sanctifying* grace, which is obtained by the process called *justification*, is given only to one whose soul has been prepared for it by the virtues of faith and hope, and who is resolved never gravely to offend God. However, it surely seems that the grace to which Davies is referring is *sanctifying* grace rather than *actual* grace, for he indicates that it is *normally* imparted through the sacraments.

Even so it is quite true that those who do not have access to the sacraments may receive sanctifying grace through extraordinary channels. But where he is either very wrong or very misleading is in suggesting that this can apply also to those who "have never had the saving word of faith proclaimed to them." For this surely suggests either:

(a) that it is possible to be in the state of grace without possessing supernatural faith; or

(b) that the act of supernatural faith is possible "in the void" – an act of belief without any specific object and therefore made by someone who does not actually believe in anything in particular, but nonetheless earnestly believes,[5] and believes on the sole authority of God revealing, although without the slightest idea of *what* God has revealed.[6]

After an irrelevant quotation from St. John Chrysostom explaining that genuinely upright non-Catholics will all be given *the opportunity of accepting the Faith*, he informs us that "the axiom 'outside the Church there is no salvation' was well explained by Cardinal Bourne in his introduction to the Catholic Truth Society edition of Pope Pius XI's encyclical on True Religious Unity (*Mortalium Animos*)."

A Cardinal Mistake

Davies then proceeds as follows, quoting Cardinal Bourne at length:

> 'While this axiom is perfectly true,' the Cardinal explains, 'it is equally true that without the deliberate act of the will there can be neither fault nor sin, so evidently this axiom applies only to those who are outside the Church knowingly, deliberately and wilfully.'

I interrupt Davies's citation of Cardinal Bourne at this point, not to refute the cardinal's *doctrine*, which may be deferred until

---

[5] The fact that these "believers" do not actually believe anything makes it necessary to use the word "believe" here as if it were an intransitive verb. Certainly in the view of those who maintain the doctrine in question, the verb "to believe" does not need an object.

[6] Against which let us note with the *Ami du Clergé*, 1925, p. 358, that "...certain knowledge of the fact of revelation is required for the act of faith." (Cf. Denzinger Nº 1171-3.)

he has stated it fully, but to expose his defective *reasoning* before his arguments are forgotten. If we reduce the logic of the passage to syllogistic form it would be stated as follows:

A

(i)   No one can be damned without sin. But ...
(ii) non-membership of the Church is sinful only for those who know of her. Therefore ...
(iii) no one can be damned for non-membership of the Church except if his non-membership is deliberate.

B

(i)   No one can be damned for non-membership of the Church except if his non-membership is deliberate. But ...
(ii) the Church teaches that all non-members of her are damned. Therefore ...
(iii) this teaching can apply only to those who deliberately refuse to become members.

With the first syllogism, no quarrel is necessary. Both premises are indubitably true and the conclusion from them is inescapable. But the second syllogism – or rather "syllogism" – is very different matter; for it sees a contradiction where none exists. Instead of drawing a conclusion from its two premises, it uses the first to emasculate the second.

It is true that no one can be damned for not being a member of the Church unless his non-membership is culpable,[7] but there is no *logical* contradiction between this and even the most literally understood statement that there is no salvation outside the Church. If the Church taught that all who are outside her communion were damned *precisely on account of, and as a punishment for*, not being Catholics, this teaching would indeed be incompatible with there being anyone who was not a Catholic through no direct[8] fault of his own. But the doctrine that all who

---

[7] Non-membership of the Church need not always be culpable.
[8] The relevance of the word "direct" is that it could be argued – correctly – that no one dies outside the Church except *in some way* through his own

die outside the Church will be damned, prescinding entirely from the question of what sin they will be damned for leads to no such incompatibility. Hence the conclusion reached in syllogism B is entirely unwarranted by the premises and the correct conclusion should be:

> Therefore (iii) any who die outside the Church without having deliberately rejected her are damned *not* for their non-membership of the Church *but for some other sin or sins*.

While His Eminence's not very eminent grasp of dialectics is under the spotlight, it should also be remarked that his introductory disclaimer, "While this axiom is perfectly true," is disingenuous; for if we accept the interpretation he offers us, the axiom is not "perfectly true" at all; in fact, it is perfectly *false*. We are told that the axiom "applies only to those who are outside the Church *knowingly* ...", but if this is so, and if language has any meaning, how can it be truthfully stated that "outside the Church there is *no* salvation." Evidently if even *one* person could be saved outside the Church by "good faith" or similar, there *would* be salvation outside the Church, and the famous, dogmatically confirmed axiom expressly denies this.

---

fault, since it is certain that, had he corresponded with the actual grace which all men receive, the necessary means of salvation (which are to be found only in the Church) would not have been denied him. However this objection would not affect my point, because ignorance of the truths necessary to be known for salvation, on the part of one who, because of his resistance to grace, has never been enlightened as to these truths, is not so much a sin as an *effect* of sin. It is a itself a punishment for resisting grace and does not itself merit further punishment. Hence no one could be damned for failure to hold the Catholic faith if he had never had the opportunity of knowing it: he could be damned for this only if he had failed to embrace it through his *direct* fault, i.e. by refusing to comply with a recognized duty to believe it or at least to study the Church's claims. One who remains outside the Church only through his *indirect* fault, i.e. because, in view of some grave sin, Divine Providence has never enlightened him on this subject, is not guilty of the sin of unbelief and will not be punished *for this*. But he remains liable to eternal punishment for those grave sins which he *has* committed.

The fact is that *no* salvation simply *cannot* mean *some* salvation, let alone a great deal. And, even allowing for the maximum amount of interpretation and "development", to say that it is "perfectly true" that there is *no* salvation outside the Church but that this applies only to *some* non-Catholics is no better than to say that it is perfectly true that all dogs have only three legs but that this applies only to three-legged dogs.

Nor, it should be added, is the plain language in which the dogma has been expressed, and, as we shall see, has often been repeated, the only barrier frustrating those who seek a legitimate weakening of its intransigence. If "no salvation outside the Church" means only that those who deliberately fail to join the Church after recognizing their duty to join it cannot be saved, the question must arise: what difference is there, in this respect, between the Catholic Church and any of the "Christian" sects or the varieties of paganism? If a man *thought* he had a grave moral duty to become a Mahometan and refused to become one because of, say, fear or human respect, he would be guilty of mortal sin just as much as would a man who recognized the grave moral duty to become a *Catholic* but did not do so out of fear or human respect. Undoubtedly the former individual would have been mistaken in what he thought was his duty, but he would have been bound nonetheless to follow his erroneous conscience. Hence one could only conclude that on Cardinal Bourne's interpretation, the words "No salvation outside the Church" have no greater validity than the words "no salvation outside Hinduism, or Islam."

Let us return to Davies and his chosen ally Cardinal Bourne in order to let them complete their case:

> And this is the doctrine of the Catholic Church on this often misunderstood and misrepresented aphorism. There are the covenanted and the uncovenanted dealings of God with His creatures, and no creature is outside His fatherly care. There are millions – even at this day the vast majority of mankind[9] – who are

still unreached or unaffected by the message of Christianity in any shape or form. There are large numbers who are persuaded that the Old Covenant still prevails and are perfectly sincere and conscientious in the observance of the Jewish law. And there are millions who accept some form of Christian teaching who ... have no thought that they are obliged in conscience to accept the teaching and to submit to the authority of the Catholic Church. All such, whether separated wholly from acceptance of Christ and His teaching or accepting that teaching only to the extent to which they have perceived it, will be judged on their own merits ....

Hence it is clear that it is no misrepresentation to say that Davies considers

(1) that salvation is available not only to heretical and schismatical Christians,[10] but also to those "separated wholly from Christ"; and

(2) that it (salvation) is available not just potentially, on the condition that they accept Christ's revelation before death, but actually, on the grounds that they "will be judged on their own merits."

The Errors Contained in Davies's Doctrine

Having allowed Davies and his selected sources to state their position, let us now list the inescapably heretical implications[11] of this position. They are as follows:

(i) That the axiom "*extra ecclesiam nulla salus* – outside the Church no salvation" – applies not to *all* of those outside the Church, but only to those who are *culpably* outside the

---

[9] I suspect that Cardinal Bourne is exaggerating wildly in this statement.

[10] Although popular usage permits the use of this term to denote all those who claim to be Christians, or at least all those who believe in the Incarnation, the Fathers are unanimously insistent that no non-Catholic can properly be called a "Christian". (See, for instance, Salvianus, *De Providentia*, lib. IV; St. Athanasius, *Disputatio Contra Arium*; and others cited by Ven. Cardinal Baronius, *Annales Ecclesiastici, ad annum* 43.)

[11] The demonstration that they are heretical will be found beginning on p. 534.

Church. (This is expressly stated in the passage Davies quotes from Cardinal Bourne.)

(ii) That faith, understood as the Church understands it, namely as supernaturally certain belief in the revelation of Jesus Christ, is not always necessary for salvation. (In the extract cited from p. 142 of *Cranmer's Godly Order*, Davies says that sanctifying grace – the condition of salvation – is given even to those "who have never had the saving word of faith proclaimed to them;" and in his telephone debate with J.S.D. he expressly said that a woman whose last action was objectively a grave sin against the natural law of self-preservation, performed in imitation of the legendary act of one of the goddesses of the Hindu pantheon,[12] not only might, but *would* be saved. Cardinal Bourne also includes Jews among those to whom salvation is available with no change of their religious positions, together with heretics and even those "separated wholly from acceptance of Christ and His teaching" – and who are therefore of course certainly not possessed of the virtue of supernatural faith as understood by the Church.)

(iii) That those who are outside the Church in "good faith" – i.e. because they are either ignorant of her or because "inculpably they have not recognized her for what she is" – and who have a "sincere desire to please God," will *automatically* "be united by 'desire', though not in fact, to the visible Church of Christ." (*Pope John's Council*, p. 173)

(iv) That all those who have never recognized the duty of embracing the Catholic Faith "will be judged on their own merits" – i.e., it would appear, their salvation or damnation will not be affected by their non-membership of the Church or their want of Faith and will not be determined in

---

[12] "But the things which the heathens sacrifice, they sacrifice to devils, and not to God. And I would not that you should be made partakers with devils." (I Corinthians 10:20.)

accordance with their observance or otherwise of Christian standards, but will depend purely on their obedience to the erroneous dictates of their misinformed consciences. (Also stated in the passage Davies quotes from Cardinal Bourne.)

Is Invincible Ignorance Possible Where the Church Is Known?

And in addition to these four heresies there is at least one other theory which it is evident, from the quotations given, that Davies entertains, and which, though not heretical, must nonetheless be drawn to readers' attention as un-Catholic. This is the opinion that even those non-Catholics – whether pagans, Mahometans, Jews or heretics – who know of the Catholic Church, who are familiar with the central facts about her, such as her claim of infallibility, her strict moral teaching and her status as the oldest body calling itself Christian, and who could have ready access to her doctrines if they so wished, may yet be readily admitted *en bloc* to the category of those who are invincibly ignorant of her true nature and of the obligation to join her.

To appreciate that this opinion is false, it must be remembered that, because "no man lighting a candle covereth it with a vessel or putteth it under a bed; but setteth it upon a candlestick, that they who come in may see the light," (Luke 8:16) so, too, Our Divine Saviour, who "was born and ... came into the world" to "give testimony to the truth," (John 18:37) ordained that His Church, "the pillar and ground of the truth," I Timothy 3:15) be indefectibly endowed with manifest marks of her Divine mission, so that the prophecy of Isaias that the path of salvation established by the Messias would be "a straight way so that fools shall not err therein"[13] might be fulfilled. Of these marks the 1870 Vatican Council teaches us that

> all those things, so many and so wonderful, which have been Divinely disposed to the evident credibility of the Christian Faith

---

[13] Isaias 35: 8.

belong to the Catholic Church alone. Indeed the Church herself, by virtue of her wondrous propagation, outstanding holiness and inexhaustible fecundity in all good things, and on account of her Catholic unity and her unconquered stability, is a great and enduring motive of credibility and an irrefragable testimony to her Divine embassy.[14]

There is nothing, it must be stressed, in the slightest degree offensive to Catholic doctrine or to the *"sensus Catholicus"* in the belief that there are many in the world who are invincibly ignorant of the obligation to join the Catholic Church and are therefore guilty of no sin in failing to do so – provided that it is not presumed that such unfortunate individuals are somehow, by virtue of their very ignorance, in the way of salvation.[15] But every Catholic instinct must rebel at the notion that *invincible* ignorance, that is to say, ignorance which is inculpable because it is not within the *power* of the person afflicted by it to emerge from his darkness into the light of truth, is *easily and often* to be found even among those who daily confront, under some aspect or other, the Church herself – that "enduring motive of credibility and irrefragable testimony to her Divine embassy." Such a conclusion seems to defy logic, for logic denies that men can *normally* remain *invincibly* ignorant of a truth of which they see compelling evidence. It is also hard to reconcile with numerous passages of Holy Writ which condemn unbelievers and attribute men's failure to be effectively enlightened by "the true light which enlighteneth every man that cometh into this world," (John 1:9) even when they had access to this light, to

---

[14] Denzinger 1794.

[15] Whether (and if so how) any such individuals could be saved without obtaining knowledge of the Church will be considered in greater detail later in this section; but what is beyond question is that invincible ignorance of the Church certainly has no salvific value in itself and that the savages of Papua New Guinea are not excused from the obligations of Faith, Hope and Charity as a condition of their salvation simply because the name of Jesus Christ may be unknown to them, nor from the obligation of perfect contrition if they should commit grave sin.

the fact that "every one that doth evil hateth the light, and cometh not to the light, that his works may not be reproved." (John 3:20)

Hence when the Second Vatican Council proposed endorsing this generalized presumption of good faith among non-Catholics, one of the Council's most acute theologians, Bishop Antonio de Castro Mayer, consistently protested, remarking, for instance:

> It ought not be thought ... that men can ordinarily be outside the way of salvation without any fault.[16]

And again :

> But the divine law is that all should embrace the true faith and enter the true Church and to achieve this God comes to the help of all by his grace in such a way that no one is damned without his own fault.[17]

Similarly the renowned moral theologian Fr. Claudius Lacroix S.J. (1642-1714), in his *Theologia Moralis* ("*De Fide*", Q. 21), observes that those who deny that there are any heretics in Germany who are only materially such, have good reason for doing so: "The heretics in Germany know of our faith," he points out;

> and they cannot or dare not claim that it is *plainly* false, but must rather judge that it is at least the more probable, since if they consider the arguments they cannot have evidence of credibility in favour of their faith. They must therefore doubt of theirs and examine ours, which, however, they do not do, because if they examined and studied the notes of the true Church and considered impartially whether they are found in their Church or in ours, they would discover that they patently support ours and not theirs. So the fact that they do not acknowledge this is due to their failure to make the enquiry they are bound to. Hence their ignorance is vincible and culpable and they are not excused from formal heresy. Nor can it be

---

[16] *Acta Synodalia*, Vol. II-V, p. 784.
[17] *Ibid*. III-II, p. 485. See also III-III, p. 161.

suggested that the idea that they are bound to this enquiry does not occur to them. The very opposite is true, for there can be *no one* who is not moved to initiate such an enquiry by the inspiration of God or by instinct or an inner scruple.

And in consequence of this, Lacroix concludes that any material heretics – i.e. any heretics whose ignorance of the true Faith was genuinely invincible – in a country such as Germany could be found only among the very simple. He also points out that even any who *are* in a state of invincible ignorance are *not*, however, in the way of salvation, though, if they were sedulously to obey their consciences throughout their lives, they would be brought to it.

But the central question is not whether non-Catholics may be invincibly ignorant, but whether they may be *saved*. Now that Davies has had his say, let us allow the Church to have hers, speaking exclusively through her Magisterium. The following passages are furnished without commentary, their clarity making further explanation unnecessary.

The Catholic Church States Her Position

(i) The Fourth Lateran Council (1215) declared in its definition "*Firmiter*" that:

There is one universal Church of the faithful, *outside of which no one at all can be saved* .... (Denzinger 430)

(ii) Pope Boniface VIII in his bull *Unam Sanctam* (1302) declares:

At the instance of faith, we are bound to believe and hold the one holy Catholic and Apostolic Church, and her we do firmly believe and simply confess, *outside of which there is neither salvation nor remission of sins* .... Hence we declare, say, define and pronounce that it is absolutely necessary for the salvation of every human creature that he be subject to the Roman Pontiff. (Denzinger 468, 469)

(iii) In its decree *Cantate Domino* for the Jacobites, the Council of Florence (1439) pronounced as follows:

> The most Holy Roman Church firmly believes, professes and preaches that *none of those who are outside the Catholic Church – not only pagans, but also Jews or heretics and schismatics – can have a share in life eternal*; but that they will go into the eternal fire which was prepared for the devil and his angels, unless before death they are joined with her; and that so important is the unity of the ecclesiastical body that only those remaining in her can profit unto salvation by the Sacraments of the Church, and that they alone will receive eternal rewards for their fasting and almsgiving, their works of piety and exercises of Christian soldiery; and that no one, no matter how great his almsgiving, and even if he shed his blood for the name of Christ, can be saved unless he remain within the bosom and unity of the Catholic Church.

(iv) In its decree on Original Sin (17th June 1536), the Council of Trent referred, in its opening words, to

> ...our Catholic Faith, without which it is impossible to please God. (Denzinger 789)

– an authoritative interpretation of St. Paul's affirmation that "without faith it is impossible to please God." (Hebrews 11:6)

(v) In his encyclical *Mirari Vos* of 1832, Pope Gregory XVI wrote the following:

> We are now proceeding against another exceedingly fertile cause of the evils by which we grieve to see the Church afflicted at present, namely indifferentism: i.e. that perverse opinion, which is everywhere gaining ground thanks to the wiles of evil men, according to which the eternal salvation of the soul can be obtained by the profession of any faith provided that the norm of upright and decent morals be observed .... (Denzinger 1613)

(vi) In his encyclical *Quanto Conficiamur* (1863), Pope Pius IX speaks as follows:

> But here ... it is necessary once more to mention and reprehend a most grave error by which some Catholics are wretchedly deluded – namely, those who think that men living in errors and as strangers to the true Faith and Catholic unity can arrive at

eternal life. Nothing indeed could be more opposed to Catholic doctrine. (Denzinger 1677)

(vii) The same pontiff in his *Syllabus of Errors* (1864) condemned the proposition that "men in any religion can find the path of, and arrive at, eternal salvation." (Denzinger 1716)

(viii) And the following protest is taken from Pope Pius XII's encyclical *Humani Generis* (1950):

Some reduce to a meaningless formula the necessity of belonging to the true Church in order to gain eternal salvation.

These statements of the Magisterium could be supplemented by many others, as well as by the unanimous voice of Holy Scripture, the Fathers, the Doctors and the saints. The doctrine thus taught, *without the smallest degree of equivocation or ambiguity*, is:

(a) that it is absolutely impossible to be saved, to have one's sins forgiven, or even to please God at all, except when united by faith to the unity of the Catholic Church and in submission to the legitimate Roman Pontiff; and

(b) that this doctrine is so firm and universal that it admits of not even a single exception – not even in the case of those who lay down their lives for Christ in a "Christian" sect.

Readers are unlikely to disagree with the above summary of the doctrine of the Magisterium on this point; for the wording of the texts is sufficient to dispel all doubt for anyone who is prepared to accept them at face value without attempting to force upon them a quite unnatural "interpretation" – or rather falsification – in order to make them accord better with what seems appropriate to him or with what he has learnt from some second-rate catechism or explanation of Catholic doctrine put together by a popularizing author rather than by a theologian of real status and merit.[18]

---

[18] Some catechisms explain this dogma better than others. Cardinal Gasparri's *The Catholic Catechism* is particularly commendable.

However it must also be made clear that these texts of the Magisterium *do not represent the complete picture*, in that a subtle theological distinction must be made before it is possible to attain a thorough understanding of how the conditions necessary for salvation may be fulfilled in practice even in exceptional situations.

Three Quite Recent Statements of the Magisterium

There have been three texts of the Magisterium[19] which, *without contradicting the other texts, or restricting the universality of their application, or even modifying their natural meaning in the slightest degree,* have nevertheless gone further than them, in broaching two subjects not expressly addressed in those earlier decrees:

(a) the reconciliation, in a manner consonant with the perfect justice of God, of the dogma that there is no salvation outside the Church with the existence of men who are invincibly and therefore inculpably ignorant of the existence of this Church, and/or of the obligation of joining her; and

(b) the exact borderline between those who are considered to be *inside* the Church, and those who are considered to be *outside* her, according to the terms of the dogma.

Long before the Magisterium had addressed these topics, some theological writers who had taken it upon themselves to address them and had reached conclusions concerning them that were simply incompatible with the dogmatic teaching of the Church already quoted. It was to correct such errors – many of them actually heretical – that the Magisterium intervened and pointed out the correct limits of orthodoxy on these questions; but, alas!, these very interventions, whether because they were studied only superficially or because they were consciously

---

[19] Excluding, of course, the irrelevant pronouncements of the Conciliar Church which readily admit salvation outside the Church.

distorted, were seized on by the liberals, the minimizers, the indifferentists, as confirmations of the very errors they had set out to correct! Although no excuse can be made to exonerate those who thus abused the teaching of the Church, it must certainly be admitted that these statements of the Magisterium contain delicate theological nuances, and that to be properly understood they must be read attentively and thoughtfully, preferably with the assistance of some trustworthy theological work specifically considering this topic.

The first of these pronouncements is Pope Pius IX's allocution *Singulari Quadam*, delivered on 9th December 1854, of which I shall quote, and then analyse, the relevant section:

> Not without sorrow have we learnt that another error, no less lethal [than the rationalistic error he has been condemning in the previous paragraphs], has taken possession of some parts of the Catholic world and lodged itself in the minds of many Catholics who think there to be good hope for the eternal salvation of all those who are by no means within the true Church of Christ ['*qui in vera Christi Ecclesia nequaquam versantur*']. For this reason they constantly wonder about the fate and condition after death of those who were not attached ['*addicti*'] to the Catholic Faith, and, convinced by arguments of not the slightest force, they await a response from us in favour of this perverse notion. (...) As our Apostolic office requires, we wish your episcopal solicitude and vigilance to be aroused so that, as far as you can, you may drive out of men's minds this opinion, no less impious than deadly, that the path of eternal salvation can be found in any religion. Use all the skill and learning at your disposal to show to the people committed to your care that these dogmas of the Catholic Faith are by no means opposed to the Divine mercy and justice.
>
> It must be held by faith that no one can be saved outside the Apostolic Roman Church, that this Church is the sole ark of salvation, and that whosoever does not enter her shall perish in the flood; but it must also be held as certain that those who are ignorant of the true religion, if their ignorance be invincible, are subject to no guilt on this account in the eyes of the Lord. But who would claim the ability to designate the limits of such ignorance in

accordance with the nature and variety of peoples, religions, characters and of so many other things? (Denzinger 1646-7)

Such are the words of Pope Pius IX on the topic we are examining, words which, according to Mgr. Joseph C. Fenton, "have all too frequently been misinterpreted by Catholic writers who have examined them superficially." (*The Catholic Church and Salvation*, p. 42)

The Doctrine of "Singulari Quadam"

Mgr. Fenton's credentials as a theologian are irreproachable. He was a Doctor of Sacred Theology and a Bachelor of Canon Law; he was professor of theology in several seminaries and at the Catholic University of America; he was editor of the *American Ecclesiastical Review*; and he was Secretary of the Catholic Theology Society of America, member of the Pontifical Roman Theological Academy, and Adviser to the Sacred Congregation for Seminaries and Universities. Nor could any reader of his excellent book *The Catholic Church and Salvation in the Light of Recent Pronouncements by the Holy See* deny that the various accolades he has thus received from the Church were well merited. Let us therefore allow him to guide us to a correct understanding of Pope Pius IX's words.[20]

> The basic thesis of *Singulari Quadam* is the assertion that the teaching 'no one can be saved outside the Apostolic Roman Church' is a dogma of the Faith. It is something to which the assent of faith itself must be given. As such, it is of course completely infallible. It is something which can never be corrected or modified. It must be received as an absolutely true proposition.
> It is interesting, incidentally, to note that Pope Pius IX was faced with a situation quite similar to that which Pope Pius XII described when he wrote his encyclical *Humani Generis* in August 1950. The attack on the dogma of the Church's necessity for salvation a

---

[20] In this and other extracts from Mgr. Fenton shortly to be quoted, I have occasionally taken the liberty of adjusting his sometimes eccentric punctuation and of adding emphases.

hundred years ago was not conducted by men who presumed to deny or to suppress the statement that there is no salvation outside the Church. Their tactic was much more subtle and dangerous: they tried to empty this statement of all real meaning. They tried to make Catholics believe that there was some hope of salvation for people who had never entered the Church in any way. *Singulari Quadam* characterizes this contention as a ruinous error.

Pope Pius XII dealt with a similar situation when he condemned the efforts of those teachers who were trying to reduce the teaching that the Church is necessary for the attainment of eternal salvation 'to an empty formula.'[21] Pius IX worked in this direction when he condemned the teaching that there is some hope for the salvation of men who have in no way entered the true Church of Jesus Christ.

Those who taught inaccurately about the necessity of the Church for salvation a century ago used still another tactic. They tried to make it appear that there was something unjust about this basic Catholic teaching. They claimed, directly or by implication, that there was some contradiction between this dogma and the assertions of the Faith which teach us that God is all-just and all-merciful. The allocution *Singulari Quadam* deals with this manoeuvre also.

A Crucial Distinction

Thus far, Mgr. Fenton's explanation will merely have expressed more clearly, and given the historical context of, what no reader of the text could have failed to note. But now he discusses that part of the text in which some readers have claimed to see a modification of the universality of the dogma excluding non-Catholics from salvation, namely the section concerning invincible ignorance; and it is here that Fenton's exegesis is of the highest importance.

> As part of their tactic, the opponents of the true Catholic teaching tried to make it appear that a genuine acceptance of the dogma that there is no salvation outside the Church implied the teaching that God would punish men for being invincibly ignorant of the true Church. Pope Pius IX set out to meet this contention also in

---

[21] In the encyclical *Humani Generis*.

Singulari Quadam. He stated simply that it is certain Catholic truth that God will blame no man for invincible ignorance of the Catholic Church, any more than He will blame anyone for invincible ignorance of anything else.

Incidentally, on this point, there have been Catholic writers who have been led astray by an incomplete translation of this portion of *Singulari Quadam*. The allocution says that people who are invincibly ignorant of the true religion 'will never be charged with any guilt *on this account* before the eyes of the Lord.' The Latin text reads ' ... *qui veræ religionis ignorantiam laborent, si ea sit invincibilis, nulla ipsos obstringi* **huiusce rei** *culpa ante oculos Domini.*' Some persons have attempted a translation of this passage which takes no account of the words '*huiusce rei*'. Such translations tend to present invincible ignorance of the true religion as a sort of sacrament, since they make it appear that the Sovereign Pontiff taught that persons invincibly ignorant of the true religion are simply not blameworthy in the eyes of the Lord.

The fact of the matter is (and this is the gist of the teaching of Pope Pius IX here and in the encyclical *Quanto Conficiamur Mærore*) that non-appurtenance to the Catholic Church is by no means the only reason why men are deprived of the Beatific Vision. Ultimately, the only fact that will exclude a man from the eternal and supernatural enjoyment of God in Heaven is sin, either original or mortal .... Any man who dies after having attained the use of reason and who is eternally excluded from the Beatific Vision is being punished for actual mortal sin which he has committed. (...)

It is perfectly possible for a man to die 'outside' the true Church and to be excluded from the Beatific Vision forever without having his ignorance of the true Church or of the true religion counted as a moral fault. That is precisely what Pope Pius IX said in *Singulari Quadam*. He said it, as the context shows, as part of his explanation of the fact that the Catholic dogma of the Church's necessity for the attainment of eternal salvation in no way involves a contradiction of the doctrines about God's sovereign mercy and justice. (Emphasis added)

In other words, Pope Pius IX would indeed have been modifying the dogma "no salvation outside the Church" if he had taught that those who are invincibly ignorant of the duty to join the Catholic Church could be saved without joining her. But popes *cannot* modify dogmas, and those who believe that he said this are simply reading what they *think* the pope *ought* to have said rather than what he *actually* said; for in reality his doctrine is simply that those who are invincibly ignorant of the Catholic Church will not be damned *for failing to join her*. But this in no way alters the fact that *unless* they enter her they *will* be lost for some *other* grave sin or sins which they have committed.

At this point the retort may occur to some readers that this does not explain the case of anyone who is invincibly ignorant of the Catholic religion and nonetheless carefully avoids mortal sins throughout his life. To such an objection I make no response at this point, as it will be considered very fully when we look at the next statement of the Magisterium advanced by the minimizers of the doctrine "*extra ecclesiam nulla salus*". But first it is worth reproducing one more part of Mgr. Fenton's commentary on *Singulari Quadam*:

> In this section of *Singulari Quadam* Pope Pius IX goes on to urge the bishops of the Catholic Church to use all of their energies to drive from the minds of men the deadly error that the way of salvation can be found in any religion. To a certain extent this is a mere restatement of the erroneous opinion according to which we may well hope for the salvation of men who have never entered in any way into the Catholic Church, the first misinterpretation of Catholic teaching reproved in this section of the allocution. Yet, in another way, the error that the way of salvation can be found in any religion has its own peculiar and individual malignity. It is based on the false implication that the false religions, those other than the Catholic, are in some measure a partial approach to the fullness of truth which is to be found in Catholicism. According to this doctrinal aberration, the Catholic religion would be distinct from others, not as the true is distinguished from the false, but only as the plenitude is distinct from incomplete participations of itself. It is this notion, the idea that all other religions contain enough of the

essence of that completeness – of truth – which is to be found in Catholicism, to make them vehicles of eternal salvation, which is thus reproved in the *Singulari Quadam*.[22]

So what of writers such as Fr. Nicholas Russo S.J., who, in his *The True Religion and its Dogmas*, asserts of one who is outside the Catholic Church in good faith and observes the natural law that "Heaven will be his home for all eternity," and appeals to the very words of *Singulari Quadam* that we have been looking at in support of this assertion? Mgr. Fenton has surely now said enough to show that such writers have not a leg to stand on.

Indeed he has said enough to confirm the opinion of Fr. Michael Mueller[23] that Fr. Russo by his scandalous words placed himself firmly in the category of those whose behaviour Pope Pius IX had deplored in his allocution dated 17th December 1847 when he indignantly exclaimed that:

> Quite recently – we shudder to say it – certain men have not hesitated to slander us by saying that we share in their folly, favour that most wicked system, and think so benevolently of every class of mankind as to suppose that not only the sons of the Church, but that the rest also, however alienated from Catholic unity they may remain, are alike in the way of salvation, and may arrive at everlasting life. We are at a loss from horror to find words to express our detestation of this new and atrocious injustice that is done to us.

The Doctrine of "Quanto Conficiamur Mærore"

Bearing these words in mind, let us now turn to the second magisterial pronouncement touching on the question of invincible ignorance in relation to the dogma that membership of the Church is universally necessary for salvation. This second one is also taken from Pope Pius IX, and it too has been seized

---

[22] *The Catholic Church and Salvation in the Light of Recent Pronouncements by the Holy See* by Mgr. Joseph C. Fenton J.C.B., S.T.D., although out of print, is easily obtainable.

[23] *The Catholic Dogma*, pp. 215-6.

upon by certain individuals – among them the far from dependable Cardinal Newman[24] – as evidence that, despite his protests to the contrary, Pope Pius IX did indeed believe that those "alienated from Catholic unity ... may arrive at everlasting life." The pronouncement in question occurs in the encyclical *Quanto Conficiamur Mœrore,* and reproducing it will entail repetition of another part of this encyclical which was already quoted earlier.

> And here, our beloved sons and venerable brethren, we must once more mention and condemn the exceedingly grave error by which some Catholics are deceived who think that men living in errors and separately from the true Faith and Catholic unity can attain to eternal life. Nothing indeed could be more opposed to Catholic doctrine. It is known to us and to you that those who labour in invincible ignorance of our most holy religion and who lead a good and upright life, carefully observing the natural law and its precepts which God has engraved on the hearts of all, being ready to obey God, can, by operation of Divine light and grace, obtain eternal life; since God, Who plainly beholds, examines and knows the minds, spirits, thoughts and habits of all, in accordance with His supreme goodness and clemency, does not allow anyone to be punished with eternal torments who has no guilt of voluntary sin. But the Catholic dogma is also very well known that no one outside the Catholic Church can be saved, and that those who stubbornly oppose the authority and definitions of the Church and are obstinately divided from the unity of the Church and from the successor of Peter, the Roman pontiff, to whom the custody of the vineyard has been entrusted by the Saviour, cannot obtain eternal salvation. (Denzinger 1677)

---

[24] Mgr. Fenton characterizes Newman's "interpretation" of *Quanto Conficiamur* (in his *Letter to the Duke of Norfolk*) as "probably the least felicitous pages of all his published works." To which I need only add that readers of Cardinal Lépicier's *De Stabilitate et Progressu Dogmatis* or of Richard Sartino's *Another Look at John Henry Cardinal Newman* would know that there are very many pages of Newman's writings indeed that rival those selected by Mgr. Fenton for this dubious distinction.

An Apparent Contradiction

It will be noted at once that Pope Pius IX repeatedly insists in this extract on the dogma that "no one outside the Catholic Church can be saved," and even tells us that "nothing could be more opposed to Catholic doctrine" than the "exceedingly grave error ... that men living in errors and separately from the true Faith and Catholic unity can attain to eternal life." And yet, not only does he assure us – as he had done also in *Singulari Quadam* – that no one is damned except for wilful sin, but this time he goes further still: he specifically envisages the possibility of salvation for some of those who are in invincible ignorance of the Catholic Church and comply with a number of other (admittedly demanding) conditions, without stating, and indeed by implication denying, that their invincible ignorance would have to be removed, before death, by their discovery of and admission into the Catholic Church, for their salvation to be obtained. However, he does not suggest that this possibility is an *exception* to the dogma; on the contrary, immediately after mentioning it he repeats the dogma just as firmly and exclusively as before.

What s to be made of this? Are we to believe that Pope Pius IX inadvertently contradicted himself, insistently proclaiming in the course of a single paragraph two mutually exclusive propositions, namely that no non-Catholics at all can be saved, but that some of them nevertheless can be – or perhaps that he was contradicting, not himself, but the dictionary, interpreting the word "none" to mean "some" and the word "never" to mean "sometimes"? Evidently no loyal Catholic can entertain either suggestion for a moment; and attentive perusal of the text will obviate any need to do so, for it will bring to light the fact that, precisely where our text superficially appears to be most paradoxical, it clearly points out for us the nature of the reconciliation needed between its two seemingly conflicting parts.

First, who are those whom Pope Pius IX indicates may be saved despite "invincible ignorance" of our most holy religion? Certainly not *all* those who are invincibly ignorant, for he lays down a number of other stringent requirements also. The individual in question must:

(a) be invincibly ignorant of the Catholic religion;

(b) carefully observe the natural law – i.e. the duty to do good and avoid evil as recognized by the light of reason;

(c) also observe "its precepts" – i.e. all those specific obligations of the natural law which are known to all men who have not stamped out the light of conscience within themselves: the obligation to adore one's Maker, not to steal or commit murder, to reserve carnal pleasure for its proper place within wedlock and without deliberate frustration of its natural fecundity, always to tell the truth – and many, many other obligations, the existence of which have been known to even uninstructed barbarians and which no one has ever in good conscience denied to exist;

(d) "lead a good and upright life" – i.e. not only observe the minimum standards known to all, but also strive to inform and obey his conscience with regard to his every action; and

(e) be "ready to obey God" – i.e. in addition to doing all that he already knows or believes to be right, he must be disposed to do whatever God should make known to him as His Will.

But the next point is the crucial one. Does the pope teach that those who comply with these conditions are *already by that very fact* in the way of salvation and that they will, provided they persevere in these admirable dispositions until death, be admitted without further ado to paradise? If so, it must frankly be admitted that he is granting in one sentence what he denies in the next. Indeed he would be making the beatific vision a reward for purely natural virtue containing no necessarily supernatural element. But this is not what the encyclical states at all. It asserts only that such a person "*can* obtain eternal life," but only by the intervention of a further factor, referred to in the essential phrase, "by operation of Divine light and grace". In other words, while the individuals described have by no personal act merited damnation, their salvation yet depends on a further specific divine intervention to raise them from natural virtue to supernatural life.

What is the nature of this Divine intervention? How will "Divine light and grace" operate to achieve the justification and salvation of a person who, despite excellent dispositions, is invincibly ignorant of the revealed faith held by the Catholic Church, outside of which, the pope repeatedly assures us, "*no one ... can be saved*"?

It is evident from the significance of the metaphor, "light", meaning supernatural faith or knowledge selected, that in some way God would enlighten such an individual as Pope Pius IX has described in order to ensure that he possessed both the requisite knowledge and the requisite actual grace to make the indispensable act of supernatural faith and the other necessary acts (of hope, charity, and, where necessary, perfect contrition) to entitle him to be numbered among the children of the Church, which is an essentially supernatural society, even if he remained in practice invincibly ignorant of almost everything pertaining to the Church herself.

He would therefore be saved just as a dying tribesman would be saved who was met by missionaries so shortly before his death that they had time only to teach him those doctrines necessary for salvation – the existence of God the Creator and Rewarder, the Blessed Trinity, the Incarnation and Redemption,[25] Heaven and Hell, the duties of faith, hope, charity and contrition – before baptizing him, without ever mentioning the Church herself because they knew that the catechumen was so disposed

---

[25] The Church has not condemned those theologians who in recent centuries have suggested the hypothesis that explicit belief in the Trinity and the Incarnation may not in all circumstances be necessary, but the contrary is the better supported view.

as *implicitly* to accept the whole of Divine revelation and was therefore undoubtedly united to the Church of which he knew nothing *explicitly*.

Extraordinary Means of Supernatural Enlightenment

Quanto Conficiamur does not address the question of how this enlightenment might be achieved beyond implying that it need not be by the normal and natural means of contact with the human missionary. But St. Thomas Aquinas goes rather further in his *Quæstiones Disputatæ*, "De Veritate", question 14, article 11, in treating the question of whether it is necessary for salvation to have *explicit* faith[26] – i.e. to believe particular, known doctrines rather than to accept, in a general way, "whatever God has revealed" or some similar formula, without actual knowledge of *what* has been revealed – a question which he answers affirmatively. In accordance with his usual practice, he begins by citing the strongest arguments he can think of *against* his position. Here is how he expresses the argument allegedly showing that there is *no* obligation for faith to be explicit:

> It seems that it is *not* necessary to believe explicitly. For nothing should be accepted, from the acceptance of which something inappropriate would follow. But if we accept that it is necessary to salvation that something be believed explicitly, something inappropriate *would* follow. For someone might have been reared in the woods, or among wolves; and such a one cannot know explicitly anything of faith, so that thus there would be a man who would necessarily be damned – which is inappropriate; hence it does not seem to be necessary to believe anything explicitly.

---

[26] The question of course is not whether it is necessarily to have *explicit* faith in the *whole* of divine revelation, which would be absurd (although some spectacularly ignorant Feeneyites have claimed it), but whether it is necessary to have explicit faith in at least *some essential parts* of it, believing the rest with merely implicit faith, i.e. the general intention to believe what God has revealed.

No doubt if Michael Davies or Cardinal Bourne had encountered that passage without being aware of its provenance, they would have felt deep sympathy with its author. They could hardly have put the argument better themselves, they might have thought ... – until they were apprised that St. Thomas was merely stating their position for them in order to demolish it. For here is his *reply* to the same argument:

> The answer to the first argument is that *nothing* inappropriate follows from acceptance of the fact that everyone is bound to believe something explicitly, even someone reared in the woods or among brute animals; for it belongs to Divine Providence to provide everyone with what is necessary for his salvation, provided that he on his part place no obstruction in the way. For if anyone thus bought up were to follow the guidance of natural reason in seeking good and shunning evil, it must be held most certainly that God would reveal to him even by an internal inspiration those things which are necessary to be believed, or would direct some preacher of the Faith to him, as he sent Peter to Cornelius. (Acts 10)

Thus in a single terse paragraph St. Thomas unravels a great part of the mystery. Some things indeed must be believed explicitly for salvation, but Divine Providence will "most certainly" ensure that these things are made known before his death to anyone who (a) has been invincibly ignorant of them, but (b) has fulfilled the conditions enumerated by Pope Pius IX to entitle him to receive this knowledge. In the normal order of His Providence this takes place by the arrival of some missionary to instruct the disposed individual, as Peter instructed Cornelius. But extraordinarily it could be done, to use Pope Pius IX's phrase, "by operation of Divine light and grace", or, in St. Thomas's words, "by an internal inspiration." And in this latter, extraordinary case, the inspiration, the supernatural instruction in question, may well be limited only to those truths which are absolutely necessary for salvation, no enlightenment being given about the Church herself, as the individual being instructed will have no opportunity to be formally received into her or to take advantage of her assistance in the path of salvation. Hence he will remain, at least to a great extent, invincibly ignorant of the Church and will still be numbered among those whom Pope Pius IX designates as labouring in "invincible ignorance of our most holy religion". But he will nonetheless, by faith and desire, be *inside* and not *outside* the supernatural society of which he knows little or nothing.

For the Church's children include, not only those whose attachment to her is formally accomplished, i.e. her baptized members, but also those who have merely a "virtual" membership effected by their desire to join her; and although this desire would be explicit in the case of catechumens, it might also be implicit in the case, perhaps, of some uneducated savage, raised in the woods among brute animals, who has ever striven to follow his conscience and has been found worthy to receive supernatural enlightenment from God. And in such a case as this last one, even an implicit desire will be taken as sufficient for the person in question to be included *within* the Church, insofar as she is the one ark of salvation, rather than outside her, despite the fact that only formal affiliation would be sufficient to allow him to take public advantage of the spiritual benefits she offers.

By contrast, if anyone who was invincibly ignorant of the Church did *not* receive before his death any enlightenment, by natural or supernatural means, enabling him to make the absolutely-necessary-for-salvation act of explicit supernatural faith, we may be sure that his ignorance of what had to be believed for the salvation of his soul was due to no defect in the perfection of God's providence, but rather to his having set his will, not upon union with God, but in defiance of the tenets of the natural law made known to him by his conscience. Hence Fr. Claudius Lacroix S.J. writes that "the faithlessness of those who have heard nothing of the Faith [not even from 'internal inspiration'] ... is not a sin, but the *penalty of sin*; because if they had done what lay within their power, God would not have concealed the faith from them." (*Theologia Moralis*, "*De Fide*", cap. 5, dub. 1.)

Concrete Examples

At this point let us allow Fr. Michael Müller to recount for us two occasions when Divine Providence has intervened – once by entirely supernatural means and once by means partly natural and partly supernatural – to bring knowledge of saving faith to souls who were invincibly ignorant of it:

> Among the holy souls of past centuries who have been loaded with signal favours and privileges by Almighty God, we must place, in the first rank, Mary of Jesus, often styled of Agreda, from the name of the place in Spain where she passed her life. The celebrated J. Goerres, in his grand work, *Mysticism*, does not hesitate to cite as an example the life of Mary of Agreda in a chapter entitled 'The Culminating Point of Christian Mysticism'. Indeed, there could not be found a more perfect model of the highest mystic ways.
>
> This holy virgin burned with a most ardent love for God and for the salvation of souls. One day, she beheld in a vision all the nations of the world. She saw how the greater part of men were deprived of God's grace and running headlong to everlasting perdition. She saw how the Indians of Mexico put fewer obstacles to the grace of conversion than any other nation who were out of the Catholic Church, and how God, on this account, was ready to show mercy to them. Hence she redoubled her prayers and penances to obtain for them the grace of conversion. God heard her prayers. He commanded her to teach the Catholic religion to those Mexican Indians. From that time, she appeared, by way of bilocation, to the savages not less than five hundred times, instructing them in all the truths of our holy religion, and performing miracles in confirmation of these truths. When all were converted to the Faith, she told them that religious priests would be sent by God to receive them into the Church by Baptism. As she had told, so it happened. God, in his mercy, sent to these good Indians several Franciscan fathers, who were greatly astonished when they found those savages fully instructed in the Catholic doctrine. When they asked the Indians who had instructed them, they were told that a holy virgin appeared

among them many times, and taught them the Catholic religion and confirmed it by miracles.' (*Life of the Venerable Mary of Jesus of Agreda*, XII) Thus those good Indians were brought miraculously to the knowledge of the true religion in the Catholic Church, because they followed their conscience in observing the natural law.

Something similar is related in the life of Father J. Anchieta S.J. (chap. VI). One day, this great man of God entered the woods of Itannia, in Brazil, without any assignable motive, and, in fact, as if he were guided by another. At a little distance he perceived an old man seated on the ground and leaning against a tree. 'Hasten your steps,' cried the old man when he saw the father, 'for I have been expecting you for some time.' The saintly missionary asked him who he was, and from what country he had come. 'My country,' said the old man, 'is beyond the sea.' He added other things, which led the father to infer that he had come from a distant province, near Rio de la Plata, and that he had either been conveyed by supernatural means from his own country to the place where he then was, or that, by the direction and guidance of Heaven, he had been led thither with great labour and fatigue, and had placed himself where the father found him, in full expectation of the accomplishment of the Divine promise. Father Anchieta then asked him why he had come to that place. 'I have come hither,' he answered, 'in order that I may be taught *the right path*.' This is the expression which the Brazilians use when they speak of the laws of God and of the way to Heaven. Father Anchieta felt convinced, from the answers of the old man, that he had never had more than one wife, had never taken up arms except in his own just defence, and that he had never grievously transgressed the law of nature. He perceived, moreover, from the arguments of the old man, that he knew many truths relative to the Author of nature, to the soul, and to virtue and vice. When Father Anchieta had explained to him several of the mysteries of our holy religion, he said: 'It is thus that I have hitherto understood them, but I knew not how to define them.' After having sufficiently instructed the old man, Father Anchieta collected some rain-water from the leaves of the wild thistles, baptized him, and named him Adam. The new disciple of Christ immediately experienced in his soul the holy effects of Baptism. He raised his eyes and hands to Heaven, and thanked

Almighty God for the mercy which he had bestowed upon him. Soon after, he expired in the arms of Father Anchieta, who buried him according to the ceremonies of the Church. (*The Catholic Dogma*, pp. 221-3)

Religious Error and Supernatural Faith

We have seen that true, salvific supernatural faith may, exceptionally, as a result of special inward or outward enlightenment, be found among some of those who are in good faith ignorant of the true Church, the bulk of her doctrines and the duty to join her. But ignorance is not error. Further difficulties undoubtedly arise when we seek to reassure ourselves that saving faith may also be found among those who are not merely ignorant of these things but positively believe falsehood about them. The difficulty is certainly not insuperable when the error is not *directly* opposed *either* to the minimum doctrines that must be believed with explicit faith *or* to the nature of the act of faith itself.

But where does this leave "Evangelical" Protestants, with their fanatical insistence that the only "faith" they have, need or want is not certitude of divine revelation, but certitude of their own salvation ? And where does it leave those who positively adhere to pagan religions, offering a multitude of divinities, like Hinduism, or no real divinity at all, like Buddhism?

Once again, the essential point is that *faith* is absolutely necessary for salvation, in accordance with St. Paul's dictum that "without faith it is impossible to please God," (Hebrews 11:6) and with the Council of Trent's explicit interpretation of this as referring to the *Catholic* Faith – "our Catholic Faith, without which it is impossible to please God" (Denzinger 789)

Ordinarily speaking the assent of "Evangelical" Protestants to Divinely revealed truths is essentially different from supernatural faith in that supernatural faith is a firm assent of the intellect, commanded by the will and assisted by actual grace, to that which the intellect, in the light of objective evidence, perceives to have been revealed by Almighty God. Instead of which "Evangelicals" use the term "faith" to denote their trust that, because they "accept Jesus as their Saviour," their sins will not be imputed to them. And this ludicrous triumph of wishful thinking has no salvific value whatever and indeed is tantamount to the sin of presumption – an unforgivable blasphemy against the Holy Ghost, as our Catholic catechisms brand it.

When it comes to their adherence to specific points of revealed doctrine, the "faith" of many "*non*-evangelical" Protestants today lacks even the essential characteristic of firmness, since most of those who still "believe" in the Incarnation and the Resurrection, for instance, regard this merely as a personal opinion rather than divinely certain. But even where there are Protestants who believe in certain Christian doctrines with a certain assent, their assent is by no means necessarily supernatural faith. On the one hand very commonly they have *not* perceived that these doctrines have in fact been revealed by God. And on the other hand they obstinately deny many points which God has very clearly revealed.[27]

It would be tedious to rehearse at length the various pronouncements of the Magisterium explaining the nature of true supernatural faith in terms sharply incompatible with the assent actually given by the mass of Protestants to such truths as they accept, and fortunately there is no need, for Denzinger's *Enchiridion Symbolorum* not only lists nearly all dogmatic pronouncements of the Magisterium but is also equipped with a "Systematic Index of Dogmatic and Moral Matters" offering a terse summary of all the principal facts about each doctrine taught by the Magisterium, systematically arranged, and followed, in each case, by the numerical references to those decrees in which the relevant doctrine is taught. Here are a few

---

[27] Probably no doctrine is taught in the New Testament so explicitly, repeatedly and emphatically as the Real Presence of Our Lord in the Eucharist.

significant extracts from it, together with the reference numbers to facilitate reference to the original decrees:

> Faith is not a religious feeling 2074 *et seq.*; but an intellectual assent 426, 798, 1789, 1791, 1814, 2145; a supernatural principle of knowledge 1789, 1795, 1814; but an act produced by the creature, not merely infused by God 1242; distinct from natural knowledge 1656, 1811 .... It is not a blind assent 1625, 1637, 1790 *et seq.*, 1812; or contrary to reason 1797 *et seq.*, 1915; but above reason 1649, 1671 *et seq.*, 1796 *et seq.* .... In fine it is an assent which is certain, infallible and immutable, based on a motive which is not an accumulation of probabilities 2025; nor anyone's private experience 2081; but the authority of God revealing 723, 1637 *et seq.*, 1656, 1789 *et seq.* ... What is called 'fiduciary faith' [i.e. the trust of Protestants that they will be saved] is not true justifying faith 802, 822 *et seq.*, 851, 922, 1383 .... Divine revelation demands a faith which is internal 1637, 1681 ... and Divine (i.e. given on account of the authority of God revealing) 1789 *et seq.*, 1811 ... Faith requires that revelations have been previously made 1622, 1650 and been known by the use of reason 1068, 1626, 1651 ... Knowledge [of the fact of revelation] does not suffice if it is only probable 1171; or merely subjective ... 1273; nor does a mere internal experience 2081; or a private inspiration 1812. Certain knowledge of the fact of revelation is required 1171, 1623 *et seq.*, 1634 *et seq.*, 1639, 1715, 1790 ... Before the acceptance of faith reason can and must certainly know, in addition to the fact of revelation, the motives of credibility of this revelation 1171, 1622 *et seq.*, 1634 *et seq.*, 1637 *et seq.*, 1651, 1790 *et seq.*, 1799, 1812, 2145.

Complementary to this is the following extract from St. Thomas's *Summa Theologiæ* II, II, question 5, article 3, in which the Angelic Doctor considers the question, "Whether a heretic who disbelieves one article of faith can have unformed [i.e. dead] faith in the other articles", and reaches a negative conclusion.

> It must be said that a heretic who disbelieves one article of faith retains no faith, whether formed or unformed. The reason for this is

that the species of any habit depends on its formal object, without which that species of habit cannot remain. But the formal object of faith is the first truth as manifested in the Sacred Scriptures and in the doctrine of the Church which proceeds from the first truth. *Hence whoever does not adhere to the doctrine of the Church ... as an infallible and Divine rule does not have the habit of faith* and holds those things which belong to faith *otherwise* than by faith." (Emphases added)

What follows from this is not that no one who adheres to a Protestant denomination can ever possess true supernatural faith. It is that his Protestant "faith" will be a hindrance rather than a help to doing so. Indeed he can only do so if (a) he is in good faith unaware of the motives of credibility of the Catholic Church; (b) he has, despite, this truly perceived that God has made a revelation and inwardly adhered to the essential truths God has in fact revealed, and (c) he has not culpably rejected any truth he perceives God to have revealed or adhered to any that he perceives God has *not* revealed.

Turning now to those who profess *no* belief in Jesus Christ and the essential doctrines of Christianity, it is almost a relief to find them unencumbered by Protestant pseudo-faith. But the relief will be short-lived for whoever adheres to St. Thomas's doctrine that:

> In the time of grace [i.e. after the coming of Christ], says St. Thomas in *De Veritate*, 14:11, everyone, greater or lesser, is bound to have explicit faith concerning the Trinity and the Redeemer.

It is true that some theologians have endeavoured to argue from St. Paul's teaching "He that cometh to God must believe that He is and is a rewarder to them that seek Him" (Hebrews 11:6) that no other doctrines need, absolutely speaking, be believed explicitly as a *means* of salvation except that God exists and rewards men according to their deserts. St. Thomas, however, devotes two separate articles of his *Summa* (II-II, Q. 2, A. 7, 8) to highlighting the no less scriptural doctrine that "There is no other name [than that of Jesus] under Heaven given to men whereby we must be saved," (Acts 4:12) and to showing that explicit faith in the doctrine of the Blessed Trinity and in Our Lord Jesus Christ as Redeemer is absolutely necessary as a means of salvation. The Church does not *require* us to follow the traditional doctrine of St. Thomas on this point, but it is certainly the position that best accords with both Scripture and Tradition. And of course it means that no Jew or Mahometan can be saved *while* adhering to his denial of the Trinity and the Incarnation.

Irrespective of this unresolved theological controversy, it is plain that belief in *no* God or in *many* "gods" is incompatible with that belief in the one God, our Creator and Rewarder, which constitutes – as no theologian has ever been authorized by the Church to question – the bare minimum object of supernatural faith necessary as a means of salvation.

The Act of Charity

There remains one error, as yet unrefuted here, which is particularly liable to ensnare those who read the teachings of the Magisterium on this subject without sufficient thought or background study. It is the notion that the act of supernatural charity necessary to vivify faith and make it salvific is compatible with the commission of grave sin against "the natural law and its precepts which God has engraved on the hearts of all."

The point here is that someone who has received – by whatever means – the necessary knowledge and grace to elicit an act of supernatural faith has received "the foundation and root of all justification" (Council of Trent, Session VI, Chapter 8), justification being "the sanctification and renewal of the inward man by voluntary acceptance of grace and gifts, by which man is made just from being unjust, a friend from being an enemy, so that he is 'an heir according to hope of eternal life' (Titus 3:7) ...[for] without ... faith ... justification does not take place." (*Ibid.*, Chapter 7)

But although faith is the necessary foundation of justification, it is by no means *all* that is necessary for justification, the other requirements being supernatural virtues which can be exercised only by one whose *will* is properly disposed as well as his intellect. "The Council of Trent[28] assigns six acts by which an adult sinner ought to dispose himself for justification; namely, acts of faith, fear, hope, love of God, penance or contrition, and the resolution to receive the sacraments instituted for the remission of sins, to begin a new life and to keep the Commandments – which resolution may be said to be included in true contrition," says Fr. Arthur Devine C.P. in his *Sacraments Explained* (p. 66). And Mgr. Fenton explains further that the man who is in the state of grace "loves God with a love of friendship or benevolence, sincerely desiring or intending to do His will and preferring to suffer anything rather than to offend Him." (*The Catholic Church and Salvation*, p. 47) It needs little enough thought, therefore, to perceive that even those who are blessed with all the advantages that come from easy access to the sacraments and other assistance offered by the Church do not always possess these and are therefore, alas, not in the state of sanctifying grace. Much more rarely would these dispositions be present among those who still have the misfortune to live in "invincible ignorance of our most holy religion," even should they have received the special enlightenment and graces needed to make an act of *faith*.

It might appear, at first sight, that such individuals have a compensatory advantage over those who have been fully instructed in the Faith, because, being invincibly ignorant of the Church's teaching, they will not be held guilty of many objectively sinful deeds that they may perform when they do not realise their sinfulness. And this is perfectly true; but it the scope of such invincible ignorance should not be exaggerated, for there are very many exceedingly demanding moral

---

[28] Session VI, chapter VI.

obligations which bind all men, and from which invincible ignorance can never excuse as it is impossible for *anyone* to be ignorant of them except by his own grave fault. It is to these obligations that Pope Pius IX refers, in the passage already quoted from *Quanto Conficiamur*, when he observes that, for one invincibly ignorant of the Catholic Church to be eligible for salvation, one of the necessary conditions is that he "carefully observe the natural law and its precepts which God has engraved on the hearts of all."

Many readers will already be aware that morally binding laws include:

(i) The *natural law*, which is the norm of right behaviour insofar as it is intrinsically immutable, is derived from the very nature of things and can be known by the light of natural reason. It includes, for instance, the obligation of parents to raise their children properly.

(ii) The *Divine positive law*, which is the norm of right behaviour insofar as it is not intrinsically immutable but is determined by the revealed will of God – e.g. the obligation of Baptism.

(iii) *Human law*, which is divided into civil law, made by governments and binding their subjects, and ecclesiastical law, made by the Church and binding the baptized.

Those who are invincibly ignorant of the Catholic Church are not bound by ecclesiastical law unless they are baptized, and even then will not be bound by those parts of it not known to them because of their invincible ignorance. And they are not bound by the Divine positive law except insofar as they have been made aware of it. But they most certainly *are* bound by the *natural* law, for whereas the Divine law binds only those to whom it has been promulgated – i.e. to whom the revelation of God, together with its corroboratory proofs have been made known – the natural law requires no promulgation, being, in Pope Pius IX's words, "engraved on the hearts of all."

This is not to say, however, that there is *no* precept of the natural law of which a man can be blamelessly ignorant, for that is not the case. But let us allow St. Alphonsus Liguori, the Church's Doctor of moral theology, to explain the necessary distinction for us:

> It is certain that in the first principles of the natural law, and no less so in its proximate conclusions, as well as in the certain obligations of one's own state, invincible ignorance does not exist, because by the light of nature itself such things are known to all except those who shut their eyes to avoid seeing. And of these very things St. Thomas[29] says:
>
>> 'There belong to the natural law, first, certain exceedingly common precepts which are known to all; but also some secondary, more particular, precepts which are conclusions closely inferred from the principles.'
>
> And he affirms that neither can be unknown except through passion or culpable ignorance. But on the other hand it is the unanimous opinion of theologians ... that, with regard to mediate and obscure conclusions, i.e. those which are remote from the principles, invincible ignorance does indeed exist and must be recognized. (*Theologia Moralis*, lib. I, n. 170 *et seq.*, Dissertation on Invincible Ignorance)

Among the "first principles" of the natural law, St. Alphonsus instances "God must be worshipped" and "Do not do to another what you would not have done to yourself." Among the "more particular precepts ... closely inferred from the principles," and which all men are therefore bound to know, he includes "the Ten Commandments." As an example of a more remote conclusion, concerning which invincible ignorance would be admissible, he mentions "the prohibition of usury." (*Ibid.*)

So it is evident that no one at all who wishes to be saved, no matter how invincible his ignorance of other things may be, is excused from the duties of worshipping the one true God,

---

[29] *Summa Theologiæ* I, II, Q. 94, A. 6.

observing all ten Commandments, and complying with many other precepts of the natural law, especially those relating to the duties of his state in life: obligations which are fulfilled by very few indeed, whether inside or outside what was once known as Christendom.

Mgr. Fenton on Precept and Necessity

At the end of this explanation of the teaching of *Quanto Conficiamur Mœrore* and refutation of the errors and objections that have arisen from its superficial reading let us once again turn to Mgr. Fenton for confirmation of the conclusions just set out. His careful exegesis of the same text is fairly lengthy, but well worth reading carefully.

> There are three most important lessons contained in this section of *Quanto Conficiamur Mœrore*: the Holy Father's insistence upon the real necessity of the Church for salvation; his implied indication of a distinction between the necessity of means and the necessity of precept; and his teaching about the possibility of salvation for a man who is invincibly ignorant of the true religion but who faithfully observes the natural law. All of these lessons must be studied carefully by a man who seeks to know the genuine doctrine of the Catholic Church on the necessity of the Church for the attainment of eternal salvation. The teaching of *Quanto Conficiamur Mœrore* has a special importance because this encyclical has been misinterpreted more than once by men who offered inadequate or inaccurate explanations of the dogma that there is no salvation outside the Church.
>
> First of all, it must be noted that the statement of the dogma that there is no salvation outside the Church is more forceful and explicit in this encyclical than in any other document except perhaps *Cantate Domino* itself. Pope Pius IX condemned as a most serious error (*'gravissimum errorem'*) the notion that 'men living in errors and apart from the true Faith and from the Catholic unity can attain to eternal life.' He denounced this false teaching as something most completely opposed to Catholic doctrine. (...)
>
> *Quanto Conficiamur Mœrore* is supremely realistic in that it recognizes religious error as an evil, and as a definite and serious

misfortune for the people who are affected by it. Its objectivity and plain speaking must have been as startling to the moderns of nearly a century ago as it is to some of the men of our own day. Some of the men of the nineteenth century and of the twentieth have been prone to lose sight of the fact that actually a man's life is vitiated by a mistake about his eternal destiny or about the means God has established for the attainment of that destiny. Thus there could be nothing more catastrophic in human life than the acceptance of the errors of atheism or agnosticism, or errors about Our Divine Redeemer, His Church, His religion, and His sacraments. It is strange that some individuals who would be first to acknowledge the calamitous nature of an error in aviation engineering, which would result in the loss of a plane, are not willing to acknowledge the inherent evil of error about Christ and His Church, which would result in man's eternal failure. (...)

Furthermore, *Quanto Conficiamur Mærore* is realistic enough to take cognizance of the fact that faith itself comes from and through the Church. We must not lose sight of the fact that the formula for the administration of Baptism, in the *Rituale Romanum*, contains this dialogue:

> 'What do you ask of the Church of God?'
> 'Faith.'
> 'What does faith offer you?'
> 'Everlasting life.'

Divine faith is definitely something which men are expected to seek and to find in the true Church of Jesus Christ. Essentially, the true Church is, and has been since the time of our first parents, the congregation of the faithful, the *'congregatio fidelium'*. A man reasonably and prudently asks the Church for faith since the Church is the society authorized and empowered by Our Lord Himself to teach His message, the doctrine we accept with the assent of Christian faith. And the Church is far more than merely the society authorized by Our Lord to teach in His name. It is actually His Mystical Body, the congregation within which He acts as the Sovereign Teacher, in such a way that the members of the hierarchy, the *'Ecclesia docens'*, are His instruments or ambassadors in the presentation of His Father's message. (...)

There have, unfortunately, been some rather serious misinterpretations of the second and third lessons contained in that portion of the encyclical *Quanto Conficiamur Mœrore* that deals with the necessity of the Catholic Church for the attainment of eternal salvation. The second lesson is to be found in the teaching of Pope Pius IX on the distinction between the Church's necessity of *means* and its necessity of *precept*. This lesson is brought out in a rather long and complicated sentence in the text. The encyclical tells us that 'it is a perfectly well known Catholic dogma that no one can be saved outside the Catholic Church, and that those who are contumacious against the authority of that same Church, and who are contumaciously separated from the unity of that Church and from Peter's successor, the Roman Pontiff, to whom the custody of the vineyard has been entrusted by the Saviour, cannot obtain eternal salvation.'

Some careless writers and teachers have tried to make people imagine that the second portion of this sentence is an expression of the *entire* meaning conveyed in the first section of that same sentence. Writers of this sort, incidentally, have even misinterpreted the Holy Office letter of 1949, *Suprema Hæc Sacra*, where the terminology is even clearer than that employed in *Quanto Conficiamur Mœrore*. In both instances there has been an attempt to give the impression that these authoritative documents were representing the Catholic Church as necessary for the attainment of eternal salvation by the necessity of precept only. In both instances the attempts were manifestly wrong. Here, however, we shall consider only the text of the encyclical written by Pope Pius IX. We shall study the *Suprema Hæc Sacra* in a later chapter.

The immediate text in the *Quanto Conficiamur Mœrore* indicates quite clearly that the Sovereign Pontiff was dealing with two distinct kinds of necessity. The context proves this point beyond any possibility of doubt. The sentence quoted two paragraphs above ['It is a perfectly well known Catholic dogma ...'] tells us of the well known dogma that no one can be saved outside the Church *and* states that people contumaciously separated from the Church and its visible head cannot be saved. The text itself indicates quite obviously that the Church is, according to its own doctrine, necessary in two distinct ways. First of all, it is represented as something necessary for all men. No one will attain to eternal salvation unless he is in some way 'within' this society at the moment of his death. Again, it is shown as necessary in still another manner. People who obstinately stay separated from it and from its visible head, the Roman Pontiff, cannot obtain eternal salvation.

Now it is immediately evident that the first statement would not be true at all if the Catholic Church were necessary for salvation merely with the necessity of *precept*. A thing is said to be necessary for salvation with the necessity of precept when God has issued a command which cannot be disobeyed except at the cost of the loss of friendship with Him. A thing which is merely the object of God's command and no more would be something necessary with the necessity of precept alone. The only persons who could be excluded from salvation on this count would be the men and women who knowingly and deliberately disobeyed the command given by God. Persons invincibly ignorant of that command would not be and could not be deprived of eternal salvation because they had not obeyed the command.

Thus, if the Church were necessary for salvation merely with the necessity of precept, or, to put the same thing in another way, if the Church were necessary for the attainment of eternal salvation only in the sense that individuals contumaciously separated from it could not be saved, it would definitely not be true to say that no man could be saved outside the Catholic Church. Yet this is precisely what the encyclical *Quanto Conficiamur Mærore*, together with many other authoritative documents of the '*Ecclesia docens*', does assert. The language of the encyclical is most explicit: '*Neminem scilicet extra Catholicam Ecclesiam posse salvari.*'

The only possible way a man could logically hold that the statement 'no one can be saved outside the Catholic Church' means nothing more than 'people who are contumaciously separated from the Church cannot be saved,' is to postulate that the only people outside of the Church are those obstinately and wilfully separated from it. Such a teaching would, of course, constitute a denial of any invincible ignorance of the Church on the part of non-Catholics. *An interpretation of this sort would run counter to the very context of the document it set out to explain*. Yet this fanciful teaching is necessarily and clearly implied in any attempt to persuade people that the Catholic dogma of the Church's necessity for salvation means only that persons who wilfully remain separated from the Church and from the Roman Pontiff cannot obtain eternal salvation. The context of *Quanto Conficiamur Mærore* makes it even more evident that we cannot explain the dogma of the Church's necessity for salvation as meaning merely that the Church is necessary with the necessity of precept. The primary point brought out in this section of *Quanto Conficiamur Mærore* is the vigorous repudiation by Pope Pius IX of the erroneous teaching 'that men living in errors and apart from the true Faith and from the Catholic unity can attain to eternal life.' Here the Sovereign Pontiff referred to *all* the people of this class. He did not restrict his statement to those who are wilfully or contumaciously dwelling and remaining apart from the Church and its teaching. It is only by doing manifest violence to the text of his encyclical that his statement could be interpreted as applying only to those who are wilfully separated from the faith and from Catholic unity.

By clear implication, though obviously not with the explicitness of *Suprema Hæc Sacra*, the encyclical *Quanto Conficiamur Mærore* brings out the fact that the dogma of the Catholic Church's necessity for the attainment of eternal salvation means that the Church is necessary in two ways. First, it is necessary with the necessity of *precept*, since God Himself has commanded all men to dwell within this society. Then it is also necessary with the necessity of *means*, since it has been constituted by God Himself as a factor apart from which men will not and cannot obtain the Beatific Vision.

Continued Explanation by Mgr. Fenton

The third and most difficult lesson of the encyclical *Quanto Conficiamur Mærore* on the subject of the Church's necessity for salvation is to be found in its teaching on the possibility of salvation for persons invincibly ignorant of the true religion. What the encyclical has to say on this point is contained in a single long and highly complicated sentence:

> It is known to Us and to you that those who labour in invincible ignorance of our most holy religion, and who, carefully observing the natural law and its precepts which God has inscribed in the hearts of all,

and who, being ready to obey God, live an honest and upright life, can, through the working of the Divine light and grace, attain eternal life; since God, who clearly sees, inspects and knows the minds, the intentions, the thoughts and the habits of all, will, by reason of His supreme goodness and kindness, never allow anyone who has not the guilt of wilful sin to be punished by eternal sufferings.

This sentence is tremendously rich in theological implication. It can never be adequately understood other than against the background and in the context of the Catholic theology of grace and of sin. Unfortunately this sentence has sometimes been explained in an inadequate manner.

In order to have an adequate and accurate analysis of this teaching, we must see clearly, first of all, what precise class of people Pope Pius IX refers to in this sentence. They are people who are described as carefully or diligently ('*sedulo*') obeying the natural law. They are prepared to obey God. They lead an honest and upright life. And they are invincibly ignorant of the true Catholic religion.

Now it is perfectly obvious that this description does not apply to all the individuals who are invincibly ignorant of the Catholic Church and of the Catholic Faith. Invincible ignorance is by no means a sacrament, communicating goodness of life to those who are afflicted with it. The fact that a man is invincibly ignorant of the true religion does not in any way guarantee that he will observe the natural law zealously, that he will be ready to obey God, or that he will actually lead an upright life.

The invincibly ignorant people described by Pope Pius IX in the encyclical *Quanto Conficiamur Mærore*, however, have attained their spiritual position by co-operating with Divine grace. It must be clearly understood, of course, that people in the state of sin, people who are not co-operating with God's grace, can perform works that are [naturally] good. *Quanto Conficiamur Mærore*, however, speaks of persons who are carefully or zealously observing the natural law and who are leading honest and upright lives. Such individuals are not turned away from God by sin. (...)

The pertinent passage of *Quanto Conficiamur Mærore* refers only to those persons invincibly ignorant of the true Catholic religion who, at the same time, are diligently observing the natural law, are prepared to obey God, and are leading honest and upright lives. Such individuals are obviously not merely avoiding some mortal sins and doing some good deeds. Rather they are continuing over a long period of time to obey the precepts of the natural law and to avoid serious offence against God. Otherwise it would not be correct to say that they were leading honest and upright lives.

But whether, as seems most probable, the individuals referred to in this section of the encyclical are in the state of grace, or they are being moved by actual grace in the direction of justification, it is important to note that *Quanto Conficiamur Mœrore* teaches that they 'can, *through the working of the Divine light and grace*, attain eternal life.' Obviously there is no hint here that these people are in a position to attain eternal life or salvation other than 'within' the Catholic Church. There is, however, a definite implication that they can be saved even though they remain invincibly ignorant of the true religion.

The 'Divine light' to which the encyclical refers is, of course, the illumination of true supernatural faith. No one is going to attain the Beatific Vision unless he has passed from this life with faith, accepting as true, on the authority of God Himself, the supernatural teaching that God has revealed.

The 'grace' spoken of in the document is ultimately sanctifying or justifying grace, the quality by which men are rendered connaturally able to act on the Divine level, and to live as adopted sons of God and as brothers of Jesus Christ. The man who possesses this quality has always, along with it, the full panoply of the supernatural or infused virtues and the gifts of the Holy Ghost. The supreme virtue in all of this supernatural organism is that of charity. No one is going to attain to the Beatific Vision unless he leaves this life in possession of sanctifying grace, charity, and the virtues of which charity is at once the crown and the bond of perfection. Actual graces tend to move a sinner toward the possession of sanctifying grace in the Church.

Now, that faith which is absolutely requisite for the attainment of eternal life is definitely not a mere willingness to believe. It is the *actual* acceptance, as perfectly true, of the supernatural message which God has revealed. Specifically, it is the acceptance of the message which God has revealed through Our Lord Jesus Christ, the teaching which theology designates as Divine public revelation.

Suprema Hæc Sacra

In the course of Mgr. Fenton's masterly exegesis of *Quanto Conficiamur* he referred more than once to another Roman pronouncement on the same subject: *Suprema Hæc Sacra*. And it is to this that we must now turn. It is a letter of the Holy Office published with the approval of Pope Pius XII as an official clarification of certain aspects of the dogma that there is no salvation outside the Church, in response to the controversy sparked off by Fr. Leonard Feeney and his St. Benedict Center in Cambridge, Massachusetts. Fr. Feeney, it may be noted by way of background, had rightly deplored the liberal understandings of the requirements for salvation that were rapidly gaining ground on the Church notwithstanding the frequent protests of the sovereign pontiffs, but he and the other members of his Center had allowed themselves to be driven into a no less heterodox position than that of their opponents by denying that *desire* (even implicit desire) for Baptism and membership of the Church can be sufficient for salvation when united with true supernatural faith, informed by Divine charity and, if necessary, accompanied by perfect contrition.[30]

This letter, *Suprema Hæc Sacra*, being originally a private letter (dated 8th August 1949) to the Archbishop of Boston, was not promulgated in the *Acta Apostolicæ Sedis*, but subsequently to its being issued its Latin text appeared in the *American Ecclesiastical Review* for October 1952.[31] The following translation of its doctrinal section is substantially Mgr. Fenton's but has been occasionally adapted to ensure close fidelity to the

---

[30] For more specific consideration – indeed I believe the most complete exposé and refutation– of the outrageous and indefensible heresies of Fr. Feeney, which still have many adherents in America, readers are referred to my article *A More Comprehensive Refutation of the Feeneyite Heresy*.

[31] It also appears in *Leges Ecclesiæ post Codicem iuris canonici editæ* Vol. II (*Leges Annis 1942-1958 Editæ*), edited by Fr. Xaverius Ochoa.

original and to change grammar and spelling from American to British usage:

> ... the Most Eminent and Most Reverend Cardinals of this Supreme Congregation, in a plenary session held on Wednesday, July 27 1949, decreed, and the August Pontiff in an audience on the following Thursday, July 28, 1949, deigned to give his approval, that the following explanations pertinent to the doctrine, and also that invitations and exhortations relevant to discipline, be given.
>
> We are bound by Divine and Catholic faith to believe all those things which are contained in the word of God, whether it be Scripture or Tradition, and which are proposed by the Church to be believed as Divinely revealed, not only by a solemn judgement but also through the ordinary and universal Magisterium.
>
> Now among those things which the Church has always preached and will never cease to preach, there is contained that infallible statement by which we are taught that there is no salvation outside the Church.
>
> However, this dogma must be understood in the sense in which the Church itself understands it. For Our Saviour gave the things that are contained in the deposit of faith to be explained by the ecclesiastical Magisterium and not by private judgements.
>
> Now, in the first place, the Church teaches us that in this matter we are dealing with a most strict precept of Jesus Christ. For He explicitly ordered His Apostles to teach all nations to observe all things whatsoever He Himself had commanded.
>
> Now, not the least important among the commandments of Christ is that one by which we are commanded to be incorporated by Baptism into the Mystical Body of Christ, which is the Church, and to remain united to Christ and to His Vicar, through whom He Himself governs the Church on earth in a visible manner.
>
> Therefore, no one shall be saved who, knowing the Church to have been Divinely established by Christ, nevertheless refuses to submit to the Church or withholds obedience from the Roman Pontiff, the Vicar of Christ on earth.
>
> But it was not only by *precept* that the Saviour required all nations to enter the Church; He also appointed the Church to be a *means* of salvation, without which ('sine quo') no one can enter the kingdom of eternal glory.

In His infinite mercy God has willed that the effects, necessary for one to be saved, of those helps to salvation which are directed towards man's final end, not by intrinsic necessity, but only by Divine institution, can also be obtained in certain circumstances when these helps are used only in *wish* or *desire* ('ubi *voto* solummodo vel *desiderio* adhibeantur'). This we see clearly stated in the Sacred Council of Trent, both with reference to the sacrament of regeneration and with reference to the sacrament of penance. (Denzinger 797, 807)

In its own way, the same thing must be said about the Church, insofar as the Church itself is a general help to salvation, because it is not always required in order that one may obtain eternal salvation that he be incorporated into the Church *actually* ('*reapse*') as a member: what is required is that he be united to it at least by intention and desire.

This desire, however, need not always be explicit, as it is in catechumens; but, when a person is handicapped by invincible ignorance, God accepts also an *implicit desire* ('*votum*') which is so called because it is included in that good disposition of soul whereby a person wishes his will to be conformed to the will of God.

These things are clearly taught in the dogmatic letter which was issued by the Sovereign Pontiff, Pope Pius XII, on June 29 1943, *On the Mystical Body of Jesus Christ.* (*Acta Apostolicæ Sedis*, Vol. XXXV, 1943, pp. 193 *et seq.*)[32] For in this letter the Sovereign Pontiff clearly distinguishes between those who are really ('*re*') incorporated into the Church as members and those who belong to the Church only in desire ('*voto*').

Discussing the members of whom the Mystical Body is composed here on earth, the same August Pontiff (*loc. cit.*, p. 202) says: 'Only those who have received the laver of regeneration, who profess the true Faith, who have not miserably separated themselves from the fabric of the Body or been expelled by legitimate authority by reason of very serious offences, are to be counted as *actually* ('*reapse*') members of the Church.'

---

[32] The encyclical *Mystici Corporis Christi.*

Towards the end of the same encyclical letter, when most affectionately inviting to unity those who do not belong to the external structure of the Catholic Church (*'qui ad Ecclesiæ Catholicæ compagem non pertinent'*), he mentions those who are 'ordered to the Redeemer's Mystical Body by a certain unconscious *wish* and *desire*,' and these he by no means excludes from eternal salvation, though he does assert that they are in a condition in which 'they cannot be secure about their own eternal salvation ... since they still lack so many and such great heavenly helps to salvation that can be enjoyed only in the Catholic Church.' (*loc. cit.*, p. 243)

With these wise words he reproves both those who exclude from eternal salvation all those united to the Church *only by implicit desire* and those who falsely assert that men can be saved equally (*'æqualiter'*) in every religion. (...)

Nor must we think that any kind of desire of entering the Church is sufficient in order that one may be saved. It is requisite that the desire by which one is ordered to the Church should be informed by perfect charity; and no *implicit desire*[33] can produce its effect unless the man have supernatural faith: 'For he who comes to God must believe that God exists and is a rewarder of those who seek Him.' (Hebrews 11:6) The Council of Trent (Session VI, Chapter 8) declares: 'Faith is the beginning of man's salvation, the foundation and root of all justification, without which it is impossible to please God and attain to the fellowship of His children.'

As it can be seen, *Suprema Hæc Sacra* simply confirms explicitly what could already be inferred from *Quanto Conficiamur Mærore*. The principal points it makes are as follows:

---

[33] By a typographical error the translation that appears in Mgr. Fenton's work (p. 102) has "explicit" instead of "implicit" here. With the correct word, "implicit", the point being made is that not only those whose intention is explicit must have faith, but also those whose intention is *implicit*.

Principal Points Taught by *Suprema Hæc Sacra*

(i) The teaching that there is no salvation outside the Church is an infallible and immutable dogma.

(ii) All men are Divinely commanded to join the Church, for which reason anyone who fails to join the Church though aware of this precept – or if unaware of it only through his own fault – is guilty of mortal sin.

(iii) But the necessity of membership of the Church for salvation is not merely one of *precept*, it is also one of *means*; so that, even when invincible ignorance excuses from moral fault in not entering the Church, nevertheless "no one" outside the Church "can enter the kingdom of eternal glory." Mgr. Fenton explains:

> A thing is said to be necessary for salvation with the necessity of *precept*[34] when it has been commanded in such a way that, if a person disobeys this order, he is guilty of mortal sin. A *means* necessary for salvation, on the other hand, is something which a man *must* have if he is to attain eternal salvation. This necessity holds *even when there is no obduracy on the part of the individual who does not possess the means* .... The Holy Office letter is the first authoritative document to bring out in full explicitness the teaching that the Church is necessary for

---

[34] In an earlier article, now out of print, I explained this distinction as follows:

"Certain of our Christian duties are termed necessary as *means* of our salvation, while others are necessary by *precept*. Examples of each will help to clarify the distinction.

"When a teacher tells a schoolboy that he will receive a prize if he has no mistakes in his homework, in order to receive the prize, top marks are necessary *by precept*. If, however, the schoolboy manages nine out of ten and has clearly done his best, the teacher *may* award him the prize nevertheless.

By contrast, if the pilot of an aircraft which is about to crash tells a passenger to put on a parachute to avoid falling to his death, the parachute is necessary as a *means* of avoiding death. No matter how vigorously the passenger searches, he cannot survive unless he succeeds in finding the parachute."

salvation both with the necessity of precept and with the necessity of means. (Emphasis added.)

(iv) Certain requirements for salvation are necessary "by *intrinsic* necessity," but others "only by Divine institution," and in the latter case their effects "can also be obtained in certain circumstances when these helps are used only in intention or desire." (Thus, for instance, Divine charity is necessary for salvation by intrinsic necessity, so that in no circumstance, no matter how exceptional, could God bestow the Beatific Vision on one who did not love Him. But sacramental absolution of a baptized person who has committed grave sin is necessary, not by *intrinsic* necessity, but only by Divine institution; and thus to an individual, who, because of exceptional circumstances, is unable to receive this sacrament, but earnestly desires to do so, there may nevertheless be granted the exceptional grace of perfect contrition by which the *effects* of the sacrament of Penance could be obtained by an extraordinary means.)

(v) The Church is necessary for salvation in two distinct ways; by necessity of *means* and of *precept*. To be within her fold is absolutely and intrinsically necessary as a *means* of salvation, for which reason there can be no exception whatsoever to the dogma reiterated by *Suprema Hæc Sacra* that "there is no salvation outside the Church."

(vi) But the *formalities* of membership of the Church, by which a person is juridically recognized as a member by ecclesiastical authority and becomes entitled to the advantages offered by the Church to her members, are not *intrinsically* necessary. "Therefore, in order that one may obtain eternal salvation, it is not always required that he be incorporated into the Church *actually* ('reapse') as a member, but it is required that at least he be united to it by intention and desire."

(vii) Catechumens possess such an intention or desire explicitly. (In the event that they die before formal affiliation to the

Church, their salvation will depend on a number of other conditions – some of which will be touched on shortly – which will be very difficult to fulfil for anyone who has no access to the sacraments which are "the principal ['*præcipua*'] means of sanctification and salvation [Canon 731]"). But from those who are "handicapped by invincible ignorance, God also accepts an implicit desire ('*votum*'), which is so called because it is included in that good disposition of the soul whereby a person wishes his will to be conformed to the will of God."

(viii) But of course this implicit desire for membership of the Church does *not* substitute for those other things which are necessary for salvation by necessity of means – such as Divine and Catholic faith, hope and charity. Hence those who are "ordered to the Redeemer's Mystical Body by a sort of unconscious desire and intuition, ... are in a condition in which they cannot be secure about their own eternal salvation."

(ix) In addition to an intention, at least implicit, of joining the Church, other conditions are essential for salvation: "It is requisite that the intention by which one is ordered to the Church should be informed by perfect charity; and no implicit intention can produce its effect unless the man have supernatural faith."

The Soul of the Church

Finally, before closing this theological exposition of the doctrine that there is no salvation outside the Church, reference ought to be made to one other false doctrine on the same topic. Because this error is not mentioned by either Davies or Bourne, it has not been touched on so far; but as it is so commonly encountered, justice could hardly be done to the subject if it were not mentioned, and the few paragraphs that follow will have the useful effect of enabling this chapter to stand alone as a defence of the true doctrine and refutation of the false doctrines concerning salvation and the Church, rather than being no more than a refutation of the errors of one particular author.

The error to which I refer is that of those who volunteer to explain away the necessity of belonging to the Church to be saved by making a distinction between the body and the soul of the Church. In addition to her body, i.e. her external structure, they explain, the Church has a soul which includes all the just, whatever their beliefs; and the dogma that there is no salvation outside the Church means simply that to be saved one must be a member of the Church's *soul*, though not necessarily of her *body*.

While the terms "body" and "soul" here are used analogically and it would be unreasonable to analyse them as if they were univocal, it is certainly permissible to comment on whether the analogy is of its nature helpful or misleading. And it is essential to stress that this explanation is certainly erroneous if taken to mean that the Church to which the dogma "no salvation outside the Church" refers is not the *visible* Catholic Church, which is in fact the only Church that exists.

In reality the analogy according to which those who are united to the external structure of the Church are referred to as being within her *body* and those who are in the state of grace are said to be within her *soul* is a perfectly sound one, for it is indeed sanctifying grace that "animates" the Mystical Body of Christ and differentiates those Catholics who are on the path to salvation from those who are dead members, living in the state of mortal sin. Moreover, it is even permissible to say of a pious catechumen, for instance, who is in the state of grace but not yet baptized, that he is in the soul of the Church without being *actually* within her body. For such an individual would, as we have seen, be within the external Church "*in voto*" – by desire – but not *actually*; whereas he would belong to the soul of the Church, i.e. would possess the life of sanctifying grace, as "actually" as would the pope himself if the pope were in a state of grace.

But this membership of the soul of the Church *cannot* be an *alternative* to membership of the body; for the dogma that there is no salvation outside the Church refers precisely to the *visible* communion of the faithful, i.e. the body, not to some invisible communion. Indeed Dr. Orestes Brownson went so far as to rephrase the dogma as follows: "Outside the (*visible*) Church there is no salvation." Nor did he fail to provide an adequate justification for his insertion of the word "visible":

> We add the word *exterior* or *visible* to distinguish the Church out of which there is no salvation from the *invisible Church* contended for by Protestants, and which no Catholic does or can admit. Without it, the dogma of faith contains no meaning. Unquestionably, as Our Lord in His humanity had two parts, His body and His soul, so may we regard the Church, His Spouse, as having two parts, the one exterior and visible, the other interior and invisible, or visible only by the exterior, as the soul of man is visible by his face; but to contend that the two parts are separable, or that the interior exists disconnected from the exterior and is sufficient independently of it, is to assert, in so many words, the prevailing doctrine of Protestants, and, so far as relates to the indispensable conditions of salvation, to yield to them, at least in their understanding, the whole question. In the present state of controversy with Protestants, we cannot save the integrity of the Faith, unless we add the epithet 'visible', or 'external'. But it is not true that by so doing we add to the dogma of faith. The sense of the epithet is necessarily contained in the simple word 'Church' itself, and the only necessity there is of adding it at all is in the fact that heretics have mutilated the meaning of the word 'Church', so that to them it no longer has its full and proper meaning. Whenever the word 'Church' is used generally, without any specific qualification, expressed or necessarily implied, it means, by its own force, the visible as well as the invisible Church, the Body no less than the Soul; for the Body, the visible or external communion, is not a mere accident, but is essential to the Church. The Church, by her very definition, is the congregation of men called by God through the evangelical doctrine, and professing the true Christian faith under their infallible Pastor and Head – the Pope.

Those who are eligible for salvation though not formally united to the Church, and even, conceivably, invincibly ignorant of her, must nevertheless belong *to her visible body* at least by desire – "*in voto*" – for outside that body no salvation is possible. Thus it is that St. Augustine, in his Sermon 267 (4:4), writes as follows:

> That which the soul is to the human body, the Holy Ghost is to the Body of Christ which is the Church; the Holy Ghost does in the entire Church what the soul does in all the members of one body. But mark well: here are grounds for wariness, for careful consideration, and for fear. It chances that from the human body, some limb, hand, finger or foot is cut off. Does the soul follow that which has been severed? While it was attached to the body, it was alive; having been cut off, it died. Likewise, too, a Christian man is a Catholic while he lives within the body; should he be severed therefrom, he becomes a heretic; the Spirit does not follow the limb that has been amputated. (Migne: *Patrologia Latina*, tom. 38, n. 1231)

This classic analogy of the "body" and "soul" of the Church has in recent times been seized upon and travestied by third-rate theological popularisers owing to a careless misreading of a passage in the works of St. Robert Bellarmine; indeed interpretations of St. Robert's words by various theologians of the seventeenth and eighteenth centuries gradually departed further and further from orthodoxy, thus giving rise to the full-scale heresies of the nineteenth and twentieth centuries reproved by the popes in the passages we have seen. A very full account of how this misunderstanding of an orthodox statement turned into a full-scale heresy which the popes had repeatedly to condemn is to be found in Part 2, Chapter 3, of Mgr. Fenton's *The Catholic Church and Salvation*, to which interested readers are referred. For the time being the following short summary from pages 126-7 of the same work must suffice:

> By all means the most important and the most widely employed of all the inadequate explanations of the Church's necessity for

salvation was the one that centred around a distinction between the 'body' and the 'soul' of the Catholic Church. The individual who tried to explain the dogma in this fashion generally designated the visible Church itself as the 'body' of the Church, and applied the term 'soul of the Church' either to grace and the supernatural virtues or to some fancied 'invisible Church'. Prior to the appearance of the encyclical *Mystici Corporis,* there were several books and articles claiming that, while the 'soul' of the Church was in some way not separated from the 'body', it was actually more extensive than this body.'

Explanations of the Church's necessity drawn up in terms of this distinction were at best inadequate and confusing and all too frequently infected with serious error. When the expression 'soul of the Church' was applied to sanctifying grace and the organism of supernatural virtues that accompany it, the explanation was confusing in that it stressed the fact that a man must be in the state of grace, and that he must have faith and charity, if he is to attain to eternal salvation; but it tended to obscure the truth that a man must in some manner be 'within' the true and visible Catholic Church at the moment of his death if he is ever to reach the Beatific Vision.

When, on the other hand, some imaginary 'invisible Church', some assembly of all the good people in the world, was designated as the 'soul of the Church', these explanations lapsed into doctrinal inaccuracy. The great paramount mystery of the Church is to be found in the fact that the visible and organized religious society over which the bishop of Rome presides as the Vicar of Christ and the Successor of St. Peter is the true and only '*ecclesia*' of the New Testament. This society, and this alone, is the true kingdom of God on earth, the Mystical Body of Jesus Christ. It holds within its membership both good men and bad. It includes those who are truly appreciative of their membership and those who are not. Nevertheless, in the mysterious and merciful designs of God's providence, this community and no other is the social entity within which men are to find salvific contact with God in Christ.

V

Davies's Doctrines Shown to be Heretical

We are now ready to return to the four propositions extracted from the writings of Mr. Michael Davies on this topic which were listed on p. 491 and there alleged to contain heresy.

The first was that the dogma that there is no salvation outside the Church is not universally applicable but denies salvation only to those who are outside the Church through their own fault. We have seen, on the contrary, (a) that the Church teaches the dogma to be universally applicable, and (b) that invincible ignorance, though excusing from sin in regard to the specific matter of which one is invincibly ignorant, is not a substitute for complying with the indispensable conditions of salvation one of which is to be, at least by desire, within the Catholic Church.

The second was that Catholic faith – i.e. belief in the Christian revelation, founded on natural recognition of the fact that God has made this revelation – is not always necessary for salvation. And we have seen that this view is directly opposed to the dogmatic teaching of the Council of Trent.

The third was that the only conditions necessary to ensure that one who is not externally united to the Church be united to her "by desire" are invincible ignorance of the true Church and the "sincere desire to please God." This we have seen to be contrary to *Quanto Conficiamur* and to *Suprema Hæc Sacra*, each of which reminds that according to Catholic dogma there are several other no less necessary requisites, such as, for instance, the theological virtues.

Finally, the fourth proposition was that those who are invincibly ignorant of the Catholic Church will be judged purely on their obedience to their own consciences, and will be saved if they have obeyed them or lost if they have not. While it is perfectly true that those who are invincibly ignorant of the Catholic Church and *fail* to observe the natural law as identified by their consciences will be *lost*, in accordance with St. Paul's assurance that "whosoever have sinned without the law shall perish without the law" (Romans 2:12), it is most certainly not true that obedience to an invincibly ignorant conscience, or to the natural law alone, could ever save anyone. Such a "doctrine of devils" (1 Timothy 4:1) is defiantly opposed to the Catholic doctrine that "without faith it is impossible to please God" (Hebrews 11:6) and that "there is no other name under Heaven [than 'the name of Our Lord Jesus Christ of Nazareth'] given to men whereby we must be saved" (Acts 4:12), as St. Peter taught the "princes of the people and ancients ... and ... all the people of Israel" (Acts 4:8, 10) and as St. Thomas, the Council of Trent and the Holy Office (*Suprema Hæc Sacra*) have each reiterated in their day.

Thus the assertion that Davies's doctrine concerning the possibility of salvation outside the Church, whether expressed in his own words or in those of his chosen mentors, is infected with multiple heresy, has been vindicated and, indeed, his errors have been shown to be so far from being in conformity with the teaching of the Church repeatedly insisted on by popes and councils, that, to quote once more the words of Pope Pius IX, "*nothing*, indeed, could be *more* opposed to Catholic doctrine." (*Quanto Conficiamur Mærore*)

CHAPTER TWELVE
DOCTRINAL EVOLUTION?

Introduction

One of the points emphasized in the preceding pages is that the teaching of the Magisterium on the subject of the requirements for salvation has been completely consistent throughout the centuries, as of course any orthodox Catholic would know that it must have been. But, as copious evidence has now shown readers of this *Evaluation*, Davies is *not* an orthodox Catholic, and he has therefore seen no difficulty in admitting that the doctrine held by the Catholic Church on this subject in the past is quite different from what Catholics are in his view entitled to believe about it today.

To explain how it may no longer be obligatory today to believe what all Catholics were formerly bound to hold he relies upon the assertion that dogmas can *evolve* or *develop*, and that this development of dogmas has taken place especially in relation to the dogma "*extra Ecclesiam nulla salus*" – a theory almost invariably maintained by those who obstinately wish to dismiss as outdated the Church's claim to be the exclusive ark of salvation.

Now there *is* a sense in which this is so – in fact more than one sense – as I intend to show shortly by analysing the orthodox doctrine on the subject, so it will be necessary to weigh carefully Davies's statement of his position in order to assess to what extent it is orthodox. This task is made easier to the extent that Davies unmistakably associates himself with the position of Cardinal Newman expressed in his famous *Essay on the Development of Christian Doctrine*;[1] but to avoid any risk of unfairness, let us as usual begin by quoting exactly what he says on the subject, whether it be original or borrowed:

(i) "Sufficient has already been written in this book to indicate that the equation 'older equals better' is facile. It does not follow that what is older expresses the Catholic Faith more clearly. In fact, the contrary is usually true as anyone familiar with Newman's *Development of Christian Doctrine* is aware. As the centuries passed the truths of the Faith were expressed more and more clearly. What had once been implicit was made explicit and what was already explicit was expressed with greater accuracy ...." (*Pope Paul's New Mass*, pp. 345-6).

(ii) "There can be a development of doctrine, but, as Newman pointed out, where a new formulation is not faithful to the idea from which it started it is an unfaithful development 'more properly called a corruption'." (*Pope John's Council*, p. 212)

(iii) "He [Newman] insists that a true development must be conservative of what has gone before it and that 'a developed doctrine which reverses the course of development which has preceded it is no true development but a corruption.'" (*Pope Paul's New Mass*, p. 256)

(iv) "By the Deposit of Faith we mean the 'stock' or 'treasure' of faith entrusted to the Church which she must faithfully preserve and infallibly expound. This original deposit is subject to development as the centuries progress, but always under the guidance of the Magisterium, and it [sic[2]] must always remain consistent with the previous stage of development. Thus the doctrine of the Trinity as defined by the councils of Nicæa (325) and Chalcedon (451) cannot be

---

[1] A work written while Newman was still an Anglican and which has never received the faintest approval from the Church.

[2] Grammatically this pronoun ought to stand for "this original deposit", which is the subject of the main verb, but it is evident that Davies intends it to refer to the new, developed doctrine.

found spelled out so exactly in the New Testament, but the doctrine of those Councils is compatible with the New Testament, and a legitimate development of its teaching."[3] (*Partisans of Error*, p. 19)

(v) "Newman shows clearly that there can never be any possibility of contradiction during the course of true development. Each stage is potentially contained in its preceding stage all the way back to the beginning." (*op. cit.*, p. 54)

(vi) "Newman listed several requirements for a true development.[4] (...) These are unity of type, continuity of principle, power of assimilation, logical sequence, anticipation of its future, conservation of its past, and, finally, chronic vigour." (*op. cit.*, p. 55)

Three principal observations are called for by Davies's doctrine of development as expounded by himself and his chosen authors. The first is that it is unacceptably vague and obscure. The second is that it is evidently inadequate to reconcile his beliefs on the necessity of membership of the Church for salvation with the declarations of the Magisterium on the same subject. And the third is that it is, in its obvious sense, heretical.

On the subject of the vagueness and obscurity of what Davies says, we suppose that few readers will disagree, particularly if

---

[3] As there is a seductive error lurking in Davies's reasoning here which is not directly concerned with doctrinal development and will therefore not be refuted by the comments I shall shortly be making on this topic, I think it necessary to draw attention to it here. It is the inference that, because the Trinitarian doctrine is not "spelled out so exactly in the New Testament" as it was by the Councils of Nicæa and Chalcedon in the fourth and fifth centuries, the Christians of those centuries must have expressed the doctrine more exactly than it was expressed by Christians of the first century. However, as the New Testament is not, and does not purport to be, either a catechism or a compendium of dogmatic theology, this inference is entirely gratuitous.

[4] 'Criteria by which legitimate development may be discerned' would be a clearer way of putting it.

they attempt to analyse exactly what "developments" would be classified by Davies as legitimate.

For instance, he tells us that "a new formulation" must be "faithful to the idea from which it started." This clause has a convincing ring about it, does it not? But what does it *mean*? If we look at some decree of an ecumenical council, who is to say which parts of it constitute the original "idea"? And who is to say to what extent it is possible to add to, diminish or alter that "idea" while remaining "faithful" to it? For instance, could the original "idea" – as Davies puts it – of charity towards one's neighbour be a starting point from which State Socialism could legitimately emerge as "a new formulation"?

Again, we are told that "a true development must be conservative of what has gone before it." But the word "conservative" is not a helpful one. The extraordinary breadth of meaning which it bears is amply illustrated by the activities of political parties which apply this epithet to themselves. In relation to doctrine we might ask whether it is possible for a development to be considered "conservative" when it is only *slightly* different from what has previously been believed: for instance, might it be that the Protestant Eucharistic doctrine of "trans-signification"[5] is to be rejected, but that the modernistic "Catholic" doctrine of "trans-finalization"[6] is sufficiently "conservative" of the old-fashioned doctrine of transubstantiation to be an acceptable stage of doctrinal progress?

The same applies to the assurance that "it [presumably the new, developed doctrine] must always remain consistent with the previous stage of development." Could it, for instance, be

---

[5] *Trans-signification* is the doctrine according to which the Eucharistic species merely *represent* the Body and Blood of Our Lord.

[6] *Trans-finalization* is the doctrine according to which the Eucharistic species become the Body and Blood of Our Lord, but only at the moment when they are sacramentally received, and only from the perspective of the communicant.

reasonably claimed that the discovery of a fourth Divine person in the Godhead is "consistent" with the old doctrine of the Trinity, on the grounds that it does not deny the presence of *three* persons, but simply adds another? Surely no one could deny that a developed doctrine would "always remain consistent with the previous stage of development" if its development consisted only of the *addition* of *detail* to an already established doctrine.

More intriguing still is Newman's assertion quoted in extract (iii): that doctrinal development must always be *in one direction*. This would indeed allow "progress" in the apparently uncompromising doctrine of "no salvation outside the Church". Such progress would start, of course, by turning "no salvation outside the Church" into "just a *little* salvation outside the Church" – a step which, alas! some otherwise sound authors – though never popes, saints, or fully approved theologians – had already taken long ago. From there it would gradually become "*plentiful* salvation outside the Church" – the position which Davies has made it clear that he, in company with Cardinal Bourne, certainly believes in. And after that, why could it not become perfectly possible one day for Catholic belief to be that there is *universal* salvation outside the Church,[7] and even that there is *no* salvation *inside* the Church? What is certain is that

---

[7] This is a position which media-idol Mother Teresa of Calcutta already seems well on her way to accepting: "We become a better Hindu, a better Muslim, a better Catholic, a better whatever we are, and then by being better we become closer and closer to Him ... What approach would I use? For me, naturally it would be a Catholic one, for you, it may be Hindu, for someone else, Buddhist, according to one's conscience. What God is in your mind you must accept ... We live that they may die, so that they may go home, according to what is written in the book, be it written according to Hindu, or Muslim, or Buddhist, or Catholic, or Protestant, or any other belief ..." Such was the "profession of faith" on this subject which she made to her biographer Desmond Doig; see p. 136 of his *Mother Teresa, Her People and Her Work*.

such a "development" would not be liable to the charge of changing direction!

Enough on that subject. Secondly I have stated that insofar as its meaning *is* clear, Davies's doctrine cannot possibly explain his new "interpretation" of "no salvation outside the Church". And here, mercifully, I can be brief; for the problem is the simple one of a direct contradiction between two mutually exclusive propositions, and it has already been shown in considerable detail that this contradiction exists.

The Church, as we have seen, has infallibly defined that there is *no salvation whatsoever* for those outside her fold, but Davies and many, many others, as we have also seen, hold that there *is* salvation outside the Church. *Both* simply *cannot* be true. And whereas a theory of doctrinal evolution as unrestricted as Darwinian biological evolution could certainly allow any one given doctrine to evolve into some other, completely different one, it is quite clear that, in theory at least, Davies does not countenance this. Whatever he means by the assertions that the new doctrine must be "compatible" and "consistent" with the old, he clearly intends them to exclude *direct contradictions* from the realm of authentic developments – or else they exclude nothing at all, which we must assume not to be intended. But on the other hand, if Davies and those who think as he does are to restrict their theory of doctrinal development to a form in which such wholesale reconstructions of Catholic theology as might please Hans Küng or Edward Schillebeeckx are excluded, their theory will by the same token be inadequate to explain how the erstwhile dogma that there is no salvation outside the Church allows Catholics of the twentieth century to believe in the salvation of Hindu women who commit suicide. The obvious reason for this is that any theory of development which allowed "*extra Ecclesiam* **nulla** *salus*" to become "*extra Ecclesiam* **copiosa** *salus*" (plentiful salvation outside the Church), which is what Davies maintains to be sound doctrine, would clearly open the floodgates to unlimited "re-interpretations" of all other dogmas, and would certainly make it impossible to reject *any* heresy as absolutely inconsistent with Divine revelation; for it would turn Divine revelation from a complex of revealed propositions to be faithfully handed down in the Church, into a protean mass of "theology" constantly writhing into new forms and never remaining the same long enough for its contradictories to be identified, let alone condemned.

Hence we may dismiss Davies's hypothesis of doctrinal development as a wholly inadequate and unsuccessful attempt to justify illusion that unbelievers are eligible for salvation.

Doctrinal Development Condemned by the Church

What now remains to be proved is the assertion that Davies's theory of doctrinal development is not only useless for his purposes, but is actually heretical. To accomplish this, let us once more allow the Magisterium to speak:

(i) The following is an extract from a letter (*Quantum Presbyterorum*), dated 9th January 476, sent by the then pope, St. Simplicius, to Acacius the bishop of Constantinople, instructing the bishop to oppose the summoning of a council on the grounds that the council in question was intended to teach *new doctrine* whereas the Church already possessed *all* true doctrine in its entirety and used councils only for the condemnation of new heresies or the clarification of ambiguities. The applicability of these words to the Second Vatican Council will have struck every reader, for this council was the first in the history of the Church to be summoned when there was no pressing need to condemn new heresies or clarify ambiguities, and to have for its motive instead the very "updating" of Catholic discipline and doctrine which Pope St. Simplicius condemns; but the main point of this extract for present purposes is the holy pontiff's explanation of the sufficiency of doctrine as it already existed, without possibility of legitimate alteration:

... as the doctrine of our predecessors of holy memory is available, against which it is unlawful to dispute, anyone who wishes to know the truth requires no new pronouncements from which to learn, *for all these things are clear and complete* [*'plana atque perfecta'*] by which it is possible to instruct one who has been deceived by heretics or to ground one who is to be planted in the vineyard of the Lord; so, beseeching the trust of the most clement prince, have him reject the call to assemble a synod .... I beseech you dearest brother, to resist the perverse attempts to call a council by every means available, as a council is never proclaimed except when there has come to light some novelty of perverse meaning or an ambiguity in the assertion of dogmas .... (Denzinger 159. Emphasis added)

(ii) The following is the teaching of the 1870 Vatican Council:

For the doctrine of faith which God has revealed is not proposed, like a philosophical discovery, for perfection [or 'completion'] by human intelligence, but as a Divine deposit entrusted by Christ to His Bride, to be faithfully preserved and infallibly declared. Hence also *that same meaning of the sacred dogmas is ever to be retained which Holy Mother Church has once declared, nor is that sense ever to be departed from on the pretext of some higher understanding.* (Denzinger 1800. Emphasis added)

(iii) The following canon of the same council reinforces this point:

If anyone should say that it is possible for dogmas proposed by the Church sometimes to receive a *new meaning* [or 'understanding'] in accordance with the advancement of knowledge, different from that which the Church has understood and does understand, *let him be anathema.* (Denzinger 1818. Emphasis added)

(iv) The following extracts from the Anti-Modernist Oath imposed by St. Pius X are no less decisive:

Fourthly, I sincerely embrace the doctrine of faith transmitted to us by the Apostles through the orthodox Fathers *always with the same meaning and interpretation*; and I therefore utterly reject *the heretical fiction* of the development [or 'evolution'] of dogmas from one meaning to another ....

... I hold most firmly the Faith of the Fathers, and shall retain it until my last breath, concerning the certain gift of truth ... not so that what may seem better and more fitting according to the culture of each period may be held, but so that neither belief *nor interpretation* may ever be different from the absolute and immutable truth preached from the beginning by the Apostles. (Denzinger 2145, 2147. Emphasis added.)

(v) And in case that is not already more than sufficient, in his 1907 Syllabus *Lamentabili Sane*, Pope St. Pius X *condemned* the following proposition:

Revelation, which constitutes the object of the Catholic Faith, was not completed with the Apostles. (Denzinger 2021)

It is clear that instead of Catholic doctrine Davies has blithely presented his readers with some hypotheses concerning doctrinal development formulated by Cardinal Newman at a time when Newman was still an Anglican. And he has never so much as mentioned the fact that doctrinal development *involving any species of change in meaning* has been condemned by the Church *as heretical*. Nor has he mentioned that *the Holy See has never once spoken of doctrinal development except to condemn it*? Nor again does he disclose that a number of *exceedingly* erudite and highly regarded theologians[8] held that Newman's

---

[8] For instance, Cardinal Franzelin (*De Divina Traditione et Scriptura, passim*, but see especially 1875 ed., p. 113), Cardinal Billot (*De Immutabilitate Traditionis contra Modernam Hærisim Evolutionismi*, passim), Cardinal Lépicier (*De Stabilitate et Progressu Dogmatis*, pp. 14, 18, 25, 90, 124, 125, 153, 159, 187, 282, 302, 349), and Dr. Orestes Brownson *passim*.

Cardinal Lépicier evidently regarded Newman's theories as so pernicious that he seized every opportunity to attack him in the work referred to; Dr. Brownson went further still, however, devoting many substantial articles to the avowed task of exposing Newman's corruptions of Catholic doctrine. The entry under "Newman" in the index to his collected works fills seven-eighths of a page, with about a hundred references. I cite only the following words: "His essay on development was not written by a Catholic and its doctrine is not Catholic." (*Brownson's Works*, Vol. VII, p. 140) Moreover, by Professor

doctrine of development flies in the face of "*de fide*" Catholic doctrine.

Out of fairness it should be mentioned that there are two genuinely authoritative writers who are sometimes invoked in support of the theory of doctrinal evolution: St. Thomas Aquinas and St. Vincent de Lérins. Let us look at what they say.

The pertinent part of St. Thomas's *Summa Theologiæ* is II-II Q. 1, A. 7. It asks "whether the articles of faith have increased ['*creverint*'] with the passage of time?" *and answers in the affirmative*. Does this sound hopeful for the Newman-Davies school? Well, it might, if taken out of its context. But in context it emerges that St. Thomas's affirmative reply relates exclusively to, and is justified only with reference to, *the period of the Old Testament*, during which God's revelation to the Hebrews was *progressive*. St. Thomas certainly does not suggest that the articles of faith have increased *since the time of Our Lord* – only that they were continually increasing in explicitness *until* His coming. His teaching on any possible increase after that time is simply expressed in the words he borrows from St. Paul according to which "God, who at sundry times and in divers manners, spoke in times past to the Fathers by the prophets, last of all, in these days, hath spoken to us by his Son."

Owen Chadwick's historical study *From Bossuet to Newman* (2nd. ed. Oxford, 1987) we are informed that Bishop Fitzpatrick of Boston agreed with Brownson that "Newman's thought was frankly heretical;" (p. 171) that Dr. Alexander Grant, rector of the Scots College at Rome, "concluded that Newman was guilty of 'material heresy'" (p. 170) and that prominent Roman theologian Fr. Giovanni Perrone summarized Newman's doctrine by the observation that "*Newman miscet et confundit omnia*" – "he muddles and confuses everything." (p. 169) Similarly, Cardinal Manning, in order to dispel Mr. J.E.C. Bodley's illusion that Newman was "a good Catholic, ... proceeded to tick off on his tapering fingers ... ten distinct heresies to be found in the most widespread works of Dr. Newman," as Bodley recorded in his *Cardinal Manning and other Essays*. (p. 17) Testimonies of Newman's Catholic contemporaries as to his heterodoxy, especially in respect of his theory of doctrinal evolution, could be multiplied almost indefinitely.

(Hebrews 1:1-2) So this has nothing to do with any alleged doctrinal development during the Christian era.

Now let us turn to St. Vincent de Lérins. The relevant passage is this:

> But perhaps someone may say: so is there to be no advancement of religion in the Church of Christ? There certainly should be, and as much as possible. For who could be so spiteful towards men and so resentful towards God as to attempt to forbid it? Nonetheless this applies only to the *advancement* of the Faith and not to *change*. The difference is that advancement occurs when something is amplified in itself, *whereas change consists in the turning of one thing into another*. So it is needful that, as the centuries and years pass, there be growth, and indeed the very maximum advancement, *in the understanding, knowledge and wisdom* of individuals and of all men, of one man and of the whole Church – but that *only* in its own kind, that is to say in *the same doctrine, the same meaning and the same judgement* ....
>
> So also is it fitting that the doctrine of the Christian religion should follow these laws of development [St. Vincent is pursuing a comparison with the way in which an organism develops, growing while retaining its identity], i.e. that it be consolidated by the years, amplified by time and exalted by age, but that it remain incorrupt and undefiled and that it be full and complete with all the proportions of its parts with all the members and senses which belong to it ....
>
> It is indeed lawful that those ancient doctrines of heavenly wisdom be trimmed, smoothed and polished with the passage of time; but it is unlawful for them to be changed, unlawful for them to be damaged or mutilated. They may increase in *clarity, perspicuity* and *distinctness*, but they must retain their *fullness, integrity* and *identity*. (*Commonitorium*, Chapter 23. Emphases added.)

It would need a very superficial reading of this passage indeed for it to succeed in reinforcing the prejudices even of an interested party; for, far from authorizing or encouraging any notion of "development of doctrine", the holy author inveighs against *the slightest change of meaning*. When he authorises "advancement of the Faith", it is *by contrast* with "change"; and his next sentence spells out that the amplification which he favours is proper, *not* to the *doctrines*, but to *men*, in whom the Faith is said to advance insofar as they increase in knowledge and understanding *of the same, unchanging doctrines.*

Indeed, his choice of terms and metaphors is such as to allow no possible hint of accretion, diminution or alteration. The doctrine, he says, may be consolidated, amplified and exalted, but remaining always "incorrupt and undefiled," not only with the same parts, but even the same proportion between them. The development to which he refers, therefore, relates exclusively to the *expression* or *formulation* of doctrine and not to its *substance*. The only features in which doctrine may develop or be improved are "clarity, perspicuity and distinctness" – all of them self-evidently proper to the *manner of stating the doctrine* rather than to the revealed propositions contained therein.

Thus in Chapter 22 of the same justifiably famous little work[9] its author writes: "*Eadem ... quæ didicisti doce, ut cum dicas nove, non dicas nova*" – "Teach the same things that you were taught, so that when you use a novel expression you will not use it to express a novelty."

Legitimate Understandings of Doctrinal Development

To be fairer still, let us admit that there *is* in fact more than one sense in which doctrine *could* be said to "develop", and it is incumbent on us to consider every possible legitimate sense, even the ones not mentioned by Davies and Newman, before we may safely reject their theory as going beyond those senses and categorically into the realm of heresy. Here is a brief classification of the ways in which it could be legitimate to refer to doctrine as developing. They are as follows:

---

[9] Now available in a bilingual English-Latin edition published by Tradibooks.com and incorporating Cardinal Franzelin's explanation of the Vincentian Canon.

(i) A doctrine can be formulated *more clearly* than it had been before, as the scholastic term "transubstantiation" was coined in the Middle Ages to express with greater lucidity the traditional doctrine of the Church on the Blessed Eucharist.

(ii) The Church may *define* a doctrine which has always been part of Divine revelation but which not everyone has *recognized* as such – as occurred, for instance, in the cases of the Immaculate Conception and the Particular Judgement.

(iii) When statements are put forward which are incompatible with Catholic belief, controversy exposes them as the errors that they are. Their condemnation by the Church thereupon increases the *number* of beliefs which every Catholic is *bound* to accept. This does not mean that the original deposit of faith revealed by God has been expanded, but that its *implications* have been manifested and authoritatively imposed on the Catholic conscience. In which regard it should be noted that no doctrine *condemned* by the Church was *ever* compatible with Divine revelation, so that the reason that Catholics have sometimes espoused such errors before their condemnation is simply that the logic showing their definite incompatibility with Catholic doctrine has not been clear to every individual.

These are the *only* species of development of the doctrinal corpus which the Church admits. And none of them is a true development of any *doctrine as such*. The first is a *linguistic* improvement; the second does not increase or expand the deposit of faith but affords Divinely guaranteed *certitude as to its contents*; and the third consists in establishing the *logical consequences* of the doctrines – which, of course, have not the slightest effect on the original revelation.

The fact that these three species of apparent development are not real developments is shown by the fact that, in none of the three cases, (a) is anything added to or taken from the original deposit, or (b) does any doctrine receive the tiniest difference of meaning from what it has always borne. Even the most extreme examples of each of the three categories retain the original doctrines entirely intact, so that *nothing* can be lawfully believed today which could not have been lawfully believed in the past, nor can anything be rightly condemned today which could not have been rightly condemned in the past – with the qualification, however, that, when man's ignorance or folly has obscured the object of Divine revelation or its implications, the judgement of the Church may determine a matter *which was always settled in objective reality* (at least since the death of the last Apostle) but on which tentative difference of opinion had been *subjectively* permissible while awaiting the definitive judgement of the Church.

V

Davies's Doctrine "Repugnant to Catholic Faith"

Now, at last, we are in a position to turn back to the passages cited on p. 538[10] in which Davies expounds his theory. Despite all efforts to help, it will be seen that they are irredeemably at odds with Catholic belief as represented by the authorities that have been quoted.

Take the following examples:

(i) " ... the truths of the Faith were expressed more and more clearly. What had once been implicit was made explicit...."

The obvious meaning of those words seems to be that some "truths of the Faith" were no more than implicit in the original deposit, and therefore not directly revealed by Our Lord, which is contrary, for instance, to the words quoted above from Pope St. Pius X's *Syllabus*. The *implications* of dogmas may become more explicit with the passage of time, but anything not revealed

---

[10] The references will be found there.

by God *in its full explicitness* before the death of the last Apostle can never become a dogma or a "truth of the Faith."

(ii) "A developed doctrine which reverses the course of development which has preceded it is no true development ...."

These words clearly envision that doctrines may develop in a particular *direction*, which cannot possibly be said of verbal clarification or of establishing the logical consequences and corollaries of doctrines. Evidently a change of meaning, however slight, is indicated – exactly what the 1870 Vatican Council and Pope St. Pius X's anti-Modernist oath anathematized. It is in fact quite irrelevant whether any "developed" version of a doctrine *reverses* the truth previously held or alters it in some degree less than a 180° *volte-face*. Given that the doctrine was already absolutely true and certain it can only remain forever on the same trajectory.

(iii) "This original deposit is subject to development ..., but always under the guidance of the Magisterium, and it [sic] must always remain consistent with the previous stage of development."

Now that which is consistent with "the previous stage of development" may, of course, be *in*consistent with the stage before *that*.[11] But let us bend over backwards as far as we can in Davies's favour, and interpret these words as meaning "*all* previous stages of development". Even then orthodoxy is not the result, for "consistent with" is quite evidently not intended to signify "identical in meaning with" (which is what, as we have seen, the Magisterium, consecrating the classic thought of St. Vincent de Lérins, insists on). Davies certainly has a sufficient command of the English tongue to have used the latter expression if that was what he meant.

And anyhow, the fact that Davies's use of the term "development" implies, or at least permits, a genuine change of

---

[11] Which would mean that a doctrine could *gradually* develop into one with an entirely different meaning.

meaning is made explicitly clear in his assurance that in a true development "each stage is *potentially* contained in its preceding stage," for *potentiality* is *opposed to actuality*. Thus if, for instance, we take the doctrine of the Blessed Trinity, which is one that Davies and Newman both consider an example of a doctrine which has developed, Davies is saying that the belief of post-Nicene Catholics in the Blessed Trinity was not *actually* held by pre-Nicene Catholics like St. Irenæus, from which it follows that the belief of second century Christians in the Trinity cannot be identical with that of the fourth century Christians, since the former contains the latter only *potentially*.

It is, incidentally, also apparent from the list of Newman's seven criteria for recognizing which developments are "authentic" and which are not, that this same heresy is contained in it – namely that even the "authentically" developed doctrine is *not* identical with the original, "undeveloped" doctrine. For if Newman had held the same belief on this subject as did St. Vincent of Lérins, surely he would have told us that the one essential criterion of true development is continuance "in the same doctrine, the same meaning and the same judgement."

In fact, Newman's doctrine, now so widely accepted, is certainly quite incompatible with the Catholic dogma that revelation ended with the Apostles. Consider, for instance, the following sentence from his *Essay on the Development of Christian Doctrine*:

> There was no *formal* acknowledgement of the doctrine of the Trinity till the fourth century.

Adequate comment on this error is provided by Dr. Orestes Brownson (1803-76), who shrewdly spotted the fact that Newman's claim was precisely the same as the claim of the Protestant Jurieu which had been refuted by Bossuet[12] in the following indignant terms:

---

[12] Bossuet, Bishop of Meaux, 1627-1704, is considered to be a profound and trustworthy theologian on subjects unconnected with the rights and

The Mystery of the Trinity, my brethren, *unformed*! Could you have believed it possible ever to have heard that from any mouth but that of a Socinian?[13] If from the beginning one only God was distinctly adored in three equal and co-eternal persons, the Mystery of the Trinity was not unformed. But according to your Minister ... Christians shed their blood for a religion not yet formed, and knew not whether they adored three Gods or only one! (Quoted by Dr. Brownson in *Brownson's Quarterly Review*, 1847, pp. 69 *et seq.*)

And Brownson, in response to those who tried to defend Newman from his learned and irresistible onslaught, observes in his own name that:

To assume ... that the doctrine of the Trinity was only imperfectly understood and believed before the Nicene Council [325 A.D.], to assert of the ante-Nicene Fathers generally that in treating this Holy Mystery they erred in thought and expression ... and to assume such a horrible doctrine as a matter of course, as a thing which will be admitted without controversy, is presuming a little too much on the ignorance, stupidity or indifference of the Catholic public. (*loc. cit.*, pp. 493-4)

He then points out:

If there be *anything* uniformly taught by our theologians, it is that the faith of the Fathers was perfect, that the revelation committed to the Church was complete and entire, and that the Church has, from the first, faithfully, infallibly, taught or proposed it. (*Ibid.*, p. 77)

Hence, Brownson concludes, and we may all conclude with him:

His [Newman's] view of Christian doctrine is sufficient to condemn his *Essay* as essentially repugnant to Catholic faith and theology.

And the same applies in equal measure to the writings on the same subject of Newman's avowed disciple Michael Davies.

---

infallibility of the papacy (not defined until after his death) and was one of the Church's most celebrated and powerful defenders against Protestantism.

[13] The Socinians were the first Protestants explicitly and completely to deny the Blessed Trinity. Their modern successors are the Unitarians.

CHAPTER THIRTEEN
OPEN LETTER TO MR. MICHAEL DAVIES

A.M.D.G.

Dear Michael,

Accompanying this Open Letter to you is a lengthy study of your writings subtitled *Evaluation on Michael Davies*, of which I am the author. This letter also comprises the last chapter of the *Evaluation*.

As you will see, the *Evaluation* constitutes a thorough examination of your theological writings and an assessment of them in the light of traditional Catholic doctrine. In the course of several hundred pages it draws attention to a vast number of clear contradictions between what you have written and correct Catholic doctrine. Further, it highlights very many examples of error, falsehood and scandal in your writings. In your expositions of Catholic theology, it convicts you of gross ignorance, indefensible errors and deliberate distortion on a huge scale. It argues – cogently in the view of those who have read it before publication – that, on the evidence it contains, to take up and read, without painstaking discrimination, a theological work bearing your name as author on the cover, is to imperil one's immortal soul. The *Evaluation* therefore amounts to a massive indictment of you in your chosen role of theological writer; unless, of course, its case is without foundation and the hundreds of statements made by yourself which it purports to expose as an affront to Our Divine Saviour and His Church – and succeeds in so exposing, in the opinion of those who have already read it – are in fact unexceptionable.

As you are of course aware, but I mention it for the benefit of all others who will read this letter, *Michael Davies – An Evaluation* is being published without your prior knowledge. There are three reasons for this:

1. You have demonstrated in the past that there is not the slightest useful purpose to be served by drawing errors and falsehoods to your attention privately. Both I and others from many different countries have done this on many occasions, a few of which are mentioned in this *Evaluation*, and the response has always been either no reaction at all, or a promise to reply in due course which is never fulfilled, or contemptuous dismissal.

2. So shamelessly unjustifiable and pernicious is much of what is exposed in the *Evaluation* and so urgent is the need, for the sake of the common good, that it be exposed, that I can think of no conceivable circumstance – not even your wholehearted admission of the *Evaluation*'s allegations and complete withdrawal from the theological arena – which could justify withholding it from publication.

3. To give you prior warning would give you the opportunity to do what you could to neutralize the *Evaluation* in advance of its being published, quite possibly by means of the sort of misrepresentations of which countless instances are documented in its pages, through the fairly numerous public channels of traditionalist communication to which you have access; and I do not believe that it is in the interests of the common good to take this risk without need.

However, it is one thing to publish without your prior knowledge, but it would be quite another not to give you the opportunity to refute my allegations and clear your name if, after consideration of the contents of the *Evaluation*, you are persuaded that you are not guilty of the charges it sets out and documents. And since it would inevitably be a lengthy and demanding task for you to answer everything in the *Evaluation* I am adding this letter to provide you with an opportunity to vindicate yourself without excessive expenditure of time and effort.

To this end is I have selected a comparatively small number of propositions defended by you in your published writings which I believe to be (a) false and (b) in open contradiction to the Catholic position on the subjects in question as found in those theological sources recognized among Catholics as authoritative; and I shall now list these propositions, briefly contrasting them with what I believe the correct Catholic position to be on each subject.

I publicly call upon you, when you have studied the list, and the relevant evidence which will be found in the *Evaluation*, to acknowledge your error in each case if you are wrong, or, if you still believe your position to be right, to substantiate your view from genuinely authoritative pre-Vatican II sources. **If you are able to refute my charges on these matters – all of which are of considerable gravity – I am happy for everything else in the *Evaluation* to be dismissed, without specific consideration, as worthless.** I do not think I could be fairer to you than that, or reasonably go further towards making it easy for you to clear your name if my censures are unjustified. But at the same time I must emphasize that my having made it so undeniably easy for you to defend yourself if I am in the wrong has a corollary which will be less agreeable to you if it is you who are in the wrong and I who am in the right. This is that if you *fail* to substantiate your position from Catholic authority on the handful of straightforward points on which I am about to challenge it, it will be impossible for me or for any other person reasonably assessing the evidence to conclude otherwise than that you *cannot* substantiate your position, because it is false. In other words, the rest of the *Evaluation*, which, as far as I am concerned can fall to the ground if you answer what follows satisfactorily, must stand if you do not. And to ensure that there is no room for quibbling over whether or not you have answered satisfactorily, I make the following clarifications:

(i) If you address some *other* point or points in the *Evaluation* instead of these which I have selected (all of which are exceedingly grave either in themselves or in the conclusions which must follow, as to your reliability, if I am right), it will be presumed that this is because you recognize that on these points you are in the wrong – in which case the *Evaluation* will be presumed substantially to have proved its case except for where you may *specifically* refute any particular stricture it makes. Evidently there is nothing to stop you from refuting other claims made in the *Evaluation as well* as the sample I have selected, but to omit the selection below and defend yourself on some other issue or issues would evidently be tantamount to an admission of guilt on the points you would be refusing to discuss.

(ii) In each of the following instances I am not merely questioning what you have written, but am directly accusing you of having made a false statement on a matter closely touching Catholic doctrine or the honour of the Church. Furthermore, I maintain (a) that in every single case listed below, if you had devoted to the topic even the barest minimum of study demanded of one who writes publicly on such topics, you would have *known* that your statement was false, and (b) that it is evident that as a generality you use such falsehoods – most of them worthy of grave theological censure and several plainly heretical – to bolster your position on points which you know are at best controversial. In respect of each item, therefore, I challenge you to refute my accusation by producing *objective, authoritative, Catholic* evidence corroborating what you have written.

Naturally to invoke in support of your position a post-Vatican II writer who agrees with you would amount to begging the question of whether or not such an individual can properly be called a Catholic authority, and would carry not the slightest weight. Nor would any reasonable person consider it acceptable for you to appeal for support to one of your notorious, anonymous theologians, not all of whom, as I have shown in the *Evaluation*, even realize that you are using them as authorities or consider themselves competent as such.

But I have neither the right nor the desire to put further restrictions on you in your use of authorities than are demanded and imposed by the nature of the issues under dispute. In each instance, therefore, I should consider that you had answered my challenge if you produced a citation from any authority of stature *equal to or greater than* the authority upon which I base my objection to your position. Thus, where I quote an *approved author*, some other *approved author* who maintains your position would suffice; but where I quote a Doctor of the Church a mere approved author would naturally *not* be adequate, although if I quote some high authority, such as a papal decree, which you believe I have *misinterpreted*, naturally I should be happy to acknowledge a contrary interpretation made by *any* approved author as sufficient to show that my case was at least not conclusive.

The only remaining scope for abuse of authority that I can think of is in relation to Canon Law, concerning which I would remark that where the 1917 *Code of Canon law* clarifies an issue – as it does, for instance, in respect of the *automatic* loss of ecclesiastical office on the part of public heretics (Canon 188§4) – it would be completely appropriate for you to use any approved commentator to support your position *provided he wrote after the Code: a pre-Code* canonist might easily have held a position which has since been altered or proved to be otherwise by the voice of authority.

I expect you already know that not all authors who have secured an "*imprimatur*" for their writings are considered to be "approved" (cf. Merkelbach: *Summa Theologiæ Moralis*, II, n.

108, note 4) and that the *"imprimatur"* is *not* indeed a reliable proof of orthodoxy at all, as St. Pius X emphasizes in *Pascendi Dominici Gregis*. The relative status of different Catholic authorities is set out, with reference to theological sources, on p.24 and in footnotes 8 and 9 to Chapter 9, Section D.

I now turn to the list of errors that I referred to earlier, in which I address the principal specific issues concerning which, in my submission, the positions you have held, committed to writing and endeavoured to propagate are indefensible.

V

1. Errors Concerning the Church's Magisterium.

ERROR 1

(See *Evaluation*, Chapter 1.) As a supplement to *Approaches* Nº 93 there was published a forty-page essay by yourself entitled *The Divine Constitution and Indefectibility of the Catholic Church*. A somewhat altered version of the same essay was subsequently published by the Neumann Press under the title *I Am With You Always*. Both versions contain heretical propositions concerning the Church's teaching authority, though I note that in the amended version you have corrected one heresy and substituted another in its place. At all events, since you have not *retracted* even the heresy which you have silently corrected, it would seem that you are content to leave it on record as your position: I shall therefore challenge you on it as well as on those heresies which you have shown *no* disposition to correct, even in this unobtrusive fashion.

In *The Divine Constitution* ..., you wrote:

> Some Catholics imagine that because the Church has the power to teach infallibly all her teaching is infallible. This is not correct. Teaching is infallible only when the special assistance of the Holy Ghost which guarantees this is invoked. *Pastor Æternus* restricts this assistance to definitions ....

This passage instructs us that, with the exception of *"definitions"*, in which "special assistance ... is invoked," the Church has no infallible teaching. By contrast, Fr. Sixtus Cartechini S.J., in his *De Valore Notarum Theologicarum* (Rome, Press of the Pontifical Gregorian University, 1951)[1] provides the following explanation:

> That there is an *infallible Ordinary Magisterium* from which a dogma can be derived is plain from the [1870] Vatican Council (Denzinger 1792) and from the bull *Munificentissimus* [Pope Pius XII's 1950 definition of the Assumption, according to which]: ' ... from the universal consent of the Ordinary Magisterium of the Church, a firm and certain argument is drawn ... that the Assumption of the Blessed Virgin Mary ... is a truth revealed by God ....' (...) The Ordinary Magisterium is exercised primarily by express teaching conveyed *outside formal definitions*, by the pope or by the bishops .... (pp. 32-3, emphasis added)

Thus for you, only definitions (Extraordinary Magisterium) are infallible; but for the Church, teaching not conveyed by definitions (Ordinary Magisterium) can be no less infallible.

CHALLENGE 1

Please produce an authority who (a) is of equal status to Fr. Cartechini, (b) wrote between the 1870 Vatican Council and the proliferation of false doctrine which began after the death of Pope Pius XII in 1958, and (c) supports your denial of the infallibility of the Ordinary Magisterium and explains why the 1870 Vatican Council and Pope Pius XII do not teach what they appear to teach on this topic. If you cannot do so, please recant your error and explain to your readers how they can dare to trust any doctrinal statement that you make.

---

[1] See also Dom Paul Nau: *The Ordinary Magisterium of the Church Theologically Considered* (translated by A.E. Slater and published by *Approaches*) and *Le Magistère Pontifical Ordinaire au Premier Concile du Vatican*. (*Revue Thomiste*, LXII, 1962)

ERROR 2

In *I Am With You Always* (p. 21) you adjust the passage I have just quoted from *The Divine Constitution* ... so that it reads as follows:

> Some Catholics imagine that all the teaching of the Extraordinary Magisterium is infallible automatically. This is not correct. Such teaching is infallible only when the special assistance of the Holy Ghost which guarantees infallibility is invoked.

Here it is noteworthy that you have added the word "such" at the beginning of the last sentence, so that you no longer deny infallibility to the Ordinary Magisterium, as the word "such" restricts the application of your remark to some teachings of the Extraordinary Magisterium.

CHALLENGE 2

Please explain why, if you had noted the error in the *Approaches* edition of your essay and corrected it by adding "such", you did not *recant* the error and draw it to the attention of *Approaches* (subsequently *À Propos*) readers. (Naturally you cannot have had any justifiable reason to think that every *Approaches/À Propos* subscriber would buy the revised Neumann Press edition and spot for him/herself the correction you had made.)

ERROR 3

(See *Evaluation*, Chapter 1.) Nonetheless, though your amendment removes one heresy it adds another in its place: "Some Catholics imagine that all the teaching of the Extraordinary Magisterium is infallible automatically. This is not correct."

I should like to avow at once that I am one of those Catholics who "imagine" that "all the teaching of the Extraordinary Magisterium is infallible automatically." Every Catholic authority I have read on the subject agrees that the Extraordinary Magisterium is exercised in each and every *solemn definition* of *pope or council* on *faith or morals* and not outside such definitions; and all agree that *every* such definition is protected by infallibility.

CHALLENGE 3

Please cite any pre-Vatican II Catholic theologian writing subsequently to the 1870 council who agrees with you that not all acts of the Extraordinary Magisterium are infallible. If you cannot, please recant your error.

ERROR 4

Moreover, you say that for the teaching of the Extraordinary Magisterium to be infallible, "the special assistance of the Holy Ghost must be invoked." The Constitution *Pastor Æternus* of the 1870 Vatican Council, however, lists four conditions for the infallible exercise of the Extraordinary Pontifical Magisterium, and the invoking of special assistance of the Holy Ghost is not among them.

CHALLENGE 4

Please refer me to any Catholic "approved author" who states that this invocation is either necessary in addition to the four conditions of *Pastor Æternus* or implied in their fulfilment.

ERROR 5

(See *Evaluation*, Chapter 1.) In a passage on the same topic, which you did *not* (alas!) revise in the latter edition of your essay, and which is found on the same page of each edition as the passage quoted above, you wrote that:

> ... no believer who pays due attention to Christ's promises can refuse to assent with absolute and irrevocable certainty to a definition of the Extraordinary Magisterium. Teaching which must be accepted with this degree of certainty is referred to as of Divine and Catholic faith ('*de fide divina et Catholica*'). A truth thus

defined is a 'Dogma of the Faith,' and its pertinacious rejection is called 'heresy.'

There is some inaccuracy of expression here which makes it difficult to determine exactly what you mean: for instance, you talk of "this degree of certainty", but the certainty you have referred to was "absolute and irrevocable," neither of which epithets denotes a degree, and the former of which is even *incompatible* with degree. (In fact, strictly speaking, certainty does not admit of *degrees*.) But I am unable to read your words without receiving the distinct impression that you are affirming that only by "a definition of the Extraordinary Magisterium" are "dogmas of faith", i.e. truths to be believed with "Divine and Catholic Faith", made known to us. And this proposition is at odds – to say the least – with the teaching of *Pastor Æternus* that "all those things are to be believed with Divine and Catholic faith which are contained in the word of God, written or handed down, and are proposed by the Church, whether by a solemn judgement *or by her Ordinary and universal Magisterium*, to be believed as Divinely revealed." (Denzinger 1792) However, a little later in the same essay you state this doctrine correctly, so I shall not press this point. What I must insist on is the indisputable implication that all truths defined by the Extraordinary Magisterium are "of Divine and Catholic faith." The definition on this subject of *Pastor Æternus* indicates that "to be believed with Divine and Catholic faith" are those truths defined by the Extraordinary Magisterium (or taught by the Ordinary Magisterium) "*as Divinely revealed.*" It says nothing of the kind about truths defined by the Extraordinary Magisterium, *not* as Divinely revealed, but simply as *true*, and as far as I am aware, although such doctrines are certainly and infallibly true and every Catholic is bound to assent to them, nevertheless, the doctrine that they are "of Divine and Catholic faith," so that to deny any of them would be *heretical*, is a doctrine peculiar to yourself. It is certainly unknown to Fr. Cartechini, for he writes as follows:

There are seen to be cases in which a canon of a council *defines a truth which has not been revealed*, such as a dogmatic fact or a theologically certain proposition. Note that I do not say, 'defines to be a dogma of faith', but simply 'defines'. In other words, not every definition is a dogma of faith. Thus the Council of Constance defined the legitimacy of the eucharistic fast and of communion under one species, saying simply that it is erroneous to deny this. (Denzinger 626) ... The pontiffs, even '*ex cathedra*', can condemn propositions not necessarily as heretical, but either as false or as scandalous. (*op. cit.*, p. 41. Emphasis as in the original)

CHALLENGE 5

Please produce an approved author of standing comparable (on the subject) to that of Fr. Cartechini who agrees with you that all doctrines defined by the Extraordinary Magisterium are necessarily dogmas of faith, propositions that contradict them being automatically in every case heretical.

ERROR 6

(See *Evaluation*, Chapter 5.) Several times in your writings, especially in the context of discussing the Vatican II *Declaration on Religious Liberty*, you have maintained that the Ordinary Magisterium (of pope or council) may err, even to the extent of affirming as true what it has earlier condemned as erroneous. In your article *The Sedevacantists* (*Christian Order*, November 1982; *The Remnant*, 15th June 1982) you wrote as follows:

> The case of the Vatican II Religious Liberty Declaration is one of the key arguments of the sedevacantists. They claim that it is heretical and that any pope endorsing it must '*ipso facto*' forfeit his office. It must be remembered that the Declaration is a document of the Ordinary Magisterium of the Church, and that the possibility of error occurs or can occur in such documents where it is a matter of some *novel teaching*. The Magisterium can certainly correct such an error without compromising itself.

Further, in your 1980 pamphlet *Archbishop Lefebvre and Religious Liberty* (pages 9-10) you wrote, of article 2 of the Vatican II Declaration, that "until it is corrected by the Magisterium, it represents ... a contradiction of consistently reiterated, and possibly infallible papal teaching ...."

Now nothing is plainer than that Pope Pius IX's condemnation of religious liberty in *Quanta Cura* is infallible, being an act of the Extraordinary Magisterium,[2] and that even if it were not infallible alone, the doctrine it teaches would have derived infallibility from having been, as you rightly observe, "consistently reiterated" by the popes. (See Dom Paul Nau's essays mentioned earlier for the fact that *re-iterated* teachings of the Ordinary Magisterium – whether universal or pontifical – are protected by infallibility.) But I refrain from pursuing this matter at present. My only concern in this letter is with the fact that you consider the Religious Liberty Declaration to be an act of the Ordinary Magisterium, exercised by a general council, and confirmed by the pope, and yet you see no difficulty in its defending as orthodox a doctrine condemned previously, and at least *perhaps* infallibly, as erroneous, nor do you have any hesitation in dissenting from this doctrine.

I accept, of course, that not every act of the pontifical or conciliar Ordinary Magisterium is protected by the charism of infallibility in such a way as to demand the assent of Divine Catholic faith or even of ecclesiastical faith; but the approved theologians I have studied on this point are all agreed that, even to non-infallible statements of the Ordinary Magisterium (and certainly no weightier act of the Ordinary Magisterium could be thought of than a doctrinal declaration of a general council approved and promulgated by the Roman pontiff, which is what you consider the Vatican II *Declaration* to be), there is due from all Catholics *a true intellectual assent* that the doctrines contained in them are at least *safe*, and that in making such

---

[2] See Cardinal Billot: *Ecclesia Christi*, thesis XXXI.

pronouncements, even if not protected absolutely and directly from error by infallibility, the Magisterium is at least protected by "the authority of universal ecclesiastical (or doctrinal) providence" from teaching doctrine which it is unsafe to hold. This is the teaching of Cardinal Franzelin:

> ... in such judgements pronounced even without '*ex cathedra*' definition there is demanded, and must be granted, *obedience* which includes *submission of the mind*, not, indeed, so that the doctrine is judged to be *infallibly* true or false ... but so that the doctrine contained in such a judgement is judged to be *safe*, and not, indeed, from the motive of Divine faith ... but from the motive of sacred authority, whose undoubted role it is to look after wholesomeness and security of doctrine, and that it must be embraced by us, and the contrary rejected, with submission of mind .... As, in theological doctrine, the proper *source*, and to that extent the proper and main reason on account of which *assent* is given, is not its intrinsically perceived truth, but the authority proposing the truth, this sacred authority of universal doctrinal providence is, by virtue of its role, an abundantly sufficient motive on the basis of which the pious will can and must command the religious or theological consent of the intellect. (*De Divina Traditione et Scriptura*, 2nd. edition, 1875, pp. 130-1)

The conflict with your position is twofold. In the first place, according to Franzelin, "universal doctrinal providence", being an abundantly sufficient motive for intellectual assent, must protect the wholesomeness and safeness even of non-infallible doctrines taught in declarations such as the Vatican II *Declaration on Religious Liberty* would be if (as you suppose) Vatican II had been a legitimate catholic council, and even pronouncements of much less authority, whereas you believe the doctrine in question *not* to be wholesome and safe. In the second place, according to Franzelin, true intellectual assent is owed to the doctrine of such declarations, whereas you do *not* assent to it, and encourage your readers not to.

CHALLENGE 6

Please cite an authority who (a) is of standing equal to or greater than that of Cardinal Franzelin, and (b) maintains that the Ordinary Magisterium, exercised by pope or general council, can teach doctrine which is not only not true but is in fact unsafe, unwholesome and unacceptable to Catholic orthodoxy, having even been condemned by the Magisterium in advance.

CHALLENGE 7

Please cite comparable authority for the proposition that Catholics may refuse to give intellectual assent to doctrine proposed by the Ordinary Magisterium (exercised by pope or council), admitting it to be at least safe and wholesome.

2. Errors Concerning the Jurisdiction of the Roman Pontiff.

ERROR 1

You wrote in *The Divine Constitution* ... :

> The faithful ... have the right to refuse to obey [the pope] if they are convinced in conscience that a particular command will harm rather than build up the Mystical Body. (p. 31)

And you have often expressed the same sentiments elsewhere. However, the approved theologians I have consulted, (Bellarmine, Suarez, Murray, Ward, St. Thomas, St. Ignatius) emphatically and to a man deny that a Catholic may disobey the pope, no matter how ill-advised and potentially disastrous his command may prove. All insist, with Fr. Patrick Murray, that "one is always bound to obey the (Roman) pontiff when he gives an absolute command, whether he does so infallibly or not, in everything which does not involve manifest sin." (*De Ecclesia*, Disp. XVII, Sect. IV, n. 90) In other words, they allow disobedience only when obedience is *forbidden* by Divine or natural law, but *not* simply because one regards the instruction as potentially harmful to souls: that judgement, they maintain, is for the pope, not the subject, to make. Moreover, when Cardinal

Newman appeared (in his letter to the Duke of Norfolk) to maintain your doctrine, he was refuted at length by Dr. W.G. Ward in the *Dublin Review* (January 1876) and issued in *The Tablet* a clarification of his position which made it clear that, whether or not he sided with you *before* Dr. Ward's article, he did not hold this position subsequently.

CHALLENGE 1

Please provide authority of status equal to, or greater than that of Fr. Murray and Dr. Ward,[3] which (a) considers the question of disobedience to the pope and when it may be justified in as much detail as they do, and (b) concludes that, when the action commanded by the pope is not intrinsically evil, or forbidden by Divine or natural law, it may nevertheless be refused on the basis of the individual's conviction that to obey would prejudice the good of souls. (In doing so, please take care not to confuse *laws* with *commands* as you have so often done in your writings.)

3. Errors Concerning the Automatic Loss of Office Incurred by Public Heretics, Particularly with Respect to Claimants to the Papacy.

ERROR 1

(See *Evaluation, passim,* but especially Chapter 5.) You are already aware of what I believe to be the clear Catholic position on this subject. It is that any person who publicly maintains heretical doctrine while knowing his doctrine to be opposed to that of the Church, in addition to incurring automatic excommunication, no less automatically forfeits all offices he may hold in the Church. If a pope were to fall into heresy – a hypothesis which never has happened and, according to a highly probable opinion, never *could* happen, but, for all that, is

---

[3] I have chosen these writers because they succinctly and specifically deny your position. St. Thomas and St. Robert Bellarmine held the same position as Fr. Murray and Dr. Ward.

nevertheless at least as permissible for us to discuss as St. Paul's impossible hypothesis that an angel from Heaven might teach false doctrine (Galatians 1:8) – he would thus automatically forfeit the papacy, and if a person *already* a heretic were to be elected to the papacy, the election would be invalid. In each case any Catholic aware of the relevant facts would be both entitled and obliged to refuse allegiance to and communion with the usurper, irrespective of any canonical admonitions or public declarations of ecclesiastical authorities of the vacancy of the Holy See.

And all this, you wholeheartedly reject. There is one detail of your own position which I do not understand. In your article *The Sedevacantists*, which I have already mentioned, you set out what you maintain are the facts as follows:

> ... a pope who pertinaciously embraced formal heresy would by the very fact be deprived of his office, as it is impossible to be a Catholic and a heretic at the same time, and the pope must be a Catholic. But the Church would need to know of this. The pope could hardly be said to have lost his office simply because one layman, one priest, one bishop, or even one Cardinal, declared that he had lost his office .... The theological consensus is that there is one certain way by which we could know that a pope has been deposed: a general council of the Church would have to declare that this was the case .... The sentence of the Council would not be judicial but declaratory, simply informing the faithful that the man occupying the See of Peter had ceased to be pope due to obdurate heresy.

When I read these words I understood you to hold that a pope who fell into heresy would lose his office immediately and automatically prior to any declarations of councils, etc., because you expressly say that he "would *by the very fact* be deprived of his office:" I thought that you were maintaining the need for a general council merely to *inform* the faithful of this, but that you acknowledged that, in such a case, the Holy See would be vacant as soon as the heresy was embraced – though, according to you, the faithful were still obliged to *treat* the heretic as pope until an authoritative declaration was made.

But when I read the introduction to *I Am With You Always* I began to doubt that I had correctly interpreted you, for there you write:

> Catholic theologians accept that a pope could loose [sic] his office through heresy .... But it would have to be such a notorious heresy that no doubt concerning the matter could exist in the minds of the faithful, and a statement that the pope had deposed in [sic] himself would need to come from a high level in the Church, most probably a general council.

Here the clear implication seems to be that until the faithful have had all doubt removed from their minds by some form of ecclesiastical declaration, the heresy is not sufficiently notorious to un-pope the miscreant. I simply do not know, therefore, whether your real position is that a pope who falls into heresy publicly, but concerning whose heresy no declaration has been made and doubt remains in some people's minds, is or is not the pope. All that is clear is that you believe he must be *treated* as pope until the declaration. Would you please clarify your position on this question? Meanwhile, I must allow, in what follows, for the possibility that you may hold either of the two different positions I have outlined.

If it is your position that a pope who publicly fell into heresy would remain pope until declared not to be so, I respond simply that some theologians, e.g. Suarez, have indeed maintained this position, but that to suggest that there is or ever has been a theological consensus in favour of this position is simply a lie. Moreover, Suarez himself based his position vis-à-vis a heretical pope on his opinion that *no* cleric would automatically forfeit his office by public heresy until sentence had been passed – a position which has been *universally* rejected since long before the 1917 *Code* explicitly declared the contrary.

CHALLENGE 1

If the above is your position, please (a) list the approved authors who hold it, together with those, such as St. Robert Bellarmine, who consider it "indefensible" (*De Romano Pontifice*), and (b) explain by what possible justification you can maintain that those who hold it are weightier than those who deny it, or represent a consensus of theologians, or justify your presenting their view to your readers as certain.

ERROR 2

Whether or not you hold that the heretical pope would remain pope until declared not to be, it is perfectly clear that you believe he must be *treated* as pope by the faithful until declared not to be. In *The Angelus* of May 1982 you wrote:

> Dr. Coomaraswamy argues that a pope can lose his office through heresy. This is correct, but if it happened, it would have to be so manifest as to be beyond any possibility of doubt and would need to be made known to the Church through the 'declaratory' sentence of a general council.

I think I can claim to have made an exceptionally extensive study of the doctrine of Catholic theologians on this topic, and I observe that the weightiest authors who consider the question (i.e. St. Robert Bellarmine and St. Alphonsus Liguori, both Doctors of the Church) unequivocally reject this supposed need for a declaratory sentence. Moreover, since Canon 188§4 of the 1917 *Code* ruled that heretics forfeit their offices automatically, I have not located a *single* author (prior to Vatican II) who defends it. The most respected commentary on the *Code* (Wernz-Vidal) considers that a pope guilty of public heresy would forfeit the papacy automatically "even before any declaratory sentence."

CHALLENGE 2

(a) Please list theologians of status equal to or greater than that of St. Robert Bellarmine and St. Alphonsus Liguori who support your thesis of the necessity of a declaration of a heretical pope's loss of office. (b) Please name any approved pre-Conciliar theologian or canonist who has maintained this position since the promulgation of the 1917 *Code*. (c) Please explain why you concealed from your readers the scantiness of support for your position and the great authority opposing it.

ERROR 3

As you know, those who today hold the Holy See to be vacant, do not – as a generality – believe that its recent usurpers *lost* the papacy by heresy, but rather that they were ineligible for it, by virtue of *prior* heresy, and thus were *never* popes. It is a fact that in his 1559 Constitution *Cum Ex Apostolatus*, which has often been drawn to your notice, Pope Paul IV expressly envisages such an eventuality and prescribes that, "the promotion or elevation, even if it shall have been uncontested and by the unanimous consent of all the Cardinals, shall be null, void and worthless; it shall not be possible for it to acquire validity ... it shall not be held as partially legitimate in any way." It is also a fact that the constitution has never been abrogated in its entirety,[4] and indeed that Pope St. Pius V confirmed it in every detail. And yet you have *never publicly referred to it*.

CHALLENGE 3

(a) Please explain why you have concealed the existence of this constitution from your readers. (b) If you maintain that this part of it is no longer in force, please ensure that your proof of this deals adequately with the evidence to the contrary mentioned in my correspondence with Dr. Glover published in the *Catholic Crusader* in 1984.[5] (c) Please name any pre-

---

[4] Although some minor canonical provisions it contains on other subjects have in fact been modified by subsequent legislation.

[5] The correspondence in question covered several topics, but the main one was Dr. Glover's contention that *Cum Ex Apostolatus* is no longer in force – a contention which was refuted in two letters from myself. If by any chance you no longer have back copies of the now defunct *Catholic Crusader*, I

Conciliar Catholic theologian writing since 1559 who has maintained that a public heretic can validly be elected to the papacy.

Error 4

As you know, Canon 188§4 of the 1917 *Code of Canon Law* declares that "If a cleric should publicly defect from the Catholic faith, any office he may hold becomes vacant '*ipso facto*' and *without any declaration* by tacit resignation accepted by the law itself."

In a letter addressed to N.M. Gwynne, dated in September 1986, you wrote as follows of this Canon:

> I am well aware of Canon 188§4, but did not include it in the study [i.e. your essay *The Divine Constitution* ...] as I understand it does not refer to heresy, the rejection of an article of the Faith, but to apostasy, defection from the Faith ....
>
> I would be very interested in seeing a photocopy of the relevant passage from Jone's commentary which, you say, interprets Canon 188§4 as referring not to complete apostasy but to heresy .... Should it transpire that you are correct, I will ensure that my booklet is amended in subsequent editions and that a correction is published in *Approaches*.

Your closing promise certainly shows that you know how you *ought* to behave in such circumstances, but a mystery remains as to why you did not keep your promise, for in our reply (8th October 1986) not only did N.M.G. and I enclose a photocopy of Fr. Jone's direct statement in his treatment of Canon 188§4 that "defection from the Faith, is contained in apostasy *and heresy*," but we also added a wad of other canonists agreeing with him. And yet *no* amendment (on this topic) was made in the subsequent edition of the same essay published by the Neumann Press, *no* correction appeared in *Approaches* or in its

---

should be happy to send you copies of the relevant letters upon request, including the final "round" of the debate which was never published owing to the collapse of the periodical.

successor *À Propos*, and you have never made the faintest attempt to show how Fr. Jone and every other canonical commentator who considers the topic made a mistake so clear in their interpretation of this canon that you and your anonymous canon lawyer friend can suppress their teaching altogether without a word of printed authority.

CHALLENGE 4

(a) If you maintain that it did not "transpire [sic] that [we] are correct," please quote your authorities equal in weight and number to those of whom you were sent photocopies, stating that Canon 188§4 applies only to apostasy and not to heresy. (b) If, on the other hand, you admit that Canon 188§4 does apply to all public heresy, as the approved commentators unanimously affirm, why did you break your promise?

4. Errors concerning the Recognition of Heresy

ERROR 1

(See *Evaluation*, Chapter 5.) On p. 48 of *I Am With You Always*, in discussing whether or not the Vatican II "popes" have been "formal heretics" you refer to some of their purportedly orthodox acts and remark: "It is only fair that we judge the orthodoxy of any Catholic by the totality of his published opinions, and not solely by particular actions or statements which appear suspect or ambiguous."

This opinion certainly sounds very sensible and "charitable", but it clashes with the Church's definition of a heretic in Canon 1325§2 of the 1917 *Code*, which is: "anyone who, after receiving baptism, while still calling himself a Christian, pertinaciously denies or doubts *any* of the truths which are to be believed with Divine and Catholic faith." Thus the Church classifies someone as a heretic who even doubts a single dogma (if he does so pertinaciously, i.e. knowing it to be a dogma), whereas you would insist, before so classifying him, on assessing his *other* statements and opinions to see if they contained sufficient evidence of orthodoxy to *outweigh* the single heretical proposition which he had espoused. The reason that the Church's attitude is correct and yours mistaken is neatly summed up in the scholastic dictum *"bonum ex integra causa; malum ex quocunque defectu"*, which means that to be considered good, or, by extension, orthodox, honest or chaste, for instance, one must be *wholly and unsulliedly* so. To be considered bad, heretical, dishonest, unchaste, etc., one need *not* be *wholly* so; it is sufficient if one is only sometimes or partly deficient in the contrary virtue.

That is why, when Our Lord admonished us to "beware of false prophets who come to you in the clothing of sheep, but inwardly they are ravening wolves," (Matthew 7:15) He did not suggest that we should include their sheep's clothing – orthodox utterances and external piety – as part of the evidence in their favour. Instead he gave us a single test to assess whether the suspected individuals be wolves or sheep: "By their fruits you shall know them." And Cornelius à Lapide, the great Jesuit Scripture commentator, remarks that the first of the evil fruit referred to is that of "false and impious doctrine."[6]

CHALLENGE 1

Please state upon what Catholic authority you made the above assertion.

ERROR 2

You affirm in *I Am With You Always* (p. 46) that "anyone in the Church who possessed the temerity to pass judgement on the Pope, and declare him a heretic, would be acting beyond the limits of his authority, *'ultra vires'*, and would himself become liable to canonical censure."

---

[6] This principle also applies to your own case, of course. When I show that something you have written is false or heretical, it is evidently no answer to reply that you have written something true or orthodox elsewhere, even on the same subject. If you had, it would merely add inconsistency to the list of your vices.

By contrast, Pope Paul IV in his constitution *Cum Ex Apostolatus* expressly enacted that, in the event of the election as Roman pontiff of one who had previously "deviated from the Catholic Faith or fallen into some heresy," *anyone*, – "the clergy, secular and religious, the laity, the cardinals, even those who shall have taken part in the election of this very Roman pontiff previously deviating from the Faith or schismatical ..., shall be permitted at any time to withdraw with impunity from obedience and devotion to those thus promoted or elevated *and to avoid them as warlocks, heathens, publicans and heresiarchs* ...."

CHALLENGE 2

(a) Do you acknowledge that if John-Paul II can be shown to have fallen away from the Faith into heresy before his putative election, anyone, *even the laity*, as Pope Paul IV and Pope St. Pius V have expressly provided, may freely withdraw from allegiance to him and may judge him not to be pope, and do so without acting *"ultra vires"* and without being liable to canonical censure? (b) If so, how is this compatible with what you wrote? (c) If not, how is your position compatible with Pope Paul IV's constitution? (d) If you claim that Catholics were entitled so to behave when Pope Paul IV promulgated his decree in 1559, but are no longer entitled to do so, please cite the subsequent legislation forbidding Catholics to do what Pope Paul IV declared they were permitted to do. (e) Finally, please cite your authority for the assertion that one becomes liable to canonical censure for judging a putative pope to be a heretic.

5. Errors and Lies Concerning the Sacrament of Ordination

ERROR 1

(See *Evaluation*, Chapter 9(A).) My next challenge relates to your article *Ordination 'Per Saltum'* which appeared in *Approaches* N° 72. In it, you twice at least misrepresent the authorities you quote, in order to make your opinion appear to your readers better supported by the theologians than it is. On p. 62 you write as follows:

> The *Dictionnaire de Théologie Catholique* also accepts that the position taken against episcopal ordination '*per saltum*' by so many theologians is because they follow St. Thomas .... The *D.T.C.* states (Vol. XI, col. 1388):
>
>> 'Once one admits that the episcopate is an order adequately distinct from the simple priesthood, one can conceive it as including eminently within itself all the powers of the priesthood. Were not the Apostles ordained as bishops without passing through the priesthood? (See *Acts*, XIII, 3) In the Apostolic Church there were only priest-bishops and deacons: see in particular Phil., I, I, and Clement of Rome, *Cor.* XLII. Many of the Popes, principally in the first centuries, were elevated immediately from the diaconate to the sovereign pontificate without receiving any other ordination but that of episcopal Consecration! One recalls also, the ordination of the antipope Constantine. See the *Liber Pontificalis*, N°s 227, 257, 292, 427, 455, 579, 264-256.'"

Here no reader could fail to suppose that the *Dictionnaire* ... is here stating its own position, whereas in reality it is doing nothing of the kind. It is simply setting out *one* of the rival positions. The questions posed in the passage are by no means rhetorical as they appear taken out of context. Immediately *after* the words you quote, the article continues:

> This is the thesis of Thomassin ... and of others cited by Gasparri ... *Undoubtedly rejoinder could be made* [to the arguments] .... Whatever the right answer may be ... there are *no peremptory arguments* for one side or the other. (Emphasis added)

Thus the *Dictionnaire* ... expressly refrains from confirming your position or expressing any definite view whatsoever. Indeed my own impression after reading the *whole* of the author's treatment was that he inclined against you.

CHALLENGE 1

How can you justify quoting the *Dictionnaire de Théologie Catholique* in such a way as to give the impression that it agrees with you when it expressly does *not* agree, and indeed *denies* your position that the matter is not open to doubt, by declaring that "there are no peremptory arguments for one side or the other"?

ERROR 2

Continuing in the same vein, you inform your readers on the very next page of the same article that, "probably the most detailed examination of the question of episcopal ordination '*per saltum*' is found in Gasparri's *De Sacra ordinatione*. The author concludes that such ordinations are valid."

After locating a copy of the work you refer to and reading the relevant part of it, I was – despite being by then somewhat hardened to your methods of pursuing theological controversy – considerably startled to discover that this assertion is simply untrue. Gasparri does *not* conclude that such Ordinations are valid. The words quoted earlier from the *Dictionnaire de Théologie Catholique* that "there are no peremptory arguments for one side or the other" were in fact borrowed from Gasparri and succinctly state his position. He considers that the more recent opinion in favour of the validity of "*per saltum*" Ordination or Consecration is sufficiently well-founded to be *probable*, but he does not even say that it is *equal* in probability to the traditional, Thomistic position against validity. Certainly he expressly declares that such a Consecration would in practice have to be repeated conditionally to be *sure* of validity: the very position you were arguing against.

CHALLENGE 2

(a) How is your statement about Cardinal Gasparri to be interpreted otherwise than as a direct lie? (b) If you maintain that it was a mistake, how is it compatible with minimal scholarly standards? (c) How is it compatible with your comment on Dr. Coomaraswamy's *Destruction of the Christian Tradition*?

This type of factual error ... makes it impossible to accept the book as a serious work of scholarship, and will provide useful ammunition for those wishing to discredit the traditional movement. (*The Angelus*, May 1982)

(d) Why should your readers trust any of the other references which fill your books any more than this one? Finally, (e) how is such indefensible misrepresentation compatible with your boast: " ... wherever possible I attempt to verify my quotations from the original sources."? (*Ibid.*)

ERROR 3

(See *Evaluation*, Chapter 9(B).) As you know, doubt has been cast on the validity of the Conciliar Church's 1968 rite of priestly Ordination owing to its omission from the form of the sacrament of the word "*ut*" ("so that") which appeared in the traditional Catholic rite. To substantiate your position that the new rite is nonetheless *certainly valid*, you pointed out that the form of the sacrament is divided into two halves, the first referring to the sacerdotal character ("*gratia gratis data*") and the second to the worthy exercise of the priestly office ("*gratia status*"). According to you, as the omission of the "*ut*" occurs in the latter half, not directly relating to the sacerdotal character, it cannot affect the validity of the form. You wrote:

> As the second part of the form is not concerned with the conferring of the sacerdotal character, the '*gratia gratis data*', but with the '*gratia status*', enabling and prompting the recipient to fulfil his office worthily, the omission of 'ut' in no way cast doubt upon the validity of the essential form of the conferral of the priesthood. (*The Roman Catholic*, 1981).

In other words, you maintain that the latter half of the form, in which the word "*ut*" appears, is not essential to the validity of the sacrament. However, as Fr. Jenkins pointed out in his follow-up article *The New Ordination Rite: An Indelible Question Mark*, this position directly contradicts Pope Pius XII's declaration in *Sacramentum Ordinis* (1947), according to which:

The form consists of the words of the 'Preface' of which the following are **essential** and therefore required for validity:

> 'Grant, we beseech Thee, Almighty Father, to these Thy servants, the dignity of the priesthood; renew the spirit of holiness within them *so that* ["*ut*"] they may hold the second rank received from Thee, O God, and may, by the example of their conduct, inculcate strict morality.'"

Thus Pope Pius XII expressly says that the latter half, which you say does *not* affect validity, is in fact "essential ... and required for validity," and he includes among the "words ... which ... are required for validity" the very "*ut*" which you maintain the Conciliar Church can omit with impunity.

CHALLENGE 3

(a) Is the second half of the form ("renew ... morality") essential and required for validity or not? (b) If not, how is this compatible with Pope Pius XII's constitution? (c) If so, how were you able to deny this despite your familiarity with *Sacramentum Ordinis*? (d) And why did you not acknowledge your error when Fr. Jenkins drew it to your attention? (e) Finally, do you consider the word "*ut*" to be essential to validity or not? (f) If so, how can you defend the validity of the 1968 Ordination rite? (g) If not, how is your position compatible with *Sacramentum Ordinis*?

6. Falsehoods Concerning Pope Liberius

Your attacks on the great anti-Arian pope St. Liberius, accused by calumniators of having subscribed to heresy, but thoroughly vindicated by Catholic scholarship, as I show in the *Evaluation*, have been so numerous as to be tedious. For a complete vindication of Liberius, I refer you to the *Evaluation* itself, as the evidence is inevitably impossible to summarize in a short space. I therefore select for consideration here only two points raised incidentally in your treatment of Pope St. Liberius.

Error 1

(See *Evaluation*, Chapter 10.) In *Pope John's Council* (page XIV) you write as follows:

> Athanasius made his stand not so much against the world, *'contra mundum,'* as against the bishops of the world – even to the point of having his excommunication confirmed by Pope Liberius – but it was the Pope who subsequently retracted and repented.

I make no comment here as to whether or not Liberius truly excommunicated St. Athanasius. My concern is with your statement that he "retracted and repented." You refer to this recantation on the part of Liberius elsewhere too (see *Pope John's Council*, p. 174; *Apologia Pro Marcel Lefebvre*, Vol. I, p. 118; *Archbishop Lefebvre – the Truth*, p. 32), and to the best of my knowledge it is *a complete invention*; for history – even including those doubtful sources which accuse Liberius of heresy and of excommunicating St. Athanasius – is completely silent about any repentance, retraction or recantation on his part.

Challenge 1

Please state your historical authority for attributing recantation or retraction to Pope Liberius.

Error 2

Secondly, you made the following observations in an article entitled "God Bless Archbishop Lefebvre!" which appeared in *The Angelus*, November 1985:

> Pope Liberius ... signed an ambiguous semi-Arian formula and excommunicated St. Athanasius ... Liberius was the first Roman Pontiff not to be canonized whereas St. Athanasius was raised to the honours of the altar.

What is remarkable about this assertion is that I can find not the faintest evidence that *any* Roman pontiff before Liberius was ever canonized! All the authorities I have consulted agree that canonization did not begin until some time after Liberius. Prior to that time, men were regarded as saints if they were included in the principal martyrologies or menologies of East and West, had a solid popular cultus and/or were referred to as saints by the Fathers. And whereas it is true that all these sources testify that all popes prior to Liberius, and St. Athanasius with them, were indeed saints, they *also* include Liberius himself as a saint. In other words, by the only means we have of identifying who was and who was not a saint prior to the institution of formal canonization, Liberius was just as much a saint as St. Athanasius or St. Clement.

CHALLENGE 2

(a) Upon what authority do you deny that Liberius received the honours of the altar? (b) Upon what authority do you affirm that popes prior to Liberius were "canonized"?

7. A Complete Invention (See Evaluation, Chapter 2.)

In *The Angelus* for May 1982, protesting at the presumption of a young priest who believed the Holy See to be vacant, you declared:

> ... the number of priests who are competent to engage in speculative theology is as limited as that of scientists who invent moon rockets .... The very idea of recently ordained priests considering themselves competent to make a credible contribution to speculative theology is absurd to the point of being grotesque .... As far as I know, there is not a single priest within the traditionalist movement in the English-speaking world who is qualified to engage in speculative theology.

This information would undoubtedly have been new to many of your readers, and some of them would no doubt have wished to find out what speculative theology *is*. If they turned to Fr. J. Herrmann's *Institutiones Theologiæ Dogmaticæ,* they would be informed that: "'Speculative' or 'dogmatic' theology consists in the contemplation of revealed truths." (Introduction, article II) If they then referred to the *Manual of Catholic Theology* by Drs.

Wilhelm and Scannel they would have learnt that: "When theology expounds and co-ordinates the dogmas themselves, and demonstrates them from Scripture and Tradition, it takes the name of Positive Theology. When it takes the dogmas for granted, and penetrates into their nature and discovers their principles and consequences, it is designated Speculative Theology .... Positive Theology and Speculative Theology cannot be completely separated."

From this, it would appear that speculative theology covers the whole field of dogma, in penetrative rather than expository fashion. It would seem, therefore, to be a very broad subject, in which every priest and many layfolk would be competent to greater or lesser extents. And yet you maintain that it is a science closed to all but the select few.

CHALLENGE 1

(a) Please refer to a single Catholic authority who holds, with you, that the vast majority of priests are not competent to engage in speculative theology. (b) If you cannot, please explain how you can justify making such emphatic and far-reaching statements on the basis of nothing but your private opinion.

ERROR 2

Even putting this difficulty aside, there remains a considerable problem. You have yourself written at length in favour of the thesis that the Holy See is *not* vacant, but you maintain that a priest is not permitted to argue that it *is* vacant because the subject pertains to speculative theology in which only a handful of priests, none of them, according to you, traditionalists, are competent. This appears to be a clear case of double standards.

CHALLENGE 2

(a) If it is forbidden to all but theologians of great stature to consider whether the Holy See might be vacant, why is it open to those such as yourself, who do not fall into this category, to argue that the Holy See is occupied? (b) If the subject is so demanding, why is it less demanding to give one answer to the question than the opposite answer?

8. Errors Concerning Participation in Religious Acts with Non-Catholics.

On p. 45 of *I Am With You Always*, you set out what you claim to be the facts about the participation of Catholics in religious acts (*"communicatio in sacris"*) with non-Catholics:

> In the Old [1917] Code of Canon law it was forbidden for Catholics to take part in the Divine worship of non-Catholics. This is an ecclesiastical and not a Divine law .... There were circumstances in which Catholics were permitted to take part in non-Catholic worship prior to Vatican II. Canon 1258 listed them as 'funerals, weddings, and other similar celebrations.' .... It was stipulated that attendance at such services should be 'passive'.

ERROR 1

The first error in this passage is your statement that the law forbidding Catholics to participate in the Divine worship of non-Catholics was an ecclesiastical and not a Divine law. Evidently this is a question of great moment, because the Conciliar Church expressly permits *"communicatio in sacris"* with non-Catholics and its "popes" habitually practise it. If, therefore, it is forbidden by the Divine law, from which even a pope cannot dispense, this would undoubtedly create a grave difficulty for the Conciliar Church's apologists such as yourself. But the voice of authority is quite clear, however, that Divine law does indeed bear on the subject. Here, for instance, is the instruction on the subject addressed to the Catholics of England by Cardinal Allen in his letter of 12th December 1592:[7]

> ... You [priests] and all my brethren must have great regard that you teach not nor defend that it is lawful to communicate with the Protestants in their prayers or services or in the conventicles where they meet to minister their untrue sacraments; for this is contrary to

---

[7] *Letters and Memorials of Cardinal Allen* (ed. T. F. Knox) Vol. II, pp. 344-5.

the practice of the Church and the Holy Doctors in all ages who never communicated or allowed any Catholic person to pray together with Arians, Donatists or what other soever. *Neither is it a positive law of the Church, for in that case it might be dispensed with upon some occasion; but it is forbidden by God's own eternal law*, as by many evident arguments I could convince .... To make all sure, I have asked for the judgement of the pope currently reigning [Pope Clement VIII] and he expressly told me that to participate with the Protestants either by praying with them or by coming to their churches or services or suchlike was by no means lawful *or dispensable* .... [I have modernized and clarified the English in one or two places and added emphases.]

Thus Cardinal Allen and Pope Clement VIII expressly hold that divine law forbids *communicatio in sacris* in the case they discuss, so that not even for the strongest of reasons could the pope himself dispense from it. Nor was there any change in the doctrine of theologians on this topic prior to Vatican II. "Active '*communicatio in sacris*' ... is *never lawful*," says Noldin-Schmitt's *Summa Theologiæ Moralis* (Vol. II, n. 38) in Fr. Heizel's 1962 edition, "because it is a denial of the Faith by internal and external profession of a false religion .... '*Communicatio in sacris*' is ... *implicitly* formal if it is done in the sacred rite itself, for instance ... by singing with the heretics in a sacred function, for *the perverse intention* of joining in a heretical *rite can never be separated from such actions*." (Emphases added.)

The issue here is not whether there can ever be cases of *communicatio in sacris cum acatholicis* which are not forbidden by divine law, but your forthright relegation of the entire range of *communicatio in sacris* to the field of mutable ecclesiastical law.

On this subject the Holy See has spoken in detail and more than once. Allow me to draw to your attention, for instance, the rescript of the Holy Office of 10th May 1753 – a document of the highest interest because it takes detailed account of the range of received theological opinion on the subject.

> We are of course not unaware that some theologians are to be found who absolve of all blame Catholics who communicate *in divinis* with heretics and schismatics who have not been denounced by name, and even receive the sacraments from them, provided that the following conditions are all simultaneously verified:
> [...]

The conditions exacted by these, the most tolerant of the Church's theologians, are as follows:

(i) a very grave and very urgent cause;
(ii) that the heretical minister be validly ordained and use exclusively Catholic rites
(iii) that the *communicatio in sacris* be not an external protestation of false doctrine as going to the Protestant churches was in England when Paul V forbad it (since the king had expressly ordered all to go to church in order to show their agreement with the Protestants)
(iv) that no scandal be given.

The rescript then notes that this lax view is far from accepted by *all* theologians either as true or as safe to act on in practice, adding that, even accepting the teaching of these theologians, since *all* the conditions must be *simultaneously* verified, "it is therefore almost impossible for it to happen that Catholics mixing in sacred rites with heretics and schismatics can be excused from grave sin [*flagitio*]."

It adds that for this reason the Roman congregations (Holy Office and Propaganda) have always considered such *communicatio* illicit and have always informed missionaries that it can *scarcely ever* [*vix umquam*] happen in practice that *communicatio in divinis* of Catholics with heretics is innocent.

CHALLENGE 1

Please produce texts of pre-Vatican II theologians, comparable in status to those I have cited, who attest the truth of your contention that "*communicatio in sacris*" with non-Catholics is forbidden only by ecclesiastical law.

Error 2

Of course it must be admitted that you do adduce evidence in the original essay that what you say is true, for you remark that "there were circumstances in which Catholics were permitted to take part in non-Catholic worship prior to Vatican II. Canon 1258 listed them ...." But this contention presents an anomaly in the light of your closing admission that "it was stipulated that attendance at such services should be 'passive'." "Passive" being the opposite of "active", it is difficult to see how one could *passively* "take part in non-Catholic worship." Plainly to "take part" in an act of worship would involve some *action* rather than mere passivity. However, you assure us that Catholics were permitted to "take part" in non-Catholic worship, and you refer us to Canon 1258 in substantiation of this, so to Canon 1258 we must turn. It reads as follows:

> (i) It is not lawful for the faithful in any way actively to be present at or to take part in the religious acts of non-Catholics.
> (ii) Passive or merely material presence can be tolerated for the sake of civil office or of honour, for a grave reason to be approved by the bishop in case of doubt at the funerals, weddings and similar ceremonies of non-Catholics, provided there be no danger of perversion or of scandal.

Thus the first paragraph of the canon absolutely forbids Catholics actively to be present at the religious acts of non-Catholics or to take part in them, and the second paragraph permits only (in certain carefully delineated circumstances) *passive presence*, which of course is *not* the same as "taking part".

Challenge 2

(a) *Does* Canon 1258 anywhere suggest, as you allege, that Catholics may "*take part* in non-Catholic worship"? (b) Were you aware, when you wrote *I Am With You Always*, of the distinction between "to take part in" a ceremony, and "to be passively present" at it? (c) How is it justifiable or excusable for you thus to invoke a canon in favour of your contention when it simply does not support you? (d) If you have some excuse, is it one that you would have taken into account if you had apprehended a notoriously modernistic priest, or a reprehensible "sedevacantist" invoking "authorities" which in fact contradict his position? (e) Finally, can you name any pre-Vatican II approved author who defends the lawfulness of "taking part in non-Catholic worship"? (f) And if not, is it not plain that the charge of authorizing what, prior to Vatican II, was universally condemned as *per se* contrary to Divine and ecclesiastical law, from which you endeavour by misrepresentation to defend the Conciliar Church, is one of which it is in fact *guilty*?

V

At this point, I close my series of challenges to you, inviting you to respond to them. What you will notice about each of the questions is that if there is any justification available for your position, it will not take you long to answer it. The argument that you have not enough time is not therefore available to you to justify declining to respond to my accusations. Hence, should you refuse to reply, therefore, or should you produce a riposte in which you evade directly answering each of my questions, the conclusion that I and, I anticipate, all impartial readers of this letter will reach, is that you *cannot* answer them without repeatedly convicting yourself, out of your own mouth, of a level of theological ignorance, dishonesty and unscrupulousness which makes you a mortal danger to the souls of all who read you as if you were a Catholic writer.

I hope you will believe me if I end this letter by assuring you that I have not enjoyed writing either it or the accompanying *Evaluation*, and have done so in no spirit of personal hostility to you, but purely in order to neutralize, as far as I may be able, your immense and pernicious influence, and only after private attempts to persuade you to justify your position or withdraw errors had been unsuccessful. For your own sake, as well as that of your readers, I earnestly pray that you may recognize the justice of the indictment this letter and the *Evaluation* comprise and take that action which alone could properly make amends for the damage you have hitherto inflicted on the Church: namely, to take up your pen one last time to renounce all your theological writings, and then to put it down forever.

Yours sincerely in the Holy Catholic Church,

John S. Daly

ALSO BY JOHN S. DALY

If you have appreciated *Michael Davies – An Evaluation* you may be interested in other books and articles by the same author:

The Theological Status of Heliocentrism
The Life of Fr. Philip Shelmerdine
"The Impossible Crisis"
"Did Vatican II Teach Infallibly?"
"Religious Liberty: Dr. Brian Harrison and the attempt to absolve Vatican II of error"
"Is the *Novus Ordo Missae* Valid?"
"Archbishop Lefebvre and Sedevacantism"
"Can Private Individuals Recognise Someone as a Heretic Before the Direct Judgment of the Church?"
"Heresy and Hylomorphism"
"Heresy in History"
"Pertinacity and Schism"
"Heresy, Schism and Their Effects"
"Have We Correctly Understood Schism?"
"A Common Fallacy"
"A Case of Confusion"
"Is the SSPX in Schism?"
"The Bishop and the Axiom"

Translations

How Grace Acts by St. Alphonsus Liguori
Cum Ex Apostolus Officio by Pope Paul IV
Jovinian 1982 by Professor Gustavo Daniel Corbi
The Christian of the Day and the Christian of the Gospel by Père Emmanuel
"Essay on Heresy" by Arnaldo Vidigal Xavier da Silveira
Economy and Interest by Professor Maurice Allais

In French

"Le Canon 2200§2 et la Pertinacité"
"L'Épikie »

"Que doit être l'éducation ? Que doit être l'homme ?"
Dion et les Sibylles (Translated from the English of Myles Keon)

www.ingramcontent.com/pod-product-compliance
Lightning Source LLC
Chambersburg PA
CBHW021128230426

43667CB00005B/64